EMERGENCY LAW IN IRELAND
1918–1925

Emergency Law in Ireland, 1918–1925

COLM CAMPBELL

CLARENDON PRESS · OXFORD
1994

Oxford University Press, Walton Street, Oxford OX2 6DP
Oxford New York
Athens Auckland Bangkok Bombay
Calcutta Cape Town Dar es Salaam Delhi
Florence Hong Kong Istanbul Karachi
Kuala Lumpur Madras Madrid Melbourne
Mexico City Nairobi Paris Singapore
Taipei Tokyo Toronto
and associated companies in
Berlin Ibadan

Oxford is a trade mark of Oxford University Press

Published in the United States
by Oxford University Press Inc., New York

British Library Cataloguing in Publication Data
Data available

Library of Congress Cataloging in Publication Data
Campbell, Colm.
Emergency law in Ireland, 1918–1925 / Colm Campbell.
p. cm.
Includes bibliographical references.
1. Internal security—Ireland. 2. War and emergency powers—
Ireland. 3. Terrorism—Ireland. I. Title.
KDK1340.C36 1993
343.415'01—dc20
[344.15031] 93–8767
ISBN 0–19–825675–2

1 3 5 7 9 10 8 6 4 2

Typeset by Best-set Typesetter Ltd., Hong Kong
Printed in Great Britain
on acid-free paper by
Bookcraft Ltd., Midsomer Norton, Avon

Acknowledgements

I am deeply grateful to Tom Hadden for his encouragement, enthusiasm, and his incisive criticisms of the many drafts of this work. I also wish to thank Professor D. S. Greer for his helpful comments on the earlier part of this research. Grateful acknowledgements are due to the staff members of the School of Law of Queen's University with whom I have kicked around ideas, to the staffs of the Imperial War Museum; the Public Record Office, Kew; the Public Record Office of Northern Ireland; the National Library Dublin; the State Paper Office Dublin; the Military Archives Dublin; to the Mulcahy Trust; and to Seamus Helferty of the University College Dublin Archives for facilitating access both to the papers provided by the latter Trust and to the O'Malley papers. Particular thanks are due to Jane Williams, Richard Hart and Dorothy McCarthy of Oxford University Press for their diligence and extra-ordinary patience.

This work was undertaken while I held the Civil Liberties Trust Research Studentship at the School of Law, Queen's University, and would have been impossible without the financial support for the studentship provided by the Nuffield Foundation.

A special word of thanks to Christine Maggs for advice on statistical analysis, helping with the typing, and so much more.

Belfast   COLM CAMPBELL
January 1994

Contents

List of Tables

List of Maps

List of Graphs

List of Figures

Abbreviations

AC	*Appeal Cases*
ADRIC	Auxiliary Division Royal Irish Constabulary
AG	Attorney-General
All ER	*All England Reports*
ASU	Active Service Unit
B & Ad.	*Barnewall and Adolphus's Reports*
BG	*Belfast Gazette*
CB	county borough
CGS	Chief of General Staff
CI	Chief Inspector
CID	Criminal Investigation Department
C-in-C	Commander-in-Chief
Crim. LR	*Criminal Law Review*
CMA	Competent Military Authority
CMO	court martial officer
CnB	Cummann na mBan
CO	commanding officer
CSJ	court of summary jurisdiction
CWS	Military Archives, Civil War Series
DCM	district court martial
DD	*Dáil Debates*
DG	*Dublin Gazette*
DI	District Inspector
DMP	Dublin Metropolitan Police
DORA	Defence of the Realm Act(s)
DORR	Defence of the Realm Regulation(s)
FGCM	field general court martial
GCM	general court martial
GHQ	General Headquarters
GL	Gaelic League
GOC	General Officer Commanding
GRO	General Routine Order
HC Deb.	*House of Commons Debates*
HCNI Deb.	*House of Commons of Northern Ireland Debates*
IFS	Irish Free State
IG	Inspector-General
ILT & SJ	*Irish Law Times and Solicitor's Journal*
ILTR	*Irish Law Times Report*

IO	intelligence officer
IO	*Irish Oifigiúil*
IR	*Irish Reports*
IRA	Irish Republican Army
IRB	Irish Republican Brotherhood
Ir. Jur.	*Irish Jurist*
IV	Irish Volunteers
IWM	Imperial War Museum
JAG	Judge Advocate General
KB	King's Bench
KBD	King's Bench Division
LCL	lower confidence limit
LJ	*Law Journal*
LQR	*Law Quarterly Review*
MLA	martial law area
MLR	*Modern Law Review*
n/a	not available
NCCL	National Council for Civil Liberties
NCO	non-commissioned officer
NILR	*Northern Ireland Law Reports*
NR	North Riding
OC	officer commanding
PRO	Public Record Office
PRONI	Public Record Office Northern Ireland
RIC	Royal Irish Constabulary
RM	Resident Magistrate
ROIA	Restoration of Order in Ireland Act
ROIR	Restoration of Order in Ireland Regulation(s)
RUC	Royal Ulster Constabulary
RUSC	Royal Ulster Special Constabulary
SCO	summary court officer
SDLP	Social Democratic and Labour Party
SF	Sinn Féin
SMA	Special Military Area
SNI Deb.	*Senate of Northern Ireland Debates*
SPO	State Paper Office, Dublin
SR	South Riding
SR & O	Statutory Rules and Orders
TD	Teachta Dála
TLR	*Times Law Report*
UCD	University College, Dublin
UCL	upper confidence limit
UPA	Ulster Protestant Association

USC	Ulster Special Constabulary
UVF	Ulster Volunteer Force
w/e	week ending
WLR	*Weekly Law Reports*

List of Cases

List of Acts

1. Introduction

COERCION: A FUTURE FOR THE PAST?

Discussion of emergency law in Ireland in the years 1918–25 inevitably invites comparison with contemporary events in Northern Ireland. If a pattern has emerged during the current 'Troubles', it must be that formed by sets of symbioses: coercion–violence (or violence–coercion) in the case of the British–republican relationship, and violence–violence (and perhaps reform–violence), in that between republicans and loyalists. Emergency legislation, by its very nature, is particularly open to abuse, and each time abuse occurs the seeds of future conflict are planted. At the initial stages, the process seems to lead inexorably towards escalation. Either the violence becomes so damaging that those resorting to coercion feel compelled to negotiate a settlement, or a situation of 'total' repression arises in which violent opposition becomes either impossible or merely gesticulatory.

Where neither outcome is arrived at (as in the case of Northern Ireland today), the result is a bloody equilibrium. In an attempt to address the causes of republican violence a reform 'package' is introduced, and security strategy becomes aimed at containing the violence until the package or packages take effect. The degree of the state's response, however, is sufficiently abrasive to generate and/or to consolidate significant resistance. And when the justification for these measures is questioned, this very resistance is claimed to necessitate the particular coercive device.

Loyalist violence and republican violence could also be said to exist, to a degree, in a symbiotic relationship, although to suggest that this offers a complete explanation of either phenomenon would be quite misleading. Many other factors are relevant to the discussion of violent loyalism, not least the degree to which this violence is spurred by perceptions of reform packages as threats to privilege, or as undermining the link with Britain.

At the start of 1994, against the background of the Anglo-Irish Joint Declaration of December 1993, and with the air filled with talk of peace, it is as yet unclear whether the 1990s will see a radical change in the situation. What is clear is that little in government policy in the last two decades has been particularly new in the context of British rule in Ireland. The 1970s and much of the 1980s have seen little more than a variant of the centuries-old recipe of conciliation and coercion—kicks and kindness. As this work may help to illustrate, many of today's prob-

lems find echoes in the past, and few of the techniques of coercion recently employed are without historical precedent. There are, of course,
massive political differences between the conflict(s) in the years 1918–25
and today's Troubles. And while there are many similarities, there are
also significant differences in the uses of law and in legal technique.

For a variety of reasons, there are limits to the degree of coercion
which the state now feels capable of resorting to (although the current
Emergency Provisions Act and Prevention of Terrorism Act probe these
limits deeply[1]). Even assuming (purely for the sake of argument) that
there might be a political will in Britain to see through a policy of
total repression as was considered in the summer of 1921, there are at
least three reasons why such a course would be politically impossible.
Firstly, there is the growing influence of international human rights and
humanitarian law norms, particularly of the European Convention on
Human Rights. Unlike many other international law mechanisms, the
European Convention incorporates relatively effective enforcement machinery. As the furore surrounding the UK's response to the *Brogan*
decision in 1988 illustrates, the cost of an adverse ruling can be high.[2] A
policy of total repression could be expected to result in many such
rulings, and were such an approach persisted with, the ultimate sanction
could be expulsion from the Council of Europe. There would also be
significant knock-on effects within the European Community, since, as
the European Parliament has put it 'respect for fundamental rights is
indispensable for the legitimacy of the Community'.[3]

---

[1] The Northern Ireland (Emergency Provisions) Act 1991 substantially re-enacts and
extends earlier Emergency Provisions legislation. It provides for trial of a schedule of
offences on indictment by single-judge jury-less 'Diplock courts' in which confessions are
admissible in circumstances in which they might ordinarily have to be thrown out, the main
test for exclusion being whether the confession was obtained by 'torture or inhuman or
degrading treatment'. In addition, there are special provisions in relation to interrogation,
internment without trial is provided for (although it has not been resorted to since 1975),
and the Army and police are given a range of stop, search, and seize powers. There are also
a battery of ancillary powers allowing organizations to be banned, roads to be closed, and
special financial investigations to be mounted. The Prevention of Terrorism (Temporary
Provisions) Act 1989 applies throughout the UK and provides *inter alia* for seven-day
detention. Such a period has been held to be inconsistent with the European Convention on
Human Rights (see fn. 2 below).

[2] In *Brogan* v. *UK*, 11 *European Human Rights Reports* 117, the European Court of
Human Rights ruled that the detention of a suspect under the Prevention of Terrorism Act
for a period of four days and six hours was inconsistent with art. 5 of the Convention
which guarantees the rights to liberty. Rather than bring its legal provisions into line
with European standards the UK retained the seven-day detention power and entered a
derogation under art. 15 of the Convention claiming that there was a 'public emergency
threatening the life of the nation'. The derogation was upheld by the European Court of
Human Rights in *Brannigan and McBride* v. *UK* (as yet unreported decision of 26 May
1993).

[3] Preamble to the 'Declaration of Fundamental Rights and Freedoms', adopted by the
European Parliament, 12 Apr. 1989, *Official Journal of the European Communities*, no. C
120/53.

Secondly, unlike the position which obtained in Ireland as a whole in the years 1918–21, the greater part of the nationalist vote in Northern Ireland now goes not to Sinn Féin, but to the constitutional nationalists in the shape of the Social Democratic and Labour Party (SDLP). A settlement involving an accommodation between a section of the Unionist parties in Northern Ireland and the SDLP—which has long been central to British strategy—therefore remains a possibility only as long as the SDLP both continues as the dominant nationalist party and remains wedded to the 'constitutional' path. The reaction which a policy of total repression would bring would almost certainly destroy the current balance.

Finally, there is the position of the rest of the island to be considered. Unlike the situation in 1920–21, the British Army now has to cope with the troublesome land frontier presented by the border with the Republic, indeed it is only in the border areas that the army has been pressed militarily. North-South security co-operation, which is seen as essential, would be unlikely to survive an iron-fist approach in the North. It is not only security co-operation with the South which is perceived as important. As the 1985 Anglo-Irish Agreement illustrates, and as the 1993 Anglo–Irish Joint Declaration re-iterates, the support of the Republic is seen as vital to any settlement in Northern Ireland, and again, such support could not survive a policy of total repression. Thus while security strategists may continue to ponder the effect of the simultaneous introduction of internment without trial on both sides of the border, a return to the militarism of the 1920s remains inconceivable.

During the current Troubles there has therefore been no formal resort to martial law whether of the statutory or non-statutory variety. Instead there has been massive reliance on 'emergency' and 'anti-terrorist' legislation. In socio-legal terms this exclusive reliance on statutory powers can be considered a reaction to the experiences of 1920–21. Then, martial law served to de-legitimate a state response which sought to portray itself as upholding constitutional standards in the face of terror and mayhem. Nevertheless, many of the functions which in the twenties would have been performed by courts martial or military courts are now carried out by Northern Ireland's jury-less single-judge 'Diplock courts'. At the detention stage, allegations of brutality (often well documented) continue to be made as they were seventy years ago. Indeed the rules on the admissibility of confessions before Diplock courts are less stringent than those which applied in trial by court martial, the law having been deliberately altered to render admissible confessions which would ordinarily have to be thrown out.[4]

Another significant difference has been a degree of awareness on the part of the authorities of the need to avoid the kind of spectacular own

[4] See fn. 1 above.

goals represented by the official and unofficial reprisals of 1920–21. There have, however, been exceptions, the most notable being 'Bloody Sunday' in 1972 when paratroopers attacked a Civil Rights march, killing thirteen people. Parallels may also be drawn between earlier reprisal killings and today's allegations of a 'shoot-to-kill' policy or under-standing, and of collusion between elements in the security forces and security services on the one hand, and loyalist paramilitary forces on the other. In the 1920s, investigation of reprisal killings was not helped by the substitution of military courts of inquiry for coroners' inquests; today, the special rules on inquests which apply only in Northern Ireland like-wise hinder meaningful investigation of suspicious killings.[5]

There have also been differences in the use of law by the opposition in 1920–21 and by today's Republicans. In the earlier period, the employ-ment of legal procedure (in the shape of the Dáil courts), and the invoca-tion of substantive international humanitarian law norms were significant factors in the matrix of legitimation. In the current Troubles, such ele-ments seem not to figure.

For lawyers there always exists the danger of overestimating the im-portance of law in any given conflict, which may result in a fixation on legal technique. This danger is likely to be especially present when dis-cussing emergencies. Law may be seen not merely as an element in the conflict, but rather as its centre-piece. With the perspective of seventy years it is obvious that the problems of Ireland in the 1920s were political rather than merely legal, and that the most important question con-cerning the role of law at that time was 'how did law impact on the wider political conflict?' Ultimately, however, political conflicts required political solutions going beyond the limits of legal discourse. The same is true of the Northern Ireland Troubles today.

---

[5] The law on inquests in Northern Ireland is governed principally by the Coroners Act (Northern Ireland) 1959, and statutory rules made pursuant to the Act: the Coroners (Practice and Procedure) Rules 1963 and the Coroners (Practice and Procedure) (Amend-ment) Rules 1980. The system thereby created differs from that in England and Wales in two crucial respects. First, only factual 'findings' rather than verdicts in the accepted sense of the word can be returned in Northern Ireland. Secondly, in that jurisdiction only there is a rule which prohibits the coroner from compelling to give evidence any person 'who is suspected of causing the death or has been charged or is likely to be charged with an offence relating to the death'. A further difference between the two systems is that in Northern Ireland coroners have adopted the practice of not opening inquests until the police and the prosecuting authorities have informed the coroner that the inquest may proceed. Often, therefore, the inquest opens years after the disputed killing. In England, on the other hand, inquests are opened and adjourned pending a decision by the prosecuting authorities, an arrangement which helps to ensure that inquests are held within a reasonable period.

APPROACHES TO EMERGENCY LAW

Standard United Kingdom constitutional law texts offer little insight into emergency law issues. The Defence of the Realm Acts may be briefly mentioned and the Irish experience is largely ignored. There will usually be a discussion of some martial law cases, but such analysis as there is usually reflects a 'black letter' approach. This approach is also taken in a few of the more specialist works concerned with an exposition of various areas of emergency law. In what aims to be 'value-free' analysis, emergency law issues are examined in an approach which might equally well be applied to taxation law or to land law. The limitation of this approach is that the notion of an 'emergency' necessarily implies a departure from the norm, and thus context is of particular importance, whereas in a 'value-free' analysis, context is formally ignored.

Because of these shortcomings, a number of other approaches have been developed. One of the most widely favoured could be termed 'the response of the liberal–democratic state to political violence and terrorism', and it is this framework that has dominated discussion in the Anglo-Irish context. Broadly, this approach can be subdivided into 'liberal' and 'authoritarian' approaches. The former focuses on adherence to an abstract 'rule of law' norm. In its purest form, emergency law is measured against this norm and any deviations are considered 'justified', if at all, only to the extent that they can be shown to be strictly required by the exigencies of the situation. In a more developed form of this approach, there will be an attempt to tie the analytical framework not only to 'rule of law' traditions, but also to obligations created by international conventions and treaties,[6] and to human rights theory generally,[7] or a critique may be combined with demands for broader legal reforms designed to eliminate factors which may have contributed to resort to violence.[8] In the authoritarian variant of this approach, attention will be

---

[6] G. Hogan and C. Walker, *Political Violence and the Law in Ireland* (Manchester, 1989), 6–7, suggest four 'pragmatic principles' to be adduced 'in order to maintain traditions as far as possible and also, when derogations are unavoidable, to mark them out as extraordinary and so avert any contamination of "normal laws"'. See also C. Walker, *The Prevention of Terrorism in British Law* (Manchester, 1986), 7–9. D. Bonner, *Emergency Powers in Peacetime* (London, 1985), 21–2, suggests six 'governing principles' in relation to resort to emergency powers. For another example of the application of this approach see C. Scorer, S. Spencer, and P. Hewitt, *The New Prevention of Terrorism Act: The Case for Repeal* (London, 1985).

[7] A developed 'human rights' approach to the South African experience of emergency law can be found in A. S. Mathews, *Freedom, State Security and the Rule of Law: Dilemmas of the Apartheid Society* (Cape Town, 1986). Although South Africa could scarcely be considered a liberal–democratic state, much of Mathews's reasoning could be applied to states which are, in form at least, liberal–democratic.

[8] See e.g. K. Boyle, T. Hadden, and P. Hillyard, *Ten Years On in Northern Ireland* (London, 1980).

focused on the nature of the 'threat', and much time may be taken up with issues such as a typology of terrorism,[9] and the development of counter-insurgency strategies.[10]

While the developed 'liberal' version of this framework succeeds well in establishing prescriptive norms for the assessment of present legislation, and generating proposals for future reform, it is less useful in providing a tool for the analysis of events in the past. Merely answering the question of whether the rule of law was adhered to in the past cannot in itself provide an answer to the really important issue as to what any lack of adherence might signify. In any case, the 'response of the liberal–democratic state' approach necessarily involves a set of presuppositions about the nature of the state, which, in the Irish situation, it might be inappropriate to make. Indeed, it may be precisely in the fact that these presuppositions are inappropriate that the significance of deviations lies.

In order to transcend the limitations of the 'response of the liberal–democratic state' model, a third approach has been developed, in which the emphasis is on relating developments in emergency law to developments in the wider political and legal arenas, and in which the presuppositions implicit in the second approach may be absent. In reality, this is a set of approaches rather than one analytical device. The wider arena may be defined by one of many points of reference—among them can be counted the class dynamics of a particular era,[11] or a generalized shift in the state from consensual to coercive forms of power.[12] In the main, these approaches have been favoured by non-lawyers, with the result that detailed questions of legal structure and form have tended to be ignored as merely 'technical'.

THE STRUCTURE OF THIS WORK

This work will attempt to draw from all three approaches, but in such a way that the analysis relates developments in emergency law to the eventual outcome of the conflict(s). The main advantage in working with historical material is precisely that, unlike the position in relation to current material, this 'outcomes analysis' is possible.

---

[9] See e.g. P. Wilkinson, *Terrorism and the Liberal State* (London, 1986).

[10] For military analyses along these lines, see e.g. R. Evelegh, *Peace-Keeping in a Democratic Society: The Lessons of Northern Ireland* (London, 1978), and F. Kitson, *Low Intensity Operations: Subversion, Insurgency, Peace-Keeping* (London, 1971). More generally, see R. Clutterbuck, *Guerrillas and Terrorists* (Chicago and London, 1977), and id. (ed.), *The Future of Political Violence: Destabilization, Disorder and Terrorism* (London, 1986).

[11] See e.g. M. Farrell, *The Apparatus of Repression* (Derry, 1986).

[12] See W. Rolston and M. Tomlinson, 'Spectators at the "Carnival of Reaction"? Analysing Political Crime in Ireland', in M. Kelly, L. O'Dowd, and J. Wickham (eds.), *Power, Conflict and Inequality* (Dublin, 1982).

In the three jurisdictions covered (pre-partition Ireland 1918–21, the Irish Free State 1922–5, and Northern Ireland 1921–5), the context is taken to be ultimately reducible to a conflict about the legitimacy of the state. In part I of each chapter, the circumstances of this conflict are described, and the broad sweep of the emergency legal response is outlined. This work is concerned only with measures relevant to the conflicts under discussion, and not with legislation, such as the Emergency Powers Act 1920,[13] designed to cope with other types of emergencies.

In part II of each chapter, three 'core' areas of emergency law—arrest and detention, special courts, and internment—are analysed in detail. A broad interpretation is given to what constitutes a provision in relation to 'special courts', so that not only statutory provisions allowing for alteration of jury trial are covered, but also non-statutory martial law military tribunals. Attention is focused not only on the strict legal provisions in this area but also on how powers in this area were used, since Draconian powers may sometimes be applied leniently, and apparently innocuous powers may be applied in a harsh manner. These issues are of particular importance in the sphere of emergency powers, since such powers are generally widely drafted, and their concrete effect may depend as much on administrative direction (or lack of it) as on positive law. The degree of departure of emergency powers from ordinary powers in these areas is noted, and the question of effectiveness is examined, but these issues are raised not in order to mount a 'rule of law' critique *per se*, or to suggest that effectiveness is of itself a valid yardstick, but rather to relate such assessments to the overall conflict of legitimacy.

Part III of each chapter is concerned with the question of judicial scrutiny of emergency powers, and examines the case law and constitutional provisions in this area in detail. This concentration is justified because the courts provided the only real forum in which legal issues arising from the use of emergency powers in the particular political context could be raised. For the most part, the cases were concerned with the operations of one or other of the three core areas of emergency powers, thus dovetailing neatly with part II. Again, an understanding of the stance of the judiciary is vital to an assessment of the relationship that adherence to the ideology of the rule of law, or the rejection thereof, bore to the overall conflict.

Finally, in Chapter 5, a typology of the emergency powers in use in the various jurisdictions is suggested, and the analysis is related to the nature of the conflict in the each jurisdiction. Overall comparisons are drawn, and an attempt is made to isolate some salient features of emergency powers.

[13] For a discussion of the Act see G. S. Morris, 'The Emergency Powers Act 1920', 1979 *Public Law*, 317, and D. Bonner, *Emergency Powers*, 211–71.

2. *Ireland 1918–1921*

PART I. LEGAL DEVELOPMENTS
IN CONTEXT

The background

Developments in the years 1918–25 can be set against a background of centuries of emergency law in Ireland.[1] The eighteenth and nineteenth centuries provide a great many examples of Irish 'coercion' Acts,[2] for the impact of the 'Irish question' was felt in many spheres of British law.[3] Most of these Acts were temporary, but eventually, in the Criminal Law and Procedure (Ireland) Act 1887, special powers that might be invoked by proclamation were placed permanently on the statute book.[4]

By 1912, it appeared that a resolution of the 'question' was at hand. A bill introduced in that year provided for a limited form of home rule for all of Ireland. Previously, similar measures had been rejected by the House of Lords, but as the power of veto of the Upper House had been effectively abolished by the Parliament Act 1911, this measure was considered to have every chance of success. The bill was broadly welcomed in nationalist Ireland, though its provisions fell far short of the demands for an Irish Republic made by the small underground Irish Republican Brotherhood (IRB) which dated back to Fenian times.[5]

In Unionist, particularly Ulster Unionist, circles the reaction to the bill was quite different, resulting in the formation in January 1913 of the paramilitary Ulster Volunteer Force (UVF) out of the various loyalist volunteer groups that had sprung up in the previous year in opposition to home rule. An establishment of 100,000 was aimed at, to be organized along British Army lines into divisions, regiments, battalions, companies, and sections. In addition, a number of 'special service' units were created.

---

[1] For historical background this part draws on F. S. L. Lyons, *Ireland since the Famine* (London, 1985), 381–468; C. Townshend, *The British Campaign in Ireland 1919–1921* (Oxford, 1975) (hereafter Townshend); R. Kee, *Ourselves Alone* (London, 1982); and J. Bowyer Bell, *The Secret Army: The IRA 1916–1979* (Dublin, 1979), 16–28.

[2] Many of these Acts are listed in Hogan and Walker, *Political Violence and the Law*, 12–14. Lists of coercion Acts since 1870 can be found in E. Mulloy, *Dynasties of Coercion* (Derry, 1986), 25–6, and Farrell, *Apparatus of Repression*, 30–1. Some of the 18th-cent. legislation is noted on pp. 127–8.

[3] See, generally, P. O'Higgins, 'English Law and the Irish Question', 1 *Ir. Jur.* 59.

[4] This Act is examined in more detail below.

[5] The Fenians were an underground movement dedicated to the establishment of an Irish Republic. In 1867 they staged an unsuccessful revolt. For a brief account of the movement, see C. Townshend, *Political Violence in Ireland* (Oxford, 1983), 24–38.

Plans were also afoot for the creation of a 'Provisional Government of Ulster' to be supported by a loyalist declaration of martial law.[6] Eventually, the British Government decided to take action against the Ulster loyalists, only to be faced with an incident that has become known as 'the Curragh Mutiny', when eighty-five Army officers offered their resignation rather than participate in the move.

The lessons of force had not been lost on the nationalists. Their response was the creation in November 1913 of the Irish Volunteers.[7] Within that movement the IRB began to expand its influence. It was against this background, and with the European war looming large on the horizon, that the eventual compromise over the Government of Ireland Bill was reached. The measure became law,[8] though it was not to be implemented until after the war,[9] and then not before amending legislation to deal with the special position of the North-East could be considered.

DORA and the 1916 Rising

The outbreak and continuation of the First World War led to the enactment of a mass of emergency legislation, much of it operative throughout Britain and Ireland.[10] For the purposes of this study, the most important enactments were the Defence of the Realm Acts (DORA).[11] Under the Defence of the Realm Act 1914, the British Government ('His Majesty in Council'[12]) was empowered 'during the continuance of the present war to issue regulations as to the powers and duties of the Army Council, and of the members of His Majesty's forces, and other persons acting on His behalf, for securing the public safety and the defence of the realm'.[13] It was specifically provided that trial by court martial could be authorized for alleged breaches of regulations designed to deal with two defined

---

[6] For a discussion of the formation and organization of the UVF and, more generally, of loyalist manœuvrings in this period see A. T. Q. Stewart, *The Ulster Crisis* (London, 1969).

[7] Its organization and development is considered below.

[8] As the Government of Ireland Act 1914.

[9] s. 1 (1) of the Suspensory Act 1914 suspended the operation of the Government of Ireland Act 1914 until the expiration of 12 months from the date of the passing of the Act, or if at the expiration of those 12 months the war had not ended, until such later date (not being later than the end of the war) as might be fixed by Order in Council.

[10] Among this legislation can be counted the Courts (Emergency Powers) Act 1914, the Special Constables Act 1914, the Local Authorities (Disqualification Relief) Act 1914, the Patents Designs and Trade Marks (Temporary Rules) Act 1914, the Execution of Trusts (War Facilities) Act 1914, the Execution of Trusts (War Facilities) (Amendment) Act 1915, the Special Acts (Extension of Time) Act 1915, the Evidence (Amendment) Act 1915, the Courts (Emergency Powers) (Amendment) Act 1916, the Summer Time Act 1916, the Courts (Emergency Powers) Act 1917, and the Local Government (Allotments and Land Cultivation) (Ireland) Act 1917.

[11] For an account of the circumstances surrounding the introduction of DORA see H. M. Bowman, 'Martial Law and the English Constitution', 15 *Michigan Law Review* 93.

[12] s. 1.

[13] s. 1.

sets of circumstances. These were: 'regulations designed—(*a*) to prevent persons communicating with the enemy or obtaining information for that purpose or any purpose calculated to jeopardize the success of the operations of any of his Majesty's forces or to assist the enemy; or (*b*) to secure the safety of any means of communication, or of railways docks or harbours.'

Later, in August 1914, amending legislation extended the powers of courts martial to try breaches of the regulations,[14] and in November 1914 the Acts were consolidated and expanded in the Defence of the Realm Consolidation Act 1914. The principal changes were threefold. First, as some doubt had arisen about the point, the formula of the regulation-making power was altered so that it was made clear that power was conferred on the Government to make regulations for the public safety and the defence of the realm, independently of regulations as to the powers of the military and naval authorities.[15] Secondly, the scope of offences triable by court martial was again enlarged,[16] and thirdly, the death penalty was introduced following trial by court martial where it was proved 'that the offence is committed with the intention of assisting the enemy'.[17]

Early in 1915 there was a reappraisal of the necessity for the power to try breaches by court martial, and this review led to the enactment of the Defence of the Realm (Amendment) Act 1915. Under section 1 of the new Act, the right of British citizens to trial by jury for alleged breaches of any of the regulations was restored (other than in respect of offences tried by a court of summary jurisdiction),[18] but provision was made for the suspension of this right by proclamation 'in the event of invasion or other special military emergency arising out of the present war'.[19] Although there was some subsequent amending legislation,[20] it was the combined effect of the Defence of the Realm Consolidation Act 1914 and the Defence of the Realm (Amendment) Act 1915 which created the framework retained by DORA for the remainder of the legislation's existence.

During the war years, the regulation-making power was used to create a vast maze of Defence of the Realm Regulations (DORR), and it

---

[14] Defence of the Realm (No. 2) Act 1914, s. 1. Principally, the scope was expanded to include regulations designed 'to prevent the spread of reports likely to cause disaffection or alarm'.

[15] See Bowman, 'Martial Law', 100.

[16] s. 1 (1).

[17] s. 1 (4).

[18] s. 1 (2).

[19] s. 1 (7).

[20] Defence of the Realm (Amendment) (No. 2) Act 1915, Defence of the Realm (Amendment) (No. 3) Act 1915.

was held that any alteration to the law made by the Regulations was equivalent to an alteration made by Act of Parliament.[21] These Regulations covered everything from food rationing to a system of internal exile.[22] Under DORR, the central figures in the administration of the Regulations were those Army (or Air Force) officers, of the rank of Field Officer or above, designated by the Army Council to be Competent Military Authorities (CMAs).[23] It appears that during the war approximately sixty-three CMAs were appointed in the UK, one of whom came from the intelligence services (M.I.5).[24]

The CMA could, if authorized by the Army Council, delegate either unconditionally or subject to such condition as he thought fit, all or any of his powers under DORR to any officer who was himself qualified to be appointed a CMA. If he did so, the delegatee was also referred to as a Competent Military Authority. It was often the practice (in Ireland at least) for an officer to be appointed a CMA for the purposes of one regulation but not for another, or for his jurisdiction in relation to the exercise of powers under a specific regulation to be limited to a certain category of cases.[25]

The breadth of these provisions meant that, particularly before the enactment of the Defence of the Realm (Amendment) Act 1915, the British Army had very extensive powers over the civilian population. As Hood Phillips has remarked, 'the United Kingdom was, in effect, placed under military law'.[26] However, although the CMA formally held these powers, in practice it appears that their exercise was subject to political control.[27]

At the outbreak of the war, the leadership of both the Ulster Volunteers and the Irish Volunteers had vouched their support for the British war effort, primarily, it would appear, in order to strengthen their respec-

---

[21] *Ernest* v. *Commissioner of Metropolitan Police* [1919] 35 *TLR* 512, per Darling J. In that case DORR 14H was upheld notwithstanding the conflict of its provisions with s. 3 of the British Nationality and Status of Aliens Act 1914.

[22] A set of the regulations revised to 31 Aug. 1918 can be found in C. Cook (ed.), *Defence of the Realm Manual* (sixth edn.). This was followed by a seventh edition in 1919 and an eighth edition covering the Regulations up to 30 Sept. 1919. The text of most of the regulations relied upon in the Irish conflict can be found in App. 3.

[23] DORR 62 (see App. 3). Competent Naval Authorities could also be appointed by the Admiralty, but for present purposes discussion will be limited to the role of the Competent Military Authorities. This latter title had a different meaning under DORR from that given to it by the Army Act. Under that Act, it meant the Army Council (s. 101) and certain high military authorities (s. 87). See *Defence of the Realm Manual*, eighth edn., 183 n. (c).

[24] These are the figures quoted by Maj.-Gen. Solly-Flood, the Military Adviser to the Government of Northern Ireland. Solly-Flood to the Minister of Home Affairs, 13 June 1922, HA 4/1/23, PRONI.

[25] Examples of this type of delegation are given on pp. 66–8.

[26] *Hood Phillips' Constitutional and Administrative Law* (London, 1987), 363.

[27] See pp. 41–2.

tive hands at the post-war bargaining table. The Irish Volunteers, however, split on the issue, with a heavily IRB-influenced minority supporting a non-participationist line. The leadership of this group began to plan an insurrection which would exploit Britain's wartime difficulties, and at Easter 1916 its Volunteers, together with those of the smaller Left-orientated Irish Citizen Army, occupied the centre of Dublin and announced the formation of a Provisional Government of the Irish Republic. The immediate British legal response was to issue two proclamations. One announced the imposition of martial law,[28] the other, under section 1 of the Defence of the Realm (Amendment) Act 1915, suspended the right to jury trial for breaches of the regulations, and thus re-created in Ireland an extensive court-martial jurisdiction.

Initially, the rebellion attracted little public support. It was swiftly crushed and its leaders tried and sentenced to death by DORA courts martial. But as the executions (fifteen in all) dragged on, public opinion became increasingly sympathetic towards the insurgents' cause. Some 1,800 prisoners had been interned in Wales after the Rising, and when in December 1916 the last were released and returned to Ireland, it was to a reception very different from that which had greeted them earlier in the year. Politicized during their detention, they spent the following year in organizational reconstruction, setting the stage for the coming conflict.

Low-level agitation continued, and the proclamation which had been issued under section 1 of the 1915 Act was not revoked. Indeed, the trend was in the opposite direction, as a collection of regulations was created which was to be in force only in an area in which section 1 was suspended. Thus the position in Ireland at the start of 1918 was that, apart from those DORRs which in any case made special provision for Ireland,[29] another group of regulations was in force, or was in force in an

---

[28] The theoretical and constitutional basis of martial law is considered in detail at pp. 123–33.

[29] As the regulations stood at 31 Aug. 1918, some simply made special provision for Ireland but their provisions applied in Britain also. Others were in force in Ireland only. Many were without political significance, concerned e.g. with agricultural issues (DORR 2L, 2M, 2O, 2P, 2R, 2T). Others related to arrangements between the Food Controller and the Local Government Board for Ireland as to the exercise of the Controller's functions (DORR 2J, 2JJ); the selection by the Lord Chief Justice of Ireland of a High Court judge to arbitrate as to the price of requisitioned output of factories (DORR 7); the charge for carrying merchandise between Great Britain and Ireland (DORR 7BB); the distribution by local authorities of venereal disease remedies (DORR 40BB); and the power of the Lord-Lieutenant in Ireland (and the Secretary of State in England) to order the early closing of business premises (DORR 10B). But others were clearly political: DORR 9E permitted drilling to be banned but was implemented in Ireland only; DORR 14E granted a power to prohibit aliens or British subjects coming to the UK after 1 Mar. 1916 from going to Ireland; DORR 27A related to prohibition on reports of the proceedings of the Irish Convention; DORR 31 imposed prohibition on the import of firearms into Ireland; and DORR 56 required the consent of the AG for Ireland for certain prosecutions.

amended form, in that country only, by virtue of the suspension of section 1.[30] A constant irritant in the life of the country, these regulations ensured (if there were any doubt about the matter) that the legacy of the preceding years would not simply fade away.

In the years 1918–21 these regulations were further developed, increasingly harshly applied, and ultimately superseded. The story is broadly one of the failure of successive strategies in the face of determined Republican insurgency. While various divisions of this period have been suggested, legal developments can be outlined in four stages. The first, from January 1918 to December 1919, saw the implementation of existing emergency statutory powers against a background of the establishment of the revolutionary Dáil and the emergence of a guerrilla campaign by the Irish Volunteers. The second, from January to July 1920, was one of considerable legal flux amid changes in tactics by the Volunteers (IRA) and a shift in the interrelationship within the Crown Forces towards Army primacy. The third, from August to November 1920, was marked by an increase in the statutory powers of the British Army in the form of the Restoration of Order in Ireland Act 1920, and the development of new and highly effective tactics by the IRA. The fourth, from December 1920 to July 1921, saw a further expansion in the British Army's powers, signalled by the proclamation of martial law in the Southern counties against a background of steadily increasing violence leading up to the truce of July 1921.

January 1918 to December 1919: the emerging conflict

By 1918 nationalist opinion was moving firmly away from parliamentary agitation for home rule towards the Republican demand for independence from Britain. The decline of the parliamentary Nationalists, preceded by the failure of the Irish Convention in 1917–18,[31] and signalled by by-election setbacks, was matched by the growth of the radical nationalist party, Sinn Féin, then undergoing extensive reorganization. Paralleling this growth was that of the Irish Volunteers, whose development was given a major boost in 1918 by the 'conscription crisis'. The British Army's shortage of manpower early in 1918 had led the British Government to introduce a measure permitting conscription in Ireland. In May,

---

[30] On 31 Aug. 1918 these were DORR 14B (special provisions in relation to internment), DORR 9A (prohibition on meetings), DORR 9AA (prohibition on wearing of uniforms, holding of assemblies, etc.), DORR 42AA (encouraging and aiding deserters), DORR 58A (trial by court martial), and DORR 58D (persons subject to military law to be subject to court martial for any offence).

[31] The Irish Convention represented a failed attempt to reach agreement between the political parties in Ireland as to the future of the country. Boycotted by Sinn Féin, it first met in July 1917 and ceased in the spring of the following year.

in anticipation of strong opposition, almost the entire leadership of Sinn Féin and the Irish Volunteers was arrested and interned on the pretext of what has become known as the 'German plot'. The conscription crisis soon faded but many of those interned remained so until the following year. Then came the 1918 general election, which in Ireland resulted in Sinn Féin winning 73 seats (many of them uncontested), the Unionists 26, and the parliamentary Nationalists 6.

In January 1919 the newly elected Sinn Féin representatives then at liberty met in Dublin and constituted their assembly as the first Dáil of the Irish Republic.[32] They then set about constructing an alternative system of government including a court system.[33] Three representatives were appointed to present Ireland's case for self-determination at the Peace Conference at Versailles, at which the map of Europe was being redrawn.[34] Although the effort to obtain a hearing proved unsuccessful, the move did have an effect on public opinion in the United States.[35]

On the day the Dáil met, and apparently coincidentally, an incident occurred which is generally taken to have been the start of the Anglo-Irish conflict. Irish Volunteers in Tipperary shot dead two policemen in an ambush designed to obtain explosives. For the remainder of the year the activities of the Volunteers, increasingly known as the Irish Republican Army (IRA), were directed principally at capturing arms, a commodity always in short supply. In the period from May to December 1919, however, eighteen policemen were killed and a number of outlying barracks evacuated. Although the Dáil in its 'Message to the Free Nations of the World' had referred to 'the existing state of war, between Ireland and England',[36] its relations with the Volunteers were for a long time problematic.

The organization which the IRA had adopted followed the lines of the British Army. The basic unit was the company; between four and seven of these formed a battalion, and three to six battalions formed a brigade. Above the brigades was a General Headquarters (GHQ) with overall responsibility. The vast majority of volunteers were initially only part-timers. While the full strength of the IRA in the 1919–21 period has been

---

[32] For a discussion of some legal aspects of the Dáil's operation see B. Farrell, 'A Note on the Dáil Constitution, 1919', 4 *Ir. Jur.* 127, and id., 'The Legislation of a "Revolutionary" Assembly: Dáil Decrees, 1919–1922', 10 *Ir. Jur.* 122.

[33] On the question of these Dáil courts, or Sinn Féin courts, see J. P. Casey, 'The Genesis of the Dail Courts', 9 *Ir. Jur.* 326; id., 'Republican Courts in Ireland, 1919–1922', 5 *Ir. Jur.* 321; and Davitt, 'The Civil Jurisdiction of the Courts of Justice of the Irish Republic 1920–22', 3 *Ir. Jur.* 112.

[34] See 'Letter to Clemenceau 1919', in D. Macardle, *The Irish Republic* (London, 1937), 963.

[35] The House of Representatives passed a motion calling for the Irish claim to self-determination to be considered favourably by the Peace Conference.

[36] 'Message to the Free Nations of the World', in Macardle, *Irish Republic*, 958–9.

variously estimated at between 4,500 and 15,000 (though some would put it much higher[37]), its active membership at any time seems to have been between 3,000 and 5,000.

Ranged against them were the two police forces then in Ireland, the armed Royal Irish Constabulary (RIC), which numbered between 9,500 and 9,700 in 1919, and the largely unarmed Dublin Metropolitan Police (DMP) which operated only in Dublin, and which in 1920 numbered approximately 1,100. British Army strength in Ireland in November 1919 stood at 37,259, but in that year its role in the conflict was not a central one.

In 1918 the growth of nationalist agitation had met with a response significantly harsher than what Lyons has characterized as the 'pin pricking coercion'[38] of the previous year. Four key regulations, or sets of regulations, under DORA provided the legal basis for the implementation of this policy. The first was DORR 9AA, a particularly broad regulation that had first been introduced in 1917 and which was strengthened four times in 1918. This Regulation enabled the CMA to impose restrictions on meetings, on the wearing of uniforms, and on the keeping of firearms and motor cycles (and later motor cars and bicycles). It also created ancillary powers of search and seizure.[39] The second was DORR 14B which authorized internment without trial, and which was likewise extended in its application in Ireland by amendment in 1918.[40] The third was the set of regulations governing trial by court martial.[41] Finally there was DORR 29B, which was also extended in 1918. This authorized the creation of 'Special Military Areas' (SMAs), which could be sealed off and searched by the military.[42]

In 1918 the number of courts martial increased, and new restrictions relating to the carrying of firearms, explosives, and ammunition were introduced in February,[43] with additional restrictions being applied later

---

[37] F. O'Donoghue, *No Other Law* (Dublin, 1986), 334, gives the paper strength of the IRA at the time of the truce as 112,650.

[38] *Ireland since the Famine*, 387.

[39] DORR 9AA was to be in force only in an area in which the operation of s. 1 of the Defence of the Realm (Amendment) Act 1915 was suspended. The text of the regulation is included in App. 3.

[40] See pp. 101–2.

[41] The operation of courts martial is considered in detail on pp. 59–85.

[42] SMAs could be created by the Admiralty or Army Council with the concurrence of the Chief Secretary.

[43] Under DORR 9AA. *DG* 22 Feb. 1918. The order prohibited the carrying of firearms, military arms, ammunition, and explosive substances generally, the only exceptions being possession by the Crown Forces, possession of shotguns by persons who were licensed to kill game, or who occupied land and used shotguns to scare birds, or possession by holders of permits from a County Inspector of the RIC or a Superintendent of the DMP. An order of the CMA made on 17 July 1916 was cancelled.

in certain areas.[44] In September tighter restrictions were introduced throughout the whole country.[45] The following month saw the introduction of a requirement that permits be obtained from the CMA or the Chief Officer of Police for the possession of motor cyles.[46] In July a blanket prohibition on unauthorized meetings, assemblies, and processions had been introduced.[47] July had also seen a ban on movement between Britain and Ireland other than by authorized routes.[48] In March, County Clare had been declared to be an SMA.[49] This was followed in June by parts of County Kerry,[50] and in September by West Cork.[51]

The other measure enforced as part of this policy was the Criminal Law and Procedure (Ireland) Act 1887 ('the 1887 Act'), a provision originally introduced in response to the land agitation of the late nineteenth century.[52] The Act incorporated a mechanism whereby all or any of its principal provisions could be brought into force by the Lord-Lieutenant in any area or areas. Such areas were then referred to as 'proclaimed districts'.[53] Special courts of summary jurisdiction under this Act had been introduced in the previous year.[54] In June the special

---

[44] In Co. Clare, Galway, Tipperary on 21 Feb. 1918 (*DG* 22 Feb.), and in Co. Cork, Kerry, Limerick, Mayo, Sligo, Roscommon, Kilkenny, Longford, Dublin, Louth, and Wexford, and the cities of Cork and Limerick on 22 Apr. 1918 (*DG* 23 Apr.). In these areas, possession was prohibited other than by members of the Crown Forces or person authorized in writing by a County Inspector of the RIC.

[45] *DG* 4 Oct. 1918. Under this order, the carrying, having, or keeping of firearms, military arms, ammunition, and explosive substances was prohibited unless 'such articles were under effective military control'. Exceptions were made in the case of members of the Crown Forces, and of persons to whom the CMA or any person authorized by him had given permission in writing.

[46] Under DORR 9AA. *DG* 15 Oct. 1918.

[47] Under DORR 9AA. *DG* 9 July 1918. The order was not to apply to 'any Meeting, Assembly or Procession authorized in writing by the Chief Commissioner DM [Dublin Metropolitan] Police, or any County Inspector, RIC, to whom seven clear days' notice of the intention to hold any such Meeting, Assembly, or Procession shall have been given'.

[48] Under DORR 14G. *DG* 2 Aug. 1918. Fifteen routes were authorized.

[49] *DG* 8 Mar. 1918.

[50] *DG* 5 July 1918. The restrictions applied to the town of Tralee. Two days later certain bars were closed. The restrictions were lifted on 23 Aug. 1918.

[51] *DG* 11 Oct. 1918.

[52] For historical accounts of this Act see L. P. Curtis, *Coercion and Conciliation in Ireland 1880–1892* (Princeton, 1963), 179–210, and Townshend, *Political Violence*, 209–15. For legal analyses see G. T. B. Vanston, *The Criminal Law and Procedure (Ireland) Act 1887* (Dublin, 1887); H. Humphreys, *The Criminal Law and Procedure (Ireland) Act 1887* (Dublin, 1887); and F. M. Feely, *The Criminal Law and Procedure (Ireland) Act 1887* (Dublin, 1888).

[53] s. 5.

[54] i.e., in 1917; see Townshend, 4. Under s. 2, persons who were alleged to have committed certain offences, which could be described as 'boycotting offences', in a proclaimed district, might be tried as provided in the Act, as might persons who were alleged to have taken part in any riot or unlawful assembly anywhere in Ireland. Summary procedure was to be governed by the Petty Sessions (Ireland) Act 1851, save that the proceedings for enforcing the appearance of the person charged and the attendance of witnesses for the

provisions of the Act relating to removal for trial on indictment and the use of special juries were introduced in fourteen counties and two cities.[55] In July the Irish Volunteers and its women's section Cummann na mBan, Sinn Féin, the Sinn Féin Clubs, and the Gaelic League were proclaimed to be 'dangerous associations' under the terms of the Act.[56] This was the first stage whereby these organizations might be prohibited and suppressed in part or all of Ireland.[57]

The response of the Irish Executive (entrusted with the day-to-day running of the country by the British Government) in 1919 was largely a continuation of the policy of the previous year. Courts martial proceeded, Westport, County Mayo was declared an SMA in April,[58] further prohibitions were imposed on unauthorized meetings, assemblies, fairs, markets, and processions in parts of Ireland in September,[59] and arrests continued. In November a requirement that a permit be obtained was imposed in respect of both motor cars and motor cyles.[60] During the course of the year, the process of development and adaptation of regulations which were to be in force only in Ireland continued.[61]

Under the 1887 Act, those associations which had previously been declared dangerous were progressively prohibited and suppressed in various parts of the country and throughout in November.[62] Dáil Eireann had been prohibited and suppressed in September on the grounds that it was 'formed and first employed' for the purposes of those associations which had previously been declared dangerous.[63] The special inquisitorial

prosecution were to be the same as if the offence were an indictable one (s. 11 (4)); evidence was to be taken as depositions (s. 11 (5)); and outside Dublin the court was to consist of two RMs, one of whom was to be a person 'of the sufficiency of whose legal knowledge' the Lord-Lieutenant was to be satisfied (s. 11 (6)). Between 11 July 1916 and 8 Apr. 1919, a total of 13 RMs were thus certified. That appointments began in 1916 might suggest that the courts were introduced in that year. In *R (Ryan and Another)* v. *Starkie and Another* (54 *ILTR* 15) (24 Nov. 1919) it was held that where a defendant had been convicted of unlawful assembly by a CSJ established under the Act, it was sufficient for the charge to state the place and date of the offence without stating the facts alleged to constitute the unlawful assembly.

[55] These provisions are considered on pp. 55–8.

[56] *DG* 2 July 1918. Under s. 6.

[57] s. 7.

[58] *DG* 11 Apr. 1919.

[59] This order, which applied in Co. Tipperary and areas of Co. Galway, included 'Fairs and Markets' in the list of other gatherings which required the authorization of the RIC. It was stated to be in response to the shooting of two RIC men, one of whom was killed. *DG* 19 Sept. 1919.

[60] Under DORR 9AA. The permit was to be issued by the CMA or the Chief Officer of Police in the district in which the applicant resided. *DG* 7 Nov. 1919.

[61] e.g. DORR 13, introduced 9 Oct. 1919, which authorized the imposition of a curfew. The text of the regulation is included in app. 3. Some other adaptations are noted on pp. 41–6.

[62] See Table 4.

[63] Second supplement to *DG* 9 Sept. 1919.

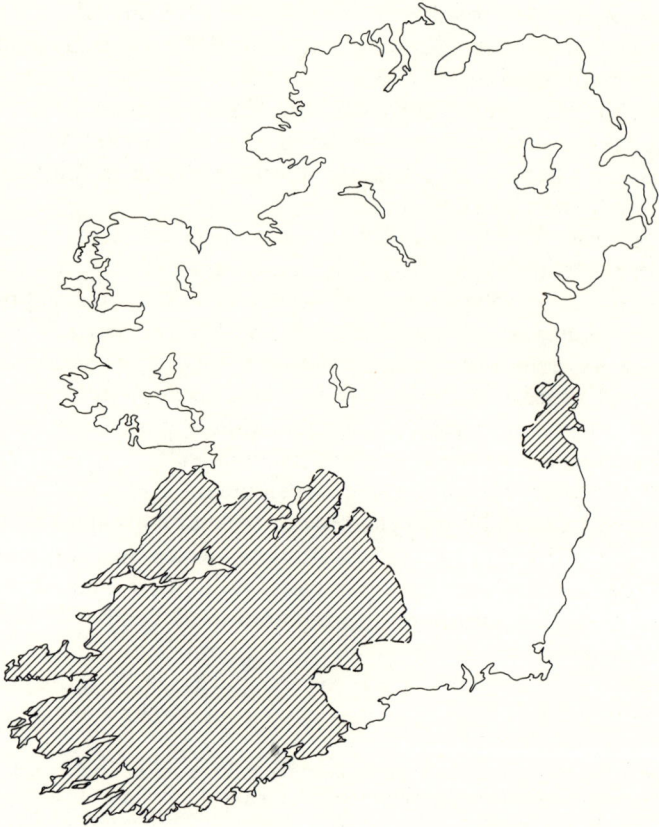

MAP A. Areas in which special inquisitorial procedures were in force, 1918–1919

Note: Proclaimed districts under s. 1 of the Criminal Law and Procedure (Ireland) Act 1887
Source: Prepared From Supplement to *DG* 10 Sept. 1919.

procedures under the Act were brought into force in a number of counties[64] (Map A), and in July and September the provisions allowing removal for trial and special juries were further implemented (Map B). This, however, marked the limit of the implementation of the Act.

[64] Under s. 1, where sworn information was made that any felony, misdemeanour, or offence under the Act had been committed in a proclaimed district, the AG could authorize an RM (of whose legal knowledge and legal experience the Lord Chancellor was to be satisfied) to summon and examine on oath any person 'whom he has reason to believe to be capable of giving material evidence concerning such offence'. See Feely, 23–9; Vanston, 5–13; Humphreys, 13–17. As Humphreys observed (p. 16), 'the holding of such inquiries . . . is a serious departure from constitutional usage', though there were precedents in Ireland, e.g. s. 22 of 'Whiteboy Act' 1775. The provisions were not much used. Quarterly returns for the period ending 31 Mar. 1920 show a total of three inquiries in two centres (Coachford, Co. Cork and the city of Dublin). In all, 32 witnesses were examined, and the result of the inquiry is marked 'pending' in each case. *DG* 20 Apr. 1920.

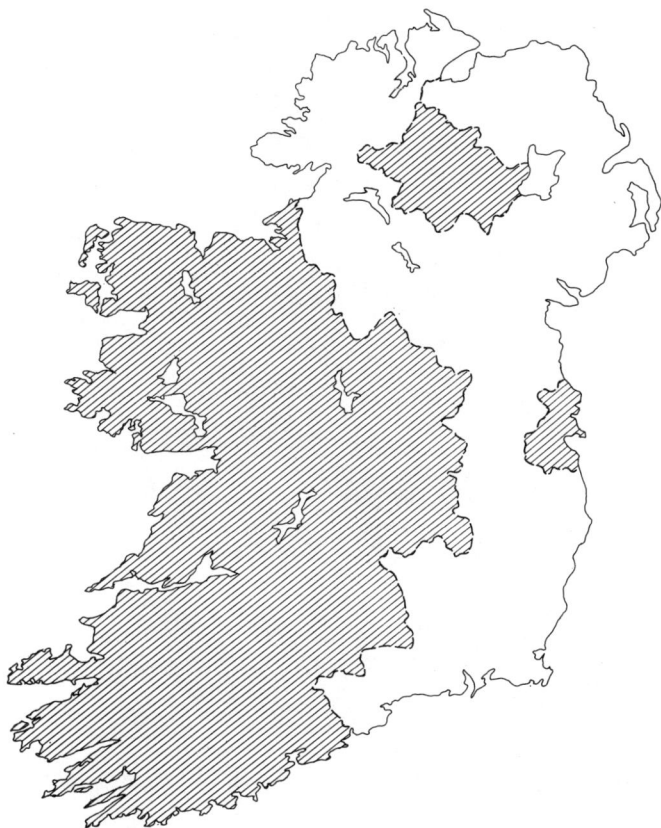

MAP B. Areas in which special juries and removal for trial operated, 1918–1919

Note: Proclaimed Districts under ss. 3 and 4 of the Criminal Law and Procedure (Ireland) Act 1887

Source: Prepared From 2nd Supplement to *DG* 14 June 1918 and *DG* 24 Oct. 1919.

January 1920 to July 1920: army primacy and police violence

The opening months of 1920 saw a change in tactics and a steady growth in IRA activities, particularly in the South, but also, as the year progressed, around Dublin and in the West (Map C). Attention was turned to attacks on outlying police stations and to individual assassinations.[65] With its very limited material resources, the IRA campaign was not geared towards the achievement of a military victory in the conventional sense. The organization's strategy was rather to increase the level of guerrilla activity to such an extent that the political, military, and financial

[65] British statistics in relation to the numbers of court-houses destroyed, persons killed, etc. can be found in Townshend, app. 5, p. 214.

MAP C. Counties in which the IRA claimed four or more operations in July 1920

Source: Derived from *An tOglach* 'War Map', in Townshend, 70.

costs of the response would be judged too heavy by the British Government. In parallel with the military campaign, political activity by Sinn Féin was designed to secure popular acceptance of the reality of the fledgeling Republic. The Volunteers now saw themselves as fighting a 'people's war',[66] a war which was justified because 'without Dáil Eireann there would, most likely, have been no sustained fight, with moral force behind it'.[67] The British characterization of events was predictably different—the issue was to crush the 'conspiracy'[68] which, in the Chief

---

[66] E. O'Malley, *Raids and Rallies* (Dublin, 1982), 1.
[67] T. Barry, *Guerrilla Days in Ireland* (Dublin, 1949), 11.
[68] A phrase used by Lloyd George at a Cabinet conference with the Irish Executive on 31 May 1920. T. Jones, *Whitehall Diary*, iii. *Ireland 1918–1925*, ed. K. Middlemas (London, 1971), 21.

Secretary's opinion, had the majority of the community 'terrorised'.[69]

The early months of 1920 also saw major shifts in British counter-insurgency strategy. There were three main strands to the new approach. On the political level, a new Government of Ireland Bill was introduced which provided for two Home Rule Parliaments in a partitioned Ireland, though few saw the measure as a final settlement. On the organizational level, there was a build-up of new paramilitary police units, and on the operational level, political approval was now forthcoming for the exercise by the CMA of his formal powers under DORA.

The police build-up came as the RIC generally was becoming increasingly militarized, and at a time when the DMP's involvement in the conflict had greatly declined as a result of continuous attacks on its intelligence ('G') division. Recruitment of ex-British Army privates to the ranks of the RIC had commenced in England towards the end of 1919. On their arrival in Ireland in March and April 1920, these men became known as the 'Black and Tans' because of their mixture of British Army and RIC uniforms. Although formally part of the RIC, the 'Tans' soon established a distinctive presence by virtue of their curious appearance and what Lyons has referred to as 'their ruthlessness and contempt for life and property'.[70] This characteristic was shared by a separate paramilitary police unit formed in July 1920, the Auxiliary Division Royal Irish Constabulary (ADRIC or 'Auxies'). This unit was composed of ex-British Army officers recruited in England, and its place in the RIC command structure was never properly defined. Over the following year, the size of the unit grew from 478 to 1,526 members. In order to accommodate this build-up in police numbers, special proclamations were issued under the 1836 Constabulary Act.[71]

The new willingness to permit the British Army to exercise its powers under DORA was complemented by moves to subordinate the police to the military effort. As one Army source put it, 'the lead in the fight . . . was henceforth to be in the hands of the military commanders instead of the police'.[72] On 9 January the acting Deputy Inspector-General RIC had issued an order that when required by the CMA, all County Inspectors were to afford police assistance in any matter in which it might be requested, and that on such occasions the police were to be under the direct orders of the military authorities.[73] GHQ issued parallel orders, the intention being that 'whenever troops and police acted together the

[69] The formulation of Hamar Greenwood, the Chief Secretary, at the conference (ibid. 17).   [70] *Ireland since the Famine*, 415.
[71] 6 & 7 William IV, c. 13. On 25 Feb. 1921 proclamations affecting the following counties were issued: Dublin, Longford, Louth, Sligo, Waterford, and Wicklow. *DG* 27 Feb. 1920.
[72] 'History of the 5th Division in Ireland, November 1919–March 1922', 20, Jeudwine papers.   [73] 'History of the 5th Division in Ireland', 20.

command of the operations devolved automatically on the military commanders of whatever rank'.[74] But despite these and other moves designed to tie in the Army and police efforts,[75] relations between the two arms remained difficult.

The British Army's appreciation was that 'Whilst the advisability of declaring Martial Law had been considered, the government decided, *before taking this extreme step*, to take fuller advantage of the powers conferred on them under the Defence of the Realm Act.'[76] The Army was not, however, placed on 'active service.'[77] Instead, as the 'Notes for Guidance of Troops when Acting in Aid of the Civil Police in Ireland'[78] which were issued in May 1920 illustrated, the British Army still saw the formal legal basis for its operations as that of acting 'in aid of the civil power', despite the effect of DORA and administrative moves towards bringing the police under military control.

The new initiative resulted in an exhaustive series of raids and arrests on military authority which began in January 1920 (Graph A). The purpose of these raids and arrests was apparently twofold. First, they were tied to a renewed reliance on selective internment.[79] Secondly, it appears to have been intended that evidence would be gathered for use in criminal proceedings. There were also other elements in the strategy: in February a curfew was imposed on Dublin, followed in July by Cork.[80]

[74] 'History of the 5th Division in Ireland', 20.

[75] On 13 Jan. the RIC issued a circular instructing County Inspectors, District Inspectors, and Head Constables to keep the CMA informed of the state of the country and to report important matters immediately to the military commander concerned. This was followed by a memo on 18 Jan. to the effect that when an 'outrage' took place, telegrams and reports were to be sent to Divisional Headquarters, to the CMA of the Infantry Brigade area concerned, and to the nearest OC Troops. Ibid. 20.

[76] Ibid. 20–1 (Army's emphasis).

[77] s. 189 (1) of the Army Act 1881 provided: 'In this Act, if not inconsistent with the context, the expression "on active service" as applied to a person subject to military law means whenever he is attached to or forms part of a force which is engaged in operations against the enemy, or is engaged in military operations in a country or place wholly or partly occupied by an enemy, or is in military occupation of any foreign country.' s. 190 (20) provided: 'The expression "enemy" includes all armed mutineers, armed rebels, armed rioters, and pirates.'

[78] Strickland papers. The Notes were mainly concerned with the question of the use of force. The following summary was included: 'Responsibility for action taken by troops must rest on the Military Commander of whatever rank he may be. Fire should only be resorted to after all other considerations for achieving the object in view have been discarded. No soldier will fire unless definitely ordered to do so by his Military Commander. Firing should be strictly limited to the number of rounds considered necessary to achieve the object. Except as described in para. 7 firing at (a) Prisoners trying to escape (b) Individuals trying to evade arrest by flight cannot be legally justified, and is therefore not permissible.' Para. 7 provided: 'It is only in the case of a grave offence, such as treason or felony and where the offender has been caught in the act, or a warrant for such offence is being executed, that he may be fired at if he attempts to escape from custody or to evade arrest. Such an extreme measure is not justified in the case of DRR offences.'

[79] Arrest and internment are considered in more detail on pp. 38–54, 101–111.

[80] Under DORR 13 which had been introduced in Oct. 1919. See app. 3.

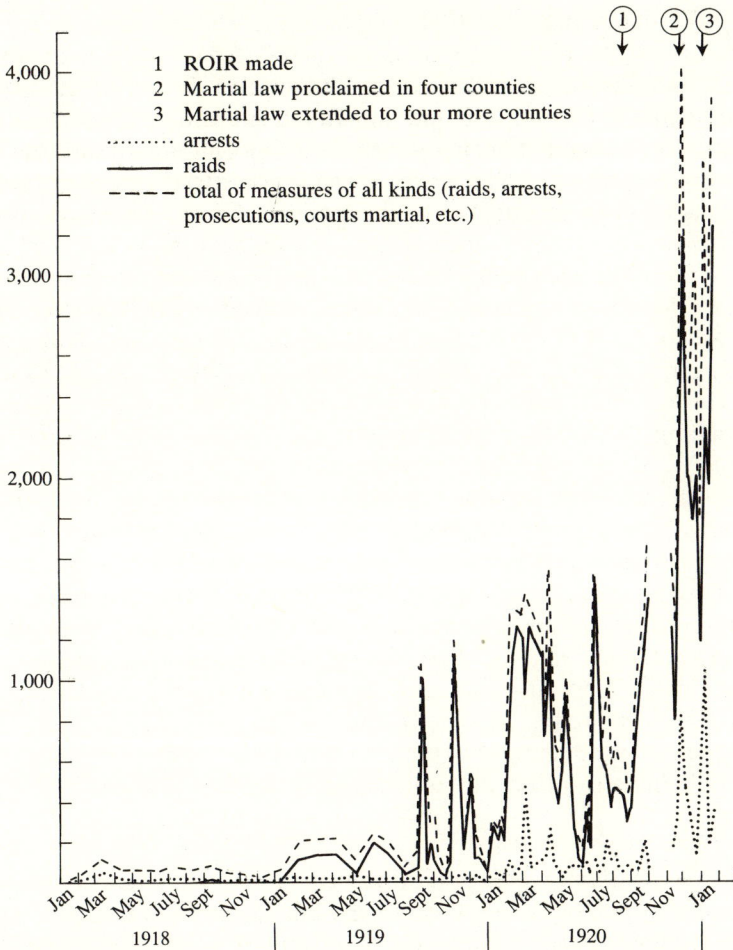

GRAPH A. Weekly totals of British counter-insurgency measures, January 1918 to January 1921 (Dáil statistics)

Source: Prepared from *Irish Bulletin*, weekly surveys from w/e 12 July 1919 to w/e 22 Jan. 1921, and retrospective figures for 1918 and Jan. to Sept. 1919 published in *Irish Bulletin* w/e 27 Sept. 1919.

But within a few months the initiative had received a major set-back. Those detained in Dublin had embarked on a hunger strike for 'political prisoner status', and in mid-April the British Government had given in and ordered their release. Although some reliance on internment powers continued from May onwards, it was at a much lower rate.

But the changes in the police were not only organizational. Tactical changes were also occurring, as the growth of 'unofficial' police reprisals is generally dated from the first half of 1920. The question of reprisals remains one of the most hotly debated issues of the Anglo-Irish conflict. There are conflicting claims as to the extent and degree of official connivance in these operations, and the full truth will probably never be known.[81] The available information seems to indicate that police reprisals can be divided into two categories: (1) random destruction of property and killings following attacks on the police; and (2) selective assassinations of suspected Republican activists (Sinn Féin and IRA). The first victim of these reprisals seems to have been Tomás Mac Curtain, the Sinn Féin Lord Mayor of Cork who was also involved in the Volunteers, and who was shot dead by masked assassins in March 1920. By July it appears that some members of the British Cabinet (notably the Prime Minister, Lloyd George, and the Secretary of State for War and Air, Churchill) were making known their tacit support for a policy later referred to as 'gunning'[82] (which apparently meant selective assassination), but that by the time this 'message' reached the end of the chain of communication, it appears to have been understood as blanket approval of police violence, even against uninvolved civilians. This was particularly true of the activities of the Black and Tans and ADRIC, both of which groups tended to exercise even less discrimination than the indigenous RIC. Even when it was apparent that many of their victims were uninvolved, there was no real political will to bring an end to these killings by rendering those responsible accountable at law. It appears, though, that a higher value was placed on property rights than on individual rights, since there was some willingness to prosecute policemen for looting offences.[83]

The search for a new strategy

By the early summer of 1920, however, the main concern of British strategists was not the issue of reprisals, but rather the perceived gaps in security strategy. Three main factors contributed to this perception. First, the spring initiative, involving as it had done greatly increased use of pre-trial powers, had ultimately yielded little in the way of concrete results. Secondly, there were 'problems' with jury trial. Jurors, it was claimed, refused to attend or to convict in political cases,[84] and even apart from the attendance issue, a very low estimate was put on the number of 'good cases'.[85] Thirdly, although the use of DORA in response to the Irish

---

[81] Figures from both sides in relation to killings by the Crown Forces are given in app. 1.

[82] A phrase used by Lloyd George in Oct. 1920; see Townshend, 120.

[83] The question of the trial of policemen by court martial is considered on pp. 77–80.

[84] See p. 58.

[85] At a Cabinet conference with the Irish Executive in May 1920 the Chief Secretary put the number of people in gaol against whom there were 'good cases' as six. Jones, *Diary*, iii. 19.

conflict after the practical cessation of hostilities in Europe had survived a challenge in the courts,[86] that legislation was nearing the end of its life. Under DORA, the power to issue regulations was exercisable 'during the continuance of the present war'.[87] The Termination of the Present War (Definition) Act 1918 had given an artificial meaning to this phrase, by providing that the British Government ('His Majesty in Council') was empowered to declare a date which was to be treated as the date of termination. But before this date was announced, the War Emergency Laws (Continuance) Act 1920 became law (March 1920).[89] This had the effect that a limited number of DORR were kept in force in Britain in a modified form until 31 August 1920,[89] but that in Ireland all DORR were kept in force (subject to the amendments introduced in respect of those regulations retained in Britain) until twelve months after the 'termination of the present war'.[90] The date of termination of the war was eventually set at midnight 31 August 1921.[91] At around this time also, doubts were being voiced about the wisdom of having prohibited and suppressed Sinn Féin, largely because the ban was proving unworkable. In fact, the party's standing was considerably enhanced by results of the local elections of January and June 1920,[92] while the activities of the IRA continued to grow (Graph B).

The debate centred on the problem of ultimate disposal of cases, particularly on the need for some mechanism which would generate convictions. At a Cabinet conference with the Irish Executive in May 1920 Churchill advocated a jury-less special tribunal for the trial of murder charges. It would have the power to impose the death penalty, its procedures would be summary, and it could be composed of three judges, or three 'Generals' if judges could not be induced to serve.[93] The Attorney-General for Ireland advised that he had put a proposal for jury-less courts to the Irish judges but that 'they didn't want to touch it'.[94] The question of martial law was discussed but the General Officer Com-

---

[86] *R v. Governor of Wormwood Scrubs Prison* [1920] 2 *KB* 305. The case is considered on pp. 117–18.

[87] s. 1 (1) Defence of the Realm Consolidation Act 1914.

[88] See Anon., 'The War Emergency Laws (Continuance) Act 1920', 54 *ILT & SJ* 121.

[89] s. 2 (1).

[90] s. 2 (4). These special provisions were to apply in any areas in which, before the passing of the Act, a proclamation suspending the operation of s. 1 of the Defence of the Realm (Amendment) Act 1915 was in force. Ireland was the only such area.

[91] By order dated 10 Aug. *DG* 16 Aug. See Anon., 'The Legal Effect of the Termination of the War', 55 *ILT & SJ* 203.

[92] Of the 127 corporation and town councils, Sinn Féin controlled 72 completely and a further 26 in collaboration with other nationalists. The party dominated 28 out of 33 County Councils, 182 out of 206 Rural District Councils, and 138 of the 154 Poor Law Boards. Lyons, *Ireland since the Famine*, 407.

[93] Jones, *Diary* iii. 19.

[94] Ibid. 19. Lord French, the Lord-Lieutenant confirmed this.

1 *Restoration of Order in Ireland Act 1920* enacted
2 Martial law proclaimed in Co. Cork (East and West Riding), the city of Cork, Co. Tipperary (NR and SR), Co. Kerry, Co. Limerick, and the city of Limerick
3 Martial law extended to Co. Clare, Co. Kilkenny, Co. Waterford, and city of Waterford, and Co. Wexford

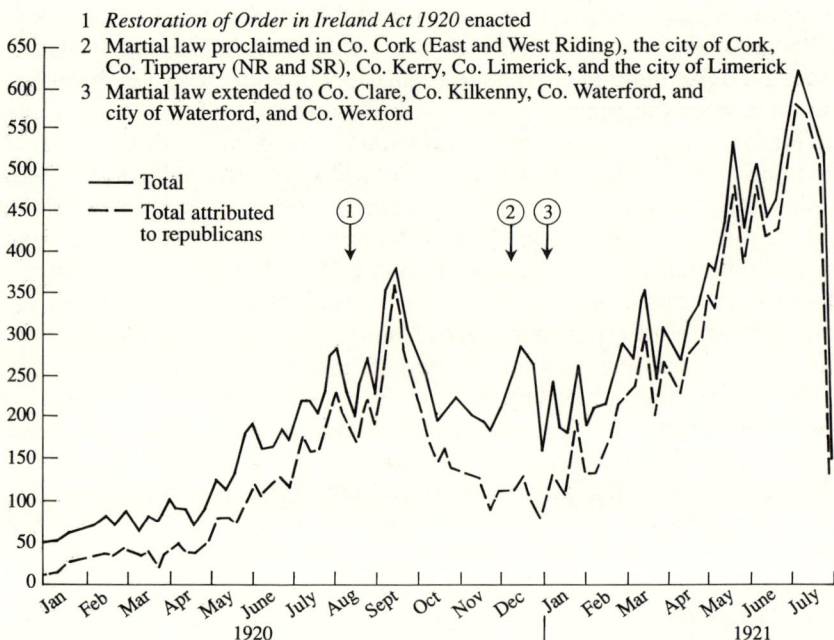

GRAPH B. Weekly totals of politically motivated crime, January 1920 to July 1921 (RIC statistics)

Source: Townshend, 123 (with indicators added).

manding (GOC), General Macready, was sceptical about whether martial law could be brought into operation in any part of the UK without legislation.[95]

Another possibility floated at around that time was the 'judicialization' of the internment process. In June 1920 it was reported that the British Government had decided to bring in a bill providing for the setting up in Ireland of a judicial tribunal to inquire whether there was any evidence, and if so, sufficient evidence, to warrant the detention of 'persons arrested on suspicion'. The tribunal was to be presided over by an Irish judge.[96] At around the same time, a measure referred to as the 'Three Judges Bill' had been prepared by the Irish Chief Crown Solicitor. This proposed to suspend trial by jury in certain cases in favour of trial by a 'Special Commission Court'.[97] The matters discussed at the May conference came

[95] The British Army's view of martial law is considered in detail on pp. 133–5.
[96] *ILT & SJ* 12 June 1920, 142. It is possible that what was under discussion was the establishment of an Advisory Committee as provided for in DORR 14B (see p. 110).
[97] The text of a draft of the proposed Criminal Justice Administration (Ireland) Bill can be found at CAB 24/109, PRO, Kew. Briefly, a 'Special Commission Court' was to consist of a President (who was to be 'such judge of the Supreme Court as may be nominated by the Lord Lieutenant' (clause 2 (1) and (2)) and two other members who were to be

up again at a British Cabinet discussion in July. The Chief Secretary (Hamar Greenwood) advised the Cabinet that he had again consulted with the Irish judges in relation to possible jury-less courts but that 'none of them thought that they should be called in for this work'.[98] In his view, the only solution was a court martial with power to impose the death penalty.[99] Lord Curzon (the Foreign Secretary) suggested that use be made of a panel of assessors,[100] but ultimately Hamar Greenwood's view prevailed, and the mechanism adopted was to be a variant of DORA specifically tailored to the Irish situation.

August to November 1920: the Restoration of Order in Ireland Act

The new measure, the Restoration of Order in Ireland Act (ROIA), became law on 9 August. Under the legislation, all the DORR which had been employed for counter-insurgency purposes in Ireland (or which might be regarded as potentially useful) were readopted as Restoration of Order in Ireland Regulations (ROIR). In the majority of cases this alteration was carried out by the substitution of the phrase 'restoration or maintenance of order in Ireland' for 'the public safety or defence of the realm'.[101] In addition, certain new regulations were made, and a power to make further regulations was given and made use of.[102]

The main features introduced by the new Act and Regulations were as follows: courts martial could now try virtually all types of crime as well as breaches of the Regulations; and they could also impose the death penalty where this was provided under the ordinary law.[103] Special

---

'persons appointed by the Lord Lieutenant' (clause 2 (2)). The jurisdiction of the Special Commission Court was to extend to a list of serious crimes including explosives offences, murder, and treason (clause 1 (1)). Where a person was committed for trial for any of these offences, the Lord-Lieutenant was empowered to refer the case for trial by Special Commission Court (clause 1 (2)). Conviction required unanimity on the bench (clause 3 (3)), and the Court could impose a sentence of death (clause 3 (13)). There were also provisions in the draft designed to prevent cases failing on technical jurisdictional grounds (clause 3 (15)).

[98] Jones, *Diary*, iii. 33. He asserted that jurors did not attend at the assizes, that they were selected by the County Councils, and he envisaged that at the next assizes there would be no jury list for a large part of Ireland.

[99] Ibid. 33.

[100] Ibid.

[101] The regulations were issued on 13 Aug. *DG* 23 Aug. 1920.

[102] s. 1 (1). The form of the legislation was that it was provided that 'Where it appears to his Majesty in Council that, owing to the existence of a state of disorder in Ireland, the ordinary law is inadequate for the prevention and punishment of crime or the maintenance of order, His Majesty in Council may issue regulations under the Defence of the Realm Consolidation Act, 1914 (hereinafter referred to as the principal Act) for securing the restoration and maintenance of order in Ireland.' On 9 Nov. 1920 a new regulation, ROIR 80A, which authorized the CMA to restrict or prohibit the carriage of passengers and articles on railways in Ireland, was created (*DG* 16 Nov. 1920), and on the same date ROIR 9AA was amended to cover 'motor spirit' (*DG* 16 Nov. 1920).

[103] The operation of these courts martial is considered in detail on pp. 59–85.

courts of summary jurisdiction of two Resident Magistrates (RMs) were created,[104] and powers were given to replace coroners' courts by military courts of inquiry.[105] In addition, provision was made for the suspension of payment of Government funds to local authorities,[106] for moving the venues of court hearings where the court-house had been destroyed,[107] and for imposing restrictions on the transport of material.[108]

Following implementation of the regulations, the number of courts martial and raids increased dramatically and the first death sentence was carried out in November. Certain restrictions on shipping had been imposed in September.[109] In the same month, the first substitution of military courts of inquiry for coroners' courts in certain areas had taken place,[110] and this was followed by further substitutions in October[111] and November.[112] The power to move the venue of court hearings was also extensively invoked in September[113] and October,[114] and in these months, steps were also taken to block funding to local authorities.[115] Other

---

[104] s. 1 (3) (a). ROIR 76. The text of this Regulation is included in App. 3. The provisions allowing exclusion of the public from courts martial (see pp. 70–1) also applied to trial by CSJ (ROIR 77).

[105] s. 1 (3) (f). ROIR 81. The text of this Regulation is included in App. 3.

[106] s. 1 (3) (i). ROIR 84.

[107] ROIR 82. Included were 'any court of assize, court of quarter sessions, civil bill court, court of petty sessions, or other court'.

[108] ROIR 80.

[109] On 10 Sept. it was ordered that no ship or vessel carrying passengers eastward bound was to enter the port or harbour of Queenstown until further notice. *DG* 14 Sept. 1920.

[110] On 1 Sept. coroners' inquests were prohibited in the counties of Cork, Clare, Galway, Kerry, Limerick, Longford, Louth, Mayo, Roscommon, Tipperary North Riding, and Tipperary South Riding, and in the county boroughs of Cork and Limerick. *DG* 3 Sept. 1920.

[111] On 5 Oct. in the counties of Donegal and Laois ('Queen's County'), and in the county borough of Waterford. *DG* 8 Oct. 1920.

[112] On 5 Nov. coroners' inquests were prohibited in the counties of Leitrim, Meath, Sligo, Westmeath, and Wexford (*DG* 5 Nov. 1920), and on 26 Nov. in the counties of Cavan, Dublin, and King's County, and in the county borough of Dublin (*DG* 26 Nov. 1920).

[113] An order made 6 Sept. in relation to the annual licensing petty sessions affected parts of 26 counties including Armagh and Fermanagh. Another order made the same day affected courts of quarter sessions and civil bill courts in 13 counties. *DG* 7 Sept. 1920. Further orders were made on 18 Sept. (2) (*DG* 21 Sept.) and on 25 Sept. (*DG* 28 Sept.).

[114] *DG* 8 and 12 Oct. 1920.

[115] On 30 Sept. an order was made that no payment was to be made to the County Council of Carlow out of the sums which otherwise would have been payable to the Council out of the Local Taxation (Ireland) Account. The order recited that orders in similar terms had been made in respect of the Councils of the county boroughs of Cork, Dublin, Limerick, and Waterford, and the counties Carlow, Cavan, Clare, Cork, Donegal, Dublin, Galway, Kerry, Kildare, Kilkenny, King's, Limerick, Longford, Louth, Mayo, Meath, Monaghan, Laois ('Queen's County'), Roscommon, Tipperary NR, Tipperary SR, Tyrone, Waterford, Westmeath, Wexford, and Wicklow. *DG* 1 Oct. 1920. On 9 Oct. a similar order was made in respect of Sligo County Council. *DG* 12 Oct. 1920. On 10 Nov. the order against Tyrone County Council was withdrawn. *DG* 12 Nov. 1920.

measures taken under ROIA were the imposition of curfews in the smaller urban centres and sometimes in whole counties,[116] and the introduction of further restrictions on the use of motor vehicles.[117]

ROIA clearly represented an intensification of the move towards Army primacy begun at the start of the year, yet sections of the police continued to operate beyond military control. Paralleling the growth of military action, reprisals by ADRIC and the Black and Tans (and to a more limited extent, by the Army) became increasingly common.

The introduction of ROIA had been followed by a general escalation in IRA activities that continued until mid-September. Thereafter, the number of incidents went into a decline which lasted until the end of November (Graph B). However, while the overall level of activities lessened, the number of British soldiers killed in the period September to December was approximately four times greater than during the period June to September, while the number of policemen killed in the same period almost doubled. This increase was largely due to the formation by the IRA in the autumn of 1920 of full-time Active Service Units (ASUs) at Brigade, or sometimes at Battalion level. In rural areas these were usually referred to as 'flying columns', and generally consisted of twenty to thirty relatively well-armed men; mobility was their essential feature and ambush their principal tactic. By the end of 1920 there were dozens of such units in operation. The IRA now also began increasingly to turn its attention to those suspected of providing information to the police or to the British Army. Such 'informers' were given summary trials by IRA drumhead courts martial, and if found guilty were swiftly killed.[118]

Another target was the British intelligence services in Dublin. On 21 November simultaneous attacks resulted in the deaths of up to fourteen agents.[119] This was followed later in the day by the deaths of twelve

---

[116] These were intended as collective punishment for specific incidents. See 'History of the 5th Division', 58–9.

[117] Under an order which came into force on 1 Dec. 1920, no motor vehicle could be used in Ireland between 8 p.m. and 6 a.m., and then only within a radius of 20 miles of its garage. Existing permits were to be renewed by 15 Jan. 1921 (later extended to 30 Jan.). Three types of exemption permit were allowed: the Special (Owner) Permit and the Special (Hire) Permit, both of which were signed by any CMA, and the Single Journey Permit which, though printed with the signature of the C-in-C, were issued by the police. Ibid. 60. The order can be found in *DG* 21 Jan. 1921.

[118] Some details of IRA courts martial for the trial of Volunteers can be found in a British Army internal briefing document entitled 'Sinn Fein and the Irish Volunteers'. Three types of court martial are described: company court martial (sentence subject to confirmation by the battalion council); battalion (or brigade) court martial (confirmation by headquarters staff); and the headquarters court martial. Strickland papers. A summary of IRA court martial procedure prepared for a specific trial can be found at MS 11406 (11), National Library, Dublin.

[119] For somewhat differing accounts see Townshend, 129, 130–1, and Lyons, *Ireland since the Famine*, 419. See also N. West, *MI5* (London, 1983), 54.

civilians when members of ADRIC fired into a crowd at a football match in the city. These two incidents gave the day the name 'Bloody Sunday'. The immediate British response was resort to internment on an unprecedented scale and an overall intensification of the counter-insurgency drive. But despite these measures, the end of November saw an ambush at Kilmichael in County Cork by the flying column of the West Cork Brigade, in which sixteen members of ADRIC died. This sequence of events prompted the decision of the British Government early in December to resort to martial law in response to the apparent failure of ROIA to curb the insurrection, though it was scarcely realistic to have expected that Act to have had a decisive effect on the conflict in only four months.

December 1920 to July 1921: martial law

On 11 December a proclamation appeared, signed by the Lord-Lieutenant, announcing the imposition of martial law in four counties in which there had been notable IRA activity: Cork, Tipperary, Limerick, and Kerry.[120] In the same month the British Army throughout Ireland was placed on 'active service'.[121] On 4 January a further proclamation extended the martial law area (MLA) to its maximum size by the inclusion of Counties Clare, Kilkenny, Waterford, and Wexford (Map D).[122] At this stage, there is no need to consider the legal principles underlying the concept; suffice it to say that, in so far as martial law was capable of being imposed in Ireland, its central feature was that during the course of its imposition the actions of the Army became non-justiciable.[123] Other events of December 1920 added to the significance of the month. On the night of the 11th, the most spectacular reprisal yet occurred, when members of ADRIC burnt down a section of Cork city centre. On the 23rd, the British Government's attempt at a political solution to the Irish question became law when the Government of Ireland Act received the Royal assent.[124] Predictably, the measure was immediately rejected by Sinn Féin, though over the following few months there were a number of behind-the-scenes peace moves.

Within the MLA, the Army proceeded to issue a number of proclamations based on those issued during the Boer War, and by the British

---

[120] The text of this proclamation, dated 10 Dec. 1920, is included in the report of *R* v. *Murphy* [1921] 2 *IR* 190, at 198, and in *DG* 10 Dec. 1920. The case is discussed on pp. 121–2.

[121] GRO 1338/1920, issued 12 Dec. 1920, WO 35/173, PRO, Kew.

[122] The text of this proclamation is in *DG* 4 Jan. 1921.

[123] The legal principles involved are examined in some detail on pp. 123–47.

[124] The provisions of the Government of Ireland Act 1920 affecting NI are considered in Ch. 4. Ch. 3, considers some provisions affecting the abortive entity of 'Southern Ireland'.

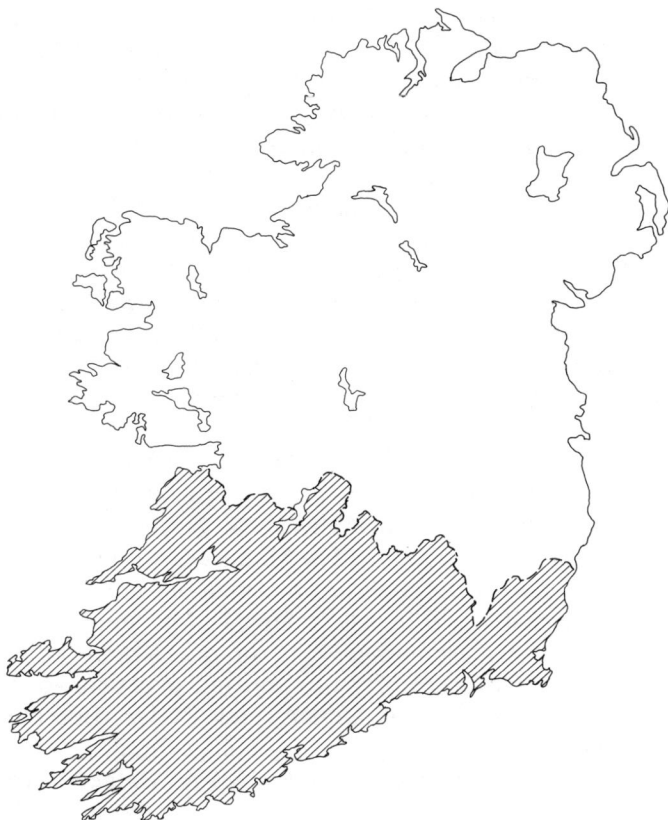

MAP D. Areas proclaimed under martial law, 1920–1921

Source: Prepared From *DG* 10 Dec. 1920 and 4 Jan. 1921.

Army of the Rhine after the First World War.[125] The first was by the Commander-in-Chief.[126] This declared that any person in 'unauthorized'[127] possession of arms, ammunition, or explosives was liable to the death penalty, as was any 'unauthorized person' wearing a British Army,

---

[125] C. F. N. Macready, *Annals of an Active Life* (London, 1924), 515. A copy of one of the proclamations issued in Germany is included in the Strickland papers. Under it, the death penalty was threatened for a variety of acts, some of which might not ordinarily amount to crimes ('If damage is done to any building . . .'), and a warning was issued that 'the sternest penalties' would be inflicted for certain other acts or omissions.

[126] The text of this proclamation is included in *R* v. *Murphy*, [1921] 2 *IR* 190, at 199–200. The case is discussed below.

[127] The preceding paragraph of the proclamation had required that 'all arms, ammunition and explosives in possession of any person not a member of His Majesty's Naval, Military, Air, or Police Forces, or who is not in possession of a permit' be surrendered by 27 Dec.

Navy, Air Force, police, or similar uniform. Persons in 'unauthorized possession' of such clothing or equipment were liable to suffer penal servitude. The Commander-in-Chief also purported to direct the continuing operation of 'all Law Courts . . . until otherwise ordered'. Three other major proclamations were then issued by subordinate authority, creating a variety of offences.[128]

Martial law measures were not uniformly imposed, however. In Wexford, in the early stages at least, the restrictions were 'lightened',[129] Macready claimed. Political considerations also affected matters, and not only in the determination of the size of the MLA: when in May peace talks were in the air, Macready received 'a hint from high quarters that . . . the death penalty should not be exacted in cases of rebels found carrying arms'.[130] During the elections of that month, Army activities were suspended for several days.[131]

The system of administering martial law was that the Commander-in-Chief had overall responsibility in his capacity as Military Governor-General. Below him were the five Divisional and Brigade Commanders within the MLA whom he appointed as Military Governors.[132] It was one of these officers who issued the three proclamations referred to above.[133] A network of martial law tribunals, referred to as 'military courts' and 'summary courts', was established, and in the administration of this system the Military Governor played a part not dissimilar to that of the CMA in the administration of DORA and ROIA. But the military tribunal apparatus, and the martial law system generally, did not entirely supersede the statutory system within the MLA. Rather it acted as an

[128] The contents of these proclamations has been summarized as follows: 'Proclamation No. 1 Made all crimes into offences punishable by Martial Law. Made tampering with official notices and proclamations an offence. Required owners of occupied buildings to keep a list of the inmates posted on the door. Required owners of hotels and boarding-houses to keep a register of guests and supply it to the police. Proclamation No. 2 Prohibited all meetings and defined a meeting as consisting of six people or more. Prohibited loitering in the streets. Prohibited sending telegrams in code or cipher. Made the possession of wireless instruments or carrier pigeons an offence. Proclamation No. 3 Required anyone having knowledge about rebels or their goings immediately to give information. Warned people who damaged or destroyed Government property that the property of such persons was liable to be confiscated or destroyed.' 'Record of the Rebellion in Ireland in 1920–21 and the Part Played by the Army in Dealing with It', i. 'Operations', 29. Jeudwine papers.

[129] Macready, *Annals*, 526.

[130] Ibid. 558.

[131] Ibid. 548.

[132] In the proclamation issued by the C-in-C referred to above, the 'Generals or other Officers Commanding 6th Division, 16th, 17th, 18th, and Kerry Infantry Brigades' were made Military Governors. A map showing the areas covered by these units is in Townshend, 86.

[133] The GOC 6th Division.

'overlay', in conjunction with which the statutory system continued to operate.[134] Military Governors not only performed functions similar to those of the CMA, but at least some of them were in fact CMAs; thus an officer might sign one document in his capacity as CMA and another as Military Governor.

Military operations within the MLA were governed by a series of special instructions and orders.[135] These covered everything from policy in relation to arrests[136] to use of forced civilian labour.[137] Perhaps the most distinctive feature of martial law was the instigation of 'official reprisals' by the Army. These required the authorization of an Infantry Brigadier and involved the destruction by explosives of the homes of those who were taken to be 'implicated' in an 'outrage'. Whether or not persons were taken to be implicated depended on an assessment of their 'proximity to the outrage or their known political tendencies'.[138] Official reprisals were not the only forms of collective punishment employed: it was also the practice for the Military Governor to order the closure of creameries and post offices in response to particular incidents.[139]

Other measures taken under martial law included the carrying of prisoners as hostages with convoys[140] and the introduction of press moni-

---

[134] The interrelationship between these two systems is considered in detail on pp. 85–9.

[135] See '17th Infantry Brigade, Summary of Important Instructions' and 'Notes on the Administration of Martial Law for the Use of Commanding Officers', Strickland papers.

[136] This is examined on pp. 51–3.

[137] The '17th Infantry Brigade, Summary' provided: 'The enforcement of civilian labour for Government purposes is only to be adopted in cases such as (i) Filling in trenches across roads. (ii) Repairs to bridges destroyed by rebels. (iii) Removal of obstacles erected by rebels. (iv) Punishment when an attack has been made on a military or police barracks. In this case it may be used to improve the defences, wiring, etc., or to demolish walls or hedges which were used as cover by the rebels. On no account is it to be used for fatigue work in Barracks' (para. 4). Strickland papers. Similar provisions were included in the 'Notes on the Administration of Martial Law', 6, para. (f).

[138] Townshend, 149. Townshend estimates the total number of such reprisals as 150 (p. 149). In 'The Irish Rebellion in the Sixth Divisional Area from after the 1916 Rebellion to December 1921' the total number of houses destroyed in official reprisals is given as 191, and the figure for 'Property Destroyed' as 20, giving a total of 211 (app. 5, p. 39). Strickland papers. Perhaps some reprisals involved the destruction of more than one house.

[139] A typical order was that issued on 1 June 1921 by the Colonel-Commandant Kerry Brigade and Military Governor, closing the creamery at Ballyhar from 6 a.m. on 3 June to 6 a.m. on 17 June. The order began with a recital: '*Whereas several* instances have recently occurred of trains being held up by armed rebels in the vicinity of *Ballyhar* and *whereas* roads have been trenched in the country surrounding the above named village and *whereas* the local inhabitants have not come forward to give information leading to the arrest of the persons responsible for these outrages . . .'. WO 36/66, PRO, Kew. In 'Rebellion in the Sixth Divisional Area' the number of creameries closed in the various martial law brigade areas in the months of May, June, and July 1921 is given as 49, and the corresponding closures of post offices as 25 (app. 5, p. 40).

[140] See ibid. 70. The 'Record of the Rebellion', i. 30, recounts that 'the fact that Sinn Fein leaders were to be so carried was made public by notices and in the Press'.

toring, which seems to have amounted to a degree of censorship.[141] In addition, an attempt (which largely failed) was also made to bring the police under effective military control by placing that arm under the orders of the Military Governors.

Some other counter-insurgency techniques employed in the MLA were also made use of outside the area. The year 1921 also saw increasing deployment of small units of plain-clothes soldiers.[142] One of their tactics was to carry out a raid, for instance demanding to examine a payroll, without giving any clue as to the objective of the exercise, and without disclosing who they were. On occasion, it seems they left the persons involved with the impression that an IRA group had carried out the operation.[143] Republicans claimed that plain-clothes units of the Crown Forces sometimes operated as assassination squads, though this allegation may have been intended to relate only to police units.[144] Less successful than other plain-clothes operations were the attempts at dropping individuals in IRA-dominated territory in the hope of their picking up useful intelligence. Some of the schemes in this regard were quite fanciful,[145] and the IRA had no difficulty in identifying and dealing with those

---

[141] The '17th Infantry Brigade, Summary' noted in relation to newspapers: 'Inaccurate and misleading reports are often published in the Press. Local newspapers should be examined daily, and reports of any occurrences likely to create any stir outside Ireland (or one serious comment on such) will be at once inquired into and Brigade headquarters informed. If the matter is of an urgent nature, this information should be wired' (para. 11). Macready, however, complained that 'On account of the partial application of martial law several essential regulations had to be considerably modified or struck out altogether, such as the institution of identity cards, an efficient control over the press, and the suspension of civil courts.' *Annals*, 516. The Army did not, however, simply monitor the press—the 'Record of the Rebellion' states: 'the newspapers were a great source of strength to the rebel cause; had it been possible to control these all over Ireland, as it was in the Martial Law area, the cause of Law and Order would have gained an advantage which is incalculable' (i. 29). On 2 May 1921 the AG for Ireland confirmed in the House that the military authorities in the MLA had prevented the correspondents of various journals of the world from sending in an account of the scenes accompanying the execution of four prisoners in Cork. He explained that this was 'caused by the fact that the area in which the censorship occurs is one where an insurrection is taking place at present'. 141 *HC Deb.*, cols. 671–2. The question of control over the reporting of trials by court martial is considered on p. 71.

[142] In the '17th Infantry Brigade, Summary' the deployment of soldiers in plain clothes was authorized in three situations. These were (i) For Protective Duties. (ii) *For a Definite Operation.* (iii) For Intelligence Work, (p. 8). Reasonably precise instructions were issued in relation to headings (i) and (iii), but in relation to heading (ii), it was merely provided that 'they will invariably be under a definite commander and closely controlled' (p. 9).

[143] 'Record of the Rebellion', ii. 'Intelligence', 26.

[144] *An tOglach*, 27 May 1921.

[145] 'Record of the Rebellion' recounts: 'The Civil Government hoped and intended at one time to flood Ireland with agents. The case of Belgium was quoted . . . It was at first overlooked that the Crown Forces in Ireland, and not the Sinn Feiners, were in the position of the Germans opposed by a national movement' (p. 28).

involved.[146] More careful placing of the agents, however, seems to have achieved better results from the British point of view.[147]

But despite these new measures, the overall number of IRA attacks continued to grow (Graph B). The number of policemen killed in 1921 up to the truce exceeded the combined total for the two previous years while the corresponding military losses doubled. Each new measure introduced by the Crown Forces resulted in fresh counter-measures by the IRA. In response to the policy of official reprisals, sections of the IRA resorted to the practice, which later became policy,[148] of destroying two loyalist homes for every nationalist home destroyed. This led the British Army to issue an order early in June prohibiting any further official reprisals. As executions both within and without the MLA became more common in 1921, some IRA units began to shoot captured members of the Crown Forces.[149] The increased emphasis on intelligence by the British Army resulted in the IRA's executing seventy-three suspected 'spies and informers' in the period January to April 1921.[150] In several instances, those killed were Southern Protestants, and the circumstances of many of their deaths served to reinforce loyalists in their belief that these were merely sectarian attacks.[151]

There were also more general developments in IRA organization and strategy, and an insistence by the Volunteers of the applicability of the 1907 Hague Convention and Rules.[152] A divisional organization was

[146] Ernie O'Malley's comment was: 'Brave men, often disguised in everything except accent, were dropped from lorries at night, but they were picked up within a few days, tried and executed.' *Raids and Rallies*, 98. O'Malley's operational area was outside the MLA.

[147] Principally in Dublin. Agents were placed 'successfully' in most of the steamship companies trading with Dublin, on the railways, as journalists or farmers, and, the British Army claimed, in the IRA. 'Record of the Rebellion', ii. 29.

[148] The text of the IRA's 'official' reprisals policy can be seen in the *Irish Bulletin*, 28 June 1921. It is also reproduced in O'Donoghue, *No Other Law*, app. 3, p. 332.

[149] For an account of one such shooting see E. O'Malley, *On Another Man's Wound* (Dublin, 1979), 333–8.

[150] According to the British Army, if a man were suspected of being an informer, he would be given false information by the IRA, and if the Crown Forces were seen to act on this information, the suspect would be immediately dealt with. 'Record of the Rebellion', ii. 25.

[151] See D. Kennedy, *The Widening Gulf: Northern Attitudes to the Independent Irish State 1919–49* (Belfast, 1988), 49–52. On the question of loyalists as a source of information, a British Army intelligence assessment concluded: 'In the south the Protestants and those who supported the Government rarely gave much information because, except by chance, they had not got it to give. An exception to this rule was in the Bandon area where there were many Protestant farmers who gave information. Although the Intelligence Officer of this area was exceptionally experienced and although the troops were most active it proved almost impossible to protect these brave men, many of whom were murdered while almost all the remainder suffered grave material loss.' 'Record of the Rebellion', ii. 26.

[152] For the IRA's arguments see 'The Laws of War', *An tOglach*, 27 May 1921, Strickland papers. This claim was not recognized by the British.

adopted in the spring of 1921 (though apparently with little practical effect), and in an attempt to broaden the conflict generally, the IRA began a campaign of arson in Britain.

The situation outside the martial law area

Most of the country, though, was not under martial law, and in these areas ROIA remained the prime counter-insurgency tool. As regards the actual conduct of operations, it was made clear that the 'Notes for the Guidance of Troops when Acting in Aid of the Civil Police in Ireland' applied only to cases where troops were dealing with riots and disturbances, and not in dealing with persons armed with firearms and explosives.[153]

By March 1921 British Army strength in Ireland stood at 39,961 while the combined strength of the police forces, apart from the Ulster Special Constabulary (which as its title suggests operated only in Ulster[154]), amounted to 16,222. This build-up, particularly in police numbers, facilitated the massive programme of raids which continued outside the MLA. The scale of operations reached its peak in May and June 1921, in a series of drives in the midlands involving a cavalry column of four regiments, backed up by infantry units. Unofficial police reprisals also continued.

There were also more mundane aspects of implementation of ROIA. Inquests were further prohibited in December 1920[155] and again in April 1921.[156] The venue of hearings in the lower courts was continuously changed,[157] and there were more blockages of funds to local authorities in February[158] and May 1921.[159] There was also a long series of orders prohibiting payment to local authorities in respect of railways, providing instead for the payment of the sums due for the upkeep of the railways

---

[153] GRO 360/1921, 8 Apr. 1921, WO 35/173, PRO, Kew.
[154] See Ch. 4.
[155] In the counties of Kildare, Kilkenny, and Waterford. *DG* 17 Dec. 1920.
[156] In Co. Monaghan.
[157] The venues of quarter sessions and civil bill courts was changed on eight occasions between Jan. and June 1921: in Co. Cork, Donegal, and Kilkenny on 18 Jan. (*DG* 18 Jan.), in Co. Longford on 21 Jan. (*DG* 21 Jan.), in Co. Sligo on 7 Mar. (*DG* 8 Mar.), in Offaly ('King's County') on 24 Mar. (*DG* 25 Mar.), in Co. Fermanagh and Monaghan on 31 Mar. (*DG* 1 Apr.), in Co. Wexford on 15 Apr. (*DG* 15 Apr.), in Co. Cork on 16 June (*DG* 17 June), and again on 25 June (*DG* 1 July). The venue of the Petty sessions was moved in 24 counties on 30 Mar. (*DG* 1 Apr.), and in Co. Offaly on 29 Apr. (*DG* 3 May). The assizes venue in Co. Wexford was moved on 27 June (*DG* 28 June). How much business was being carried out, even at these changed venues, is difficult to say, as it seems that the Dáil courts succeeded in taking over much of this type of work in many areas.
[158] On 28 Feb. 39 Urban District Councils had their funds blocked. *DG* 4 Mar. 1921.
[159] On 13 May orders were made against one Urban District Council, three Town Commissions, against the Boards of Guardians of 116 Unions, and against 129 Rural District Councils. *DG* 17 May 1921.

directly to the relevant train companies.[160] The process of developing new regulations and adapting old ones also continued, and in April one of these new regulations was used to prevent the taking of a census.[161] The imposition of curfew restrictions in towns became increasingly common; the system was that the local CMA was authorized to impose the curfew, but the order could be withdrawn only by sanction from GHQ.[162] Sometimes these curfews were clearly intended as a form of collective punishment.[163] Another form of such punishment was the issuing of orders forbidding the holding of fairs and markets within a certain radius of the scene of an 'outrage'.[164] Among the other powers over the civilian population invoked under ROIA were those to impose restrictions on the use of bicycles,[165] and to close roads.[166]

Political and legal constraints

In the MLA the effective implementation of the new regime depended not least on the degree to which it would prove acceptable to the judiciary. In a number of decisions the High Court in Ireland had accepted its validity[167] but the very fact that the cases had been brought amounted to a brake on the operation of the military court system.[168] Eventually in July, the Master of the Rolls ruled against the validity of martial law,[169] and when the Army refused to comply with the relevant order, he ordered

[160] See *DG* 14 Jan. (5 orders), 21 Apr. (2 orders), 27 May (2 orders), 8 July (1 order), and 15 July (1 order).

[161] *DG* 15/4/1921. The regulation in question, ROIR 85, had been made on 5 Apr. (*DG* 15 Apr.). Other new ROIRs created in 1921 were ROIR 71A (fines at courts martial) (*DG* 15 Feb.), ROIR 79A (recognizances on suspicion) (*DG* 15 Feb.), and ROIR 72A (evidence at court martial) (*DG* 25 Feb.). Amendments were made to the following regulations: ROIR 9AA (*DG* 15 Feb.), ROIR 84 (*DG* 15 Feb. and 18 Mar.), ROIR 57 (*DG* 25 Feb.), ROIR 69 (*DG* 25 Feb.), ROIR 79A (*DG* 25 Feb.), and ROIR 81 (*DG* 15 Apr.).

[162] 'Record of the Rebellion', i. 30.

[163] 'History of the 5th Division', 58.

[164] The Army considered that this had 'a very marked effect in setting farmers against the rebel extremists'. 'Record of the Rebellion', 30.

[165] ROIR 9AA had been amended in Feb. 1921 to bring bicycles within its scope (see above). In the 5th Division area, the system adopted in relation to restrictions on bicycles was that a memo was sent by Divisional HQ on 29 May pointing out that permission to enforce restriction on ordinary bicycles could be applied for in the following order of severity: (1) no bicycle or tricycle to be used during curfew hours; (2) at other times none to be used except where provided with a military permit; (3) all bicycles, except those whose owners had permits, to be requisitioned and retained; (4) total prohibition (without exception) of the use of all bicycles and tricycles. 'History of the 5th Division', 82.

[166] e.g. the order of the CMA dated 2 July 1921, closing the lane passing to the westward of the recreation ground and to the southward of Portobello barracks in Dublin. WO 35/66, PRO, Kew.

[167] These cases are discussed on pp. 136–40.

[168] Macready recorded that an appeal was made in every case where military courts passed sentences of death. *Annals*, 518.

[169] *Egan* v. *Macready* [1921] 1 *IR* 265. The case is discussed on pp. 140–4.

a writ of attachment to issue against the GOC. The GOC, however, refused to accept the authority of the Court and was prepared to arrest the Master.[170] A way out of the impasse was found when the British Government, without consulting the GOC, ordered the release of the two men on whose behalf the case had been brought. The releases were made, it was explained, 'solely on the basis of the existing circumstances in Ireland . . . civil courts have no power to overrule the decisions of military courts in the Martial Law Area'.[171] As the decision had come shortly after the truce, no effort was made to test its full implications.

Political developments had also been proceeding quickly. The elections under the Government of Ireland Act for the two Home Rule Parliaments took place in May. The Dáil chose to adopt them as elections to the second Dáil. One hundred and twenty-four seats in the South went to Sinn Féin and four to (non-party) Unionists. In the North, Unionists won 40 out of the 52 seats. The Northern Ireland Parliament was opened in June, but as the Sinn Féin representatives ignored the entity of 'Southern Ireland' created under the Government of Ireland Act, plans were drawn up to rule the south of Ireland as a Crown colony[172] with martial law imposed throughout on a much harsher basis than had hitherto been the case.[173] Peace moves were afoot, however, and on 11 July the fighting ceased when a truce came into effect.[174]

PART II

SECTION (A) ARREST AND DETENTION

Developments in relation to use of arrest and detention powers corresponded closely with successive British counter-insurgency strategies. In

---

[170] Macready, *Annals*, 589.

[171] Quoted in Townshend, 194.

[172] Under s. 72 (1) of the Government of Ireland Act 1920, provision was made that if less than half the number elected to either House of Commons actually took part in proceedings, the dissolution of the House could be ordered and the power of the Government of Southern or Northern Ireland as the case many be, exercised by the Lord-Lieutenant with the assistance of a special committee.

[173] Macready had spoken in terms of 100 executions per week (Townshend, 189). Full martial law was initially to come into force on 12 July, but because of the association of that date, 14 July was substituted. The draft proclamation for martial law in the 26 counties made provision for, among other things, closure of ports, identification cards for all males between 16 and 50, confiscation of all means of conveyance following ambushes, requirement of a passport signed by the CMA for travel to Great Britain and abroad, suppression of newspapers by the Military Governor, trials by drumhead military courts, and a declaration that membership of Dáil Eireann or the IRA amounted to an act of treason. CAB 27/107, PRO, Kew.

[174] The British and Irish versions of the terms of the truce were published as a White Paper at Cmnd. 1534 (1921). As to the dispute between the Irish and the British sides as to the terms, see Townshend, 196–9.

the years 1918 and 1919 it appears that the bulk of arrests were carried out by the police. The new initiative of January to May 1920 saw a much greater role for the army. This process continued under the ROIA initiative, and reached its full development under martial law.

Introduction: the ordinary law of arrest and detention

In order to assess the significance of the emergency arrest and detention provisions introduced under DORR and ROIR, it is first necessary to summarize briefly the ordinary law on arrest and detention.[175] The main division in the ordinary law in this area was between arrest on foot of a warrant and arrest without warrant. Arrest under warrant required the issuing of a warrant by a judicial authority on the basis of 'information' laid. This information had to allege that a person had committed an offence for which an arrest warrant could be issued. Powers of arrest without warrant fell under two main headings: common law powers and those granted by statute. Within the former category, there was a further subdivision between powers exercisable in relation to (1) treason and felony, (2) misdemeanours, and (3) breaches of the peace.

In the category of common law powers exercisable in relation to felonies and treason, there was an important distinction to be made between those exercisable by 'peace officers' (which term included justices, constables, sheriffs, and coroners, but not soldiers) and others. Peace officers could arrest a person found in the actual commission of a felony or treason, or a person who was reasonably suspected of being on the point of committing or attempting to commit or having committed such crimes. Provided the suspicion was reasonable, the arrest would be lawful even if it subsequently transpired that no felony or treason had been committed, or was about to have been committed, as the case may be. The position in relation to other classes of arrestor was that although every person who was present when any treason or felony was committed, or attempted to be committed, was entitled to arrest the offender, and although once a felony had been committed any person was entitled to arrest a person reasonably suspected of having committed the felony, the arrest would be unlawful if it should subsequently transpire that no felony had in fact been committed.

There was some confusion about the law of arrest in relation to misdemeanours. It is clear that there was no general power of arrest available either to peace officers or to others in relation to this class of crime. But it appears that there were two exceptions to this rule: (1) a power of arrest existed where the offence was 'of a character publicly scandalous

---

[175] This summary is based on J. O'Connor, *The Irish Justice of the Peace* (Dublin, 1911), 146–9, and R. M. Hennessey, *Molloy's Justice of the Peace for Ireland* (Dublin, 1910), 34–9.

and prejudicial to morals', and (2) a constable could effect an arrest where a misdemeanour was committed in his presence. In relation to a breach of the peace, any person was justified in arresting a person committing a breach of the peace in his presence, but not after the breach and danger of any renewal had ceased.

A variety of statutes created a number of powers of arrest without warrant in relation to specific offences, but there were not in existence at that time the sort of blanket statutory powers of arrest without warrant with which the modern lawyer will be familiar.[176] Whichever power of arrest was invoked, whether under common law or by statute, any arrested person was to be brought before a justice and formally charged as soon as possible. The common law did not envisage the intensive interrogation of detained persons,[177] though not all questioning was unlawful, and confessions made in custody were admissible in certain circumstances.[178]

For the purposes of comparison with emergency powers of arrest and detention, six salient features of ordinary powers in this area can be noted: (1) powers of arrest were always linked to the commission or apprehended commission of a specific offence; (2) the range of offences in relation to which such powers were exercisable was limited; (3) a requirement of 'reasonable' or 'good suspicion' was the norm for the exercise of these powers; (4) only peace officers (for practical purposes this meant constables) could exercise powers of arrest different from those of the ordinary citizen; (5) the period of detention following arrest was limited to that reasonably required to bring a person before a justice and to charge him; and (6) powers of questioning were entirely incidental to detention for the purposes of bringing a person before a justice.

---

[176] Among the statutory powers of arrest without warrant listed by O'Connor the following are germane to the present discussion: s. 57 and s. 61 of the Malicious Damage Act 1861, s. 66 of the Offences against the Person Act 1861, s. 2 of the Unlawful Drilling Act 1819, and s. 78 of the Explosive Substances Act 1875. For a discussion of judicial interpretation of this kind of arrest power see G. Williams, 'The Interpretation of Statutory Powers of Arrest without Warrant', [1958] *Crim. LR* 73.

[177] C. Molloy, *The Justice of the Peace for Ireland* (Dublin, 1890), 90, wrote: 'Constables cannot be too cautious in abstaining from interrogating prisoners in their custody . . . The practice of questioning prisoners by police officers is entirely opposed to the spirit of our law, for by the law of this country no person ought to be made to criminate himself.'

[178] The English 1912 Judges Rules do not appear to have been expressly adopted by the Irish judiciary at this stage, although clearly similar approaches were taken to the admissibility of confessions. See O'Connor, *Irish Justice*, 272–5, and W. A. Breakey, *Handbook of the Common and Statute Law of Ireland* (Dublin, 1895), 317–19. It must be remembered that at this time the accused was not a competent witness in his own defence in Ireland. This matter would have been related to the whole question of interrogation/admissibility of confession evidence. It appears that there was a general debate on these issues in progress; see Anon., 'Statements by Prisoners or Suspects', 52 *ILT & SJ* 242, and 'Confession and Admissions Allowable in Evidence', 52 *ILT & SJ* 89.

Arrest and detention under DORR 55 and ROIR 55

The arrest

DORR 55 and ROIR 55 each introduced a cluster of powers of arrest and detention without warrant[179] which marked a radical departure from ordinary powers in this area (Tables 1 and 2).[180] Each empowered four classes of arrestor—any police constable, an officer of customs and excise, an aliens officer (from 1919 an immigration officer[181]), and any person authorized by the CMA. The inclusion of constables among those empowered is unremarkable, while inclusion of customs officers and aliens officers was presumably intended to provide special 'port powers' of arrest.

The most significant feature about the list of arrestors under DORR 55 was that the power given to the CMA meant that arrests could be carried out under military orders, though in practice the exercise of these powers was subject to political approval. It appears that prior to 1920 this approval was not forthcoming. There were large numbers of arrests in the preceding years (Table 3) but the bulk of these would have been carried out by the RIC, and many may have been under ordinary powers.[182] The position changed early in 1920, and between 7 January and 27 February a series of orders was issued by GHQ authorizing the use of arrest powers by troops when on duty and when acting under the orders of a CMA.[183] In the Army's view 'expression was given to the new policy of the Government'.[184] Where possible, the arrests were still to be carried out by the police, but in practice it was often the troops who made the arrests.[185] This policy persisted for as long as did the new counter-insurgency initiative, of which the changed approach to arrests was a part. But with the collapse of that policy early in May 1920, Army arrests were

---

[179] Arrest under these powers could also be on foot of a warrant since s. 27 of the Criminal Justice Administration Act 1914 provided that where 'under any Act whether passed before or after the commencement of this Act there is power to arrest a person with a warrant a warrant for his arrest may be issued'. Under s. 42 this provision applied to Ireland; see Cook (ed.), *Defence of the Realm Manual*, eighth edn., 170 n. (b).

[180] The only other arrest power given by DORR appears to have been that under DORR 45F, which regulation empowered the Admiralty, the Army Council, and the Air Council to make orders authorizing 'the arrest and custody of members of any force of an Ally alleged to have been guilty of offences'.

[181] Aliens Order 1919; see *Defence of the Realm Manual*, 170 n. (a).

[182] Some other available British figures indicate a total of 14,676 arrests in Ireland in relation to all types of offence in 1918, 13,130 in 1919, and 1,955 in Jan. 1920 (126 *HC Deb.*, col. 1503, 138 *HC Deb.*, cols. 945–6). The figure for Jan. 1920 represented an 82 per cent increase on the monthly average for the previous year.

[183] 'History of the 5th Division', 21.

[184] Ibid. 21.

[185] Ibid. 22.

TABLE I. DORR 55

Arrester	Grounds for Arrest
(Reg. as at 1 January 1918)	(Reg. as at 1 January 1918)
Any person authorised for the purpose by the competent naval or military authority, or any police constable, or officer of customs and excise or aliens officer	. . . may arrest without warrant any person whose behaviour is of such a nature as to give reasonable grounds for suspecting that he has acted or is acting or is about to act in a manner prejudicial to the public safety or the defence of the Realm, or upon whom may be found any article, book, letter, or other document, the possession of which gives ground for such a suspicion, or who is suspected of having committed an offence against these regulations, or of being in possession of any article or document which is being used or intended to be used for any purpose or in any way prejudicial to the public safety or the defence of the Realm;

cont.

ordered to be stopped temporarily, an order specifically confirmed in relation to DORR 55 on 21 May.[186]

The key element of the new policy had been the reintroduction of selective internment under DORR 14B,[187] and the use of DORR 55 as a first step in the internment process was facilitated by the criteria in the Regulation for the making of arrests. There were three sets of grounds (Table 1). The first was where a person's behaviour was 'of such a nature as to give reasonable grounds for suspecting that he has acted or is acting or is about to act in a manner prejudicial to the public safety or the defence of the Realm'. The significance of this provision is that it permitted arrest where there was no suspicion of the commission of a specific offence. The word 'behaviour' in this context was held to include 'all such acts as the competent naval or military authority may be credibly informed of',[188] including material from intelligence dossiers. The link with DORR 14B is emphasized by the fact that the phrase 'public safety or the defence of the Realm' was also included in the criteria for the exercise of internment powers in the latter Regulation.[189]

---

[186] 'History of the 5th Division', 39.

[187] See pp. 101–11.

[188] *Michaels* v. *Block* [1918] 34 *TLR* 438. The case is discussed on pp. 114–15. Ordinarily, in an action for false imprisonment, the burden of proving the existence of reasonable and probable cause lay on the defendant. See W. T. S. Stallybrass, *Salmond's Law of Torts* (London, 1936). 378.

[189] See pp. 101–2.

TABLE I. *Continued*

Provisions governing Detention

(Reg. as at 1 January 1918)

On a person being taken into custody under this regulation he may apply to the competent naval or military authority for release on bail, and, if the competent naval or military authority so directs in writing, any officer of police, who under the Summary Jurisdiction Acts has power to release on bail any person apprehended without warrant, may discharge the person so in custody upon his entering into a recognizance, or, in Scotland, finding caution, with or without sureties, for a reasonable amount to appear at such time and place, to be named in the recognizance or caution, as may be fixed by the competent naval or military authority. Provided that a person so taken into custody as having committed a summary offence against these regulations may be released on bail in manner aforesaid without application to or direction from the competent naval or military authority.

Added 14 January 1919

The power given by this regulation to an officer of the police to discharge any person in custody shall in Ireland be exerciseable by a resident magistrate or in the police district of Dublin Metropolis by a divisional justice of that district.

Any person so arrested may be detained either in civil custody or in military custody; and without prejudice to any other power of detention any such person may, on the order of the competent naval or military authority, be detained in any of His Majesty's prisons as a person committed to prison on remand, or, in Scotland, for further examination, until it has been determined whether or not he is to be proceeded against for an offence under these regulations and, if the offence for which he is to be proceeded against is not a summary offence, until it has also been determined in what manner he is to be tried.

Misc.

(Reg. as at 1 January 1918)

Any person so arrested shall, if so ordered by the competent naval or military authority, or by the chief officer of police for the district, be photographed and finger-print impressions of the fingers and thumbs of both of his hands taken, and if any person refuses to allow such photograph or impressions to be taken, or obstructs the taking thereof, he shall be guilty of a summary offence against these regulations:

Provided that:

(a) no photograph of a person so taken shall be published except for the purpose of tracing that person, nor shall a copy of any such photograph be shown to any person except a person officially authorised to see it; and

(b) if the person arrested neither has been nor is subsequently convicted of an offence against these regulations, all photographs (both negatives and copies) and finger-print impressions so taken shall be destroyed as soon as they are no longer required for the purposes of these regulations, and in any case forthwith after the termination of the present war.

. . . and anything found on any person so arrested which there is reason to suspect is being so used or intended to be used may be seized, and the competent naval or military authority may order anything so seized to be destroyed or otherwise disposed of.

Added 28 August 1918

If any person assists or connives at the escape of any person who may be in custody under this regulation, or knowingly harbours or assists any person who has so escaped, he shall be guilty of an offence against these regulations.

TABLE 2. ROIR 55

Arrester	**Grounds for Arrest**
(Reg. as at 13 August 1920)	(Reg. as at 13 August 1920)
Any person authorised for the purpose by the competent naval or military authority, or any police constable, or officer of customs and excise or aliens officer	... may arrest without warrant any person whose behaviour is of such a nature as to give reasonable grounds for suspecting that he has acted or is acting or is about to act in a manner prejudicial to the restoration or maintenance of order in Ireland, or upon whom may be found any article, book, letter, or other document, the possession of which gives ground for such a suspicion, or who is suspected of having committed a crime or an offence against these regulations, or of being in possession of any article or document which is being used or intended to be used for any purpose or in any way prejudicial to the restoration or maintenance of order in Ireland;

cont.

Under DORR 55, the requirement that 'reasonable grounds' exist for the suspicion opened the possibility for meaningful judicial scrutiny. The 'reasonableness test' was an objective one, and it appears that the courts were prepared to consider the nature of the grounds creating the suspicion.[190] But the possibility of effective scrutiny was reduced by the fact that suspicion need not relate to the commission of a specific offence. As the case law in relation to the question of *vires* illustrated,[191] the courts were prepared to give a very wide interpretation to the phrase 'public safety or the defence of the Realm'.

The second set of criteria for an arrest was where a search of an individual disclosed 'any article, book, letter or other document', the possession of which gave rise to the suspicion mentioned earlier. The main effect of this provision was to clarify that mere possession of one of these articles could in itself be sufficient to create the required suspicion.

In the third set of grounds the test was a subjective one. The formula 'who is suspected' included no requirement for reasonableness; thus in any judicial challenge to the use of these powers, it would be sufficient for the arrestor to prove the existence of a 'real' suspicion—in distinction from a 'reasonable' suspicion—a lower hurdle to mount.[192] This again

[190] *Michaels* v. *Block* [1918] 34 *TLR* 438. The case is discussed below.
[191] See pp. 112–16.
[192] See *R* v. *Denison* [1916] 32 *TLR* 528, and *Ronnfeldt* v. *Phillips* [1918–19] 35 *TLR* 46, where this construction was put on the similar wording of DORR 14 (see App. 3).

TABLE 2. *Continued*

Provisions governing Detention

(Reg. as at 13 August 1920)

Any person so arrested may be detained either in civil custody or in military custody; and without prejudice to any other power of detention any such person may, on the order of the competent naval or military authority, be detained in any of His Majesty's prisons as a person committed to prison on remand, or, in Scotland, for further examination, until it has been determined whether or not he is to be proceeded against for a crime or an offence under these regulations and, if the offence for which he is to be proceeded against is not a summary offence, until it has also been determined in what manner he is to be tried.

On a person being taken into custody under this regulation he may apply to the competent naval or military authority for release on bail, and, if the competent naval or military authority so directs in writing, any officer of police, who under the Summary Jurisdiction Acts has power to release on bail any person apprehended without warrant, may discharge the person so in custody upon his entering into a recognizance, or, in Scotland, finding caution, with or without sureties, for a reasonable amount to appear at such time and place, to be named in the recognizance or caution, as may be fixed by the competent naval or military authority. Provided that a person so taken into custody as having committed a summary offence against these regulations may be released on bail in manner aforesaid without application to or direction from the competent naval or military authority.

The power given by this regulation to an officer of the police to discharge any person in custody shall in Ireland be exerciseable by a resident magistrate or in the police district of Dublin Metropolis by a divisional justice of that district.

Misc.

(Reg. as at 13 August 1920)

Any person so arrested shall, if so ordered by the competent naval or military authority, or by the chief officer of police for the district, be photographed and finger-print impressions of the fingers and thumbs of both of his hands taken, and if any person refuses to allow such photograph or impressions to be taken, or obstructs the taking thereof, he shall be guilty of a summary offence against these regulations:

Provided that:

(a) no photograph of a person so taken shall be published except for the purpose of tracing that person, nor shall a copy of any such photograph be shown to any person except a person officially authorised to see it; and

(b) if the person arrested neither has been nor is subsequently convicted of an offence against these regulations, all photographs (both negatives and copies) and finger-print impressions so taken shall be destroyed as soon as they are no longer required for the purposes of these regulations,

... and anything found on any person so arrested which there is reason to suspect is being so used or intended to be used may be seized, and the competent naval or military authority may order anything so seized to be destroyed or otherwise disposed of.

If any person assists or connives at the escape of any person who may be in custody under this regulation, or knowingly harbours or assists any person who has so escaped, he shall be guilty of an offence against these regulations.

marked a departure from the ordinary law. The 'real' suspicion could be either that a person had committed an offence against the regulations, or that he was in possession of 'any article or document which is being used or intended to be used for any purpose or in any way prejudicial to the public safety or the defence of the Realm'. This latter provision differed from the second set of grounds for arrest in that it was designed to permit arrest where a person was suspected of being in possession of the material in question, whereas the second set of grounds was intended to cope with a situation where a person was searched prior to arrest, and such material was found on him.

In August 1920, ROIR 55 was created from DORR 55, principally by the substitution of the phrase 'restoration or maintenance of order in Ireland' for 'public safety or the defence of the Realm', and by the inclusion of the words 'a crime or' before the words 'an offence' (Table 2). Crime for the purposes of the regulations was defined as:

Any treason, treason felony, felony, misdemeanour or other offence punishable whether on indictment or summary conviction by imprisonment or by any greater punishment other than offences against the Defence of the Realm Regulations or these regulations.

Thus all but the most petty crimes were rendered arrestable under the new Regulation. This innovation was designed to permit use of ROIR 55 as a first stage in the newly expanded courts martial jurisdiction, which under ROIA covered all of these crimes.

But this was only one of the intended uses of the Regulation. The provisions allowing arrest where no specific crime was suspected were also incorporated, thus facilitating use of ROIR 55 in connection with the mass internment policy (under ROIR 14B) initiated in November 1920.[193] Although there is considerable divergence between British and Dáil statistics in relation to the numbers arrested (Table 3), both sets of statistics are agreed that the new policy resulted in an increase.

Detention

It would be a mistake, however, to assume that all arrests under ROIR 55 were carried out with a view to trial by court martial or to internment. The Regulation contained no provision to the effect that it was to be used only for these purposes, though it did clearly envisage investigation of the case of a detained person by the CMA. Several provisions in the Regulation (and in DORR 55) in relation to detention allowed the collection of information which could provide useful intelligence material whether or not the detainee were tried or interned. First, detainees could

[193] See pp. 105–9.

TABLE 3. Number of arrests in relation to political offences, January 1918 to January 1921

Dáil figures[1]		British figures	
Weeks ending		Weeks ending	
1918 (full year)	1,107	n/a	
1 Jan. 1919–27 Mar. 1920[a]	2,096	1 Jan. 1919–29 Mar. 1920[2]	210
3 Apr. 1920–7 Aug. 1920	1,748	n/a	
14 Aug. 1920–4 Sept. 1920	253	14 Aug. 1920–4 Sept. 1920[3]	117
11 Sept. 1920–2 Oct. 1920	464	11 Sept. 1920–2 Oct. 1920	333
9 Oct. 1920–30 Oct. 1920	n/a	9 Oct. 1920–30 Oct. 1920	271
6 Nov. 1920–27 Nov. 1920	1,231	6 Nov. 1920–27 Nov. 1920	485
4 Dec. 1920–25 Dec. 1920	1,139	4 Dec. 1920–25 Dec. 1920	320
1 Jan. 1921–22 Jan. 1921	1,977	Not to hand	

[a] Incomplete—figures for w/e 23 Aug., 30 Aug., 8 Sept. and 15 Nov. 1919, 20 Mar. and 27 Mar. 1920 not available.

Sources: (1) *Irish Bulletin*, weekly surveys from w/e 12 July 1919 to w/e 22 Jan. 1921, and retrospective figures for 1918 and Jan.–Sept. 1919 published in *Irish Bulletin*, for w/e 27 Sept. 1919, National Library, Dublin; (2) 128 *HC Deb.*, col. 864; (3) Townshend, 221.

be photographed on the orders of either the CMA or the appropriate Chief of Police, a facility which seems to have been widely used in Ireland.[194] Secondly, they could be fingerprinted on the same authority. Thirdly, there was the provision that certain items 'found on any person' could be seized. This provision implicitly assumes a power to search, though the regulation did not explicitly incorporate such a power. Fourthly, and perhaps most importantly, it was the practice to interrogate detainees. There were no specific powers of interrogation in the Regulation,[195] but neither was there any general bar on questioning.

[194] A collection of photographs of suspects can be found in 'Some Types of the Sinn Fein, Compiled by Intelligence Branch 6th Division', Strickland papers. The suspect is shown standing beside a chalked description giving the following details: date, name, address, age, description of eyes, hair colour, and complexion. On the photograph is written the suspect's IRA rank, and his brigade, battalion, and company. Ernie O'Malley, in his account of his arrest and detention by the British Army, records being photographed and being shown photographs of other suspects during interrogation. *On Another Man's Wound*, 221–58.
[195] A general power to interrogate of the type which might be used by military sentries was given by DORR 53, the text of which is given in App. 3.

In December 1920 the Chief Secretary informed the House of Commons that 'owing to the difficulties in regard to obtaining evidence which exist in many parts of Ireland, it has been necessary to make numerous arrests on suspicion and many so arrested have been detained for a short time for examination or pending further inquiry and then released'.[196] Similarly, it was the practice in the Chief Secretary's weekly reports to the Cabinet not to record 'the very considerable number of persons arrested and temporarily detained in military custody'.[197] In modern parlance what were being described were 'screening operations'. It may have been an earlier reliance on this practice which explains the disparity between Dáil and British arrest figures for 1919 (Table 3).

By 1920 at the latest, the Army had developed two sets of interrogation techniques. One was geared towards intelligence gathering, but 'where a man was of importance or where his evidence was important in order to secure a conviction, a different procedure was necessary and the legal branch had to be consulted before interrogation'.[198] The reason for this was that 'The claims of the law and of intelligence were bound to conflict because from a civil and legal point of view trial and conviction were all important; while, from the point of view of military intelligence, information, which might lead to operations in the field, was the first consideration.'[199] The Army placed a high premium on interrogation as a source of intelligence: 'The best information, i.e., that on which the most successful operations, where the heaviest loss was inflicted on the IRA, were based, was that given by IRA deserters and prisoners under interrogation.'[200] The recommended technique was to get a man who was worried about the position in which he found himself and then 'to try to obtain some hold over him—for instance, a man who had given a false name might easily imagine that this was likely to get him into serious trouble out of which his questioner alone could extricate him'.[201] The man being interrogated was to be separated from his fellow prisoners, and it was generally found best to commence interrogation by a general conversation about such things as the man's food, his home, or his life and pursuits. From this seemingly innocent start,

It was an easy transition to the people who lived near him, and he could be asked whether he was acquainted with some one whom the interrogator knew to be locally prominent in the IRA. This placed a prisoner in rather an awkward

---

[196] 136 *HC Deb.*, col. 261. Written answers, 14 Dec. 1920.
[197] Chief Secretary's weekly survey, w/e 28 Feb. 1921, CAB 24/120, PRO, Kew.
[198] 'Record of the Rebellion', ii. 27.
[199] Ibid.   [200] Ibid. 26.   [201] Ibid. 27.

predicament, for if he denied knowledge of such a one he was an obvious liar, while he did not realise where the admission that he knew the man would lead.[202]

Complaints of ill-treatment, often of severe ill-treatment, during interrogation were common from the second half of 1920 onwards. In one case in County Cork it was claimed that a man had been driven insane after he and a fellow prisoner had been tortured by members of the Essex Regiment, by having their nails crushed and their hair pulled out using pincers and pliers.[203] In an affidavit submitted to the Labour Commission on Ireland, another prisoner described how, following arrest by the Army, he was beaten, stripped, searched, and had his mouth forced open with knife handles while rum was poured down. He alleged that he was then beaten again, tied to a chair, and partly burned using petrol.[204]

Ernie O'Malley's account of his detention describes a mixture of casual brutality and formal interviews leading up to a session in the 'Interview Room' at Dublin Castle. During this, he alleged that when he refused to give satisfactory answers he was first beaten in the chest and face by one of his two Army interrogators, both of whom were officers. As he began to bleed he was told to drop his coat in order to keep the floor clean. His description of what followed was that one of his interrogators

walked in front of me to a stove and picked up a poker from the floor. He dug the poker between the bars. He pulled it out, the point was a soft crimson; he shoved it back. The Major looked at me, then turned to the stove. I felt a hollow in my stomach. The Captain looked at the poker; it was bent, the crimson glow ran up close to the handle. 'Now you'll talk.' He held the poker in front of my face. I moved back from the heat. 'By God, you'll talk.' He held one of my arms tight, then angled the point forward as if to dig it into my eyes. He swung it horizontally until it was on a level with my eyes. My eyebrows were singed; the heat made my eyes burn. He brought the poker nearer, I tried to move back, the smell made me cough dryly. My eyelashes curled up; the lids smarted . . . 'Will you answer?' I shook my head. He raised the poker as if he was going to hit me. He put it back between the bars of the stove.[205]

O'Malley alleged that he was then partly choked by hand, and that a blank cartridge was fired from a gun which was pointed at him and which he had been told was loaded. The threat of being shot could not have been assumed to have been an empty one, since, as Lyons notes, 'shot while attempting to escape' was 'frequently enough used as a euphemism for murder'.[206]

---

[202] Ibid.   [203] Barry, *Guerilla Days*, 15.
[204] The text of the affidavit is reproduced in the *Report of the Labour Commission to Ireland* (London, 1921), 84.
[205] O'Malley, *On Another Man's Wound*, 250.
[206] *Ireland since the Famine*, 419. Some further accounts alleging ill-treatment can be found in L. Deasy, *Towards Ireland Free* (Dublin, 1973), 335–47.

An Army Intelligence summary of the Irish campaign later concluded: 'Brutal methods are a Mistake.—Many innocent men were imprisoned because brutal interrogators, who believed that every Irish man was a Sinn Feiner, so treated them that, in the hope to escaping further ill-treatment, they confessed that they were soldiers of the IRA.'[207] That brutality could be counter-productive was considered one of the 'golden rules for interrogation'. Another was that detailed local knowledge was essential. 'For senior intelligence officers to conduct interrogations was, with few exceptions, generally a waste of time of all concerned.'[208] The final one was that a man should be interrogated alone by one Intelligence Officer because detainees feared being overheard by someone else on account of the risk of being denounced as an informer.[209]

Interrogations could be conducted over a period stretching into weeks. Initially, DORR 55 had contained no express provisions in relation to detention. It may or may not have been intended that the position under military law was to apply, whereby Commanding Officers were to investigate cases within forty-eight hours after the committal of the person into custody was reported to them, unless investigation within that period seemed 'impracticable with due regard to the public service'.[210] In any case, an amendment introduced in January 1919 expressly permitted an arrested person to be detained in civil or military custody, and authorized the CMA to order the detention of the person in prison 'until it has been determined whether or not he is to be proceeded against for an offence under these regulations' (Table 1). This provision was carried through in ROIR 55, and by January 1921 the delays had become so long that GHQ began to express concern. In that month it was ordered that every CMA was to ensure that charges against civilians were investigated within seven days of the date on which the committal into custody of the prisoner was reported to him.[211] As was the position under military law, delays were permissible where investigation within the time limits seemed impracticable 'with due regard to the public service'.[212] Cases in which the person was detained beyond a period of seven days without investigation were to be reported by the CMA to his immediate superior authority giving the reasons for the delay.

---

[207] 'Record of the Rebellion', ii. 27.
[208] Ibid.
[209] By and large, the conclusions reached in relation to military interrogations in Ireland corresponded with those arrived at as a result of the British Army's interrogation of prisoners during the First World War. For an assessment of this latter experience see M. Occleshaw, *Armour against Fate* (London, 1989), 99–109.
[210] Rule of Procedure 2. *Manual of Military Law* (London, 1914), 571.
[211] GRO 54, 14 Jan. 1921, WO 35/173/2, PRO, Kew.
[212] Ibid.

If the case were one which the CMA had authority to deal with, he was to convene a court martial[213] or to refer the matter to his superiors within three days of the completion of the investigation. If more than twenty-one days elapsed between the day of arrest and the date at which the case was disposed of, either by the assembly of a court martial or by orders for internment being received, the CMA was to report the cases with the reasons for delay direct to GHQ, and a similar report was to be forwarded every ten days until a court martial was assembled, an internment order received, or the suspect released. There may well have been some tardiness in complying with these time-limits, as GHQ found it necessary to issue further orders in which the limits were re-enforced.[214]

It was open to a person in custody under the regulation to apply for bail. In the case of a suspect taken into custody as having committed a summary offence against the regulations, provision was initially made under DORR 55 that the suspect could apply directly to any officer of police who under the Summary Jurisdiction Acts had power to release on bail. Under an amendment introduced in January 1919, this power was made exercisable in Ireland by an RM or in Dublin by a divisional justice (Table 1). ROIR 55 also incorporated this provision, and under both regulations special provisions applied in the cases of those taken into custody other than in relation to summary offences against the regulations. In such cases the prisoner was to apply first to the CMA, and if the CMA gave a written direction, the suspect could then apply for bail in the same way as a person suspected of a summary offence. This enabled the CMA to prevent the granting of bail where further interrogation was planned, or indeed for any other reason he deemed appropriate.

Martial law powers

Under martial law, all legal remedies were effectively suspended. Thus there could be said to have been no immediately operative legal limitations on the powers of arrest and detention open to the Army. Despite this, the martial law legal system generally corresponded in many respects with, and overlapped with, the statutory system.[215] While there were a number of special orders in this field in the MLA, the Army seems to have viewed

---

[213] See pp. 61–9.

[214] GRO 313/1921, 22 Mar. 1921, ordered that when transmitting the proceedings of the trial, in all cases in which the accused had been in arrest awaiting trial for a period exceeding 21 days, a detailed explanation of the delay was to be forwarded to GHQ with the proceedings. GRO 509/1921, 10 May 1921, ordered that delays as set out in GRO 54/1921 were to be shown on the CMA's weekly report. WO 35/173/2, PRO, Kew.

[215] See pp. 85–7 below.

the length of detention at least as being governed by the General Routine Orders issued in relation to detention under ROIR 55.[216]

In the MLA military arrests were to be carried out on the orders of an officer.[217] In that area generally, expediency was given pride of place in military calculations, thus in relation to arrests it was ordered that 'care must be taken to discriminate between those worthy of detention and those whose detention will not only be of no value to us, but also will congest our prison camps'.[218] This was because 'the number of arrests are no criterion of the importance of operations, but rather the *value* of the arrests'.[219] Another factor was the status of the suspect. If 'anyone who claims to be an alien' was thought to be 'misbehaving', a wire was to be sent to GHQ at once, and beyond arrest no action was to be taken without order from GHQ.[220]

Special instructions were also issued in relation to round-ups: 'When a general "round-up" of the male population takes place, it will be held, if possible, at such an hour as will not prevent persons from attending Divine Service.'[221] The round-up, though, could take place immediately after Mass, because this 'gives no ground for enemy propaganda to the effect that the crown Forces are interfering with the religion of the people'.[222] Where a round-up took place, men were to be held for identification by the Intelligence Department if the slightest grounds for suspicion as to their identity existed.[223]

As regards detention, it was ordered that 'a small cage' was to be erected in every barrack, hutment, or camp, to take a limited number of persons 'arrested for a short time'.[224] But a time-limit was always to be ordered by a Military Governor beyond which prisoners were not to be detained in such local cages. In the MLA, the range of additional powers available to the Army made it easier for interrogators to establish the vital hold over the suspect. One Army account of an interrogation reads:

A man who had been employed as an agent, but who had joined the IRA and ceased to give information was arrested by RIC in Cork, and found to be in possession of a revolver. He at once claimed to be a Secret Service Agent, and gave the name of the Intelligence Officer whom he was supposed to work under.

---

[216] The 'Notes on the Administration of Martial Law' provided: 'Attention is drawn to General Routine Orders 54 and 509 of 1921 which deal with the question of delay in disposing of persons who have been arrested.'
[217] Ibid.
[218] '17th Infantry Brigade, Summary', 1.
[219] Ibid. (original emphasis).
[220] 'Notes on the Administration of Martial Law', 3.
[221] '17th Infantry Brigade, Summary', 3.
[222] Ibid. 3.
[223] Ibid. 7.
[224] 'Notes on the Administration of Martial Law', 3.

This officer was sent for, and denied all knowledge of the man, who was then informed that he would be tried by Drumhead Court-martial and shot. This had the desired effect, and the Police Officer and Intelligence Officer proceeded to interrogate him carefully. Seven hours were spent in interrogation and cross-examination, and at the end of that time the ex-agent broke down and gave a great deal of information.[225]

Arrest and detention powers: conclusion

DORR 55 and ROIR 55 created powers of arrest and detention which were significantly different from those of the ordinary law. The main points of departure from normal standards were: (1) arrests were permitted on military authority; (2) arrests were authorized where no specific offence was suspected; (3) if a specific offence was suspected, there was no requirement of reasonableness; and (4) extended detention for the purpose of investigation of the case against the accused was permitted.

These four points of departure facilitated the use of the regulations as a device for the screening of suspects. It appears that the Army first began to use DORR 55 as the initial stage of the internment process in January 1920, but it was only when ROIR 55 was introduced and political control over the use of arrest and detention powers was all but removed that full use was made of the flexibility of the provisions. Under martial law even greater flexibility was introduced, so that expediency became the guiding principle.

The position at the end of 1920 seems to have been that use of the regulation involved three separate value judgements. The first was arrest. This could be on the merest suspicion and was in effect a screening process. If the detainee were not 'filtered out' at this stage, the decision would be made as to whether the case was suitable for trial by court martial or it should be otherwise dealt with. If it were deemed a suitable case, the Army's legal branch would be consulted, and the interrogation of the suspect would be conducted in a manner designed to produce evidence which would be admissible at the trial. In other cases the interrogation would be geared towards intelligence gathering, with a view to possible internment. Particularly from the second half of 1920 onwards, the conduct of interrogations was not infrequently marked by the ill-treatment of suspects. On occasion, this ill-treatment seems to have been so intense, and so purposefully inflicted, as to have amounted to

---

[225] 'Rebellion in the Sixth Divisional Area', 96. The Army claimed that the information which the man gave led to the deaths of six of the Cork Active Service Unit ('Murder Gang'). Following the deaths, he was further interrogated, and his information led to the discovery of two munitions dumps and a large dug-out. He was eventually given £150 and shipped out of the country in a destroyer.

torture.[226] The chances of ill-treatment occurring were increased by the nature of the powers given under the regulation, in particular by the provisions allowing detention in military custody with no time-limits other than those which the Army decided to impose, and more generally, by the lack of external scrutiny of the treatment of prisoners.

SECTION (B) SPECIAL COURTS

The story of special courts in the years 1918–21 is largely the story of trials by the military, involving a variety of statutory and non-statutory tribunals. While the provisions of the Criminal Law and Procedure (Ireland) Act 1887 in this area are of interest (and are examined immediately below), they seem to have had little practical effect. The experience of trials by the military was broadly one of progressive degradation of procedure as, with each new initiative, simplified procedures were introduced in an attempt to render the system more effective. The process began with formal DORA and then ROIA general courts martial, and was taken a step further with introduction of the less formal ROIA field general courts martial. The third step was the introduction of martial law military courts, and the nadir was reached with the institution of trial by martial law drumhead court.

Introduction: the ordinary court system and the 1887 Act

Under the ordinary system of criminal administration, summary offences were tried before courts of summary jurisdiction (CSJ) at the Petty sessions, and indictable offences at quarter sessions, or, in the case of more serious offences, at the assizes.[227] The bench at the trial of summary cases often consisted of lay magistrates (Justices of the Peace) and stipendiary magistrates. Outside Dublin, the latter resided in their districts and held the title of Resident Magistrate. This latter office was a nineteenth-century creation, the existence of which was due to dissatisfaction with the system of unpaid magistrates. By 1912 there were sixty-four RMs who between them covered the whole country apart from Dublin. In the case of a conviction at the Petty sessions, an appeal usually lay to quarter sessions.

The system of dealing with indictable offences was that, following charging, a magistrate would conduct a preliminary examination to decide

---

[226] For discussions of the meaning of 'torture' see B. M. Klayman, 'The Definition of Torture in International Law', 51 *Temple Law Quarterly* 449, and R. Maran, 'Against Torture', 4 *Human Rights Review* 85.

[227] This description is based on V. T. H. Delany, *The Administration of Justice in Ireland* (Dublin, 1970), 19–31.

on the sufficiency of evidence. If he decided there was sufficient evidence he returned the prisoner for trial at quarter sessions or at the assizes. If not, the prisoner was discharged. Historically, 'all felonies of a political and insurrectionary character' were tried only at the assizes. The next stage was that a 'bill of indictment' was preferred to the grand jury by the prosecutor. The grand jury then considered whether there was a prima-facie case against the accused. If so, they returned a 'true bill' which then became an indictment, and if not they 'ignored' it. If an indictment were found, the final stage was trial by a judge and 'Petty' jury. There existed no full appeals system in relation to convictions on indictment, but the Court of Crown Cases Reserved could hear questions of law only which might be reserved at any criminal trial.

Special juries and removal for trial under the 1887 Act

If the ordinary court system could be said to have functioned effectively when dealing with ordinary crime, at least prior to 1920, the situation in relation to politically motivated crime had long been quite different.[228] The reluctance of juries to enter convictions in such cases, either through sympathy with the accused or because of intimidation, had led to the introduction of a variety of temporary measures altering jury trial in the eighteenth and nineteenth centuries. Eventually, as noted in part I, permanent provisions were introduced in the Criminal Law and Procedure (Ireland) Act 1887 which allowed jury trial to be altered in any district which might be 'proclaimed'.

Under the Act, criminal procedure in relation to trial on indictment could be altered in two respects. In both instances this was to be primarily at the behest of the Attorney-General. In the case of a district proclaimed under section 3, provisions permitting use of a 'special jury' could be invoked, and in the case of a district proclaimed under section 4, the venue of the trial could be moved. In Ireland in the period in question, the practice was to proclaim districts under both sections simultaneously (Table 4).

Section 3 provided:

Where an indictment for a crime committed in a proclaimed district has been found against a defendant, or a defendant has been committed for trial for such crime, and the trial is to be by a jury before a court in Ireland other than a court of quarter sessions, the High Court shall on an application by or on behalf of the Attorney General for Ireland or a defendant make an order, as of course, that the trial of the defendant or the defendants if more than one shall be by a special jury.

---

[228] See, generally, Vanston 16–18; Humphreys, 20–1; and Feely, 15–16.

TABLE 4. Implementation of the Criminal Law and Procedure (Ireland) Act 1887, 1918–1919

District (counties unless otherwise indicated)	14 June 1918 ss. 3 and 4 in force	3 July 1918 SF, SF Clubs, IV, CnB, and GL declared dangerous	4 July 1919 SF, SF Clubs, IV, CnB, and GL prohibited and suppressed	13 Aug. 1919 SF, SF Clubs, IV, CnB, and GL prohibited and suppressed	9 Sept. 1919 s. 1 in force	10 Sept. 1919 Dáil Eireann prohibited and suppressed	10 Sept. 1919 SF, SF Clubs, IV, CnB, and GL prohibited and suppressed	15 Oct. 1919 SF, SF Clubs, IV, CnB, and GL prohibited and suppressed	24 Oct. 1919 ss. 3 and 4 in force	25 Nov. 1919 SF, SF Clubs, IV, CnB, and GL prohibited and suppressed
Antrim		+				+				+
Armagh		+				+				+
Belfast CB		+				+				+
Carlow		+				+				+
Cavan		+				+				
Clare	+	+		+	+	+	+			
Cork	+	+			+	+	+			
Cork CB		+				+				
Donegal		+				+				+
Down		+				+				+
Dublin		+			+	+		+	+	+
Dublin CB		+			+	+		+	+	+
Fermanagh		+				+				+
Galway	+	+				+				+
Kerry	+	+				+				+
Kildare		+				+				+
Kilkenny		+				+				+
King's	+	+				+				+
Leitrim		+				+				+
Limerick	+	+			+	+				+
Limerick CB	+	+			+	+				+
Londonderry		+				+				+
Londonderry CB		+				+				+
Longford	+	+				+				+
Louth	+	+				+				+
Mayo		+				+				+
Meath		+				+				+
Monaghan		+				+				+
Queen's	+	+				+				+
Roscommon	+	+				+				+
Sligo	+	+				+				+
Tipperary NR	+	+	+		+	+				
Tipperary SR	+	+	+		+	+				
Tyrone	+	+				+				
Waterford		+				+				+
Waterford CB		+				+				+
Westmeath	+	+				+				+
Wexford		+				+				+
Wicklow		+				+				+

Sources: Supplements to *DG* 14 June and 2 July 1918, *DG* 4 July 1918, *DG* 4 July 1919, Supplements to *DG* 12 Aug. and 9 Sept. 1919, Supplement to *DG* 9 Sept. 1919, 2nd Supplement to *DG* 9 Sept. 1919, Supplement to *DG* 14 Oct. 1919, *DG* 24 Oct. 1919, Supplement to *DG* 25 Nov. 1919.

The distinguishing feature of special juries was that those entitled to serve on them had to meet a higher than usual property qualification.[229] Otherwise, special juries were to be chosen like other juries.[230] Under the rules of procedure made under the Act, the number of special jurors to be summoned, returned, and empanelled was set out,[231] and it was provided that a copy of an order for trial by special jury obtained by or on behalf of the Attorney-General was to be served on the defendant ten days before the trial.[232]

In relation to removal for trial, section 4 provided:

Where an indictment for a crime committed in a proclaimed district has been found against a defendant, or a defendant has been committed for trial for such crime, and the trial is to be at a court of assize for any county in a proclaimed district, or at a court of quarter sessions for any county or borough in a proclaimed district, the High Court on an application by or on behalf of the Attorney General for Ireland, and upon his certificate that he believes that a more fair and impartial trial can be had at a court of assize in some county to be named in the certificate, shall make an order as of course that the trial shall be had at a court of assize in the county named in the certificate.

In the case of an order for removal made before an indictment had been found, the crime was to be 'inquired of' by a grand jury in the county named in the order for removal, and if the order was made after the indictment had been found, it was to be tried as if the indictment had been found in the court to which the trial was removed.[233] There was a safeguard for the defendant in that section 4 also provided:

The defendant or any defendant, if more than one, may in the prescribed manner and within the prescribed time apply to the High Court to discharge or vary any

---

[229] Under the Juries (Ireland) Act 1871, those entitled to serve on special juries were 'the sons of peers, baronets, knights, magistrates, the eldest sons of baronets, of knights, or of magistrates' and every person who met the property qualification of owning land with a rateable valuation of between £30 and £100 depending on where the potential juror lived (s. 11 and the fifth schedule). Otherwise, the rateable valuation for service on juries was between £12 and £20 (fourth schedule). By the Juries (Ireland) Act 1873, the qualification for service on special juries was raised to between £40 and £150, and that for other jury service to between £12 and £30 (s. 2 and the first and second schedules). The Jurors Qualification (Ireland) Act 1876, which was to be in force until 1880 (s. 6) altered the qualification for service to between £30 and £150 in the case of special juries, and between £6 and £40 in the case of other juries. See, generally, J. F. McEldowney, 'Irish Jury Trial: A Survey of Some Eighteenth and Nineteenth Century Statutes', *Warwick Law Working Papers*, 3/4 (1979).

[230] s. 9, i.e. under s. 19 of the Juries Procedure (Ireland) Act 1876.

[231] Rule II. In a county where the special jurors did not amount to 200, all were to be summoned, and in counties where there were 200 or more special jurors, 200 were to be summoned.

[232] Rule I (a). These Rules, which were made on 23 July 1887, are included as an appendix in Feely, 53–61.

[233] s. 10 (1).

such order for the removal of a trial, upon the ground that the trial can be more fairly and impartially had in a county other than the county named in the order of removal, and thereupon the High Court may order that the trial shall be had in any county in which it shall appear that the trial can be most fairly and impartially had.

An application by a defendant to discharge or vary any such order was to be made within four days from the service of the order.[234] The section was interpreted as being mandatory and not merely permissive. Thus it was held that where a defendant satisfied the court that the trial could be more fairly and impartially had in a county other than the county named in the order of removal, the court was obliged to order the trial to take place in the county in which it appeared that the trial could be most fairly and impartially held.[235]

By April 1920 some satisfaction was being expressed about the operation of the amended procedures, though not in relation to murder charges. At a conference in that month, the Attorney-General for Ireland reported that 'at the last winter Assizes there had been a good many convictions obtained but in the murder cases it has difficult [*sic*] to get evidence. The venue of the trials had been repeatedly changed.'[236] In some instances the Attorney-General obtained orders for removal of trial from Southern counties to Belfast and Derry, but such orders were successfully challenged by the defendants under section 4 of the Act.[237]

Within a few months the situation had considerably worsened from the British point of view. No conviction for murder had been obtained in any political case, a fact which advocates of the death penalty found particularly irksome. By July the military were also convinced of the failure of the court system; in Macready's view 'the civil courts of the country . . . as shown by the last assizes, have completely lapsed'.[238] Intelligence reports likewise indicated 'the assizes were a failure in most places, jurors, witnesses, civil plaintiffs and defendants being afraid to attend'.[239] A few weeks later, ROIA became law and the jurisdiction of courts martial was greatly expanded.

---

[234] Rule of Procedure III (c).
[235] *R* v. *Fitzgerald and Others* [1920] 2 *IR* 428 (23 and 24 June 1920), and *R* v. *Maher and Others* [1920] 2 *IR* 440 (26 and 27 Feb. 1920).
[236] CAB 23/21, PRO, Kew.
[237] This was what happened in *R* v. *Fitzgerald and Others* [1920] 2 *IR* 428, and in *R* v. *Maher and Others* [1920] 2 *IR* 440.
[238] Memorandum by Gen. Macready 26 July 1920, CAB 24/110, PRO, Kew.
[239] 'Report on Revolutionary Organizations in the UK', 29 July 1920, CAB 24/110, PRO, Kew. Similarly, the 6th Division's 'Weekly Intelligence Summary' of 12 July 1920 complained about the absence of jurors at the Waterford assizes, and reported that 'the business before the court was adjourned to "the next Assizes"—but there is no guarantee that the next assizes will be held'. Included in the summary is a threatening letter purportedly sent to a juror and signed 'Competent Military Authority IRA'. Strickland papers.

Courts martial under DORA and ROIA

The Army Act 1881 and the 1907 Rules of Procedure formed the foundation upon which the DORA and ROIA court-martial systems were constructed.[240] The main difference between the two systems was that under DORA only alleged breaches of DORR could be tried by court martial, whereas the jurisdiction of ROIA courts martial extended not only to ROIR but to virtually all types of crime. While the provisions setting out the procedures of these courts martial were, in the main, precise and legalistic, it would perhaps be a mistake to imagine that in their actual operation 'technical' legal considerations were always paramount. In general, courts martial had been developed as a means of enforcing discipline in the Army rather than in an attempt to mimic civil judicial proceedings. Accounts of front-line field general courts martial conducted by the British Army in the First World War (and therefore immediately before the period in question), paint a picture of procedures which were sometimes unfair and heavy-handed, with scant regard being paid to legal niceties.[241] But not all trials by courts martial, particularly by general courts martial, may have fitted this description.

Not only is it difficult to be definite about the ethos of courts martial in Ireland in this period; it is also difficult to be precise about the numbers that took place, as there are significant differences between British and Dáil figures in this regard (Table 5). British statistics indicate a drop in 1919 on the 1918 figure whereas Dáil figures indicate the exact opposite— a doubling in 1919. It is not easy to explain how, as British statistics indicate, the number of trials in 1918 could have been so much greater than in the following year. One possible explanation is that some of the trials in 1918 related not specifically to the 'Troubles' but were in respect

---

[240] Discovering the applicable provisions is not an easy task. In the case of ROIA courts martial, there were no fewer than eight layers of relevant material. First there was the 1881 Act. The Rules of Procedure formed the second layer. The third was DORA, and the fourth DORR (as amended) which, with minor alteration, became ROIR. ROIA and the original ROIR (apart from those which were simply amended DORR) formed the fifth and sixth layers, while the seventh consisted of the new regulations issued after Aug. 1920 (including amendments). Lastly there were the GRO concerned with the operation of courts martial, which amounted to practice directions. Description of the procedures of Army Act courts martial can be found in the 1914 *Manual of Military Law*, 35–54, and in Cmnd. 7608 (1946), 'Report of Army and Air Force Courts-Martial Committee', 9–15 (hereafter Lewis Report). This report is relevant, as it came before the radical changes introduced by the Courts Martial (Appeals) Act 1951, and the Army Act 1955. The description of court-martial procedures herein is based on these two sources. References to other sources are indicated in the footnotes. For comparative purposes, a description of American court-martial procedures can be found in J. W. Bishop, *Justice under Fire* (New York, 1974), 19–44.

[241] See, generally, A. Babington, *For the Sake of Example* (London, 1983), in which procedures are described on pp. 12–22. For a much less critical account see P. H. Winfield, 'Courts-Martial from the Lawyer's Point of View' 34 *LQR* 143.

TABLE 5. Operation of DORA courts martial in
Ireland, January 1918 to July 1920

Period	British figures	Dáil figures
1918	202	137
1919	138	260
Jan.–July 1920	94	50[a]

[a] Incomplete figures for w/e 20 Mar., 27 Mar. and 10 Apr. 1920. Figures for w/e 5 June 1920 not available.

Sources: (British figures) Townshend, app. 10, p. 221; (Dáil figures) *Irish Bulletin*, weekly surveys from w/e 12 July 1919 to w/e 7 Aug. 1920 and retrospective figures for 1918 and Jan.–Sept. 1919, published in *Irish Bulletin*, w/e 27 Sept. 1919, National Library, Dublin.

TABLE 6. Operation of ROIA courts martial
from week ending 14 August 1920 to week ending
25 December 1920

Weeks ending	No. tried	No. convicted
14 Aug.–4 Sept.	39	37
11 Sept.–2 Oct.	167	124
9 Oct.–30 Oct.	223	192
6 Nov.–27 Nov.	160	120
4 Dec.–25 Dec.	220	182
TOTAL	809	655[a]

[a] *i.e.* 81%.

Source: Derived from Townshend, app. 10, p. 221 (British official figures).

of breaches of DORR relating to food rationing etc., a category which might have declined with the ending of hostilities in Europe.

What is not disputed is that the introduction of ROIA courts martial in August 1920, with greatly increased jurisdiction, led to a corresponding rise in the volume of trials. The rate trebled in the first four-week period of the operation of the new Act (Table 6) only to quadruple in the second. It remained at roughly this level for the rest of 1920. January 1921 saw an increase in the numbers court-martialled with the highest

weekly total for the whole period occurring at the end of January 1921.[242]
For the remainder of the period up to the truce, the numbers court-
martialled averaged approximately 250 per month, a slight increase on
the figure for August–December 1920.

The procedures of both courts martial systems are illustrated by flow-
chart in Figures 1 and 2. Since an attempt to describe the procedures of
both systems separately would involve a great deal of repetition, the
description below is limited (with some exceptions) to the more complex
ROIA system; differences between the two systems are indicated in the
footnotes.

Pre-trial: initiation

Proceedings before a ROIA court martial could be commenced in a
number of ways. Alleged breaches of ROIR declared to be summary
offences were to be tried before a special court of summary jurisdiction
(CSJ). In the cases of alleged breaches of other regulations the case was
to be referred to the appropriate CMA[243] who was to investigate the
case.[244] Ordinarily, a suspect would have been in detention under ROIR
55 while this investigation was taking place, though proceedings could
also be instituted by summons.

In cases of alleged breaches of the ordinary law, the Regulations
provided that the case of any person alleged to be guilty of any crime
punishable summarily or on indictment by imprisonment or any greater
punishment 'may' be referred to the CMA.[245] The Regulations are silent
both as to who was to refer the case and as to the criteria to be employed
in the making of the decision on referring. It seems likely that the
decision would have lain with the Attorney-General for Ireland or with

---

[242] See Table 9.

[243] ROIRs 60, 61, 61A. Strictly speaking, a case was to be referred to the Competent
Naval or Military Authority, but in practice the function seems to have been exclusively a
military one. The CMA was usually a Brigade Commander and in some cases was a
Divisional Commander (Townshend, 49), and jurisdiction in any particular case could
depend on the offence charged. The question of jurisdiction is examined in more detail
below in relation to powers to convene courts martial and to confirm sentences. Under
DORR, special provisions applied in relation to breaches of regulations which were taken to
amount to 'press offences' (DORR 56 (13)) and 'munitions offences' (DORR 56 (14)). In
both instances, instead of being referred to the CMA, the case was to be referred to the AG
for Ireland (or if in Britain, to the Director of Public Prosecutions or the Lord Advocate),
who was to investigate the case and determine whether it was to be proceeded with, and if
so, the manner of its trial. In the period in question, the options in Ireland were trial by CSJ
or by court martial. Special provisions for these classes of offence were dropped in ROIR.

[244] ROIR 56 (3).

[245] ROIR 68 (2). Under ROIR 67, crime was defined as 'any treason, treason felony,
misdemeanour or other offence punishable whether on indictment or summary conviction
by imprisonment or by any greater punishment other than offences against the Defence of
the Realm Regulations or these regulations'.

Ireland 1918–1921

| Offence against DORR |

| Non-summary offence | | Summary offence |

| Case referred to CMA | | Trial by CSJ |

| Investigation of case by CMA and preparation of Summary of Evidence |

| Case not proceeded with | | Case to be proceeded with by court martial | | Case to be proceeded with by CSJ |

| Proceedings terminated |

| Convening of court martial. Copies of charge sheets and Summary of Evidence furnished to accused |

| Trial by court martial |

| Decision of court martial |

| Not guilty | | Guilty |

| Confirmation |

| Revision of finding or sentence ordered | | Finding and sentence confirmed | | Finding upheld sentence commuted or mitigated |

| Promulgation |

| Proceedings to JAG |

| Proceedings upheld | | Proceedings quashed |

| Execution of sentence |

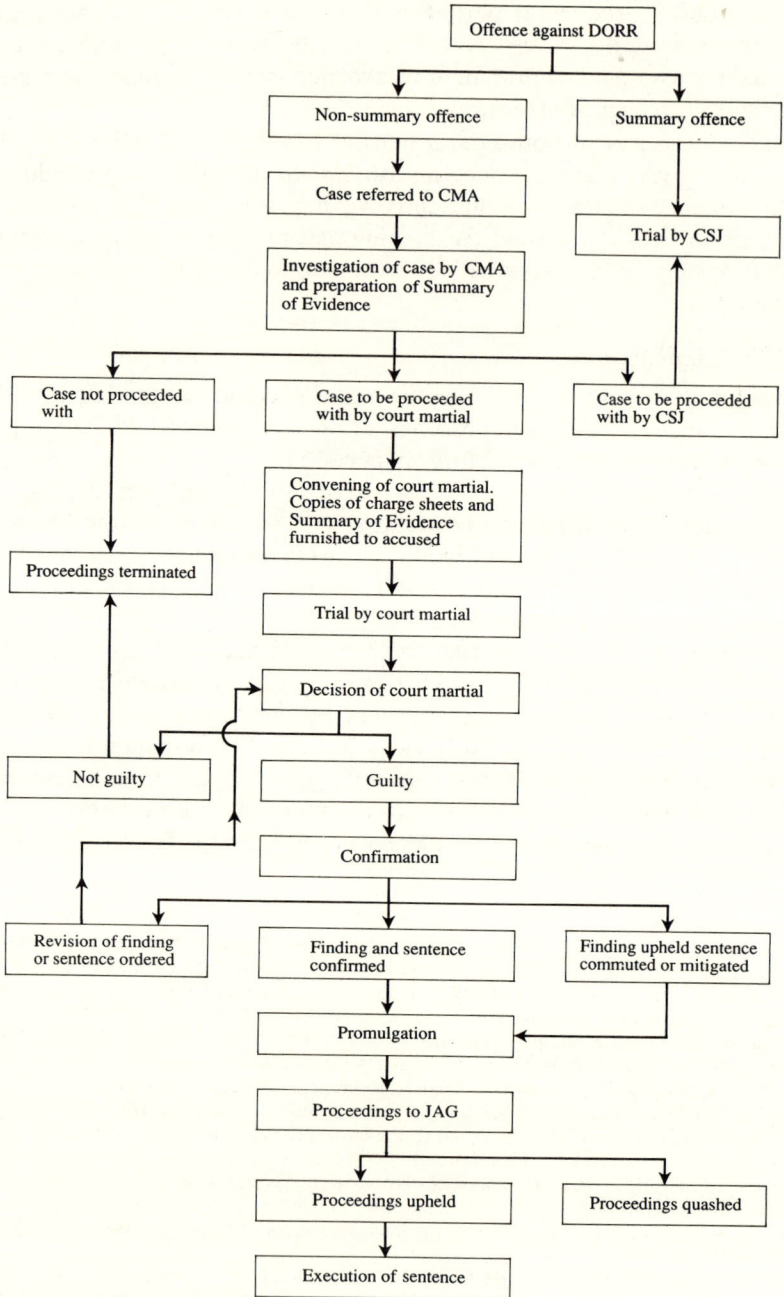

FIG. I. The DORA court martial system

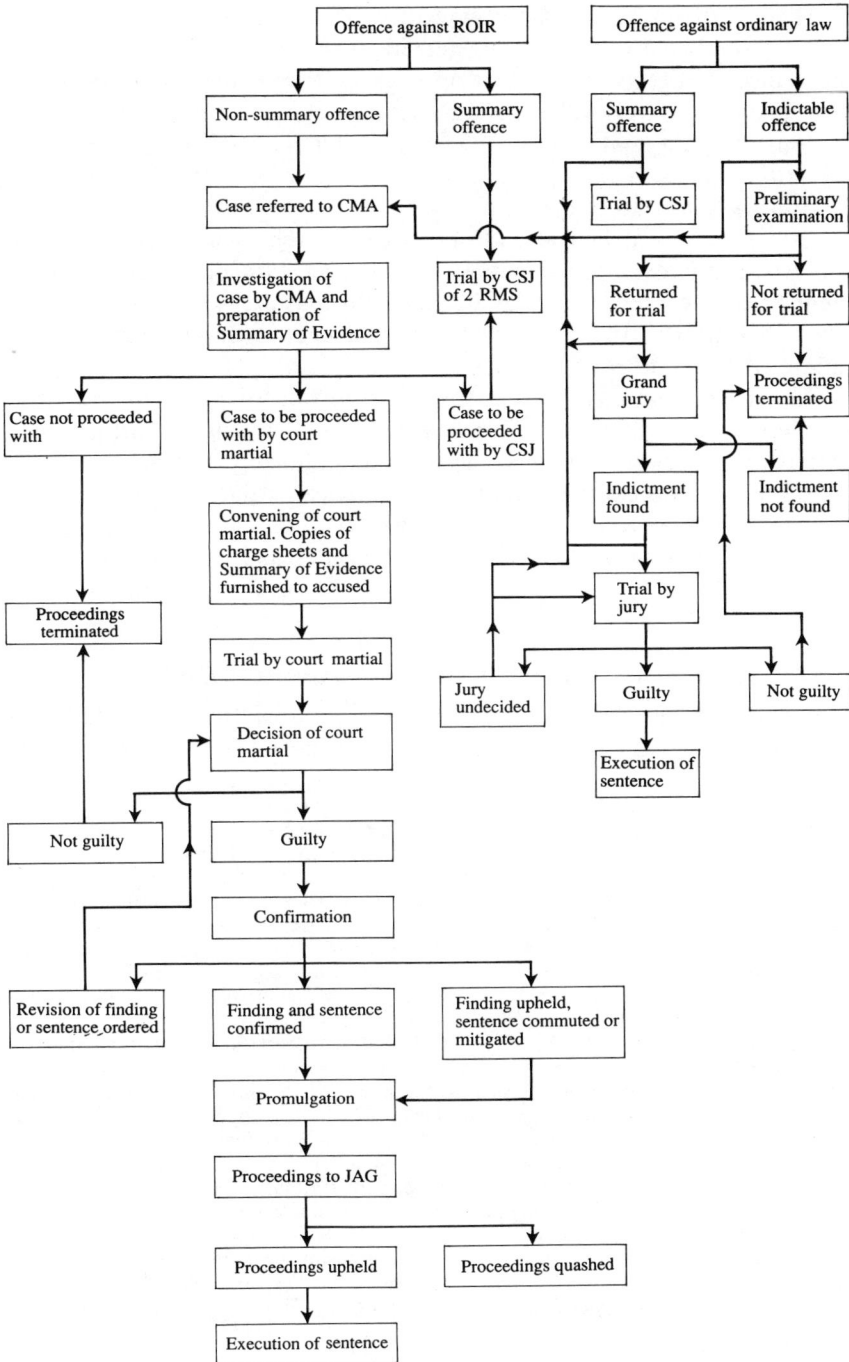

FIG. 2. The ROIA court martial system

the Law Adviser to the Irish Executive.[246] Initially however, the case would have had to have been referred to the civil authorities by either the police or the Army, and it appears that immediately following the introduction of ROIA, there was considerable confusion as to whose responsibility the matter was.[247] The referring of a case was not limited to the initial stages of the investigation, but might be done after committal for trial or upon an indictment having been found in the civil courts.[248] Where the accused had already been before the civil courts, the CMA was to obtain the original depositions and any attached statutory statement of the accused.[249] It was further held that a case could be referred where a retrial in the ordinary courts had been ordered because of the failure of a jury to reach a decision.[250]

The absence of any criteria for the referring of cases to the CMA, coupled with the extensive jurisdiction of ROIA courts martial, meant that persons other than those accused of politically motivated offences were liable to be court-martialled. In practice, while it appears that the majority of those appearing before ROIA courts martial appeared on charges relating to politically motivated crimes and offences, some non-politically-motivated offenders and significant numbers of policemen also appeared as defendants.[251]

Pre-trial: investigation and preparation of Summary of Evidence

Under the Army Act, the initial investigation of the case would have been conducted by the Commanding Officer (CO) to whose unit the

---

[246] In relation to breaches of DORR, Hamar Greenwood advised the British Cabinet in July 1920 that 'courts-martial are now sitting daily, Wylie the Public Prosecutor decides whether the cases should go to a court martial Assize or RM'. Jones, *Diary*, iii. 34. Wylie was at that time the Law Adviser to the Dublin Castle Executive. Townshend, 97. Since some acts which constituted breaches of DORR (and ROIR) also amounted to crimes under the ordinary law (e.g. DORR 32—prohibition on discharge of firearms—and DORR 9E—prohibition on drilling), it may be that Wylie had the task of deciding how charges in such instances should be framed. It seems likely that a similar function would have been performed by the Law Adviser in relation to ROIA courts martial. The 'History of the 5th Division' states in relation to the introduction of ROIA courts martial that 'directions for the prosecution would continue to be issued by the government' (p. 57).

[247] 'History of the 5th Division' records that following the introduction of ROIR 'there were two channels of communication with General headquarters, by military channels and police channels, and there was some uncertainty as to how reports on cases should be communicated to General Headquarters. On occasion the Police were under the impression that the Military had reported the case, and the Military that the Police had taken action, with the result that no action of any kind was taken.' App. 8, para. 6.

[248] ROIR 68 (2). There was no corresponding DORR.

[249] GRO 241, WO 35/173, PRO, Kew. Application was to be made to the Clerk of the Crown and Peace of the county in which the accused had been returned for trial.

[250] *R (Rodgers)* v. *Campbell and Others*, [1921] 55 *ILTR* 192. This case is discussed on pp. 122–3.

[251] The point is discussed below.

alleged offender belonged. Depending on the view taken by the CO of the evidence, he would dismiss the case or deal with it summarily or remand the case for trial by court martial and prepare a 'Summary of Evidence' (discussed below). It would seem that the investigation of the case by the CMA under ROIA would have followed similar lines. Under ROIR, the CMA, after making his investigation, was to decide either to proceed with the case or to dismiss it, and if a decision were taken to proceed, whether the case was to go before a special CSJ or a court martial.[252]

If the decision were taken to proceed by court martial the next stage would have been the preparation of a Summary of Evidence,[253] except in the instances of those who had been committed for trial or against whom an indictment had been found in the ordinary courts and whose cases had been referred to the CMA. In these cases, the depositions and any attached statutory statement of the accused were to be deemed a Summary of Evidence duly taken under the Army Act.[254]

Under ROIR, one of three types of court martial could be ordered: a general court martial, a district court martial, or a field general court martial. The Army Act set out clear directions for the taking of a Summary of Evidence in relation to trials by general and district courts martial, but the Rules of Procedure are less clear on the preparation of the Summary of Evidence in relation to trials by field general courts martial. This latter form of court martial was normally used only when troops were on active service and thus in circumstances which might mean that the formal preparation of a Summary of Evidence was impossible. In Ireland, field general courts martial were introduced when the British Army was put on active service in December 1920,[255] a change which apparently had the effect that 'the whole administration of Military Law, was much simplified'[256] (though this did not result in any marked increase in the numbers court-martialled). Thus, although the *Manual of Military Law* noted in relation to trials by field general courts martial that 'speaking

---

[252] ROIR 56 (3), 56 (5), 56 (6), 68 (2). Summary punishment of soldiers by the CO was permitted under the Army Act, but was expressly prohibited under ROIR (ROIR 69 (3)).

[253] ROIR 69 (3) provided 'an investigation of the case by the competent naval or military authority in such manner as he shall see fit and a written summary of the evidence taken by him or by his direction shall be deemed to be an investigation of the charge and a written summary of the evidence taken by the proper military authority in accordance with the provisions of the Army Act and the Rules of Procedure made thereunder'. In view of the complexity of the procedures involved in the preparation of a Summary of Evidence, it would appear that this regulation should be construed as requiring the preparation of a summary of evidence only in cases where the Army Act required the preparation of a Summary of Evidence and not in cases where the CMA had decided to proceed by CSJ. See also ROIR 57.

[254] ROIR 69 (4). There was no corresponding DORR.

[255] GRO 1338, WO 35/173, PRO, Kew.

[256] 'History of the 5th Division', app. 8, para. 10.

generally, the rules which govern the procedure of ordinary courts-martial should be observed as far as practicable',[257] it seems clear that the responsible officers were given considerable latitude in such matters as the taking of the Summary of Evidence.

The full procedures involved in taking the Summary of Evidence corresponded in some respects with those of committal proceedings in the civil courts. They are described in the Lewis Report as follows:

Witnesses are examined in the presence of the accused, and if the accused so requires or the commanding officer so directs, the examination is on oath. The evidence is taken down in writing by the officer in charge of the proceedings, and read over to each witness at the end of his evidence. The witness then signs the statement. The accused has the right personally to cross-examine any witness and may call witnesses on his own behalf. He is not, however, entitled to be legally represented at the taking of the Summary of Evidence.[258]

The provisions covering the compelling of the attendance of witnesses and of the accused at trials by court martial (discussed below) applied also to the taking of the Summary of Evidence.[259] The taking of the summary could, however, proceed in the absence of the accused if he failed to appear to a summons.[260]

Under the Army Act, the commanding officer might, after completion of the Summary of Evidence and notwithstanding that he had previously remanded the case with the intention of applying for trial by court martial, decide to proceed summarily or to dismiss the case. It may be assumed, therefore, that the CMA could, after the taking of the Summary of Evidence, either dismiss the case or order trial by a special CSJ rather than by court martial.[261]

If he decided to proceed by court martial he issued a 'Direction for Trial'.[262] Copies of the charge or charges and the Summary of Evidence were furnished to the accused who was to be given proper facilities for preparing his defence, communicating with his legal adviser, and procuring the attendance at the trial of any witnesses he might require.

The next stage was for the 'convening officer' (see Table 7) (in practice, it appears, the CMA) to set about arranging for the sitting of one of the three types of court martial. Because of the differing sentencing powers

---

[257] Rule of Procedure 106, 632 n. 1.

[258] Lewis Report, para. 50. Under normal Army Act procedures, the accused was entitled to make a statement and to give evidence on oath at the taking of the Summary of Evidence. This provision would not have applied to ROIA courts martial because, as noted above, the accused was not, in Ireland, a competent witness in his own defence.

[259] ROIR 72 (1), 73 (4). There was no corresponding DORR.

[260] ROIR 72 (1). There was no corresponding DORR.

[261] For this reason, the investigation by the CMA and the taking of the Summary of Evidence have been shown as one stage on the flow-charts.

[262] ROIR 68 (5).

TABLE 7. Courts martial under the Army Act 1881 (excluding regimental courts martial)

Title of court	Composition	Convening authority	Sentencing power	Method of reaching decision
General court martial	At least 9 officers, each of whom must have held a commission during not less than 3 years, and one of whom acts as President. President never below the rank of Field Officer,[a] save exceptionally when no such officer is available. Not less than 5 members of the court must be of the rank of Captain or above.	HM or GOC by warrant.	Death; penal servitude.	Sentence by majority, but no death sentence unless two-thirds majority in favour. Majority decision on conviction.
District court martial	At least 3 officers of at least two years' standing, one of whom acts as President. President must not be under the rank of Field Officer unless no such officer is available. Normally not more than 1 member of court is a subaltern.[b]	GOC or other officer having a warrant to convene a DCM.	2 years.	Majority decision on conviction and sentence.
Field general court martial	Consists as a rule of at least 3 officers, 1 of whom acts as President. President normally a Field Officer unless such is not available. The members of the court must have held commissions for not less than 1 year, but if officers are available who have held commissions for not less than 3 years, they are to be selected in preference. Exceptionally, FGCM could consist of 2 officers only, but see 'Sentencing power'.	OC detach, on active service if GCM not possible, or no superior, authority.	If composed of 3 officers, it can award same punishment as a GCM. If composed of 2 officers, 2 years' imprisonment.	Sentence by majority but no death sentence unless vote is unanimous. Majority decision on conviction.

[a] Commissioned officer above the rank of Captain and under that of General.
[b] Commissioned officer of lower rank than Captain.

of the various types of court martial, the choice of one type or other was obviously crucial. Prior to January 1920, convening powers in relation to DORR courts martial were confined to Divisional Commanders,[263] but in that month certain Brigade Commanders were granted this power 'in case of emergency'[264] only. In September 1920, following the introduction of ROIA, it was ordered that general courts martial were not to be convened without General Headquarters' instructions.[265] At that time also, the level within the military hierarchy at which the power to convene a court martial rested could depend on the particular ROIR which the accused was alleged to have breached.[266] With the introduction of field general courts martial in December the position was considerably simplified, so that in May 1921 the position was that Brigade Commanders had practically full power to deal with all cases.[267]

Throughout the procedures described above, the accused may have been in custody or at liberty;[268] in the latter case he would have been summoned to appear at the taking of the Summary of Evidence.[269] A person in custody could be held in civil or military custody or could be transferred from one to the other.[270] If a determination for trial by court martial had issued, the accused might, on the order of the CMA, be detained in prison 'as a person committed for trial for felony'.[271] Such an order could be made at any stage of the court-martial process after the determination for trial had issued, but such detention without the making of the requisite order was impermissible.[272] Where there was a delay in dealing with the case of a suspect detained in custody, the CMA was to indicate this in his weekly progress report, with a note of the action taken since the previous report.[273]

A person in custody could apply to the CMA in relation to bail, and if the CMA signified in writing that the case was in his opinion a proper one

---

[263] 'History of the 5th Division', app. 8, para. 2.

[264] Ibid., para. 2.

[265] Ibid., para. 4.

[266] e.g. the GOC 5th Division was empowered to order trial in cases under ROIR 9AA and 27, but not apparently in others. In Sept. 1920 powers were given to all Brigade Commanders to try cases under ROIR 9AA. Ibid., paras. 6, 8.

[267] There remained, however, certain reservations in respect of confirmation (discussed below). Ibid., para. 2.

[268] ROIR 68 (6), 56 (10). Under DORA, the accused could not be kept in military custody after a decision had been taken to proceed for trial by CSJ (DORR 56 (10)).

[269] ROIR 72 (1).

[270] ROIR 68 (6). For a stark account of conditions in military prisons around the time of the First World War see Babington, *For the Sake of Example* 87.

[271] ROIR 68 (6).

[272] *R* v. *Fitzgerald Edwards and Hooper*, [1921] 55 *ILTR* 60. This case is discussed on p. 120.

[273] GRO 509, WO 35/173/2, PRO, Kew. See pp. 50–1.

for bail, the accused could then apply to an RM who might then admit him to bail 'in like manner as if he had been committed . . . for trial for a felony'.[274]

Trial

The next stage in the court-martial process was the trial proper. The composition of the various types of court martial under the Army Act is shown in Table 7.[275] Macready was at pains to claim that those involved in the trials did not personally take part in raids and searches, and that they were thus devoid of any 'trace of bitterness',[276] but there was no attempt at a complete separation of court martial from other duties—for instance service on a military court of inquiry was not sufficient to disqualify an officer from court-martial work.[277]

Apart from the normal Army Act requirements in relation to courts martial composition, under ROIA a court martial for the trial and punishment of a person alleged to be guilty of a crime punishable by death was to include as a member of the court a person nominated by the Lord-Lieutenant and certified by the Lord Chancellor of Ireland or by the Lord Chief Justice of England to be a person of 'legal knowledge and experience'.[278] Such a person did not have to be an officer, but if he was he did not have to meet all the normal requirements of the Army Act for service in court martial.[279] The record of the case, known as the

---

[274] ROIR 68 (7), 56 (10). In the police district of Dublin Metropolis the power was exercisable by a divisional justice of that district. Under DORR 56 (10), the same provision applied save that it was provided that 'nothing in this regulation shall affect any power of the High Court, or any power of any court of summary jurisdiction, to admit any person to bail'. This latter provision was dropped in the drafting of ROIR.

[275] The Army Act 1881 made provision for a fourth type—the Regimental Court Martial. This form of court martial was not incorporated into the DORA or ROIA systems. Its role in the British Army's court-martial system was in decline in the period under discussion. As the 1914 *Manual of Military Law* notes: 'As Commanding Officers can now . . . award 28 days detention for any description of offence, and as a Regimental Court Martial cannot award any punishment higher than 42 days detention, the assembly of Regimental Courts-Martial will be of rare occurrence' (p. 426). Under DORR, trials by court martial were originally limited to general or district courts martial (DORR, 28 Nov. 1914), but subsequently (26 Apr. 1916 and 23 Mar. 1915) provision was made for trial by field general courts martial in areas where s. 1 of the Defence of the Realm (Amendment) Act 1915 was suspended. Regimental courts martial were abolished in 1920.

[276] Draft of interview with the *Evening Standard*, Strickland papers. The text of the interview published in the edition of 25 Jan. 1921 is also included in the papers.

[277] GRO 227, WO 35/173/2, PRO, Kew.

[278] ROIR 69 (5). There was no corresponding DORR.

[279] Ibid. See Army Act 1881 s. 48 (3). The Regulations do not specifically state that such a person was to be a member of the Army, but it seems highly unlikely that any private would have held the necessary qualifications. It may be that civilian lawyers were induced to join the Army specifically to perform this function, but if that were the case, it seems unlikely that they would have joined as privates.

'Proceedings', had to show compliance with this provision,[280] but it was unnecessary formally to put in evidence either the nomination by the Lord-Lieutenant or the certificate of the Lord Chancellor or Lord Chief Justice.[281] It was apparently these appointees who formed the corps of courts martial officers (CMOs),[282] whose presence at courts martial Macready was keen to highlight as a safeguard.[283] Courts martial officers had first been introduced during the First World War in September 1916, in response to allegations of injustice against front-line tribunals.[284] These wartime CMOs were all temporary officers who belonged to the legal profession. In Ireland, the duties of the CMO have been described as:

the preparation of cases to go before Courts-martial or military courts and advice on legal matters generally. He was responsible for collecting and recording the evidence to be produced and for ensuring that the Rules of Procedure were properly carried out by the Court and every defendant had a fair trial.[285]

A Judge Advocate might also be present but his presence was not essential. His functions were not, as his title might suggest, to act both as prosecutor and judge, but to advise the court on points of law and to prepare the Proceedings.[286] But despite the presence of these members, there were frequent mistakes in paperwork at courts martial,[287] and serious legal errors continued to be made.[288]

A court martial had the limited powers inherent in any court to exclude

[280] ROIR 69 (5).

[281] *Whelan* v. *Rex* [1921] 2 *IR* 310. This case is discussed on p. 122.

[282] In the 'History of the 5th Division' the appointment of CMOs was linked to the great expansion in the operation of courts martial brought about by ROIA (p. 57).

[283] Interview with *Evening Standard* (n. 276).

[284] See Babington, *For the Sake of Example*, 119–120. Babington claims that 'the conduct of British courts martial in France was considerably improved at this time by the introduction of the CMO'.

[285] Draft reference for one Maj. R. J. Clarke who had served as a CMO in Ireland. Strickland papers.

[286] Rule of Procedure 95A. For a brief discussion of the role of the Judge Advocate and of how his title may have arisen, see Lewis Report, para. 30. In Ireland it appears that civilian lawyers were used as Judge Advocates. Answering a question in the Commons in relation to the case of *R* v. *Murphy* [1921] 2 *IR* 190 Worthington Evans (Secretary of State for War) informed the House that the Judge Advocate at the trial was a civilian barrister of 18 years' standing with great experience of criminal cases both before civil courts and courts martial. 138 *HC Deb.*, col. 737. Hamar Greenwood, the Chief Secretary, later informed the House that Judge Advocates at courts martial in Ireland were persons approved by the JAG as having a sufficient degree of legal training (138 *HC Deb.*, col. 1989), but he later stated that he could not undertake to put a barrister in every court martial (139 *HC Deb.*, col. 2589). It is perhaps possible that there was a degree of confusion between the CMO and the Judge Advocate.

[287] e.g. GRO 298 drew attention to failures to record certain details on the Proceedings, GRO 334 to delays in transmitting the Proceedings to GHQ, and GRO 510 to 'careless mistakes' generally. WO 35/173/2, PRO, Kew.

[288] e.g. that described in *R* v. *Murphy* [1921] 2 *IR* 190. The case is discussed below.

the public if the court deemed it necessary for the administration of justice, and it was held that possible risk to witnesses justified the holding of the court martial in camera.[289] In addition, under ROIR it was provided that if application were made by the prosecution, in the public interest, that all or any portion of the public should be excluded during any part of the hearing, the court might make an order to that effect.[290] The Army was also acutely sensitive about any attempt by the accused to use the trial to make a political point, and this sensitivity was reflected in a willingness to invoke exclusion powers in an attempt to influence, and effectively to censor newspaper reporting.[291] It was not the general practice to exclude all of the public from all courts martial, but in certain instances reporters were to be admitted and other members of the public excluded provided 'they [the Press] are willing to exercise an intelligent discrimination, or to act on suggestions from the Court'.[292] Other circumstances where the Army considered exclusion justified were: '(1) If disturbance has occurred or is likely to occur owing to the presence of spectators, or (2) If the safety of witnesses is likely to be endangered, or (3) When for other special reasons, it is clearly against the public interest that the evidence or some part of it should be published'.[293]

Where several accused persons were charged before a field general court martial on separate charge sheets, they were not to be tried together except with their consent, and only where all the charges arose out of the same 'transaction'.[294] Where several persons were jointly charged with an offence alleged to have been committed by them collectively, and there were separate charges against one or more, there was to be a separate trial in respect of each of these separate charges.[295] Trial under ROIA could take place in the absence of the accused, provided service of a summons to attend were proved, but in such cases the court could impose no sentence greater than a fine.[296]

---

[289] Per Viscount Reading CJ (with whom Avory J., Rowlatt J., Bailhacke J., Atkin J., and Sankey J. concurred) in *R* v. *Governor of Lewes Prison, ex parte Doyle* [1917] 2 *KB* 254. The case involved a DORA court martial sitting shortly after the 1916 Rising.

[290] ROIR 57, 77. There was no equivalent DORR.

[291] GRO 709 provided: 'In the newspaper reports of several recent Courts-Martial, undue prominence has been given to statements made by the accused, where the statements were made not by way of defence, but for the deliberate purpose of preaching sedition through the medium of the Press and of throwing odium on the Crown Forces. It is not in the public interest that this abuse should continue . . . As a rule it will be sufficient for the President to indicate what portions of the proceedings it is not in the public interest to make public, and to obtain from the reporters present an undertaking that such portions will not be published.' WO 35/173, PRO, Kew.

[292] GRO 1375, WO 35/173/1, PRO, Kew.

[293] Ibid.

[294] GRO 748, WO 35/173, PRO, Kew.

[295] Ibid.

[296] ROIR 72 (2).

Trials ordinarily began with the bringing of the accused before the court and the reading of the convening order. The accused was asked if he objected to the President or any other member of the court, and if so, the grounds for his objection. If there were no objection, the charges were read to the accused and he was asked to plead. If he refused to recognize the court, a plea of 'not guilty' was entered.[297] Initially, this appears to have been the course adopted by many Republican defendants, but from January 1921 this seems to have changed, at least where a death sentence was feared.[298] In any case, where such a sentence was possible, the court would not accept a plea of 'guilty', but would instead enter a plea of 'not guilty'.

The accused would then be asked whether he required an adjournment on the grounds that the Rules of Procedure had not been complied with at the pre-trial stage, or that he had not had sufficient opportunity to prepare his defence. If there were no such application, or if the application were refused, the trial began with the prosecutor (who was often an English barrister[299]) making an opening address. He then proceeded with the examination-in-chief of his witnesses, who were then subject to cross-examination by the defence. Any remark which the court wished to make about the 'conduct' of a witness was to be attached to the Proceedings.[300] It appears that civilian witnesses who gave evidence did so at considerable risk, and one proposal put forward was that such people should be assisted as informers had been, that is 'recompensed out of a special Intelligence Fund and transferred to England'.[301]

Ordinarily, of course, the onus of proof rests upon the prosecution. Under ROIR, however, the burden was reversed in certain instances. Thus ROIR 58B provided:

Where under these regulations any act if done without lawful authority or without lawful authority or excuse is an offence against these regulations, the burden of

---

[297] See e.g. account in the *Cork Examiner*, 15 Dec. 1920, 'Cork Courtmartial', which recounts that 'the accused declined to recognize the court and a plea of "not guilty" was entered'.

[298] The GOC's report for the w/e 29 Jan. 1921 commented: 'It is perhaps to some extent significant that in the series of trials now proceeding on charges of murder of officers in Dublin, the Accused has been defended by Counsel and has not as in previous cases (one of which resulted in the execution of a prisoner), declined to recognize the court.' CAB 24/119, PRO, Kew.

[299] See *ILT & SJ* 20 Nov. 1920, p. 280; 4 Dec. 1920, p. 292; 11 Dec. 1920, p. 298. The employment of English barristers led to a complaint from the Irish Bar Council, some of whose members were apparently eager for the work. The Bar Council claimed that under Rule of Procedure 93, they (and Irish solicitors) were the only persons apart from Army officers, properly qualified for the task.

[300] GRO 668, WO 35/173, PRO, Kew.

[301] This proposal is made in an unattributed Army document headed 'Draft', Strickland papers.

proving that the act was done with lawful authority or with lawful authority or excuse shall rest on the person accused.

Similar provisions covered the possession of documents relating to the affairs of unlawful associations.[302] As was then the case under the ordinary law in Ireland, the accused (and his wife) was not a competent witness in his own defence.[303] The reversal of the onus of proof was therefore particularly burdensome in such cases. The practical effect of these provisions can be taken to have been significant, as 'possession of seditious literature' was the second largest class of offence tried by court martial (Table 8).

Another situation where the provision that the accused was not a competent witness in his own defence could have resulted in serious injustice was where the prosecution sought to rely on an incriminating statement made by the accused under interrogation. In the previous section, the conclusion of an intelligence summary that confessions obtained by brutal interrogation methods had resulted in the imprisonment of many innocent men was noted. 'Imprisonment' in this context may have referred to internment or to conviction by court martial. If a forced confession were put in evidence, the provision that the accused was not a competent witness greatly reduced the possibility of the defence's mounting an effective challenge to its admissibility.

The reversal of the burden of proof was not the only special rule in relation to evidence at ROIA courts martial, though in general the rules of evidence at courts martial corresponded with those of the civil law.[304] Under an amendment introduced in February 1921, the statement on oath of any witness included in the Summary of Evidence was to be admissible in evidence 'if it is proved that the statement was signed by the witness and taken in the presence of the accused and that the witness is dead or has been forcibly and unlawfully carried away or is unable to attend owing to sickness or injuries'.[305]

[302] See ROIR 79 (2), app. 3. DORR 58B corresponded with ROIR 58B, but there was no DORR equivalent to ROIR 79 (2).

[303] Apart from the single statutory exception provided in s. 19 (4) of the Motor Cars Act 1903 (which provided that ss. 1–4 of the 1898 Act extended to Ireland in the case of a person charged with an offence under the 1903 Act), the provisions of the Criminal Evidence Act 1898 (making the accused a competent witness in his own defence) did not apply to Ireland.

[304] On the evidence question see *Manual of Military Law*, 55–84. The Army appears to have been quite attentive about the collection of forensic evidence, as illustrated by the issuing of GRO 299 which related to the production of the clothes of the accused where these were required as evidence by the prosecution. WO 35/173/2, PRO, Kew.

[305] ROIR 72A, introduced 14 Feb. *DG* 25 Feb. 1921. At the same time ROIR 57 was amended with the addition of the provision that 'the statement on oath of any witness which is included in the summary may be given in evidence on the trial of the person by court martial, if it is proved that the witness has been forcibly and unlawfully carried away, in the

cont.

TABLE 8. Sentences of ROIA courts martial

During week ending 18 January 1921

Attacks on military and police

one to penal servitude for life

Being in possession of arms and ammunition

one to 10 years' penal servitude
one to 7 years' penal servitude
six to 2 years with HL
one to 18 months with HL
one to 18 months without HL
one to 1 year with HL
one to 6 months with HL
one to 3 months without HL
one to 14 days without HL (unexpired portion of sentence remitted)
one fined £25 or in default 2 months with HL
one fined £2 or 1 month without HL
one bound over in sum of £1 to keep the peace for 1 month or in default 1 day's
    imprisonment

Being in possession of seditious literature

one to 5 years' penal servitude
one to 18 months with HL
four to 12 months with HL
one to 9 months with HL
four to 6 months with HL (one not confirmed)
two to 6 months without HL (one not confirmed)
one to 6 months without HL and enter into own recognizances in £10 to keep the
    peace for 12 months or in default 3 months without HL
one to 4 months with HL
two to 112 days with HL
one to 84 days with HL (not confirmed)
one fined £50 or in default 6 months without HL

Miscellaneous offences

one to 10 years' penal servitude (not confirmed)
seven to 5 years' penal servitude
four to 4 years' penal servitude
two to 3 years' penal servitude
two to 18 months with HL
three to 1 year with HL
one to 6 months with HL
one to 1 month without HL (unexpired portion remitted)
one fined 21*s.* (105p) or in default 1 month without HL

TABLE 8. *Continued*

During week ending 25 January 1921

Being in possession of arms and ammunition

three to 10 years' penal servitude
two to 7 years' penal servitude
one to 5 years' penal servitude
three to 2 years' HL
one to 2 years without HL
two to 1 year with HL
one to 1 year without HL
four to 6 months' HL
two to 3 months' HL (one not confirmed)
one fined £20 or in default 4 months without HL
one fined £10 or in default 6 months with HL
one fined £10 or in default 3 months without HL
two fined £2 or in default 1 month without HL
one fined 10s. (50p) or in default 7 days without HL

Being in possession of seditious literature

one to 2 years with HL
one to 2 years without HL
one to 21 months' HL
three to 18 months' HL
five to 1 year with HL
one to 1 year without HL
one to 9 months with HL
one to 6 months with HL (one not confirmed)
two to 6 months without HL
two to 3 months with HL (one not confirmed)
one to 14 days without HL
one to 18 months without HL

Miscellaneous offences

four to 18 months with HL
one to 1 year without HL
one to 6 months with HL
three to 56 days with HL
three to 1 month with HL
one to 1 month without HL

Note: Categories and abbreviations as in GOC's reports.

Source: GOC's Weekly Reports on the State of Ireland, CAB 24/118–25, PRO, Kew.

Once the prosecution case was completed, it was the turn of the defence. In those cases in which IRA suspects decided to recognize the court, they were represented by counsel.[306] There was a certain tradition of antipathy in the British Army towards the defence advocate. During the First World War, many members of the court had apparently considered him 'superfluous', and 'could not stomach the sight of him' if he attempted any true advocacy.[307] This antipathy, together with a generalized distrust of the legal profession, was reflected in an intelligence briefing prepared for officers serving in Ireland, which commented in relation to the 'defence of rebels on trial':

When a rebel is being tried for a serious offence Sinn Fein pays for his defence. King's Counsel or Barrister is employed and dozens of witnesses are brought forward to swear to the innocence of the prisoner, and, if necessary, an excellent *alibi* will be set up. The solicitor tells the various witnesses just what to say and what not to say and, knowing the consequences involved by disobedience to Sinn Fein, they do as they are told.[308]

Republicans, on the contrary, claimed that courts martial were biased against the accused and unwilling to believe legitimate alibis, and that in at least one case this refusal resulted in a wrongful execution.[309]

Although the accused was not a competent witness in his own defence, newspaper accounts of the period record statements by the accused made in the course of the trial, and the Army's sensitivity in relation to such statements has been noted above. Thus, while it appears that the accused was given some hearing during courts martial, the exact evidential status of such a statement is unclear. It could not have the same evidential value as that of a competent witness, and the court would presumably be free to attach to it whatever value it thought fit.

IRA suspects were not the only defendants to appear before ROIA courts martial. Non-politically-motivated offenders were also tried, and (according to British figures), this category[310] amounted to 3–7 per cent

---

like circumstances and manner in which it could be given in evidence on such trial if it were proved that the witness was dead'. ROIR 69 was also amended so that in a case which had originated in the civil courts and was then referred to the CMA, the depositions and any statutory statement of the accused were likewise made admissible. *DG* 25 Feb. 1921. S. 2 (1) of the Evidence (Amendment) Act 1915 had permitted statements on oath taken for the Summary of Evidence to be put in evidence in certain circumstances.

[306] GOC's report for w/e 29 Jan. 1921, CAB 24/119, PRO, Kew.

[307] Herbert, *The Secret Battle* (a fictionalized account), quoted in Babington, *For the Sake of Example*, 14.

[308] 'Notes on the Organization and Methods of Sinn Fein', Strickland papers.

[309] That of Thomas Whelan who was hanged in Dublin on 14 Mar. 1921. For an account of the circumstances surrounding the trial of Whelan, see K. Villiers-Tuthill, *Beyond the Twelve Bens* (Galway, 1986), 202–7. See also Macardle, *Irish Republic*, 440–1.

[310] In the Chief Secretary's weekly surveys this category is referred to as 'ordinary crime' or is defined by its distinction from 'offences connected with the Sinn Fein movement' and 'offences concerned with the disturbed state of the country'. CAB 24/118–25, PRO, Kew.

of the total (Table 7).[311] The other significant group was policemen, members of the Army being subject to the slightly different procedures of Army Act courts martial.[312] The trial of policemen by courts martial is related to the generalized breakdown of police discipline at the time; the most frequently occurring charges upon which policemen appeared before courts martial are described in the Chief Secretary's surveys as 'looting' and 'robbery'.[313] Details of the trial of policemen by ROIA courts martial in the period January to June 1921 are shown in Table 9 . Depending on how the figures are read, it appears that police defendants amounted to between 6 per cent and 10 per cent of the total.[314]

The largest category of police defendant shown in the Chief Secretary's surveys is the RIC (Table 9). This category would include the many English ex-Army members recruited to the RIC from the spring of 1920—the Black and Tans. The second largest category is 'constable'. This may refer to members of the Dublin Metropolitan Police or it may again refer to the RIC. Thereafter comes ADRIC and 'special

[311] The Chief Secretary's weekly survey of the state of Ireland for w/e 24 Jan. 1921 shows that 21% of those tried by court martial in that week came within the category of non-politically-motivated offender. Thereafter this category declined as a percentage of the total. In the weekly surveys following that for w/e 4 Apr. 1920, no mention is made of it. It may be that the trial by court martial of non-politically-motivated offenders had then ceased, or it may be that such trials continued but statistics were simply not included in the reports. If the former is the case, then during the first six months of 1921 this category amounted to 3% of the total tried, while during those weeks for which figures are given, it amounts to 7% of the total.

[312] Under ROIR 58D, persons subject to military law alleged to have committed any offence were, unless the CMA otherwise directed, to be tried only by Army Act courts martial. DORR 58D contained the same provisions but was to be in operation only in areas where s. 1 of the Defence of the Realm (Amendment) Act 1915 was suspended. In the period 1 Jan. to 14 Apr. 1921 a total of 221 members of the Crown Forces were arrested in Ireland for offences against the criminal law. By 14 Apr. 1921, 165 had been brought to trial. Of these, 124 were convicted and 41 acquitted. The sentences imposed on those convicted were as follows: 12 sentences of penal servitude from three to ten years, 26 sentences of imprisonment for periods from one month to two years, 5 sentences of reduction to the ranks, 1 discharge under the Probation Act, 1 bound over to keep the peace, 7 sentences not at 14 Apr. 1921 promulgated. 140 *HC Deb.*, col. 1272. A point worth noting is that soldiers appearing before Army Act courts martial in Ireland were competent witnesses in their own defence, whereas policemen (and others) appearing before ROIA courts martial were not. See *Defence of the Realm Manual*, 9 n. (b).

[313] CAB 24/118–25, PRO, Kew.

[314] In some of the Chief Secretary's weekly surveys the numbers of policemen convicted and the numbers acquitted are expressly set out. In others, mention is simply made of the fact that a certain number of policemen were convicted (or acquitted as the case may be). It may be that for those weeks for which only the number of policemen convicted is shown, no policemen were acquitted and that therefore the number of policemen shown as convicted represents the total number tried in that week. Alternatively, other policemen may have been tried and acquitted, in which case the numbers shown would not represent the total tried. If the former is the case, then for the period Jan. to June 1921 policemen formed 6% of the total. In those weeks for which the numbers convicted and acquitted are expressly set out, policemen formed 10% of the total.

TABLE 9. Trial of policemen by ROIA courts martial from week ending 24 January 1921 to week ending 27 June 1921

Week ending	No. tried	No. convicted	No. acquitted	Breakdown[a]					
				RIC	ADRIC	Special constable	Constable	Temporary constable	Cadet
24 Jan.	n/a	n/a	3		3				
31 Jan.	n/a	1	n/a						1
7 Feb.	4	1	3	4					
14 Feb.	5	2	3	2			3		
21 Feb.	n/a	n/a	n/a						
28 Feb.	4	2	2	4					
7 Mar.	7	4	3	2	4				1
14 Mar.	n/a	2	n/a	2					
21 Mar.	n/a	5	n/a	4			1		
28 Mar.	n/a	n/a	n/a						

4 Apr.	6	4	2	3		1	2	2
11 Apr.	4	2	2	2			2	2
18 Apr.	8	5	3	2		6		
25 Apr.	n/a	5	n/a		1	4		
2 May	3	n/a	n/a	3	1			
9 May	13	7	6	12				
16 May	n/a	5	n/a	5				
23 May	n/a	n/a	1	1				
28 May	7	3	4	2	1		4	4
6 June	n/a	1	n/a	1				
13 June	n/a	n/a	1	1				
20 June	n/a	n/a	4	4				
27 June	n/a	3	n/a	1	1		1	1
TOTALS[b]	58	30	28	55	11	11	12	2

[a] Classifications are those used in the weekly surveys.
[b] Totals for weeks for which full figures are available. The conviction rate, based on these figures, was 52%.

Source: Chief Secretary's Weekly Surveys of the State of Ireland, CAB 24/118–25, PRO, Kew.

constables'—presumably either ADRIC or the Ulster Special Constabulary. Of the remaining categories, 'cadet' refers to ADRIC, and
'temporary constable' probably to the Black and Tans.

At the completion of the evidence, the defence might make a closing
address to which the prosecution could reply. The Judge Advocate, if one
were present, then summed up the evidence and advised the court upon
the law relating to the case. The court then closed for consideration of its
findings. The method of reaching decisions is shown on Table 7. A finding
of 'not guilty' was announced in open court and was not subject to
confirmation; a finding of 'guilty', and the corresponding sentence, were
not so announced. The sole exception was where only a fine was imposed,
or where the accused was ordered to enter into recognizances. In such
instances, the imposition of the fine or the requirement to enter into
recognizances could be announced in open court, but only if special
permission to this effect had been given by the Army Council.[315]

Given the fact that many of those involved in the taking of evidence
and the conduct of courts martial must have had little or no legal experience, it might have been expected that there would have been some
inconsistency in relation to findings. There is some evidence that this was
the case, as percentage conviction figures show considerable variation. In
the first four-week period of the operation of ROIA courts martial, an
abnormally high percentage conviction of 95 per cent occurred (Table 6),
thereafter the percentage dropped, levelling out for the whole five-month
period of 1920 at 81 per cent. Variations are more apparent if the weekly
figures for January to June 1921 are examined (Table 10). Large variations
(from 60 to 88 per cent) occur although no clear pattern emerges. The
overall percentage conviction figure for the first six months of 1921 (78
per cent), however, corresponds closely with the figure for 1920 (81 per
cent).

There is also some evidence of lack of consistency in relation to the
trial of policemen. The percentage conviction recorded in their cases (52
per cent overall in those weeks for which full figures for those convicted
and acquitted are expressly given; 58 per cent if the totals shown convicted are compared with the totals shown acquitted) is statistically significantly different from the overall percentage conviction for the same
period (78 per cent).[316]

---

[315] This was under an amendment (ROIR 71A) introduced on 7 Feb. 1921. *DG* 15 Feb.
The sentence or requirement was still subject to confirmation and the accused was to be
informed that notice of confirmation was to be sent to him by post.

[316] The analysis was conducted using three groups of samples: (1) all those tried in Table
9; (2) those policemen tried in the weeks for which full figures are expressly shown on Table
10; (3) all the policemen shown as having been convicted or acquitted in Table 10 on the
hypothesis that in those weeks for which *y* number of policemen are shown as having been

TABLE 10. Operation of ROIA courts martial from week ending 24 January 1921 to week ending 27 June 1921

Week ending	No. tried	No. convicted	% conviction	No. of non-politically-motivated offenders[a]	Non-politically-motivated offenders (% of total)
24 Jan.	72	60	83	15	21
31 Jan.	142	122	86	5	4
7 Feb.	84	67	80	7	8
14 Feb.[b]	52	38	73	1	2
21 Feb.[b]	43	34	79	1	2
28 Feb.	75	63	84	n/a	n/a
7 Mar.	67	48	72	4	6
14 Mar.	84	61	73	8	10
21 Mar.	56	43	77	n/a	n/a
28 Mar.	31	19	61	0	0
4 Apr.	60	36	60	1	2
11 Apr.	34	27	79	n/a	n/a
18 Apr.	65	49	75	n/a	n/a
25 Apr.	54	35	65	n/a	n/a
2 May	56	44	79	n/a	n/a
9 May	73	56	77	n/a	n/a
16 May	66	53	80	n/a	n/a
23 May	49	36	73	n/a	n/a
28 May	50	36	72	n/a	n/a
6 June[b]	53	47	88	n/a	n/a
13 June	49	44	90	n/a	n/a
20 June	70	58	83	n/a	n/a
27 June	66	56	85	n/a	n/a
TOTAL	1,451	1,132	78		

[a] Not including police.
[b] In these weeks, due to typing errors in the weekly surveys, the figure for total number tried does not correspond with the totals of those convicted and acquitted. The figures shown here are estimates.

Source: Chief Secretary's Weekly Surveys of the State of Ireland, CAB 24/118–25, PRO, Kew.

acquitted (or convicted as the case may be) and none are shown as having been convicted (or acquitted as the case may be) only y policemen were tried. The analysis consists of a transformation of percentage data (to give normal distribution) by 'angular' transformation $(\sin^{-1}\sqrt{p})$ of the groups of samples. Group (a) yielded the following results: (no. of samples) $n = 23$, (mean) $\bar{x} = 77.6\%$, UCL (upper confidence limit) = 80.9, LCL (lower confidence limit) = 74.1. Group (b) yielded the following results: $n = 5$, $\bar{x} = 50.7$, UCL =

While this might be taken to indicate bias by the military in favour of policemen in that courts martial might have been more ready to acquit policemen than other defendants, it does not conclusively prove the issue. First, it might also be taken to show military bias against policemen, in that charges were being brought against this class of defendant on evidence that was less compelling than in the general run of cases (though this seems highly unlikely). Secondly, there may have been significant differences in the approach of different classes of defendant to the trial. Policemen presumably always recognized the court and conducted a defence, whereas some IRA suspects refused to recognize the court and did not mount a defence. It might be expected that the latter strategy would result in a greater number of convictions of this class of defendant. Thirdly, there may have been significant differences in patterns of pleas. It is impossible to establish this from the available statistics, as these do not differentiate between contested and uncontested cases.

There is also some evidence that practice in relation to sentencing displayed inconsistency. A person found guilty of a crime was liable to the punishment assigned to the crime by statute or common law[317] (including the death sentence and the imposition of fines[318]), although the limitation on the sentencing power of a district court martial (see Table 7) was expressly retained.[319] In relation to breaches of ROIR, a court martial could impose any sentence from a fine to penal servitude for life,[320] or it could, whether or not it found the accused guilty, require him

---

63.6, LCL = 37.8. Group (c) yielded the following results: $n = 7$, $\bar{x} = 58.1$, UCL = 73.6, LCL = 41.7. A comparison of group (a) and group (b) shows that the 95% confidence limits do not overlap. This indicates that the two groups are significantly (p less than 0.05) different. A comparison of group (a) and group (c) shows that the 95% confidence limits do not overlap but that they are not widely separate. A further treatment was necessary to make a conclusive comparison. This was a t-test (comparison of means of 2 small samples). (1) Data was transformed by $\sin^{-1}\sqrt{p}$. (2) Using Σx and Σx^2 of Transformed data, variations were compared by t-test. (3) The result was $t = 4.160$ with 28 degrees of freedom (30 samples). t is highly significant (p less than 0.001) with more than 99.9% probability that the means of the two samples are different. Therefore the two groups are significantly different.

[317] ROIR 69 (1). There was no corresponding DORR.

[318] ROIR 69 (1), 70 (1). There were no corresponding DORR. Fines imposed on civilians by courts martial were, when realized, to be forwarded by cheque to the Cashier, Irish Command, accompanied by a statement showing the names of the persons fined, the amounts received from each of them, and the authority. GRO 269, 11 Feb. 1921, WO 35/173/2, PRO, Kew. A pro-forma statement is set out in the order.

[319] ROIR 69 (2).

[320] ROIR 57, 70 (1). Under DORR, breaches of the regulations apart from those described below were punishable by a sentence of penal servitude for life or any less punishment, unless the court found that the offence was committed with the intention of assisting the enemy, in which case the offence was punishable by death or any less punishment (DORR 57). In the case of a breach of regulations 12, 13, 21, 22, 24, 25, 26, 28A, 53, 60, or 61, if the offender proved that he acted without any intention of assisting the enemy and, in the case of a breach of regulation 27, if the offender proved that he acted without any intention of causing any such disaffection interference or prejudice as is

to enter a recognizance to keep the peace and to be of good behaviour.[321] In practice, courts martial had difficulty deciding on the appropriate sentence.[322] Mistakes were not infrequently made,[323] and there was very wide variation in sentencing. Offences relating to the possession of arms and ammunition could attract any penalty from a 10 shilling (50p) fine to ten years' penal servitude (Table 8), while possession of seditious literature might be punished by anything from a £50 fine to a sentence of five years' penal servitude.

Post-trial

After reaching its decision on sentence, the Proceedings (prepared by the President, or perhaps by the CMO if no Judge Advocate was present) with the sentence marked thereon, were forwarded to the officer authorized to confirm the sentence. Ordinarily, in the case of a district or field general court martial, the confirming officer would have been the officer who convened the court (Table 7), and in the case of a general court martial, the confirming officer would have been the GOC. In Ireland the position was that the power to confirm (as with the power to convene) could depend on the crime or offence tried, and the sentence imposed. In September 1920 it was ordered that all courts martial of civilians were required to be confirmed by the Commander-in-Chief,[324] but the following November, Divisional Commanders were given powers

---

mentioned in that regulation, the maximum sentence permissible was six months' imprisonment with hard labour (DORR 57).

[321] ROIR 57, 71 (1). There were no corresponding DORR. A regulation introduced on 7 Feb. 1921 empowered the CMA to require any person 'suspected of acting or of having acted or being about to act in a manner prejudicial to the restoration or maintenance of order in Ireland' to enter into recognizances before the CMA to 'keep the peace and be of good behaviour' even if no prosecution had been initiated. ROIR 79A, *DG* 15 Feb 1921. What appear to have been drafting errors in the regulation were corrected by amendment on 14 Feb. 1921. *DG* 25 Feb. 1921.

[322] GRO 270, 11 Mar. 1921, commented: 'A review of the proceedings of certain recent Courts-Martial held under the Restoration of Order in Ireland Act for the trial of civilians discloses the fact that, especially as regards offences against the ordinary criminal law, Courts have sometimes a difficulty in coming to a conclusion as to what the appropriate punishment ought to be.' The 25th edn. of *Archbold* was referred to, and it was recommended that 'The facts which the Court should take into consideration are the character and age of the accused, provocation, temptation, etc., and the effect which the punishment may have on the community in general, either on account of its lightness or on account of its severity. In the case of offences under the "Restoration of Order in Ireland Regulations" the latter consideration is of the highest importance, as an act otherwise innocent may, as an offence under the Regulations, and as being prejudicial to the restoration of order in Ireland, become a crime of the gravest magnitude.' WO 35/173/2, PRO, Kew.

[323] GRO 334, 23 Sept. 1921, commented: 'In several recent cases Courts have awarded Penal Servitude in respect of crimes which by Statute or Common Law are punishable by fine of imprisonment only.' WO 35/173/2, PRO, Kew.

[324] 'History of the 5th Division', app. 8.

of confirmation in respect of any convictions for breaches of ROIR 9AA, and all cases involving violence, except treason and murder. Although the manner of exercise of delegated powers of confirmation seems to have been a cause of concern to GHQ,[325] in May 1921 all Infantry Brigade Commanders obtained such powers in all cases except those in which death sentences had been imposed.[326] The latter sentences, it seems, still required confirmation by the GOC-in-Chief Ireland.[327]

The confirming officer could confirm the sentence or finding or direct the reassembly of the court for the purpose of revising the finding or sentence or both, or could mitigate, remit, commute, or in some cases suspend the sentence. The sentence, as confirmed, was then promulgated to the accused.[328] Overall, it appears that confirmation of sentence was refused in respect of 7 per cent of sentences (for all types of crime or offence) imposed by ROIA courts martial, and that in a further 2 per cent of cases the confirming officer used his powers to remit the unexpired portion of the sentence.[329]

The Proceedings were then to be forwarded to GHQ, though in practice considerable delays sometimes occurred.[330] At least in relation to death sentences (and possibly in relation to other types of sentence), the Proceedings were sent to the office of the Army's senior law officer, the Judge Advocate General (JAG) in London for scrutiny.[331] If he formed the opinion that an irregularity or miscarriage of justice had occurred, he so advised the Secretary of State for War who had power to quash the

---

[325] In GRO 334, 29 Mar. 1921, it was thought necessary to order that 'Confirming Officers should take care that they do not confirm sentences which are wholly illegal.' WO 35/173/2, PRO, Kew.

[326] 'History of the 5th Division', which comments: 'No doubt had experienced Legal Officers been available to advise Brigade Commander, these delegations would have been made earlier.'

[327] This was the case in the reported cases relating to GCMs.

[328] Where it had been ordered during the trial that the names of witnesses and members should not be published in the press, the President was not to sign his name on the form communicating the sentence to the accused. GRO 226, 1 Mar. 1921, WO 35/173/2, PRO, Kew.

[329] In Table 8, of the 117 cases in which convictions were obtained, confirmation was refused in seven instances (6%), and in two instances (1.7%) the unexpired portion of the sentence was remitted.

[330] GRO 334, 29 Mar. 1921, drew attention to such delays, and ordered that in future a full explanation of the reasons for a delay was to be submitted to GHQ. WO 35/173/2, PRO, Kew.

[331] In May 1921 Sir Dennis Henry, the AG for Ireland, in reply to the question 'whether his attention has been called to a statement made by General Macready, in an interview published in the Press, that, in every case of conviction for murder, the case goes to the Judge Advocate-General in London, and that the latter has to be convicted of the legality of the findings before the military authorities went any further?', answered in the affirmative, and added: 'I understand that the statement made by the Commander-in-Chief referred only to the cases of courts-martial under the Restoration of Order in Ireland Act.' 141 *HC Deb.*, cols. 1204–5.

conviction. In practice, it appears that this power would have been used very sparingly, if at all.[332]

As was then the case in Ireland in relation to indictable offences tried in the ordinary courts,[333] the court-martial system incorporated no appeals procedure of the type with which the modern lawyer would be familiar,[334] although a petition could be submitted to the confirming or reviewing authority. Courts martial were also subject to a very limited scrutiny by the superior civil courts through the issue of prerogative writs.[335]

In the case of a death sentence, the execution was to be carried out at such time and place and by such person as the confirming authority might order, and the order of that authority was to serve as a warrant for execution.[336] In all, ten persons were executed following sentence by ROIA courts martial. All of these executions took place in Dublin, and all were by hanging.[337]

Martial law military tribunals: introduction

The system of trial by ROIA courts martial was distinct but not entirely separate from the system of military tribunals that was established in the MLA. The basic document establishing these tribunals was the Army's 'Circular Memorandum on Martial Law'.[338] This was amended by subsequent Army orders and supplemented by guide-lines issued by GHQ[339] and by local units.[340]

The tribunals were to try breaches of martial law. But since, under martial law proclamation no. 1, not only were specific martial law offences created, but all crimes were also made offences against martial law, the jurisdiction of these tribunals extended not only to alleged breaches

---

[332] The weekly results of ROIA courts martial for Jan. 1921 shown in Table 8 do not disclose the quashing of any proceedings, though this may have been because there would have been a considerable time-lag between confirmation and scrutiny by the JAG. In *R* v. *Murphy* [1921] 2 *IR* 190, (discussed below) the High Court held that a court martial had erred in law but that the matter was not reviewable by the Court. The proceedings were not, however, quashed by the JAG although the confirming officer (the GOC Ireland) commuted the sentence from death to penal servitude for life.

[333] Under the Supreme Court of Judicature (Ireland) Act 1887, five judges of the High Court sat to hear questions of law only, which might be reserved at a criminal trial. See Delaney, *Administration of Justice*, 26, and *Defence of the Realm Manual*, eighth edn., 196 n. a (iii).

[334] In Britain a Courts-Martial Appeals Court was established by the Courts-Martial (Appeals) Act 1951.

[335] The issues arising under this heading are considered on pp. 118–23.

[336] ROIR 69 (1).

[337] A list of these executions can be found in Macardle, *Irish Republic*, 1023–4.

[338] WO 35/66, PRO, Kew.

[339] e.g. by the 'Notes on the Administration of Martial Law'.

[340] e.g. '17th Infantry Brigade, Summary', issued by Maj. B. L. Montgomery, Cork, 1921.

of martial law orders and regulations, but also to offences under the ordinary law and under ROIR.[341] The intersection between the ordinary law and martial law did not end there, since in June 1921 the Army ordered that acts contrary to martial law proclamations could also be dealt with (presumably in the civil courts or courts martial) as breaches of ROIR 50,[342] which Regulation provided:

If any person does any act of such a nature as to be calculated to be prejudicial to the restoration or maintenance of order in Ireland and not specifically provided for in the foregoing regulation, he shall be deemed to be guilty of an offence against these regulations.

Not only could statutory (and common law) offences be tried as martial law offences, but martial law offences could also be tried as statutory offences. This overlap is indicative of the confusion surrounding the whole area of martial law. One of the reasons for the duplication was that those sentenced by martial law tribunals could serve their sentences only in the MLA, as such sentences had no validity outside that area, and this resulted in overcrowding of the gaols in the MLA. The imprisonment of those sentenced under statutory powers, however, was not so restricted.

Immediately following the proclamation of martial law, two types of tribunal were introduced: military courts and summary courts. The former initially corresponded closely in procedure and jurisdiction with field general courts martial, while the latter consisted of a summary court officer (SCO) sitting alone, and was concerned only with minor offences. Military courts did not immediately completely supersede ROIA courts martial,[343] but they did function extensively in the period January to June 1921. In June, however, it was ordered that 'trial by Military Court will not be ordered as a rule in any case where there was no likelihood that a death sentence will be awarded and carried out'.[344] In other serious cases, trial was to be by ROIA courts martial.[345] The rationale for this move was the same as that which had led to reliance on ROIR 50. Thus one ironic result of congestion in the gaols of the MLA was that under the developed form of martial law, the majority of serious cases was dealt with under statutory powers.

In early 1921 the Judge Advocate General had advised that all legal

---

[341] 'Circular Memorandum on Martial Law, Martial Law—Legal Procedure', para. 2, WO 35/66, PRO, Kew.

[342] Ibid., para. 26 (a), as inserted by GRO 641, 21 June 1921, WO 35/173/2, PRO, Kew.

[343] e.g. *R* v. *Murphy* [1921] 2 *IR* 190 concerned a trial by ROIA court martial held in the MLA immediately after the proclamation of martial law. The case is discussed below.

[344] 'Martial Law—Legal Procedure', para. 32, as substituted by GRO 641, 21 June 1921, WO 35/173, PRO, Kew.

[345] Ibid.

formalities could be dispensed with in trial under martial law.[346] This did not mean that legal procedure was abandoned in trials by military courts and summary courts, but in late spring and early summer 1921 there began the introduction of a third type of military tribunal, the less formal drumhead courts for the trial of those captured in arms.[347]

The system

How the developed form of the martial law system operated is illustrated by flow-chart in Figure 3. The first stage in the process would usually be arrest, though proceedings might instead be instituted in less serious cases by the issuing of a summons. If the suspect were caught carrying arms after an ambush, the decision might be taken (apparently by the nearest officer of the rank of Field Officer or above) to proceed summarily by drumhead court. Otherwise the case would normally first be submitted to the SCO.[348]

If the case involved one of the offences punishable by death under proclamation no. 1, or civil offences of a serious nature, or if the SCO was in any doubt whether or not to deal with a case, he was to refer it to the 'OC Troops' appointed by the Military Governor.[349] If the SCO decided to deal with the case summarily he would either proceed to trial by summary court (in which case he could also recommend internment) or he could refer the case for trial by CSJ.

Cases might also be referred in the first instance to the OC Troops.[350] In such an event, or where the case had been referred thus by the SCO, the OC Troops would first decide whether or not to proceed with the case.[351] If the decision were to proceed, then he would either send the case to the SCO to be dealt with summarily, or submit an application for trial to the Military Governor.[352] Applications for trial were to be accompanied by witness statements and 'proposed charges',[353] but these witness statements were not taken in the presence of the accused.[354]

The Military Governor would also have been a Competent Military Authority under ROIA. He was empowered to order trial by military court where it was likely that a sentence of death would be awarded and carried out; in other cases trial was to be by ROIA court martial.[355] He

---

[346] Quoted in Townshend, 147.   [347] These courts are discussed below.
[348] 'Circular Memorandum on Martial Law', 2, para. 13, WO 35/66, PRO, Kew.
[349] Ibid., para. 9.   [350] Ibid., para. 13.
[351] Ibid., para. 9.   [352] Ibid., para 9; p. 3, para. 14.
[353] Ibid.   [354] This point is discussed below.
[355] 'Circular Memorandum on Martial Law', 1, para. 3, as substituted by GRO 641, 21 June 1921, WO 35/173/2, PRO, Kew. The order simply provides that the Military Governor could order trial *inter alia* by ROIA court martial, but presumably in making such an order, he would have been acting under his statutory powers as CMA rather than under martial law.

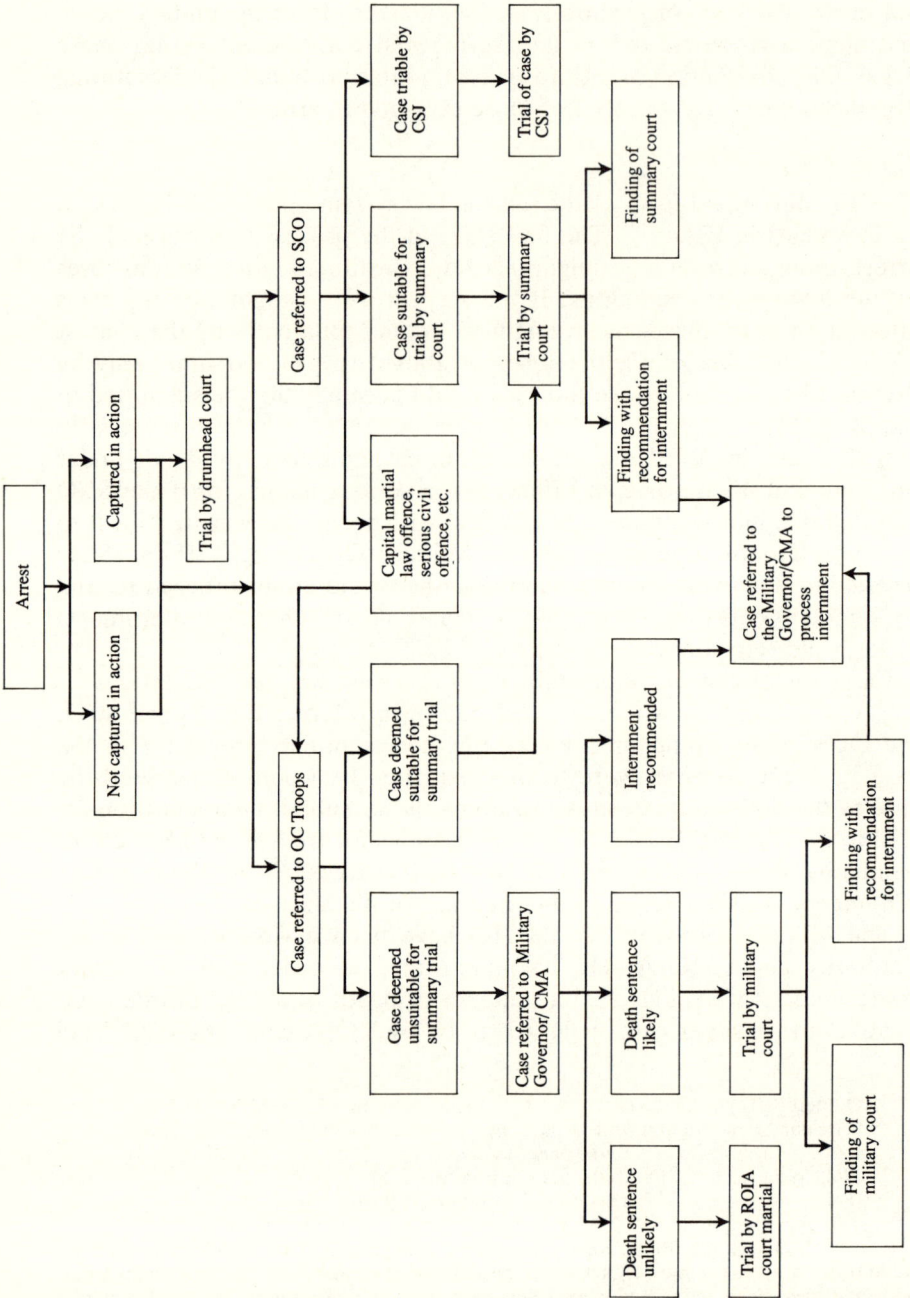

FIG. 3 The martial law legal system (June 1921)

could also recommend internment under ROIR 14B. A military court could, as well as issuing a finding, also recommend internment, and in such cases the matter would have been referred back to the Military Governor/CMA. Consideration can now be given to the detailed workings of these three types of tribunal.

Summary courts

Summary courts,[356] which, as noted above, were to consist of an SCO sitting alone, were established 'to effect the speedy trial of civilians . . . charged with less serious offences against martial law'.[357] This also covered lesser offences against the ordinary criminal law and against ROIR. They were the most widely used form of martial law tribunal, and over 1,000 cases were processed through them.[358] Summary courts were intended partly to assume the function of CSJs which, because of the insurrection, were unable to operate,[359] but where possible, minor offences against the ordinary law were to be left to be dealt with at the Petty sessions, or by the RM.[360] The types of offences tried by summary courts are shown in Table 11. They are a curious mixture of offences against martial law regulations ('failing to have a list of occupants on back of door'), offences against ROIR ('driving motor car without owner's permit'), offences against the ordinary law ('assault'), and 'offences' which do not appear to come within any of these categories such as 'being a suspected person' (though this may be a reference to a breach of an order under ROIR 14[361]).

The attendance of the accused for trial would be secured either by summons or by bringing him before the court under arrest. If he failed to appear to a summons, the trial could proceed *in absentia* provided that in such circumstances only a fine could be imposed with the alternative of imprisonment without hard labour in default of either payment or distress.[362] Women were not to be arrested without reference to the

---

[356] The rules governing the procedures of summary courts are set out in paras. 8–16 of the 'Martial Law—Legal Procedure', and in the separate section headed 'Summary Court Procedure'. WO 35/66, as amended by GRO 641, 21 June 1921, WO 35/173/2, and GRO 857, 23 Aug. 1921, WO 35/173/2, PRO, Kew.

[357] 'Summary Court Procedure', para. 1.

[358] In 'Notes on the Administration of Martial Law', app. B, the number of cases stated as having been disposed of by summary courts is shown as over 1,000, but the exact numerals are illegible. This included 447 cases in which sentences of imprisonment were imposed. In addition, fines of £2,532 were imposed. The document appears to have been issued in mid-1921.

[359] 'Summary Court Procedure', para. 1, WO 35/66, PRO, Kew.

[360] Ibid., para. 10.

[361] See App. 3.

[362] 'Summary Court Procedure', para. 6, WO 35/66, PRO, Kew. A scale setting out the terms of imprisonment to be awarded in default of payment of fines was included at schedule 1 of 'Summary Court Procedure', para. 20 (f). For example, for a fine between 10s.

TABLE 11. Types of offences dealt with by martial law summary courts

Breach of Curfew Regulations.
Possession of Arms and Ammunition.
Possession of Seditious Documents.
Possession of Uniform of the Irish Republican Army.
Possession of equipment of HM Forces.
Loitering.
Driving a Motor Car without Owner's permit.
Using a bicycle without a permit.
Giving false name when arrested.
Being a Member of an Unlawful association, i.e. IRA.
Collecting money for Arms.
Refusing to give name to a Military Officer.
Failing to have a list of occupants on back of door.
Failing to give information concerning rebels.
Failing to report removal of Proclamations posted by military in the window of his
    house.
Harbouring rebels.
Attempting to avoid arrest.
Failing to clear an obstruction from the road.
Being a suspected person.
Having seditious writing on the wall of his house.
Unlawful assembly.
Failing to report information concerning an ambush.
Conveying IRA despatches.
Having licensed premises open after prohibited hours.
Making defamatory statements against the Forces of the Crown.
Attempting to obtain money by threats.
Communicating contagious disease to the troops.
Refusing to halt when called upon to do so.
Theft.
Drunkenness.
Assault.
Driving a vehicle without a light.
Maliciously damaging private property.

Source: As described in 'Summary Courts: Class of Offences Dealt With', app.
B, 'Notes on the Administration of Martial Law for the Use of Commanding
Officers', Strickland papers.

CMA or the Military Governor unless there was a serious risk of their absconding, and they were not to be tried by summary court for any offence for which a fine was not an adequate penalty.[363]

If the accused wished to be legally represented at the trial, 'reasonable facilities' were to be allowed to him for obtaining such assistance'.[364] The prosecution was to be conducted by the branch of the Crown Forces that had effected the original arrest.[365] In the case of the Army, the prosecutor was to be an officer detailed by the OC Troops appointed by the Military Governor.[366] Summary court procedure was generally to follow that of military courts.[367] It was specifically provided that the accused was to be given the opportunity of giving evidence on oath in his defence, or of making a statement not on oath, and of calling witnesses.[368]

If after hearing the evidence, the SCO was of the opinion that the case was too serious for him to deal with, he was to refer the case to the OC Troops for instructions.[369] In addition, apart from a finding of 'guilty' or 'not guilty', the SCO might also make recommendations to the Military Governor as to internment.[370] The sentencing power of a summary court was limited to imprisonment with or without hard labour for six months and to fines not exceeding £100.[371] In general, fines were to be imposed rather than short terms of imprisonment.[372] A power was also given to compel the accused, with or without conviction, to enter into recogniz-

(50p) and £1, the period was 14 days; between £50 and £100, it was six months. In the event of non-payment, a warrant for distress was to be signed by the SCO (form B in 'Summary Court Procedure'). Action for distress was to be carried out by the military. In default of distress, a committal order (form C in 'Summary Court Procedure') was to be completed by the SCO in respect of the convicted person. In Aug. 1921 it was ordered that 'because of the difficulty of disposing of the goods distressed . . . warrants for distress should not normally be ordered'. GRO 875, 23 Aug. 1921, WO 35/173/2, PRO, Kew.

[363] 'Summary Court Procedure', paras. 6, 9, and '17th Infantry Brigade, Summary', Rule 29 (b).

[364] 'Summary Court Procedure', para. 11. Representation could be by solicitor, counsel, or by the accused's friends. 'Martial Law—Legal Procedure', para. 11, WO 35/66, PRO, Kew.

[365] 'Summary Court Procedure', para. 11, WO 35/66, PRO, Kew.

[366] Ibid.

[367] 'Martial Law—Legal Procedure', para. 11, WO 35/66, PRO, Kew. The procedures of military courts are considered in detail below.

[368] 'Summary Court Procedure', para. 15, WO 35/66, PRO, Kew. In theory at least, the defendant was therefore in a somewhat better position than before DORA and ROIA courts martial, since in the case of these latter tribunals, the accused was not a competent witness in his own defence. See p. 73.

[369] 'Summary Court Procedure', para. 16. The Military Governor could presumably then order trial by military court or court martial. The record of the witness's statements could then serve in place of a Summary or Statement of Evidence. See 'Notes on the Administration of Martial Law', 11.

[370] 'Martial Law—Legal Procedure', para. 10, WO 35/66, PRO, Kew.

[371] Ibid.

[372] 'Summary Court Procedure', para. 20 (a). This probably reflected the problem of overcrowding in the gaols. WO 35/66, PRO, Kew.

ances with or without sureties.[373] In the case of breaches of the ordinary law, the sentencing power was not limited to that of a civil court, but it was considered 'very desirable that, for the sake of uniformity and as a matter of policy the maximum penalty according to the ordinary law should not be exceeded'.[374] There was some equivocation on the issue of sentencing policy. One source indicated that the sentence should not be based on the political character of the accused if that person was considered 'a dangerous person in the political sense' a sentence which was 'just for the offence charged' should be imposed but a recommendation for internment should be added.[375] Elsewhere, it was provided that 'discretion in dealing with breaches [of martial law] can and should be exercised, and in awarding punishment it is desirable to draw a distinction between loyalists and persons known to be disaffected'.[376]

A note of the case, known as the 'Record', was to be kept in duplicate by the SCO.[377] This was to include the name and description of the accused, the charges, the plea, the names of the witnesses, a short account of the evidence, the finding and sentence, and any remarks (for example in regard to internment) the SCO might wish to make.[378]

No confirmation of the Proceedings of summary courts was necessary,[379] but the duplicate copy of the Record was to be sent to the Military Governor who was authorized to 'issue such orders as he may think fit with regard to quashing, remission, mitigation, or commutation of imprisonment to a fine'.[380] Any such alteration was to be marked on the record before it was forwarded to GHQ. There was no provision for appeals to any higher tribunal, but the prisoner was entitled to make submissions about the decision of the SCO to the Military Governor.[381]

Military courts

The procedures of military courts were 'so far as practicable' to follow that of field general courts martial set out in the Army Act and the Rules of Procedure.[382] Contemporary orders provided that 'in practice they will be conducted on the lines of field general courts-martial held during the late war'.[383] Much of the material in the earlier section on statutory

---

[373] 'Martial Law—Legal Procedure', para. 10, WO 35/66, PRO, Kew.
[374] 'Summary Court Procedure', para. 21 (a), WO 35/66, PRO, Kew.
[375] Ibid., para. 21 (b).
[376] Copy of letter issued from headquarters 5th Division on 19 Jan. 1921, included at app. A, 'Notes on the Administration of Martial Law'.
[377] 'Martial Law—Legal Procedure', para. 12, WO 35/66, PRO, Kew.
[378] Ibid.
[379] Ibid., para. 11, WO 35/66, PRO, Kew.
[380] Ibid., para. 12.
[381] 'Summary Court Procedure', para. 23, WO 35/66, PRO, Kew.
[382] 'Circular Memorandum on Martial Law', 1, para. 3, WO 35/66, PRO, Kew.
[383] Ibid. 1, para. 3.

courts martial would therefore also apply to military courts. This section will therefore only be concerned with points that were emphasized specifically in relation to military courts.

Pre-trial

The initial investigation of cases which might be tried by military court was, as noted above, to be conducted by the SCO or the OC Troops, and it appears that it was on them that the burden of preparing the Summary of Evidence fell. Such Summaries were not, 'as a rule', to be taken in the presence of the accused,[384] though in practice they sometimes were.[385] In general, every effort was to be made to expedite cases at all stages.[386]

Once the Military Governor had taken the decision to proceed to trial by military court, the OC Troops submitted recommendations on the composition of the court,[387] and it was convened by one of the officers specifically empowered to do so by orders of the Military Governor-General. The Form of Proceedings of a Military Court (upon which various details of the trial were to be noted) was then prepared at the office of the Military Governor.[388]

In an 'ordinary case', the court was as far as practicable to consist of a Field Officer, a Captain, and a Subaltern.[389] In no case were there to be fewer than three officers.[390] A Judge Advocate was to be appointed in capital cases,[391] and in such trials the President was not to be below the rank of Lieutenant-Colonel.[392] A Judge Advocate could also be appointed by the convening officer 'in any case of great importance or difficulty',[393] and as has been noted above, a court martial officer might also be involved.

Copies of the Summary of Evidence and the Charge were to be furnished to the accused sufficiently before the trial to enable him to prepare his defence.[394] But preparation was hindered by the provision that the names of witnesses (and of the officers concerned in the preliminaries) were not to be included.[395] If the accused asked for the names of witnesses, the decision on the matter lay with the Military Governor.[396] It also appears

---

[384] Ibid. 3, para. 17.

[385] In *R* v. *Allen* [1921] 2 *IR* 241, a case which concerned a military court, it is clear that the Summary of Evidence was taken in the presence of the accused (per Molony CJ, at p. 262). This was also true of the pre-trial proceedings described in *R (Garde and Others)* v. *Strickland* [1921] 2 *IR* 317 (per affidavit of accused's solicitor set out at pp. 318–19). These cases are discussed on pp. 136–8.

[386] 'Circular Memorandum on Martial Law', 1, para. 7, WO 35/66, PRO, Kew.

[387] Ibid 3, para. 15.   [388] Ibid.   [389] Ibid 4, para. 25.

[390] Ibid.   [391] Ibid.   [392] Ibid.   [393] Ibid.

[394] Ibid. 3, paras. 17, 18.   [395] Ibid. 3, para. 17.   [396] Ibid.

to have been the practice at the eventual trial for members of the military court not to give their names.[397]

Proper charge sheets were 'unnecessary'.[398] The document referred to as 'the charge' could be 'in any form, provided that it clearly states the nature of the charge'.[399] In practice, extremely vague wording such as 'improper possession of arms' was frequently used (Table 12).[400] These charges appear generally to have arisen when the accused had been stopped and found in possession of some contraband article rather than following a long period of careful investigation (in Table 12 this is reflected in the fact that incident date and arrest date coincide in all cases).

If the accused wished to be legally represented, all reasonable steps were to be taken to comply with the request,[401] and in practice it is clear that at least in some cases legal representation was obtained.[402] In capital cases, an officer was to be appointed for the defence if the accused so wished and if he had employed no legal representative.[403] If the accused wished to be assisted by a person other than an officer or counsel, the request was to be granted 'unless there are special reasons to the contrary'.[404]

Trial

Trials by military court took place quickly, usually about two and a half weeks after the date of arrest (Table 12). As 1921 progressed, the tendency was for this period to become shorter. In capital cases, if the accused refused to recognize the court, an officer was to watch the case on his behalf, taking no part in the proceedings but reporting directly to the Military Governor.[405] But since prisoners appear generally to have been legally represented in serious cases, it is doubtful if this procedure was much used. Pleas of guilty were not to be accepted in any case in which a death sentence was likely to be awarded.[406]

---

[397] This was one of the points relied on in *R (Garde and Others)* v. *Strickland* [1921] 2 *IR* 317, at 318.

[398] 'Circular Memorandum on Martial Law', 5, para. 26, WO 35/66, PRO, Kew.

[399] Ibid. 5, para. 26.

[400] e.g. in *Egan* v. *Macready* [1921] 1 *IR* 265, where this lack of precision was severely criticized by O'Connor MR. The case is discussed below. 'Improper possessions' of arms etc. was an offence created by Proclamation no. 1, and this is the wording used in one of the specimen charges included at p. 5, para. 26, in the 'Circular Memorandum on Martial Law', WO 35/66, PRO, Kew.

[401] Ibid. 4, para. 19.

[402] e.g. the reports of *R* v. *Allen* [1921] 2 *IR* 241, at 262, and *R (Garde and Others)* v. *Strickland* [1921] 2 *IR* 317, at 318, make it clear that the accused was represented by counsel at the trial.

[403] 'Circular Memorandum on Martial Law', 4, para. 19, WO 35/66, PRO, Kew.

[404] Ibid. 4, para. 20.

[405] Ibid. 4, paras. 19, 22.

[406] Ibid. 6, para. 31.

TABLE 12. Reported cases on operation of military courts in 1921

Title of case	R v. Allen[a]	R (Garde and Others) v. Strickland[b]	Egan v. Macready[c]	In re Clifford and O'Sullivan[d]
Date of reported case	9–24 Feb. 1921	23 Mar.–25 Apr. 1921	6–26 July 1921	28 July 1921
Date of arrest	19 Jan. 1921	20 Feb. 1921	26 May 1921	23 Apr. 1921
Incident date	19 Jan. 1921	20 Feb. 1921	26 May 1921	23 Apr. 1921
Date of trial	7 Feb. 1921	8–19 Mar. 1921	11 June 1921	3 May 1921
Period between arrest and trial (weeks)	2.7	2.3	2.3	1.4
Charges	Improperly in possession of arms. Improperly in possession of ammunition. Improperly in possession of a document prejudicial to the restoration of order in Ireland.	Levying war against HM.	Improperly in possession of ammunition.	Improperly in possession of arms and ammunition.
Sentence	Death	Death	Death	Death

[a] [1921] 2 IR 241.
[b] [1921] 2 IR 317.
[c] [1921] 1 IR 265.
[d] [1921] 2 AC 570.

It was expressly provided that the accused could in his defence (1) give evidence as a witness in court, in which case he was liable to be cross-examined by the prosecutor and examined by the court, or (2) make or hand in a statement not on oath, in which case he was not liable to be questioned in any way, or (3) say nothing, or (4) hand in a written statement on oath, in which case he could be cross-examined on it.[407]

Generally, the rules of evidence were to apply 'as strictly as in any other court',[408] though there are indications that practice fell short of this standard.[409] Death sentences could originally be imposed only where the court was unanimous both as regards finding and sentence,[410] but later this was altered to allow for such decisions by a two-thirds majority where the court consisted of five or more members.[411] In other cases, decisions were apparently to be reached by a simple majority.[412] It appears that trials were, at least sometimes, conducted in a very rushed manner. One prisoner in Cork gaol in 1921 described his experience and that of another prisoner as follows:

After a week or so both he and I were called out, and marched across the square to the courtmartial quarters. He was led in while I was kept outside the door. He was in for less than fifteen minutes when he came out, and was put on a lorry bound for Cork jail: he had been sentenced to death. I was marched back to the hut without being asked a question. This happened about three times in all, and on each occasion the prisoner was sentenced.[413]

The 'Circular Memorandum on Martial Law' provided that 'in awarding punishment, the Court . . . is not restricted to any limitation of punishment imposed for any offence either by the Army Act or by the General Criminal Law'.[414] The sentencing options open to the court were, in order of severity, death by hanging, death by shooting, penal servitude for between three years and life, imprisonment for up to two years, fines not exceeding £1,000 with any other punishment, and with a period of

---

[407] 'Circular Memorandum on Martial Law' 9, para. 44.

[408] Ibid. 9, para. 66.

[409] e.g. in *R (Garde and Others)* v. *Strickland* [1921] 2 *IR* 317 it was claimed that the overt acts of treason alleged by the prosecution at the trial by military court were not proved upon the oaths and testimony of two lawful witnesses, and therefore that no powers existed to indict or try the prisoners as required by 1 & 2 Geo. 4, c. 24, s. 1. This claim was not contradicted by the respondent.

[410] 'Circular Memorandum on Martial Law', 10, para. 48, WO 35/66, PRO, Kew.

[411] Ibid. 10, para. 48, as substituted by GRO 641, 21 June 1921, WO 35/173/2, PRO, Kew.

[412] At least the 'Circular Memorandum on Martial Law' provided that 'in the case of an equality of votes, the finding is entered as one of "Not Guilty" ' (p. 10, para. 49), so presumably a simple majority was all that was required to bring in a guilty verdict. WO 35/66, PRO, Kew.

[413] Statement of Timothy O'Connell, included in app. D, in Deasy, *Towards Ireland Free*, at p. 340.

[414] p. 12, para. 56, WO 35/66, PRO, Kew.

imprisonment in default of payment.[415] Thus it would appear that a military court could impose the death penalty for any offence. It is difficult to be precise about the types of charges tried and the sentencing record of military courts.[416] Initially, it appears that a variety of sentences were being handed down,[417] and that the charges on which death sentences were usually awarded were 'improper possession of arms' and treason ('levying war against his Majesty') (Table 12). By June 1921 these were probably the only type of offence being tried by military court. This specialization is reflected in the pattern of executions for political offences carried out in 1920–1. There were twenty-four in all: ten carried out pursuant to sentences of ROIA courts martial and fourteen pursuant to sentences of martial law tribunals. Of these fourteen, eleven were imposed by military courts, and three by drumhead courts.[418]

Sentences of military courts were subject to confirmation, usually by the officer who convened the court,[419] but in the case of death sentences, by the Military Governor-General.[420] The confirming officer might before confirmation, 'if there is any doubt about the legality of the Finding or about any other point', send the proceedings to superior authority or to the Deputy Judge Advocate General, GHQ, direct.[421] The proceedings were to be returned directly with a ruling on the point in question.[422]

In addition to or without any punishment, the court was empowered to compel the accused to enter into recognizances with or without sureties, and could also recommend internment.[423] Any such recommendation would presumably be referred to the CMA/Military Governor.

Drumhead courts

On 1 May 1921 one Patrick Casey was arrested immediately after an ambush on a military patrol in the MLA. He was 'tried' the following

---

[415] Ibid. 11, para. 54. Originally, fines could be imposed 'with or without any other punishment', but 'or without' was deleted by GRO 857, 23 Aug. 1921, WO 35/173/2, PRO, Kew.

[416] Relevant information is not readily extracted from the separate weekly reports on the state of Ireland submitted to the British Cabinet by the Chief Secretary and by the GOC. CAB 24/118–25, PRO, Kew. The Chief Secretary's reports for 1921 apparently do not cover the operation of martial law tribunals, while the GOC's weekly reports after 5 Feb. do not distinguish between military courts and courts martial.

[417] e.g. in the GOC's report for w/e 25 Jan. 1921 six trials by military are recorded. These resulted in two releases and four convictions, details of which are as follows: (1) possession or arms and ammunition, 1 bound over to keep the peace for eight months in £50 and 2 sureties of £25 each, (2) miscellaneous offences, 1 to two years with hard labour, 1 to 18 months with hard labour, and 1 fined £5.

[418] Macardle lists 24 executions in 1920–1, 14 of which were in the MLA (13 in Cork and 1 in Limerick), and 10 outside (all in Dublin). *Irish Republic*, 1023–4.

[419] 'Circular Memorandum on Martial Law,' 15, para. 73, WO 35/66, PRO, Kew.

[420] Ibid. 15, para. 75.   [421] Ibid. 15, para. 77.

[422] Ibid.   [423] Ibid. 11, para. 55.

morning for his alleged involvement and executed that night, twenty-five or twenty-six hours after his arrest. When questioned about the affair at Westminster, the Attorney-General (Sir Denis Henry) replied: 'Patrick Casey, who was caught in the act of attempting to shoot an officer and was in arms joined with others in rebellion against His Majesty, was tried by a military court in the martial law area, sentenced, and convicted. The sentence was confirmed by the Military Governor.'[424] In reply to the question as to whether 'there was any reasonable opportunity for those who were assigned to defend the accused to master and state the case?',[425] he replied evasively: 'I am sure that if any application were made, it would be duly considered by the court.'[426] This seems to have been the first instance of trial by drumhead court.

The decision must have been taken to adopt the most summary procedures in trials of IRA suspects captured in action. The matter does not appear to have been covered in the General Routine Orders, and the earliest available GHQ order authorizing such action is that of August 1921.[427] It could have been claimed that such trials were authorized by the orders governing military courts, but this seems unlikely, as the latter orders expressly allowed for legal representation and time to prepare a defence, whereas the time-limits involved in drumhead trial would have precluded obtaining such assistance. It seems likely that one reason for the adoption of these procedures was that the speed and the circumstances of the process prevented the accused from obtaining legal representation and thus from challenging the proceedings in the civil courts. Thus, the principal clog on the martial law court system—application for prerogative writs to the civil courts[428]—was circumvented.

Macready asserted that these courts were used on only three occasions before the truce, but that had martial law been extended, it was his intention 'to use these courts alone for men taken in arms'.[429] He pressed the demand for drumhead courts at a meeting of the Irish Situation Committee (of the British Cabinet) in June 1921,[430] and it was presumably with a view to the possibility of a breakdown in the truce that the order setting out the procedures for drumhead courts was issued in August 1921.

[424] 141 *HC Deb.*, col. 1502, 9 May 1921.

[425] Ibid. 1205, 5 May 1921.

[426] Ibid.

[427] The order of Aug. 1921 (CRIC, no. 2/54340, GHQ Ireland, 22 Aug. 1921) is marked 'confidential'. It is included in the 'Circular Memorandum on Martial Law', WO 35/66, PRO, Kew.

[428] The reported cases on these applications and the Army's response are considered in detail on pp. 136–47.

[429] Quoted in Townshend, 518.

[430] 'Record of Meeting of the Irish Situation Committee', 15 June 1921, CAB 27/107, PRO, Kew.

That order provided that where (1) persons are captured in action with arms, bombs, or explosives whether in uniform or not, (2) persons are captured with arms, bombs, or explosives in their hands or on their person, or (3) persons are captured where there is clear evidence that they had arms, bombs, or explosives on their person immediately before capture, application was to be made at once to the nearest officer not under the rank of Field Officer in command of a body of troops to convene a drumhead court. This was only to be done 'where the evidence appears to be clear beyond possibility of doubt'.[431] The court was to be convened at the 'nearest convenient place',[432] and was to consist of three officers of whom the President was ordinarily to be of field rank. The convening officer could, if no other Field Officer were available, appoint himself President, and this post could be held by a Captain if no other field-ranking officer were available.

The assembly of the court was to take place 'with the utmost expedition'.[433] No adjournments were to be allowed, and nothing was to be permitted to delay the commencement and conclusion of the trial. Subject to any order to the contrary which might be issued by superior authority, the sentence of the court was to be confirmed either by the senior officer of field rank on the spot, other than the President, or by the nearest Field Officer available.

If the sentence were one of death, the confirming officer was to give instruction for its immediate execution. He was then to send a telegram to GHQ giving the name of the man, the nature of the offence, and the place, date, and time of execution. Apart from these special provisions, the instructions issued for ordinary military courts were to apply 'so far as is practicable, according to the circumstances of the case'.[434]

Suspects were to be tried by drumhead court only 'where the evidence appears to be clear beyond possibility of doubt'.[435] The purpose of such proceedings could not therefore be said to be the adjudication on the guilt or innocence of the accused, since the decision to convene a drumhead court effectively prejudged the substantive issue, but rather to share responsibility for the fate of the captive. Thus the pseudo-judicial procedure of drumhead courts approximated even less to courts in the true sense of the term, than did other martial law tribunals.

Trials by the army: conclusions

It would be pointless simply to measure the operation of courts martial and military courts in Ireland against a 'rule of law' standard. Courts martial generally were never intended to function exactly as the ordinary

---

[431] CRIC, no. 2/54340, 22 Aug. 1921, WO 35/66, PRO, Kew.
[432] Ibid.   [433] Ibid.   [434] Ibid.   [435] Ibid.

courts, since so to operate would involve a duplication of functions. In any case, trial by court martial was incompatible with the basic rule of natural justice *nemo iudex in causa sua*. The British Army was frequently not only the 'injured party', but also performed the functions of judge, jury, and sometimes prosecutor and executioner as well.

Historically, courts martial were seen as a means of enforcing discipline in the Army, and, analogously, in Ireland their function was seen as that of obtaining convictions and coercing the 'enemy'. But it might be asked: within this framework were their procedures fair? The answer would have to be in the negative. Fairness in procedure was severely compromised by the arbitrary powers of referring cases to the CMA, and in the reversal of the burden of proof in certain instances, especially when it is borne in mind that the accused was not a competent witness in his own defence at DORA and ROIA courts martial. This incapacity also meant that the opportunities open to the accused to challenge the admissibility of confessions obtained in dubious circumstances were greatly reduced. Another provision which could tend to result in unfairness was that permitting statements from the Summary of Evidence to be admissible in evidence at the trial in certain instances. Such statements could not, at the trial, be the subject of cross-examination by the defence and could not be rebutted adequately by the accused owing to the latter's incapacity in relation to the giving of evidence. The possibility of fairness in sentencing was reduced by the virtually unlimited range of sentences available for breaches of the regulations, a feature more marked in the case of ROIA courts martial than in DORA courts martial.

In practice there is evidence that wide sentencing powers resulted in very wide variation in sentencing and that the widespread use of the ROIA courts-martial system resulted in a lack of consistency either in charging or in relation to findings, that bias was evident in the cases of policemen and that review procedures were inadequate. Generally, these criticisms (apart from those relating to the accused's competence as a witness) apply with even greater force to trial by military court.

If courts martial and military courts could never approximate to the 'rule of law', and if their procedures could not be said to have been fair, could they yet be said to have achieved their primary function? Again, the answer would probably have to be in the negative. Their operation appears to have had little or no braking effect on the IRA—the IRA leadership seems to have been almost entirely unaffected by them. Indeed, not only does the operation of courts martial and military courts appear to have been ineffectual, the executions policy which was central to the exercise appears to have been entirely counter-productive. The dates of forthcoming executions were well publicized, and the waiting periods became occasions for massive public displays of support for the condemned men. Just how counter-productive the policy was can be gauged from the description of the events of one morning in Dublin when six prisoners were due to be hanged:

A general stoppage of work was called for by the Irish Transport and General Workers Union between the hours of six a.m. and noon. Throughout the morning blinds and shutters were down and business premises kept their doors closed, not only in Dublin but throughout the country . . . Shortly after five a.m. crowds began to gather outside the prison. As the hour progressed the crowd was estimated to be near forty thousand.[436]

SECTION (C) INTERNMENT

Internment under DORR 14B and ROIR 14B

The phases in the use of powers to detain indefinitely without trial or to 'intern' in Ireland in the years 1918–21 correspond closely with those delineated above in relation to arrest powers. The broad picture is one of lessening political control, increasing if uneven use, and a growing militarization of the process.

The powers and the decision to intern

DORR 14B gave authority to the Secretary of State to order that a person reside in a named area or that he be interned. From April 1918, these powers were made exercisable in Ireland by the Chief Secretary,[437] and from February 1920 by the Lord-Lieutenant or the Chief Secretary[438] (Table 13). In exercising these powers he was to act on the recommendation of a CMA or of a specially constituted 'advisory committee'. Initially, the criteria for the making of an internment order against a person was that such a course of action appeared expedient 'for securing the public safety or the defence of the realm' in view of the 'hostile origin or association of any person'. There was no requirement of 'reasonable suspicion' for the making of an order and thus the possibility of meaningful judicial review of the ministerial action was minimized.[439] Also in April 1918, powers of internment became exercisable in Ireland only, 'in relation to any person who is suspected of acting or having acted or of being about to act in a manner prejudicial to the public safety of

---

[436] *Irish Independent*, 14 Mar. 1921, quoted in Villiers-Tuthill, *Beyond the Twelve Bens*, 206.

[437] *DG* 26 Apr. 1918.

[438] *DG* 13 Feb. 1920.

[439] For a failed judicial challenge to DORR 14B see *R* v. *Halliday* [1917] *AC* 260, though the issue of the factual basis of the Secretary of State's opinion was not challenged therein. The case is discussed on pp. 113–14.

TABLE 13. DORR 14B

Criteria for Use

(Reg. as at 1 January 1918)

When on the recommendation of a competent naval or military authority or of one of the advisory committees hereinafter mentioned it appears to the Secretary of State that for securing the public safety or the defence of the Realm it is expedient in view of the hostile origin or associations of any person that he shall be subjected to such obligations and restrictions as are hereinafter mentioned . . .

Powers Granted

(Reg. as at 1 January 1918)

. . . the Secretary of State may by Order require that person forthwith, or from time to time, either to remain in, or to proceed to and reside in, such place as may be specified in the order, and to comply with such directions as to reporting to the police, restriction of movement, and otherwise as may be specified in the order,
or
to be interned as may be directed in the order.

Added 20 April 1918

In any area in respect of which the operation of Section one of the Defence of the Realm (Amendment) Act, 1915, is for the time being suspended, this regulation shall apply in relation to any person who is suspected of acting or having acted or of being about to act in a manner prejudicial to the public safety or the defence of the Realm, as it applies in relation to persons of hostile origin or association.

If any person in respect of whom any order is made under this regulation fails to comply with any of the provisions of the order he shall be guilty of an offence against these regulations, and any person interned under such order shall be subject to the like restrictions and may be dealt with in like manner as a prisoner of war, except so far as the Secretary of State may modify such restrictions . . .

Added 4 Sept. 1918

The Secretary of State may make any such order as aforesaid with respect to any alien in any case where in his opinion the making of the order is calculated to secure the safety of any British subject in any foreign country.

---

cont.

the defence of the Realm',[440] a formulation which was likewise not susceptible to judicial challenge.[441] This laid the ground for the arrest in May 1918 of seventy-three Sinn Féin and Irish Volunteer activists on the pretext of the 'German plot'. These were then interned in England, the regulation having been appropriately amended.[442] Because of this

---

[440] *DG* 26 Apr. 1918.

[441] See *R* v. *Governor of Wormwood Scrubs Prison* [1920] 2 *KB* 305. The case is discussed below.

[442] *DG* 26 Apr. 1918. Those interned (under DORR 14B) after the 1916 Easter Rising had been interned at Frongach camp in Wales. There was some doubt about the legal validity of this move, and a legal challenge was planned. The internees were released, however, before the issue was raised in court. The amendment was presumably designed to forestall such a move. See J. McGuffin, *Internment* (Tralee, 1973), 28–9.

TABLE 13. *Continued*

Appeals

(Reg. as at 1 January 1918)

Provided that any such order shall, in the case of any person who is not a subject of a state at war with His Majesty, include express provision for the due consideration by one of such advisory committees of any representations he may make against the order.

The advisory committees for the purpose of this regulation shall be such advisory committees as are appointed for the purpose of advising the Secretary of State with respect to the internment and deportation of aliens, each of such committees being presided over by a person who holds or has held high judicial office.

> **Amended** 20 April 1918
>
> The advisory committees for the purpose of this regulation shall be such advisory committees as are appointed for the purpose of advising the Secretary of State with respect to the internment and deportation of aliens, or any committee specially appointed by the Secretary of State for the purposes of this regulation, each of such committees being presided over by a person who holds or has held high judicial office.

> **Amended** 4 September 1918
>
> Provided that any order made under this regulation shall, in the case of any person who is not a subject of a state at war with His Majesty, include express provision for the due consideration by one of such advisory committees of any representations he may make against the order.

Miscellaneous

(Reg. as at 1 January 1918)

. . . and if any person so interned escapes or attempts to escape from the place of internment or commits any breach of the rules in force therein, he shall be guilty of an offence against these regulations.

Nothing in this regulation shall be construed to restrict or prejudice the application or effect of Regulation 14, or any power of interning aliens who are subjects of any State at war with His Majesty.

In the application of this regulation to Scotland, references to the Secretary for Scotland shall be substituted for references to the Secretary of State.

> **Amended** 20 April 1918
>
> In the application of this regulation to Scotland and Ireland, references to the Secretary for Scotland and the Chief Secretary respectively, shall be substituted for references to the Secretary of State

> **Added** 20 April 1918
>
> but an order under this regulation may require the person to whom the order relates to reside or to be interned in any place in the British Islands.

> **Amended** 9 February 1920
>
> In the application of this regulation to Scotland and Ireland, references to the Secretary for Scotland and references to the Lord Lieutenant or Chief Secretary shall respectively be substituted for references to the Secretary of State.

practice, internment orders were frequently referred to as 'deportation orders'.

The decision to proceed with the arrests and internments appears to have been taken by the British Government as a pre-emptive move to facilitate the introduction of conscription in Ireland, rather than in response to any particular German threat, but despite the unconvincing pretext, the policy was persevered with, and at least twenty more people were interned before the internees were released in March 1919.[443] What is significant about this phase is that the decision on internment was clearly a political one.

The next round of internments came with the fresh counter-insurgency drive at the start of 1920. On 30 and 31 January a series of arrests took place which the Army considered to be the 'first arrests by military authority'.[444] Initially, it appears that seventy-four people were targeted for arrest and internment in the various divisional areas, and of these fifty-seven were held. Seven more were held who were 'known to the police as dangerous', and early in February sixty-one people were shipped to England and interned.[445]

As implementation of the new policy developed, it can be seen that it operated on three different levels of suspicion or evidential requirement, thus laying the foundation for what came later in the year.[446] The first stage in the process was arrest under DORR 55,[447] a step which required a lower level of suspicion than that required under the ordinary law,[448] and could be simply a military decision. Those ordered to be arrested were 'any officer or prominent member of the Irish Volunteer organization or other persons responsible for the existing lawlessness'.[449] The practice in relation to a detainee was, 'if sufficient evidence could be obtained against him, to deport him under DORR 14B'.[450] Divisions were assigned quotas on internments,[451] but the decision on the sufficiency of 'evidence' for internment was not simply a military one. Before the order was made it appears that it was the practice for the 'evidence' to be put before the Attorney-General and the Lord-Lieutenant.[452] This was the second level. The third level was where sufficient evidence was available to mount a prosecution against a detainee. Decisions on the sufficiency of evidence at this level rested with the civil prosecuting authorities in respect of alleged crimes, and with the appropriate CMA in the case of alleged breaches of DORR.

---

[443] See, generally, McGuffin, *Internment*, 28–32.
[444] 'Record of the Rebellion', vol. i.
[445] Ibid.
[446] See pp. 46–51.
[447] 'History of the 5th Division', 21.
[448] See pp. 41–6.
[449] 'History of the 5th Division', 21–2,
[450] Ibid. 22.
[451] e.g. the 5th Division was given a quota of 80 suspects to be deported to England (ibid. 22).
[452] Note of conversation between the Prime Minister, the Viceroy, the Chief Secretary, and the AG on 30 Apr. 1920, CAB 23/21, PRO, Kew. Presumably the reference is to the AG for Ireland.

By mid-April a total of 317 had been held, and by the beginning of May over 250 people whom the Army considered 'rebel leaders' had been deported and interned in England.[453] Those held in Dublin combated the new strategy by the use of the hunger strike, and on 14 April the strikers were released. On 3 May the initiative received another major set-back as orders were issued to suspend all arrests.[454] But by the end of the month deportations to England were again proceeding, though at a greatly curtailed rate.[455]

ROIR 14B was introduced in August 1920 (Table 14). As with the bulk of ROIR, it had been created by amendment to DORR, so that under the new regulation internment could be ordered if it appeared to the Chief Secretary expedient 'for securing the restoration or maintenance of order in Ireland that a person who is suspected of acting or having acted or of being about to act in a manner prejudicial to the restoration or maintenance of order in Ireland' should be interned. The power to make internment orders was not limited to the Chief Secretary but, as had been the case with DORR 14B, it could also be exercised in Britain by the Secretary of State, and by the Secretary of State for Scotland. It is unclear whether, in Britain, the power to order internment under ROIR 14B was used in 1920–1, but if it was, it would probably have been ordered that internees be held in Ireland.[456]

Following 'Bloody Sunday' (21 November 1920)[457] full use was made of the new Regulation. Orders were given 'to arrest all leaders of the IRA and other "wanted men" and if sufficient evidence was not available to secure a conviction, to forward their names for internment in Ireland'.[458] These guide-lines were interpreted much more freely than those issued earlier in the year had been, and by 23 December, 1,002 orders under ROIR 14B had been made.[459] The system of internment in force at that time has been described as follows:

Divisions submitted to GHQ lists of men they wished to intern, giving their believed rank in the IRA. These lists were examined at GHQ and forwarded to the Chief Secretary with application for internment warrants. Owing to delay in the issue of warrants and the congestion which would have occurred in divisional

---

[453] 'Record of the Rebellion', vol. i. The ranks of those held were given as: Brigade Commandants 27, Brigade staff 13, Battalion Commander 16, Battalion officers 116, other prominent officials 145.

[454] Ibid. 38.

[455] See Townshend, 77.

[456] See *R* v. *Governor of Wormwood Scrubs Prison* [1920] 2 *KB* 305 for a failed judicial challenge to the use of DORR powers in Britain to order internment in Ireland. In *R* v. *Home Secretary, ex parte O'Brien* [1923] 2 *KB* 361, an order under ROIR 14B that a person be interned in the south of Ireland after the creation of the Irish Free State was ruled void.

[457] See pp. 29–30.

[458] 'History of the 5th Division', 58.

[459] 136 *HC Deb.*, col. 2104.

TABLE 14. ROIR 14B

Criteria for Use

(Reg. as at 13 August 1920)

When on the recommendation of a competent naval or military authority or of one of the advisory committees hereinafter mentioned it appears to the Secretary of State that for securing the restoration or maintenance of order in Ireland it is expedient that a person who is suspected of acting or having acted or of being about to act in a manner prejudicial to the restoration or maintenance of order in Ireland shall be subjected to such obligations and restrictions as are hereinafter mentioned . . .

The Secretary of State may make any such order as aforesaid with respect to any alien in any case where in his opinion the making of the order is calculated to secure the safety of any British subject in any foreign country.

Powers Granted

(Reg. as at 13 August 1920)

. . . the Secretary of State may by Order require that person forthwith, or from time to time, either to remain in, or to proceed to and reside in, such place as may be specified in the order, and to comply with such directions as to reporting to the police, restriction of movement, and otherwise as may be specified in the order, or
to be interned as may be directed in the order.

If any person in respect of whom any order is made under this regulation fails to comply with any of the provisions of the order he shall be guilty of an offence against these regulations, and any person interned under such order shall be subject to the like restrictions and may be dealt with in like manner as a prisoner of war, except so far as the Secretary of State may modify such restrictions . . .

cont.

areas had the arrested men been retained until the warrants were received, divisions were authorized to ship to Ballykinlar [Internment Camp] batches of men whose internment had been approved, as and when shipping facilities became available, the internments warrants were then sent direct from GHQ to the Commandant of the internment camp.[460]

Army documents at this time give the impression that the role of the Chief Secretary was simply to rubber-stamp GHQ approvals of Divisional decisions on internment. In many instances the civilian authorities did not know enough about the suspect to get the name right on the requisite documentation, with the result that the camp commandant sometimes experienced difficulty in fitting the the warrants received from GHQ to the individuals received from the Divisions.[461] As one source rather contemptuously put it:

The main difficulty experienced throughout was found to be one of identity. Thus in the process from arrest to confinement in an Internment Camp, an internee originally arrested as say Michael Collins of Rascarbery became Sean Lehone of Ballydibob owing to varying identification. Later the internee stated that he was neither one nor the other, but Frank Doherty of Ballinrobe, and demanded his

[460] 'Record of the Rebellion', i. 27.   [461] Ibid.

Table 14. *Continued*

Appeals

(Reg. as at 13 August 1920)

Provided that any order made under this regulation shall, in the case of any person who is not a subject of a state at war with His Majesty, include express provision for the due consideration by one of such advisory committees of any representations he may make against the order.

The advisory committees for the purpose of this regulation shall be such advisory committees as are appointed for the purpose of advising the Secretary of State with respect to the internment and deportation of aliens, or any committee specially appointed by the Secretary of State for the purposes of this regulation, each of such committees being presided over by a person who holds or has held high judicial office.

Miscellaneous

(Reg. as at 13 August 1920)

. . . and if any person so interned escapes or attempts to escape from the place of internment or commits any breach of the rules in force therein, he shall be guilty of an offence against these regulations.

Nothing in this regulation shall be construed to restrict or prejudice the applicaton or effect of Regulation 14, or any power of interning aliens who are subjects of any State at war with His Majesty.

In the application of this regulation to Scotland and Ireland, references to the Secretary for Scotland and references to the Lord Lieutenant or Chief Secretary shall respectively be substituted for references to the Secretary of State, but an order under this regulation may require the person to whom the order relates to reside or to be interned in any place in the British Islands.

immediate release. While this was going on, the internee's number had been changed from the original Brigade Number to the GHQ Internment Number, and as reference to the Brigade concerned might not result in identifying the man, endless correspondence ensued.[462]

The Army itself also experienced internal administrative difficulties. Initially, at Divisional level, staff work in connection with internment involved both the General Staff and the Adjutant-General's branches. In some areas at least, the position was rationalized so that the Adjutant-General's branch was given sole responsibility in administrative matters. In the 5th Division, for instance, these duties included responsibility 'for ensuring that every case was dealt with correctly, that arrest reports were received, checked and forwarded to GHQ, and that the machinery for internment generally ran correctly and smoothly'.[463] Reference to the General Staff was only to be 'with regard to recommendations as to internment or release as the case might be'.[464] A similar division of responsibility was made in the 6th Division, with the General Staff

---

[462] 'History of the 5th Division', app. 16.   [463] Ibid.   [464] Ibid.

TABLE 15. Numbers interned from January
1921 to July 1921

Week ending	Cumulative total no. of internments[a]	No. of fresh internments during period
17 Jan.	1,478	n/a
7 Feb.	1,857	379
21 Feb.	1,985	128
5 Mar.	2,317	332
21 Mar.	2,569	252
2 Apr.	2,756	187
30 Apr.	3,005	249
21 May	3,689	684
4 June	3,839	150
18 June	4,139	300
2 July	4,287	148
16 July	4,454	167

[a] This does not give the actual number interned at any one time.

Source: Derived from Townshend, app. 12, p. 223.

retaining responsibility 'for all questions affecting individuals from an Intelligence point of view'.[465]

The Army insisted on attributing an IRA rank to all those interned,[466] and members of the British Government were likewise keen to claim that all of them were 'believed to be active members of the Irish Republican Army',[467] but in view of the interrogation methods involved in obtaining admissions of membership, these designations and claims were probably far from accurate in many instances. However selective or otherwise, internment powers continued to be used on a massive scale in the period leading up to the truce, with the maximum intensity of use occurring in May 1921 (Table 15). In the MLA, statutory internment powers continued to be used, sometimes on the recommendation to the CMA of a military court. This was despite the fact that under martial law, habeas corpus was effectively suspended, so that indefinite detention without statutory authority would have been possible.[468] The reason for this

---

[465] 'Policy on dealing with all matters concerning Internees, Political Prisoners, Prisons in the field, Gaols and Detention Barracks', CR, No. GS 429, issued by General Staff, 6th Division, 31 May 1921, Strickland papers.

[466] A breakdown by rank of all those interned from w/e 17 Jan. 1921 to w/e 16 July 1921 can be found in Townshend, app. 12, p. 223.

[467] 136 *HC Deb.*, cols. 2103–4.

[468] Issues under this heading are discussed on pp. 123–47.

course of action appears to have been that any such detentions without statutory authority would have had no validity outside the MLA, and keeping internees within that area was impossible owing to overcrowding in the gaols and the fact that no internment camp existed in the MLA.

Treatment of internees

It appears that the practice prior to the introduction of ROIA of deporting the bulk of the internees to England was felt to present few problems as long as internees and prisoners of war were being held in Britain anyway for reasons unrelated to the Irish conflict. The system in early 1920 was that 'Deportees, as they were called, were kept in military custody (guard-room cells or huts erected specially for the purpose at the larger military stations) until their deportation orders were signed in Dublin, when they were sent under military escort to Dublin or Belfast for transfer to England.'[469] With the phasing out of DORA in Britain in 1920, this procedure appears to have been ended. A large internment camp was established at Ballykinlar, County Down, and in March 1921 a second camp was established at the Curragh.[470] The huts were wooden and some were bugged, though the practice was not particularly effective.[471] Neither were the interrogations which were conducted by intelligence officers in the camps considered a fruitful source of information. This was apparently because of lack of local knowledge on the part of the interrogators, but 'a certain amount of unimportant information' was gleaned through this process.[472] A more useful source of information was found to be the secret posts organized by the internees—a source which was found to be 'particularly useful especially to the branch compiling the Order of Battle and Irish Republican Army List'.[473]

Under both DORR 14B and ROIR 14B, internees were 'subject to the like restrictions and may be dealt with in like manner as a prisoner of war, except so far as the Secretary of State may modify such restrictions'. The pamphlet issued as a guide to camp commandants was, however, considered inappropriate by the Army precisely because it had been 'drawn up primarily in connection with the administration of Prisoners of War Camps'.[474] The atmosphere in the camps was not good, with

---

[469] 'History of the 5th Division', 22.

[470] Ibid. 85.

[471] 'Record of the Rebellion' commented: 'Microphones and detectaphones were used to a certain extent. Their value depended on the type of building in which they were situated and they were useless in buildings such as wooden huts where every noise was magnified. Consequently, they were not effective in internment camps, but the prisoners believed they were installed everywhere' (ii. 29).

[472] Ibid.

[473] Ibid.

[474] 'History of the 5th Division', app. 16, p. 2.

frequent accusations by the prisoners of brutality. In retrospect, one Divisional history was prepared to admit, in what was probably an understatement, that 'a few isolated cases took place of harassed officers and men treating internees with some roughness'.[475] And there were other problems—in an attempt to cut down on the many escapes by tunnelling from the Curragh, a ditch was constructed all around the camp. This filled with stagnant water, a development which 'produced vehement protest from medical authorities and much activity on the part of the local Fire Engine'.[476]

Advisory committees

Internees could make representations against their internment to an Advisory Committee. This could be one specially created for the purpose and presided over by a 'person who holds or has held high judicial office', or it could be one 'appointed for the purpose of advising the Secretary of State with respect to the internment and deportation of aliens'. It appears that in April 1920 no special committee had yet been appointed, as the suggestion was at that time being put forward by the Chief Secretary that one be created, consisting of a judge and two Members of Parliament.[477] But by January 1921 at the latest, a committee had been appointed, the composition of which was entirely judicial.[478] It appears to have attracted little interest from internees—by the end of June 1921 there were only twenty-four appeals awaiting hearing, a figure which represents approximately 0.6 per cent of those interned.[479]

Conclusions

Powers of internment under DORA and ROIA marked a radical departure from normal legal standards. Three broad phases can be delineated in their use in the period in question. The first lasted from May 1918 to March 1919. During this period internment powers were under political control, and were exercised for a political purpose. The second period covered the first few months of 1920. At this stage internment powers were used for military purposes under political control. The third ran

---

[475] 'History of the 5th Division'. Internees, the Army claimed, engaged in obstruction, which 'took the form of refusing to answer roll call, refusing to obey orders given by Section Officers, destruction of government property, and incessant clamour and complaint. The obvious and only remedy for such a course of action was to enforce obedience and good behaviour by physical violence, but such a course was not permitted by the regulations governing the treatment of internees.'

[476] Ibid.

[477] Cabinet Conclusions, 26 Apr. 1920, CAB 23/21, PRO, Kew.

[478] This consisted of Mr Justice Ross, His Honour Judge Doyle KC, Recorder of Galway, and Mr W. Sullivan RM. Chief Secretary's weekly survey, w/e 17 Jan. 1921, CAB 24/118, PRO, Kew.

[479] Chief Secretary's weekly survey, w/e 20 June 1921, CAB 24, PRO, Kew.

from November 1920 to the truce of July 1921. During the last period, both purposes and control appear to have been military, with only nominal political scrutiny.

This giving of a free hand to the Army resulted in mass use of internment powers, based in many instances, it would appear, on quite doubtful evidence. The injustices which thus occurred could not have been remedied by the Advisory Committee, as evidenced by the small number of appeals heard. Internment was used by the Army not only as a form of preventive detention, but also in an attempt to gather intelligence, despite there having been no specific power to interrogate internees. Accusations of brutality were common, and in view of the Army's comments in relation to such claims, were probably at least partly justified.

As to the question of effectiveness, what has been noted above in relation to courts martial could also be said to apply to the use of internment powers. Neither device seems to have greatly impeded the IRA. It is significant that British Army sources were not uniform in the endorsement of the effectiveness of internment. Some claimed that the internments of February, March, and April 1920 'had considerable effect on the country'[480] but another hinted at counter-productive effects in that the mass arrests towards the end of 1920 prompted the introduction of organizational improvements in the IRA:

As was to be expected, after the first shock of the arrests the rebel leaders who had escaped internment urged on the IRA to new efforts. It was not long before substitutes were provided for the lost leaders, and the flying columns received an impetus from the influx of the greatly increased number of rebels who found it necessary to go 'on the run'.[481]

PART III. JUDICIAL SCRUTINY OF EMERGENCY POWERS

In theory, all the remedies ordinarily available to the individual who felt that his rights had been infringed by executive action remained available during an emergency unless expressly excluded. Thus actions might be brought in tort for the recovery of damages, or injunctive relief sought. Unlawful detention might be challenged in habeas corpus proceedings, and the actions of inferior courts might be challenged by application for the prerogative writs of *certiorari*, mandamus, and prohibition. These writs might also be utilized to exert a degree of control over administrative

---

[480] 'History of the 5th Division', 38.
[481] 'Record of the Rebellion', i. 27.

action.[482] In addition, the validity of all subordinate legislative instruments could be tested by the superior courts by reference to the test of *vires*.[483] Any statutory instrument or regulation made outside the powers conferred by the principal Act would, if tested, be held to be invalid. An order purportedly made under subordinate legislation could likewise be challenged.

In practice, the position in emergencies tended to be somewhat different.[484] Emergency powers were typically drafted in a manner designed to minimize the possibility of judicial scrutiny, reflecting a desire that emergency powers should, above all else, be seen to be effective. It was felt that this effectiveness might be enhanced by removing any clogs on the exercise of emergency powers caused by meaningful judicial or parliamentary scrutiny. In the Defence of the Realm Consolidation Act 1914, for instance, there was no provision that regulations made under the Act require parliamentary approval. In such situations the judiciary tended to place special emphasis on context, invoking the particular circumstances as justifying (or requiring) self-imposed limitation.

DORA and the English courts

With the introduction of DORA, the above viewpoint was expressed in a substantial body of legal opinion which took the view that the normal rigid judicial approach to the scrutiny of legislation, particularly by the test of *vires*, should not apply to these Acts and Regulations. This approach was forcefully expressed in the frequently quoted remarks of Scrutton LJ in *Ronnfeldt* v. *Phillips*[485] (29 October 1918), a case which involved a failed challenge to the making of an order excluding a person from an area under DORR 14:[486]

It has been said that a war could not be conducted on the principles of the Sermon on the Mount. It might also be said that a war could not be carried on according to the principles of Magna Carta. Very wide powers had been given to the Executive to act on suspicion on matters affecting the interests of the state.[487]

---

[482] See S. A. De Smith, *De Smith's Judicial Review of Administrative Action* (London, 1980), 381–428. During the 1920s the law on judicial review of administrative action was very much less developed than it currently is.
[483] See S. A. De Smith, *Constitutional and Administrative Law* (Harmondsworth, 1985), 571–625.
[484] See, generally, Bonner, *Emergency Powers*, 50–71.
[485] 35 *TLR* 46. For another failed challenge to an order under DORR 14 see *R* v. *Denison* [1916] 32 *TLR* 528 (22 May 1916).
[486] See App. 3.
[487] *Ronnfeldt* v. *Phillips* [1918–19] 35 *TLR* 46, at 47. Similar views were expressed by the bench in *Norman* v. *Matthews* [1916] 32 *TLR* 303 and 369, a case in which DORR 27 and DORR 51A were held to be *intra vires*.

This relaxation of the *ultra vires* doctrine was evident in the leading case on DORA, *R* v. *Halliday*[488] (1 May 1917) in which a German-born naturalized British citizen challenged his detention under DORR 14B by seeking to have the regulation declared *ultra vires* the Act. The applicant's main contention was that since the Act contained no provision for imprisonment without trial, a regulation purporting to make provision for such imprisonment must, on a strict construction, be repugnant to the Act.

The House of Lords split on the issue: the dissenting judgment of Lord Shaw insisted on adherence to the rule of law even in an emergency; the majority judgment adopted a frankly instrumentalist interpretation. In the words of the Lord Chancellor (Finlay):

it may be necessary in a time of great public danger to entrust great power to His Majesty in council, and that Parliament may do so feeling certain that such powers will be reasonably exercised . . . One of the more obvious means of taking precaution against dangers . . . is to impose some restriction on the freedom of movement of persons whom there may be some reason to suspect of being disposed to help the enemy. It is to this that Reg. 14B is directed. The measure is not prohibitory but precautionary.[489]

This formulation glosses over the fact that there is a difference in kind, and not just in degree, between imposing some restrictions on a person's movement, and preventing that person from engaging in any movement at all by interning him or her.

As to the argument that there was no express provision in the Act allowing internment without trial, Finlay LC stated: 'the legislature has selected another way of achieving the same purpose probably milder as well as more effectual than those adopted on the occasion of previous wars'.[490] Whether the measures adopted were, or were not, 'milder' or 'more effectual' than those relied upon in previous wars is, strictly speaking, irrelevant. The issue was not the relative merits of the measures, but rather whether Parliament could have been said to have made proper provision for them.

C. K. Allen, however, considered the case 'notable for the vigorous dissenting judgment of Lord Shaw in which the principles of the liberty of the subject were forcibly asserted and an impressive warning was uttered concerning the extensions of executive action'.[491] In Lord Shaw's view:

This and this alone is what regulation means: it constitutes *pro tanto* a code of conduct: in following the code the citizen will be safe; in violating it the citizen will become an offender and may be charged and tried . . . This is perfectly simple: it squares with all the rest of the legislation and destroys none of it.

---

[488] [1917] *AC* 260.   [489] At pp. 268–9.   [490] p. 270.
[491] *Law and Orders* (London, 1965), 44.

It sacrifices no constitutional principle; it introduces nothing of the nature of arbitrary condemnation or punishment.[492]

It was also his view that 'if Parliament had intended to make this colossal delegation of power it would have done so plainly and courageously and not under cover of words about regulations for safety and defence'.[493]

It should be noted that the applicant did not challenge the assertion that he was a person of hostile origin or association.[494] Lord Wrenbury in his concurring judgment stated that 'if his case were that he had neither hostile origin nor association he could have his writ of habeas corpus on the ground that that was so, and if he established the fact he would be discharged'.[495]

The majority view depended on a rigidly teleological approach. As Lowry has observed:

The purpose of the legislation, in the opinion of Lord Finlay, overrode the principles of construction and the requirement of meaningful judicial review in emergency situations. The majority opinion showed that the House of Lords was prepared to assume that Parliament had intended to devolve to the Executive complete and unfettered discretion to implement whatever means the Executive might deem to be necessary for defence.[496]

Pollock, in a private comment on Lord Shaw's dissenting judgment, adopted a more extreme approach to the question of the correct judicial assumptions to be applied in consideration of these Acts: 'It is my private opinion that in time of war there is no such thing as the liberty of the subject.'[497]

This revised judicial approach applied not only in relation to the test of *vires*, but also to the interpretation of specific regulations. Thus in *Michaels* v. *Block*,[498] a case on false arrest which turned on the wording of DORR 55,[499] it was claimed that the plaintiff's 'behaviour' (as the word was used in the regulation[500]) was 'a question of fact, and must be proved by the best evidence'.[501] Consequently, it would not be sufficient for the defendant to rebut the plaintiff's claim that he had been falsely

---

[492] [1917] *AC* 260, at 286.

[493] pp. 291–2.

[494] Per Lord Finally LC, at p. 267.

[495] p. 308.

[496] D. R. Lowry, 'Terrorism and Human Rights: Counter-Insurgency and Necessity at Common Law', 53 *Notre Dame Lawyer* 49, at 55.

[497] Correspondence with Justice O. W. Homes, quoted in Allen, *Law and Orders*, 45 n. 30. Allen was at pains to point out that the remarks were not to be taken literally.

[498] [1918] 34 *TLR* 438.

[499] At the time of the arrest the relevant regulation was DORR 13, but by the time of the hearing, this had become DORR 55 of the consolidated regulations.

[500] See pp. 42–4.

[501] [1918] 34 *TLR* 438.

imprisoned simply by a chief constable's giving evidence that he gave the military authorities certain information concerning the plaintiff's antecedents: 'the dossier system, which might include information picked out of the gutter, was foreign to English justice'.[502] The assertion was roundly rejected in a very brief judgment by Darling J., for reasons which echoed previous cases on DORA. In his view the regulation was 'part of legislation passed hurriedly while the country is at war, and I think one ought to construe it according to the maxim, *salus populi suprema lex*'.[503]

There were, however, other judgments in which a more restrictive approach was taken by the judiciary to reliance on emergency powers by the executive. In some instances these arose out of the application of the test of *vires*,[504] but more significantly, for present purposes, the courts were not prepared to endorse resort to non-statutory powers where statutory powers existed in the same area. In *Attorney-General* v. *De Keyser's Royal Hotel Ltd.*[505] (10 May 1920), a case which was to have a powerful impact in relation to martial law in Ireland, it was asserted on behalf of the Attorney-General that apart from the provisions of DORA authorizing the acquisition of land, there existed a prerogative right of the Crown to take property, which was also exercisable during wartime. The Law Lords rejected this claim, doubting whether such a prerogative power existed, but in any case holding that both sets of powers could not be exercisable at the same time. In the words of Lord Atkinson:

> where such a statute, expressing the will and intention of the King and of the three estates of the realm, is passed, it abridges the Royal Prerogative while it is in force to this extent: that the Crown can only do the particular thing under and in accordance with the statutory provisions, and that its prerogative power to do that thing is in abeyance . . . after the statute has been passed, and while it is in force, the thing it empowers the Crown to do can thenceforth only be done by and under the statute, and subject to all the limitations, restrictions and conditions by it imposed, however unrestricted the Royal Prerogative may theretofore have been.[506]

Lowry has suggested that property rights were placed in a relatively advantageous position in comparison with individual rights.[507] It can also

---

[502] At p. 438.
[503] At p. 438.
[504] See *AG* v. *Wilts United Dairies Ltd.* [1921] 37 *TLR* 884, a case in which the Court of Appeal held that the Food Controller (under DORR) had acted *ultra vires* in imposing a levy on the price of milk. See also *Chester* v. *Bateson* [1920] 1 *KB* 829, in which a regulation (DORR 2A) which required that the consent of the Minister of Munitions be obtained before the institution of proceedings for the recovery of certain property, was held to be *ultra vires*.
[505] [1920] *AC* 508.
[506] At pp. 539–40.
[507] 'Terrorism and Human Rights', 60. One of the very few non-political Irish cases, if not the only one, on DORA was also concerned with property rights but, unlike the English

be pointed out that the more critical decisions were all handed down after the termination of actual hostilities in Europe.[508]

Apart from these exceptional cases, it can be said that DORA generally led to a threefold diminution of the judicial role. The first was the self-imposed restriction on the review of the executive's delegated legislative powers at least in relation to individual rights. As Allen has observed, the effect of the UK's emergency legislation of this century was to lead to a great attenuation, and in some cases the virtual extinction of, the doctrine of *ultra vires*.[509] The second arose from the particular 'judge-proof' manner in which powers under DORR were generally structured. This meant that even had the judges been disposed to examine the use of these powers critically, the opportunities for such examination would not have presented themselves unless the courts were prepared to display a degree of activism which would have been unusual even by normal standards. The third way in which the judicial role was diminished was by the granting under DORR of judicial and quasi-judicial powers to the executive. This was particularly true of powers to intern (by the use of which the judicial process could, in effect, be entirely circumvented) and the power to try by court martial, thereby removing the trial of relevant offences from the judicial process (though leaving the issue of judicial review of courts martial open).

The definition of the Irish emergency

Generally, the courts displayed no greater willingness to intervene in the Irish emergency than they had in the earlier cases, and the minimalist stance of the judiciary in the interpretation of DORA generally also applied to the application of DORA to the Irish situation, even after the end of the fighting in the European conflict. In Ireland litigation (or at least reported litigation) in relation to DORA was of a trivial nature, typically concerned with such issues as breaches of orders on the maximum prices of food, but without raising the question of *vires*.[510] While issues of

cases noted above, the plaintiff was not successful. See judgment of O'Connor MR in *Rooney v. Department of Agriculture and Technical Instruction for Ireland* [1918] 53 *ILTR* 49.

[508] The date of *AG v. Wilts United Dairies Ltd.* [1921] 37 *TLR* 884 was 5 July 1921, that of *Chester v. Bateson* [1920] 1 *KB* 829 was 26 and 29 Jan. 1920, and that of *AG v. De Keyser's Royal Hotel Ltd.* [1920] *AC* 509 was 10 May 1920.

[509] *Law in the Making* (London, 1964), 564–5.

[510] See *Wallace v. Burrows* [1918] 2 *IR* 127 (22 Nov. 1917) which concerned the Flour and Bread (Prices) Order 1917; *R (O'Shea) v. O'Neill* [1918] 2 *IR* 395 (11 and 30 Apr. 1918) which concerned the Bacon Ham and Lard (Provisional Prices) Order 1917; *R (M'Entee) v. Smyth* [1918] 2 *IR* 402 (15 and 30 Apr. 1918) which was concerned with the Butter (Maximum Prices) Order 1917 (as amended); *R (Taylour) v. M'Donnell* [1918] 2 *IR* 398 (15 and 30 Apr. 1918) which concerned the Bread Order 1917; and *Spicer v. Murnane* [1919] 2 *IR* 57 (7 May 1918) which was concerned with the Flour and Bread (Prices) Order 1917. All

broader significance were occasionally raised,[511] it was in the English courts that the more important issues relating to Ireland were decided.

In *R* v. *Governor of Wormwood Scrubs Prison*[512] (8 March 1920) a person from Ireland who had been interned in England under DORR 14B (as amended) on the grounds that 'he was a person suspected of acting, having acted, or of being about to act in a manner prejudicial to the public safety and the defence of the realm', challenged his detention on two main grounds. First, that as the war with Germany had ended and as the Regulation had been designed for the protection of that state from foreign forces rather than from rebellion or from internal disorder, the Regulation had no longer any validity in any part of the UK. Secondly, that as the military emergency which had led to the suspension of section 1 of the Defence of the Realm (Amendment) Act 1915 (the fear of a German invasion) had passed, the suspension of section 1 was no longer in force and that in so far as the application of DORR 14B in Ireland was dependent upon the suspension of section 1,[513] it was, to that extent, no longer in force.

The English High Court rejected both contentions. As regards the first point, it was held that as the requisite order under the Termination of the Present War (Definition) Act 1918 had not been made, the war had not come formally to an end, and the regulations therefore were still in force. The Earl of Reading CJ had this to say:

> So long as the war continues . . . acts of rebellion which are in effect military operations against the executive power, must be acts which have the effect of weakening the forces which this country can oppose to the enemy, and as such must be acts endangering the public safety and the defence of the realm.[514]

---

these Orders seem to have been made under DORR 2FF which vested certain powers in a Food Controller. Perhaps the only point of general interest which can be extracted from these cases is Gibson J.'s comment in relation to the Order in *R (O'Shea)* v. *O'Neill*, that its phraseology was 'loose and dangerously wide' and that generally it was the case with such orders that 'literal compliance is practically impossible' (at p. 398).

[511] In *Maire Nic Shiublaigh* v. *Love* [1919] 53 *ILTR* 137, it was held that the search power under DORR 51 authorized the CMA or any police constable to take immediate action where they considered that any premises or anything therein was being used or kept for any purpose prejudicial to the public safety or the defence of the realm, while that under DORR 51A applied in cases where no such urgent necessity arose, and where more ordinary legal procedure was sufficient (see App. 3). It was also held that property could be validly seized during a search even though a small portion of it was not 'seditious'. In *Rooney* v. *Department of Agriculture and Technical Instruction for Ireland* [1918] 53 *ILTR* 189 (30 Apr. 1919) it was held that under DORR 2L the fact of the defendant's being 'of opinion' that use of land was being 'unreasonably withheld' was not reviewable by the court. For the eventual settlement of the compensation issue in the case, see *Rooney* v. *Department of Agriculture* [1924] 58 *ILTR* 83.

[512] [1920] 2 *KB* 305.

[513] See pp. 101–4.

[514] At pp. 310–11.

As regards the second contention, the court took the view that it had no
jurisdiction to consider the matter: 'even if it is material to consider
whether the military necessity has come to an end, it is not a matter this
court can consider; whether the emergency continues to exist or not it is
for the executive alone to determine.'[515]

The applicant had also averred that he could not reasonably be suspected of acting in a manner prejudicial to the defence of the realm as he
had never taken part in any 'political controversy'.[516] As noted above, in
Halliday's case Lord Wrenbury had suggested that judicial review of the
substantive reasons for the making of an internment order would be
possible. In the present case, however, the court took the opposite view:
'It is not competent for this court to enquire whether there are grounds
for so suspecting him. That is a matter which, as *R* v. *Halliday*[517] points
out, is left to the Secretary of State alone to decide.'[518] Of course,
Halliday's cases clearly did not provide authority for that proposition.

Judicial review of courts martial

The power to try civilians by court martial given by DORA raised fundamental questions about the relative legal position of the British Army.
It has been suggested that 'the United Kingdom was in effect placed
under military law' in 1914.[519] In the past in Britain, trial of civilians by
courts martial (other than in the cases of those civilians attached to the
armed forces who were in any case subject to military law) had taken place
only in situations of civil war or armed rebellion under non-statutory
martial law powers. Some have considered the trial of civilians by court
martial under DORA to have amounted to a 'statutory imposition of
martial law'.[520]

There was, however, this important distinction between the Army's
operating under martial law powers and statutory military law powers.
In the former case, once the courts had accepted the validity of the
imposition of martial law, the actions of the military were non-justiciable
during the course of the war or armed rebellion.[521] In the latter case, the
actions of the Army were subject to a degree of judicial scrutiny.

As DORA provided that 'for the purposes of the trial of a person for
an offence against the regulations by court-martial and the punishment
thereof, the person may be proceeded against and dealt with as if he were

---

[515] Earl of Reading CJ, at p. 111.
[516] Per Bray J., at p. 314.
[517] [1917] *AC* 260.
[518] Per Bray J., at p. 314.
[519] M. Supperstone, *Brownlie's Law of Public Order and National Security* (London,
1981), 223.
[520] Lowry, 'Terrorism and Human Rights', 51. See also Bowman, 'Martial Law'.
[521] See below.

a person subject to military law and had on active service committed an offence under section 5 of the Army Act',[522] the degree of judicial review over DORA courts martial trying civilians was to be the same as that exercisable under Army Act courts martial trying soldiers.

The law in this area, which had been in some degree of confusion, was clarified in the leading 1919 case of *Heddon* v. *Evans*.[523] Therein McCardie J. set out the principles governing judicial review of *inter alia* the operation of courts martial as follows:

Firstly . . . a military tribunal or officer will be liable to an action for damages, if when acting in excess of or without jurisdiction, they or he do or direct that to be done to another military man, whether officer or private, which amounts to assault, false imprisonment, or other common law wrong, even though the injury inflicted purport to be done in the course of actual military discipline. Secondly, that if the act causing the injury to person or liberty be within jurisdiction and in the course of military discipline, no action will lie upon the ground only that the act has been done maliciously and without reasonable and probable cause.[524]

The remedies available to a person who claimed that a court martial acted in excess or without jurisdiction were not limited to an action for damages, however. Elsewhere in the judgment he noted 'with respect to writs of prohibition it seems clear that they may be granted with respect to military proceedings',[525] and also 'that a writ of certiorari may be issued to military authority in appropriate cases seems also to be clear in principle'.[526] Thus although the scope for judicial review was less in the case of court martial than in relation to the inferior courts, there did exist a clear legal basis for judicial intervention in trials by court martial under DORA and ROIA.

ROIA courts martial and the courts in Ireland

Following the enactment of ROIA, the issue of emergency powers came before the courts in Ireland in the shape of applications arising out of the increased jurisdiction of ROIA courts martial. In effect, the judges whose refusal to participate in jury-less courts had led the British Government to expand court martial jurisdiction, now found themselves reviewing the operation of these bodies. In legal and political terms this was, even by

---

[522] s. 1 (5) Defence of the Realm Consolidation Act 1914.

[523] A shortened report of the judgment in *Heddon* v. *Evans* can be found at 35 *TLR* 642. What appears to be a full report is reproduced (with annotations) in R. O'Sullivan, *Military Law and the Supremacy of the Civil Courts* (London, 1921), 42–119. The case, in the opinion of O'Sullivan, 'demonstrates and establishes once for all that the right of a soldier to seek—and the corresponding duty of the judges to afford—the protection of the Civil Courts against officers acting without or in excess of jurisdiction, whether as individual or as members of a military tribunal' (p. 2).

[524] Ibid. 87. [525] Ibid. 70. [526] Ibid. 71.

emergency law standards, a more than usually difficult situation. And the awkward position of the judges was not helped by the fact that the errors which the Army was making in court martial procedure were in some instances quite elementary, thus leaving the courts with no easy way of avoiding quashing the proceedings. The central judicial figure in this litigation was Molony CJ. As was later the case in the litigation arising out of the imposition of martial law, the position he adopted was formally to assert a judicial role, often in ringing tones, and then generally to implement this role in a manner designed to cause minimum conflict with the military.

This line of authority began with a strongly worded judicial assertion of individual liberty. In *R* v. *Fitzgerald Edwards and Hooper*[527] (9, 10 December 1920), what was at issue was not the actual conduct of courts martial, but the documentation requirement in relation to detention. The case took the form of an application for habeas corpus of the owners (Fitzgerald and Edwards) and the editor (Hooper) of the *Freeman's Journal*, a 'mainstream' nationalist newspaper. The application in respect of Fitzgerald and Edwards was dropped, leaving the net issue (on the evidence presented) whether the remaining defendant, who had been at liberty before his trial, could be detained in civil custody (Mountjoy Prison) in the interval between the conclusion of the trial and the pro-mulgation of the finding and sentence without the making of any order by the CMA. Molony CJ decisively rejected any such assertion:

I desire in the clearest way possible to repudiate on behalf of this Court the doctrine . . . that the Governor of a prison, without any written warrant or auth-ority, is entitled to receive and retain in custody any of the King's subjects who is brought to the prison by a military officer. To sanction such a course would be to strike a deadly blow at the doctrine of personal liberty, which is part of the first rudiment of the constitution.[528]

Unusually, Gibson J. also delivered a judgment, in which, in less strident tones, he concurred with the Chief Justice. The court made the writ returnable for the Tuesday following the hearing, but in view of the full facts which later emerged, the case can be considered more a monument to a dismissive military attitude towards the civil courts than a landmark of judicial activism.[529]

---

[527] [1921] 55 *ILTR* 60.
[528] At p. 63.
[529] A 'Note' included with the report of the case reads: 'At the time fixed for making the return to the writ in the above case, the body of the defendant, Hooper, was duly produced in Court by the Governor of the prison, but no formal return to the writ had been made. The Court ordered the immediate production of the writ and return thereto, which order was subsequently complied with. It appeared from the return that the defendant had been

In *R* v. *Murphy*[530] (15, 17, 24, 25, 31 January 1921) Molony CJ expressly asserted the right of the superior courts to interfere with the workings of courts martial by the issue of prerogative writs:

If a court-martial acts without, or in excess of jurisdiction, this court can exercise its controlling authority against the tribunal by writs of prohibition or certiorari, and against the governor of the prison or who ever detains a person by means of a writ of habeas corpus.[531]

But, surprisingly, *Heddon* v. *Evans*[532] was nowhere cited in the judgment (nor in any of the other decisions in relation to courts martial in Ireland in this period).

In Murphy's case a prisoner sought writs of habeas corpus and *certiorari* that his conviction by a court martial might be quashed, because *inter alia* counsel for the accused had not been allowed to contradict essential witnesses for the prosecution on portions of their evidence, by proving that the witnesses in question had made statements on oath at a military inquiry held in lieu of an inquest at variance with their evidence at the trial. In giving the unanimous judgment of the King's Bench Division, Molony CJ first decided that the court martial had indeed made a mistake in law in ruling against the admissibility of the evidence in question and then proceeded to consider the consequences of this error.

The first point turned on whether or not the evidence was part of the record of the case. Counsel for the accused had argued that, as under the Army Act rules of procedure a record was to be kept of the transactions of the court, the evidence was thereby made part of the record and was examinable by the court. The Chief Justice, however, considered that 'the object of requiring a note of the evidence to be taken at a court-martial is not to make such evidence part of the record, but to assist the Court, accused and the confirming authorities, and in the last resort, the King or his representative'.[533]

Even were the evidence to be looked at, Molony CJ noted:

The court-martial must, however in the exercise of its jurisdiction, decide questions, not only of fact, but of law, including the admissibility of evidence . . . When the Court has jurisdiction to decide a matter, its jurisdiction is

---

committed to the custody of the Governor of Mountjoy on a written order signed by the Competent Military Authority, which order was annexed to the return. The arguments and judgments in the case, however, proceeded on the assumption that no such order existed. The Court stated that their duty, on the form of the return before them, was to remand the defendant in custody, but in the interval the military authorities had agreed that the defendant, Hooper, should be released from custody on his personal undertaking to appear when required; so after consideration, and counsel for the defendant consenting, the Court discharged the original order of December 10' (p. 64).

[530] [1921] 2 *IR* 190.   [531] At p. 224.   [532] 35 *TLR* 462.   [533] At p. 225.

not ousted because it happens to give an erroneous decision, and it certainly cannot be deemed to exceed or abuse its jurisdiction merely because it incidentally misconstrues a statute, or admits illegal evidence or rejects legal evidence.[534]

Thus 'although the court-martial gave an erroneous decision in point of law, it was a decision made *intra vires* and does not entitle the accused to the relief sought in the present application'.[535]

This remarkable decision would seem to indicate that courts martial could depart from the law of evidence in any way and yet be immune from scrutiny by the superior courts. One commentator has suggested, however, that if the error took the form of a refusal to hear the defence *in toto* a writ of prohibition would be granted.[536] The decision is very difficult to reconcile with modern notions of the circumstances in which a writ of prohibition would issue, as an error in law appeared on the record of the proceedings.[537]

In *Whelan* v. *Rex*[538] (9 February 1921) a prisoner sentenced to death by a court martial applied for a writ of *certiorari* to quash the conviction on the ground that *inter alia* no certificate as to the legal knowledge and experience of a member of the court had been handed in. In refusing the application, Molony CJ said: 'in the absence of any objection at the trial it seems to us to be clear that this is a case where the maxim *omnia praesumuntur rite esse acta* applies. The general presumption of law is that a person acting in a public or judicial capacity is duly authorised to do so.'[539] In dealing with the case on its merits, the court had of course implicitly accepted that a writ might issue.

In *R (Rodgers)* v. *Campbell and Others*[540] (8 November 1921) an attempt was made to have the power to refer cases for trial by court martial made reviewable by the court. The applicant had been tried in the ordinary courts and as the jury had disagreed on a verdict, he was sent

---

[534] At p. 226.

[535] At p. 228.

[536] R. O'Sullivan, *Military Law*, 15 n. The question was left open by the court (see p. 228 of the report).

[537] Murphy was, however, not executed. It was announced that 'in view solely of the repeated postponements of his execution and of the distress of mind which has been caused to him thereby, as an act of mercy the General Officer Commanding-in-Chief has commuted the sentence to one of penal servitude for life'. See note attached to report of case at p. 229. The Chief Secretary was also keen to make this point in his reports to the British Cabinet (Weekly Survey of the State of Ireland, w/e 7 Feb. 1921, CAB 24/119, PRO, Kew). It is worthwhile to note that although it was clear to all that a mistake in law had been made, there is nothing to indicate that the JAG moved to quash the proceedings.

[538] [1921] 2 *IR* 310.

[539] p. 313.

[540] [1921] 55 *ILTR* 192. The report of the case merely gives the pleadings of counsel for the prosecution and for the respondent and the information that 'the court refused the motion with costs'. Either the report is incomplete or no reasons were given by the court for the refusal.

forward for trial at the next assizes. The case was then referred to the CMA who ordered trial by court martial. At that trial the prisoner was found guilty. He then sought to have his conviction quashed and his liberty restored on an application for writs of habeas corpus and *certiorari*. His main contention was that once his case had been tried by judge and jury there was no jurisdiction either to refer the case for trial by court martial or thus to try the case. Relief was refused by the court which apparently took the view that 'the status of the prisoner remained the same after disagreement of the jury as before the trial',[541] and that consequently the powers conferred by ROIR had not been exceeded.[542]

In this line of decisions on ROIA courts martial, while the High Court expressly stated its right to review the conduct of ROIA courts martial, its posture was such as to ensure that this right would be exercised in the narrowest possible circumstances. An analogy can be drawn between the approach adopted by the judiciary generally towards the question of *vires* in relation to DORA, and that adopted by the High Court in Ireland to the question of *vires* and procedural irregularity generally in relation to ROIA courts martial. This approach was also in line with that taken by the English judiciary in relation to ROIA.[543]

Martial law: the background

The cases on ROIA courts martial could be said to have defined the posture of the judiciary under 'statutory martial law'. From December 1920 new issues arose when the question of non-statutory (or true) martial law came before the courts. In order to assess this case law, it is first necessary to examine some of the theories of martial law roughly contemporaneous with the period under discussion, together with two cases from the Boer War germane to the debate. The view of the British Army in the period leading up to the imposition of martial law will also be examined.

The meaning of martial law

The term 'martial law' as opposed to military law is used in two distinct senses: (1) in international law to refer to the law administered by a military commander in occupied territory in time of war, and (2) to refer

---

[541] This is what is written in the headnote at p. 193.

[542] Rodgers remained in prison even after the Treaty. Eventually he escaped and fled to the Free State, where in *O'Boyle and Rodgers* v. *AG* [1929] *IR* 558 he brought a successful action to ensure that he would not be surrendered to Northern Ireland. See Ch. 3.

[543] In *R* v. *Cannon Row Police Station, ex parte Brady* [1922] 91 *LJ* 98 (25 July 1921) the Court of Appeal in England held that ROIR 14B could be used to order the internment in Ireland of a person resident in England. The applicant in the case was Irish. In a dissenting judgment, Scrutton LJ held that ROIA did not show with sufficient clearness that the Act was intended to apply to persons resident in England.

to the exceptional, non-statutory powers excercisable in situations of war or armed rebellion.[544] It is with the latter meaning of the term that this work is concerned.

The history of martial law can be traced back to the Norman Conquest and beyond.[545] For the past 300 years the circumstances in England have been such that there has been no impetus to develop a legal response to rebellion or civil war (although there have been developments in response to lower levels of disturbance). The situation in Ireland, in the colonies, and in the Empire was considerably different, however, and in these areas martial law has frequently been a matter more of immediate practical concern than of abstract constitutional theory.[546]

At the start of this century the question of martial law was provoking renewed academic debate in Britain. The immediate spur to these developments was the outbreak of the Boer War, the legacy of which had an impact on several levels in Ireland. The war presented certain new problems for the legal theoreticians of response to insurrection. First, there was the fact that the Boers did not limit themselves to conventional warfare—the conflict saw perhaps the first modern guerrilla campaign. Secondly, and related to the first issue, technological developments were occurring which were profoundly influencing the shape of non-international armed conflicts. Increasing mobility, and access to portable yet highly effective armaments, gave the guerrilla fighter an advantage which he could not previously have possessed. In such circumstances there might be no front line, and an area which was on the surface peaceful could suddenly erupt into violence, only just as quickly to subside into relative peace. Apologists for military action might advance this factor as justification for the adoption of Draconian measures in an apparently peaceful district. Yet just as these technological changes might tend to extend the geographical scope of martial law, improvements in communications could tend to impose limits on the extent of the measures which the Army could adopt. Put simply, there was a difference between what the Army might like to do, and what it could afford to be seen to have done. These latter considerations do not appear to have had a decisive influence in the Boer War, where the British Government seems to have been not unduly concerned about reports of the terrible conditions in the camps in which the Boers were interned but, as will be

---

[544] Wade and Bradley, *Constitutional and Administrative Law* (London, 1985), 550–1.

[545] For some recent writing on early martial law see J. V. Capua, 'Early History of Martial Law in England from the 14th Century to the Petition of Right', 36 *Cambridge Law Journal* 152; D. A. Schlueter, 'Courts-Martial: An Historical Survey', 87 *Military Law Review* 129. R. Higham, *A Guide to the Sources of British Military History* (London, 1972), provides a list of source material on martial law.

[546] See C. Townshend, 'Martial Law: Legal and Administrative Problems of Civil Emergency in Britain and the Empire, 1800–1940', 25 *Historical Journal* 167.

discussed below, they did have an influence on the British Army's activities in Ireland. In order to assess what happened in Ireland it is first necessary to examine the theoretical debate on these issues which was then current.

Contemporary theories of martial law: prerogative and common law

As part of the contribution to the renewed debate, Holdsworth, writing in 1902, outlined two alternative theories of martial law.[547] To borrow the classification suggested by Greer,[548] these can be described as the prerogative theory and the common law theory.

Holdsworth traced the origin of the theory to the medieval Court of the Constable and the Marshal which sat by virtue of the Royal prerogative and the jurisdiction of which covered *inter alia* 'the offences and miscarriages of soldiers contrary to the laws and rules of the army'.[549] As the division between the professional soldier and the citizen emerged (a division which did not exist in medieval times), so emerged the distinction between military law which related to soldiers, and martial law which related to all subjects in time of war. Confusion in this area was, as Holdsworth pointed out,

increased by the policy pursued by the Tudors and the earlier Stuarts. They did not consider themselves bound by the legal definition of 'a time of war'. They considered that they might submit ordinary citizens to the jurisdiction of the Marshal or his deputies whenever in their opinion such a measure was necessary to the preservation of order.[550]

The response to these pretentions towards absolutism was the adoption of the Petition of Right 1628, an instrument indistinguishable from a statute. The Petition recited that 'of late times divers Commissions under Your Majesty's Great Seal have issued forth, by which certain Persons have been assigned and appointed Commissioners, with Power and Authority to proceed within the land according to the Justice of Martial law'[551] and continued:

They do therefore humbly pray Your most excellent Majesty . . . that no Freeman, in any such Manner as is before mentioned, be imprisoned or detained; and that Your Majesty would be pleased to remove the said Soldiers and Mariners; and that Your People may not be so burthened in time to come; and that the said

---

[547] W. S. Holdsworth, 'Martial Law Historically Considered', 18 *LQR* 117.

[548] S. Greer, 'Military Intervention in Civil Disturbances: The Legal Basis Reconsidered', 1983 *Public Law* 573. This article is mainly concerned with civil disturbances falling short of war or armed rebellion, but the analysis of theory is equally applicable to both sets of circumstances.

[549] 'Martial Law', 117.

[550] Ibid. 123.

[551] Clause 7.

Commissions for proceeding by Martial Law, may be revoked and annulled; and that hereafter no Commissions of like nature may issue forth to any Person or Persons whatsoever to be executed as aforesaid.[552]

Holdsworth asserted in relation to the Petition of Right that:

The clauses contained in it with reference to martial law enact nothing new. They assume that martial law was perfectly legal in time of war—a fact which the parliamentary lawyers did not dispute. And in later times the Petition of Right has generally been taken to deal simply with the recent extensions which martial law had received, and to declare them illegal, leaving martial law only applicable to armies in time of war. The question what was a time of war was also clearly settled. 'The time of peace is when the Courts of Westminster are open'.[553]

Other commentators have differed. Kohn (1932) considered that the Petition of Right 'was not in its effect limited to a "condition of peace".'[554] On the contrary, he took the view that 'the essential object of the Petition was to protect the citizens against trial by the military in times of internal disturbances'.[555] Keir and Lawson's (1979) view was that 'it is a moot point whether the Petition of Right prohibited Martial Law altogether or only in time of peace'.[556] The other major development in the seventeenth century germane to this discussion was the adoption of the Bill of Rights 1689[557] which, among other things, made the raising or keeping of a standing army within the kingdom in time of peace without the consent of Parliament illegal.

Holdsworth pointed out that although the jurisdiction of the Court of the Constable and the Marshal had declined in the seventeenth century and disappeared after 1737, 'It might however be argued that if the Crown had once had a prerogative to govern ordinary citizens by martial law in the case of a rebellion which amounted to a war, and if that prerogative had never been taken away, it still existed.'[558] To any such attempt to explain contemporary views on the meaning of martial law in the light of the Royal prerogative, he raised two objections:

1. Suppose that the Constables and Marshal's Court would have had jurisdiction to try by martial law any persons actually combatant in case of rebellion, would this necessarily give the Crown power to subject to martial law all citizens combatant or non-combatant? To contend that this was so would seem to be an extension of the term martial law similar to that made by the Tudors, and

---

[552] Clause 10.

[553] 'Martial Law', 121.

[554] L. Kohn, *The Constitution of the Irish Free State* (London, 1932), 140.

[555] Ibid. 141. Cf. Greer, 'Military Intervention': 'The Petition of Right 1628 made it unconstitutional for the Crown to impose martial law upon civilians' (p. 580).

[556] D. Keir and F. Lawson, *Cases in Constitutional Law* (Oxford, 1979), 223.

[557] 1 Will. & M., sess. 2, c. 2.

[558] 'Martial Law', 126.

condemned by the Petition of Right . . . 2. If the Constable and Marshal's Court had jurisdiction and if therefore the right of the Crown to try persons by martial law could be established, we should have the anomaly of a law without a court to administer it.[559]

Ireland's turbulent history provides plenty of examples of resort to martial law in various guises,[560] and the debate on which of these powers could be said to have arisen out of the prerogative and which by process of common law is, if anything, more involved than in relation to England. First, there was the complicating factor that the Petition of Right 1628 applied only in England and not in Ireland, thus leaving open the question of the degree to which prerogative powers in relation to martial law were exercisable in peacetime.[561] Secondly, the Bill of Rights 1688 likewise did not apply to Ireland. In 1692, in the first Irish Parliament held after the 'Glorious Revolution', the heads of a bill containing the chief provisions of the Bill of Rights were sent to England, but were never returned.[562]

Thirdly, powerful support for the prerogative theory was to be found in some of the legislation enacted by the Irish Parliament in response to the 1798 Rebellion,[563] and following the Act of Union, in that passed by the United Kingdom Parliament in response to insurrection in Ireland. Thus in 39 Geo. III, c. 11 (1799), it was provided that 'nothing in this act contained shall be construed to take away, abridge or diminish, the acknowledged prerogative of his Majesty, for the public safety, to resort

[559] Ibid. 127.
[560] L. Irwin, 'Irish Presidency Courts 1569–1672'. 12 *Ir. Jur.* 106, and J. C. Crawford, 'Origins of the Court of Castle Chamber: A Star Chamber Jurisdiction in Ireland', 24 *American Journal of Legal History* 22, contain some references to the medieval history of martial law in Ireland.
[561] A. Finlason (1866) considered that the application of the Petition of Right was to 'England, the realm, meaning this country alone, within the four seas, according to the legal phrase. It is to that alone the Petition of Right relates, which declares that martial law shall not be proclaimed within the realm in time of peace, which implies that it may be, here, in time of war, civil or foreign, and that it may be out of the realm, in Ireland or in any colony or dependency, if there is a case for it by the common law, or any local law, statutable or otherwise (as there may be, by some imminency of public peril, through a conspiracy to levy war to raise a rebellion) although there is no actual rebellion or levying of war' (*A Treatise on Martial Law* (London, 1886), 18–19 n. (b)). See also p. 3 n. (a). It is, however, arguable that if the Petition of Right merely declared what was already the existing law, and if the law in Ireland was, in this area, the same as in England, then the position in Ireland remained the same as in England, even after the adoption of the Petition of Right.
[562] See J. G. Swift Mac Neill, *Studies in the Constitution of the Irish Free State* (Dublin, 1925), 38.
[563] For an account of some of the measures taken on behalf of the Crown in the suppression of the rebellion, and an analysis of the issues arising out of some of the Acts of Indemnity passed in response to the Rebellion, see P. O'Higgins, 'Wright v. Fitzgerald Revisited', 25 *MLR* 413. See also K. P. Ferguson, 'The Army in Ireland from the Restoration to the Act of Union' (Ph.D. thesis, Trinity College, Dublin, 1980).

to the exercise of martial law against open enemies or traitors'.[564] A similar reservation was included in 43 Geo. III, c. 117, of the United Kingdom Parliament (1803),[565] and as late as 1833, 3 Will. IV, c. 4 ('An Act for the more effectual Suppression of local Disturbances and dangerous Associations in Ireland') provided:

nothing in this Act contained shall be construed to take away, abridge, or diminish the acknowledged Prerogative of His Majesty, in respect of appointing and convening Courts-martial according to the Provisions of the Act for punishing Mutiny and Desertion, or the undoubted Prerogative of his Majesty, for the Public Safety, to resort to the Exercise of Martial Law against open Enemies or Traitors.[566]

Another issue to be taken into account in considering the special position of the legal basis of martial law in Ireland was that Wolfe Tone's case had given some support to the contention that martial law could not be imposed while the ordinary courts were open, though it had not decided the point.[567]

Despite this evidence (mainly from Ireland), there was no shortage of support for the alternative, common law theory. Holdsworth described this theory, quoting from *R* v. *Nelson and Brand*[568] as follows:

Martial law as a distinct code of rules does not exist. It is merely the application of the common law principle 'that life may be protected and crime prevented by the immediate application of any amount of force which, under the circumstances, may be necessary'.[569]

He compared and contrasted the two theories as follows:

There are many points of agreement between the two theories. Moreover we shall see that in practice their results are not materially different. Both demand as conditions precedent of a proclamation of martial law a state of war, i.e. a condition of affairs in which it is absolutely necessary to use force. The great point

---

[564] s. 6.   [565] s. 5.   [566] s. 40.

[567] The case is reported at 27 *Howell's State Trials* 613. Tone, one of the leaders of the United Irishmen, and a holder of a commission in the service of the French Republic, was tried by a court martial and sentenced to death by hanging on charges of high treason. An application for habeas corpus was brought by Tone's father in the Court of King's Bench. This application rested on 'this sacred and immmutable principle of the constitution—*that martial law and civil law are incompatible*; and that the former must cease with the existence of the latter' (p. 625). The Lord Chief Justice ordered a writ to issue and ordered the sheriff to see to it that Tone be not executed. When Tone's father returned, he informed the Court that the officer responsible, Gen. Craig, refused to obey the writ. The Court was then informed that Tone was not in a condition to be removed as his throat was cut, apparently by his own hand. Tone died some days later without the matter having been resolved. The events took place between 12 Nov. and 19 Nov. 1798. On 25 Mar. 1799, 39 Geo. III, c. 11 (see above), which authorized trial by court martial of non-military personnel, received the Royal assent.

[568] *Special Report*, 99–100.   [569] 'Martial Law', 128.

of difference consists in the consequences to the persons acting under such a proclamation. On the first [prerogative] theory the person so acting cannot be made civilly or criminally responsible unless he has acted with malice. On this theory it is only in cases of riot as distinguished from cases of rebellion that a person is civilly or criminally responsible unless he accurately apportions the degree of force used to the necessity of the case. On the second theory there is no such distinction to be drawn between cases of riot and cases of rebellion. The same principles apply to both: for rebellion is but riot 'writ large'.[570]

Dicey's view (1885) accorded with the common law theory: '"Martial law" in the proper sense of that term, in which it means the suspension of ordinary law and the temporary government of a country or parts of it by military tribunals, is unknown to the law of England',[571] but he noted:

Martial law is sometimes employed as a name for the common law right of the Crown and its servants to repel force by force in the case of invasion, insurrection, riot, or generally of any violent resistance to the law. This right, or power, is essential to the very existence of orderly government, and is most assuredly recognised in the most ample manner by the law of England.[572]

But

it is a power which has in itself no special connection with the existence of an armed force. The Crown has the right to put down breaches of the peace. Every subject, whether a civilian or a soldier, whether what is called a 'servant of the government', such for example as a policeman, or a person in no way connected with the administration, not only has the right, but is, as a matter of legal duty, bound to assist in putting down breaches of the peace. No doubt policemen or soldiers are the persons, who, as being specially employed in the maintenance of order, are most generally called upon to suppress a riot, but it is clear that all loyal subjects are bound to take their part in the suppression of riots.[573]

Thus Dicey viewed rebellion as differing in degree rather than quality from riot. In both cases there was not only a right but also a duty to 'repel force by force'. Finlason (1866), another proponent of the common law theory, echoed this view:

no man has a right by law to be neutral in a time of rebellion. The law imposes upon all able-bodied subjects in time of rebellion the obligation and duty of doing their utmost to serve the Crown, and suppress the rebellion. Hence it is that, by common law, the Sheriff can call out the whole *posse comitatus* the whole power or force of the county to assist him in quelling a rebellion, and those who neglect or refuse to do so are deemed criminal, and are indictable and punishable for the refusal. This is the true origin and theory of martial law. It takes its origin from

[570] Ibid. 128–9.
[571] A. V. Dicey, *The Law and the Constitution* (London, 1885), 294.
[572] Ibid. 295.   [573] Ibid. 295–6.

the principle of the common law: the right and duty of every subject in time of rebellion to assist the Crown in putting it down.[574]

There was some dispute as to the actual extent of the measures envisaged by the common law theory. Dicey laid stress on individual acts of restraint: 'during the effort to restore peace rebels may be lawfully killed just as enemies may be lawfully slaughtered in battle, or prisoners may be shot to prevent their escape, but any execution (independently of military law) inflicted by a court-martial is illegal and technically murder',[575] whereas Pollock (1902), whose views were in line with the common law theory, took a more attenuated view of the notion of necessity:

So-called 'martial law', as distinct from military law, is an unlucky name for the justification by the common law of acts done by necessity for the defence of the Commonwealth where there is a war within the realm. Such acts are not necessarily acts of personal force or restraint. They may be preventative as well as punitive.[576]

Erle-Richards (1902) outlined these measures as follows:

1. Military operations cannot be conducted in time of war without interference with rights of property, and the authorities show that interference in such cases is not contrary to law.

2. Interference with personal liberty is equally a matter of necessity, and the same principle must apply as in the case of property.

3. Such interference must include the right of trial and the infliction of punishment.[577]

There were therefore two streams of authority offering different theoretical bases for the phenomenon of martial law, and particularly within the common law theory there was considerable difference of opinion as to what measures might be adopted. In Ireland the implications of these divergent streams were fully tested. The result was not an academic argument but a crisis in relations between the courts and the Army.

Boer War case law

Legal analysis of martial law in Ireland was much influenced by the decisions of the Privy Council in two cases arising out of the Boer War: *Ex parte Marais*[578] and *Tilonko* v. *AG*.[579] Surprisingly, in view of the influence which these cases have had on the development of the theory of martial law, the decisions in both cases are notable for the lack of precedents cited.

---

[574] *Treatise on Martial Law*, 5.   [575] *Law and Constitution*, 300.
[576] F. Pollock, 'What is Martial Law?' 18 *LQR* 152, at p.156.
[577] H. Erle-Richards, 'Martial Law', 18 *LQR* 133, at p. 139.
[578] [1902] *AC* 109.   [579] [1907] *AC* 93.

In Marais's case, the applicant, who had been detained without trial under martial law regulations, applied for special leave to appeal from the order of the Supreme Court in Cape Town refusing an application for his release brought 'on the ground that his arrest and imprisonment were in violation of the fundamental liberties secured to the subjects of Her Majesty'.[580] The advice of the Privy Council, which was adverse to the applicant, was couched by the Lord Chancellor in broad language:

They [the members of the judicial committee] are of opinion that where actual war is raging acts done by the military authorities are not justiciable by the ordinary tribunals . . . the fact that for some purposes some tribunals have been permitted to pursue their ordinary course is not conclusive that war was not raging.[581]

Pollock's comment on the case was that 'The only point it really decided . . . was that the absence of visible disorder and the continual sitting of the courts are not conclusive evidence of a state of peace'.[582] Dodd considered that the propositions advanced in Marais's case were 'stated in general terms which, as stated, can hardly be reconciled with what has hitherto been supposed to be the law'.[583] He agreed that the propositions that the fact that some courts are open was not conclusive that war was not raging, 'may it would seem, be accepted at the present day as a sound statement of the law'.[584] But he considered that the proposition that, where war is raging, acts done by military authority are not justiciable by the ordinary tribunals

was probably intended to be taken as limited to the actual facts of the case, to ordinary tribunals sitting in time of war, and to acts such as were complained of by Marais. Thus limited, it might probably not be open to serious criticism. But if it is intended thereby to affirm that military authorities cannot in any case when the war is ended be sued for acts of violence inflicted upon citizens during war, or done to their property whilst hostilities are raging, then it is a proposition at variance with what has long been, and what is still believed to be, the law. Apart from the protection afforded by Acts of Indemnity usual in such cases, the military authorities can be sued in the Courts for such acts, and are legally liable therefore unless they can prove that they were necessary acts, acts necessary, that is, for the public defence or for the proper prosecution of the war. The only defence for them is their necessity, the proclamation of martial law is not *per se* a defence, though it may be a circumstance to be considered. The proclamation is not to be taken as proving of itself the necessity.[585]

---

[580] p. 109
[581] Ibid. 114.
[582] 'What is Martial Law?', 157.
[583] C. Dodd, 'The Case of Marais', 18 *LQR* 143, at p. 148.
[584] Ibid. 148.
[585] Ibid. 148–9.

O'Sullivan (1921) took a similar view:

acts done by military authorities and others during a state of insurrection are examinable in the ordinary Courts. The proposition that the acts of the military authorities during a state of insurrection may be challenged in the civil Courts (if the civil Courts are sitting) is admittedly inconsistent with the principle which is supposed to have been established by the judgment of the Privy Council in *Marais' Case*, the principle, namely, that 'where actual war is raging,' no acts done by the military authorities (even though they be done maliciously, or without jurisdiction, or in excess of jurisdiction) are justiciable by the ordinary tribunals. This principle does *not* signify (what it has been sometimes taken to mean) that the acts of the military authorities are not examinable by the ordinary Courts *when the war is over*. It only means that *whilst war is actually raging* the ordinary Courts will not entertain proceedings against military men for acts done in purported execution of martial law.[586]

In Tilonko's case, a petitioner sentenced by a military court sitting under declaration of martial law sought special leave to appeal from the judgment of the court. An Act of Indemnity had been passed approving of the sentences of these military courts. The Earl of Halsbury, giving the decision of the committee, held that the circumstances of the case were covered by the Act of Indemnity and that therefore judicial review was impossible. There are, however, important dicta in the decision:

If there is war, there is the right to repel force by force, but it is found convenient and decorous, from time to time, to authorise what are called 'courts' to administer punishments, and restrain by acts of repression the violence that is committed in time of war, instead of leaving such punishment and repression to the casual actions of persons acting without sufficient consultation, or without sufficient order or regularity in the procedure in which things alleged to have been done are proved. But to attempt to make these proceedings of so-called 'courts-martial', administering summary justice under the supervision of a military commander analogous to the regular proceedings of courts of justice is quite illusory. Such acts of justice are justified by necessity, by the fact of actual war, and that they are so justified under the circumstances is a fact that is no longer necessary to insist upon, because it has been over and over again so decided by Courts as to whose authority there can be no doubt.[587]

O'Sullivan considered that in its decision in this case the Privy Council had 'suggested that the existence of a state of war may be a matter of fact which the Court will if necessary determine'.[588] He then drew attention to the fact that in Marais's case the arrest complained of by the petitioner had taken place at least 150 miles or more from the area of 'actual hostilities'.[589] On the impact of technological development on the theory

---

[586] *Military Law*, 34–5 (O'Sullivan's emphasis).
[587] p. 95.   [588] *Military Law*, 50.   [589] Ibid.

of martial law, he quoted with approval the view of Pollock that 'nowadays, telegraphic communication has given an extreme importance to acts far from the seat of war that, while they might have a great effect on military operations, the place where they were committed may yet enjoy perfect peace and the Courts there remain open'.[590] Dodd also drew attention to the impact of the 'new technology':

it may be fairly considered that the area now affected by a war, the area in which martial law is a necessity, and because of that necessity, lawful or excusable, is much larger, much more extended, than was the case prior to the increased facilities afforded for locomotion by railways and other improved modes of travel, and prior to the improved modes of transmitting information and orders by telegraph and the like. So that whilst in primitive times the area of disturbance was little more than the locality occupied by the rival encampments of the two bodies in conflict, in which area no Court could or would be found to sit for any purpose, in modern times it extends to long distances and comprises a large, it may be a vast, area.[591]

As the eagerness of commentators to limit the application of the Boer War cases illustrated, the debate in this area was very much open. And the debate was not limited to civilian lawyers—examination of the Army's approach reveals few certainties and much confusion.

The martial law option: the British Army's view

The 1914 *Manual of Military Law* provides little insight into the British Army's view of the measures which could be taken under the type of martial law imposed in Ireland in 1920–1. It notes generally that 'Martial law in the proper sense of the term, can be established in the UK or in a self-governing British Possession only by an Act of Parliament or of the local legislature'[592] and elsewhere that 'English law . . . never presupposes the possibility of civil war, and makes no express provisions for such contingencies'.[593] It does, however, state that 'in times of invasion or rebellion, or in expectation thereof, exceptional powers are often assumed by the Crown, acting usually (though by no means necessarily) through its military forces, for the suppression of hostilities or maintenance of good order within its territories (whether in the UK or British possessions)'[594] and that 'the intention to exercise such exceptional powers and to take such exceptional measures is generally announced by the issue of "proclamation of martial law"'.[595] As to the measures which could be taken in such circumstances the Manual merely notes:

[590] 19 *LQR* 231, quoted ibid.   [591] 'Case of Marais', 147.
[592] p. 4.   [593] p. 3.   [594] p. 4.   [595] p. 4.

when a proclamation of martial law has been issued, any soldier who takes, in
accordance with the official instructions laid down for the guidance of those
administering martial law, such measures as he honestly thinks to be necessary for
carrying to a successful issue the operation of restoring peace and preserving
authority, may rely on any question as to the legality of his conduct being
subsequently met by an Act of Indemnity.[596]

By mid-1920 the problem of lack of clarity in relation to the applicability
of martial law in Britain and Ireland was no longer an abstract constitutional one. Developments in Ireland had made it a pressing practical
concern of British strategists. At the May 1920 Cabinet conference with
the Irish Executive, General Macready had expressed doubts both as to
its legality and as to the willingness of the politicians fully to support the
military: 'the question is can martial law be brought into operation in any
part of the UK without legislation . . . The difficulty behind martial law is
that you would put certain persons in prison and they would hunger
strike. What would the people in England say?'[597]

This diffidence was shared by the Army's legal officers. When, in July
1920, the Judge Advocate General prepared a memorandum on the
subject for the Chief Secretary, the result was not a model of clarity.[598] It
began by mentioning *Marais* and then noted: 'It has to be remembered
that a form of Statutory Martial Law already exists in Ireland under the
Defence of the Realm Acts and Regulations made pursuant thereto.'[599] It
was suggested, though, that 'the proclamation and enforcement of martial
law'[600] would extend the executive's powers in six areas: (1) military
courts could inflict the death penalty in circumstances in which DORA
courts martial could not; (2) military courts would not be restricted to the
trial of breaches of the regulations but could try 'all offences of disorder
and violence connected with the rebellion';[601] (3) military courts could
take the form of field general courts martial; (4) there would be a 'greater
sense of confidence in using lethal weapons';[602] (5) the military commander would have greater powers of issuing and varying any order he
might think necessary; and (6) the troops could be declared to be on
active service.

The Judge Advocate General then outlined the historical precedents
for the imposition of martial law in Ireland and drew the conclusion that:

The precedents in Ireland therefore rather point to the introduction of Martial
Law by legislation though the *Prerogative* power without Parliamentary sanction
is undoubted. If it were not thought desirable to proclaim martial Law under the

---

[596] p. 5.   [597] Jones, *Diary*, iii. 20.
[598] Copy of letter from the JAG to the Chief Secretary for Ireland, 19 July 1920, CAB
24/109, PRO, Kew.
[599] Ibid., para. 4.   [600] Ibid.
[601] Ibid., para. 4 (b).   [602] Ibid., para. 4 (d).

Prerogative, any special additional powers required e.g. that of inflicting death sentences by Military Courts might perhaps be obtained by Statute.[603]

In fact, all but the second last of the six additional powers which were seen as accruing from martial law were achieved under ROIA.

Macready later complained that the attitude of the politicians on the subject of martial law was characterized by 'their ignorance of the whole question',[604] but given the Army's own uncertainties, this was not surprising. In mid-1920 the GOC considered that:

any form of martial law that might be imposed would be a very diluted draft, but even so it would have the effect of abolishing several anomalies and would ensure unity of command, the abolition of the civil courts, the control of the press, and above all would give greater control over the city which was the headquarters of the rebel organisation.[605]

General Jeudwine (who commanded the 6th Division in the MLA) saw greater advantages arising from martial law:

1. Unity of command (control of police, reprisals, etc.).
2. Promptitude in action and administration.
3. Heavy sentences for carrying or being in possession of arms.
4. Heavy sentences for harbouring known rebels.
5. Restriction of movement.
6. Identification of individuals.
7. Control of the press.
8. Internment of *suspects* at discretion of Military Governor.
9. Moral effect.[606]

Macready, in considering the necessity for the introduction of martial law, felt that the reputation of the Army had to be above all political considerations. In September 1920 he advised that if army and police reprisals were not to get out of hand it was necessary either to declare martial law throughout the country or 'for the government to acknowledge publicly that a state of insurrection exists in Ireland, that organised rebel forces are in active opposition to the Government, and that peace cannot be restored without military measures such as would be taken under martial law'.[607] This proposal, he noted, 'had little or no effect, the Chief Secretary being optimistic that reprisals would not affect public opinion in England or the stability of the Government, two objects which to me personally were of minor importance in comparison with the good name of the Army'.[608]

---

[603] Ibid., para. 7 (my emphasis).   [604] *Annals*, 515.
[605] Ibid. 538.   [606] Townshend, 134 (Jeudwine's emphasis).
[607] Macready, *Annals*, 500–1.   [608] Ibid. 502.

Martial law and the courts in Ireland

The question of martial law first came before the King's Bench Division in *R* v. *Murphy*,[609] a case which, as noted above, related to a ROIA court martial. The court, however, had sat in Cork five days after the proclamation of martial law in that city, and it was pleaded on behalf of the Crown that because the court had sat in the MLA the conduct of the trial could not be enquired into by the court. In reply to the question from Molony CJ, 'Do you say that every court assembled in a martial law area is a martial law Court?',[610] the Attorney-General replied, 'No, I say it is consistent with Commander-in-Chief's adopting a Court that may not be strictly a martial law Court, and putting it there as a martial law Court.'[611] In giving the unanimous judgment of the court, Molony CJ held that:

As however, all the proceedings were conducted on the basis that the court-martial was held on the statutory authority and as our judgment is adverse to the prisoner on that assumption it becomes unnecessary to consider the broad question of the effect and application of martial law, as to which our opinion would be in the nature of an *obiter dictum*.[612]

This decision (which was in line with the precedent set following the 1916 Rising[613]) would seem to leave open the question as to whether the High Court would have had to consider whether or not its jurisdiction had been ousted, had it found for the prisoner on the substantive points raised in relation to the conduct of the court martial.

In *R* v. *Allen*[614] (9–24 February 1921) application for writs of *certiorari*, prohibition, and habeas corpus was made by a prisoner sentenced to death in the MLA by a martial law military court for an offence for which the death penalty was not available at common law or by statute.[615] The

---

[609] [1921] 2 *IR* 190.   [610] At p. 213.   [611] Ibid.   [612] p. 217.

[613] In *R* v. *Governor of Lewes Prison, ex parte Doyle* [1917] 2 *KB* 254 a prisoner captured during the 1916 Rebellion and convicted by a DORA field general court martial sought to have his conviction quashed on a number of grounds. Though the court martial had sat after the proclamation of martial law, no point in relation to the declaration was pleaded by the respondent. Viscount Reading CJ stated: 'It is not necessary for us to pronounce any opinion upon the proclamation of martial law. It must not be taken that we are implying any doubt as to the validity of the proclamation but we only say that it becomes unnecessary to consider whether it was good or bad' (p. 272).

[614] [1921] 2 *IR* 241.

[615] In his memoirs Macready included what purported to be an IRA communication in relation to the trial of Allen, in which the prisoner was described as a Company Captain and an 'FC [Flying Column] man'. Macready claimed that, when captured, Allen had been in possession of dumdum ammunition (*Annals*, 517–18). The significance of this is that such ammunition was prohibited by a Declaration adopted at the First Peace Conference of the Hague of 1899; see F. Kalshoven, *Constraints on the Waging of War* (Geneva, 1987), 15, 30. But if, as the British Army claimed, international humanitarian law was not applicable in the conflict, why draw attention to acts of the IRA which would have been in breach? It is perhaps worth pointing out that Republicans frequently claimed this type of ammunition

procedure adopted by the military court had been that of a field general court martial.[616] It was pleaded by the Attorney-General, relying on an affidavit of General Macready, that owing to the conditions of war then existing the civil court had no jurisdiction to interfere with the military in the suppression of the insurrection. Macready's affidavit referred to attacks on police barracks and on policemen and soldiers. He also averred that the mails had been continually raided, that trains had been held up and that Government officers had been attacked throughout the country. The organization of the IRA was described, and its members were stated to be

continuously engaged in levying guerrilla warfare against the forces of the Crown. The scheme of the said warfare does not entail fighting in distinctive uniforms, or in accordance with the laws of war, but under a system of guerrilla attacks, in which inhabitants, apparently pursuing peaceful avocations, suddenly come together, and carry out guerrilla operations.[617]

He did not, however, claim that ROIA courts martial, or indeed that the ordinary courts, had been unable to function.

In giving the judgment of the court, Molony CJ considered the conditions of guerrilla warfare described in the General's affidavit and concluded that these conditions amounted to a state wherein 'the Government is entitled and indeed bound to repel force by force',[618] and he rejected the contention that martial law could not be in force because the ordinary courts were open. Following *ex parte Marais*,[619] he stated:

it is also clear on the authorities that when martial law is imposed and the necessity for it exists, or in other words, while war is raging, this court has no jurisdiction to question any acts done by the military authorities, although after the war is over persons may be made liable, civilly and criminally, for any acts which they are proved to have done in excess of what was reasonably required by the necessities of the case... unless these acts have in the meantime been covered by an Act of Indemnity.[620]

Thus the Chief Justice qualified some of the bare propositions advanced in *Marais* and *Tilonko* in a manner which was consistent with contemporary commentators' views of those cases. It was made clear that actions of the military carried out in the execution of martial law could be held to

had been captured from the Black and Tans. At Allen's trial his counsel claimed that 'The prisoner in this case was what might be called a manufactured rebel. His father's house had been burned down, and his case was that he had a revolver to defend himself.' He also stated that one of the witnesses at the trial had asserted 'that the accused said that he had been hounded out of the town by the police, and carried the revolver and ammunition for his protection'. [1921] 2 *IR* 241, at 249.

[616] See pp. 65–6, 92–7.   [617] *R* v. *Allen* [1921] 2 *IR* 241, at 244.
[618] Ibid. 268.   [619] [1902] *AC* 109.   [620] p. 269.

be justiciable after the conclusion of the war or armed rebellion, unless covered by an Act of Indemnity. Although the imposition of martial law was not specifically stated to depend on a common law right or duty, the view expressed was clearly in line with the common law theory.

In Allen's case the court had asked itself the question, 'Was there a state of war in the area included in the Lord Lieutenant's proclamation justifying the application of martial law?',[621] and had answered this in the affirmative. But it had not specifically insisted on the necessity of the court's deciding the point in any proceedings which might be brought before it, though it seems that the Chief Justice intended this to have been implicit in the judgment. This very issue was brought before the court in *R (Garde and Others)* v. *Strickland*,[622] a case also arising out of the operation of a military court, and again involving an application for writs of *certiorari* and habeas corpus. The pleadings differed from those in Allen's case in two material respects. First, a series of affidavits of prominent people in the city of Cork (the venue of trial by military court) was submitted on behalf of the applicants, in which the assertion in the affidavit submitted by General Macready that a state of war existed, was contradicted. Secondly, the respondent pleaded that the court was bound to accept Macready's affidavit as decisive of the matter.

The first ground was quickly dismissed by an examination of military and police losses which showed marked increases even since the decision in Allen's case. But although the judgment therefore went against the prisoners, Molony CJ typically combined the rejection of their case with a formal assertion of judicial independence. The contention advanced on behalf of the respondent was also to be rejected because it was 'absolutely opposed to our judgment in Allen's Case, and is destitute of authority, and we desire to state, in the clearest possible language, that this Court has the power and the duty to decide whether a state of war exists which justifies the application of martial law'.[623] Although none of these applications were proving successful, the very fact that they were being brought operated as a clog on the military court system, and was a constant source of annoyance to the military authorities.[624] Grounds for bringing further applications continued to be found. In *R (Ronayne and Mulcahy)* v. *Strickland*[625] (2 April 1921) explicit reliance was placed on behalf of the applicants on the prerogative theory, and an attempt was made to test its implications. It was pleaded that there was a prerogative right of the King to proclaim martial law, but that as this right had been surrendered or released by ROIA, martial law could not therefore be proclaimed without the consent of Parliament. Molony CJ, however, chose to evade the issue

---

[621] [1921] 2 *IR* 264.   [622] [1921] 2 *IR* 317.   [623] p. 329.
[624] See pp. 37–8, 144–5.   [625] [1921] 2 *IR* 333.

as to whether the imposition of martial law was justified by virtue of the common law or by the Royal prerogative, saying:

It is quite unnecessary for us to entangle ourselves in an academic enquiry as to the use of the term 'prerogative'. It is sometimes used in one sense sometimes in another. The King is head of a standing army with the consent of Parliament. He cannot it is conceded, merely by proclamation declare war inside his own dominions. It is also conceded that without such proclamation a state of things may exist when the military forces of the Crown may be employed 'in executing martial law'. We hold that when a state of things does exist which justify the 'execution of martial law' and such is proved to our satisfaction, our hands are tied.[626]

He added, however, that

when the state of war is over, the acts of the military during the war, unless prohibited by an Act of Indemnity may be challenged before a jury: in that event even the King's command could not be an answer if the jury are satisfied that the acts complained of were not justified by the circumstances and the necessities of the case.[627]

In *Higgins* v. *Willis*[628] (26 April 1921) it was held by the King's Bench Division that the same test was to be applied after the war in relation to damage caused during the British Army's official reprisals. The action which the plaintiff had brought claiming damage for loss of property caused during a reprisal was ordered to be stayed until 'the state of war was no longer present'.[629]

This series of cases, all unanimous judgments of the King's Bench Division delivered by Molony CJ, has provoked polemical comment. Heuston (1964) was clear in his approval of the Chief Justice's 'masterly judgments'.[630] On the question of the court's insistence of its right to adjudicate on the existence or otherwise of the circumstances justifying the imposition of martial law, he wrote:

Molony CJ brought the law on this point into line with the law governing the exercise of discretionary powers generally, namely, that it was for the courts to determine whether or not the state of facts justifying the existence of martial law had been established, but that once such a state of affairs had been shown to exist to the satisfaction of the ordinary courts they could not interfere with the action of the military authorities *durante bello*.[631]

Kohn (1932), bringing a Continental lawyer's insight to the issue, considered the judgment in Allen's case 'truly revolting'.[632] The fault lay in

---

[626] p. 334.   [627] p. 334.   [628] [1921] 2 *IR* 386.   [629] p. 387.
[630] R. F. V. Heuston, *Essays in Constitutional Law* (London, 1964), 154.
[631] Ibid.   [632] *Constitution*, 141.

following Marais's case, a decision which Kohn considered 'not a statement of established Common Law, but a naked pronouncement of the
neo-absolutist doctrine of State Necessity'.[633] The most objectionable
feature of the judgment in Allen's case was 'the toleration accorded by
the Civil Courts to the assumption by the Military Authorities of judicial
powers over civilians and to the application of this arbitrary and irregular
jurisdiction to capital cases'.[634]

The validation by the King's Bench Division of the imposition of
martial law did not receive explicit endorsement from any other court.
The matter of martial law military courts came before the House of Lords
in *In re Clifford and O'Sullivan*[635] (28 July 1921), which case involved an
application for a writ of prohibition against a military court. It was held
that as the military court was not in fact a court at all, a writ of prohibition
could not lie against it. In the words of Viscount Cave:

> They [the members of the military court] sat not as a tribunal for hearing charges
> of a crime, but as a military committee for considering a matter arising under the
> proclamation and advising the commanding officer thereon; and although in the
> interest of prisoners brought before them they followed the form of law, their
> proceedings were in no sense criminal proceedings.[636]

Thus the case turned on a procedural point, and following the rejection of
the application fresh habeas corpus proceedings were commenced in the
Chancery courts.[637]

Almost simultaneously with *In re Clifford and O'Sullivan*,[638] a case was
proceeding before the Master of the Rolls in Ireland, which led to the
Army/judiciary crisis of July 1921. *Egan* v. *Macready*[639] involved a habeas
corpus application brought on behalf of a prisoner tried by a military
court. In making a conditional order for the issue of a writ absolute,
O'Connor MR, in an explicit endorsement of the prerogative theory,
distinguished the case from Marais's case on the grounds that the present,
unlike the latter, involved a military emergency for which a specific mode
of action had been provided by Parliament in ROIA. Refusing to follow
Allen's case, he quoted with approval from Lord Atkinson's judgment in
the De Keyser case, holding that the Royal prerogative to deal with
situations of war expressed in the use of martial law could not exist
alongside the very extensive powers to deal with the same problem
contained in ROIA:

---

[633] *Constitution* 141.   [634] Ibid. 142.   [635] [1921] 2 *AC* 570.   [636] p. 582.

[637] Macready, *Annals*, 587. Macready records that, owing to the truce, the case was not
fought, as the military gave an undertaking not to carry the sentences into effect during the
continuance of the truce.

[638] [1921] 2 *AC* 570.   [639] [1921] 1 *IR* 265.

This is the case of a military emergency for which a specific mode of action is provided by Parliament. The Act is not merely enabling, but prohibitory, The military authority, like any other department of the State, is subject to the Supreme Court of the realm. To hold that, notwithstanding the Restoration of Order Act [*sic*], the military authority can waive aside Courts-martial, and sweep away the limitations as to punishment, would really involve the proposition that express legislation that the existing rebellion was not to warrant the holding of military Courts would not be binding. This would be a new development of British Constitutional Law, for which I can find no authority.[640]

The Master of the Rolls did not, however, entirely dismiss the relevance of arguments based on military necessity:

Once the military are called into action no precise regulations can be laid down prescribing the amount of force to be used; when and when not there should be firing; the exact circumstances in a conflict in which a man should be shot or captured . . . But there is no difficulty in the way of legislating that any person not killed in conflict shall be tried according to law. This is exactly what the Act of Parliament has done.[641]

Arguments based on necessity might also have a bearing on the mode of trial, but not in this instance since 'the evidence offered by the military in this case seems to me to negative the necessity for bringing the prisoner before a military Court rather than a Court-martial'.[642]

The crisis which resulted from the decision was eventually solved only by the intervention of the civil Government.[643] Commentators initially reacted unfavourably to the decision in Egan's case, both in relation to procedural aspects of the case,[644] and on the substantive issues. Kelly (1961) considered that the decision 'did not, however deprive the earlier

---

[640] p. 275.   [641] pp. 276-7.

[642] p. 277.

[643] See pp. 37–8 above. On the day for which the writ was made returnable, counsel for the defendant informed the court that an appeal was being lodged, whereupon O'Connor MR ordered a writ of attachment to issue against the named defendants. On the following day counsel stated that the Government had decided to release the prisoners pending the hearing of the appeal. O'Connor MR then put a stay on the writ of attachment and dispensed with any return to the writ of habeas corpus. See p. 280 of the report of the proceedings. It can be assumed that the appeal was not heard because of the truce.

[644] Heuston writes that 'it is extremely doubtful whether the court had jurisdiction to hear an application for habeas corpus as the applicant had already applied unsuccessfully to the King's Bench Division, which had followed its own previous decision in *R* v. *Allen*' (*Constitutional Law*, 159). Macready claimed that in making the writ returnable for the day on which he did, the Master ignored the provisions of 'Statutes 21 & 22 Geo. III', as the prisoners were at the time in the Limerick and Cork gaols respectively (*Annals*, 587). The citation given by the General is incomplete. It seems likely that he was referring to 21 & 22 Geo. III, c. 11, 'An Act for Securing the Better Liberty of the Subject' (the Habeas Corpus Act), but it is not immediately clear why the Master's action could be said to have been procedurally incorrect by reference to that Act.

cases of authority'.[645] Keir and Lawson (1979) attack the decision in *Egan*
v. *Macready* on two main grounds: (1) the execution of martial law does
not involve the exercise of the Royal prerogative, and (2) the provisions
of ROIA were enabling only and not prohibitory. As regards the first
point, the authors write: 'it is not necessary to derive the powers of the
military in time of insurrection from the prerogative',[646] because 'the
term "execution of martial law" is now nothing more than a convenient
label for the state of affairs which exists when the military takes exceptional measures to suppress an insurrection'.[647] While the right to repel
force by force might be seen to justify actions taken in the field by the
military, it is less easy to see how the right of the military to be free from
judicial scrutiny during the course of the rebellion necessarily arises from
this common law right. On this point Keir and Lawson write:

It is submitted that what has happened is that the courts have recognized frankly
that when a state of war exists—and they have not relinquished the right of
adjudication on this point—they must accept the consequences. One of these
consequences is that the executive with the aid of the military must conduct warlike operations without liability to interference.[648]

The authors, however, state: 'if the right not to be interfered with is still a
part of the prerogative, probably the latter case [Egan's] is right. But if so
it is the only portion of the prerogative as to martial law which still
survives.'[649] Keir and Lawson's view is supported by Heuston who writes
of Egan's case: 'it appears to depend on the view that the right to use
martial law is a prerogative right. The better view appears to be that it is
not a prerogative right but simply an extension of the ordinary common
law power to meet force with force.'[650]

On the second ground (ROIA being enabling and not prohibitory) Keir
and Lawson write:

In these circumstances it is most unlikely that Parliament intended by the passing
of the act to deprive them of their right to justify their acts on the pleas of
absolute necessity. The Act no doubt narrowed the sphere within which the
defence of necessity needed to be relied on, but it surely did not take it away
entirely.[651]

This point is echoed in the comment on the case in the seventh edition of
Wade and Phillips (1965): 'The better opinion is that inadequacy of
statutory powers does not disable the military from taking whatever steps
are necessary in good faith to restore order.'[652] To this it must be

---

[645] J. M. Kelly, *Fundamental Rights in the Irish Law and Constitution* (Dublin, 1961), 241.
[646] *Cases*, 228.   [647] Ibid. 226.   [648] Ibid.   [649] Ibid. 225.
[650] *Constitutional Law*, 159.   [651] *Cases*, 228.
[652] *Constitutional Law* (London, 1965), 406.

answered that in the line of authority discussed above, it was never claimed that the statutory powers given by the ROIA were inadequate, nor was it explained how these powers might have been inadequate— although successive affidavits by Macready did disclose increasing losses. It will be recalled that DORA, and therefore *a fortiori* ROIA, have been considered to have amounted to a 'statutory imposition of martial law'. The Master of the Rolls did not entirely dismiss the possibility that military necessity might require a mode of trial beyond that authorized by statute, but he did suggest that the clearest proof would be required to justify the existence of such necessity.

More recently there seems to have been something of a reappraisal of the merits of the decision in Egan's case. In the tenth edition of Wade and Bradley (1985) the authors write: 'If Parliament is sitting but refuses to pass emergency legislation there would seem to be great difficulty from a democratic or a constitutional standpoint, in accepting that extra-ordinary powers of the military arise by a process of common law',[653] and Egan's case is cited as a footnote to that proposition. De Smith (1985) wrote in relation to Egan's and other cases: 'It is arguable that public policy does not require a total abdication of judicial review during a state of martial law.'[654]

Further support for O'Connor MR's decision might be also be found in the House of Lords' decision in *Johnstone* v. *Pedlar*[655] (24 June 1921), a case which, although it preceded *Egan* v. *Macready*,[656] was not cited in the judgment. The case involved a naturalized American citizen of Irish birth (Pedlar) who had taken part in the 1916 Rising and been interned, and who, following his release, had been arrested by the DMP for illegal drilling. A large sum of money which was found on him on his arrest was retained by the police, and the seizure was subsequently ratified by the Chief Secretary. When Pedlar sought to recover the money through the courts the defence was that the money (and cheque) had been taken and detained by 'an officer of the Crown by the direction of the Crown as an act of State for the defence of the realm and for the prevention of crime',[657] 'act of State' being a term used to describe actions done under the prerogative in the sphere of foreign affairs.[658]

This argument was rejected by the majority of the Court of Appeal (in Ireland)[659] and was unanimously rejected by the House of Lords. In the words of Lord Phillimore:

---

[653] *Constitutional and Administrative Law*, 552.
[654] Ibid. 526 n. 23.   [655] [1921] 2 *AC* 262.
[656] [1921] 1 *IR* 265.   [657] [1921] 2 *AC* 263.
[658] See Wade and Bradley, *Constitutional and Administrative Law*, 316.
[659] *Pedlar* v. *Johnstone* [1920] 2 *IR* 450.

To begin with the alien takes his character from his State . . . If his State is in amity with ours he is considered an alien ami even though his personal intentions are hostile. His individual hostility does not entitle him to the character of an alien enemy . . . But an alien ami is never exlex, he is never subject to the arbitrary dispositions of the King. His rights may be limited, but whatever rights he has he can enforce by law just as an ordinary subject can . . . The alien ami, once he is resident within the realm, is given the same rights for the protection of his person and property as a natural born or naturalised subject.[660]

Consequently, since the property of a subject could not be confiscated as an 'act of State', neither could that of a friendly alien be, at least not until the Crown chose to withdraw its protection: 'If it should be necessary, as counsel for the appellant suggest, that in the disturbed state of Ireland there should be special provisions in respect of aliens this must be effected by legislation.'[661] Lord Sumner expanded on this point:

The prerogative of the Crown for the defence of the realm in time of war is one thing; the powers of the executive for the maintenance of order and the punishment of crime quite another. The difference does not disappear merely because the offence is an offence against public tranquillity, or because it is committed in time of war. The Executive, which holds office and wields power, thanks to the support of Parliament, ought constitutionally to seek wider powers from Parliament, if the existing law is insufficient, nor, if so, would the enactment of wider powers be refused.[662]

In the opinion of Keir and Lawson, 'if the view of Lord Sumner is to be accepted, there can never be any such thing as martial law, and there can never be any room to apply the rule in Marais's Case.'[663] It is arguable that this would be the case whether the common law or the prerogative theory were relied upon.

Constraints on martial law: military perspectives

Once martial law had been proclaimed, General Macready considered that its effective implementation depended above all else on the Army's having complete discretion to do what it deemed necessary without having to seek prior sanction from any source. He was not prepared to comply with decisions of the Irish High Court adverse to his view of martial law (at least once the validity of martial law had been accepted) and objected generally to having to answer applications brought on behalf of prisoners.[664] His response to the decision in Egan's case has been noted in part I. Earlier, he had ordered his Generals not to accept service of writs arising out of official Army reprisals.

Despite his comments on the relative importance of the reputation of

---

[660] [1921] 2 *AC* 262, at 296.   [661] At p. 298.
[662] At p. 294.   [663] *Cases*, 230.   [664] Ibid. 517.

the Army versus the stability of the Government, he was prepared to submit to political control. At best he hoped that 'the full force of martial law would have been applied so far as was permissible in the courts within telephonic range of Whitehall'.[665] Such political control, however, he considered defeated the whole purpose of martial law. When, in 1921, the Chief Secretary explained to him that 'martial law in Ireland means martial law that is supported by the House of Commons',[666] he wrote:

In other words, a soldier charged with the administration of martial law, instead of being a free agent to employ such measures as he might consider necessary, always bearing in mind that such acts must be justified to his Government after the event, must consult and obtain the concurrence of Government before taking any step which he, as the man on the spot, considered should be taken to save the situation. For the soldier such a position was impossible.[667]

What emerges (not surprisingly) is that the British Army's view of martial law derived not from an understanding of the the the law of the land but from military experience. For Macready, martial law in Ireland should mean the same thing as martial law in Germany after the First World War, and as it had meant to Wellington in the mid nineteenth century: 'the will of the general'.[668] This is not to say that he was totally ignorant of the legal problems involved. His observations in that regard at a Cabinet conference in May 1920 have been noted. When on 3 July 1921 he received an order (apparently from the Chief Secretary) to delay an execution in the MLA, his view was that 'it justified the suspicion I had always had that martial law in any part of the British Isles could never be brought to a logical conclusion'.[669]

The problem of theory and practice

If the actual prosecution of martial law in Ireland in 1920–1 is considered, its reconciliation with the common law theory presents certain difficulties. First, apologists for the common law theory generally insist that, in times of war or armed rebellion there is not only a right but a duty to take exceptional martial law measures. Thus in Allen's case Molony CJ held that 'during the continuance of such a state of affairs as is described in Sir Nevil Macready's affidavit the Government is entitled and, indeed, bound to repel force by force, and thereby to put down the insurrection and restore public order'.[670] In practice, reference to 'duty' in this context was meaningless since no sanction was feared for any breach of such duty. The decision to opt for martial law was a political one, made not because

---

[665] Ibid. 514.   [666] Ibid. 564.   [667] Ibid.
[668] 1851 Hansard, 115, col. 880, quoted in Keir and Lawson, *Cases*, 217.
[669] Macready, *Annals*, 564.   [670] [1921] 2 *IR* at 268.

a sanction was feared for the non-adoption of that course, but as part of an overall strategy. And it is clear that those involved in the administration of martial law saw it as a discretionary matter, as evidenced by the refusal to sanction the imposition of martial law in Dublin, despite its operational importance for the IRA.

Supporters of the strict common law view argue that there is a duty not only on the Government but on every able-bodied citizen to 'resist force by force'. They insist that 'soldiers as civilians', and civilians generally, may be under a duty to act, irrespective of the wishes of the Government. But in Ireland it is clear that the British Army was unwilling to impose or to extend martial law without the sanction of the British Government, and that all martial law measures were taken under the auspices of the British Army.

But perhaps the most significant legal flaw in the common law theory is that it failed to provide a mechanism whereby the law on the deployment of the British Army in an insurrection in what was regarded as part of the United Kingdom could be reconciled with constitutional norms of parliamentary sovereignty. Instead, it appeared to allow such norms to be flouted by permitting, or perhaps insisting, that force be used without statutory authority, not only by the British Government acting through the British Army, but indeed by any loyalist. Partly, this can be considered to have been a result of the shortcomings of the constitutional arrangements of the seventeenth century, shortcomings which were particularly acute in relation to Ireland. It is this 'constitutional' or 'democratic' failure which contemporary critics of the common law theory have been particularly critical of. Indeed, some have regarded the common law theory as having failed not only by modern standards, but also by reference to those of the past. In the words of Greer:

The establishment of the constitutional principle of military subordination to the civil executive in the seventeenth century effectively rendered the common law theory an anachronism. Unfortunately since then judges and jurists have signally failed to acknowledge that this has happened.[671]

On the other hand, there is the prerogative theory, a theory for which particularly strong support can be found in Ireland. In terms of derivation, the essential difference between prerogative powers and other common law powers is that the former, unlike the latter, are vested solely in the Crown. If resort to martial law were founded on the prerogative it would follow that such powers were exercisable only at the behest of the Government (usually acting through the Army), and this was what actually happened in relation to martial law in Ireland. Commentators are

_____

[671] 'Military Intervention', 592.

generally agreed that the 'disposition' of the British Army is a prerogative matter.[672] Keir and Lawson, as noted above, have suggested that the non-justiciability of Army action during the imposition of martial law may arise from the prerogative. Since prerogative powers are by their nature discretionary, it would be logically consistent that in so far as 'martial law' involved the exercise of these powers, it might be imposed on a discretionary basis (as was the case in Ireland), and its enforcement might be tempered with political considerations.

If, then, martial law involves the exercise of the prerogative, it follows that the application of the De Keyser principle in Egan's case was correct (an interpretation strengthened by *Johnstone* v. *Pedlar*[673]). This leads to the conclusion that the principal strength of the prerogative theory is that it provides a means of circumventing the principal weakness of the common law theory, that is it provides a mechanism for the reassertion of contemporary notions of parliamentary supremacy over all military action.[674] This can be considered another facet of 'modernist' trends which led to Macready's ultimate frustration with martial law.

Judicial scrutiny of emergency powers: conclusions

The relaxation of the *ultra vires* test in relation to DORA evident in cases such as Halliday's signalled a significant shift in judicial posture. Instead of interpreting legislative provisions in terms of what the ordinary rules of construction would have indicated, interpretation was geared towards validating whatever claims the executive might make that a particular exercise of delegated legislative powers was necessary for the public safety or the defence of the realm. Within this framework, what was important was not what the statutes said, but what the Executive Government chose to interpret Parliament as having intended to say. As Bonner has written of the judiciary: 'their role in emergency powers situations may be more one of giving the seal of legal legitimacy to government action.'[675] Implicit in this is an effective abandonment of judicial independence, if only a temporary one. This did not mean the complete abandonment of the ideology of the rule of law, though as the constant recourse to Latin maxims illustrate (*salus populi suprema lex* etc.), it very nearly did so. Adherence to legal form could be important in the process

---

[672] See Ibid. 577.

[673] [1921] 2 *AC* 262.

[674] More recently, though, the direction of contemporary theory is becoming less clear. In *R* v. *Secretary of State for the Home Department, ex parte Northumbria Police Authority* [1988] 2 *WLR* 590, it was held that prerogative powers to 'maintain the Queen's peace and to keep law and order' were still exercisable notwithstanding the provisions of the Police Act 1964. See also *Council of Civil Service Unions* v. *Minister for the Civil Service*, [1984] 3 *All ER* 935.

[675] *Emergency Powers*, 50.

of legitimation, whatever the substance.[676] There were, in any case, some notable dissents, and in some cases a more stringent approach was taken (though these cases typically involved property rather than individual rights and were heard after the end of the actual fighting in Europe). And the courts always insisted on their right to adjudicate on the substantive issues in cases involving statutory interpretation, even if this adjudication was frequently trite, and obviously geared towards the achievement of a particular result.

This analysis applies equally to the response to the Irish emergency. The British courts were unwilling to assume responsibility for the definition of that emergency, and as the cases on courts martial illustrate, the courts in Ireland were likewise loath to interfere with the exercise of emergency powers. But if the courts in Britain were by and large unwilling to question delegated legislative powers, they were prepared to place some brake on Executive Government, by insisting in the De Keyser case that prerogative powers were not exercisable where statutory powers existed in the same area.

In Ireland the position was somewhat different. When martial law was imposed in December 1920, the existence of two streams of authority in this area (the prerogative theory and the common law theory), coupled with the effect of the De Keyser decision, meant that two courses were open to the courts in Ireland. Reliance on the common law theory would lead to a non-interventionist posture, and this was the course taken by the King's Bench Division in Allen's and subsequent cases. This degree of judicial abdication can be considered an intensification of trends already manifest in the case law on ROIA courts martial (and indeed on DORA).

Reliance on the prerogative theory (which seems to have been regarded as the correct one by the Army's own lawyers) would involve an interventionist posture, and this was the course taken in Egan's case. The modernism of the Master of the Rolls' decision contrasted sharply with what Kohn has referred to as the 'naked pronouncement of the neo-absolutist doctrine of State Necessity'[677] in Allen's case. The decision is of importance, not only because of its substance, but also because of its immediate practical effect—a constitutional crisis arising out of a martial law death sentence. The refusal of O'Connor MR to grant Bonner's 'seal of legal legitimacy' to the imposition of martial law was bound to be profoundly damaging. The incident served to highlight in the starkest manner possible the shortcomings of an approach which readily invoked the law in order to stigmatize opposition in Ireland, but whose ultimate response to emergency seemed to be to abandon all legal standards.[678]

---

[676] See Ch. 5.   [677] See above.
[678] The point is discussed further in Ch. 5.

3. The Irish Free State 1922–1925

PART I. LEGAL DEVELOPMENTS
IN CONTEXT

The Irish Civil War is generally taken to have begun at the end of June 1922, and to have ended in May the following year.[1] There were three main phases in the conflict. The first, from the end of June until the end of August, saw the fighting between the anti-Treaty (Republican) and pro-Treaty (Free State) forces waged largely on conventional lines. Defeat in the field led to a readoption of guerrilla tactics by the Republicans and in the second phase, a military stalemate ensued which began in September 1922 and lasted for much of the year. The third phase began in December and saw the development of an increasingly ruthless, and ultimately victorious, counter-insurgency strategy by the Free State. Though victory came in May, this period can be considered to have lasted until the end of July 1923, as it was only then that martial law came to an end.

From August 1923 until mid-April 1925 a variety of emergency Public Safety Acts were in force, and then in June 1925, during the final period under discussion (the end of April to December 1925), severe penalties were prescribed for political crime in the Treasonable Offences Act 1925. But before describing legal developments during the Civil War proper, mention must be made of the circumstances leading up to it.

July 1921 to June 1922: truce, treaty, and the descent into Civil War

In order to ensure that the truce would operate smoothly, both the British Army and the IRA appointed Liaison Officers throughout the country. Disputes did occur, however, and one such dispute centred on the British practice of attempting to deal with the appropriate Republican liaison officials without according them formal status, and thus attempting to avoid any 'recognition of belligerency' in international law.[2] In the MLA this led to particular difficulties, and these were compounded by a

---

[1] This part draws on M. Hopkinson, *Green against Green: The Irish Civil War* (Dublin, 1988); C. Younger, *Ireland's Civil War* (London, 1970); E. Neeson, *The Civil War in Ireland* (Dublin, 1989); J. M. Curran, *The Birth of the Irish Free State* (Tuscaloosa, Ala., 1980); and S. M. Lawlor, 'Civil–Military Relations in Ireland 1921–23' (MA thesis, UCD, 1976).

[2] 'Recognition of belligerency' is an acceptance that what is taking place is a 'war' or 'armed conflict' as the phrase is used in international humanitarian law. Such a recognition triggers the applicability of that body of law, though during the period with which this work is concerned, the applicable norms were much less developed than they currently are. See Kalshoven, *Constraints*, 26–7.

British insistence that martial law restrictions on fairs, post offices, and creameries be lifted only gradually, a policy which local IRA officers saw as a breach of the truce. The British responded with claims that the armed drilling and manœuvres of the IRA were in breach, that some violence still continued, and that Republican Liaison Officers were not acting in good faith.[3] Ultimately, however, the political need to provide the conditions for dialogue overrode the difficulties caused by the inevitable frictions, so that even when military communication channels broke down, alternative civil channels were found.

In fact, both sides continued with preparations for a possible resumption of hostilities. The British Army finalized plans for drumhead courts, which were to be widely employed under extended martial law powers.[4] The IRA proceeded with arms importations, and enlisted thousands of new recruits—the 'trucers'—some of whom were of doubtful quality. In many areas policing functions were performed by the IRA's Republican Police. Guerrilla fighters came out of hiding, generally to an enthusiastic welcome from the civilian population, but with the removal of the constraints of an ongoing campaign, discipline and security inevitably declined.

There also remained the vexed question of the formal relationship between the Dáil and the IRA. During the guerrilla period, military efficacy had seemed more important than constitutional context, but with the switch of attention from the military to the political arena, these issues gained a fresh importance. The result was that towards the end of November 1921 the Army (which retained the title 'IRA') was formally subordinated to the Republican Government, and the procedures for the granting of new commissions by that Government were formalized.

The new political context was provided by the Treaty negotiations. Initial contacts were made in mid-July when de Valera visited Lloyd George in London, but the negotiations proper began only in October. It soon emerged that the sticking points were partition and the question of Ireland's position *vis-à-vis* the Empire. The British side was prepared to accept a break over the latter issue, but calculated that a break on the former would be much less likely to attract imperial support. Eventually, however, the deal which was struck on 6 December 1921 under threat of a resumption of hostilities provided for an Irish Free State with dominion status within the Commonwealth. Under the 'Articles of Agreement for a Treaty between Great Britain and Ireland',[5] Northern Ireland was to have the right to exclude itself from the new state and if it did so, the eventual border between the two jurisdictions was to be decided by a

---

[3] For the British GOC's complaints see Macready, *Annals*, 580–1.
[4] See pp. 97–9.
[5] Cmnd. 1534 (1921).

Boundary Commission.[6] Other articles concerned the thorny question of the oath to be taken by Members of Parliament of the Irish Free State legislature,[7] and for the retention of naval bases by the British and the provision of other facilities 'in time of war or of strained relations with Foreign Powers'.[8] Article 17 made provision for transitional arrangements pending the 'constitution of a Parliament and Government of the Irish Free State'. A meeting was to be summoned of MPs elected for constituencies in 'Southern Ireland' since the passing of the Government of Ireland Act 1920 and for constituting a 'Provisional Government'. The British Government was to take the 'steps necessary to transfer to such Provisional Government the powers and machinery requisite for the discharge of its duties, provided that every member of such Provisional Government shall have signified in writing his or her acceptance of this instrument'. The Treaty was to be submitted for approval to the British Parliament and to a meeting summoned for that purpose of the members elected to sit in the House of Commons of Southern Ireland, and if approved, was to be ratified by the necessary legislation.

In Britain parliamentary approval was quickly forthcoming, but in Ireland the situation was quite different. Whatever the terms of the Treaty in relation to ratification, the *realpolitik* of Dublin required consideration of the document by the Republican organs of the Dáil. Opinion immediately polarized; indeed there was a move, which was successfully resisted, to have the negotiators arrested for treason on their return. On 8 December the Dáil Cabinet approved the terms on a 4:3 vote, and on 8 January 1922, after a long and acrimonious debate, the Dáil likewise voted its approval on a 64:57 division.

Establishment of the Free State necessarily involved the disestablishment of the Republic, a step which, Republicans asserted, the Dáil was constitutionally precluded from taking. Indeed it was claimed that no authority for such a step could be found, since as de Valera was later to put it, 'the people had never a right to do wrong'.[9] The immediate effect of such considerations was that the Dáil Cabinet was placed in an anomalous position. De Valera resigned as President and sought re-election, but was rejected by a margin which was even narrower than that which had rejected the Treaty, and in his place a new pro-Treaty President and Cabinet were elected. Then on 14 January, in accordance with the terms of the Treaty, the Members elected for Southern Ireland assembled to vote their approval, and to elect a Provisional Government. Republicans boycotted this assembly and took no part in the election by the pro-Treaty faction of this government. In practice, its membership

---

[6] Art. 12.   [7] Art. 4.   [8] Art. 7.   [9] Quoted in Curran, *Birth*, 174.

overlapped considerably with that of the Dáil Government, resulting in a dual system. Thus the pro-Treaty faction was able to claim organizational continuity with the institutions of 1919 while staying within the terms of the Treaty, and thus to straddle two essentially conflicting constitutional arrangements.

Whatever the constitutional niceties, the real issue was the acquisition and consolidation of power, and this entailed not only obtaining formal transfers from the British, but also the creation of institutions at home which would act as power bases. The IRA GHQ was dominated by pro-Treaty members, and little time was lost by this group in creating a new, and exclusively pro-Treaty, military force from IRA cadres who supported the Treaty. Initially, however, the impression was given that continuity with the IRA of 1919–21 was being maintained, and the new force retained the IRA's Gaelic title of 'Oglaigh na hEireann' (the Irish Volunteers). It was only later that the distinction between this new 'National Army' or 'Free State Army' and the IRA became absolutely clear.

In January also, GHQ ordered the disbandment of the old Republican Police and recruitment for a new police force, the Civic Guard, was begun. As with the new Army, police recruitment concentrated on pro-Treaty IRA members, so that 97 per cent of its early membership came from this source.[10] By the end of January, ADRIC had been withdrawn to England, and at the end of March the disbandment of the RIC proper began, its policing role having effectively ended a month earlier.[11] An attempt was made to integrate some former RIC men of nationalist sympathies into the Civic Guard, but this was abandoned within a few months when a virtual mutiny erupted. In contrast, the DMP was permitted to continue to function in Dublin, a reflection of the fact that that force had never attracted the degree of nationalist ire that the RIC had. The British Army had also begun to withdraw, and in March Macready began concentrating his remaining troops at the Curragh and around Dublin,[12] the Provisional Government having earlier decreed a 'general amnesty' for the Crown Forces.[13]

Initial preparations for the formal transfer of power had begun in December 1921 with Lloyd George's appointment of a Provisional Government of Ireland Committee to oversee the transfer. Early in February the terms of the transfer were agreed between British and Irish officials, and the following month British legal requirements were attended

[10] See R. Fanning, *Independent Ireland* (Dublin, 1983), 66.
[11] Legal aspects of the disbandment were attended to when the British Parliament enacted the Constabulary (Ireland) Act 1922, on 4 Aug.
[12] See P. Canning, *British Policy towards Ireland 1921–1941* (Oxford, 1985), 32.
[13] The text of the amnesty, dated 10 Feb. 1922, can be found at SR & O 1922–38, i. 23.

to with the enactment of the Irish Free State (Agreement) Act 1922. The legislation provided that the Treaty (which was scheduled) was to have 'the force of law' from the date of the Act's passing,[14] and set out the mechanism whereby Orders in Council might be made transferring to the Provisional Government 'the powers and machinery requisite for the discharge of its duties'[15] as provided in the Treaty.[16] It also specified that a new election to a parliament to which the Provisional Government was to be responsible was to be held within four months.[17]

On 1 April, the Provisional Government (Transfer of Functions) Order 1922 was made, which, as its title suggests, provided for the investment with legal powers of the various Departments of the Provisional Government, and most of the relevant powers were transferred on that day.[18] What were being transferred were not 'services' as in the case of the Government of Ireland Act 1920,[19] but merely 'the *functions* in connection with the administration of public services in Southern Ireland heretofore performed by existing [British] Government Departments and officers'.[20] And the functions thus transferred were by no means all-embracing; there was, for instance, a specific reservation in respect of 'the existing naval, military or air forces of the Crown',[21] and although it was envisaged that the Parliament which was to be elected might legislate for the creation of an Army as provided for in the Treaty, there was no provision for the establishment of an Army by the Provisional Government pending the enactment of such legislation.[22]

Of more immediate concern to the pro-Treaty faction was the attitude of the Republicans, particularly those in the IRA, who persisted in their opposition to the Treaty. One of the few unifying influences between the former comrades was the pressing necessity of action in support of Northern nationalists, a necessity underlined by the arrival of refugees

[14] s. 1 (1).   [15] Treaty, art. 17.   [16] s. 1 (2) and (3).   [17] s. 1 (2).
[18] It is perhaps a measure of the sensitivity of the question of derivation of power that the Order was not gazetted in the *Dublin Gazette*. Instead, the Provisional Government published a 'Public Notice No. 6 concerning the Constitution of Ministries and Departments of Government, and the Allocation of National Service' which recited the Dáil's approval of the Treaty, and provided that 'the several services of the Nation hitherto controlled by the British Parliament shall be and the same are respectively allocated and assigned to the Departments in the manner and under the Ministers particularly mentioned in the said Schedule hereto annexed'. *DG* 4 Apr. 1922. A further notice advised that the date on which most powers provided for in the order were to be transferred was 1 Apr. *DG* 14 Apr. 1922. The text of the Provisional Government (Transfer of Functions) Order 1922 can, however, be found in *BG* 7 Apr. 1922.
[19] See Ch. 4.
[20] Provisional Government (Transfer of Functions) Order 1922, para. 1 (my emphasis).
[21] Ibid., para. 9.
[22] This question is discussed further on pp. 243–7.

in Dublin.[23] These concerns led Collins to enter into two successive Agreements with Sir James Craig, the Northern Ireland Prime Minister, in the early part of 1922, and ultimately to a degree of covert collusion with the Republicans in the development of an armed strategy against Northern Ireland.[24] But these moves were not, in themselves, sufficient to restore unity.

Divisions had surfaced at the Sinn Féin Ard Fheis (National Conference) in February 1922, but a split was avoided on the basis that no general election would be held until the Constitution of the new state could be put before the electorate. The following month, however, de Valera and other anti-Treaty members broke with the pro-Treatyites to form a new Republican party, Cummann na Poblachta. The split in the IRA was also becoming clear. In January a meeting attended by a majority of Divisional officers and a minority of GHQ officers had affirmed that the Army had been established under its own executive, and that allegiance to the Dáil had been granted only on the condition that the Republic be upheld. An Army Convention was demanded, and a new leadership body was established. The pro-Treaty faction attempted to stall the holding of the Convention, and eventually to ban it, but at the end of March it went ahead anyway. The allegiance of the IRA to the Republic was confirmed, and a new Executive, which was to exercise exclusive control over the Army, was elected. Throughout the country, barracks vacated by the British were falling into the hands of rival IRA factions and small armed clashes began to mount. In Dublin, Republicans occupied the Four Courts and other buildings in Dublin city centre. It was around this time also that some of the worst sectarian attacks of the conflict in the South occurred. Over two nights in April eight Protestants were shot in West Cork, apparently in reprisal for the shooting of an IRA man in Bandon and the murder of Catholics in Belfast. Although both sides were keen to repudiate such action, sectarian attacks did not immediately cease.[25]

A final attempt at nationalist political unity was made in the Collins–de Valera pact of 20 May. Under its terms, the forthcoming election was to be contested by a reunited panel, with the strengths of the existing factions reflected in the nominations. Afterwards, a coalition executive was to be formed, the composition of which would also reflect the relative strengths. No reference was made to the Treaty, the pro-Treaty faction

---

[23] For some correspondence between the Provisional Government on this issue and on the question of refugees from the South arriving in Britain see Cmnd. 1684 (1922), 'Correspondence between His Majesty's Government and the Provisional Government of Ireland relating to the Liability for the Relief of Irish Refugees'.

[24] See Ch. 4.

[25] See, generally, Kennedy, *Widening Gulf*, 114–29.

still apparently hoping to secure British acceptance of a Constitution which would be sufficiently 'republican' to satisfy, or at least to neutralize, the domestic opposition.[26] These hopes proved illusory. At the end of May the British rejected the version which had been submitted in no uncertain terms. In Lloyd George's view it was republican with 'a thin veneer'.[27] The result was a hasty redrafting in an attempt to have the Constitution ready before the election date which had been set at 16 June. Just before polling date, the fragile unity which had been established a month earlier was shattered when Collins made a speech which seemed to repudiate his pact with de Valera.

It was in this clouded atmosphere that the poll took place, informed debate on the issues not having been helped by the fact that the Constitution was published only on the day of the election. The result, though, showed that the pro-Treaty faction had clearly out-polled the anti-Treatyites, with groupings favourable to the Treaty from outside the old Sinn Féin organization also doing well.[28] But before the election result was announced, news came that Sir Henry Wilson, a Unionist Westminster MP, had been assassinated in London. The anti-Treaty IRA was blamed, but commentators now seem to favour the view that the killing had been ordered by Collins as a reprisal for attacks on Northern Catholics. On 24 June the British Government decided on its response: the British Army was ordered to attack the Four Courts garrison the following day. The plan was cancelled at the last minute, but events were in any case moving towards a climax. A Republican officer was arrested in Dublin, and the anti-Treaty IRA responded by kidnapping the Deputy Chief of Staff of the National Army and detaining him in the Four Courts. The National Army surrounded the building and at 3.30 a.m. on 28 June an ultimatum was delivered to the garrison. As no response was forthcoming, shelling began forty-five minutes later using artillery borrowed from the British.

28 June 1922 to August 1922: open conflict

The strength of the pro-Treaty forces at the start of the Civil War has been estimated to have been in the region of 7,000 to 14,000 men, while

---

[26] On the question of the drafting of the new Constitution see D. H. Akenson and J. F. Fallin, 'The Irish Civil War and the Drafting of the Free State Constitution', 5 *Eire-Ireland* 2, p. 42; 4, p. 28; T. Towey, 'Hugh Kennedy and the Constitutional Development of the Irish Free State 1922–23', 12 *Ir. Jur.* 355; and B. Farrell, 'The Drafting of the Irish Free State Constitution', 5 *Ir. Jur.* 115.
[27] Quoted in Hopkinson, *Green*, 106.
[28] Of the 128 seats, 58 went to pro-Treatyites from the old Sinn Féin party, 35 to the anti-Treatyites, 17 to Labour, 7 to Independents, 7 to the Farmers' Party, and 4 to members from Dublin University.

that of the anti-Treaty forces has been put at four times that number.[29] The split in the old IRA was not, however, simply a two-way one. A significant section remained neutral throughout the conflict, while others remained neutral for some of it. The initial numerical disparity between the two forces is misleading in that it disguises important differences in armaments. It appears that the anti-Treaty forces, though strong on paper, could muster only 3,000 rifles, whereas even before the start of the fighting the pro-Treaty forces had received nearly 12,000 rifles, together with ammunition, machine guns, and armoured cars from the British.[30] And once the conflict erupted there was little shortage from the same source of the material necessary to arm the rapidly expanding National Army. Recruitment was not limited to old IRA men, but relied heavily on demobilized British soldiers and the urban unemployed. In contrast, the Republicans (henceforth referred to as the IRA) refused to enlist ex-British soldiers despite the fact that some of their most effective personnel in the earlier conflict came from that background. The organization and outlook of that force remained firmly tied to its guerrilla past, a factor which militated against effective strategy formulation in the first phase of the Civil War during which the fighting approximated to conventional warfare. The National Army, on the other hand, was developed as a regular Army from its inception. But perhaps its biggest advantage during the first phase came less from its capacity for strategic manœuvring than from the simple fact that it alone possessed artillery, and was thus able to reduce Republican strongholds with relative impunity.

The Four Courts garrison surrendered after three days' bombardment, and by the end of the first week of July most of the other IRA strongholds in the city centre had been captured. After some fighting in County Wicklow, the Republicans concentrated their strategic efforts on holding the southern portion of the country—the 'Munster Republic'. In County Limerick the National Army advance was for a while successfully resisted, but elsewhere resistance began to crumble. The IRA evacuated the towns of Enniscorthy and Wexford on 8 July, and by the 21st of the month Republican troops had been driven from Limerick city. On 7 August a National Army force set sail for Cork and the city was soon captured in a sea-borne landing which caught the Republicans off their guard. Although the IRA was able to launch a successful attack on Dundalk, by the end of the month, at the latest, most of the urban centres in the jurisdiction were in National Army hands as the advance, aided by aerial reconnaissance, continued.[31]

---

[29] Neeson, *Civil War*, 119.
[30] See Fanning, *Independent Ireland*, 16.
[31] See e.g. 'Aerial Reconnaissance Report', 14 Aug. 1922, of C. Russell, Mulcahy papers, P7/B/39.

If the military position was becoming clear, the legal position was much less so. For reasons outlined above, the National Army could not derive legal status under the Irish Free State (Agreement) Act 1922, at least without the enactment of further legislation. Merely issuing a decree, as the Government did, setting out the position in regard to commissions in the new Army, could not of itself be sufficient,[32] and the continual post-ponement, on the Provisional Government's insistence, of the opening of Parliament rendered the enactment of such legislation impossible. Neither could the National Army derive legality within the Dáil con-stitutional arrangement, since the Army was clearly not the army of the Republic. A legal challenge to the holding of prisoners by the National Army within that latter framework was dealt with by the abolition of the Dáil Supreme Court, and ultimately by the detention of a judge of that Court,[33] though Dáil Parish and District courts sitting outside of the city of Dublin were permitted to continue to function.[34]

When the legality of such powers eventually came to be considered within the court system inherited from the British, they were upheld as martial law powers, on the same basis as the martial law had been upheld under British rule.[35] There was this important distinction though, that in July and August there were no formal proclamations of martial law from central authority, with the result that the exact extent of the Army's powers remained unclear.

At the start of the fighting, the Provisional Government had taken a number of steps which covered areas dealt with or touched upon by the British under ROIA and under martial law powers. In relation to inquests, the Government had decided on the day after the outbreak of the fighting in Dublin that inquests should be held on all dead civilians, and also on all military killed whose deaths did not occur in definite military action.[36] The number of bodies soon built up, however, so that

---

[32] The decree, dated 2 Aug. 1922, began with the recital: '*We, the Provisional Govern-ment*, duly constituted pursuant to the provisions of the Treaty between Great Britain and Ireland signed at London on the 6th day of December, 1921, by virtue and force of all and every the powers and authorities us hereunto enabling do hereby *decree* and *order* as follows . . .' *DG* 29 Sept. 1922.

[33] The case was brought before Judge Crowley by way of a habeas corpus action. For a brief discussion see Neeson, *Civil War*, 147.

[34] Notice of 25 July 1922, *DG* 1 Aug. 1922. Abolition was stated to be on the authority of the 'Aire um Ghnóthaí Dúithche [Minister for Home Affairs] with the concurrence of the Cabinet of Dáil Eireann', and not therefore on the authority of the Provisional Government. This was because the Dáil court system was not cognizable within the Provisional Govern-ment framework.

[35] The reported cases are considered on pp. 247–52. In Sept. 1922, in *ex parte Beaumont*, a habeas corpus application brought by a prisoner in military custody failed on the grounds that 'a state of war existed in Dublin'. A brief description of the proceedings (though not a report) can be found at *ILT & SJ* 16 and 23 Sept. 1922.

[36] Minutes of Meeting of the Provisional Government, 29 June 1922, SPO.

on 1 July it was decided that in view of the impossibility of holding inquests on them all, the coroner be authorized to have the bodies formally viewed and then issue orders for their burial.[37] Afterwards, it seems that in principle inquests were to be held, though to what extent this occurred in practice, it is difficult to say.[38]

Another area covered was censorship. Early in July it was ordered that 'no newspaper or publication shall be permitted to be imported, distributed, published, or sold in the area of the jurisdiction of the Provisional Government which, or the contents of which, have not been submitted to the Official Censors of the National Army, and passed by them for publication'.[39] In addition, 'all communication, reports, correspondence and other press matter referring to operations of the National Army' was to be submitted to the censors, and 'no such communication, report, correspondence or other press matter was to be transmitted by the Irish postal, telegraph or telephone services' until it had been passed by the censors. It appears that the National Army authorities had been particularly dissatisfied with reports appearing in the English press.[40] These powers were used to ensure that only the pro-Treaty picture of events would be published. The Republicans, for instance, would henceforth be referred to as the 'Irregulars'. There was soon dissatisfaction with the way the powers were being used, and the Provisional Government decided that censorship should be eased.[41] And this was not the only example of media manipulation by the National Army; civilian photographers were issued with military passes which authorized them to photograph only 'at the discretion of the officer commanding operations in any particular area'.[42] Another move taken by the Provisional Government was the issuing of a decree placing restrictions on the importation of a variety of goods which might be useful to the Republicans, including petrol, car parts, and wirelesses.[43]

In a move which was presumably intended to improve the decision-making process in relation to the conflict generally, a War Council was established on 12 July, consisting of General Mulcahy, who combined the posts of Minister of Defence and Chief of Staff; O'Duffy, the Assistant Chief of Staff; and Collins, who left his civil post on a temporary basis to

---

[37] Minutes of Meeting. 1 July 1922. A suggestion made the following day that bodies be buried after simply taking 'certain particulars in each case' was rejected. Ibid. 2 July 1922.

[38] The question of inquests is briefly touched upon below in relation to the question of extra-judicial executions.

[39] *DG* 4 July 1922.

[40] Minutes of Meeting of Provisional Government, 2 July 1922.

[41] Acting Chairman to C-in-C, 28 July 1922, Mulcahy papers, P7/B/1.

[42] C-in-C to CGS, 15 July 1922, ibid. Pro forma 'Photographer's Permit' and 'Press Permit' can be found at Mulcahy papers, P7/B/53.

[43] Decree No. 7, 22 July 1922, *DG* 25 July 1922.

become Commander-in-Chief. On the same day, the new division of the National Army into five Commands was made.[44] Collins then formally wrote to the Provisional Government, seeking direction on issues such as use of arrest and detention powers, and policy in relation to hunger strikes.[45] A few weeks later, in a move which harked back to the use of SMAs by the British, Collins suggested that where incidents such as train ambushes occurred, the districts in question might be designated a 'military area' and special punishments would be announced for any-body carrying arms 'without due authority' in such a district.[46] The Government's decision was that it would 'support the military authorities in whatever steps they consider necessary to restore order in districts where military operations have ceased but in which outbreaks of violence still continue'.[47] This was not, however, interpreted as blanket approval for whatever the National Army might choose to do in the future. Both the Government and the Army seem to have seen it as an indication that whatever suggestions the Army put forward would meet with approval. For instance, the Government still found it advisable to write specifically to the Commander-in-Chief on the questions of use of force and of the deployment of plain-clothes troops in covert operations in Dublin,[48] and the Commander-in-Chief to submit an outline in advance of his plans for vehicle stops and searches in the capital.[49] And where subordinates acted on their own initiative without the Commander-in-Chief's having obtained prior sanction from the Government, friction ensued within the Army. Attempts by the local Army authorities to restrict opening times of public houses caused trouble,[50] and when General O'Duffy issued a

[44] For a general discussion of the nuts and bolts of the creation of the National Army see D. Long, 'The Army of the Irish Free State, 1922–24' (MA thesis, UCD, 1983).

[45] The position with regard to arrest and detention powers is discussed on pp. 179–80. On 21 July 1922 the Government decided that 'captured Irregulars on Hunger Strike should not be released and that no exception should be made to this rule'. Minutes of Meeting of Provisional Government, 21 July 1922.

[46] C-in-C to Government, 25 July 1922, Mulcahy papers, P7/B/29. A copy of the letter can also be found at S1 376, SPO.

[47] Minutes of Meeting of Provisional Government, 25 July 1922. The Government then wrote to Collins in these terms. Acting Chairman [Provisional Government] to C-in-C, 25 July 1922, S1 376, SPO.

[48] Ibid. 27 July 1922, S1 376, SPO. In relation to use of force, the C-in-C was informed that 'It is considered, therefore, that a Proclamation should be issued warning all concerned that the troops have orders to shoot persons found sniping, ambushing or in the possession of bombs, or interfering with Railway or Road communication, in areas in which military operations have ceased.' Earlier, the Provisional Government had decided that 'officers in charge of military parties should be given full discretionary powers to deal with persons found carrying or throwing bombs'. Minutes of Meeting of Provisional Government, 7 July 1922.

[49] C-in-C to Government, 25 July 1922, Mulcahy papers, P7/B/29. The public notice eventually issued in relation to vehicle stops and searches was gazetted in *DG* 28 July 1922.

[50] A copy of one such order issued on 27 July 1922 and affecting the area of the 2nd Eastern Division is at S1 376, SPO.

proclamation in Limerick threatening to try offenders by military court,[51] the Commander-in-Chief protested that the General had no power whatever to try offenders thus and that 'such action will not be taken without express direction of government'.[52]

If the leadership of the National Army was eager to emphasize ultimate civil supremacy in the larger legal or quasi-legal issues, this was not true of its approach to operational decisions. As Government complaints over lack of reports indicated, the military saw no pressing need to involve, or even to inform, the Provisional Government at this level.[53] And despite the overall successes of the National Army, and moves in August towards formalizing clear procedures in such areas as arrest and detention,[54] there were operational difficulties. The Army proved unable to comply with some aspects of the General Orders on military operations, which had been intended to put the Army on a more regular footing,[55] and early attempts at joint police–military operations foundered over police objections that they were being 'used simply as Black and Tans'.[56] In this, it seems that what was being referred to was the division of responsibilities rather than the attitude to the civilian population generally. Significantly, the National Army displayed an awareness of the need to avoid the British mistake of alienating this body of opinion. Collins, for instance, specifically ordered that 'anything that would be construed by the people as militarism must be kept out of the action of our troops'.[57]

End of August 1922 to November 1922: the response to guerrilla warfare

Despite these difficulties, the National Army's military position improved as August progressed. In many areas, however, the IRA had been displaced rather than destroyed, and the overall result was not surrender but reorganization. The tactics that had proved so successful against the British were now employed against the Provisional Government. On 19 August the IRA's Adjutant-General ordered the re-formation of ASUs, which were to operate both in the countryside and in the towns. The best men and adequate supplies of arms were to go to these units; others were

[51] The relevant portion is extracted in C-in-C to Government, 28 July 1922, Mulcahy papers, P7/B/29.

[52] C-in-C to CGS, 28 July 1922, Mulcahy papers P7/B/1.

[53] See e.g. Acting Chairman [Provisional Government] to C-in-C, 27 July 1922, complaining of the lack of reports. S1 376, SPO.

[54] Provisions in relation to detention and internment are discussed on pp. 266–7. Other areas covered included the internal distribution of pro forma raid reports (including records of any evidence found) and barracks inspection reports. Mulcahy papers, P7/B/41.

[55] C-in-C to CGS, 5 Aug. 1922, Mulcahy papers, P7/B/1. This related to General Order No. 11 which governed the issuing of military search warrants.

[56] Note of Civic Guards at Wellington, attached to Commissioner Gárda Siochána to C-in-C, 24 July 1922, Mulcahy papers, P7/B/39.

[57] GROs issued by C-in-C, 14 Aug. 1922, Mulcahy papers, P7/B/41.

to be relegated to back-up roles. In areas in which significant Republican
support existed the pressure from the new units soon began to be felt,
with ambushes a commonplace occurrence. In areas such as the midlands, though, activity was more limited. Overall, a military stalemate
developed which lasted for much for the remainder of the year. The
National Army could control the towns but could not eradicate the IRA
from the countryside; the IRA could not defeat the National Army,
though it could quite visibly prevent the pro-Treaty side from achieving a
total victory.

The most striking example of the effectiveness of the new tactics came
on 22 August, when Collins died, in disputed circumstances, in an ambush
in County Cork. General Mulcahy now became Commander-in-Chief,
and Cosgrave was elevated from Acting Chairman to Chairman of the
Provisional Government. The ambush seems to have marked a turning
point in attitudes to the conduct of the conflict. A British Army intelligence summary for the week ending 2 September 1922 reported that
'several leading Republicans have been murdered under very revolting
circumstances, probably as a reprisal for Collins although the P.G. [Pro-
visional Government] endeavour to put the blame on the Republicans
themselves',[58] and subsequent reports contained fresh allegations.[59] Some
of these reports came into Republican hands, and their publication induced a crisis in relations between the Provisional Government and
London. The British claimed, unconvincingly, that the summaries were
merely reporting allegations which were not stated to be true. In any
case, this was only part of the problem. Provisional Government dis-
comfiture seems to have owed as much to the fact that the reports were
signed by 'C. M. Boyd, Major General, Commanding Dublin District' as
to the substance of the allegations. The latter rank was taken to amount
to an insensitive claim to operational jurisdiction. The British responded
that it was solely of administrative importance, and applied only to the
5,000 to 5,500 troops, who remained in barracks in Dublin on what
Macready was to refer to as a 'watching brief'.[60]

Allegations also surfaced from other sources, and in some instances it
appears that a special Army unit ('the squad'), was involved, and that a
degree of approval from the highest ranks of the Army was forthcoming.[61]

---

[58] Dublin District Weekly Intelligence Summary No. 176, for w/e 2 Sept. 1922, SI 784,
SPO.
[59] Intelligence summaries for w/e 26 Aug., 2 Sept., 9 Sept., 16 Sept., 7 Oct. 1922.
[60] *Annals*, 660.
[61] In one case, the shooting of a prisoner in West Cork led to a near mutiny, and when
reporting the matter to the C-in-C, the GOC Maj.-Gen. Dalton, stated: 'This shooting was
the work of the Squad. Now I personally approve of the action but the men I have in my
Command are of such a temperament that they can look at seven of their companions being
blown to atoms by a murderous trick without feeling annoyed—but an enemy is found with

Initially, though, even Republicans found this difficult to believe.[62] And as the number of incidents grew, there was renewed concern about inquests.[63] The total number killed in these assassinations and unofficial executions, many of which were carried out as reprisals, is difficult to gauge. One source puts the figure for the whole conflict at about 150.[64]

Apart from certain Army units, the other force implicated in these killings was the Criminal Investigation Department (CID).[65] This was not, as its name might suggest, a regular police unit, but rather began life as a semi-military force composed largely of pro-Treaty ex-IRA men, and only came under the control of the Ministry of Home Affairs towards the end of August 1922.[66] The CID was based in Oriel House in Dublin, and its interrogation practices there soon earned it a fearsome reputation.[67] There were also a number of more shadowy organizations. In November 1922 a new force, the Protective Corps, was formed, with Government approval, as an 'auxiliary' to the CID.[68] Initially, it consisted of twenty ex-soldiers of the National Army who had also seen pre-truce service with the IRA. Later it expanded to a maximum complement of 175. Yet another force to be established by the Provisional Government in November 1922 was the Citizens' Defence Force.[69] This was composed mainly of ex-British soldiers, and was organized 'on military lines on a semi-secret basis'.[70]

The development of more conventional forces was also progressing. By

a rifle and amm. they will mutiny if he be shot. On this account I think it would be better if you kept the "squad" out of my area.' The C-in-C's reply expressed no dissatisfaction, merely informing Dalton that 'you are at perfect liberty to return here any Officer you think well of so returning'. O'Conlain to Dalton, 18 Sept. 1922; Dalton to C-in-C 19 Sept. 1922; C-in-C to Dalton, 21 Sept. 1922, Mulcahy papers, P7/B/82.

[62] In Oct., David Robinson of HQ 1st Southern Division IRA wrote to 'GD' of the National Army complaining about the killing of a prisoner in Kerry: 'Could you ask a question about it. I cannot believe that Mulcahy would tolerate it for a moment, but I wonder would he take enough trouble to find out the real truth.' Robinson to GD, 10 Oct. 1922, Mulcahy papers, P7/B/86.

[63] GRO 1, 1 Nov. 1922, reads: 'Cases have occurred in which, owing to the ordinary operation report not having been rendered at once, or in fact not having been rendered at all, verdicts have been returned at inquests arising out of such operations which have reflected upon the army as a whole as well as upon individual Officers and men.' In future, the appropriate reports were to be forwarded 'without the slightest delay'. Mulcahy papers, P7/B/167.

[64] Fanning writes that about twice as many were killed in unofficial reprisals as in official executions, and puts the number of offical executions at 77. *Independent Ireland*, 21. On the numbers officially executed, however, see App. 2.

[65] The British Army intelligence reports referred to above for w/e 9 and 16 Sept. 1922 specifically suggest CID responsibility. S1 784, SPO.

[66] Minutes of Meeting of Provisional Government, 24 Aug. 1922.

[67] See pp. 183–8.

[68] O'Muireadhaigh to McGrath, 12 Oct. 1923, S3 331, SPO.

[69] Minutes of Meeting of Provisional Government, 24 Nov. 1922.

[70] O'Muireadhaigh to McGrath, 12 Oct. 1923, S3 331, SPO.

November, the strength of the National Army stood at 30,000 men, and this increased to 50,000 by the end of the War. The Civic Guard had been reconstituted in September, largely as an unarmed force, and at that time numbered approximately 1,500. Initial moves were made towards dispersing the force throughout the country, but the continuing violence ensured that the policy was not pressed very far. Where deployed, the civil nature of the force was to be preserved. Army encroachments in this sphere led the Provisional Government to insist in November that 'the Civic Guard is, and must remain a purely Civil force, taking orders only from its own officer, and having no connection with the Army'.[71]

At regular intervals during July and August 1922 the assembly of the new Parliament had been postponed, but eventually on 9 September it met as the 'third Dáil'. From that day, announced Cosgrave, the dual system of government ended.[72] Republican Teachta Dála (members of parliament) abstained, and refused to recognize the assembly. The extent of the legislative competence of the Dáil was a matter for debate; the formula eventually adopted was that it was to act solely as a constituent assembly for the adoption of the new Constitution.[73] To this end, the Constitution Bill was introduced on 18 September and received final approval on 25 October. During the course of the debates the draft Constitution was revised in a number of spheres. Most importantly from the point of view of emergency law, provisions touching upon martial law were altered so as to take account of the reality of the continuing conflict.[74]

The other major business occupying that session of the Dáil arose out of the National Army's insistence that it be granted new powers to combat the IRA. The Provisional Government had been wary of sanctioning powers such as the British Army had employed in the MLA without the sanction of Parliament,[75] yet the question of how this sanction might be granted was far from unproblematic in law.[76] On 15 September Mulcahy had outlined to the Government the powers sought by the Army, and the law officer was instructed to draw up the necessary measure.[77] On 27 September the Army Emergency Powers Resolution

[71] Minutes of Meeting of Provisional Government, 13 Nov. 1922. Some National Army officers had been instructing Civic Guard officers to submit reports to them.
[72] For a discussion see Kohn, *Constitution*, 70.
[73] The issue of the legislative competence of the third Dáil is considered on pp. 243–7.
[74] These alterations are discussed on pp. 253–6.
[75] e.g. when on 6 and 7 Sept. 1922 the question of the proclamation of martial law in Cork was discussed by the Provisional Government, it was decided that the matter should be dealt with by the Chairman in Parliament. Minutes of Meeting of Provisional Government, 6 and 7 Sept. 1922.
[76] The issue is discussed on pp. 246–7.
[77] Minutes of Meeting of Provisional Government, 15 Sept. 1922.

was introduced in the Dáil, and following minor amendments, it was adopted the following day. As its title makes clear, this was not intended as an Act of Parliament. Rather, it consisted of a number of recitals followed by a ratification clause.[78] Among the matters sanctioned were the establishment of military courts or committees with powers to impose the death sentence on non-Army personnel,[79] indefinite detention without trial,[80] and control of the dealing in firearms by the Army Council of the National Army.[81] In addition to the special offences specified in the Resolution as being triable by military court or committee, the Army Council was authorized to create new orders or regulations thus triable,[82] provided that any such order or regulation was to be laid before the Dáil.[83]

Before bringing the Resolution into force, the Provisional Government decided first to offer an amnesty.[84] Two proclamations were issued: one, by the Government, offered a 'full amnesty and pardon' until 15 October;[85] another, by the Army Council, announced that the new powers would be exercised from that date.[86] At around the same time the remaining jurisdiction of the Dáil courts was abolished.[87] Earlier, powers similar to those under ROIA had been assumed to allow sittings of the quarter sessions and the civil bill courts to be held outside their normal areas.[88] When the first executions under the Army Emergency Powers Resolution took place on 17 November 1922, their announcement led to a storm of protest, not least because no prior warning had been forthcoming. Then on 24 November came the execution of Erskine Childers after a failed challenge to the military court system in the civil courts.[89]

The IRA response to the killings came when its Chief of Staff (Lynch) wrote to the speaker of the pro-Treaty Dáil on 27 November threatening

[78] Para. 4. The relevant text can be found on p. 247.
[79] Para. 3. These military courts and committees are examined in detail later in this chapter.
[80] Para. 3 (c). These powers are considered later.
[81] Para. 3 (d).
[82] Paras. 3 (b) and 4.
[83] Such order or regulation was to take effect four days thereafter, unless the Dáil had, in the mean time, passed a resolution disallowing it.
[84] Minutes of Meetings of Provisional Government 12.45 p.m. and 9.30 p.m., 3 Oct. 1922.
[85] SR & O, 1922–38, i. 93–5.
[86] Ibid. xix. 533–7.
[87] Notice of 26 Oct. 1922, *Iris Oifigiúil*, 27 Oct. 1922. The notice was stated to be by the 'Aire um Ghnóthaí Dúithe [Minister for Home Affairs], with the concurrence of the Cabinet of Dáil Eireann'. The significance of this is that the step was not taken formally by the Provisional Government but by the Dáil Government.
[88] Provisional Government (Courts—Emergency Provisions) Decree No. 9, 21 Sept. 1922, *Iris Oifigiúil*, 3 Oct. 1922.
[89] *R (Childers)* v. *Adjutant-General* [1923] 1 *IR* 5. This, and the other relevant case, *R (Johnstone)* v. *O'Sullivan* [1923] 2 *IR* 13, are analysed on pp. 247–52.

'very drastic measures to protect our forces'.[90] Three days later, an order was issued to IRA battalion OCs authorizing the shooting on sight of TDs who had voted for the Resolution, and of thirteen other categories of persons. Earlier, in a move designed to add legitimacy to the campaign, Republican TDs had met, claiming that their assembly constituted the only legitimate Dáil. On 26 October a Council of State was appointed, with IRA approval, and de Valera became President of the Republic and Chief Executive of the state. A Cabinet was appointed, the rival pro-Treaty Dáil was 'proclaimed', and the Treaty rescinded. But despite these manœuvrings, there was no real attempt to establish an effective alternative administration, as there had been in 1919–21. Nevertheless, the move did indicate a determination to continue on the part of the Republicans, and this, together with the Army Emergency Powers Resolution and the IRA 'shoot-on-sight' order, meant that the most bitter phase of the conflict was yet to come.

December 1922 to July 1923: terror

On 6 December 1922 the Constitution of the Irish Free State came into force. In Irish constitutional law, the enactment by the third Dáil, sitting as a constituent assembly, of the Constitution of the Irish Free State (Saorstát Eireann) Act 1922 provided the Constitution's 'one and all-sufficient root of title'.[91] In British law, however, it derived its validity from the Irish Free State Constitution Act 1922, to which the Irish Act was scheduled.[92] What is not disputed is that the Constitution was, in both Irish and British law, formally subordinated to the Treaty.[93]

The main provisions of the Constitution can be outlined as follows: the Irish Free State was to be a 'coequal member of the Community of Nations forming the British Commonwealth of Nations'.[94] Its legislature (Oireachtas) was to consist of the King, the Dáil, and a Senate, and in it was vested the 'sole and exclusive power of making laws for the peace order and good government' of the state.[95] Formal executive authority was vested in the King and was to be exercisable by the representative of the Crown in accordance with the law, practice, and constitutional usage governing the exercise of the executive authority in the case of the dominion of Canada.[96] An Executive Council (in effect the Government), consisting of members of the Dáil, was to advise on the exercise of this authority. The President of the Executive Council was to be nominated

---

[90] Quoted in Neeson, *Civil War*, 277.
[91] Per Meredith J., in *Cahill* v. *AG* [1925] *IR* 70, at 76.
[92] For discussions of the derivation of the validity of the Constitution see Kelly, *Fundamental Rights*, 6–7, and Kohn, *Constitution*, 90–2.
[93] See p. 253.
[94] Art. 1.   [95] Art. 12.   [96] Art. 51.

by the Dáil, and he in turn nominated the other members of the Council.[97] Judges were to be appointed by the representative of the Crown on the advice of the Executive Council.[98] All judges were to be independent in the exercise of their functions,[99] and the 'judicial power' of the High Court was to extend to the question of the validity of any law having regard to the provisions of the Constitution.[100] Under the Constitution there also existed an ambiguous right of appeal to the judicial committee of the Privy Council. The relevant article (66) incorporated what Kohn has described as 'a formal self-contradiction'.[101] Decisions of the Supreme Court were to be 'final and conclusive' and not 'capable of being reviewed by any other Court, Tribunal, or Authority whatsoever', but nothing in the Constitution was to 'impair the right of any person to petition His Majesty in Council or the right of His Majesty to grant such leave'.

Under article 12 of the Treaty, Northern Ireland was to be given one month (the 'Ulster month') from the passing of the Act of Parliament for the ratification of the instrument to opt out of the Free State, and until the expiration of that month, the powers of the Parliament and the government of the Irish Free State were not to be exercisable as respects Northern Ireland.[102] By agreement, the relevant date was made 6 December 1922,[103] and on the following day both Houses of the Northern Ireland Parliament made the required resolution, thus leaving the eventual border between the two parts of Ireland to be decided by a Boundary Commission.[104] Earlier, the British Irish Free State (Consequential Provisions) Act 1922 had provided for further amendments to the Government of Ireland Act 1920, consequent upon the establishment of the Irish Free State.

The Constitution did not prohibit the imposition of martial law, though it could be interpreted as having limited its applicability.[105] In practice, no additional constraints were applied, indeed developments were in quite the opposite direction. On 7 December 1922 the IRA took the first step in the implementation of its reprisal orders when its members assassinated one pro-Treaty TD and wounded another (the Deputy

---

[97] Arts. 51, 52, and 53.
[98] Art. 68.
[99] Art. 69.
[100] Art. 64.
[101] *Constitution*, 355. For a discussion of the results of this provision see ibid. 355–63.
[102] Art. 11 of the Treaty.
[103] Under s. 1 (5) of the Irish Free State (Agreement) Act 1922, that Act was not to be deemed to be the Act of Parliament for the ratification of the said Articles of Agreement as from the passing whereof the month mentioned in art. 11 of the Treaty was to run. Instead, the Irish Free State Constitution Act 1922 became the legislation from which the month was to run. See Kohn, *Constitution*, 61–5.
[104] The workings of the Boundary Commission are considered in Ch. 4.
[105] See pp. 253–6.

Speaker). The response was swift. Following approval by the Executive Council, four leading Republicans who had been captured in the Four Courts garrison (and therefore well before the adoption of the Army Emergency Powers Resolution) were executed without trial in what was officially stated to be a reprisal.[106] In the Dáil, Cosgrave sought to justify the action by explaining that it was 'really a psychological question'.[107] A conspiracy was afoot and the only way to deal with it was to show those involved 'that terror will be struck into them'.[108]

The killings were clearly outside the terms of the Resolution, but later that month a way was found of introducing the threat of reprisal execution within the terms of the Resolutions when sentences of death imposed on four IRA prisoners tried by military court in Kerry were suspended with a threat that if there was a resurgence of IRA activity the executions would be carried out. In that month also, the National Army first established the new summary committees provided for in the Resolution, and as time progressed, the sentences of these tribunals also began to be carried out as reprisals.[109] There were other moves in this new tougher policy, for instance the town of Sligo was placed under a curfew,[110] but a suggestion by the Minister for Home Affairs that 'middle class Irregular families' be put out of their homes did not meet with military approval.[111] Then in January a new General Order of the Army Council greatly expanded the jurisdiction of the military courts and committee in a way which was designed to bring IRA back-up personnel and supporters within the net of those triable.[112] In the words of Mulcahy, it was a 'Stand-Clear Order'.[113] Waverers in the National Army were also being sent a clear message. In January and February a number of soldiers who had been

---

[106] The document which was apparently handed to each of the four read: 'You —— are hereby notified that being a person taken in Arms against the Government, you will be executed at 8 a.m. on Friday 8th December as a reprisal for the assassination of Brigadier Sean Hales, TD in Dublin, on the 7th December, on his way to a meeting of *Dáil Eireann* and as a solemn warning to those associated with you who are engaged in a conspiracy of assassination against the representatives of the Irish People. Mulcahy papers, P7/B/85.

[107] 2 *DD*, col. 94.

[108] 2 *DD*, col. 95.

[109] The question of reprisal executions following disposal of cases by military courts and committees is examined on pp. 219–23.

[110] Minutes of Meeting of the Executive Council, 15 Dec. 1922, SPO.

[111] C-in-C to O'Hegarty, 13 Dec. 1922, had the following handwritten suggestion on it: 'Put about 10 middle class families out of their homes and close a few business places establishing a post in each case.' The C-in-C's comment was: 'This is a suggestion of O'Higgins regarding the question of burnings. I am inclined not to agree with it at all—apart altogether from difficulties in providing men for such posts.' What appears to have been O'Hegarty's reply was: '. . . O'Higgins's suggestions are not likely to be practicable. Our people have more property for destruction than the Irregulars have.' Mulcahy papers, P7/B/101.

[112] The text of the order is reproduced in n. 251 below.

[113] 2 *DD*, col. 887.

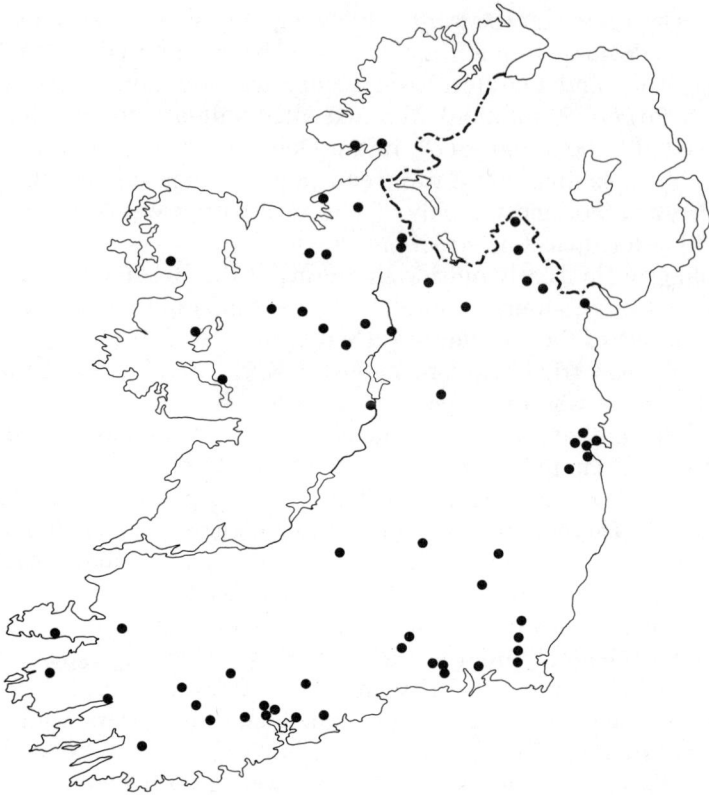

MAP E. Republican successes during four weeks of November and December 1922

Source: Derived from maps attached to National Army reports of incidents for the period: w/e 25 Nov. to w/e 16 Dec. 1922, Mulcahy papers, P7/B/123. The incidents shown are those indicated on the original maps as 'Irregular successes'.

captured after going over to the Republican side were executed following trial by court martial.[114]

The initial effect of the executions had been to stir the IRA into renewed activity. At the end of November and the start of December 1922, the pattern of IRA activity corresponded with that established at the start of the guerrilla phase. There were successes in the South, parts of the West, in the border counties, and around Dublin (Map E). In mid-December a Republican offensive led to the capture of a number of towns in Counties Kilkenny and Tipperary. But these successes were short-lived. The executions had a demoralizing effect, and the numerical superiority of the National Army forced the IRA to operate in ever

[114] Details are given in App. 2.

smaller numbers. But the key issue was that of popular support. Support for the Republicans was very much lower than it had been in the 1919–21 conflict and, correspondingly, the National Army enjoyed a degree of support that had never been available to the British Army or to the RIC. The National Army also knew the countryside well, and its officers were familiar with the tactics and the mentality of those against whom they were fighting, having been their comrades only a year previously. The pro-Treaty side could also count on good intelligence, the key to any successful counter-insurgency campaign.

Increasingly, arson, particularly of the houses of Government supporters, became the main IRA tactic. In more than one instance, uninvolved family members met their deaths in such attacks. Republican morale received a bad blow with the capture of Deacy, a Divisional Commander and Deputy Chief of Staff on 19 January 1923. He was rapidly tried, convicted, and sentenced to death, and escaped with his life only by agreeing to a call for an immediate surrender. Dissension in Republican ranks was rife, and a further amnesty period in February served to heighten divisions. In many areas Republican resistance began to crumble. The exception was Kerry where IRA columns continued to operate and where in March 1923 some of the worst incidents of the conflict occurred, many of them laid at the door of the National Army's 'Dublin Guards' brigade.

In December 1922 the National Army in Kerry had resorted to the practice of forcing IRA prisoners to clear road obstructions which it was feared might be mined. On 6 March 1923 five National Army troops were killed by a mine in the county. This led to the GOC's (Daly) reissuing orders about the use of prisoners for mine-clearing. On 7 March eight prisoners died in what was claimed to have been such an exercise. The following day four were killed, and on 12 March five prisoners died. One survived the incident of 7 March to claim that the prisoners had been tied together and the mine deliberately detonated by the National Army. There was similar disturbing evidence about the episode of 12 March. A military court of inquiry into the event cleared the Army personnel involved,[115] but the Gardaí (police) later reported that after being taken by the Army from the workhouse in which they were being held 'the five prisoners were subsequently shot and their bodies blown up by a mine'.[116] Although Mulcahy defended the Army in the Dáil, behind the scenes there were moves to tighten up the procedures for dealing with

---

[115] Extracts from the report of the court of enquiry can be found at S1 369/12, SPO.

[116] Extract from Gárda Report, quoted in report of E. O Frighil, attached to Secretary of Ministry of Home Affairs to Each Member of the Executive Council, 10 Jan. 1924, S1 369/12, SPO.

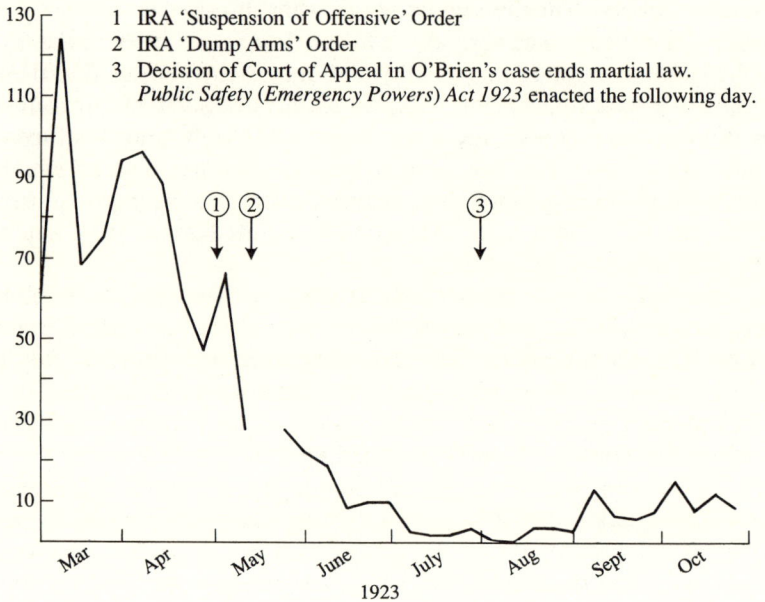

1 IRA 'Suspension of Offensive' Order
2 IRA 'Dump Arms' Order
3 Decision of Court of Appeal in O'Brien's case ends martial law.
   Public Safety (Emergency Powers) Act 1923 enacted the following day.

GRAPH C. Weekly incident totals, March 1923 to October 1923

Source: Prepared from Statistical Summaries of Official Reports for the period w/e 2 Feb. to w/e 26 Oct. 1923 (report for w/e 18 May 1923 not available), Mulcahy papers, P7/B/127. The total is obtained by adding the returns for the following categories: attacks on troops (including ambushes), attacks on posts, destruction of property (houses etc.), stations burnt, cabins burnt, bridges destroyed, lines taken up, wire destruction, minor acts of rail destruction, burnings (incendiarism), houses attacked, post offices attacked, civil guard barracks destroyed, house robberies, road robberies. From 6 Apr. 1923 onwards, the figures were recorded slightly differently on pre-printed forms, but the relevant totals have been adjusted accordingly.

prisoners.[117] The controversy served to heighten tensions which were becoming apparent within the Executive Council. On 27 March 1923 a Supreme War Council was established with considerable powers over the Army, and with a majority of civilian members. Mulcahy's response was to resign, but though he was persuaded to rescind his resignation, the work of the Council went ahead. One of its actions was the setting up of the Special Infantry Corps which was entrusted with the task of clearing illegally occupied land, and with support for the civil administration generally. Earlier, emergency civil law powers had been provided in the Enforcement of Law (Occasional Powers) Act 1923, which legislation was to have a life of six months.[118]

[117] These are discussed on pp. 183–4.
[118] s. 16 (2). Among the matters covered was the holding of courts of quarter sessions and civil bill courts outside their normal areas (s. 13). Retrospective validation was given to such removals from 6 Dec. 1922 (s. 13 (1)).

On the Republican side, there were plans to widen the conflict by carrying out attacks in England, but these were scrapped when during March approximately 100 suspects were rounded up in Britain. Orders were made in that jurisdiction (illegally as it subsequently transpired) for their internment in the Free State under ROIA.[119] On their arrival in Ireland, they were interned under martial law powers. Overall IRA decline was becoming increasingly apparent from mid-March (Graph C), and the killing, on the 10th of the following month, of the Republican Chief of Staff underlined the futility of continuing the campaign. On 30 April, the new Chief of Staff (Aiken) issued a Suspension of Offensive order, and once this was circulated, IRA actions plummeted. Pressure from the National Army continued—there were two more executions on 2 May—but on 24 May orders for a cease-fire and the dumping of arms were published, and it is this date that is generally taken as marking the end of the Civil War.

The end of the conflict proper led to a sharp decline in the number of incidents rather than to an immediate return to normal conditions (Graph C). Nor did it result in the immediate ending of martial law, as June 1923 saw a number of unsuccessful judicial challenges to its continuing imposition.[120] That martial law would soon end, though, was apparent to all, and with a view to this occurring, the task of preparing emergency legislation was proceeded with. The matter had first been addressed in mid-April,[121] and by the end of May the Executive Council had decided on the general lines of the measure, including that provision would be made for internment without trial.[122] At the start of June a draft skeleton bill was approved,[123] so that when on 31 July 1923 the Court of Appeal ruled that the state of war or armed rebellion had come to an end, and that martial law powers could no longer be made use of,[124] it seemed that keeping the internees in the camps by rushing through fresh legislation would pose few problems.

August 1923 to April 1925: the Public Safety Acts

On 1 August 1923 the new measure, the Public Safety (Emergency Powers) Act 1923, received the Royal assent, but a ruling by the Court of Appeal held that its mode of enactment was defective.[125] The result was that the Public Safety (Emergency Powers) (No. 2) Act 1923 was rushed through. The new Act contained a declaration the absence of which had

---

[119] A successful challenge to the orders was mounted in England in *R* v. *Home Secretary, ex parte O'Brien* [1923] 2 *KB* 361. The ruling prompted the enactment in Britain of the Restoration of Order in Ireland (Indemnity) Act 1923 (7 June 1923).

[120] See *ILT & SJ*, 23 June 1923, 152–3 for a brief account of some such cases.

[121] Minutes of Meeting of Executive Council, 16 Apr. 1923.

[122] Ibid. 28 May 1923. There had been some doubts about the constitutionality of internment powers (see p. 262).

[123] Minutes of Meeting of the Executive Council, 2 June 1923.

[124] See pp. 256–9.   [125] See pp. 259–61.

led to the impeachment of the first Act,[126] and became law on 3 August. Its form was to incorporate the earlier Act *in toto* as a schedule.[127] In its substantive provisions, it granted special powers of arrest, detention, and internment without trial, and permitted the venue of jury trials to be changed.[128] The death penalty was permitted for a number of special offences,[129] and flogging was prescribed for certain others.[130] Powers were given to allow the seizure of animals found trespassing,[131] to place restrictions on the possession and sale of firearms,[132] and District Justices were granted a special jurisdiction in respect of property suspected of having been stolen,[133] including money lodged in banks.[134] There was also a saving clause, designed to ensure that the measure would not place a brake on possible resort to non-statutory martial law powers in the future.[135]

The Act was to have a life of six months,[136] and its provisions were clearly not intended as mere paper powers. Arrests continued, and although some internees were released, fresh internments were still being made. The ending of martial law meant that not only the *powers* which had been resorted to were open to legal challenge, it also meant that the *institutions* which had been entrusted with the execution of these powers were now subject to legal scrutiny. The result was a rash of legislation designed to regularize the bodies which had been created *ad hoc* during the fighting. The National Army was legislated for,[137] and so was the Garda Siochána (Civic Guard).[138] An Indemnity Act was passed to cover the activities of the pro-Treaty forces during the Civil War[139] (a previous Act had covered the earlier activities of the Crown Forces[140]), and the

---

[126] s. 2 (1).

[127] Reference to sections of the Act below are to be taken to refer to sections in the schedule to the Act. For a discussion of the Public Safety Acts in general see J. Hanna, *The Statute Law of the Irish Free State* (Dublin, 1929), 37–44, and D. O'Sullivan, *The Irish Free State and its Senate* (London, 1940), 126–33.

[128] These are discussed in part II.   [129] s. 5 (1), schedule, pt. 1.

[130] s. 5 (4).   [131] s. 6.   [132] s. 8.   [133] ss. 9 and 10.   [134] s. 11.

[135] s. 15 provided: 'Nothing in this Act shall be deemed to revoke, annul, derogate from or prejudice the exercise by the Military Forces of Saorstát Eireann of any of the powers or authorities exercisable by them by virtue of military necessity arising in the course of the performance of their duty to suppress rebellion or vested in them by virtue of their having been entrusted by the Executive Government with the duty of securing the public safety and restoring order throughout the country.'

[136] s. 17 (2).

[137] Defence Forces (Temporary Provisions) Act 1923 (3 Aug. 1923).

[138] Gárda Siochána (Temporary Provisions) Act 1923 (8 Aug. 1923). Earlier, the acquisition of premises had been provided for in the Civic Guard (Acquisition of Premises) Act 1923 (6 July 1923).

[139] Indemnity Act 1923 (3 Aug. 1923).

[140] Indemnity (British Military) Act 1923 (10 Feb. 1923).

Dáil courts were formally wound up.[141] Later came an Act of Indemnity designed to cover the activities of local authorities during the struggle against the British,[142] and later still came legislation covering the activities of the Irish Volunteers during the same period.[143]

Military defeat of the IRA did not result in the political annihilation of the Republicans, a fact made clear by Sinn Féin's surprisingly good showing in the August 1923 general election.[144] For a time, the form, though not the substance, of an alternative administration was persevered with, as Republican TDs refused to take their seats in the Dáil created by the 1922 Constitution. Nor was there an end to violence that related to the political conflict, or at least arose out of the unsettled conditions. The number of 'incidents' began to rise again in August, and the trend continued in September and October (Graph C). This, however, did not signal the start of any coherent campaign. Rather, as the high incidence of robberies indicated, many of these offences had little political motivation,[145] and responsibility for a significant amount could probably be attributed to demobilized members of the National Army. A new edge was given to the political conflict, though, by the mass hunger strike of Republican prisoners which began in October 1923. No concessions were forthcoming, and the protest came to a demoralized end with the deaths of two prisoners the following month.

In the country at large, the involvement of the National Army in internal security duties continued, though at a Cabinet conference on the maintenance of order in September 1923, it had been stressed that in situations of riot or 'organised violence beyond the powers of unarmed police' the military would act only when requested to do so by the civil authorities.[146] This was at the time of the disbandment of the Special Infantry Corps, and therefore at a time when the Army was itself re-assessing its role. Henceforth ordinary Army units would be assigned to what the Army chose to term 'protection duty'.[147] Under the Army's

---

[141] Dáil Eireann Courts (Winding-Up) Act 1923) (8 Aug. 1923). This was subsequently amended by the Dáil Eireann Courts (Winding-Up) Act 1923. Amendment Act 1924.

[142] Local Authorities (Indemnity) Act 1923 (28 Dec. 1923).

[143] Indemnity Act 1924 (1 Aug. 1924).

[144] The pro-Treaty party, now called Cummann na nGaedhael, won 63, the Republicans (Sinn Féin) 44, and others 46. Eighteen of the Sinn Féin TDs were either imprisoned or interned.

[145] The returns for serious crimes reported to the DMP from 1 July to 31 Dec. 1923 were as follows: murders, 10; raids, hold-ups, robbery, larceny with use of arms, 137; aggravated assaults, 79; interference with police in the execution of their duty, 17. The corresponding figures for the Gárda Siochána were as follows: murder and manslaughter, 30; attempted murder, 29; firing into houses, 36; robbery with arms, 260; armed raids, 119. S3 527, SPO.

[146] Conference re Maintenance of Order, Proposals to be discussed, S3 306, SPO.

[147] 'General Staff Memorandum No. 14, Employment of Troops to Aid Civil Authorities', CWS, Prisoners' Files, P/6.

system, troops were to be detailed for such duty on the requisition of the Civic Guard only. An Army officer in charge of a post or a unit was then to supply such troops as he saw fit. In general, these were to be under the command of an Army officer, but where one was not available a 'competent NCO' was to be placed in charge.

The general situation was reviewed in detail at a meeting of the Executive Council held at the end of November, at which the respective roles of the police and the military were redefined. It was decided that the state could, at that time, be broken up into three classes of area ('(a), (b), & (c)'), and that in general 'the Military and Civic Guard should co-operate in rounding up and arresting armed criminals'.[148] As regards the regional breakdown, class (a) consisted of thirteen counties in which conditions could be said to be normal. Class (b) consisted of six counties in which the Civic Guard could accept responsibility for the maintenance of order 'provided they had the moral support of military garrisons stationed at the larger centres'.[149] In these areas the military were to be in readiness to assist the police when called upon for the suppression of aggravated disorder and for the protection of those engaged in the recovery of debt. Class (c) consisted of seven counties or portions of counties, where 'owing to the presence of bands of armed men, the civic guard could not take responsibility for the prevention of crime'.[150] Here, the military was to take the initiative and to 'operate intensively until order had been restored'.[151] Details of co-operation between the two forces were to be settled at an Army–police conference, and lists of ex-Army men 'demobilised with bad character' were to be supplied to the police to facilitate surveillance.

But the National Army and the regular police were not the only elements of the security forces to have been active since the end of the fighting—the CID and the other undercover forces had also continued to function. And it appears that the range of their activities was not limited simply to arrests and to preventive patrol work. When, two months after the end of the fighting, the body of a prominent Republican was found in the Dublin mountains, responsibility for his disappearance and killing was widely attributed to the CID.[152] In October the Executive Council decided on a scheme for the winding up of these organizations, which involved integrating some members in the regular police.[153] But the

---

[148] Minutes of Meeting of Executive Council, 30 Nov. 1923.
[149] Ibid.
[150] Ibid. The areas were Cork, Leitrim South, Galway south of the MGWR line, Clare, Tipperary, Offaly, and Roscommon.
[151] Ibid.
[152] See E. O'Malley, *The Singing Flame* (Dublin, 1978), 249–50.
[153] Minutes of Meeting of Executive Council, 16 Nov. 1923.

scrapping of these units did not mean the abandonment of undercover activities. Indeed, following their disbandment, ex-members of the Protective Corps themselves became subject to the unappreciative surveillance of the National Army's Intelligence Department.[154]

The new year saw little change in the overall situation, and the lapse of the Public Safety Act in January 1924 did not result in the abandonment of reliance on emergency legislation. Instead, that month saw the enactment of the Public Safety (Powers of Arrest and Detention) Temporary Act 1924, which was to last for one year.[155] The measure was considerably narrower than its predecessor, as it was concerned solely with powers of arrest, detention, and internment.[156] But despite the retention of internment powers, mass releases meant that the number of internees greatly declined in the winter of 1923/4, and by the summer all had been released.

The attention of the Executive Council had remained focused on the threat from the IRA,[157] but in March 1924 a challenge emerged from a new source. A significant section of the officer corps of the National Army had supported the Treaty on the basis that it offered what Collins had referred to as 'the freedom to win freedom'. By 1924 it was becoming apparent that this 'stepping stone' policy was no longer being pursued by the Government. Indeed the trend seemed to be quite in the opposite direction. As peacetime demobilization in the National Army continued, pro-Treaty IRA veterans of the struggle against the British were being removed, and ex-British Army officers were being retained. These veterans formed a secret organization within the Army, styling itself the 'Old IRA'. This was in opposition to the revived 'New IRB' which operated as a focus for pro-Treaty sentiment, and in which it appears that Mulcahy was involved.

On 6 March 1924 the President received an ultimatum from this Old IRA group demanding that demobilization be suspended and reiterating the claim that the Treaty had been accepted only as a step towards the Republic. A Government minister who supported the demands resigned,

---

[154] Report, Activities of Ex-Member of Protective Corps, 29 Nov. 1923, Office of Director of Intelligence. The Department's comment was that 'as there are a number of ne'er-do-wells in this crowd who would only be prevented from carrying out hold-ups on their own behalf by the fact that it is not a very healthy occupation at present, in fact the only interest the Minister for Home Affairs should take in the matter is to put the Detective division after them'. Mulcahy papers, P7/B/140. For an equally critical assessment of the CID by the Ministry of Home Affairs see p. 185.

[155] s. 10 (2).

[156] These are examined in detail on pp. 186–91, 232–8.

[157] In Feb. 1924 the Minister for Home Affairs requested that 1,000 armed police be dispatched to cope with trouble in the areas of Leitrim, Sligo, Mayo, Kerry, Cork (East and West), Tipperary, and Clare. Consideration of the proposal was postponed for two months and ultimately the matter seems to have been dropped. Minutes of Meeting of Executive Council, 26 Feb. 1924.

and some Army officers, absconded with their arms. The signatories of the ultimatum were arrested, but the Government's overall strategy was to deal with the matter by diplomacy rather than by confrontation. Then on 16 March the Army mounted an unauthorized raid on a Dublin bar, and following a fire-fight, ten of the 'mutineers' were arrested. A Government-sponsored purge was soon under way. The Chief of Staff, the Adjutant-General, and the Quartermaster-General were dismissed, and Mulcahy, the Minister for Defence, resigned.[158]

In what seems to have been a related incident, an IRA team dressed in National Army uniforms mounted a fatal machine gun attack on a party of British soldiers in County Cork on 21 March. The attackers were never caught, but the attempt, if such it were, to forge links between Republicans and National Army dissidents failed. An Army inquiry committee was established to examine the administration of the Army, and thereafter the National Army's political role faded away. Like the police forces, it became one of the institutions of state to be legislated for in the usual way.[159] At this time generally, the final form of many of these institutions was being shaped, perhaps the most important example of this process being the Courts of Justice Act 1924 that set the pattern of the new state's court system for nearly four decades.[160] The following year the final form of the new state's police force emerged, when the DMP and the Garda Siochána were merged under the Police Forces Amalgamation Act 1925.

In April 1924 yet more emergency legislation had been enacted in the form of the Public Safety (Punishment of Offences) Temporary Act 1924. In essence, those powers which had been incorporated in the 1923 Public Safety Act but dropped from the Public Safety (Powers of Arrest and

---

[158] Historians have reason to be thankful for the incident. When Mulcahy left, he removed from the Army masses of documents relating to matters in which he had been involved. These documents, which stretched back several years, were to provide the bulk of the Mulcahy papers in the UCD Archives. Had he not removed the papers at that time, it is reasonable to assume that many of these documents, some of which were quite sensitive, would have been destroyed in the great burning of Civil War material which occurred just before Cummann na nGaedhael lost power in 1932.

[159] Defence Forces (Temporary Provisions) Act 1923 (Continuation and Amendment) Act 1924 (1 Aug. 1924). The police forces were legislated for in the Gárda Siochána Act 1924 (17 July 1924), and in the Dublin Police Act 1924 (28 July 1924).

[160] At the base of the system created by Courts of Justice Act 1924 was the jury-less District Court with limited criminal and civil jurisdiction, presided over by a District Justice. Grand juries were abolished. Appeals lay from the District Court to the Circuit Court of Justice, which could, by judge and jury, try all felonies and misdemeanours other than murder, treason, or piracy. Those accused of the most serious crimes were to be tried by the Central Criminal Court which consisted of a judge or judges of the High Court and which sat with a jury. Appeals lay to the Court of Criminal Appeal. The High Court had six judges and had all the jurisdiction of the old High Court of Justice in Southern Ireland transferred to it, together with the jurisdiction created by the Constitution. The Supreme Court was composed of three judges, one of whom was the Chief Justice. See, generally, Delaney, *Administration of Justice*, 35–45.

Detention) Temporary Act 1924 were re-enacted for one year. Thus District Justices were given a renewed special jurisdiction in relation to property suspected of having been stolen,[161] flogging was prescribed for certain offences,[162] provision was made for the change of venue of jury trials,[163] and powers were given to order the seizure of animals found trespassing.[164] The main change from the earlier provisions was that the death penalty was no longer specially permitted; instead the maximum penalty permitted under the Act was that of penal servitude for life.[165] Special temporary powers in relation to the enforcement of civil remedies were also provided in the Enforcement of Law (Occasional Powers) Act 1924, which was enacted in June.

April 1925 to December 1925: the pattern is set

The period from the end of April to 6 June 1925 was almost unique in the history of the Irish state. During these six weeks the Public Safety Acts had lapsed and not been replaced, thus there was no legislation on the statute books designed to cope with political violence. The enactment in June of the Treasonable Offences Act 1925 brought this interregnum to an end. Unlike the Public Safety Acts, the new legislation was concerned almost solely with the redefinition and creation of special offences. No provision was made for alteration of the mode of trial, and no broad powers of arrest, detention, or internment were included.[166] And unlike the Public Safety Acts, the Treasonable Offences Act 1925 had no defined lifespan, and was to be permanently in force.

The thrust of the Act was threefold: treason was given a wide statutory definition,[167] penalties were prescribed for any attempt at the creation of an alternative system of government and for 'certain offences against the state',[168] and the creation of secret societies in the police or the Army

---

[161] ss. 5 and 6.
[162] s. 1 (4).
[163] s. 8. These provisions are discussed on pp. 195–6.
[164] s. 2 (1).
[165] s. 1 (1).
[166] The Act did include one narrow arrest power, described on pp. 192–3. There were also special provisions in relation to search warrants (s. 10 (1)).
[167] The Act provided that 'Every person who commits in Saorstát Eireann any of the following acts, that is to say: (*a*) levies war against Saorstát Eireann, or (*b*) assists any state or person engaged in levying war against Saorstát Eireann, or (*c*) conspires with any person (other than his or her wife or husband) or incites any person to levy war against Saorstát Eireann, or (*d*) attempts or takes part or is concerned in an attempt to overthrow by force of arms or other violent means the Government of Saorstát Eireann as established by or under the Constitution, or (*e*) conspires with any person (other than his or her wife or husband) or incites any person to make or to take part or be concerned in any such attempt, shall be guilty of treason and shall be liable on conviction thereof to suffer death' (s. 1 (1)). Other relevant provisions are s. 1 (2) to (5) and s. 2 (misprision of treason).
[168] s. 3.

was outlawed.[169] The provisions in relation to the establishment of an alternative administration were clearly aimed at the Republicans' shadow Government. Activities prohibited included the usurpation of executive authority,[170] the formation of an assembly claiming to exercise the powers of the Oireachtas,[171] the formation of military or police forces not established by law,[172] and the holding of unauthorized military exercises.[173] In the following month permanent restrictions on the possession of firearms were imposed in the Firearms Act 1925. The pattern in relation to emergency law had been clearly set. Over the next decade there were a number of new pieces of emergency legislation, and from 1939 onwards there was no period during which such legislation would not be in force.

The pattern of irredentist Republicanism was also emerging. In November 1925 an IRA General Army Convention withdrew the allegiance of the organization from the political leadership of de Valera, and decided that it would be subject only to its Executive. Then later in the month came a big IRA gaol break. The final element of the picture slotted into place with the agreement between the British, Free State, and Northern Ireland Governments on the rejection of the Boundary Commission recommendations. Instead, the original partition settlement was to be consolidated, a move legislated for in December 1925 in the Treaty (Confirmation of Amending Agreement) Act 1925.[174]

PART II

SECTION (A) ARREST AND DETENTION

In operation terms, the main divisions during this period in the use of arrest, detention (and internment) powers were those between the first 'conventional' phase of the Civil War, the second 'guerilla phase', and the third 'emergency' period which followed the cessation of the fighting. During the first phase the issues were essentially strategic in that the criteria for taking and holding a prisoner were dictated by the requirements of the fighting, and were thus the same as in any other conventional conflict. During the second phase, arrest and detention powers became central elements in the counter-insurgency process and became keyed to other elements in that process, most notably to the military court and committee systems and the internment process. During the third phase, arrest powers no longer functioned as a feeder system for the military

---

[169] s. 8.   [170] s. 4.   [171] s. 5.   [172] s. 6.   [173] s. 7.
[174] See Ch. 4. Earlier provision was made for Northern Ireland's refusal to appoint its representative in the Treaty (Confirmation of Supplemental Agreement) Act 1924.

court process but for much of this phase, they remained tied to the internment mechanism.

In legal terms, the principal division was between extraordinary non-statutory powers and the later emergency legislation. The ordinary law in relation to arrest and detention in the Irish Free State remained, as it had been under British rule, based on the common law as supplemented by specific statutory provisions. The 1922 Constitution incorporated certain provisions in this area, which were broadly in line with British law as it then stood, but the safeguards introduced by these provisions were held inapplicable during the course of the actual fighting, and immediately thereafter.[175] Thus the position from the end of June 1922 until the end of July 1923 was that the special powers of arrest and detention relied upon were, in effect, martial law powers, although, as has been noted in part I, there had been no formal proclamation of martial law. Following the ending of martial law, temporary emergency statutory powers of arrest and detention were incorporated in the Public Safety (Emergency Powers) (No. 2) Act 1923 and the Public Safety (Powers of Arrest and Detention) Temporary Act 1924, but before examining these enactments in detail, the use of martial law powers must be discussed.

Arrest and detention from June 1922 to July 1923

The decision to arrest

During the first phase of the Civil War, issues relating to the arrest of Republican combatants seemed relatively clear in that the conditions approximated to conventional warfare.[176] The question of arrest of non-combatant Republican activists, particularly the Republican political leadership, proved a more problematic one for the National Army. In July 1922 Collins, in his capacity of Commander-in-Chief, wrote to the Provisional Government requesting 'a clear instruction as to whether it is the intention to ask for the arrest and detention of what are purely political suspects'.[177] The Government's decision was that 'members of Parliament, persons engaged in political propaganda for the Irregulars, or mere political suspects, should not be arrested, except of course, those actually captured in arms'.[178]

By August, provisions for dealing with the captives during their initial

---

[175] The relevant constitutional provisions and the case law in this area are considered on pp. 253–9.

[176] See pp. 226–8 for a discussion of the status issue which inevitably arose and the question of the number arrested.

[177] Collins to Government, 16 July 1922, S1 369/3, SPO.

[178] Minutes of Meeting of the Provisional Government, 17 July 1922, SPO.

period of detention had been formalized,[179] but the ending of the first and 'open' phase of the conflict in that month meant that the relative clarity of the first phase faded. The second stage was marked by the IRA's resort to guerrilla tactics and the introduction of the Army Emergency Powers Resolution. That Resolution sanctioned

The removal under authority of the Army Council of any person taken prisoner arrested or detained by the National Army to any place or places whether within or without the area of jurisdiction of the Government and the detention or imprisonment of any such persons in any place or places within or without the area aforesaid.[180]

No criteria for arrest or detention were therefore set out in the Resolution, but the language used, with its reference to 'any person taken prisoner', implied that military necessity or perhaps military expediency would be the guiding principle.

These provisions would of themselves change little in the way in which arrest and detention powers were used. But the opening of a new phase in the conflict did result in changes, principally in an increased involvement of the Intelligence Department. Involvement was increased for two reasons: first, the end of conventional warfare meant that there was in many cases no longer an easily identifiable 'enemy'. Consequently, pinpointing the opposition became an intelligence exercise. Secondly, the introduction of military courts entailed a new emphasis on the gathering of evidence, a task which was also assigned to the Intelligence Department.[181]

In April 1923 the role of intelligence in relation to the making of arrests was spelled out in a 'General Staff Intelligence Memorandum' which specified that the Command Intelligence Officer was to recommend to the GOC of the Command, or other officer concerned, the arrest of all individuals whom he had reason to believe were a danger to the state while at large. He was to collect any available evidence against such persons 'whether in custody or not'.[182] This arrangement did not necessarily preclude others from ordering arrests. In any case, not all arrests would be pre-planned; some were bound to occur in the course of operations in circumstances in which the Intelligence Department would have no involvement. In the following July, however, the role of the Depart-

---

[179] 'The Reporting of the Capture of Prisoners to Local HQ and Arrangements at Local Headquarters', Mulcahy papers, P7/B/41. These instruction appear to have been issued by Collins in Aug. 1922. Although they are undated, they are included in the section of the Mulcahy papers belonging to Collins, and are alongside GROs issued by the C-in-C on 14 Aug. 1922. These instructions are considered in more detail below.

[180] Clause 3 (c).

[181] See pp. 201–2.

[182] 'General Staff Intelligence Memo. No. 3, Prisoners', by the CGS, CWS, Prisoners' Files, P/4.

ment in relation to arrests was restated in a directive which provided that '*All* correspondence in connection with the activities the arrest and the release of prisoners is now being dealt with by the Director of Intelligence'.[183] The other aspect of the increased work-load of the Intelligence Department, the collection of evidence which might be used before military courts, needs to be examined in the context of detention.

Detention and interrogation

The first formalized procedures in relation to detainees, those of August 1922, made general provision in relation to the treatment of detainees, including a provision that they be treated with 'utmost military respect',[184] but set no time-limits on detention. Towards the end of the Civil War it could take three or four weeks after arrest for a person whose innocence had been established to be released.[185] The authorization of the Adjutant-General was required, and this could be a time-consuming process.[186]

Significantly, the August document also anticipated the introduction of the military court system. The cases of prisoners who were found in possession of arms or munitions 'not in harmony with the usages of war' were to be examined by a specially assembled court of inquiry. The prisoners were to be interrogated 'very closely' and evidence was to be taken down by a person 'not seen', a proviso which harked back to the British experience that interrogation could be effective only if conducted in an atmosphere of privacy. This inquiry was not only for propaganda purposes, but the exercise aimed to ensure that 'if the person responsible came within the jurisdiction of Military Law later he could be suitably dealt with'.

As the military court and committee system eventually developed, prisoners were brought before committees as a matter of course, sometimes within twenty-four hours of arrest.[187] But when military courts were first instituted in November 1922, only prisoners against whom cases could be assembled were brought to trial. This affected detention in two ways. First, the possibility of trial raised the issue of legal representation, and this led to the issuing of orders in relation to visits by legal advisers.[188] Secondly, the need to assemble evidence resulted in specific instructions in that regard being issued which were applicable immediately on arrest and during pre-trial detention.

[183] Office of Director of Intelligence to GOC Commands and All Prison Governors, 28 July 1923, CWS, Prisoners' Files, P/4 (my emphasis).
[184] 'Reporting of the Capture of Prisoners to Local HQ', Mulcahy papers, P7/B/41.
[185] These were the time-limits described in District IO Brennan-Whitmore to Command IO, Dublin Command, 18 Apr. 1923, CWS, Prisoners' Files, P/4.
[186] Ibid.
[187] See pp. 217–19.
[188] GRO 3, 23 Nov. 1922, Mulcahy papers, P7/B/167.

The General Routine Order dealing with access to legal advisers provided that a prisoner charged and awaiting trial by military court, or in respect of whom an application for a writ of habeas corpus was made, might be allowed at any reasonable time to receive a visit from his solicitor, or counsel, or both. The General Officer of any Command could, however, still refuse admission to any solicitor whom he considered inadvisable 'for military reasons' to admit.[189] And any legal adviser granted permission was required to sign a declaration that he would not take advantage in any way of the permission accorded him to interview the prisoner except to discuss and prepare his defence or his habeas corpus application, as the case might be.

Where a visit was granted, the prisoner could be interviewed alone, and documents could be passed between him and his legal advisers. But immediately before and after every such visit he was to be subjected to a careful search. Any other visits required the specific authorization of the Adjutant-General.[190] How effective these provisions were in practice it is difficult to say;[191] in any event they were not stated to be applicable in cases which were being disposed of by committee.

On the question of assembling evidence, a further General Routine Order specified that in every case where a prisoner was taken in possession of arms, ammunition, or explosives, a written record was to be made and signed by the officer or NCO in charge of the party effecting the arrest, in which such details as circumstances of the arrest, description of weapons in the possession of the prisoner, etc. were to be noted.[192] Any such weapons were to be labelled, and a copy of the record was to be sent to the Command Adjutant. Any voluntary statements made by the prisoner were to be taken down in writing, together with a record of the circumstances in which such statement was made and the questions leading up to such statement, but the prisoner was to be 'duly warned'[193] before making any such statement.

It would be a mistake, however, to assume that the only purpose behind the questioning and interrogation of prisoners was the collecting of evidence which would be admissible at their trials. The Command Intelligence Officer was specifically empowered to order interrogation in cases where it was thought advisable.[194] In many instances this would have been in connection with his decision on the internment or otherwise

---

[189] GRO 3, as amended by GRO 4, 24 Nov. 1922, Mulcahy papers, P/7/B/167.
[190] GRO 3 and GRO 25, 9 Mar. 1923, Mulcahy papers, P7/B/167.
[191] The point is discussed further on pp. 203–4.
[192] GRO 6, 4 Dec. 1922, Mulcahy papers, P7/B/167.
[193] Ibid.
[194] 'General Staff Intelligence Memo. No. 3', 13 Apr. 1923, from the CGS, CWS, Prisoners' Files, P/4.

of the prisoner, but in others, interrogation would have been geared towards gathering operational intelligence.

Allegations of ill-treatment

Although the rules as to the detention of prisoners, which seem to have been issued in August 1922, specifically provided that 'there must be no ill-treatment of prisoners in any shape whatsoever',[195] partly on the grounds that such treatment would be counter-productive ('brutal treatment will always fail'[196]), allegations of ill-treatment during interrogation soon surfaced. These centred mainly, though not exclusively, on the activities of two groups: the Dublin-based CID, and the Dublin Guards brigade of the National Army during their operations in Kerry in the spring of 1923.[197]

As mentioned above,[198] the Dublin Guards achieved some notoriety for their activities in Kerry, and responsibility for many of the atrocities of the Civil War has been attributed to the brigade. One account from a Republican source describes an interrogation in Kerry in the following terms:

'Interrogation' . . . in Ballymullen Barracks was an ordeal under which reason might give way. The prisoner, in the usual practice, was first blind-folded, then his arms were tied to his sides and 'interrogation' began. This time a hammer was used. The prisoners were taken in separately. When Shanahan came out his head was covered with blood and his spine was injured, but he was still able to walk . . . The Prisoners were taken out to be shot, and shots were fired about their head.[199]

This kind of allegation was quite common. If true, the behaviour of the troops clearly amounted to torture, and was comparable with that described in Chapter 2. It may have been in response to these types of criticism that in March the Commander-in-Chief expressly reiterated that General Officers Commanding Commands were responsible for the custody of prisoners until such time as their detention in a prisoner or internment camp was ordered by the Adjutant-General, or until they were definitely committed to a prison under sentence of a military court or committee 'or otherwise disposed of'.[200] Later in the month the Adjutant-General took the further step of directing the GOC of each

---

[195] These are attached to the instruction re 'Reporting of the Capture of Prisoners to Local HQ', Mulcahy papers, P7/B/41.
[196] Ibid.
[197] The Dublin Guards had originated as an eight-man column, closely associated with Michael Collins. Long, 'Army', 17.
[198] pp. 169–70.
[199] Long, 'Army', 17.
[200] GRO 25, Mar. 1923, Mulcahy papers, P7/B/167.

Command to appoint a special officer to assist the Command Adjutant, and whose only duties were to be to attend to the disposal of prisoners taken in the Command.[201] He was to report daily direct to the Adjutant-General. The main function of this officer seems to have been to ensure the smooth running of the system, but he may also have been intended to exercise a more general supervisory role, as it was later specifically set out that the Adjutant-General's Department was to have responsibility for issues such as health of prisoners, at least in relation to interness.[202] Another significant move was the appointment of Colonel Fred Henry as Provost-Marshal, a Military Police post, with responsibility for the investigation of allegations of ill-treatment and murder.[203] Initial military inquiries exonerated the Army of the murder allegations, but public pressure persisted, and following a further inquiry, Major-General Daly, the Guards' Commanding Officer, was removed from his post.[204]

The other allegations concerned the CID which, as has been stated in part I, was an organization which operated outside normal police and Army channels, but which from August 1922 onwards was formally under the control of the Ministry of Home Affairs. One suspect gave the following description of his experiences of the CID following arrest:

I was taken to Interrogation Office and questioned re running of trains and replied that my job consisted of lighting of fire on an engine when so instructed, and that beyond that I had no information on these matters. I was struck on the face with clenched fists by CID men and called a liar, qualified with the foulest adjectives, made to kneel down and my shirt torn open baring my chest. A cocked revolver was rammed down my throat till my mouth bled freely and another used to dig me in the chest. I was threatened all the while to be shot unless I admitted having given information to IRA, about a certain train and that I advocated refusal of men to light fires on Troop Trains at a Transport Workers meeting— that never took place—which of course I steadfastly refused.

I was then alternately beaten on the head and gripped by the throat till half chocked [*sic*] so that my hearing was almost completely gone and is still defective. This treatment was kept up for three quarters of an hour by four men who then kicked me out of the door to a cell where I was left in a state of collapse.[205]

A CID officer was later to acknowledge that 'the average irregular really believed that the terrors of the Spanish Inquisition were mere lullabys to the treatment meted out to prisoners by the Officers of the CID', but insisted that this was due to the fact that 'Irregular propagandists spread

[201] Adj.-Gen. to GOC, CWS, Prisoners' Files, P/4.

[202] Office of Director of Intelligence to GOC Commands and All Prison Governors, 28 July 1923, ibid.

[203] See Neeson, *Civil War*, 257.

[204] See Curran, *Birth*, 269.

[205] Statement of James Kelly, attached to Sheehy-Skeffington to Town Clerk [Dublin], 11 Sept. 1922, S1 369/3, SPO.

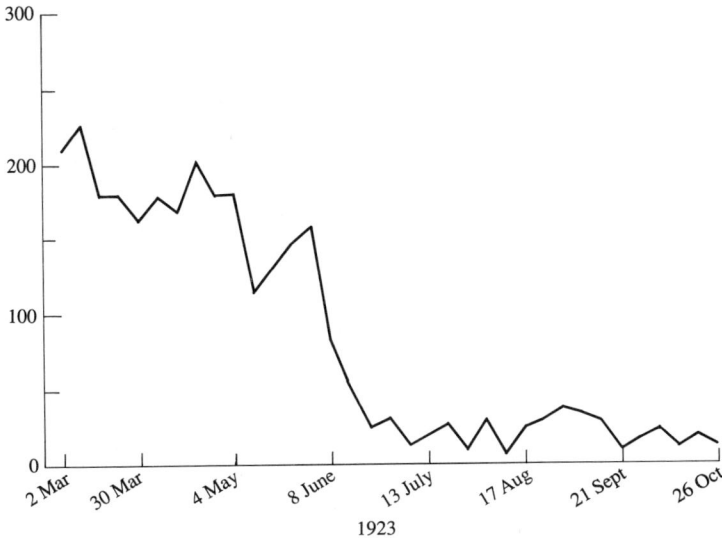

GRAPH D. Weekly arrest totals, March 1923 to October 1923

Source: Prepared from Statistical Summaries of Official Reports from w/e 2 Mar. to w/e 26 Oct. 1923, Mulcahy papers, P7/B/124. Figures for w/e 18 May 1923 are estimated.

such lying reports about these interrogations'.[206] Instead, he claimed that 'the interrogation of any prisoner was at least as humane as that form at present extensively used in America and known as the Third Degree'.[207] Of the staff of 88 Merrion Square (the CID headquarters) he declared, 'I cannot speak too highly. I found each of them very painstaking and diligent and always ready to give every assistance even in matters which were outside their regular duties.'[208] When the issue of the disbandment of the CID eventually arose in May 1923, the Minister of Home Affairs displayed a very different assessment of the organization. Of its complement, as it then was, of 86 men, he estimated that only 25 were of a 'good type' and could be absorbed into the 'G' Division of the DMP, 31 were 'hopeless', and would have to be 'got rid of', while 30 constituted a middle group whose cases could be dealt with by disbandment with a bonus, with a possibility of future employment 'in the event of suitable vacancies occurring'.[209]

There appear to have been no further allegations of gross ill-treatment after the ending of martial law at the start of August 1923, and by then

[206] O'Muireadhaigh to McGrath, 12 Oct. 1923, S3 331, SPO.
[207] Ibid.
[208] Ibid.
[209] Minutes of Meeting of Executive Council, 25 May 1923.

TABLE 16. Arrest and detention powers under the Public Safety (Emergency Powers) (No. 2) Act 1923 and the Public Safety (Powers of Arrest and Detention) Temporary Act 1924

Act/section	Person empowered to arrest	Detention period	Grounds for arrest
1923 Act s. 2 (1)	It shall be lawful for a responsible officer to arrest *Responsible officer defined as:* an officer of the Military Forces of Saorstát Eireann not below the rank of commandant or an officer of a police force established by or under the control of the Minister for Home Affairs not below the rank of superintendent (s. 16).	and to detain in custody for any period not exceeding one week	any person found committing or attempting to commit or whom such [responsible] officer suspects of having committed any of the offences mentioned in part II of the schedule to this Act.

1924 Act s. 2 (1)	It shall be lawful for a responsible officer to arrest	and to detain in custody for any period not exceeding one week	any person found committing or attempting to commit or whom such [responsible] officer suspects of having committed any of the offences mentioned in part II of the schedule to this Act.
	Responsible officer defined as: an officer of a police force established by or under the control of the Minister for Home Affairs not below the rank of superintendent or any member of a police force particularly authorised by him or an officer of the military forces of Saorstát Eireann not being below the rank of Commandant who may be specifically empowered in any particular case by the Minister for Defence to delegate his powers under this Act to any member of the military forces of Saorstát Eireann not below the rank of sergeant save and except in such cases where a military force has been detailed by the order of a person so empowered to arrest any person or persons, in which case every member of such force shall be deemed to possess the powers granted by this Act (s. 9).		

the weekly arrest totals had declined considerably (Graph D). Reliance then switched to statutory emergency powers.

Arrest and detention under the Public Safety (Emergency Powers) (No. 2) Act 1923 and the Public Safety (Powers of Arrest and Detention) Temporary Act 1924

Persons empowered to arrest

Apart from the question of arrest powers which were strictly ancillary to internment powers,[210] both the Public Safety (Emergency Powers) (No. 2) Act and the Public Safety (Powers of Arrest and Detention) Temporary Act 1924 (the '1923 Act' and the '1924 Act' respectively) incorporated powers of arrest and limited detention which were very similar in terms (Table 16). Each vested arrest powers in a 'responsible officer', a figure whose role may have been derived from the CMA under DORA. As had been the case with the CMA, the powers of the responsible officer were not limited to the spheres of arrest and detention, but also, in the Irish legislation, extended to the exercise of powers in relation to stolen property.[211] The term was, however, defined somewhat differently in the Acts of 1923 and 1924.

Under the 1923 Act, the responsible officer was to hold the rank of Commandant or higher in the National Army, or to be of a rank not lower than that of superintendent in a police force 'established by or under the control of the Minister for Home Affairs'.[212] This latter phrase was sufficiently broad to cover both the Garda Síochána and the DMP; it probably also covered the CID, and in addition may have extended to the Protective Corps and the Citizens' Defence Force, assuming the latter two forces could be counted as 'police forces'. There was, however, no provision in relation to delegation of authority by the officer empowered to arrest, nor was the Army willing to assume that the power to delegate was implicit.[213] Thus it would appear that under the 1923 Act the only person physically empowered to carry out an arrest was an officer of the appropriate police or Army rank.

In contrast, under the 1924 Act, there was express provision for delegation in respect of both police and Army powers. Police arrest powers under section 2 (1) became exercisable by any member of a police force

---

[210] See pp. 232–7.

[211] 1923 Act, s. 7.

[212] s. 16.

[213] GRO 48, 6 Sept. 1923, which dealt with the exercise of the Army's powers under the 1923 Act, simply stated that an officer of a rank not below that of Commandant was entitled to arrest in the appropriate circumstances, and gave no authorization in respect of delegation. Mulcahy papers, P7/B/168.

'particularly authorised'[214] by a superintendent. The phrase 'particularly authorised' presumably meant that delegation could only be in respect of specific cases rather than amounting to a blanket handing over of authority. An alternative construction would be that the phrase was intended to permit blanket delegation to some member of the police forces but not to others, thus a superintendent might delegate to members of the detective branch but not to the uniformed branch. But this construction would seem to make the word 'particularly' redundant, since if a superintendent was simply allowed to delegate his powers, there would be nothing to prevent him delegating to one class of policeman rather than another.

In relation to the Army, there was twofold provision in respect of delegation. First, the person primarily empowered to arrest, as had been the case under the 1923 Act, was 'an officer of the military forces of Saorstát Eireann not below the rank of Commandant',[215] but there was specific provision that such officer 'may be specifically empowered in any particular case by the Minister of Defence to delegate his powers . . . to any member of the military forces of Saorstát Eireann not below the rank of sergeant'.[216] The phrase 'any particular case', as had been the case with the phrase 'particularly' when used in relation to police powers, was presumably meant to place a bar on blanket delegation.[217]

The second provision in relation to delegation of Army powers was that where arrest powers were 'in any particular case' delegated to a sergeant, and where such a sergeant detailed members of a military force for the task (such members would be NCOs of lower rank and privates), then 'every member of such force' was to be deemed to have the powers granted by the Act.

Within the Army's internal structures, the Intelligence Department still claimed a supervisory role in the use of statutory arrest powers by the Army, as it had done in relation to martial law powers. This was evidenced by an insistence that on the switch to statutory powers 'no man should be arrested except he is a danger to the peace of *An Saorstat* [the Free State]',[218] and this tightening up reflected the relatively narrow criteria for arrest under statutory powers, criteria which must now be examined in detail.

---

[214] s. 9.   [215] s. 9.   [216] s. 9.

[217] GRO 67, 23 Feb. 1924, in relation to the Army's powers under the Public Safety (Powers of Arrest and Detention) Temporary Act 1924, simply provided that 'In a particular case the Minister for Defence may specifically empower a responsible Officer to delegate his powers of arrest to any Officer or to any NCO not below the rank of Sergeant.' Mulcahy papers, P7/B/168.

[218] Office of Director of Intelligence to IO Claremorris Command, 3 Aug. 1923, CWS, Prisoners' Files, P/4.

Criteria for arrest

Under both the 1923 and the 1924 Acts, those whose arrest was authorized were 'any person found committing or attempting to commit or whom such [responsible] officer suspects of having committed'[219] a range of offences. The list of offences thus rendered arrestable was slightly different in the two Acts. Both covered not only typical examples of political crime such as what could be termed 'firearms and munitions offences',[220] 'malicious damage offences',[221] illegal use of police or Army uniforms etc.,[222] armed robbery,[223] arson,[224] but also 'offences' against property which would normally come only within the realm of the civil law.[225] But whereas the 1924 Act included 'Inciting persons to engage in an attempt to overthrow by violence the established form of Government

---

[219] 1923 Act, s. 2 (1); 1924 Act s. 2 (1).

[220] 1923 Act, schedule, pt. 2, para. 1, and 1924 Act, schedule, para. 3, incorporated identical provisions defining an offence in the following terms: '1. Having possession without lawful authority of (a) any lethal firearm or other weapon of any description from which any shot, bullet or other missile can be discharged; or (b) any ammunition for any such firearm or weapon; or (c) any grenade, bomb or other similar missile, whether capable of being used with any such firearm or weapon or not; or (d) any land mine or other similar explosive machine; or (e) any dynamite, gelignite or other explosive substance; or (f) any component part or ingredient of any such article or substance aforesaid.'

[221] 1923 Act, schedule, pt. 2, para. 8; and 1924 Act, schedule, para. 10. 'Unlawfully injuring or destroying or attempting to injure or destroy any house, factory, barn, haggard, workshop, or other building, or any agricultural property, food supplies for man or beast, or any other property of any nature or kind, movable or immovable, public or private, including standing trees and crops'.

[222] 1923 Act, schedule, pt. 2, paras. 2, 3, 4, and 1924 Act, schedule, paras. 4, 5, 6, incorporated the following identical provisions: 'Having possession without lawful authority of any article of clothing, equipment or accoutrement or any arms or ammunition belonging or issued to any member of the military or police forces of Saorstát Eireann . . . Putting on or assuming without authority the uniform or any part of the uniform of any branch of the military or police forces of Saorstát Eireann . . . Assuming the name, designation or description of any rank, or of any member, of the military or police forces of Saorstát Eireann for the purpose of doing or procuring to be done any act which the person assuming such name, designation or description would not by law be entitled to do or procure to be done of his own authority.'

[223] 1923 Act, schedule, pt. 2, para. 6, reads: 'Robbery under arms; that is to say, robbing or attempting to rob while armed with any offensive weapon or instrument'. The corresponding wording of the 1924 Act, schedule, para. 8, differs slightly: 'robbery under arms; that is to say, robbing or attempting to rob while armed with any offensive or apparently offensive weapon or instrument'.

[224] 1923 Act, schedule, pt. 2, para. 7, and 1924 Act, schedule, para. 9: 'Arson; that is to say, unlawfully setting fire or attempting to set fire to any house, factory, barn, haggard, workshop, or other building, or any agricultural property, food supplies for man or beast, or any other property of any nature or kind, movable or immovable, public or private, including standing trees and crops'.

[225] 1923 Act, schedule, pt. 2, para. 5; 1924 Act, schedule, para. 7: 'Wrongful entry on and retention of possession of land without colour or pretence of title or authority'. 1923 Act, schedule, pt. 2, para. 9: 'Interfering with or preventing without lawful authority the lawful occupation, use or enjoyment of any land or premises'. The corresponding provisions of the 1924 Act were in schedule, para. 11: 'Unlawfully interfering with or preventing the lawful occupation, use or enjoyment of any land or premises'.

of Saorstát Eireann or organising or otherwise assisting or encouraging any such attempt'[226] among the list of arrestable offences, the 1923 Act did not, although that Act did include some offences relating to the illicit distillation of alcohol[227] which were not included in the 1924 Act. Under both Acts, 'Knowingly aiding abetting, assisting in, or encouraging the commission of any of the offences mentioned . . . or helping in the concealment or escape of any person guilty of any such offence' was also an arrestable offence.[228]

The wording used in defining the criteria for an arrest under both Acts, 'found committing or attempting to commit or whom such [responsible] officer suspects of having committed' any of the relevant offences, differed from its British predecessor, DORR 55, in that it permitted arrest only in connection with the commission of a specific offence and not on such general grounds as that the behaviour of the suspect might be considered 'prejudicial to the public safety or the defence of the Realm'.

The formula used in the Irish Acts incorporated three separable grounds for arrest (Table 16): (1) and (2) were exercisable where a person was 'found committing or attempting to commit' an offence, and (3) was exercisable in respect of a person whom the arrester 'suspects of having committed' an offence. Ground (3) was exercisable in respect of a person whom the arrester 'suspects of having committed' a relevant offence, and the Army interpreted this as meaning having committed an offence since 1 August 1923,[229] thus refraining from claiming an effect retrospective to the martial law period. One significant feature about this power was that, unlike common law powers, there was no requirement that the suspicion be 'reasonable'. Consequently, all that was required for a valid arrest under this provision was a 'real' suspicion, and thus the scope for judicial scrutiny of the use of such powers was diminished. But this diminution was not as marked in relation to the use of the Irish powers as had been the case in relation to DORR 55, since, as noted above, all the powers under the Acts of 1923 and 1924 were exercisable only in relation to the commission of specific offences.

Detention

The powers under section 2 (1) of the Irish Acts were not limited to arrest but also included a power 'to detain in custody for any period not

---

[226] Schedule, para. 1. Para. 2 included 'unlawfully inducing or attempting to induce any officer of the Government of Saorstát Eireann to refuse, neglect or omit to discharge his duty as such officer'.

[227] Schedule, pt. 2, para. 10: 'Illicit distillation, or having possession or control of any illicitly distilled spirits or any illicit still or any articles or materials for illicit distillation'. Para. 11: 'Selling or offering exposing or having for sale any illicitly distilled spirits'.

[228] 1923 Act, schedule, pt. 2, para. 12; 1924 Act, schedule, para. 13.

[229] GRO 48, 6 Sept. 1923, Mulcahy papers, P7/B/168.

exceeding one week'. Such detainees became subject to the provisions of section 2 (3) of both the 1923 and 1924 Acts. These subsections provided in identical terms that unless an order for their indefinite detention was made by an Executive Minister, such detainees were, not later than one week after their arrest, to be either released or charged with one or more of the offences mentioned in the schedule to the Act or with any other offence or offences and dealt with according to law. Detainees in military custody were to be delivered into civil custody for the purposes of charging. During the week-long detention, the prisoner would presumably be interrogated although there was no specific power of interrogation in either the 1923 or the 1924 Act.

Under internal Army orders, the system adopted was that following arrest, the officer who effected it was immediately to report it and to forward all available information respecting the prisoner and the reason for his arrest by the quickest available means of communication directly to the Adjutant-General, as well as to the General Officer Commanding the Command. If, within one week of the arrest, orders for the disposal or otherwise of the prisoner were not received from the Adjutant-General, the prisoner was either to be handed over to the civil authorities and charged with an offence or else released from custody.[230] The handing over to civil custody of prisoners was to be done only by the Military Governor where the prisoner was detained, or by the Command Assistant Provost-Marshal (a senior Military Policeman), and the necessary arrangements were to be made directly with the civil police.[231] These provisions caused some initial confusion,[232] but by November 1923 the Army had standardized a 'Temporary Detention Warrant' to be filled in in respect of arrests. This was a simple document recording such details as prisoner's name and address, and date, time, and reason for arrest.[233]

The 1924 Act lapsed on 1 February 1925, and with it all emergency powers of arrest and detention. This meant reliance on ordinary common law and statutory powers in dealing with politically motivated violence, which had, by that time, considerably diminished. The introduction of the Treasonable Offences Act in June 1925 did not signal a return to wide-ranging powers of arrest and detention, since the only arrest power contained in the Act was that exercisable in respect of a person who refused to give his name or address, or who gave a name or address which

---

[230] These provisions in respect of the 1923 Act were first issued under GRO 48, in Sept. 1923, and were restated in respect of arrests under the 1924 Act in GRO 67, Feb. 1924. Ibid.

[231] GRO 52, 12 Oct. 1923, ibid.

[232] DAAG Dublin Command to Director of Intelligence, 24 Nov. 1923, CWS, Prisoners' Files, P/4.

[233] A pro forma warrant can be found attached to the communication, ibid.

an officer conducting a search under the terms of the Act knew or suspected to be false or misleading.[234]

Arrest and detention powers: conclusions

At the start of the Civil War, martial law powers of arrest and detention were used which corresponded closely with the powers to take prisoners invoked by all armies in conventional warfare. With the resort to guerrilla tactics by the IRA, and the introduction of the Army Emergency Powers Resolution, the position changed, and arrest and detention powers came to be used in a manner similar to that resorted to by the British Army in the MLA in 1920–1.

This development led to an ever increasing involvement of the National Army's Intelligence Department in the making of arrests and to an increasing emphasis on interrogation. The purpose of such interrogation was probably not the obtaining of incriminating statements which could be adduced in trial by military court, since most cases tried by this method involved 'possession' charges in which special rules of evidence applied,[235] but rather was geared towards the decision on internment and the collection of fresh operational intelligence.

Allegations of ill-treatment during interrogation were common. In relation to the allegations which were made against some (though not all) National Army units, it seems clear now in view of the widespread nature of these allegations and the fact that there is clear evidence of Army atrocities in Kerry, that some of these allegations were substantially true. Similarly, in view of the fact that the CID was prepared to admit that it engaged in 'third degree' tactics, and considering that over a third of the complement of the force was deemed 'hopeless' and unsuitable for normal police work, there are grounds for suggesting that the allegations made against the force may also have been substantially true.

The ending of martial law and the switch to statutory powers saw the institution of the 'responsible officer' with powers of arrest, a position which may have been derived from the DORA post of CMA. And as had been the case with British emergency arrest powers, there was no requirement of 'reasonable suspicion' in the Irish measures, although unlike the British provisions, arrest powers in the Irish Free State were exercisable only where suspicion related to the commission of a specific offence.

There were therefore clear parallels between the measures taken in this area under the last phase of British rule and in the early years of the Irish Free State. There were also differences—principally arising out of the unique nature of the conflict at the start of the Civil War, and secondarily

---

[234] s. 10 (3).   [235] See p. 207.

in that Irish statutory powers were more tightly drawn than their British counterparts.

SECTION (B) SPECIAL COURT PROVISIONS

The operation of military courts and committees can be said to have constituted the central element of the counter-insurgency policy of the Provisional Government and then of the Free State authorities from November 1922 to May 1923. National Army military courts were first introduced as a response to the IRA's readoption of guerilla tactics. The overall strategy therefore corresponded closely with that adopted by the British Army in the MLA from December 1920. And as had been the British Army's experience, once trial by the military was introduced, the desire for 'results' led to a progressive degradation of procedure, so that in the spring of 1923 captured prisoners were having their cases disposed of not by military court but by summary Army committees as a matter of course.

With the ending of martial law, and therefore of trials by the Army, security strategy became based on resort to statutory internment powers. Reliance on these powers meant there was less emphasis on the trial process generally as a means of combating political crime, though the Public Safety Acts did incorporate provisions in relation to removal of jury trial (discussed below) which were taken almost verbatim from the Criminal Law and Procedure (Ireland) Act 1887.

The ordinary courts and change of venue under the Public Safety Acts

The provisions of the Government of Ireland Act in relation to the Supreme Court of Judicature were virtually the only elements of the measure to have any effect in the South.[236] At the lower levels of the court system, the County courts and courts of Petty session continued to function in some parts of the jurisdiction prior to the Civil War, but the assizes apparently did not.[237] In the South and West particularly, it was the Dáil courts that handled much of the day-to-day business. When the War broke out the Dáil courts were progressively abolished and the Provisional Government began the task of reforming the court system it had inherited from the British. In October 1922 District Justices were appointed by decree under the Constabulary (Ireland) Act 1836. That Act properly made provision for the appointment of Resident Magistrates. The position of the new justices was strengthened by the Adaptation of

---

[236] The relevant provisions of the Act are discussed briefly on p. 308.

[237] In an affidavit filed in *R (O'Brien)* v. *Military Governor NDU* [1924] 1 *IR* 32 in June 1923, the Adj.-Gen. of the National Army averred that 'owing to the conditions prevailing in the country it has not been possible to hold an assize since July 1921' (at p. 34).

Enactments Act 1922 which made all powers conferred on Justices of the Peace and Resident Magistrates exercisable by District Justices, and the position was further regularized by the District Justices (Temporary Provisions) Act 1923.

In the mean time the new Constitution had come into effect. A new court system was to be created (and was eventually provided for in the Courts of Justice Act 1924[238]), but pending its establishment the Supreme Court of Judicature, County courts, courts of quarter sessions, and courts of summary jurisdiction were to continue to function. It was within this framework that the removal for jury trial under the Public Safety Acts operated.

Change of venue in criminal cases under the Public Safety (Emergency Powers) Act 1923 and the Public Safety (Punishment of Offences) Temporary Act 1924

In both the Public Safety (Emergency Powers) Act 1923 and the Public Safety (Punishment of Offences) Temporary Act 1924 identical provisions were introduced which enabled cases to be removed for trial to areas other than those in which they would normally have been heard. Specifically, the Acts provided:

1. Where an indictment for a crime committed at any place in Saorstát Eireann has been found against any person, or any person has been committed for trial for such crime, the High Court on an application by or on behalf of the Attorney-General of Saorstát Eireann and upon his Certificate that he believes that a more fair and impartial trial can be had at a court and in a county to be named in such Certificate, shall make an order as of course that the trial shall be had at the court and in the county named in the Certificate.

2. Whenever an order for the removal of the trial of a crime is made under this section before the indictment has been found, such crime may be inquired into by a grand jury of, and the trial thereof may be had in, the county named in the order of removal in like manner as if the crime had been committed in such county.

3. Whenever an order for the removal of the trial of a crime of a crime is made under this section after the indictment has been found, such trial may be had as if the indictment had been found in the court to which the trial is removed.[239]

These provisions were taken directly from sections 4 and 10 of the Criminal Law and Procedure (Ireland) Act 1887 which related to removal for trial. The principal difference between the British measure and those of the Irish Free State was that in the former removal powers were available only in 'proclaimed districts', whereas in the latter the powers were available throughout that jurisdiction. And the criticism that could be

---

[238] The main provisions of the Act are outlined in n. 160 above.
[239] 1923 Act, s. 12, and 1924 Act, s. 8.

levelled at the British measure, that it created the possibility of the Attorney-General's attempting to manipulate the trial process in order to obtain a conviction which would not otherwise be obtained, could also be made of the Free State measure. Indeed, added validity might be given to such criticisms by the omission from the Irish measure of any provision corresponding to that of the British Act, that the defendant was at liberty to apply to the High Court to have the order discharged or varied on the ground that the trial could be more fairly and impartially had in a county other than that named in the order for removal. But whereas introduction of the 1887 Act in 1918 was followed within two years by a great expansion of trials by the military, the corresponding provisions of the Irish Free State came into existence only once trials by the military had ended.

Military courts and committees: introduction

The basic document providing for the trial by the National Army of persons other than its own members was the Army Emergency Powers Resolution of 28 September 1922. The Resolution had sanctioned the establishment of both military courts and committees but it had not set out what the differences between these two types of tribunal were to be. On 2 October 1922 the Army Council of the National Army issued its 'General Regulations as to Trial of Civilians by Military Courts'[240] (the 'General Regulations'). As its title suggests, these regulations were concerned solely with trial by military courts, and made no mention of committees. Many aspects of military court procedure were covered in the General Regulations, but apart from these specific rules, every military court was to determine its own procedure,[241] subject to the proviso that 'where practicable' every military court was to 'have regard to the procedure provided by the General Regulations as to discipline in the case of Courts Martial'.[242] A proclamation on behalf of the Army Council set 15 October 1922 as the date at which the General Regulations would come into effect. But it was not until 3 November 1922 that military courts actually began to operate.[243]

In December 1922, following the execution without trial of four members of the Four Courts garrison, the Army took the further step of establishing committees with more summary procedures, though in the case of these bodies no general regulations were issued, and consequently the task of piecing together a picture is not an easy one. Indeed, the area is so obscure that many historians seem to have overlooked the fact that committees functioned at all.

A proclamation issued on behalf of the Army Council warned that certain categories of offence listed in the Resolution were liable to be

---

[240] SR & O, 1922–38, xix. 515.   [241] reg. 15 (1).
[242] reg. 15 (4).   [243] 1 *DD*, col. 2057.

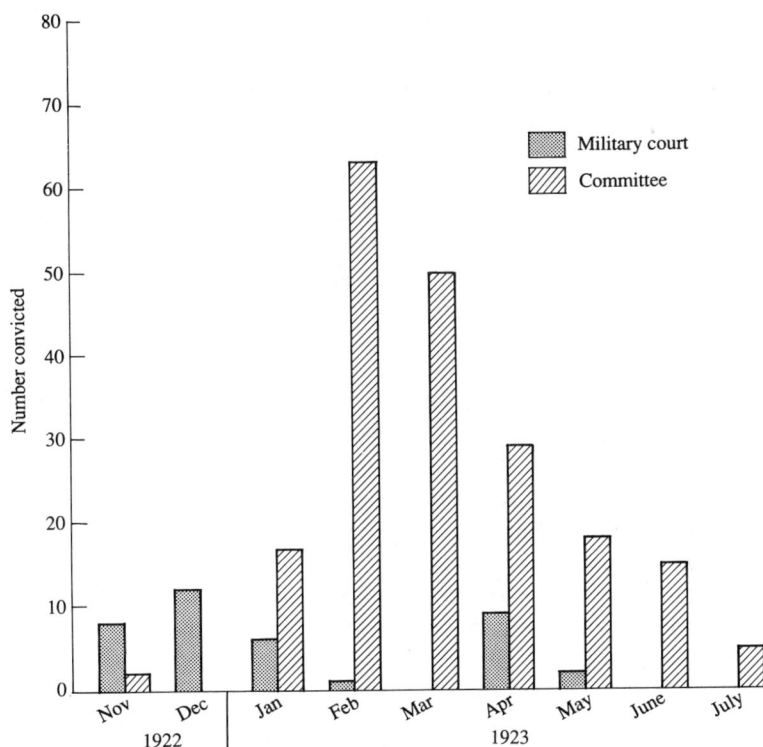

GRAPH E. Monthly totals of convictions by military courts and committees, November 1922 to July 1923

Note: Because these figures are based only on the cases in which the Judges recommended a full remission of sentence, they do not provide a full picture of convictions by military courts and committees. Not included are (1) those in which the death sentence was carried out, (2) those in which the prisoners had already been released or escaped at the time the Judges conducted their review, and (3) those in which the Judges did not recommend a full remission. There are, however, no reasons to believe that the pattern indicated in the graph is unrepresentative of the total picture.

Source: Prepared from schedules 1–10 of the Military Court and Committee cases, reviewed by Judges Doyle and Dromgoole, Army Archives, Civil War Series, Prisoners Files, P/2, Dublin.

tried by such committees.[244] The offences triable by committee over-lapped therefore with those triable by military court, and the rather confused system of dividing the work-load between these two types of tribunal is considered below. What is clear is that the work-load of committees soon came to exceed that of the military courts (Graph E). In all, around 140 people were tried by military court, while just over 1,000 had their cases disposed of by committee.

[244] A copy of the proclamation (with 'pretty hot' pencilled on it) can be found in the Jeudwine papers, and a newspaper cutting of the proclamation at S1 376, SPO.

In January 1923 the Army Council issued a General Order, which greatly widened the range of offences triable by military courts and also increased, though to a lesser extent, the jurisdiction of the committees.[245] This new order came into force from 20 January 1923.[246] A further order relating to the control of arms on foreign vessels in Irish ports was drafted and submitted by the Commander-in-Chief to the Government in April 1923. But this was not proceeded with, not surprisingly perhaps, both because the fighting in the Civil War was coming to an end, and because the measure had the potential to cause conflict with foreign Governments. The end of the fighting, however, did not lead to an immediate end to trials by the military—the tribunals continued to sit as late as June 1923.[247]

The full story of the operation of these tribunals will never be known because the Cummann na nGaedhael administration destroyed vital papers on leaving office in 1932. This action has always been assumed to have been taken because of extreme sensitivity over the question of reprisal executions. But even if a complete account is impossible, a reasonably comprehensive picture can be put together, and the discussion below examines in some detail military courts, committees, and the eventual Government review of the sentences of both of these tribunals.

Military courts

Pre-trial: jurisdiction and initiation of proceedings

The original jurisdiction of military courts was set by the list of offences thus triable in Regulation 2 of the General Regulations.[248] These were:

A. *Taking part* in the or aiding or abetting any attack upon or using force against the National Forces.

B. Looting, arson, destruction, seizure, unlawful possession or removal or damage to any public or private property.

C. *Having possession* without proper authority of:
    1. *any bomb* or article in the nature of a bomb;
    2. *any dynamite* gelignite or other explosive substance;

---

[245] The text of the order can be found in *IO* 2 Feb. 1923.

[246] Proclamation on behalf of the Army Council, 2 Feb. 1923.

[247] In a case arising out of the murder of one Patrick Shally in Apr. 1922, the Executive Council decided on 5 June 1922 that the case should be tried by military court, the view having been expressed that 'owing to the state of the country it was useless to expect an impartial verdict from a jury'. It was also agreed, however, that the matter should be postponed pending the result of the habeas corpus application which was then being brought on behalf of Mrs Connolly O'Brien (for the eventual result in this case see pp. 256–9). On 16 June the Executive Council reversed its decision, and ruled instead that the matter should be dealt with through the ordinary criminal courts. See Minutes of Meetings of Executive Council, 4, 5, and 16 June 1923.

[248] Gen. Regs. 1 and 5.

3. *any revolver* rifle gun or other firearm or lethal weapon or any ammunition for any such firearm.

D. *The breach of* any general order or regulation made by the Army Council.[249]

The wording of these offences ('possession without proper authority') followed that of British martial law proclamations, wording which had been so trenchantly criticized for its vagueness by O'Connor MR in Egan's case. If anything, it marked a further movement along the road to imprecision by utilizing such phrases as 'using force against the National Forces'.

The order of January 1923 expanded the jurisdiction of military courts in a number of ways. First, there was the provision that murder, attempts to murder, conspiracy to murder, and other similar offences[250] became triable by military court. Secondly, a large array of inchoate offences defined in relation to the offences originally set out in paragraph 2 of the General Regulations (see above) became triable by military court, as did possession of plans and official uniforms in certain circumstances.[251] And thirdly, offences relating to the sending of threatening letters and escaping from lawful custody became similarly triable.[252]

The first stage in the military court process would normally have been arrest, no provision having been made for appearance by summons. The decision would then be made whether or not to prosecute, though in certain cases the decision to prosecute preceded the arrest. The Regulations did not provide for any civil input into this decision, but while it was therefore formally a military matter, in at least some instances political considerations applied.

Frequently, not even token respect to notions of 'due process' was shown in relation to the decision on prosecution. A communication from the Commander-in-Chief might not only indicate that trials should be held arising out of some incident which happened to have come to his attention, but also suggest that convictions be obtained, and even prescribe the sentence to be imposed.[253] Much seems to have depended on

---

[249] Gen. Reg. 2.

[250] Under para. 1 (c), those triable included 'any person who shall . . . command, procure, incite, counsel, solicit, encourage, persuade or endeavour to persuade any person to murder any person'.

[251] For instance, para. 2 of the General Order of 8 Jan. 1923 provided *inter alia* 'From and after the date hereof any person who shall . . . Command, procure, incite, counsel, solicit, encourage, persuade or endeavour to persuade any person to commit an offence specified in sub-paragraphs (a) (b) or (c) or paragraph 2 of the said General Regulations as to the Trial of Civilians by Military Courts . . . shall upon trial and conviction thereof by Military Court be liable to suffer death or any less punishment.'

[252] Para. 3.

[253] e.g. on 26 Nov. 1922 the C-in-C wrote to the GOC Kerry Command in the following terms: '1. Press Report "Irish Times" 25/11/22 that—"Documents were found on one person giving the names of those to whom four taken from a looted boat at Dingle was

the attitude of the local GOC. In Cork, for instance, the local officer was able to resist Headquarters' pressure for trials.[254]

In other cases the decision on prosecution was clearly a political one. Thus in October 1922 the Provisional Government decided that 'the Commander-in-Chief should be asked to arrange for the immediate trial' of the men arrested in connection with a recent attack on Oriel House.[255] In another incident the Dáil was informed about certain executions in a way which clearly hinted at a forthcoming execution and strongly suggested that the process had been manipulated for political effect.[256]

Once the decision had been taken to prosecute, the General Officer Commanding the Command area in which the offence was alleged to have been committed was to have the task of convening the military court[257] and affixing the time and place of its sitting[258] (see Figure. 4). In certain instances, however, the Army Council made special orders (despite there being no authority do this in the General Regulations) removing the trial to a different Command area.[259]

The mechanics of military court trials was the responsibility of the Judge Advocate General's Department, and the system began to operate only after the National Army's Judge Advocate General had been in communication with each of the legal staff officers in the jurisdiction

distributed". 2. I want to suggest that two or three people of definite irregular sympathies, or otherwise objectionable . . . be arrested, and charged before a Military Court with the possession of this loot and sentenced to imprisonment *and fined*, and that the others be left for three or four days after this to see what the effect will be on them.' Mulcahy papers, P7/B/72. Another example is C-in-C to GOC Eastern Command, 26 Nov. 1922, in which Mulcahy wrote in relation to an attack on a mail car: 'A case of this kind should be followed up at once and person against whom a charge like this can be sustained should be brought before a military court and in an instance as wanton as this one, the death penalty should be imposed.' Mulcahy papers, P7/B/111.

[254] The Review of Work of the JAG's Department for w/e 2 Dec. 1922 notes: 'Cork Command (Trial of Civilians). The command Legal Staff Officer reports that General Officer Commanding and General Ennis have intimated that in the present state of affairs in the Area, no trials of Civilians are to be held at present, and that General officer Commanding has reported decision to General Headquarters.' Mulcahy papers, P7/B/135. See also Hopkinson, *Green*, 239–40.

[255] Minutes of Meeting of Provisional Government, 31 Oct. 1922.

[256] Commenting on the first four executions, the minister explained to the Dáil: 'it was better at first to take the average case, to take the cases which had nothing particular' (1 DD 2267). A few days later came news of the execution of Erskine Childers, a matter which was clearly not the 'average case'. *R (Childers)* v. *Adj.-Gen.* [1923] 1 *IR* 5, is considered on pp. 247–52.

[257] Gen. Reg. 3 (1).

[258] Gen. Reg. 7.

[259] e.g. in the case of the trial of Michael Kilroy who was taken prisoner near Newport, Co. Mayo on 24 Nov. 1922, and though the offences with which he was charged were alleged to have been committed near Newport, the Army Council made a special order on 12 Feb. 1923 transferring the case to Dublin. For the Dáil debate on the issue see 2 *DD*, cols. 1933–6.

```
┌─────────────────────┐
│ Offence against     │
│ regulations         │
└─────────────────────┘
          │
          ▼
┌─────────────────────┐
│ Convening of military│
│ court, copies of    │
│ charge sheet,       │
│ abstract of evidence,│
│ and list of members │
│ of the court        │
│ furnished to accused│
└─────────────────────┘
          │
          ▼
┌─────────────────────┐
│ Trial by military   │
│ court               │
└─────────────────────┘
          │
          ▼
┌─────────────────────┐
│ Decision of military│
│ court               │
└─────────────────────┘
```

Offence against regulations

Convening of military court, copies of charge sheet, abstract of evidence, and list of members of the court furnished to accused

Trial by military court

Decision of military court

Acquittal | Conviction | Detention recommended

Confirmation

Revision of finding or sentence ordered | Finding and sentence confirmed | Finding upheld, sentence commuted or mitigated | Finding upheld, execution of sentence suspended | New trial ordered

Promulgation

Non-suspended sentence | Suspended sentence

Suspension revoked | Suspension maintained

Execution of sentence

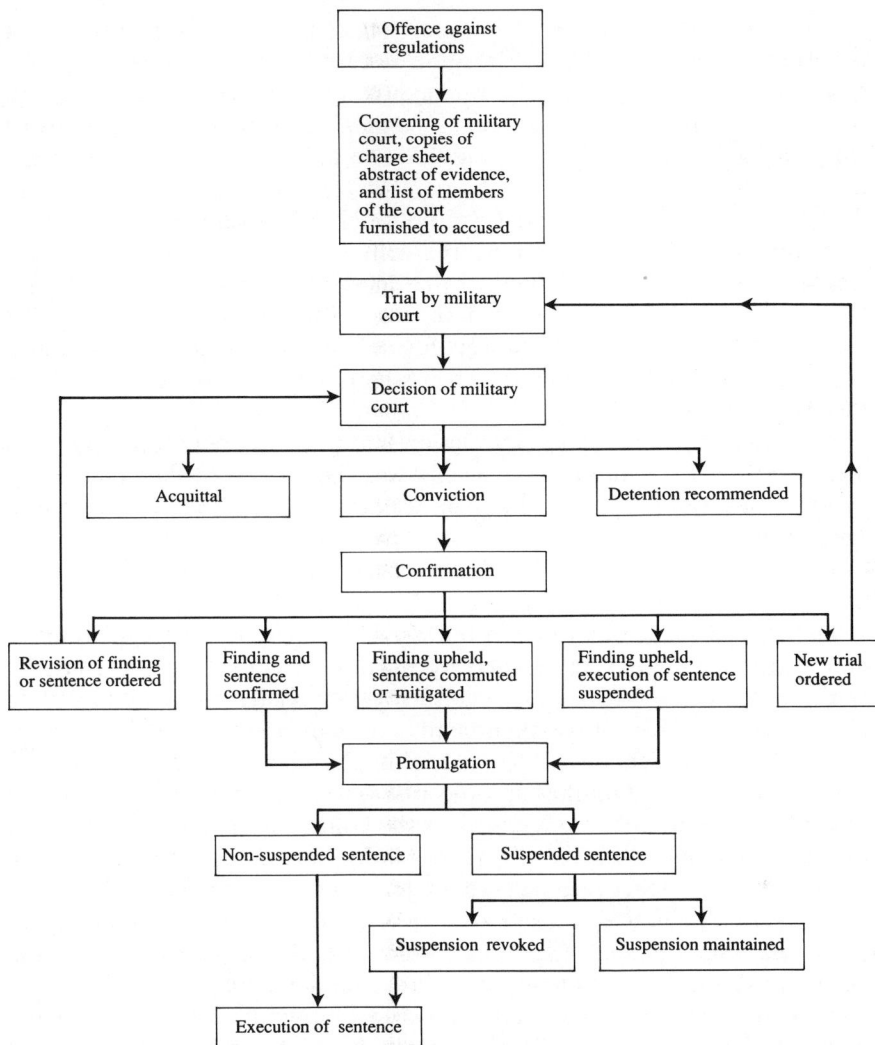

FIG. 4. The National Army military court system

in order to establish procedures.[260] The assessment of the validity of evidence with a view to prosecution was presumably the responsibility of the latter Department, but as early as September 1922 it was made clear that the Director of Intelligence at GHQ had overall responsibility for

[260] Review of Work of JAG's Dep. for w/e 4 Nov. 1922, Mulcahy papers, P7/B/135.

'compiling charges' against prisoners, which phrase presumably meant collating the evidence.[261] Later some decentralization appears to have taken place, as in April 1923 it was expressly set out that the Command Intelligence Officer was to collect any available evidence against persons whether in custody or not.[262] In addition to the involvement of the intelligence and the Judge Advocate General's Department in the process, the Adjutant-General's Department (as noted above) assumed a greater role from the end of March 1923 onwards with an order that a special officer whose only duty was 'to attend to the disposal of prisoners taken in the Command' was to be appointed to assist the Command Adjutant.[263] He was to 'make himself thoroughly acquainted with the procedure governing the trial and disposal of prisoners' and was to report daily to the Adjutant-General.[264]

A period of at least forty-eight hours had to elapse between a person's arrest and trial,[265] and at least twenty-four hours before the commencement of the trial the arrested person was to be given a copy of a charge sheet listing the charges against him, together with an abstract of the evidence to be given against him and a list of the names, rank, and corps of the officers constituting the court.[266]

The charge sheet was to be in the form specified in the Regulations[267] and was to be settled and signed by the officer convening the court.[268] Initially, the Judge Advocate General was personally involved in settling charge sheets.[269] The sheet might contain one or more 'charges or accusations'[270] but each 'charge or accusation' might allege only one offence.[271]

Other than providing that an officer who took or prepared the abstract of evidence could not be a member of the court, the regulations are silent on the preparation of the abstract. Under the British Army Act, an Abstract of Evidence was served in place of a Summary of Evidence in cases in which the accused was an officer. Unlike the Summary of Evidence, the Abstract of Evidence was not taken in the presence of the accused. It may be assumed, therefore, in the absence of an explicit statement to the contrary, and given the time-limits involved, that the National Army's Abstract did not have to be prepared in the presence of the accused. Ernie O'Malley, in his description of the events prior to his intended trial, recounts that an officer simply arrived one day at his prison sick-bed handed him 'the papers for your trial'.[272] Similarly,

[261] Office of the Director of Intelligence to the Military Governor of Newbridge Prison, 13 Sept. 1922, CWS, Prisoners' Files, P/6.
[262] 'General Staff Intelligence Memo. No. 3, Prisoners', CWS, Prisoners' Files, P/4.
[263] Adj.-Gen. to GOC, 22 Mar. 1923, CWS, Prisoners' Files, P/4.
[264] Ibid.   [265] Gen. Reg. 7.   [266] Ibid. 10.   [267] Ibid. 11 (1).   [268] Ibid. 11 (3).
[269] Review of Work of JAG's Dep. for w/e 11 Nov. 1922, Mulcahy papers, P7/B/135.
[270] Gen. Reg. 11 (2).   [271] Ibid.   [272] *Singing Flame*, 210.

TABLE 17. Operation of military courts, mid-November to mid-December 1992

Week ending	No. of cases tried	No. awaiting trial	No. of cases where Summary taken
11 Nov. 1922[a]	10	36	13
18 Nov. 1922[b]	8	31	1
25 Nov. 1922[c]	6	71	—
2 Dec. 1922[d]	13	77	1
9 Dec. 1922[e]	11	69	4
16 Dec. 1922[f]	4	102	11

[a] No figures available for Limerick Command.
[b] No figures available for 3rd Southern and Curragh Commands.
[c] No figures available for Limerick, 3rd Southern and Curragh Commands.
[d] This appears not to include material from 3rd Southern Command and Curragh Command.
[e] No reports available from Cork Command, 2nd Southern and 3rd Southern Commands.
[f] No reports available for 3rd Southern and Cork Commands.

Source: Weekly Reviews of Work of JAG's Department, from w/e 11 Nov. to w/e 16 Dec. 1922, Mulcahy papers, P7/B/135.

Liam Deasy, in his account of his trial, makes no mention of pre-trial proceedings.[273] But even though these procedures were relatively simple, the preparation of the Abstract seems to have placed a clog on the system, and a backlog soon built up (Table 17).

The officer delivering the charge sheet was to inform the accused that upon his (the accused's) furnishing the names of witnesses he wished to call in his defence all reasonable precautions would be taken to secure their attendance.[274] 'Every reasonable facility consistent with military exigencies' was to be afforded the accused in the preparation of his defence and this included the right to interview and instruct a solicitor or counsel or both.[275] It is difficult to gauge what the practical effect of this provision was as the decision to proceed by military court was not publicized.[276] O'Malley records being offered (and declining) the services

---

[273] L. Deasy, *Brother against Brother* (Dublin, 1982), 108–18.
[274] Gen. Reg. 10.
[275] Ibid. 9.
[276] Gen. Mulcahy (Minister for Defence) advised the Dáil on 29 Nov. 1922 that 'we are not making any arrangements at the present time to appraise the relatives of people taken

of a solicitor,[277] while Deasy writes that a National Army officer came to see him in custody and informed him that he would be defending him at his trial.[278] Refusal of legal assistance seems generally to have followed from the policy of non-recognition which Republican defendants adopted, but it appears that at least by February 1923, IRA GHQ was prepared in some cases to intervene in order to have prisoners defended.[279]

The trial

Then followed the actual trial. The court was to be constituted of a President holding the rank of Commandant or above and appointed by the convening officer, a legal officer nominated by the Minister for Defence and certified by the law officer to be a person of legal knowledge and experience and detailed by the convening officer for service on the court, and one other officer not below the rank of Captain appointed by the convening officer.[280] The provisions in relation to the 'Legal Officer' were derived from those under ROIA, whereby courts martial trying charges which carried the death penalty were to include a person certified by the Lord Chancellor of Ireland or the Lord Chief Justice of England to be a person of 'legal knowledge and experience'.[281] In the military court system however, the legal officer might also be appointed as President[282] in which case it may be that the court would consist of two members only. Excluded from membership of the court were the convening officer, the officer who took or prepared the abstract of evidence, the prosecuting officer, and any officer who either had a 'personal interest' in the case or who was not subject to military law.[283] The Judge Advocate General was

under such circumstances before we bring them before the military courts, or before we execute them . . . We do not under our present circumstances propose that when we get men in ambushes, or destroying these things that are the life of the country, to find out who their people are before we deal with them.' 1 *DD*, cols. 2442–3. See also 1 *DD*, cols. 2263–83 in relation to the secrecy surrounding the first four executions. Ernest Blythe, a member of the Executive Council, informed the Dáil on 17 Nov. 1922 that every person tried under the Resolutions passed by the Dáil would have a full opportunity for conducting his defence. 1 *DD* 2273. On 4 May 1923 R. O'Deaghaidh TD alleged in the Dáil that two defendants at a military court had been refused the right to obtain legal representation and to call witnesses. The Minister for Defence denied this and claimed that the defendants accepted the service of an officer for their defence. 3 DD 603.

[277] *Singing Flame*, 210.
[278] *Brother against Brother*, 110.
[279] In that month the Adj.-Gen. of the IRA wrote to Sean O'hUadaigh solicitor, in connection with the trial of Maj.-Gen. Kilroy (IRA) which it was believed was then forthcoming, stating that although Kilroy had said that he did not wish to consult a solicitor, it was the wish of GHQ (IRA) that a solicitor should meet him. Adj.-Gen. (IRA) to Sean O'hUadaigh, 16 Feb. 1923, O'Malley papers, P 17 a/38.
[280] Gen. Reg. 4 (1).
[281] ROIR 69 (5). See pp. 69–70.
[282] Gen. Reg. 4 (2).
[283] Ibid. 12.

personally present at some important trials, though presumably he did not take part in the hearings.[284] The accused had the right to challenge 'for cause shown' any member of the court except the legal officer.[285] Any vacancy arising from such challenge was to be filled from a panel of properly qualified officers detailed by the convening officer.[286]

The accused was formally entitled to be represented by counsel or by solicitor or both,[287] but it appears that IRA prisoners were ordered not to recognize the courts.[288] In some cases a National Army officer was appointed to conduct the defence. The prosecution was to be conducted by an officer detailed by the convening officer or by a solicitor or counsel or both appointed by the convening officer.[289] But even after state solicitors had been appointed in March 1923, it was ordered that these were not to be employed on military court or military committee work. The services of the Command legal officer were to be utilized instead.[290]

It is not stated in the Regulations whether the court was to sit *in camera* or not and in practice it seems that trials took place in secrecy or semi-secrecy.[291] In the case of the first four executions, relatives received no prior warning either of their trial or of their executions. For those four prisoners, there was obviously no opportunity for the kind of build-up in public sympathy for the condemned men of the kind which executions by the British had generated. Towards the end of November 1922 the Provisional Government decided that rather than having relatives discover the facts from newspapers, they would be advised immediately after the execution, but a proposal for prior notification was specifically rejected.[292] The press was also excluded from trials.[293]

At the commencement of the trial it appears that the prosecuting officer read out the charges.[294] The accused was then presumably called

---

[284] e.g. Review of Work of the JAG's Dep. for w/e 18 Nov. 1922 records: '*E. Childers*. Taking evidence herein, drawing Charge sheet, and order convening Court. Interviewing Witnesses for Prosecution, Counsel and Solicitor for Accused and attending trial'. Mulcahy papers, P7/B/135.

[285] Gen. Reg. 14.

[286] Ibid. 3 (2).

[287] Ibid. 8; however, see n. 276 above.

[288] On 22 Nov. 1922 the Provisional Government instructed the Minister of External Affairs to arrange for the publication of the directions given to 'Irregulars' by their Chief of Staff on 1 Nov. not to recognize either civil or military courts even where such recognition might save them from the death penalty. Minutes of Meeting of Provisional Government, 22 Nov. 1922.

[289] Gen. Reg. 3 (3).

[290] GRO 25, 9 Mar. 1923, 105: 'Employment of State Solicitors'. Mulcahy papers, P7/B/167.

[291] See n. 276 above.

[292] Minutes of the Meeting of Provisional Government, 22 Nov. 1922.

[293] See 2, *DD* cols. 36–7.

[294] Deasy, *Brother against Brother*, 110.

TABLE 18. Military courts: charges and outcome

Cases/charges[a]	Cases		Finding		Adjourned generally		Guilty		Not guilty		Not available
	No.	%	No.	%	No.	%	No.	%	No.	%	No.
Possession of Firearms and/or Ammunition Without Proper Authority	81	60[b]	6	7[c]	5	6[d]	51	88[e]	7	12	12
Using Force against National Forces	25	18	2	8	0	0	23	100	0	0	0
Armed Robbery or Robbery and Possession of Firearms Without Proper Authority	8	6	0	0	0	0	5	63	3	38	0
Possession of Bombs (including Mills bombs) without proper authority	4[f]	3	0	0	0	0	3	100	0	0	1
Miscellaneous	18	13	1	6	0	0	11	65	6	35	0
TOTAL	136	100	9	7	5	4	93	85	16	15	13

[a] Each case represents one individual, and the charges shown are the most serious with which that person was tried.

[b] This indicates total charges of this kind as a percentage of the total tried (136).

[c] This indicates 'no findings' as a percentage of the total number of offences of this category tried (81).

[d] This indicates cases 'adjourned generally' as a percentage of the total number of offences of this category tried (81).

[e] This indicates cases in which a verdict of 'not guilty' was reached as a percentage of the total number of cases in this category in which a finding was made (58), i.e. excluding 'no finding', 'adjourned generally', and 'not available'.

[f] In one of these cases a retrial was ordered but the outcome is not available.

Source: Prepared from list of military court trials, attached to Deputy JAG to Director of Intelligence, 15 Nov. 1923, Military Archives, Civil War Series, Prisoners Files, P/7, Dublin. Although this was stated to be a complete list, it was not so. In the schedule attached to Adjutant-General's Department to Minister of Defence, 8 Apr. 1924 at Military Archives, Civil War Series, Prisoners Files P/2, a total of 143 cases are mentioned, and that probably understates the position as only 11 executions are listed whereas the true figure was higher (see App. 2). In the above table, one case in which the sentence imposed was listed as penal servitude in the letter of 15 Nov. 1922 (that of Peter Cassidy), has, in accordance with other definite information, been reclassified as a death penalty case.

upon to enter a plea (although no specific stipulation in that regard was contained in the Regulations), and the prosecutor would begin his evidence-in-chief.

On the question of what evidence was relied upon at military court trials, it was made clear in the General Routine Orders that statements made by prisoners would be admissible only if 'purely voluntary'.[295] A pointer as to the type of evidence adduced was the provision that, as had been the case before DORA and ROIA courts martial, the burden of proof was reversed in certain circumstances. For instance, where the accused was charged with firearms offences or with offences relating to possession of documents, or National Army or police uniforms, it was for him to prove that he had not acted 'without lawful authority'.[296] This was reflected in the fact that cases of possession of firearms and/or ammunition without proper authority accounted for 60 per cent of the total tried (Table 18). In two other categories of offence—armed robbery or robbery and possession of firearms without proper authority; and possession of bombs without proper authority—which together accounted for a further 9 per cent of cases tried, the reversal of the burden of proof could have been a significant factor. In all other cases, every military court was to be bound by the ordinary law of evidence.[297]

The accused might give evidence on his own behalf.[298] This contrasted with the position under the ordinary law, under which, prior to the enactment of the Criminal Justice (Evidence) Act 1924, an accused was not a competent witness in his own defence. In giving such evidence, however, the Regulations provided that

it shall be no objection to a question put to him in cross-examination that it may tend to criminate him as to the offence with which he is then charged; but he shall not be asked, and if asked shall not be required to answer any question tending to show (a) that he has committed, been convicted of, or charged with any offence other than that with which he is then charged; (b) that he is of bad character; unless (a) the proof that he has committed or been convicted of such other offence is admissible to show that he is guilty of the offence with which he is then charged, or (b) he has personally or by his advocate asked questions of the witnesses with a view to establishing his own good character, or has given evidence of his own good character, or (c) the nature of conduct of the defence is such as to involve imputations upon the character of the prosecutor, or any of the witnesses for the prosecution.[299]

---

[295] GRO 4, 24 Nov. 1922, 22: 'Prisoners in Possession of Arms etc. Procedure as to on Arrest', para. 6, Mulcahy papers, P7/B/167.
[296] e.g. see paras. 2 (e) and 2 (g) General Order 8 Jan. 1923.
[297] Gen. Reg. 15 (2).
[298] Ibid. 16.
[299] Ibid. 17.

This rule differed from that introduced by the 1924 Act in that the accused was not entitled to refuse to answer questions on the ground that his answer might incriminate him.

During the course of the trial, the legal officer was to advise the court on points of law, procedure, and evidence.[300] He was also to make a record of all evidence and 'transactions' of the court.[301] The hearings do not seem to have been elaborate legal spectacles. Deasy's description of his trial (which he admits was 'hazy') (and which may in any case have been by committee) was that:

Very little was said apart from the reading of the charges by the prosecuting officer who asked for the maximum penalty. I remained silent. The findings were apparently transmitted immediately by the special wireless telephone system used by army units to maintain communication with their headquarters in Dublin.[302]

At the conclusion of the trial, this record, known as the Proceedings, with the decision of the court marked thereon, was to be sent to the Adjutant-General.[303] The military court might acquit or convict on any charge, or instead of either a conviction or acquittal, might not bring in a finding, and might instead recommend the accused's detention within or without the jurisdiction of the Provisional Government.[304] This latter provision was derived from the similar rule which applied at trials by British military courts. In the National Army's military court system, this result was arrived at in 7 per cent of trials. In these cases the accused were ordered to be detained for periods ranging from 135 days to two years, in what was the equivalent of the imposition of a sentence of imprisonment.[305] In addition, a further 4 per cent of cases were adjourned generally without a result having been reached (Table 18).

The Regulations do not explicitly state whether decisions of the court were to be arrived at by majority or unanimously. An acquittal on any charge was to be announced in open court[306] and was not subject to confirmation.[307] A conviction was, however, subject to confirmation. The following range of sentences (listed in order of decreasing severity) was (subject to confirmation) available for most offences: death, penal servitude, imprisonment, deportation, internment, or fine.[308] For some of the lesser offences, however, the death penalty was not available.[309]

---

[300] Gen. Reg. 15 (3).   [301] Ibid. 18.   [302] *Brother against Brother*, 110–11.
[303] Gen. Reg. 20.   [304] Ibid. 26.

[305] Schedule of complete list of trials by military court, attached to Deputy JAG to Director of Intelligence, 15 Nov. 1923, CWS, Prisoners' Files, P/7.

[306] Gen. Reg. 26.   [307] Ibid. 21.   [308] Ibid. 5 and 6.

[309] For instance, under para. 3 General Order 8 Jan. 1923, assisting in escape from military custody or sending threatening letters was punishable by 'penal servitude for any period or any lesser punishment'.

Post-trial: confirmation and reprisals

Every sentence and every finding of the court other than a finding of 'not guilty' was to be subject to confirmation by a confirming authority consisting of two members of the Army Council.[310] The Confirming Authority might confirm or refuse confirmation in whole or in part of the original or revised finding or sentence[311] or direct the reassembly of the court for revision of the finding and sentence or either of them. It might also order a new trial or suspend execution of the sentence or reduce or commute the sentence but not increase it,[312] and where a sentence was sent back to the court for revision, the court might not increase the original sentence.[313] Where confirmation was sought, it was the practice of the Judge Advocate General to issue an 'advice on confirmation',[314] a procedure which was presumably designed to ensure that he exercised a scrutinizing function in relation to these trials.

Overall, convictions were sustained in 85 per cent of cases in which a finding was reached. The major category of offences in which the highest percentage of convictions was reached was that of 'using force against National Forces'. On this charge no defendant was acquitted (Table 18). One possible explanation for this unusually high percentage conviction was that those tried on this charge had been captured in the course of an ambush, and that accordingly evidence was readily available. A percentage conviction which was slightly higher than the average was also obtained in respect of charges of possession of firearms without proper authority, probably reflecting the effect of the reversal of the burden of proof in these cases.

A wide variety of sentencing options were made use of. Death sentences were imposed and confirmed in 29 per cent of the total number of cases tried, but the bulk of these sentences were imposed on charges of possession of firearms without proper authority, and overall 46 per cent of those tried on this charge were sentenced to death (Table 19). It is surprising that the death sentence was employed much less frequently on what would seem to be the more serious charge of 'using force against National Forces'. One noticeable difference in patterns of sentencing in relation to these classes of offence is that while the death sentence was much more likely to be imposed on 'possession' charges, much heavier custodial sentences were imposed on 'use of force' charges—87 per cent of those convicted on the latter charge received sentences varying from six years to life, whereas only 12 per cent of sentences for the latter class of offence came within this category. It seems to have been the case that if a 'possession' charge were deemed serious, the heavier custodial sentences

[310] Gen. Reg. 21.   [311] Ibid. 23.   [312] Ibid. 24.   [313] Ibid. 23.
[314] See Review of Work of JAG's Dep. for w/e 18 Nov. 1922, Mulcahy papers, P7/B/135.

TABLE 19. Military courts: charges and sentencing

Cases/charges[a]	No. found guilty	Sentence imposed														Not available
		Non-custodial		Internment		0–2 years		3–5 years		6–10 years		11 years–life		Death		
		No.	%	No.	%	No.	%	No.	%	No.	%	No.	%	No.	%	No.
Possession of Firearms and/or Ammunition Without Proper Authority	51	0	0[b]	0	0	4	10	13	32	5	12	0	0	19	46	10
Using Force against National Forces	23	0	0	0	0	0	0	1	4	19	83	1	4	2	9	0
Possession of Bombs (including Mills bombs) without proper authority	3	0	0	0	0	0	0	0	0	0	0	0	0	0	0	2
Armed Robbery or Robbery and Possession of Firearms Without Proper Authority	5	0	0	0	0	0	0	2	67	1	33	0	0	2	100	1
Miscellaneous	11	1	10	6	60	0	0	2	20	0	0	1	10	0	0	1
TOTAL	93	1	1	6	8	4	5	18	23	25	32	2	3	23	29	14

[a] Each case represents one individual, and the charges shown are the most serious with which that person was tried.
[b] This indicates the number of non-custodial sentences imposed as a percentage of the total number of convictions in respect of this class of offence for which details of sentence imposed are available (41 i.e. total no. (51) less no. not available (10)).
Source: See Table 18.

were overlooked and a death sentence was imposed, while in 'using force' charges, the reverse obtained.

Other sentencing options were much less frequently made use of. Only one instance can be traced in which a fine was imposed,[315] though provision was expressly made in the General Routine Orders that where this was the punishment decided upon, the money was to be collected by the military and eventually forwarded to the Army finance officer 'for crediting to the Public'.[316] Internment as a sentencing option was employed in only six cases, all of which trials were held in Cork in July 1923, and therefore after the end of the fighting. In all cases the charge was one of possession of 'seditious documents'.[317] It appears that if any sentences of deportation were recommended by military courts, none was confirmed (though there is some dispute about the matter),[318] although there were instances in which the Intelligence Department was prepared to recommend deportation rather than detain the prisoner in military custody.[319]

The most notorious feature of the military court system was the way in which the provisions allowing suspension of sentence were used to create the threat of reprisal executions. This process, and the parallel operation of military committees, remain the most controversial measures taken by the winning side in the Civil War, and it is therefore worth examining in some detail.

Some days after the execution without trial of four prisoners from the Four Courts garrison (who were publicly stated to have been shot as a reprisal), the matter of the confirmation of sentence in the cases of four prisoners tried in Kerry Command came up for consideration. Instead of simply agreeing to the confirmation of the sentence of death that had been passed on the prisoners, the Commander-in-Chief proposed a suspension of the sentences and the issuing of a public notice of the following terms:

[315] This was a fine of £50 imposed on a charge of 'unlawful possession of property' at a trial held in Athlone. Schedule of trials by military court, attached with Deputy JAG to Director of Intelligence, 15 Nov. 1923, CWS, Prisoners' Files, P/7.

[316] GRO 22, 4 July 1923, 224: 'Fines Imposed by Military Courts, Procedure re Collection', Mulcahy papers, P7/B/168.

[317] Schedule of trials by military court, attached with Deputy JAG to Director of Intelligence, 15 Nov. 1923, CWS, Prisoners' Files, P/7.

[318] J. M. Kelly writes that deportations took place during the Civil War on the orders of military courts (*Fundamental Rights*, 81), but in the schedule referred to in n. 317 there is no record or any sentence of deportation having been confirmed.

[319] e.g. in the case of eight individuals from Belfast captured in Dundalk in Feb. 1923, the Intelligence Dep. advised that 'while ostensibly assisting the "Irregulars"', the men had 'indulged in looting and plundering rather than in any other form of activity', and that rather than holding the men in military custody 'a much better course would be to release them, and arrange if possible, for their deportation back to the Six County Area'. Intelligence Dep. to Ministry of Home Affairs, 28 May 1923, CWS, Prisoners' Files, P/8.

In accordance with paragraph 23E of the 'General Regulations as to the Trial of Civilians by Military Courts' the execution of the sentence has been suspended, with a view to seeing whether the attitude of the Irregulars still at large in County Kerry, may not have sufficiently changed or be changing sufficiently to warrant that without endangering the lives and the properties of the people of Kerry generally—clemency may not be exercised in these cases.[320]

The threat was clear—the prisoners were to be shot in the event of a resurgence of IRA activity in Kerry. In effect, they were to become hostages. The Judge Advocate General clearly recognized the departure which such a step marked. His view was that

There are only two considerations which justify this course; firstly that the circumstances of the nation at present justify almost anything that would serve to end the present campaign of murder and arson of the Irregulars; secondly that the execution of persons tried and convicted in pursuance of a resolution of an Dail as a reprisal, is preferable to the execution of persons untried and unconvicted.[321]

Nevertheless, he indicated a considerable degree of unease about the policy:

There is no other justification whatever for the course which cannot be called humane. In no criminal or court-martial code can a death sentence be suspended and normally the course indicated is foreign to all ideas of fair play and humanity.[322]

This latter comment raises the question as to whether the proposed course was *ultra vires* the Army Emergency Powers Resolution. In stating that 'In no criminal or court-martial code can a death sentence be suspended' the Judge Advocate General cannot be taken to have meant that in ordinary circumstances death sentences could never be suspended, because they obviously could (for example, in Murphy's case, the British GOC had repeatedly suspended execution pending appeal in the civil courts).[323] Rather, he must be interpreted as having meant that no power ordinarily existed to use the power to suspend in order to force persons other than those directly involved in the proceedings to do, or desist from doing, some act. Perhaps in anticipation of this sort of argument he added the following postscript in his communication with the Commander-in-Chief:

The course is however clearly not inconsistent with the Army Emergency Powers Resolution of the 28th September 1922, except in so far as that Resolution must be understood to be interpreted with due regard to humanitarian considerations.[324]

---

[320] Copy draft statement attached to JAG to C-in-C, 12 Dec. 1922, Mulcahy papers, P7/B/101.
[321] JAG to C-in-C, 12 Dec. 1922, Mulcahy papers, P7/B/101.
[322] Ibid.   [323] See Ch. 2.
[324] JAG to C-in-C, 12 Dec. 1922, Mulcahy papers, P7/B/101.

In any case, the question of *vires* could not be raised in the civil courts,[325] nor was there any appeals structure within the military court system.

The proposed course of action was approved by the Executive Council on 12 December, the minutes of the meeting recording as follows:

The Minister of Defence [who was also the Commander-in-Chief] reported that in view of the improved situation in the Kerry area, he proposed to adopt a certain procedure in regard to the cases of four men who had been captured in arms, and tried before a military court. His proposal was approved.[326]

The next step taken was that the Commander-in-Chief wrote on 13 December 1922 to the GOC Kerry Command, informing him that confirmation of the finding and sentence in the four cases would be sent to him, with an instruction that 'the execution of the sentence has been suspended for the present with a view to seeing whether clemency may not ultimately be exercised in each of these four cases'.[327] The scheme was explained as follows:

What we have in mind is that should, within the next two or three weeks, a serious ambush take place, or 'spy' case occur, or should the work on the railways in Kerry be interfered with, or should there be any other serious evidence that the irregulars are going to continue their activity in Kerry, it will not be possible to extend clemency in these four cases.[328]

While it was stressed that the ultimate decision in the matter rested with the Army Council, that body informed the GOC that it would be 'guided very much by your appreciation of the general situation and significance of events'.[329]

Thus apart from the formal mechanism for disposing of cases, an informal parallel mechanism, whereby the Commander-in-Chief dealt directly with the local GOC, was also being created. The formal mechanism was attended to when the Commander-in-Chief wrote to the Chief of Staff on the same date, enclosing the letter to the GOC, requesting signature of the Findings Sheet and the Certificate of the Confirming Authority in the four cases.[330]

Later in the month the GOC issued posters which announced that the case of the four would be dealt with as follows:

Whereas the confirming authority, influenced by the favourable reports of the General Officer Commanding Kerry Command, as to the general tendency of the situation in Kerry, has suspended the execution of the sentences in each of these

---

[325] See pp. 257–9.
[326] Minutes of Meeting of Executive Council, 12 Dec. 1922.
[327] C-in-C to GOC Kerry Command, 13 Dec. 1922, Mulcahy papers, P7/B/101.
[328] Ibid.
[329] Ibid.
[330] C-in-C to Chief of Staff, 13 Dec. 1922, Mulcahy papers, P7/B/101.

cases on certain conditions—if, after Thursday 21st December (1) ambushes or attacks on national troops, (2) interference with railways or roads, and (3) interference with private property are committed, the stay on the execution of the sentences will be removed and the sentences of death on each of the above named men will be forthwith carried out.[331]

In the event, the sentences of all of the prisoners were commuted to ten years' penal servitude on 18 January 1922.[332] On 19 February 1923 the GOC Kerry Command sent a message to the Commander-in-Chief, advising that 'In view of Pierce's surrender I would strongly recommend that Death Sentences be not carried out on members who have been tried on capital charges.'[333] This may have been because other Kerry prisoners faced execution, or it may have been done in ignorance of the decision to commute the earlier sentences.

It is not clear what subsequently happened in the case of death sentences handed down by military courts, though it is clear that many more reprisal executions took place. There is also uncertainty as to the numbers actually executed.[334] What seems to have happened was that military committees, rather than military courts, were favoured as a mechanism whereby executions might be carried out as reprisals (though perhaps not exclusively so), and it is to these committees that attention must now be turned.

Military committees

There was no uniform committee system. Instead, the rules under which these committees operated seem to have been changed on a number of occasions for strategic rather than for legal reasons. Three main organizational proposals can be identified and are examined below. The key strategic considerations centred around the question of death sentences and this issue is also examined in detail.

The first proposal: December 1922

The starting point in the discussion of these committees, as with the military courts, is the Army Emergency Powers Resolution of September

---

[331] A cutting from *Irish Times*, dated 20 Dec. 1922 and carrying the text of the notice, is included in S1 884, SPO.

[332] A handwritten list of military court cases listing the sentences in the cases of the four as having been commuted can be found at CWS, Prisoners' Files, P/3. Further confirmation can be had in the fact that the names of the four do not appear on any lists of executed prisoners (see App. 2).

[333] Intelligence Dep., translation of cipher message, 19 Feb. 1923, GOC Kerry Command to C-in-C, Mulcahy papers, P7/B/284.

[334] Macardle, in *Irish Republic*, lists 77 executions, including the four executed without trial from the Four Courts garrison. One list prepared by the National Army lists a total of 75, including the Four Courts prisoners, while another lists 81, again including the Four Courts prisoners. The best available details from all sources are given in App. 2.

1922. Under the Resolution, committees were given the same jurisdiction as military courts, and as with the Courts, it was stipulated that they were to include at least one person nominated by the Minister of Defence and certified by the law officer to be a person of legal knowledge and experience.[335] Likewise, there was a requirement that no sentence of death imposed by a committee be executed except under the counter-signature of two members of the Army Council.[336] But it appears that it was only after the proclamation of 7 December 1922 that steps were taken to establish such committees, and in the Reviews of Work of the Judge Advocate General's Department, the first record of the operation of the committees came in the week ending 16 December 1922.[337] It is not clear from the report, however, what role the Department played in the operation of the committees, and as time progressed these types of tribunal seem to have come increasingly under the auspices of the Adjutant-General's Department.

The proclamation of 7 December had warned that any person arrested in possession of (1) any bomb, portion of a bomb, or article in the nature of a bomb; or (2) any dynamite, gelignite, or other explosive substance; or (3) any revolver, rifle, gun, or other firearm, or lethal weapon, or any ammunition for such firearm, was to be brought before a committee of officers and charged and the charges investigated. Upon consideration of the report of such a committee the confirming authority, which was to be any two members of the Army Council, might order the person 'to suffer death or such other punishment as they shall see fit', and such order was to be carried out summarily. In these provisions, there was no pretence that the proceedings were to amount to a trial. Instead, what was to take place was an 'investigation', and a 'report' rather than a 'finding' was to be arrived at.

As all offences that could be investigated by the committees might instead be tried by military court (though not all offences triable by military court could be investigated by committee), the question arises as to how cases were to be divided between the two types of tribunal. By 13 December 1922 a draft Army Council Order had been prepared for trans-mission to the GOC Eastern Command, setting out that upon the arrest of any person in possession of any one or more of the articles specified in the proclamation, the officer to whom such person was given charge was immediately to report the matter in full to the GOC, charging such person with possession of the item in question.[338] The GOC could then

---

[335] Cl. 3 (a).
[336] Cl. 3 (b).
[337] Mulcahy papers, P7/B/135.
[338] 'Draft Order by the Army Council to The General Officer Commanding Eastern Command', attached to memo. of C-in-C, 13 Dec. 1922, Mulcahy papers, P7/B/232.

convene a committee of officers to investigate the charge or charges.[339] Thus under this proposed scheme, the decision to convene a committee lay at the same level in the military hierarchy as the decision to convene a military court.

A committee was to consist of at least three officers of whom at least one was to be of a rank not lower than Captain. There was provision that if the accused so wished, the convening officer was to detail an officer to defend him, but there was no provision that representation could be by solicitor or barrister. Nor was there any provision that the prisoner could either consult with a solicitor before the investigation or attempt to arrange for any witnesses to be present.

The senior officer on the committee was to act as President, and another officer, who could be one of the members of the committee, was to make a written record of the investigation. After the members of the committee had been sworn in, the President was to state to the accused the charge(s) he faced. The witnesses for the prosecution were then to give their evidence on oath, and were subject to cross-examination by the accused.

At the conclusion of the prosecution case, the accused was to be entitled to give evidence in his own defence, but there was no specific provision for him to call witnesses although he, or any officer he chose to represent him, was to be permitted 'to make his defence'.[340] Upon the conclusion of the evidence, the accused, or his representative, could address the committee. The investigation was then to conclude, and the President was to record the recommendation of the committee and transmit the record to the appropriate GOC. Presumably this 'recommendation' was to indicate a conclusion as to the question of guilt or innocence, and a sentence, though this was not expressly stated.

The GOC, if he was satisfied that the committee was 'duly convened',[341] was to endorse upon the record a certificate to that effect and transmit the record to the Adjutant-General. In the case of a death sentence, the case would then presumably be referred to another member of the Army Council for signature.

The second proposal: early January 1923

It is not clear whether the procedures contained in the draft order of December 1922 were ever generally implemented. Under the General Order of the Army Council of 8 January 1923 the jurisdiction of committees was expanded to include the investigation of charges of murder and related inchoate offences.[342] On 18 January 1923 a memorandum was

---

[339] Draft Order, para. 3.   [340] Ibid., para. 11.   [341] Ibid., para. 15.
[342] Those facing investigation by committee under the January Order were 'any person who shall: (a) Murder any person or aid or abet the murder of any person, or attempt in any

issued by the Commander-in-Chief which sought to clarify the position in relation to distribution of cases between military courts and committees. In future, cases would be divided into two classes.[343] Class (a) was to consist of 'persons caught red-handedly guilty of any of the offences indicated in paragraphs 2 A, B, & C of the general Regulations' (the same offences as listed in the proclamation of December 1922); while class (b) was to consist of all other cases. Class (b) cases were to be brought to Command Headquarters, and were to be dealt with at that level, presumably by military court, whereas class (a) cases were to be brought to Battalion Headquarters and the cases were to be investigated by a committee. They were then to be kept at Battalion Headquarters until notification of sentence had been received, and in the event of a sentence of death, the execution was to take place at Battalion Headquarters.

As had been the case with British Army drumhead courts, the decision to refer cases to committees of officers involved a prejudgement of the substantive issues, in that resort was to be had to investigation by committee only in the case of persons caught red-handed. Thus, as had been the case with their British predecessors, the accused was placed at maximum risk of a death sentence in situations in which the minimum safeguards were to apply.

The third proposal: 23 January 1923

The memorandum of 18 January 1923 had specifically rejected a suggestion that all cases be tried before a committee and that in 'non red-handed' cases GHQ should return the case for trial by military court as 'not feasible', but in the eventual orders of 23 January 1923 it was provided that the cases of all arrested prisoners should be brought before a Battalion committee of officers,[344] and it was later specified that this should be within 24 hours of capture.[345] What eventually seems to have happened in these cases is illustrated by flow-chart in Figure 5. It appears that prisoners were brought before committees as of course, but in those cases reserved for trial by military court, the committee presumably did not conduct an investigation, but instead referred the case to the appropriate GOC who then handed the matter over to his legal officer for possible trial by military court.[346]

way to murder any person; (*b*) Conspire to murder any person; (*c*) Command, procure, incite, counsel, solicit, encourage, persuade or endeavour to persuade any person to murder any person' (para. 1).

[343] C-in-C's Memo. No. 4, 18 Jan. 1923, Mulcahy papers, P7/B/169.

[344] A copy of the order is not available and is probably not extant, but reference to the order is made in Ministry of Defence to Director of Intelligence, 21 Nov. 1923, CWS, Prisoners' Files, P/2.

[345] Adj.-Gen. to GOC, 22 Mar. 1923, ibid., P/4.

[346] Special Instructions (No. 1): Prisoners had ordered that 'cases in which a Committee

```
                                    ┌──────────────┐
                                    │    Arrest    │
                                    └──────┬───────┘
                                           │
                                    ┌──────▼───────┐
                                    │  Appearance  │
                                    │   before     │
                                    │  committee   │
                                    └──────┬───────┘
                                           │
                  ┌────────────────────────┴────────────────────────┐
          ┌───────▼────────┐                              ┌──────────▼────────┐
          │ Committee has  │                              │  Committee has    │
          │ jurisdiction   │                              │  no jurisdiction  │
          │ per            │                              └──────────┬────────┘
          │ instructions   │                                         │
          │ issued to GOCs │                              ┌──────────▼────────┐
          │ 27 Jan. 1923   │                              │ Case referred     │
          └───────┬────────┘                              │ to GOC            │
                  │                                        │ Command           │
          ┌───────▼────────┐                              └──────────┬────────┘
          │ Investigation  │                                         │
          │ by committee   │                              ┌──────────▼────────┐
          └───────┬────────┘                              │ Case referred     │
                  │                                        │ to Command        │
          ┌───────▼────────┐                              │ Legal Officer for │
          │ Record of      │                              │ possible          │
          │ investigation  │                              │ disposal by       │
          │ sent to        │                              │ military court    │
          │ Adjutant-      │                              └───────────────────┘
          │ General's      │
          │ Department     │
          └───────┬────────┘
          ┌───────┴──────────────────────────┐
   ┌──────▼───────┐                    ┌──────▼───────┐
   │ Non-trivial  │                    │ Trivial      │
   │ cases        │                    │ cases        │
   └──────┬───────┘                    └──────┬───────┘
   ┌──────┴────────┐                          │
┌──▼────────┐ ┌────▼─────────┐         ┌──────▼────────┐
│ Offences  │ │ Other        │         │ Cases referred│
│ covered by│ │ offences     │────────▶│ to Intelligence│
│ Army      │ │ specified in │         │ Department to │
│ Council   │ │ instructions │         │ be considered │
│ Proclam-  │ │ of           │         │ for release or│
│ ation     │ │ 27 Jan. 1923 │         │ otherwise     │
│ 7 Dec.1922│ └──────────────┘         │ dealt with    │
└──┬────────┘                          │ without       │
┌──▼────────┐                          │ reference to  │
│ Case      │                          │ Army Council  │
│ referred  │                          └───────────────┘
│ to Army   │
│ Council   │
│ for       │
│ adjudic-  │
│ ation and │
│ sentencing│
└───────────┘
```

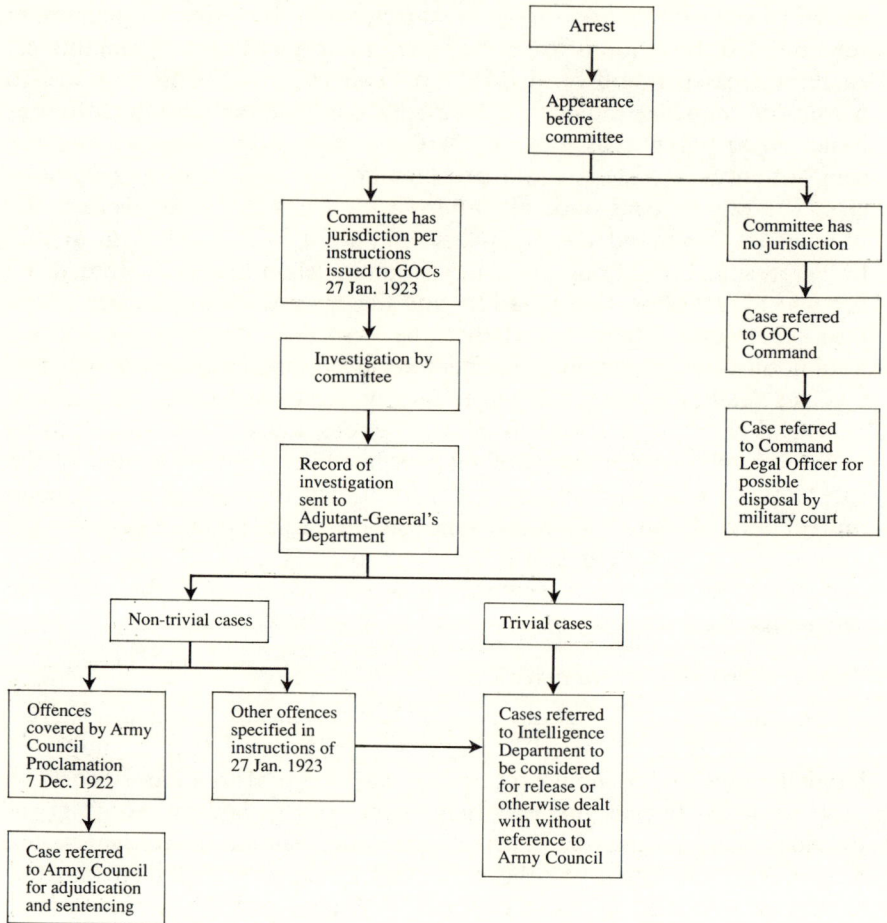

FIG. 5. The committee and military court systems (final form)

In cases in which an investigation was carried out, the record was sent to the Adjutant-General's Department. From March 1923 onwards, that Department was to have been informed of any investigations in the daily reports of the special officer detailed at Command level to oversee the disposal of prisoners' cases. In the Adjutant-General's Department, it was the practice to separate trivial cases on receipt of records of investi-

of Officers have not jurisdiction will be reported to the GOC Dublin Command who will place such cases in the hands of the Legal Officer'. The instructions are undated but seem to be attached to an Intelligence Dep. Memo. of 20 Dec. 1923, in CWS, Prisoners' Files, P/5.

gations, and to refer them to the Intelligence Department to be considered for release, or otherwise dealt with, without reference to the Army Council. Non-trivial cases were, however, to be referred to two members of the Army Council for adjudication and sentencing. In practice, a considerable backlog of cases which had not been considered by the Army Council built up, and in November 1923, months after investigations had ceased, it was decided that committee cases other than those falling within the terms of the proclamation of 7 December 1922 should also be referred to the Intelligence Department for disposal; in effect, they were to be dealt with as internees. Other cases were still proceeded with, thus many prisoners knew of their conviction and sentence only months after capture, and some claimed that they did not even know that they had been tried.

Work-load and types of charge

The lack of discrimination in bringing cases before committees resulted in much lower conviction rates being obtained by these tribunals than was the case with military courts. Overall, only 46 per cent of those investigated by committee were convicted, or strictly speaking were 'reported guilty' (Table 20). The most usual charge on which convictions were obtained was 'possession of firearms without proper authority'. A sample of cases in which convictions were obtained by committee shows this charge to have been brought in 88 per cent of cases (Table 21), a figure considerably higher than the corresponding percentage for military courts. The burden of proof would have been reversed in these cases, as in the second largest category of offence tried by committee, that of possession of bombs without proper authority.

Sentencing and reprisals

In almost half the cases in the sample the accused was sentenced to death (48 per cent), and in 'possession of firearms' charges a majority was so sentenced (Table 21). It was the manner in which these death sentences were reached and carried out that illustrates most clearly the parody of due process that trial by committee entailed. On 23 January a further order was issued by the Commander-in-Chief which because of its singular ruthlessness deserves extensive quotation. The order recited that it was the Government's intention to stop the practice of kidnapping of certain defined categories by the IRA, and continued:

There are in the various Commands quite a large number of prisoners taken since 15th October and chargeable with offences under the Military Courts. Steps should be taken at once to schedule those cases and to tabulate the evidence against those prisoners.

TABLE 20. Work-load of committees

Total no. investigated	1039
Outcome of investigations	
Acquitted	563 (54%)
Convicted	476 (46%)
Recommended for internment	0 (0%)
Outcome of Convictions	
Executed	64
In custody on 8 Apr. 1924	274
Escaped by 8 Apr. 1924	31
Released by 8 Apr. 1924	107

Source: Derived from schedule attached to Adjutant-General's Department to Minister of Defence, 8 Apr. 1924, CWS, Prisoners' Files, P/2.

3. On the kidnapping of any of the above mentioned persons, the G-O-C of the area shall immediately issue a printed Proclamation, within whatever radius of the place of kidnapping he thinks well, ordering the return within 48 hours of the person kidnapped. He shall, in the meantime remove to the Battalion Head-quarters of the area, 10 or 12 persons chargeable with an offence punishable by death since 15th October, and against whom definite evidence has been tabulated. He shall arrange that a Committee of Officers sit on those cases forthwith, with a view to being in a position to execute one or more in respect of each kidnapped person not later than 6 hours after the expiration of the 48 hours should the kidnapped person not be released by that time. In case of non-release, a second Proclamation giving a second period of 48 hours should be given when double the number should be executed within 6 hours after the expiration of the notice in case of non-return of the kidnapped persons.

A third Proclamation should then be issued, giving a fresh period of 48 hours, and a responsible Officer despatched to the Adjutant General, GHQ with a report and for further instructions.[347]

On 31 January 1923, following the kidnapping of Senator John Bagwell, one such proclamation was issued, which warned that if the Senator was not permitted to return to his own home within forty-eight hours of the date and hour of the proclamation 'punitive action will be taken against several associates in this conspiracy now in custody and otherwise'.[348] Bagwell was released, and it appears that no reprisals were exacted in this instance.

January had seen the most extensive series of executions since the start of the conflict. At least thirty-four people were officially shot following

[347] C-in-C to GOC Each Command, 23 Jan. 1923, Mulcahy papers, P7/B/177.
[348] Quoted in the Dáil debate on the proclamation. 2 *DD*, col. 1196.

TABLE 21. Committees: patterns of charges and sentences

Charge[a]	No. of cases		Sentence									
			0–2 years		3–5 years		6–10 years		11 years–life		Death (commuted)	
	No.	%	No.	%	No.	%	No.	%	No.	%	No.	%
Poss. f/a and/or ammunition	177	88[b]	18	10[c]	34	19	24	14	6	3	95	54
Poss. bombs, Mills bombs, etc.	15	7	8	53	4	27	2	13	0	0	1	7
Taking part in armed attack	8	4	0	0	0	0	5	63	2	25	1	13
Misc.	2	1	0	0	1	50	1	50	0	0	0	0
TOTAL	202[d]	100	26	13	39	19	32	16	8	4	97	48[e]

[a] Each case represents one individual, and the charges shown are the most serious with which that person was tried.

[b] This figure indicates the number of cases of this type as a percentage of the total sample.

[c] This figure indicates the number of sentences coming within this band as a percentage of the number of charges of this kind in the sample.

[d] This sample amounts to 19% of the total number of cases/prisoners investigated by committee, or to 42% of the total convicted. It is not wholly representative as it includes no cases in which fines or very short sentences were imposed, nor those in which the death penalty was imposed. These are, however, the best figures available at present.

[e] Breakdown of commuted death sentences—0–2: 4 (4%); 3–5: 28 (29%); 6–10: 29 (30%); 11–life: 36 (37%).

Source: Prepared from schedules 1–10 of the military court and committee cases reviewed by Judges Doyle and Drumgoole, CWS, Prisoners' Files, P/2, Dublin.

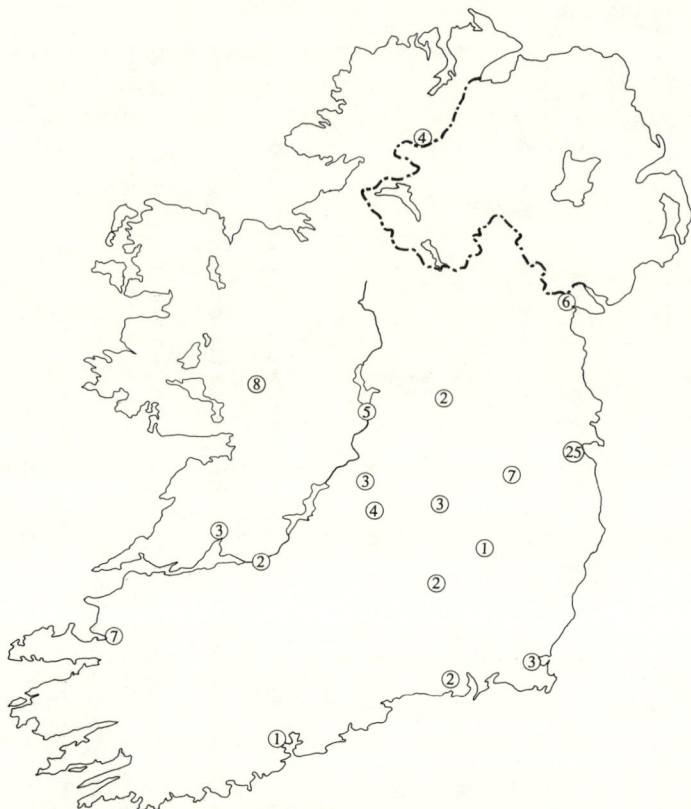

MAP F. National Army executions, 1922–1923

Source: Prepared from lists of 'Executions' and 'Executed Irregulars' at S1 184, SPO, Dublin; list of 'Executed Republicans' in Macardle, *Irish Republic*, 1023–4; copies of press releases issued by the National Army after the executions, in Military Archives, A/0770, Dublin, and list of military court trials attached to Deputy JAG to Director of Intelligence, 15 Nov. 1923, Military Archives, P/7, Dublin. For further details see App. 2.

disposal of their cases by military courts or committees.[349] One effect of the introduction of committees at Battalion level was that the resulting executions were geographically much more widely distributed than would probably have been the case had disposal of cases been limited to trial by military court which were organized at Command level (Map F). This practice of decentralized executions was certain to have maximum localized effect, and also meant that a lower stratum of the National Army was directly involved in the executions policy.

In February there was only one execution, the break being due, it seems, to the amnesty offer which had followed Deasy's (the captured

[349] Extracted from list of executions, at s1 884, SPO.

IRA Deputy Chief of Staff) call for an end to the struggle. Deasy had avoided execution by signing a document in those terms, and it appears that some other prisoners, in a move which caused considerable dissension within Republican ranks, avoided, or sought to avoid execution, by signing similar documents.[350]

The cessation, though, was clearly envisaged as being temporary only, and on 12 February the Army Council decided that 'bad cases' were to be prepared for execution, and that after 18 February 'it must be anticipated that no clemency will be shown in any case'.[351] In every case of outrage in any Battalion area, three men were to be executed. To this end, at least nine men per Battalion area were to be immediately concentrated at the Command centre. The executions continued—eleven in March and fourteen in April, when Republican resistance was clearly facing collapse. The final executions took place in May 1923.

Review of military court and committee cases

The decision in O'Brien's case in July to August 1923 deprived the sentences of the various military tribunals of any continuing validity,[352] but this did not result in the release of sentenced prisoners, since the rapidly enacted Public Safety (Emergency Powers) Act 1923 provided that such prisoners would have to serve out the remainder of their sentences.[353] Then, under the Indemnity Act 1923, explicit retrospective validation was given to the sentences of any 'military court, committee or tribunal' established since 27 June 1922,[354] but it was further provided that a Board of Commissioners was to be established of not less than two members, all of whom were to hold specified judicial office.[355] The Board was to have power to review sentences of the various military tribunals, and could confirm or reduce, but not increase a sentence.[356]

In January 1924 rules of procedure for the Board were made by the Minister for Defence.[357] Hearings began on 27 February 1924 and continued until 19 May,[358] but the response from the prisoners was disappointing, due no doubt to a refusal to recognize any official bodies. Of the 323 persons described as 'political prisoners' on 27 February, only seventeen applied to the Board. In nine of these cases there was a

---

[350] See Hopkinson, *Green*, 232, and O'Malley, *Singing Flame*, 224.

[351] Army Council Decision, 12 Dec. 1923, Mulcahy papers, P7/B/178.

[352] See part III.

[353] s. 3 (2).

[354] s. 3 (1).

[355] Those entitled to appointment were a judge of the Supreme Court of Judicature in Ireland, a Recorder or County court judge, a judge of the Supreme Court, High Court, or Circuit Court of Saorstát Eireann, or of the late Supreme Court of Dáil Eireann (s. 2 (2)).

[356] s. 3 (3).

[357] SR & O 1922–38, xiii. 485.

[358] 'Review of Sentences Imposed by Military Tribunals by Commissioners Appointed under the Indemnity Act 1923', S1 369/4, SPO.

total remission of sentence, and in the remaining eight cases a partial remission.

The Board had more success in attracting interest from 'military prisoners'. Of the forty-four prisoners in this category, all applied to the Board, with the result that eighteen had their sentences partially remitted, and seventeen totally remitted, while nine had their sentences confirmed.

The lack of interest from the political prisoners left the Government in an embarrassing position, and in May 1924 a further review process was begun. Two judges were instructed to examine the cases not already reviewed, and to re-examine those in which a portion of the sentence had yet to run.[359] The co-operation of the prisoners was not necessary for this exercise and the result was that 295 of the political prisoners had their sentences totally remitted, eight had theirs partially remitted, and in only one case was there a non-remission. The main reason given for treating these latter cases differently from the others was that the crimes in question had 'no political connection'.[360] The Government did not, however, immediately act on all the recommendations of the judges, and on 30 June 1924 seventy-seven political prisoners were still being held, fourteen because there were 'military objections to release' and sixty-three because civil charges were possibly pending (that is charges which could be heard in the ordinary criminal courts).

Military courts and committees: conclusion

From their inception, the military court and committee systems were envisaged as being the vehicle for a specific policy of executions. The development of the systems was therefore intimately tied in with the attitude of the Provisional Government (and later the Executive Council) and of the National Army Council towards executions.

Two broad phases can be delineated. The first was from November until early December 1922. During this phase, the National Army's military courts operated on lines similar to the British Army's formal military courts, upon which they were based. From the beginning, however, it was clear that the choice of cases for trial (and ultimately for execution) was dictated by a desire for political effect rather than by any ideological adherence to an approximation to legal process.

The spur for the development of the second phase was the four reprisal executions without trial in early December 1922. Administrative reprisal executions left the Free State Government open to obvious criticism even within its own terms of reference, as such measures clearly fell outside the

---

[359] Those conducting the examination were Judges Doyle and Dromgoole, ibid. 1.
[360] Ibid., schedule 14.

terms of the Army Emergency Powers Resolution. Two ways were found to enable the threat of reprisal executions to be generated within the framework of the Resolution. The first was the suspension of death sentences imposed by military courts conditional on the cessation of local IRA activities. The genesis of this distortion of the confirmation process can be traced to the manipulation of the prosecutorial power evident in the first phase of the military court system.

The second was the introduction of committees, and the resort to these tribunals as a means of generating death sentences which could be carried out as reprisals. The work-load of these committees eventually expanded so that captured prisoners were brought before them as a matter of course. In effect, hostages were being created—the difference between the committee system and the military court system in this regard being that under the former all prisoners captured under arms became hostages, whereas under the latter the hostages were the sentenced prisoners.

The rationale for this course was the same as that advanced by Cosgrave for the executions without trial: terror was to be struck into the Republicans. A feeling of terror was indeed created in some quarters, though at a cost of decades of damage to Irish political life. As Lyons has remarked of the attacks and reprisals of the latter half of the Civil War, they 'more than anything else led to estrangements persisting sometimes to this day'.[361] Demoralization did ensue in the ranks of the IRA, but only because the Republicans were facing defeat in any case through lack of popular support. As the experience of 1920–1 had illustrated, the execution tactic would be entirely counter-productive against an adversary with a reasonable chance of victory. Thus the execution policy cannot be said to have been decisive of the Civil War, though more than any single factor other than the Treaty, it did serve to mould the political climate at the end of the conflict.

SECTION (C) INTERNMENT

Developments in relation to internment corresponded closely with those in the fields of arrest and detention, the big operational division being between resort to internment powers out of strategic necessity, and their use as a counter-insurgency tool. The overlapping legal division was that between non-statutory martial law powers and statutory powers under the Public Safety Acts of 1923 and 1924. Under martial law powers, the trend from July 1922 to July 1923 was towards greater formalization, whereas under statutory powers, after an initial increase in the numbers interned,

---

[361] *Ireland since the Famine*, 466. To this day the Civil War divide is still reflected in the domination of the political life of the Republic of Ireland by the Fianna Fáil and Fine Gael parties, both descendants of the opposing sides in the Civil War.

there was a gradual winding down and ultimately an abandoning of the internment process.

Internment under martial law

The system

As has been pointed out above, considerations relating to the taking of prisoners in the first phase of the Civil War were essentially strategic, and by the end of July 1922 at least 2,000 such prisoners were being held.[362] It appears that it was not until August 1922 that formal provisions on the treatment of prisoners were drawn up, though there had earlier been a number of Government decisions on the matter.[363] The August provisions covered many mundane issues, such as food and letter allowances, and set out a pro forma 'Form of Commitment to Prison of Prisoners in the Irregular Forces'.[364]

Further formalization of these powers came with the Army Emergency Powers Resolution of September 1922, which authorized indefinite detention, though without specifying the relevant criteria, and without stating how the internment process was to operate other than specifying that removal of prisoners was to be 'under authority of the Army Council'.[365] A staff meeting in November hammered out the details of the new system. The Adjutant-General would be authorized by the Army Council to order the internment of prisoners. Each order would issue in triplicate: one for headquarters, one for the camp OC and one for the prisoner.[366]

By December 1922 the Judge Advocate General had approved the details of the new internment forms.[367] The first, the 'Order for the Detention of a Person taken Prisoner (Arrested), (Detained), by the National Forces', recited the Order of the Army Council and the Army Emergency Powers Resolution, and ordered 'the removal to and the detention at —— during such period as the Army Council shall determine, of —— a person taken prisoner, (arrested), (detained), by the National Forces'.[368] The second, the 'Order for the Committal of the Person above-mentioned', was addressed to the Officer in Command of the Detention Camp (Barrack) and provided: 'You are hereby ordered to

---

[362] C-in-C to Acting Chairman, Provisional Government, 'Statement No. 6, Statement of Prisoners in Custody on 31 July 1922', listed a total of 1,986 prisoners, but added that 'There are probably a few hundred more'. It also listed 122 releases but this was again qualified with the comment that 'It is also probable that there have been very many more'. Mulcahy papers, P7/B/29.

[363] See pp. 179–80.

[364] 'Reporting of the Capture of Prisoners to Local HQ'. Mulcahy papers, P7/B/41.

[365] See pp. 180–1.

[366] Lawlor, 'Civil–Military Relations', 340 n. 82.

[367] Review of Work of JAG's Department for w/e Dec. 1922, Mulcahy papers, P7/B/135.

[368] Proforma copies of these orders can be found at CWS, Prisoners' Files, P/3.

receive and detain in your custody during such period as the Army Council may determine, the person above mentioned, and for so doing this shall be your warrant.'[369]

The making of the decision on internment required up-to-date intelligence, and this was especially true in the case of those not captured in action. Particularly from September 1922 onwards, the role of the Intelligence Department in this field was expanded,[370] so that in April 1923 it was provided that the Command intelligence officer was to keep a file for every prisoner taken in his area, and was to keep this record up to date by the addition of all information as it came to hand.[371] It was he who was to decide whether any prisoner who was not chargeable should be released or interned, though the actual act of release required the authorization of the Adjutant-General's Department.[372] Later, even the cases of those charged before committees whose cases were deemed 'trivial' were referred to the Intelligence Department.[373]

The issue of status

The circumstances in which prisoners had been captured at the start of the Civil War ensured that the status issue was certain to become a bone of contention. Early in July 1922, Republican prisoners held in Mountjoy Gaol (which was made a military prison by Government order), were informed that they would be treated as 'military captives, still within the area of operation'.[374] This was to be 'without prejudice to any status that may be subsequently accorded, as soon as military operations in Dublin have ceased'.[375] The prisoners replied that their rightful status was that of prisoners-of-war and not military prisoners, and backed this up with a number of specific demands,[376] demands which, their supporters claimed,

[369] Ibid.
[370] On 13 Sept. 1922 the Officer of the Director of Intelligence set out that the Director of Intelligence was now handling such matters as the location of prisoners, the release of prisoners, applications for parole and visits, compiling of charges, and dealing with all queries relative to each individual prisoner. Letter to the Military Governor or Officer in Charge of Military Prisoners at Newbridge Prison, CWS, Prisoners' Files, P/6. Later, some functions were transferred to the Adj.-Gen.'s Department, though responsibility for the decision to intern remained with Intelligence. Officer of Director of Intelligence to Military Governor, Newbridge, 5 Dec. 1922, CWS, Prisoners' Files, P/6.
[371] 'General Staff Intelligence Memo. No. 3, Prisoners', 13 Apr. 1923, ibid., P/4.
[372] Office of Director of Intelligence to GOC Commands and All Prison Governors, 28 July 1923, ibid.
[373] See pp. 218–19.
[374] 'Order No. 1', by Diarmuid O'Hegarty, 3 July 1922 (handwritten), S1 369/1, SPO.
[375] Ibid.
[376] McKelvey ('Chief of Staff, IRA') to Governor, Mountjoy Military Prison, July 1922, s1 369/1, SPO. The demands were expressed as follows: 'No. (1) Our being kept in a camp under our own officers. No. (2) The allowing of parcels containing articles not to be used for the purposes of escape. No. (3) Adequate medical supplies and attendance. No. (4).

were essentially the same as those which had been made on the British.[377]

These demands received some support from the pro-Treaty side when Gavan Duffy, a Minister in the Dáil Cabinet, suggested to his colleagues the applicability of the resolution passed at the tenth International Red Cross conference of April 1920 that 'political prisoners in time of civil war ought to be considered and treated by the belligerent parties as prisoners of war, that is to say, according to the principles of the Hague Convention of 1907'.[378] Although Gavan Duffy resigned following disagreements in August 1922, and later became a stern critic of the executions policy, the results of a subsequent Red Cross investigation tend to suggest that his views may have had some effect.[379]

Ulterior use of internment powers

There was another sense in which Civil War prisoners had special status, and that was the manner in which conditions of detention were used as a means of punishment, both individually and collectively, for the way in which the conflict was waged. In August 1922 the Provisional Government decided that a public notice should be issued to the effect that persons found in possession of expanding bullets, or 'employing devices contrary to the accepted usages of civilized warfare' should, when arrested, be placed in solitary confinement and 'deprived of all privileges at present enjoyed by captured Irregulars'.[380] At the same time, the Government imposed what appears to have been the first collective punishment on prisoners when it was decided that all privileges should be withdrawn for a fortnight from the prisoners in Dundalk Prison 'as a deterrent against repetitions of the recent attack on the prison'.[381] Then in December 1922 this approach was extended when it was decided that 'in view of the continuance of outrages in Dublin, . . . the privileges currently enjoyed by Irregular prisoners should be considerably curtailed

---

Suitable accommodation. No. (5). Issuing of adequate food supplies by our own men. No. (6) Supplies of cooking utensils. No. (7) No interference with internal organization or work of prisoners, in addition we require three visits per week per man.' McKelvey was apparently unaware that he had been replaced as Chief of Staff following his capture.

[377] Sheehy-Skeffington to Town Clerk, Dublin, 11 Sept. 1922, S1 369/3, SPO. Sheehy-Skeffington listed seven demands: 'Right to free association with fellow-prisoners. Right to one visit and one letter per day. Right to receive books, papers, etc. Right to receive parcels of food from outside. Right of prisoners to choose their own officers, responsible for their discipline, and to have the usual internment camp conditions, such as prevailed in Frongoch and other camps. No compulsory labour to be enforced. Prisoners dry canteen to be set up where food might be purchased (as done at Ballykinlar).'

[378] A note of the resolution is enclosed with S. Ghabhain Ui Dhubhaigh (Gavan Duffy) to the Minister of Defence, 20 July 1922, Mulcahy papers, P7/B/217.

[379] This investigation is considered below.

[380] Minutes of Meeting of Provisional Govt., 3 Aug. 1922, SPO.

[381] Ibid.

pending a marked improvement in the situation'.[382] This state of affairs persisted until the end of March 1923.[383]

Conditions of detention could also be used as a means of creating distrust among the prisoners, and this, it was hoped, would facilitate intelligence gathering. For instance, the instructions issued in August 1922 provided that the more prominent prisoners were to be isolated so that 'the rank and file would ... regard any special treatment the others may get with a certain amount of doubt. Doubt leads to discontent and possibly information of a useful nature may be gleaned in this way'.[384] It was also thought advisable 'to have a couple of Intelligence men "captured" as well'.[385]

The Red Cross visit

Much dissatisfaction was voiced about such use of internment powers, and to this were added complaints alleging overcrowding, poor food and sanitation, ill-treatment, and indiscriminate use of firearms by prison guards. Concern was voiced not only by Republican supporters, but also by a number of pro-Treaty Senators, among them W. B. Yeats.[386] Eventually, the complaints prompted the International Committee of the Red Cross to request permission to inspect prisons, internment camps, and hospitals, and in April 1923 the request was granted.[387] This intervention was based not on hard-and-fast rules of international humanitarian law, but on a then newly developing area of involvement in situations of 'internal disturbances and tensions'. Indeed the Irish involvement was one of the first such investigations.[388]

Between 18 and 25 April R. A. Haccius, the ICRC delegate, visited the Newbridge internment camp, Mountjoy Gaol, 'Tintown' internment camp at the Curragh, and Gormanstown camp. In general his reports were favourable and he concluded that 'the Government refuses the status of "prisoners-of-war" to the prisoners, but in reality treats them as such'.[389] He did, however, register some concern about congestion and ventilation at Mountjoy. And there was an important proviso in his reports, typical of which was his comment in relation to Tintown that

---

[382] Ibid. 29 Dec. 1922, SPO.

[383] Ibid. 29 Mar. 1923, SPO.

[384] 'Reporting of the Capture of Prisoners to Local HQ', Mulcahy papers, P7/B/41.

[385] Ibid.

[386] Guinness to Cosgrave, 9 May 1923, attaching memorial signed by Senators Jameson, Jackson, Lord Granard, Yeats, Sir Bryan Makon, Goodbody, and Guinness. S1 369/3, SPO.

[387] Minutes of Meeting to Executive Council, 18 Apr. 1923.

[388] See ICRC, 'The International Committee of the Red Cross and Internal Disturbances and Tensions', 6.

[389] 'Report of International Committee of the Red Cross Mission in Ireland, April–May 1923', S1 369/3, SPO.

'I have not had any complaints to register concerning the food, medical care, or treatment, not having been authorised to question the prisoners'.[390] A further limitation in the report was that, because it limited itself to an investigation of conditions of detention, no attempt was made to consider whether the executions policy then current amounted to a violation of prisoner-of-war status.

In an obvious expression of pleasure, the Executive Council published the report, even going to the length of stating that 'prisoners actually receive full prisoner-of-war treatment'.[391] Critics of the Government were considerably less enthusiastic about the report, and were highly critical of the fact that some of the prisons in relation to which the most serious complaints had been made were not investigated, whereas what it was claimed were 'show' internment camps were.[392] Other complaints were that the prisoners were not questioned, that statements by Republican representatives were not considered in the drawing up of the report, and that the terms of reference were set by the Government.

Undertakings and releases

Apart from the question of conditions of detention, another prime source of irritation for the prisoners was the issue of release on entering into undertakings. As early as July 1922 the Provisional Government had ruled that prisoners might be released on their signing an appropriate undertaking.[393] Exceptions were to be made in the case of those who in the opinion of the CID or the military authorities were regarded as important leaders, or those who had a previous criminal record. A General Order was therefore issued, which provided for an undertaking in the following terms:

I promise that I will not use arms against the Parliament elected by the Irish people, or the Government for the time being responsible to that Parliament, and that I will not support in any way any such action. Nor will I interfere with the property or the persons of others.[394]

Recommendations for release were to go to the Adjutant-General for submission to the Minister for Defence who had the final decision on release. The prisoners' command structure reacted strongly against this

---

[390] 'Report of Visit to Internment Camp at Tintown, 20 Apr. 1923', included in ICRC Report, ibid.

[391] Communiqué from the Publicity Department, June 1923, attached to ICRC Report, ibid.

[392] A newspaper cutting of a published letter from C. Despard, Maud Gonne MacBride, Mary Mac Swiney, Marion K. Malley, Albinia Brodrick, Kate Boland, and Sarah Mellows, which was highly critical of the Red Cross Report, can be found in the Mulcahy papers, P7/B/223. It is stamped 11 July 1923, but the newspaper in question is not noted.

[393] Minutes of Meeting of Provisional Government, 17 July 1922.

[394] 'General Order No. 6', Mulcahy papers, P7/B/165.

system, seeing it as an attempt to break down their political organization, but the system must have prompted not a few applications, as within a few months there were a number of moves to tighten it up.

The first was in November 1922. Intelligence input was increased when a man from that Department was detailed to report to the Adjutant-General in connection with releases.[395] Forms were to be provided which would require the signature of the Command intelligence officer and the GOC before release could be granted.[396] If either refused, the prisoner was to be kept in custody, and even if both concurred on release, the Director of Intelligence could refuse to liberate the prisoner, though in such cases he was to communicate his reasons to the Command GOC.

Later the system was further altered. During the amnesty period which followed Liam Deasy's surrender call, the Executive Council decided that internees were to be given the chance of declaring themselves in favour of Deasy's call, and that those who failed to avail of that opportunity should not be given any further chance of securing release by signing a form.[397] Another change was that a system of guarantors was introduced in some cases, under which persons from the prisoner's area were required to guarantee that the prisoner was a person 'who will faithfully observe the undertaking he has signed'.[398]

The ending of the actual fighting, though not of the martial law regime, in May 1923 prompted a loosening up of the release system, though the numbers held continued to grow. The Executive Council decided that 'With a view to expediting the release of Irregular prisoners of the more or less harmless type' the Minister of Defence should arrange for the setting up of a committee of officers in the various Commands to whom lists of selected prisoners should be referred. Such committees were to consult with the local state solicitor and where desirable with the County Committee of Order, and in Dublin with the CID, and to report to the Minister.[399] Internal Army communications were also eased with the provision that the Command IO was to send reports in this regard directly to the Director of Intelligence. Delays had previously occurred because reports passed from the Command IO to the Command Adjutant, then to the GOC Command, and then on to the Adjutant-General (Prisoners' Department) before reaching the Director of Intelligence for his recom-

---

[395] Office of Director of Intelligence to C-in-C, 16 Nov. 1922, Mulcahy papers, P7/B/177.
[396] What appear to be copies of such forms can be found at S1 369/3, SPO. The Command IO was required to provide a detailed report of the activities of the prisoner, and the circumstances of his arrest.
[397] Minutes of Meeting of Executive Council, 16 Feb. 1923.
[398] A pro forma Guarantee can be found at S1 369/3, SPO. See also 'Circular Memorandum from Adjutant General to GOC All Commands and All Military Governors', 26 Feb. 1923, CWS, Prisoners' Files, P/8.
[399] Minutes of Meeting of Executive Council, 16 June 1923.

mendation.[400] Under the new system, cases were being dealt with at the rate of more than a hundred per day, with releases at the rate of thirty-five per day.[401] Although Intelligence retained responsibility for individual cases, and insisted on an extension of the guarantors scheme,[402] overall release strategy was decided upon by the Army Council. In July 1923 that body decided that all prisoners' cases were to be divided into four classes. The first consisted of those who could be released immediately: 'i.e. those who are no longer a danger to the State'.[403] The second consisted of those who might be released on signing the form of undertaking, or when conditions in any particular area had returned to normal, or when 'the Prisoner has shown that he intends to become a law-abiding citizen'.[404] The third class consisted of those prisoners who were to be held until the country was 'absolutely normal',[405] and the fourth of those prisoners against whom a serious charge had been or was to be preferred, and who were to be held indefinitely.

The switch to statutory internment powers led to a review of release procedures, but before examining these revised arrangements, the powers under the Acts of 1923 and 1923 must be examined in detail.

Internment under the Public Safety (Emergency Powers) (No. 2) Act 1923 and the Public Safety (Powers of Arrest and Detention) Temporary Act 1924

System and procedures

The powers in both Acts can be divided into three broad categories: (1) those exercisable in respect of persons at liberty, (2) those exercisable in respect of persons detained under the seven-day power, and (3) those exercisable in respect of persons already detained in military custody or held as military captives. In the discussion below, the phrases 'internment' and 'indefinite detention' are used interchangeably. Although the relevant power conferring sections of the legislation refers to 'detention', those detained are referred to as having been 'interned' in the provisions covering Appeals Councils.[406] Use of the phrase 'internment' also has the

---

[400] Office of Director of Intelligence to Minister of Defence, 21 June 1923, CWS, Prisoners' Files, P/4.

[401] Ibid.

[402] Office of Director of Intelligence to All Command IOs, 20 July 1923, provided that 'it would be desirable wherever possible to obtain Guarantors for every prisoner who signs the Form', CWS, Prisoners' Files, P/4.

[403] Office of Director of Intelligence to IO Cork Command, 4 July 1923, ibid.

[404] Ibid.

[405] Ibid.

[406] See below.

advantage of avoiding confusion with detention under the seven-day power included in the Acts.

All internment powers in the first category were exercisable by an 'Exeuctive Minister', which expression was defined as 'a Minister who is a member of the Executive Council'.[407] Although any Minister from the Executive Council was thereby empowered to order detention, contemporary documents leave the impression that in practice, it was only the Minster of Defence who exercised such powers. An ancillary arrest power was also included. The procedure adopted by the Army was that a warrant, which did not have to be under seal,[408] issued from the Minister for Defence to the GOC of the appropriate Command. He entrusted it for execution to any officer of his choice, and when carrying out the arrest, that officer was to have the warrant in his possession and to show it on demand to the person being arrested.[409] Once effected, the arrest was to be reported immediately to the Adjutant-General and to the Command GOC.

Although formally warrants issued from the Minister, in practice they were prepared by the Intelligence Department.[410] The switch to statutory powers led to a renewed insistence on accuracy in compiling intelligence reports by that Department. A directive to Command IOs stressed that 'Henceforth, the vague generalities and rumours which in the absence of more definite evidence, were accepted at a time when we were compelled by circumstances to make a virtue of necessity must now be replace by *Facts*.'[411] Implicitly, doubt was cast on the selectivity of use of internment powers during the martial law period, and indeed one sample suggests that as many as 43 per cent may have been unjustifiably interned.[412]

The first category: internment of persons at liberty

A tightening up was considered necessary by Intelligence because 'in future every statement or assertion put forward by this department in connection with any individual may be questioned, possibly in a law

---

[407] 1923 Act s. 16; 1924 Act, s. 9.

[408] *R (Burke)* v. *Governor of Mountjoy Prison*, [1924] 58 *ILTR* 106. For a discussion of the case see p. 266.

[409] GRO 48, issued 6 Sept. 1923 in relation to the 1923 Act, and GRO 67, issued 23 Feb. 1924 in relation to the 1924 Act. Mulcahy papers, P7/B/168.

[410] e.g. Office of the Director of Intelligence to CGS, 17 Dec. 1923, reads: 'I have the honour to forward to you attached lists of wanted irregulars still at large for whom Warrants for arrest have been issued from this Department in respect of Forms 1 (a) and 1 (c) of the Public Safety Act.'

[411] Office of Director of Intelligence to Command IO, all Commands, 28 Sept. 1923, CWS, Prisoners' Files, P/4.

[412] This was in the case of Government employees. See below.

TABLE 22. Powers of indefinite detention under the Public Safety (Emergency Powers) (No. 2) Act 1923 and the Public Safety (Powers of Arrest and Detention) Temporary Act 1924

Act/section	Person empowered to order detention	Grounds for detention
1923 Act s. 1	It shall be lawful for an *Executive Minister* to cause the arrest and, subject to the provisions of this Act, to order the detention in custody in any place in Saorstát Eireann of any person . . .	(a) in respect of whom such Minister shall certify in writing that he is satisfied that there is reasonable ground for suspecting such person of being or having been engaged or concerned in the commission of any of the offences mentioned in Part 1 of the Schedule to this Act, or (b) in respect of whom such Minister shall have received a report from the military authorities that the detention of such person is a matter of military necessity arising out of the existence of a state of war or armed rebellion, whether local or general, or (c) in respect of whom such Minister shall certify in writing that he is satisfied that the public safety is endangered by such person being allowed to remain at liberty.
s. 2 (2)	It shall be lawful for an *Executive Minister* subject to the provisions of this Act to order the detention in custody in any place in Saorstát Eireann . . .	of any person arrested under this section in respect of whom such Minister certifies in writing that he is of opinion that the public safety would be endangered by such person being set at liberty.
s. 3	*The military authorities defined as*: the Army Council for the time being of the National Army, or a General Officer commanding a district or any other officer, not being below the rank of commandant, having executive command of troops (s. 16).	Every person who is now detained in military custody or held as a military prisoner or captive and has not before the passing of this Act been sentenced to a term of imprisonment or penal servitude by any tribunal established by the military authorities may be detained in custody under this Act (a) by the military authorities if those authorities are of opinion that his detention is a matter of military necessity arising out of the existence of a state of war or armed rebellion, whether local or general, or
	Executive Minister	(b) under an order of an Executive Minister if such Minister is of opinion that the public safety would be endangered by such person being set at liberty.

T ABLE 22. *Continued*

Act/section	Person empowered to order detention	Grounds for detention
1924 Act s. 1	It shall be lawful for an *Executive Minister* to cause the arrest and, subject to the provision of this Act, to order the detention in custody in any place in Saorstát Eireann of any person . . .	in respect of whom such Minister shall certify in writing that he is satisfied that there is reasonable ground for suspecting such person of being or having been engaged or concerned in the commission of any of the offences mentioned in the schedule to this Act.
s. 2 (2)	It shall be lawful for an *Executive Minister* subject to the provisions of this Act to order the detention in custody in any place in Saorstát Eireann . . .	. . . of any person arrested under this section in respect of whom such Minister certifies in writing that he is satisfied that there is reasonable ground for suspecting such person of being or having been engaged or concerned in the commission of any of the offences mentioned in the schedule to this Act.
s. 4	*Executive Minister*	Every person who is now detained in military custody or held a military prisoner or captive and has not before the passing of this Act been sentenced to a term of imprisonment or penal servitude by any tribunal established by the military authorities, may be detained in custody under this Act under an order of an Executive Minister if such Minister is of opinion that the public safety would be endangered by such person being set at liberty.

court.'[413] This concern reflected the particular grounds for internment under the Acts of 1923 and 1924 (Table 22). In the first category, both Acts authorized an Executive Minister to order the detention of any person 'in respect of whom such Minister shall certify in writing that he is satisfied that there is reasonable ground for suspecting such person of being or having been engaged or concerned in the commission' of certain offences.[414] This form of words is open to at least two interpretations. Were an internee to challenge his detention by pleading that there were no grounds for suspecting him of being or having been involved in the

[413] Office of Director of Intelligence to Command IO, All Commands, 28 Sept. 1923, CWS, Prisoners' Files, P/4.
[414] 1923 Act. s. 1, para. (a); 1924 Act, s. 1. The relevant offences differed slightly in the two Acts. In the 1923 Act they were set out in pt. 1 of the schedule, and in the 1924 Act in the schedule to that Act (for scheduled offences, see fn. 220–7, pp. 190–1).

commission of a specified offence, a court might have insisted that the substantive evidence which led the Minister to his decision be examined on the basis that the Acts required that there be a 'reasonable ground' for the suspicion. Since the 'reasonableness' test was an objective one, the Minister's judgement might be measured against this standard, and in order to do this, the evidence against the internee would need to be examined. In the alternative interpretation, it might be held that all that was required was that the Minister be 'satisfied' about certain matters. The fact that the matter about which he had to be 'satisfied' was that there was a 'reasonable ground' for suspecting a person's involvement in the commission of an offence was irrelevant to the issue that the 'satisfied' test was a subjective one. Consequently the court could not look behind the Minister's decision, at least in the absence of *mala fides*.[415]

Whichever interpretation is accepted, a significant feature of this ground was that it clearly envisaged use of internment powers as a substitute for prosecution rather than as a preventive device. The suspicion related to the commission of an offence in the past, and was presumably intended to 'cover' a situation in which intelligence reports indicated a person's guilt, though insufficient admissible evidence was available to secure the suspect's conviction in a court of law. A factor which may have influenced this course was that during the operation of the Acts of 1923 and 1924 there were no special courts in existence.

The 1923 Act incorporated two other grounds which came within the first category, and which were not retained in the 1924 Act. One was where the Minister certified in writing that 'he is satisfied that the public safety is endangered by such person being allowed to remain at liberty'.[416] A Minister's action under this provision would almost certainly be held to be non-reviewable by the courts, at least in the absence of *male fides*, and the overall thrust of this ground seems directed at the use of internment powers in a precautionary or prohibitive manner, rather than as a substitute for prosecution.

The third ground was more problematic in that it authorized a Minister to order detention where he had 'received a report from the military authorities that the detention of such person is a matter of military necessity arising out of the existence of a state of war or armed rebellion whether local or general'.[417] The difficulty with this ground was that it was a decision by the courts that a state of war or armed rebellion no longer existed which led to the introduction of the 1923 Act. That Act specifically contained a saver clause designed to ensure that its powers were not to prejudice the exercise of non-statutory powers, should there

[415] See *Liversidge* v. *Anderson*, 1942 AC 206. For a discussion of this kind of interpretation see C. K. Allen, 'Regulation 18B and Reasonable Cause', 58 *LQR* 232.
[416] s. 1, para. (c).   [417] s. 1, para. (b).

be a fresh outbreak.[418] Consequently, the powers given under this ground would be exercisable only where identical non-statutory powers would also have been available, and they might therefore be viewed as superfluous.

One explanation for this duplication could be that it was designed to cover a situation where there was a localized outbreak of sufficient intensity to justify resort to martial law powers, but where it was thought advisable to hold prisoners taken in the outbreak elsewhere. Since, bearing in mind the British experience with the MLA in 1920–1, such prisoners could not be held under martial law powers outside the affected area, statutory powers would be necessary if they were to be interned elsewhere. Another explanation could be that it was simply an example of a 'belt and braces' approach, designed to guard against any eventuality. In any case, the evidence suggests that other powers of detention tended to be relied upon, and consequently, it may be that this latter power was never invoked.[419]

The second category: internment of persons detained under the seven-day power

In the case of persons arrested and detained under the seven-day power,[420] both Acts authorized an Executive Minister to order internment within the seven days, although the criteria set out in the two Acts were different. In the 1923 Act the ground was that the Minister was satisfied that the public safety would be endangered by the suspect being set at liberty. This was essentially the same as one of the grounds discussed above in relation to persons at liberty, and was clearly intended to be prohibitory, though arrest in the first instance required suspicion of the commission of an offence. In contrast, the 1924 Act empowered the Minister to order internment of a detainee where he certified in writing 'that he is satisfied that there is reasonable ground for suspecting such person of being or having been engaged or concerned in the commission'[421] of a specified offence, criteria which envisaged use of internment as a substitute for prosecution, and thus as a punitive measure.

The third category: power exercisable in respect of persons already detained in military custody or held as military captives

Both the 1923 and the 1924 Acts incorporated internment powers designed to allow the continuation of the detention of those already held. In both

---

[418] The relevant text is included in n. 135.

[419] e.g. in the Office of Director of Intelligence to the Chief of Staff, 17 Dec. 1923, on the subject of 'Warrants for Wanted Irregulars still at large', warrants in respect of grounds (a) and (c) were specified but none on ground (b) (see Table 22). CWS, Prisoners' Files, P/2.

[420] See pp. 188–93.   [421] s. 2 (2).

cases these powers were stated to be exercisable in respect of 'Every person who is now detained in military custody or held as a military prisoner or captive and has not before the passing of this Act been sentenced to a term of imprisonment or penal servitude by any tribunal established by the military authorities'.[422] In the 1923 Act this was clearly intended to cover the cases of prisoners detained under martial law powers. Similarly, in the 1924 Act these provisions must have been intended to apply to those previously held under the 1923 Act, but it is curious that a form of wording was not adopted which more clearly referred to detention under the earlier Act, since the words 'detained in military custody or held as a military prisoner or captive' had clear connotations of martial law.

Both Acts also made these powers exercisable on the order of an Executive Minister 'if such minister is of opinion that the public safety would be endangered by such person being set at liberty',[423] but only the 1923 Act additionally authorized the military authorities to detain a person 'if those authorities are of opinion that his detention is a matter of military necessity arising out of the existence of a state of war or armed rebellion, whether local or general',[424] a phrase the anomalous nature of which has been remarked upon above. Surprisingly also, the decision on internment could be made at a relatively low level of the military hierarchy, since 'military authorities' was defined as 'the Army Council for the time being of the National Army, or a General Officer commanding a district or any other officer not being below the rank of commandant, having executive command of troops'.[425] Thus no authority higher than that required to authorize an arrest under the Act (that of a Commandant) might be required to order internment. But in line with the general policy in this area, there was also a tightening up in the procedures involved in extending detention, and in October 1923 it was ordered that in future, before a recommendation for future detention was made by the Intelligence Department, the case should be reviewed by an officer of that Department in consultation with a legal officer. Furthermore, whenever Intelligence recommended the further detention of a prisoner, it was to be stated whether the new procedure had been followed and whether the legal officer concurred with the recommendation.[426]

---

[422] 1923 Act, s. 3 (1); 1924 Act, s. 4.
[423] 1923 Act, s. 3 (1); 1924 Act, s. 4.
[424] s. 3 (1).
[425] s. 16.
[426] Office of CGS to Director of Intelligence, 17 Oct. 1923, CWS, Prisoners' Files, P/4.

Appeals councils, releases, and reviews

The release review procedure developed under martial law continued to be made use of in the period immediately following the switch to statutory powers,[427] but dissatisfaction with the system soon became apparent. Camp governors complained that the practice of ordering the release of prisoners provided they signed the form of undertaking was futile 'unless they approached us on this matter themselves'.[428] The prisoners' own (IRA) officers insisted that they sign nothing, and the system was being undermined owing to the fact that 'some prisoners who admit having been active irregulars and being captured with arms are released unconditionally, while others taken merely on suspicion are asked to sign forms of undertaking'.[429] A reassessment led to a decision in September 1923 at a conference of the Minister for Defence, the Chief of General Staff, the Adjutant-General, and the Director of Intelligence, that forms of undertaking and guarantors' forms were to be discontinued as a precedent to the release of the prisoners.[430]

In any case, both the 1923 and 1924 Acts contained virtually identical provisions in respect of the establishment of Appeals Councils, which were presumably intended to amount to an alternative to the undertaking/guarantee system. 'As soon as may be' after the passing of the 1923 Act, one or more such Councils was to be established by an Executive Minister.[431] Each was to consist of not less than three members of whom one was to be a practising barrister or solicitor of not less than five years' standing.[432] It appears to have been envisaged that consideration of cases would be initiated only on application of the internee, since the Act provided that 'Any person detained in custody under this Act, whether under an order of an Executive Minister or by the military authorities, may in the prescribed manner request that an enquiry into the matter of his detention be made.'[433] It might be argued, however, that since this wording did not expressly prohibit either a Minister or an Appeal Council from initiating an investigation, then investigations could be begun without application by the prisoner.

---

[427] See e.g. Office of Director of Intelligence to Governor of Hare Park Camp, 18 Aug. 1923, requesting forms of undertaking, completed guarantee forms, reports and recommendations of camp staff, and prisoners' statements. Ibid., P/3.
[428] Military Governor of Hare Park Camp to Prisoners' Department, Office of the Adj.-Gen., 21 Sept. 1923, ibid.
[429] Ibid.
[430] Note of conference, 21 Sept. 1923, ibid., P/4.
[431] 1923 Act, s. 4 (1), the corresponding provision of the 1924 Act was s. 5 (1), which provided that existing Appeals Councils established under the 1923 Act were to be kept in force and additional Councils could be established.
[432] 1923 Act, s. 4 (1); 1924 Act, s. 5 (2).
[433] 1923 Act, s. 4 (2); 1924 Act, s. 5 (4).

Any inquiry was to be furnished with the reports or certificates in virtue of which the person whose case was being inquired into was being detained,[434] and was to report to the Executive Minister who had ordered the internment.[435] Surprisingly, the grounds upon which an Appeals Council could uphold an internment order were narrower than those upon which internment might be ordered in the first instance. The legislation provided that:

when . . . an Executive Minister shall receive a report from an Appeal Council that there are no reasonable grounds for suspecting the person interned of having committed or being engaged or concerned in the commission of any of the offences mentioned in the schedule to this Act he shall, within one calender month from the receipt of the report, order his release unless:

    (*a*) he shall refer back the report to the Appeal Council for the consideration of further evidence, or

    (*b*) the person be charged with any offence punishable by imprisonment.[436]

The significance of this was that both the 1923 and the 1924 Acts permitted internment of a person where an Executive Minister was of the opinion that 'the public safety would be endangered by such person being set at liberty' (Table 22), and without any requirement that the person be suspected of involvement in the commission of an offence. Presumably this apparent anomaly was intended to act as a safeguard against arbitrary use of internment powers, but it nevertheless begs the question as to why internment could be ordered in the first instance in circumstances in which such use might not be upheld by an Appeals Council. The other significant feature of this provision was that unlike the analogous provisions applying at that time in Northern Ireland, the decision of the Council was binding on the Minister, rather than being merely advisory.[437] But, as in Northern Ireland, a person might under the 1924 Act be obliged to enter into recognizances to be of good behaviour and to keep the peace, in order to secure his release.[438]

In view of the attitude of the internees towards the question of undertakings, it seems unlikely that a high percentage would have been willing to submit applications to the Appeals Councils. Nevertheless, releases steadily increased in the latter half of 1923, particularly after the ending of the October–November hunger strike, reaching a peak of 3,574 in January 1924 (Table 23). It seems to have been the case that the bulk of these releases took place because of the Army's own continuing review,

---

[434] 1923 Act, s. 4 (3); 1924 Act, s. 5 (5).

[435] 1923 Act, s. 4 (2); 1924 Act, s. 5 (4).

[436] 1923 Act, s. 4 (4). S. 5 (6) of the 1923 Act contained identical provisions save that a period of 14 days was substituted for that in the earlier Act of one calendar month.

[437] See pp. 297–8.

[438] s. 6 (1). There were no corresponding provisions in the 1923 Act.

TABLE 23. Release of internees, June 1923 to
May 1924

Date	No. in custody	No. released during previous month
1 June 1923	10,884	n/a
1 July 1923	11,480	284
1 Aug. 1923	n/a	427
1 Sept. 1923	n/a	521
1 Oct. 1923	9,697	944
1 Nov. 1923	8,023	1,780
1 Dec. 1923	5,494	2,304
1 Jan. 1924	1,852	3,574
1 Feb. 1924	1,306	539
1 Mar. 1924	1,076	248
1 Apr. 1924	941	138
1 May 1924	772	143
21 May 1924	618	165

Source: List of 'Number of Prisoners (Political)', S1
369/4, SPO.

though with the establishment of the new police force, the question
of release was no longer exclusively a military matter, and the recommendation of the Garda Siochána,[439] and in Dublin the CID,[440] was also
sought. The difficulties in conducting these investigations mirrored the
problems the British Army had earlier experienced with its internment
policy. The CID reported that 'The performing of this particular duty has
been found to be a most arduous one owing to the extreme difficulty in
obtaining information relative to the men who are imprisoned. In many
cases it was found next to impossible to even verify the addresses given by
the prisoners.'[441] Its main sources of information were individual National
Army and CID officers who were at one time attached to the old IRA
battalions situated in the areas in which the prisoners had resided, that is
ex-comrades of the internees. In approximately 20 per cent of the cases
investigated by the CID, continued detention was recommended.

Of the 618 prisoners still in custody on 21 May 1924, twenty-four were

---

[439] Ministry of Defence to Director of Intelligence, 21 Mar. 1924, CWS, Prisoners' Files,
P/4.
[440] O'Muireadhaigh to McGrath, 12 Oct. 1923, S3 331, SPO. By the date of the report,
the CID had investigated over 1,100 cases, and recommended continued detention in
approximately 20% of them.
[441] Ibid.

classified as 'releases waiting execution', and in ninety-six cases civil charges were being investigated by the Gardaí, elaborate procedures having been devised for dealing with this latter category of case.[442] Internees had earlier reacted strongly against what they saw as 'an attempt of the enemy to convict us all as criminals',[443] and in order to combat this policy, the IRA was prepared to 'prevent civilians from giving evidence'.[444] Releases continued, however, so that at the start of July 1924 the number of prisoners in military custody was put at 226, and by the 21st of the month, this figure had dropped to two.[445] Eventually, in November 1924, the Executive Council resolved that

no useful purpose could be served by the institution or continuation of prosecutions in respect of criminal acts committed, or alleged to have been committed between the 6th day of December, 1921, and the 12th day of May 1923, in any case in which it appears that the act was committed or purported to be committed in connection, directly or indirectly, with the state of rebellion and public disturbances.[446]

Government employees

A final point which should be mentioned in relation to the use of internment powers is the special case of interned Government employees. At a meeting of the Executive Council in November 1923 it was decided that any person who had been interned or imprisoned in connection with the 'Irregular campaign', and who had as a result been absent without leave from his official duties at any period since 1 July 1922 should be dismissed.[447] A review was conducted of the 159 cases which came within this category, and the results of this re-examination could be said to have cast considerable doubt as to the degree of selectivity exercised in the use of internment powers. Sixty-eight cases, or 43 per cent of the total, were classified as 'arrested, released and completely exonerated'[448] while a further 18 cases (11 per cent) were deemed 'arrested and released with no comment or such comment as "nothing definite against him"'.[449] Eventually, yet another review was instigated.[450]

---

[442] 'General Staff Intelligence Memo. No. 6', 5 Dec. 1923, CWS, Prisoners' Files, P/2.

[443] Divisional Adj., 1st Southern Division IRA to Deputy. Adj., IRA, 16 Oct. 1923, O'Malley papers, P 17 a/38.

[444] Ibid.

[445] Returns of Prisoners in Military Custody, 2 June to 21 July 1924, S1 369/4, SPO.

[446] Minutes of Meeting of Executive Council, 4 Nov. 1924.

[447] Ibid. 13 Nov. 1923.

[448] Ibid. 18 Dec. 1923. It is not entirely clear whether the figure of 43% referred only to those who appealed against their dismissal or whether it referred to all interned Government employees.

[449] Ibid.

[450] 'Ministry of Finance Circular No. 12/24', 7 Mar. 1924; 'Arrested or Interned Employees Paid out of Public Funds', S3 406A, SPO.

Internment: conclusions

Under martial law, internment powers were first resorted to out of strategic military necessity, and later as a counter-insurgency tool primarily designed to take Republican activists 'out of circulation'. Eventually, these powers were used on a scale which was approximately three times greater than that used by the British under ROIA, and there is evidence that use on such a wide scale resulted in large numbers of unjustified detentions. Subsidiary uses of internment powers were as a means of imposing collective punishments as reprisals, and for intelligence-gathering purposes.

The switch to statutory powers saw the form of internment change from being a military process to one primarily under civilian control. This process was accentuated in the 1924 Act, though in practice power continued to lie with the Army's Intelligence Department. The grounds for the exercise of internment powers under both Acts make it clear that internment was to be used in some cases as a substitute for prosecution, and in others as a preventive device. As was the case with the military court and committee systems, the criteria employed by the authorities in assessing use of internment powers was simply effectiveness. And effective the system was, though, as with the military court and committee systems, this was at a terrible cost.

PART III. JUDICIAL SCRUTINY OF EMERGENCY POWERS

Emergency powers and the Provisional Government

The unique constitutional position of the Provisional government presented particular problems in the field of emergency law. Within the Dáil system, the Provisional Government had no standing, and when the military actions of the pro-Treaty faction were challenged in the Dáil courts, the Provisional Government's response was to abolish the courts' jurisdiction rather than to argue the case on its merits.[451]

Within the Treaty-based constitutional framework, while it was clear that some powers were legally vested in the Provisional Government, the extent of these powers was a matter for dispute. The starting point of this debate was the Treaty itself. Under article 17, it was provided that 'By way of provisional arrangement for the administration of Southern Ireland' a Provisional Government was to be established. The limits of the powers of this Government were not defined in advance. Instead it

---

[451] See p. 157.

was simply provided that 'the British Government shall take the steps necessary to transfer to such Provisional Government the powers and machinery requisite for the discharge of its duties'.[452] The Treaty, however, clearly envisaged that the Irish Free State, when legally established, would eventually maintain an army, since article 8 incorporated provisions designed to limit the size of any such 'military defence force'.[453]

The mechanism for the transfer of powers was created by the Irish Free State (Agreement) Act 1922, and it was under this legislation that the Provisional Government (Transfer of Functions) Order 1922 was made, under which a variety of functions were actually transferred.[454] In addition to executive authority, the Act also purported to define the extent of the authority of the legislature to which the Provisional Government was to be responsible since it provided that the 'Parliament shall, as respects matters within the jurisdiction of the Provisional Government, have power to make laws in like manner as the Parliament of the Irish Free State when constituted'.[455]

As Mc Colgan has pointed out in relation to the transfer of 'functions': 'The terminology underscored the temporary nature of the provisional government. Even "departments" technically remained organizations of the imperial government, but their "functions" for the time being were carried out by the provisional government and paid for by its exchequer.'[456] In the spheres of defence and public order the position was doubly complicated. No transfer of defence functions was made, indeed it was specifically provided that the administration of any of the existing naval, military, or air forces of the Crown was not to be affected,[457] though it was set out that 'nothing in this Article shall be construed as prejudicing the exercise by the Provisional Government in respect of any military defence force which may, in accordance with Article 8 of the said Agreement, be raised in pursuance of an Act of the Provisional Parliament of such powers as may be conferred on the Provisional Government by such Act.'[458] Thus, rather than directly investing the Provisional Government with the power to establish an army, a power was given to create a power (by legislation) to create an army. The position in relation

---

[452] Art. 17.

[453] Art. 8 provided: 'With a view to securing the observance of the principle of international limitation of armaments, if the Government of the Irish Free State establishes and maintains a military defence force, the establishments thereof shall not exceed in size such proportion of the military establishments maintained in Great Britain as that which the population of Ireland bears to the population of Great Britain.'

[454] See p. 153.

[455] s. 1 (2).

[456] *British Policy and the Irish Administration 1920–22* (London, 1983), 99.

[457] See p. 153.

[458] Art. 9.

to policing was more straightforward. The functions assigned to the Provisional Government's Ministry of Home Affairs included 'The administration of services in connection with Law, Justice, Police and Home Affairs generally'.[459] Control of the DMP was explicitly granted,[460] but control of the RIC was specifically excluded.[461]

If there existed authority to legislate for the National Army from April 1922, the question needs to asked as to why this power was not made use of. The answer seems to involve a complex mixture of legal and political considerations. The question of the 'legislative powers of the Provisional Government' was the subject of an opinion of the Provisional Government's law officer on 13 September 1922.[462] In this, the power to legislate was summed up as follows:

(a) The laws must relate to matters of administration and that administration must be:
   (i) concerned only with functions which at the moment under consideration have been actually transferred to the provisional government,
   (ii) concerned only with 26 counties,
   (iii) provisional only that is to say concerned only with matters of administration during the period which began on the 6th December 1921 and will end upon the constitution of a Parliament and government of the Irish Free State, or the 6th December, 1922, whichever be the sooner.
(b) The Parliament cannot make laws:
   (i) for imposing taxation, or
   (ii) of a permanent character or operating beyond the limit of time already mentioned, or
   (iii) affecting the six North-Eastern Counties, or
   (iv) relating to functions or Departments not yet transferred.

No mention was made of the specific power granted in relation to a 'military defence force', nor was the question of the Royal assent addressed. This latter issue was covered in a supplemental opinion of 15 September:

I am of opinion that the office and functions of the Lord Lieutenant as such have ceased in the 26 counties since the passing of the Irish Free State Agreement Act. The time for appointment of a Governor General has not yet arrived. For the purpose of administering the twenty-six counties during the present interval, the Provisional Government is in my opinion in the position of both these functionaries.

[459] Provisional Government (Transfer of Functions) Order 1992, schedule, p. 1.
[460] Ibid., para. 10 (i).
[461] Ibid., para. 10 (ii).
[462] 'Opinion, Legislative Power of Provisional Government', attached to Gniomh Runaí d'on Rialtas [Secretary to the Government] to C-in-C, 16 Sept. 1922, Mulcahy papers, P7/B/249.

3. But legislation raises the difficult question of assent. By whom is assent to be given? It may well be argued by the British that the King's personal assent is requisite.[463]

The question of the Royal assent also involved delicate political considerations since, in the view of the pro-Treaty faction, the Dáil was acting on its own authority, as a constituent assembly for the adoption of a Constitution. Consequently, to request the Royal assent prior to the coming into force of the Constitution could be seen as compromising this stance. The position was explained in the Dáil by Ernest Blythe as follows:

There is no power in this Dáil to legislate without the Royal Assent; so far as the Free State Agreement goes, that is the only power it has, unless it chooses to exercise the inherent, inalienable and indefeasible power it has to repudiate the Treaty. There is no power unless we choose now to have this Royal Assent given, other than the matter that we laid down in our own Constitution, and we are not prepared to do that. And consequently for all practical purposes the Dáil has not the power.[464]

The law officer had suggested that the difficulties in this field could be got around by 'confining the legislative work of the parliament to resolutions on the subjects within the powers of the Parliament',[465] and introducing confirmatory legislation when the Constitution was enacted. Such resolutions could, he suggested, be introduced in the following terms: 'The Provisional Government with the concurrence of the Provisional Parliament hereby resolve and decree that etc'.[466] The particular problems posed by defence issues were not addressed, specifically those arising from the provision that the powers of the Provisional Government in this sphere were to be exercisable in respect of an army created by an Act of Parliament. Nevertheless, in the Army Emergency Powers Resolution, the Dáil proceeded by resolution, and without legislation, in precisely this sphere. It is perhaps significant that the ratification clause of the Resolution did not correspond exactly with the formula originally suggested by the law officer in relation to resolutions generally. Instead, the form of words read:

---

[463] 'Supplemental Opinion, Legislative Powers of the Provisional Parliament', attached to Aodh Ua Cinneide to the Secretary, Provisional Government, 15 Sept. 1922, Mulcahy papers, P7/B/249.

[464] 2 *DD*, col. 2040.

[465] 'Supplemental Opinion, Legislative Powers of the Provisional Parliament', attached to Aod Ua Cinneide to the Secretary, Provisional Government, 15 Sept. 1922, Mulcahy papers, P7/B/149.

[466] Aodh Ua Cinneide to the Secretary, Provisional Government, 15 Sept. 1922, Mulcahy papers, P7/B/249.

Now this Dáil being of opinion that the doing by or under the Authority of the Army Council of the several matters aforesaid is a matter of military necessity doth hereby ratify and approve of the sanction given by the Government and of the doing by or under the Authority of the Army Council of all or any of the acts and matters aforesaid.[467]

In this, the Dáil was merely indicating its approval of the taking of steps already sanctioned, thus leaving open the interpretation that these steps could in any case be sanctioned without Dáil approval on the basis of 'military necessity'.

The martial law regime challenged

Whatever the niceties surrounding the wording of the Resolution, it is clear that in November and December 1922 the military court system (and the Provisional Government's emergency apparatus generally) was open to challenge on a number of grounds. Statutory authority could be found neither for that system nor for the creation of the National Army, and the fact that there were statutory provisions in existence under which the Army might have been created might be taken to preclude reliance on any other authority. If statutory authority could not be found, reliance would have to be placed on common law or prerogative powers, and in this regard, the Provisional Government could not, as Kohn (1932) has remarked, 'be certain whether its provisional status would entitle it in the eyes of the judges of the preceding regime to those prerogative powers which had been accorded in so generous a measure to their predecessors'.[468] Even if justification might be sought in the area of non-statutory emergency powers, ROIA remained on the statute books and its continued existence might be held to have the same prohibiting effect as in Egan's case.[469]

These issues were variously raised in two reported cases heard immediately after the military court executions began: *R (Childers)* v. *Adjutant-General of the Provisional Forces*, and *R (Johnstone)* v. *O'Sullivan*.[470] In deciding these cases, the judges of the 'preceding regime' found themselves in a particularly awkward position. The legal framework which had provided their points of reference was in the process of dismantlement, and they were being asked to adjudicate on the actions of people whom only eighteen months previously they had castigated as 'rebels'. In addition, while both the Provisional Government and the British Government were agreed on the legitimacy of the temporary apparatus of state, there were significant differences in

---

[467] Para. 4.
[468] *Constitution*, 143.
[469] *Egan.* v. *Macready* [1921] 1 *IR* 265. See discussion above.
[470] [1923] 1 *IR* 5; [1923] 2 *IR* 13.

approach between the two parties on the derivation of this legitimacy, differences which could lead to disputes as to the powers inherent in these institutions.

In Childers' case (20–3 November 1922) the prisoner tried but not yet convicted by a military court applied to O'Connor MR for a writ of habeas corpus.[471] Not surprisingly, reliance was placed on O'Connor's own decision in *Egan v. Macready*.[472] It was pleaded that as the Dáil Resolution was not law, and that as ROIA had not been repealed, the effect of the decision in Egan's case was to prohibit the National Army from establishing non-statutory military courts. Childers' solicitor submitted an affidavit in which he described the circumstances surrounding his client's trial by military court and in which he exhibited the written objections which had been entered for the prisoner. Among these objections was a claim that 'Under the resolutions of the International Red Cross Conference 1921, which have been accorded international recognition, it is laid down that in civil war political prisoners are entitled to be treated as prisoners of war.'[473] Childers described himself as 'an officer of the Irish Republican Army' and consequently as entitled to belligerent rights. The defendant submitted an affidavit which was remarkably similar to those of General Macready in 1921.[474] In it, he described the armed Republican campaign, exhibited copies of some IRA documents captured in the possession of Ernie O'Malley, and recited the Army Emergency Powers Resolution.

In his judgment, the Master of the Rolls distinguished Egan's case from the case at issue on the grounds that the former 'turned entirely on the effect of the Restoration of Order Act 1920 [*sic*] . . . But that Act has no application to the circumstance of the present time. It applied only to the British Army as controlled and regulated by the Army Act.'[475] ROIA was not 'without express legislation . . . adaptable to the Irish Constitution as it is provisionally established'.[476]

In relation to the powers of the Provisional Government O'Connor held that it was now

de jure as well as *de facto* the ruling authority, bound to administer the law, to preserve the peace, and to repress by force, if necessary, all persons who seek by

---

[471] Childers agreed to proceed with the habeas corpus application only in order that it might benefit eight other condemned prisoners whose names the Government would not divulge. See Curran, *Birth*, 257.

[472] [1921] 1 *IR* 265.

[473] [1923] 1 *IR* 8–9. See pp. 227–8.

[474] See Ch. 2.

[475] At p. 15.

[476] Ibid. See also *O'Boyle and Rodgers v. Attorney-General and General O'Duffy*, 1929 IR 558.

violence to overthrow it. Those duties carry with them the right to organize an army for the protection of the people in any case of emergency. It is a right inherent in any Government. No Government can exist unless there is some physical force behind it.[477]

In support of these propositions and in relation to the issue of justiciability, he cited exactly those precedents which he had either distinguished or refused to follow in his earlier decision:

However doubtful the law may have been in the past, it is now clearly established that once a state of war arises the civil Courts have no jurisdiction over the acts of the military authority during the continuance of hostilities. The matter has been so recently and frequently discussed, I do not consider it necessary to do more than refer to Marais' Case, Tilonko's Case, and Allen's Case.[478]

He accordingly held that as the existence of a state of war had been proved he was bound to refuse the application. The question of the applicability of international law standards was not even mentioned. In any case, it is not clear that the point was expressly pleaded, though it had been mentioned in the objections set out in the Childers solicitor's affidavit. *Sub silentio*, the 'dualist' British approach to such questions, was being maintained.[479]

On the main issue, this decision amounted in some respects to a remarkable volte-face. As Kohn has remarked:

The most objectionable feature of the judgment in Allen's case, the toleration accorded by the Civil Courts to the assumption by the Military Authorities of judicial powers over civilians and to the application of this arbitrary and irregular jurisdiction to capital cases, was thus in principle not rejected.[480]

That writer also questioned O'Connor's interpretation of his previous decision:

It is not easy to reconcile this interpretation of the judgment [in *Egan v. Macready*][481] with the official report of the decision. The latter would seem to indicate that the Master of the Rolls regarded the criticism to which the Marais judgment had been subjected by Egan's counsel as 'very proper'. He further expressed himself 'immensely struck' by the latter's contention that the judgment

---

[477] p. 14.

[478] pp. 14–15.

[479] The 'monist' theory holds that national law and international law are one, while the 'dualist' theory sees them as separate. Whereas the former theory sees a state's international law commitments as binding in national law without further ado, the latter sees obligations created by international law as binding in the national legal system, only if given effect to by domestic legislation. For an account of the UK's approach see Wade and Bradley, *Constitutional and Administrative Law*, 10–11, 68–9.

[480] *Constitution*, 142

[481] [1921] 1 *IR* 265.

in that case, which referred merely to the arrest of a prisoner during a state of war—'a minor punishment, if a punishment at all, possibly a mere act of precaution'—ought not to be held to govern one in which the death sentence had been imposed.[482]

It could, however, be argued that the decision in Childers' case was consistent with that in Egan's case. If martial law arose from a prerogative, and if the prerogative were in abeyance only where statutory powers existed in the same area, it is not illogical to assert that when these statutory powers no longer applied, the prerogative was no longer in abeyance.

Virtually simultaneously with Childers' case, the legal shortcomings of the Provisional Government's measures were being argued before the King's Bench Division (22–3 November 1923) and on appeal before the Court of Appeal of Southern Ireland (27 November to 4 December 1923), in Johnstone's case. The applicants, who were detained in military custody, and were awaiting trial by military court, sought writs of habeas corpus and an injunction to restrain the military authorities from proceeding with the trial.

At first instance, as had become usual, Molony CJ delivered the unanimous judgment of the Court. In relation to the National Army, he noted that it was not an army formed in accordance with clause 8 of the Treaty and that it had not been established by an Act of Parliament. This, however, did not necessarily deprive the Army of status: 'When the Government of a country is attacked it has, apart from any statutory or other provisions, an inherent right to organize a force and to take such other steps as it may deem necessary to quell the insurrection.'[483] Taking notice of the Emergency Powers Resolution and subsequent proclamations, he considered that the National Army had indeed been entrusted with the task of quelling the rebellion the existence of which was judged to have been proven to the Court by an affidavit filed on behalf of the Army authorities. Consequently, following Allen's case, the application was refused: 'we have no jurisdiction *durante bello* in inquire into or pass judgment upon the conduct of the military authorities in repressing the rebellion.'[484]

The applicants met with no greater success before the Court of Appeal. Significantly, though, that Court split 2 : 1 on the issue—the only Irish decision in the long line of martial law cases in which a court divided. Unfortunately, the dissenting judge, Ronan LJ, was 'prevented by indisposition from attending to deliver his own judgment'.[485] Only his findings were announced: a limited injunction and a writ of habeas corpus should be granted.

---

[482] p. 142 n. 4.   [483] p. 15.   [484] p. 17.   [485] p. 21.

The majority judgments are available. O'Connor LJ, on the basis of
the affidavit filed by the military authorities, took the view that a state
of war existed in that county (Donegal) in which the applicants were
arrested. In any case, proof of the existence of a war in the jurisdiction
generally was sufficient: 'where a state of war exists in a particular unit of
territory I cannot discriminate between one portion of that territory and
another.'[486] The test he formulated to decide whether or not war existed
was: 'Is the forcible resistance to authority so continuous, so formidable,
of such duration that the help of the army must be invoked, not merely in
one or two instances, but habitually or constantly lest the state shall
perish?'[487]

This test differed in tone at least from that advanced in Allen's case.
Therein Molony CJ had spoken in terms of conditions in which 'the
Government is entitled and indeed bound to repel force by force'[488]
thereby implicitly recognizing the primacy of the Army. The test in
Johnstone's case, with its reference to the 'help of the Army', has connotations of the Army's acting in aid of the civil power. There have been
many situations world-wide where the 'help of the Army' has been invoked
on a continuous basis, yet there has been no formal assertion of martial
law. The example of the current emergency in Northern Ireland can be
given, though this would have to be subject to certain qualifications.[489]
These examples might suggest that if the role of the Army was to act in
aid of the civil power, martial law might not be the appropriate legal
mechanism.

Presumably O'Connor LJ's formulation was advanced to take account
of the particular nature of the IRA campaign at the time—an intensive
series of sporadic attacks lacking in centralized direction. Rhetorically, he
asked:

Is it war? I suppose there are many people who would say it was not—hesitating
to dignify by the title 'war' a state of circumstances in which there is little or no
open clash of arms, and in which the attempt to coerce the will of others is carried
on, not in the field, not in battle, but mainly, at any rate, in a surreptitious way by
the commission of multiplied crimes. But we have to consider the question from
its legal aspect; and, from that point of view, it is undoubtedly war—guerilla war,
a sort of war perhaps, but war.[490]

---

[486] p. 25.
[487] Ibid.
[488] [1921] 2 *IR* 268.
[489] See T. Hadden, K. Boyle, and C. Campbell, 'Emergency Law in Northern Ireland:
The Context', 17, in Jennings (ed.), *Justice*, and C. Palley, 'The Evolution Disintegration
and Possible Reconstruction of the Northern Ireland Constitution', 1 *Anglo-American Law
Review*, 368 n. 214.
[490] p. 24.

There still remained the question of the status of the National Army. Noting that the Army was acting 'under the eyes and to the knowledge of the King's representative—the Lord Lieutenant of Ireland' he took the view that

The fair and obvious inference is that to the Free State army was entrusted the work of quelling the rebellion. It is unnecessary to consider what form the delegation or transfer took, or what it should be called—call it what you will. I shall put it in terms that, I hope, will not offend the susceptibilities of any man, when I say that a mutual arrangement between the two countries was come to whereby the task of restoring order in Ireland was given to a body of Irishmen—to wit the Free State army.[491]

At the very least this position amounted to a remarkable extension of the doctrine of judicial notice coupled with an equally remarkable willingness to draw inferences. The argument does not appear to have been pleaded on behalf of the military authorities, indeed to have done so would have amounted to a severe political embarrassment to the Provisional Government, anxious as it was to assert its own authority.

Pim J., delivering the second majority judgment, saw the status of the Provisional Government and its army in much the same light as O Connor MR had in Childers' case:

I cannot imagine any person denying the right of every Government, no matter whether absolute or limited in power, to protect itself, and, in case of hostile attack, to meet force by force. On the contrary, not only its right, but its duty is clear; and if Courts were authorized to interfere with the acts which any such Government thinks it right to take during a war, it would make it impossible for it to carry out that which is its paramount duty.[492]

The applications were therefore refused.

Perhaps the real significance of these decisions lies not in the reasoning advanced but in the position adopted. As Bishop (1978) has remarked, in the context of emergency powers in other jurisdictions, 'It is more instructive to look at what the courts do than what they say.'[493] What the courts did was to strain legal rules and principles almost beyond recognition so as to accommodate the Provisional Government. That perhaps is not surprising in the circumstances of the time. Legal niceties were not very high on the Government's list of priorities: Childers began an appeal against his refusal but was shot before it could be heard.

---

[491] p. 26.
[492] p. 30.
[493] 'Law in the Control of Terrorism and Insurrection: The British Laboratory Experience', 42 *Law and Contemporary Problems* 187.

The Constitution: martial law and judicial power

With the coming into force of the Constitution in December 1922 a whole new set of issues was raised. In order to assess the significance of reported cases after that date it is necessary first to examine the constitutional provisions relating both to the judiciary and to martial law.

The courts

The doctrine of the separation of powers was given explicit recognition in article 2: 'All powers of government and all authority, legislative, executive and judicial in Ireland are derived from the people of Ireland'. In defining the scope of judicial authority, the key phrase used in the Constitution was 'judicial power'. In article 64 it was provided: 'The judicial power of the Irish Free State (Saorstát Eireann) shall be exercised and justice administered in the public Court established by the Oireachtas by judges appointed in manner hereinafter provided'. The phrase was vague, presumably purposefully so, and was ripe for judicial interpretation.

There were, however, certain definite guide-lines set out for the exercise of this power. Article 65 provided that 'the judicial power of the High Court shall extend to the question of the validity of any law having regard to the provisions of the Constitution', and the appellate jurisdiction of the Supreme Court in that regard was specifically enshrined (article 66). As Kohn has remarked, 'The terms of the Irish Constitution invest the power of judicial review with a formal authority which it lacks in the American Constitution.'[494] An additional ground for review was implicitly provided in section 2 of the Constitution of the Irish Free State (Saorstát Eireann) Act 1922 which provided:

the . . . Constitution shall be construed with reference to the articles of agreement for a Treaty between Great Britain and Ireland . . . and if any provision of the said Constitution or of any amendment thereof or of any law made thereunder is in any respect repugnant to any of the provisions of the Scheduled Treaty, it shall, to the extent only of such repugnancy be absolutely void and inoperative.

Martial law

As Swift Mac Neill (1925) has observed, 'the framers of that [1922] Constitution took as their model, like the framers of the American Constitution, the British Constitution of their own times and endeavoured to improve on that model'.[495] Thus, in many spheres, the Constitution incorporated as positive law not only the statutory underpinning of the British Constitution, but also its conventions and that body of binding

---

[494] *Constitution*, 352. See Kelly, *Fundamental Rights*, 244 n. 5.
[495] *Constitution*, p. ix.

precedent found in case law. This process is well illustrated in articles 6 and 70 which relate to martial law.

Article 6 of the draft constitution of June 1922 had provided as follows:

The liberty of the person is inviolable, and no person shall be deprived of his liberty except in accordance with law. Upon complaint made by or on behalf of any person that he is being unlawfully detained, the High Court and any and every judge thereof shall forthwith enquire into the same and may make an order requiring the person in whose custody such person shall be detained to produce the body of the person so detained before such Court or judge without delay, and to certify in writing as to the cause of the detention and such Court or judge shall thereupon order the release of such person unless satisfied that he is being detained in accordance with the law.

The Civil War broke out in the interval between the publication of the draft constitution[496] and the meeting of the Constituent Assembly, and practical experience led to the addition of the following ouster clause to article 6:

Provided, however, that nothing in this Article contained shall be invoked to prohibit, control or interfere with any act of the military forces of the Irish Free State (Saorstát Eireann) during the existence of a state of war or armed rebellion.

Kohn's view was that 'The proviso attached to Article 6 is not to be interpreted as a sweeping authorisation for the establishment of military rule during war or rebellion in the sense of the doctrine in the Marais case. The clause . . . refers exclusively to the question of arrest and detention.'[497] Indeed, on a strict reading, the clause does not authorize arrest and detention by the military during a war or armed rebellion but merely prohibits any person the subject of such arrest or detention from relying on the provisions of the article. Its content is therefore procedural rather than substantive.

These special provisions were not without historical precedent since the Irish Habeas Corpus (Ireland) Act of 1781[498] incorporated a power to suspend the Act by proclamation during such times as there should be an actual invasion in Ireland or Great Britain, a power which as Swift Mac Neill has pointed out 'bears a very striking resemblance to the proviso contained in the last paragraph of Article 6'.[499]

The other relevant constitutional provision (article 70) provided as follows:

---

[496] The text of the draft constitution can be found in D. Figgis, *The Irish Constitution* (undated). See also Kohn, *Constitution*, 136.

[497] Ibid. 145.

[498] 21 & 22 Geo. III, c. II. See Ch. 2.

[499] *Studies*, 51. For a general discussion of the roots of habeas corpus in Ireland see ibid. 35–52.

No one shall be tried save in due course of law, and extraordinary courts shall not be established, save only such Military Tribunals as may be authorised by law for dealing with Military offenders against Military law. The jurisdiction of Military Tribunals shall not be extended to or exercised over the civil population save in time of war, or armed rebellion, and for acts committed in time of war or armed rebellion, and in accordance with regulations to be prescribed by law. Such jurisdiction shall not be exercised in any area in which all civil courts are open or capable of being held, and no person shall be removed from one area to another for the purpose of creating such jurisdiction.

In the opinion of Kelly (1961):

The collective effect of Articles 6 and 70 was therefore to halt the trend of judicial decisions on the matter, and, while preserving the right of the executive to repel force by force through the 'decorous' agency of military courts not subject to supervision by the ordinary courts, to limit more narrowly the circumstances in which such courts might act.[500]

Kohn likewise considered the joint effect of the articles to be:

to impose effective limitations on the wide discretionary powers previously claimed for the Military Authorities on the strength of an undefined prerogative. The common law authority of the Executive in time of internal disturbance to repress force by force in open conflict retains its latent validity. Its military organs are, under the terms of the proviso of Art. 6, entitled to arrest and detain civilians, but the power to subject civilians to military jurisdiction which had latterly been claimed on the strength of executive prerogative was, by the provision of Art. 70, effectively subjected to the authority of Parliament.[501]

The test for the invocation of emergency powers in article 70 differed from that in article 6. In the former, military courts were permitted only 'in time of war, or armed rebellion' and not in any area 'in which all civil courts are open or capable of being held'. In the latter, remedies for extra-legal detention are set aside only 'during the existence of a state of war or armed rebellion'. This point is adverted to by Kelly who writes:

The military forces of the State were not precluded by these Articles from exercising an uncontrolled discretion in a time of war or armed rebellion in matters falling short of operating military courts, such for example as the taking and keeping prisoners.[502]

It may have been due to bad drafting, but it would appear that martial law under the Constitution incorporated a two-stage test: in any particular geographical area it would be open to the superior civil courts to hold that their jurisdiction to inquire into military detentions was ousted while their jurisdiction to prevent military tribunals operating remained. In

---

[500] *Fundamental Rights*, 244.   [501] *Constitution*, 147.   [502] *Fundamental Rights*, 244.

another important respect, the provisions of the Constitution in relation to martial law marked a departure from previous theory. Only military tribunals and the 'military forces of the Irish Free State' were specifically referred to, whereas on the strict common law theory, the 'right to repel force by force' was vested in every citizen and was not therefore specifically a military matter. In practical terms this was not really an innovation since, as was discussed in Chapter 2, the carrying out of martial law measures in 1920–1 was entirely the responsibility of the British Army.

Case law

The coming into force of the Constitution does not appear to have been marked by any legal challenges to the martial law powers then being exercised.[503] This is perhaps surprising, in that article 70 had spoken in terms of military tribunals established by law, whereas the military courts and committees which operated in December 1922 clearly were not established by law. Their authority was based on a Dáil Resolution, and the law officer had warned that confirmatory legislation would be necessary in respect of such resolutions, once the Constitution came into force. Secondly, there was the fact that the Constitution incorporated a two-stage test. The operation of military courts and committees might be challenged on the basis that all the civil courts in a given area were operating, though this of itself would not be sufficient grounds for impugning the detention of prisoners. When the continuing operation of military tribunals was queried in the Dáil in March 1923 on this basis, Mulcahy replied: 'No military tribunals are exercising jurisdiction over the civil population in any area in which all the Civil Courts are open or capable of being held, and in respect of charges which may suitably be tried by those Courts.'[504] But the Constitution created no jurisdiction for military tribunals on the basis of charges which might be unsuitable for trial in the civil courts, and Mulcahy's answer was open to the interpretation that military tribunals were trying such charges in areas in which all the civil courts were open.

Following the cessation of hostilities, the summer of 1923 saw a number of habeas corpus applications brought on behalf of martial law detainees. All were refused on the grounds that a state of war existed,[505] but eventually in *R (O'Brien)* v. *Military Governor NDU*[506] (15 June–1 August 1923) the Court of Appeal took a different view. The case involved a habeas corpus application brought on behalf of a military detainee.

---

[503] At least there is no reported case law on the subject to be found.

[504] 2 *DD*, col. 1933.

[505] These decisions are not reported, but a brief account can be found in [1923] 57 *ILT & SJ* 152.

[506] [1924] 1 *IR* 32.

O'Connor MR at first instance had refused the application on the grounds that the state of war had not ceased. In giving the judgment of the Court of Appeal, Molony CJ first considered the effect of article 6:

The Article (Article 6) of the Constitution is only declaratory of the pre-existing law and accords with the decisions of the King's Bench Division in *The King* v. *Allen*,[507] *The King (Garde & Others)* v. *Strickland*,[508] *The King (Johnstone)* v. *O'Sullivan*[509] affirmed by the court. To the same effect is the decision of the MR in *The King (Childers)* v. *Adj. Gen. Provisional Forces*.[510] The court is bound when its jurisdiction is invoked to decide whether or not there exists a state of war or armed rebellion, but once it so decides, it has no power to prohibit, control, or interfere with any act of the military forces, whether it is a matter of detention as in the present case, or the execution of a capital sentence after trial by a so-called military court as in Allen's case and Childers's case, or the execution of a person without trial as in Rory O'Connor's case.[511]

Upon consideration of the various affidavits filed, the Chief Justice came to the conclusion that 'it has not been proved that a state of war or armed rebellion at present exists in the city of Dublin'.[512] The court then set a return date for the production of the prisoner. When the matter again came up the prisoner's detention fell to be defended on the basis of statutory powers which had by then come into force. The issues arising under this heading are considered below.

In relation to martial law powers the only issue directly at stake was detention; consequently what was said in relation to military courts and executions can be regarded as *obiter*. It is submitted, however, that what was said on the latter subjects was not in accordance with the express terms of the Constitution. The military tribunals provided for in article 70 were not the 'so-called military courts' of Allen's case but courts created by positive law. By making special provision in the Constitution for the operation of military tribunals it was surely intended that these tribunals were to be the only bodies with powers to order the execution of prisoners. Consequently, and contrary to what the Chief Justice had to say in relation to the execution of Rory O'Connor, neither article 6 nor article 70 could oust the jurisdiction of the Court to inquire into planned executions without trial.

The Chief Justice's view, particularly in relation to military courts, is tenable only if article 70 is seen as enabling and not prohibitory. It is further necessary to assert that common law/prerogative powers of the kind resorted to by the British under martial law were carried through under the new Constitution. If so, they would have to depend for their continuing validity on article 73 which provided:

---

[507] [1921] 2 *IR* 241.   [508] [1921] 2 *IR* 317.   [509] [1923] 2 *IR* 13.
[510] [1923] 1 *IR* 15.   [511] p. 38.   [512] p. 42.

Subject to this Consitution and to the extent to which they are not inconsistent therewith, the laws in force in the Irish Free State (Saorstát Eireann) at the date of the coming into operation of this Constitution shall continue to be of full force and effect until the same or any of them shall have been repealed or amended by enactment of the Oireachtas.

Since, however, there was an express provision that this carrying through was to be subject to the Constitution, it would seem to have been intended that common law/prerogative powers in the martial law sphere could be exercised only through the channels set out in the Constitution. Some support for an alternative interpretation might be found in the views which commentators have expressed of article 70. Both Kelly (explicitly) and Kohn (implicitly) regard the actual workings of the military tribunals mentioned in the article as non-justiciable. This apparently is to be implied from article 70 since the question of justiciability is not specifically adverted to therein and is in certain ways difficult to reconcile with the wording of the article: as Swift Mac Neill has pointed out: 'The military law and the military tribunals referred to in this Article are institutions created by law.'[513]

Clearly this view is predicated on the continuing validity of at least part of the the common law/prerogative martial law doctrine. Keir and Lawson's (1979) view of the earlier Irish cases was that non-justiciability in such circumstances might be the only aspect of the prerogative to survive in modern times.[514] However, as has been discussed above, both Kelly and Kohn are clear that martial law powers could, under the 1922 Constitution, be exercised only through the channels thereby created.[515] It flows from this interpretation that non-justiciability might have been carried through under article 73, but that other aspects of the martial law doctrine were carried through only to the extent prescribed by the Constitution. This would correspond with the approach taken in other areas, as prerogative powers generally were not always assumed to have been carried through under the new Constitution.[516]

In effect, what the Chief Justice did was to give so wide a construction to article 6 as to nullify any curbing effect of article 70. He thereby glossed over the fact that the National Army's military courts and com-

---

[513] *Studies*, 219.

[514] See p. 142.

[515] M. Forde suggests, in relation to the 1937 Constitution, that art. 50 of that instrument (which was similar to art. 73 of the 1922 Constitution) may have carried through common law martial law powers similar to those employed by the British under martial law, though he leaves the point open (*Constitutional Law of Ireland* (Dublin, 1987), 776–9). There are, however, some important differences in this field between the two Constitutions. See arts. 38.4.1, 38.3, and 28.3.3, of the 1937 Constitution.

[516] See Kelly, *Fundamental Rights*, 200–23.

mittees were not established by law, and therefore could fairly be said to have been wholly illegal under the terms of the Constitution.

Statutory emergency powers before the courts

Under the British emergency statutory provisions, judicial scrutiny had been limited to applying the test of *vires* in respect of delegated legislation, and examining practice in individual cases to check its conformity with specific statutory requirements. With the coming into force of the 1922 Constitution, a further ground for challenge presented itself: repugnance of the statutory measures in questions to the Constitution. No time was lost in taking advantage of the new possibilities.

In the first part of the case of *R (O'Brien)* v. *Military Governor NDU*[517] the Court of Appeal of 31 July 1923 held that a state of war no longer existed in Dublin and set a return date for the production of the prisoner. In the interim period the Public Safety (Emergency Powers) Act 1923 was rapidly enacted (1 August 1923) and a detention order was made against the applicant. When the matter again came before the Court the central issue turned on the mode of enactment of the Public Safety Act with reference to article 47. That article provided:

Any Bill passed or deemed to have been passed by both Houses may be suspended for a period of ninety days on the written demand of two-fifths of the members of Dáil Eireann or of a majority of the members of Seanad Eireann presented to the President of the Executive Council not later than seven days from the day on which such a Bill shall have been so passed or deemed to have been so passed. Such a Bill shall in accordance with regulations to be made by the Oireachtas be submitted by Referendum to the decision of the people if demanded before the expiration of the ninety days either by a resolution of Seanad Eireann assented to by three-fifths of the members of Seanad Eireann, or by a petition signed by not less than one-twentieth of the voters then on the register of voters, and the decision of the people by a majority of the votes recorded on such Referendum shall be conclusive. These provisions shall not apply to Money Bills or to such Bills as shall be declared by both Houses to be necessary for the immediate preservation of the public peace, health or safety.

Counsel for the applicant contended that the Act could only have become binding not earlier than seven days after its passage by both Houses, since within that period a written demand for its suspension could have been made. Article 47 applied in full because the Act had not been declared by both Houses to have been necessary for the immediate preservation of the public peace.

The Attorney-General replied first, that once the bill had received the Governor General's assent, the Court was bound to assume that article

[517] [1924] 1 *IR* 32.

47 had no application; secondly that even if the demands by the requisite number of members of the Oireachtas had been made, the President of the Executive Council still had a discretion to disregard the demand and submit the bill at once to the Governor-General; thirdly, that the third recital in the Act amounted to a declaration as envisaged in the last paragraph of article 47.[518]

The Court rejected these assertions. The Chief Justice's judgment was concerned with careful examination of article 47. The use of the word 'may' in the first part of the article in the view of Molony CJ cast a duty on the President of the Executive Council. The duty arose if the demand were made, but

A written demand requires time. What time is to be given for that written demand? The Article says seven days. Consequently the scheme of the Article so far is this: A Bill passes both Houses, but notwithstanding that it passes both Houses two-fifths of the members of the Dail or the majority of the Seanad may think that there should be a referendum and may express their thoughts in a constitutional manner under Article 47 by presenting a petition to the President of the Executive Council.[519]

Therefore the Act could not become binding within that period. As regards the complicance of the recital and bill with the last sentence of article 47:

One has only to put side by side the recital and the concluding words of Article 47 to see that that recital does not comply with the provisions which, according to the Constitution, the declaration should contain if it is to be held that immediate operation is to be given to the measure.[520]

Consequently, the prisoner should be released.

Ronan LJ, in agreeing with the Chief Justice, subjected the anti-democratic nature of the Attorney-General's arguments to some trenchant criticism:

A referendum is a most important element in a democratic Constitution, and the substance of the referendum is that in certain cases and in certain circumstances the people themselves are to have a vote to determine whether a law shall be passed or not—that the law shall be finally submitted in the words of this Article, 'to the decision of the people . . . I reject as ridiculous and absurd a construction that the existence of the referendum is to depend on the *ipse dixit* of the President

---

[518] That recital provided: 'Whereas it is desirable that the civil authorities should be endowed with such powers as will enable them lawfully to co-operate with the military forces in the work of restoring and maintaining order and of re-establishing the supremacy of the law and civil government with or without military co-operation as may be possible as soon as the success of the military operations and circumstances of each district will permit.'

[519] At p. 48.

[520] p. 49.

of the Executive Council. The Constitution provides that the written demand of two-fifths of the Dail or of the majority of the Seanad to ensure a referendum can be effectively given within seven days. If any Bill can be made a binding law two minutes after the commencement of the period, that reduces the provisions as to a referendum to a farce.[521]

The significance of the decision lies in its having been the first example of a statutory emergency provision to be rendered inoperative by reference to the new written Constitution. Both parts of the O'Brien case could be taken to indicate a change towards a more activist judicial stance in relation to emergency powers, but as later cases illustrated, this promise was to remain unfulfilled. In any case, the two parts of the decision were, in effect, immediately overruled by legislation, the first part by the Public Safety (Emergency Powers) Act 1923, and the second by the Public Safety (Emergency Powers) (No. 2) Act 1923 which incorporated the declaration required to bring it outside the delaying provisions of article 47.[522]

An attempt to impugn the validity of these Acts, again by reference to procedural constitution provisions, was made in *R (Murphy)* v. *Military Governor, Mountjoy Prison*[523] (6 November 1923). The prosecutor in this habeas corpus action had been interned under the Acts and had been elected to the Dáil.[524] On his behalf it was claimed that the Acts had not been validly enacted, first because the Parliament, which had purported to legislate from 6 December 1922 to 9 August 1923, had not been summoned in accordance with article 24 of the Constitution and was therefore incapable of enacting any legislation;[525] secondly, because the effect of article 47 was to require that legislation be passed more than seven days before the end of the parliamentary session, since otherwise the time allowed for the demand for suspension would be curtailed. Both of the Public Safety Acts had been passed within that time-limit and were therefore, it was claimed, invalid.

O'Connor MR dismissed the first argument by holding that article 24

---

[521] pp. 50–1. The referendum provisions were abolished in 1928 by the Constitution (Amendment No. 10) Act 1928.

[522] See part I.

[523] [1924] 58 *ILTR* 1.

[524] O'Connor MR in his judgment stated that 'this man is admittedly in custody under the authority or presumed authority of the Public Safety (Emergency Powers) Acts (Nos. 1 and 2) 1923' ([1924] 58 *ILTR* 1, at 2). The question of any differences in standing between the first and second Acts was not gone into; it was, in any case, irrelevant to the argument before the court.

[525] Art. 24 provided: 'The Oireachtas shall hold at least one session each year. The Oireachtas shall be summoned and dissolved by the Representative of the Crown in the name of the King and subject as aforesaid Dáil Eireann shall fix the date of re-assembly of the Oireachtas and the date of the conclusion of the session of each House: Provided that the sessions of Seanad Eireann shall not be concluded without its own consent.'

'was not intended to apply until the Oireachtas to be called into being under the Constitution was created and did not apply to the legislature which was to operate under the transitory provision of the Constitution'.[526] In any case:

even if there were irregularity in the summons [of the Governor-General], which I am far from saying, the Senate met in response to it, and the three Estates in the Parliament—the King the Senate and the Dáil—present together in Parliament treated the summons as good and waived the irregularity if any there was.[527]

The argument under article 47 was also dismissed:

this proceeds from the misconception that the demand should be presented to the legislature, whereas the demand may be presented to the President of the Executive Council. It would certainly be a curious Constitution under which a Parliament should continue to sit for seven days doing absolutely nothing.[528]

A further challenge to the constitutionality of the use of indefinite detention powers, this time on substantive grounds, was made before the old King's Bench Division in *R (O'Connell)* v. *Military Governor of Hare Park Camp*[529] (8 April 1924). The Executive Council had privately displayed some concern about the general issue, but eventually had come to accept the opinion of the Attorney-General that 'deterrent detention as distinct from punitive imprisonment is not debarred by the Constitution'.[530] The judiciary was to show no greater degree of legal creativity; indeed the case well illustrates Kelly's contention that the function of judicial review of the constitutionality of legislation was one 'entirely new to the Irish judges and for which by their traditions and experience they were not very well conditioned'.[531]

The action involved a habeas corpus application brought on behalf of a person interned under a detention order made pursuant to the Public Safety (Powers of Arrest and Detention) Temporary Act 1924.[532] Four points appear to have been pleaded on his behalf: (1) section 4 of the Act amounted to a deprivation of habeas corpus as enshrined in article 6; (2) the Executive Minister was not acting in due course of law and was therefore in breach of article 70 and article 72; (3) in making such an order the Minister was acting as an extraordinary court in contravention

---

[526] p. 2. The transitory provisions of the Constitution were contained in arts. 73 to 83. As their title would suggest, they were concerned with ensuring a legally smooth transition of power to the new institutions of state created by the Constitution.

[527] p. 3.

[528] Ibid.

[529] [1924] 2 *IR* 104.

[530] Minutes of Meeting of Executive Council, 28 May 1923.

[531] *Fundamental Rights*, 13.

[532] See pp. 232–8.

of article 70; (4) the making of a detention order was an exercise of 'judicial power' within the meaning of article 64.

Molony CJ, in dealing with the first ground, held that 'The powers of the Oireachtas cover the whole area of self-government within the whole area of the Irish Free State, and do include power to make such a provision as is sought to have been impeached.'[533] The contrary argument, in the Chief Justice's opinion, was based on the view that 'the Oireachtas cannot do what the Imperial Parliament might do, and this argument is based on the assumption that it is not a free and unfettered legislature'.[534] But the 1922 Constitution placed specific limits on the powers of the Oireachtas, limits which did not apply in the British system with its doctrine of the supremacy of Parliament. Consequently, the Oireachtas could not be considered an unfettered legislature on the British model.[535]

Having stated his view in the widest possible terms, Molony CJ then adopted a significantly narrower formulation: 'there is nothing in the Treaty or the Constitution, or the statutes confirming same, which limits the power of the Oireachtas to make such a provision as is hereby impugned.'[536] In dealing with article 6, the Chief Justice nowhere analysed the phrase 'in accordance with law'. Implicitly he accepted a strict positivist view. This was made clear when he dealt with the contention based on articles 70 and 72 simply by noting, 'the phrase "in due course of law" simply means in accordance with the law then in force: see *King* v. *Halliday*'.[537]

The issues thereby raised were similar to those at the root of the split decision in Halliday's case. Did the power to make laws given by the Constitution, and the power to make regulations under DORA, mean that any type of law/regulation, even one providing for indefinite detention without trial, could be made, or did it mean that a power was given to create a code, the infringement of which would result in the imposition of sanctions? The conflict was essentially that between the 'due process' and the 'instrumentalist' view of law. It might well be argued that the former was the one envisaged by the Constitution. Article 6 guaranteed personal liberty except during the existence of 'a state of war or armed rebellion'. Otherwise, deprivation of liberty could only be 'in accordance with law'. Various articles in the Constitution established the mechanism for this deprivation in accordance with law. There would seem to be little point in adding the ouster clause relating to war or armed rebellion if indefinite

---

[533] p. 110.   [534] At p. 111.
[535] As Kelly has commented: 'The judges were used to the idea of the sovereignty of parliament, and notions of fundamental law were foreign to their training and tradition' (*Fundamental Rights*, 14). See also the discussion of *R (O'Hanlon)* v. *Governor of Belfast Prison* [1924] 56 *ILTR* 170, at pp. 334–6.
[536] p. 111.
[537] p. 113. Cf. *State (Burke)* v. *Lennon and AG* [1940] *IR* 136.

detention without trial could in any case be 'in accordance with law'. If such were the case, then the ouster clause in article 6 merely removed the necessity for the existence of statutory powers, and in essence was enabling but not prohibitory. The contrary argument is that the addition of a specific ouster clause in article 6 had both an enabling and a prohibitory effect: enabling in that it permitted detention other than that provided for in the ordinary law, but only during the existence of a state of war or armed rebellion, prohibitory in that it prevented detention other than that provided for in the ordinary law, except during the existence of a state of war or armed rebellion. The structure of these arguments closely follows those underlying the conflict between Egan's case and Allen's case. Given that Molony CJ delivered the judgment in Allen's case, it is not surprising that a non-prohibitory argument was implicitly accepted in O'Connell's case.

In response to the contention that the Minister was acting as an extraordinary court, the Chief Justice adopted the definition of a court as 'a place where justice is judicially administered':[538]

What is necessary in order to have justice judicially administered? The answer will be found in the judgment of Lord O'Brien in *The King (Martin)* v. *Mahony*:[539] 'In all matters of procedure the essentials of justice must be observed. It is one of the essential requirements of justice that a charge shall be duly formulated, that an accused person shall have notice of it, and that he should be given an adequate opportunity of defending himself. Such matters are not mere formalities; they are the essential requirements of justice'. It is in my opinion impossible to say that the minister in making the order in the present case was acting as a court, ordinary or extraordinary, and Article 70 has no application.[540]

With reference to the arguments previously advanced, it might well be suggested that since the courts alone were to adjudicate on guilt or innocence in particular cases and as a consequence of that process to order the detention or otherwise of persons, there was implicit in that a prohibition on any other body arriving at the same result (detention), all the more so if that body did not act judicially.

To the argument that in making a detention order, the Minister was exercising 'judicial power', Molony CJ replied:

what are judicial powers? A statutory definition will be found in sect. 3 of the *Vice-Admiralty Courts Amendment Act, 1867*, which prescribes that 'judicial powers' shall mean all powers and authorities which may be lawfully exercised by, and all duties by law imposed upon, any such judge in the trial, hearing, and progress of any cause. Within this definition, or anything like it, the order of the Executive Minister certainly does not come. He is to form an opinion on whatever

---

[538] p. 113.   [539] [1910] 2 *IR* 695.   [540] p. 113.

materials he deems sufficient; but there is no cause, no trial, no hearing, nothing except the inner consciousness of the minister expressed in the written order. The power given by sect. 4 is not judicial power. It is a power, in its nature arbitrary, conferred by the legislature to meet a threatened danger to the State, and limited to particular persons and for a limited time, and in this connexion I may repeat the words of Lord Finlay in *The King* v. Halliday: 'It seems obvious that no tribunal for investigating the question whether circumstances of suspicion exist warranting some restraint can be imagined less appropriate than a Court of law'.[541]

It is submitted that to define judicial powers as what judges can lawfully do amounts to little more than a tautology. In any case, it might be said that by choosing a definition of 'judicial power' with such a high degree of specificity, Molony CJ was in danger of effecting a distortion. An argument could be presented that the exercise of the judicial processes set out in the definition of 'judicial power' presupposed the existence of 'judicial authority'. The existence of such a uniquely judicial authority was guaranteed by article 2 of the Constitution in which Government authority is said to be tripartite. Taken to its logical conclusion, Molony CJ's choice of definition could lead to a permanent encroachment in certain areas of judicial authority, for example a legislative enactment allowing indefinite detention without trial of all potential criminals could spell the end of the criminal justice system. Therefore, since Molony CJ's view was based on a definition of 'judicial power' insufficient to protect the existence of the 'judicial authority', it was inadequate.[542]

It was perhaps with a view to this type of argument, that Pim J., while concurring with the Chief Justice, added a proviso:

It would be possible, I think, to argue successfully that a permanent law giving the Executive power to deprive any citizen of his liberty without trial was contrary to the spirit of Article 6, and therefore a violation of the Constitution; but that is a very different thing from a temporary law made in abnormal times and for a temporary purpose.[543]

This view was echoed in the concurring judgment of Dodd J.:

In a land of settled government the liberty of the subject is the prevailing note. In a land unsettled and turbulent, the duty of the Legislature is to continue as far as may be to reconcile personal liberty with safety to the persons and property of the citizens.[544]

To these views it might be replied that article 6 did permit the liberty of the individual to be set aside during abnormal times—narrowly defined as

---

[541] p. 112.
[542] Cf. *State (Burke)* v. *Lennon and AG* [1940] *IR* 136, but also In re Article 26 of the Constitution and the Offences against the State (Amendment) Bill 1940 [1940] *IR* 470.
[543] p. 118.   [544] p. 116.

'during the existence of a state of war or armed rebellion'. For there to have been any other occasions permitting departure from the safeguards contained in article 6 would have required an amendment to that article. It was impermissible to say that a permanent enactment providing for indefinite detention without trial would have been in breach of article 6 while a temporary one was not, since no provision in the Article differentiated between temporary and permanent Acts. The result of the interpretation put on the Constitution in that case was that the habeas corpus application failed.

All of these decisions had been handed down by the court system inherited from the 'preceding regime' and therefore the question as to whether a more stringent approach in the sphere of emergency law might be taken by an indigenous system remained open. In *R (Burke)* v. *Governor of Mountjoy Prison*[545] (7 July 1924) the first reported emergency law decision of a court established under the Courts of Justice Act 1924, this question was answered firmly in the negative.

In that case, the issue of the validity of a detention order made under the Public Safety (Powers of Arrest and Detention) Temporary Act 1924 came before the new High Court on a habeas corpus application. Procedural rather than substantive issues were raised. It was pleaded (1) that the authorization for the original arrest of the applicant given by a superintendent under section 2 should have been in writing; (2) that the fact of the making of the detention order should have been communicated to the prisoner within the seven-day period provided for its making; (3) that the order of the Minister should have been under seal.

The application was rejected with costs.[546] In a laconic judgment, the President of the High Court, Sullivan, held:

In this Court we are only concerned with the interpretation of the law . . . The words 'unless an order for his detention is made by an Executive Minister' are quite clear, and cannot be construed as meaning that the order should be communicated to prisoner. The arguments brought forward by Mr Lynn [for applicant] might be very powerful arguments if addressed to the Oireachtas to convince them of the desirability of this course, but they cannot assist us now. We are of opinion that the prisoner was arrested by responsible officers, and is now detained in due course of law.[547]

Murnaghan J. concurred, merely adding, 'I certainly cannot read the Ministries and Secretaries Act to assume that every act of a Minister must be under seal'.[548]

[545] [1924] 58 *ILTR* 106.
[546] On other occasions the courts could be more considerate in relation to the question of costs. See *R (O'Sullivan)* v. *Military Governor of Hare Park Internment Camp* [1924] 58 *ILTR* 62, a case involving an internee which was concerned only with the issue of costs.
[547] p. 107.   [548] Ibid.

Judicial scrutiny: conclusions

The decisions in Childers' and Johnstone's cases represented a continuation and if anything an extension of the judicial interpretation of martial law in Allen's case. Military necessity overrode any statutory shortcomings. Following the coming into force of the Constitution, its provisions were interpreted so as to conform with the previously accepted view of martial law. The dicta in O'Brien's case gave a degree of retrospective validation to executions without trial and to the operation of military tribunals not established by law. As alternative interpretations were clearly open (as evidenced by Ronan LJ's dissent in Johnstone's case), the question needs to be asked as to why this judicial abnegation took place.

Ultimately, the answer is probably political rather than legal. While the judiciary maintained a formal commitment to legal standards, the purpose of this commitment was to put some legal construction, which would be intelligible within the framework of previously accepted values, on the actions of the Provisional Government, rather than to provide an objective standard by which the actions of that Government could be measured. They were therefore reflecting the realities of political power rather than attempting to assert any meaningful degree of judicial independence. In view of the fate of the Dáil courts, and of Erskine Childers, this attitude is perhaps not surprising. The Provisional Government was unlikely to have tolerated any challenge to its authority, particularly by an institution which remained closely identified with the previous regime.

It was only when the new Constitution had been in place for eight months, and the institutional structures of the new state had been set, that the courts were prepared to challenge Government assertions in this sphere. And then, it was only in a manner which seemed to validate some earlier, and highly questionable, official activity. Where this happened, the other new institutions were prepared to step in, in order effectively to overrule the courts by legislative action.

O'Connell's case made clear that the ending of martial law by the courts did not signal a new dawn of judicial activism, and this approach was carried through by the indigenously created court system in Burke's case. Overall, therefore, the pattern of judicial scrutiny of emergency powers in the formative and the early years of the new state remained much as it had been under British rule.

4. *Northern Ireland 1921–1925*

PART I. LEGAL DEVELOPMENTS IN CONTEXT

The conflict in the North-East prior to partition differed significantly from that in the rest of the country.[1] Perhaps it would be more correct to speak of 'conflicts' because, apart from IRA activity which was an extension of the campaign in the South, the North alone saw massive rioting and civil disorder, most of it instigated by loyalists. From June 1921 to March 1922 the apparatus of the Northern Ireland state was in the process of creation, and for much of this period, responsibility for security matters remained with the British Government. By April 1922 much of the new machinery (including the Civil Authorities (Special Powers) Act (Northern Ireland) 1922), had been created and the months up to the end of June saw its most intense application. The third period, from July 1922 to November 1923, was one of consolidation, at the end of which the future course of developments in Northern Ireland had clearly been set. The final period, from December 1923 to December 1925, saw the gradual winding down, though not the scrapping, of the emergency apparatus.

The North-East prior to partition

The IRA's 1919–21 campaign had been much less effective in the six North-Eastern counties which were to comprise Northern Ireland than in the rest of the country.[2] In the view of one Republican commentator, 'Every problem in the organization, training and arming of Volunteers which had to be overcome in every brigade was intensified a hundred fold in these counties.'[3] There were two main reasons for this: first the density of loyalists in the North was very much higher than in the South, thus presenting obvious operational difficulties for the IRA; secondly, as the failure of Sinn Féin to eclipse the Irish Parliamentary Party in the North illustrated, the Republicans did not achieve that degree of dominance over their nationalist rivals which had been one of the most striking developments of political life elsewhere on the island.

---

[1] This section draws on the following historical works: P. Buckland, *A History of Northern Ireland* (Dublin, 1981); M. Farrell, *Northern Ireland: The Orange State* (London, 1980); Lyons, *Ireland since the Famine*; and D. Harkness, *Northern Ireland since 1920* (Dublin, 1983). Reference to primary sources and to other works is made in the footnotes.

[2] Partition is taken to have commenced on 26 June 1921, the day on which the King opened the Northern Ireland Parliament.

[3] O'Donoghue, *No Other Law*, 247.

The IRA campaign in the South had depended to a large extent on the sympathy or neutrality of the civilian population. This was particularly true of the full-time flying columns, units which by virtue of the relatively large numbers of volunteers involved were both particularly effective in an ambush, and particularly vulnerable in a hostile environment. IRA activities in the North-East tended therefore to be concentrated in solidly nationalist territory, and while it appears that there was some flying-column activity in Tyrone, Armagh, and South Down in April 1921,[4] the North saw none of the large-scale ambushes that had been a feature of the conflict elsewhere.

One response of Northern loyalists to the IRA campaign was the formation of vigilante groups, often based loosely on the pre-war UVF. This development was regarded as benign by some British strategists. As early as July 1920 the Irish Situation Sub-committee of the British Cabinet had reached the conclusion that 'In view of the urgent need of concentrating all available troops . . . advantage ought to be taken of the willingness of the North to protect themselves and steps taken at once to enlist volunteers on a special constabulary basis'.[5] Others were less enthusiastic—General Macready saw it as 'the raising of Carson's army from the grave'.[6] It was not until October that formal details of the new force, which was to become known as the Ulster Special Constabulary (USC), were announced.[7] There were to be three classes: full-time 'A' Specials with an establishment initially set at 1,500 but quickly raised to 2,000; part-time 'B' Specials (19,500); and a reserve of 'C' Specials (over 8,000). During the following month recruiting for the USC began under the Special Constables (Ireland) Act 1832. The force which emerged was based mainly on the reorganized UVF and other vigilante groups,[8] a fact which caused alarm among Northern nationalists. And the creation of this force did not result in the ending of other loyalist paramilitary activities, as evidenced by the emergence in May 1921 of the Ulster Brotherhood, better known as 'Crawford's Tigers', a group which operated with official tolerance if not outright endorsement.[9]

July 1920 had seen intense rioting in Belfast.[10] Thousands of nationalists had been driven from their homes, and over 10,000 had been expelled

---

[4] P. Buckland, *The Factory of Grievances* (Dublin, 1977), 182.

[5] Note by Walter Long, CAB 27/107, PRO, Kew.

[6] Quoted in Townshend, 124.

[7] For detailed (different) histories of the force see M. Farrell, *Arming the Protestants* (London, 1983), and A. R. Hezlett, *The 'B' Specials: A History of the Ulster Special Constabulary* (London, 1972).

[8] See D. W. Miller, *Queen's Rebels* (Dublin, 1978), 127.

[9] See M. Farrell, *Arming the Protestants*, 55–6.

[10] See A. Boyd, *Holy War in Belfast* (Belfast, 1987), 181–95. See also G. B. Kenna (pseud.), *Facts and Figures of the Belfast Pogrom* (Dublin, 1922).

from their jobs. There had been more rioting the following month, and the Dáil responded with a boycott of Belfast goods. In September 1920 a further twenty-three people were killed in disturbances. To many nationalists it seemed that those who had been involved in the attempted destruction of their community were now being armed and regularized by the state.

In many respects, the USC in the North performed much the same role as the Black and Tans and ADRIC in the South, with the significant difference that the USC possessed a degree of local knowledge which the imported forces did not. ADRIC also operated in the North and, as in the South, elements of the RIC seem to have been involved in a number of unofficial reprisal assassinations, some of the victims of which appear to have been targeted as Republican activists, others to have been chosen at random from the nationalist community.[11]

Many of the emergency statutory measures which were applied in the South were also applied in the North-East, for example ROIA courts martial functioned in Belfast,[12] an internment camp was established at Ballykinlar in County Down,[13] and curfews were enforced in response to outbreaks of violence.[14] Generally, however, the steps taken in the North were less severe: none of the 'six counties' were proclaimed under section 1 of the Criminal Law and Procedure (Ireland) Act 1887 (special inquisitorial procedures). Only County Tyrone was proclaimed under sections 3 and 4 of the Act (special juries and removal for trial); and none of these counties was placed under martial law. But those involved in the operation of the legal system were familiar with the workings of DORA and ROIA, a factor which was to have a significant impact on the future development of emergency legislation in the new jurisdiction.

The Government of Ireland Act 1920 ('the 1920 Act') which provided for partition, had received the Royal assent in December 1920, but as early as September of that year, the groundwork for partition had already been laid when a separate Under-Secretary for Ireland had been placed in Belfast.[15] When the results of the first elections to be held under the

[11] See M. Farrell, *Arming the Protestants*, app. 2, pp. 298–300, and Buckland, *Factory of Grievances*, 182.

[12] e.g. *R (Rodgers)* v. *Campbell and Others* [1921] 55 *ILTR* 192 (discussed on pp. 122–3) involved a ROIA court martial held in Belfast.

[13] See, generally, McGuffin, *Internment*.

[14] See FIN 18/1/162 PRONI for details of representations made by theatre owners in Belfast complaining of the effects on their businesses of a curfew which they claimed began at 10 p.m. Their efforts appear to have met with little success—the Assistant Under-Secretary commented: 'it must be borne in mind that the [previous] curfew was taken off with a warning that it would be re-imposed in the event of further disturbances; and that 9 days after, a policeman was shot and two others wounded at about 11:30 at night, and that as a result of this and the following consequent disturbances, the curfew was re-imposed.' Clark to Anderson, 16 Nov. 1920.

[15] Townshend, 124.

1920 Act were announced on 25 May 1921 they confirmed the Unionist majority in the North, with that group winning forty seats in the House of Commons of Northern Ireland, as opposed to six seats each for Sinn Féin and the Nationalists.

June 1921 to March 1922: the emerging framework

On 26 June 1921 the King formally opened the Northern Ireland Parliament, and event boycotted by Sinn Féin and by the Nationalists. Under the 1920 Act the constitutional position of Northern Ireland was that of a subordinate jurisdiction within the United Kingdom. While the Northern Ireland Parliament (which consisted of a Senate, a House of Commons, and notionally the monarch) was granted a general power to make laws 'for the peace order and good government' of the jurisdiction, this right was limited in three important respects. There was a prohibition on legislation in respect of certain matters which were declared to be 'excepted', and in respect of other matters which were (temporarily) 'reserved'. And there was also a bar on legislation which would have certain specified effects, for example taking property without compensation. Executive authority was similarly limited to the sphere of 'Irish Services' defined as 'all public services in connection with the administration of civil government in . . . Northern Ireland' other than with respect to the reserved or excepted matters.[16]

Services in relation to the enforcement of law and order and the administration of justice were not initially transferred. Thus the position in June 1921 was that responsibility for this area remained with Westminster, and in practice this meant with Dublin Castle—a situation much resented by Belfast.[17] In addition, since the armed forces remained an excepted matter, control of the British Army also lay outside of the hands of the Northern Ireland Government. Tensions between the two Governments in this area were heightened by the truce between the Crown Forces and the IRA which came into force throughout Ireland on 11 July and had been negotiated over the heads of the Northern Ireland Government. During its continuance, the implementation of ROIA was suspended, and the USC (whose strength then stood at 3,515 'A' Specials, 15,903 'B' Specials, and 1,310 'C' Specials[18]) was all but demobilized.

On 9 July, the day on which the truce terms had been agreed upon, the IRA shot dead a policeman in Belfast, and this incident was followed by rioting which continued around the loyalist celebrations of 12 July. On the 11th, the Northern Ireland Government was demanding the reimposition of the curfew because of 'the situation which has arisen in Belfast

---

[16] These issues are discussed in more detail on pp. 317–19.
[17] See Buckland, *Factory of Grievances*, 182.
[18] See M. Farrell, *Arming the Protestants*, 53–4.

through attacks on Constabulary',[19] and on the 15th it was requesting the GOC that ROIA be 'again re-established'.[20] The GOC replied that although the Act was still in force, his instructions were that 'as far as Troops are concerned they will be guided by the spirit [of] the agreement entered for the cessation of activities'.[21] On 22 July the Northern Ireland Cabinet agreed on steps to be taken in the event of a breakdown in the truce including the introduction throughout Northern Ireland of identification cards (with photographs), and provision for the internment of 'five or six hundred people'.[22]

At this point the British Government was proving largely unresponsive to demands from Belfast. Particularly when the Treaty negotiations opened, British concerns focused on reaching an accommodation with Sinn Féin (or a section thereof), and the chances of a settlement were not to be scuttled by the adoption of abrasive security measures in Northern Ireland. The fact that the Dáil Cabinet refused to operate the 1920 Act in 'Southern Ireland' (as the twenty-six-county area was referred to under the Act) meant that the transfer of services by the British Government was delayed not only in the South, but also in the North. Thus for much of 1921 the administration of law and order remained outside the competence of the Northern Ireland Government.

The IRA used the truce to build up its strength in Northern Ireland as elsewhere. Its nominal membership in that area at the time of the truce has been estimated at not more that 4,500, of whom the great majority were poorly armed and only a fraction of whom would have been active.[23] Experienced Volunteers were drafted in from other areas to assist in training, and in July and August the 'Republican Police' began operating in nationalist areas of Belfast.

August also saw increased activity by loyalist paramilitaries, including the Ulster Protestant Association (UPA). This group, which had originally been formed as a vigilante force in East Belfast in the autumn of the previous year, eventually came to specialize in the random assassination of nationalists. Rioting broke out on the night of 29 August and

---

[19] CAB 4/8, PRONI, report of conclusions reached after conference of members of the Cabinet of Northern Ireland with the Government, military, and police authorities on 11 July 1921.

[20] CAB 4/9, PRONI.

[21] Note of correspondence attached to Ministry of Home Affairs, Northern Ireland, Memorandum, 10 Sept. 1921, HA 20/A/1/2, PRONI.

[22] CAB 4/10, PRONI. Draft conclusions of Cabinet meeting of 22 July 1921. Objections were also raised to the use of the Ballykinlar camp for the internment of Southerners.

[23] M. Farrell, *Arming the Protestants*, 64. Details of the establishment of the three IRA Divisions which operated almost exclusively in Northern Ireland in July 1921 (the 2nd, 3rd, and 4th Northern), and of four Divisions whose operational areas straddled the border (the 1st and 5th Northern, the 1st Midland, and the 3rd Western) can be found in O'Donoghue, *No Other Law*, app. 5, p. 334; see also map on p. 198.

eventually, on the 30th and 31st, the British Army intervened, though Macready was careful to limit military involvement and there was no attempt at a full-scale reliance on ROIA. Northern Ireland Ministers still complained of a lack of military willingness to use their powers under the Act, and of confusion between the Crown Forces, with the result that 'the Police and Military are still uncertain as to the extent to which they may use these powers'.[24]

In the following month, the Northern Ireland Parliament met for its first real session amid rumours that the UVF was yet again being reorganized. On the 29th, the third round of rioting of the year broke out in Belfast, and on this occasion the response was harsher. Craig announced that the USC was being mobilized, and that four Catholics and four Protestants were being detained by the British Army under ROIR 55, a step which fell short of the reintroduction of internment (ROIR 14B), but which led to vociferous loyalist protest at the detention of the Protestants.[25] Then on midnight, September 29, the military assumed control of the police in Belfast, including the USC.

This brought a temporary lull in the disturbances, but there was more rioting in November. There were also more loyalist paramilitary displays of strength, the latest group to appear publicly being the Imperial Guards who staged a 13,000-strong parade in Belfast.[26] With pressure from Unionists mounting, an Order in Council was made on 9 November transferring 'Irish Services in connection with the maintenance of Law and Order and the Administration of Justice'[27] as and from the 22nd.

Planning continued on measures to be taken in the North in the event of a breakdown in the truce. It had apparently been agreed that if martial law were re-established in the South, a 'Senior Military Officer should be appointed as Military Advisor to the Cabinet of Northern Ireland',[28] and a large quantity of arms would be brought in.[29] Early in December the Northern Ireland Government decided on the enactment of fresh emergency powers. On the 14th of that month, the Local Government (Emergency Powers) Act (Northern Ireland) 1921 became law, a measure which permitted the Minister of Home Affairs to dissolve local authorities in certain circumstances, and in their place to appoint 'such person as the Ministry thinks fit to exercise and perform all the powers and duties of the local authority'.[30]

---

[24] Ministry of Home Affairs, Northern Ireland, Memorandum for Circulation to the Cabinet, Dawson Bates, 10 Sept. 1921, HA 20/A/1/2, PRONI.

[25] Buckland, *Factory of Grievances*, 193.

[26] See M. Farrell, *Arming the Protestants*, 72.

[27] Schedule to Order of 9 Nov. *BG* 18 Nov. 1921.

[28] Spender to Worthington Evans, 1 Dec. 1921, HA 20/A/1/2, PRONI. This is first of a series of four letters of the same date sent by Spender to Worthington Evans on this subject.

[29] Ibid. (second letter), HA 20/A/1/2, PRONI.

[30] S. 1 (1).

Events in the South were also proceeding apace. On 6 December the Treaty had been signed, which, as outlined in Chapter 3, allowed Northern Ireland to opt out of the Free State, and provided for the establishment of a Boundary Commission to settle the eventual borders between the two jurisdictions. On 7 January 1922 the Provisional Government was formed, and in an attempt to regularize the position between the two new Governments, a meeting was held under British auspices on 21 January out of which came the first Craig–Collins pact. Under its terms, the border was to be settled not by the Boundary Commission envisaged by the Treaty, but by direct negotiation between the two Governments. Craig was to arrange the return of Catholics expelled from the shipyards, and Collins to end the Belfast boycott.

The pact quickly collapsed amid mutual recriminations, and the violence continued. On 14 January members of the Monaghan Gaelic football team, who were also in the IRA, were arrested and detained when documents concerning a plan to release condemned Republican prisoners held in Derry were found on them. In the event, the Derry prisoners were saved when, against the wishes of the Northern Ireland Government, their sentences were commuted.[31]

The effect of the arrests of the 'Monaghan Footballers' was to shore up the divisions in the IRA caused by the Treaty, at least in relation to Northern policy. A new united Ulster Council Command was established,[32] and in early February the IRA responded with the kidnapping of forty-two loyalists who were then held as hostages on the southern side of the border. Then came the 'Clones incident'—a fire-fight between the IRA and a party of Specials in transit through County Monaghan.

By mid-February relations between North and South were at their lowest ever ebb. On 13 February Craig sent an irate telegram to the Secretary of State at the War Office requesting him to 'ask the law officers of the Crown whether there is any legal obstacle to our sending a flying column of five thousand men to recover the kidnapped loyalists'.[33] Churchill, from the Irish Office, replied that 'violent measures would do more harm than good and might entail the resignation of the Irish Provisional Government thus creating chaos and leaving the extremists in control'.[34] He followed this up with another telegram later in the day informing Craig that 'The despatch of Northern Ireland Constabulary to Southern Ireland to recover kidnapped Loyalists would be illegal and

---

[31] The legal implications of this move are considered on pp. 319–23.
[32] For an account of Republican manœuvrings during this period see Hopkinson, *Green*, 77–88.
[33] Craig to Secretary of State, War Office, 13 Feb. 1922, (telegram) CAB 11/1, PRONI.
[34] Churchill to Craig, 14 Feb. 1922, received 8.30 a.m., CAB 11/1, PRONI.

would result in immediate civil war'.[35] The flying column was not sent, but in an attempt to pour oil on troubled waters, a 'Border Commission' with British, Northern, and Southern representation was established on 16 February to monitor developments on the frontier. It proved a failure, and within a couple of months had completely broken down.

Republican and loyalist violence continued in March as the IRA renewed its attacks on Crown Forces in Northern Ireland. Reprisals followed, in the course of which it appears that the USC was responsible for the deaths of several innocent nationalists.[36] Unionist demands for military intervention were becoming more insistent, but Macready remained unimpressed: early in the month he wrote, 'All this talk about ROIA and Martial Law is perfect nonsense . . . The fact remains that if they did so a greater number of Protestants would probably have to be executed than Catholics, and we all know what that means.'[37] This was because, in his view, 'the balance for making trouble is due to the so-called Protestants',[38] yet simultaneously he could state 'four fifths of the trouble in the Six Counties is entirely due to the presence there of recognized Divisions of the IRA who owe allegiance to Griffith'.[39] Craig was only too aware of the problems which the enforcement of martial law would pose for his administration: 'I feel instinctively that if we hand over any part of the affairs of this city to the military, who would be controlled through Dublin from Westminster, we would get back to the same old chaos and confusion in which we were before.'[40] There would also have been legal and constitutional problems with such a course.[41] Instead, the Northern Ireland Government was to arm itself with emergency powers under its own control, and, under the auspices of the British, there was to be a new agreement with the Provisional Government in Dublin designed to bring an end to the IRA campaign.

The new security policy was signalled by the introduction of the Civil Authorities (Special Powers) Bill (Northern Ireland) on 21 March, and by the move of Field Marshal Sir Henry Wilson from his post as Chief of the Imperial General Staff to advise the Northern Ireland Government on security matters. The new agreement took the form of the second Craig–Collins pact, signed on 29 March 1922.

[35] Churchill to Craig, 14 Feb. 1922, received 4 p.m., ibid.
[36] See M. Farrell, *Arming the Protestants*, 100, and P. Canning, *British Policy*, 34.
[37] Quoted ibid. 58.
[38] Ibid. 57.
[39] Ibid. 58.
[40] 2 *HCNI Deb.*, col. 15.
[41] These problems are considered in detail on pp. 319–25.

April 1922 to June 22: the Special Powers Act

'*Peace* is to-day declared',[42] announced the pact. Its central provisions were that the IRA was to cease activity 'in the six counties',[43] and the 'Northern Signatories' were to use every effort to secure the reinstatement of expelled workers.[44] A Catholic Advisory Committee was to be set up to assist in the selection of Catholic recruits for the USC,[45] and a mixed committee was to be established 'to hear and investigate complaints as to intimidation, outrages, &c.'[46] In addition, a jury-less court for the trial of serious offences was to be introduced,[47] and 'in cases agreed upon between the Signatories', political prisoners in prison for offences committed before the date of the pact were to be released.[48]

The issue of jury-less courts was tackled with the introduction of the Criminal Procedure Bill (Northern Ireland) which provided for trial of a range of offences by two judges sitting without a jury.[49] It was immediately apparent that the competence of the Northern Ireland Parliament to enact such legislation, limited as it was by the terms of the 1920 Act, was doubtful.[50] But even before the bill was introduced, there were pledges that the Imperial Parliament would cover any shortcomings by fresh legislation.[51] The measure received the Royal assent on 13 April and confirmatory British legislation was drafted,[52] but its practical effect came to nil as no use was made of the Act's provisions. The Northern Cabinet later considered a different proposal suggested by the constabulary and military authorities 'for the establishment of special courts leading to the more speedy conviction and punishment of the "outrage offenders"'. But this was not proceeded with because 'the establishment

---

[42] Clause 1. The text of the Agreement is included in K. Boyle, 'The Tallents Report on the Craig–Collins Pact of 30 March 1922', 12 *Ir. Jur.* 148, at pp. 173–5.

[43] Clause 6.

[44] Clause 9.

[45] Clause 3.

[46] Clause 5.

[47] Clause 4.

[48] Clause 10.

[49] The terms of the eventual Act, the Criminal Procedure Act (Northern Ireland) 1922, are considered in detail on pp. 313–15.

[50] Telegram from Prime Minister of Northern Ireland to Secretary of State, Irish Office, London, 3 Apr. 1922, CAB 6/56, PRONI. The substantive issues involved are considered on pp. 325–7.

[51] Telegram from Secretary of State for the Colonies to Prime Minister of Northern Ireland, 3 Apr. 1922, ibid.

[52] A draft of the proposed Criminal Procedure Act (Northern Ireland) (Confirmation) Bill 1922 is enclosed with Greer to Spender 1 May 1922, CAB 6/56, PRONI. The Northern Ireland Act was included as a schedule, and it was provided that 'The Act set out in the Schedule . . . shall have effect, and shall be deemed as from the passing thereof to have had effect, as if the subject matter thereof were a matter with respect to which the Parliament of Northern Ireland has power to make laws' (clause 1 (1)).

of Special Courts would have a bad effect in England where it would not be understood'.[53]

The other provisions of the pact had little more practical impact. Expelled Catholics were not returned to their jobs. The mixed Reconciliation Committee met on a number of occasions, but ceased to function after its sixth meeting of 1 May. The Catholic Advisory Committee likewise collapsed amid recriminations after its third meeting of 7 June.[54] The political prisoners issue also proved to be a bone of contention. Collins interpreted the term broadly and submitted a list of 169 persons convicted or awaiting trial for such offences as murder, riot, and possession of arms and ammunition.[55] Craig chose a narrow definition stating that the Northern Ireland Government 'could not countenance the liberation of those convicted of grave civil offences'.[56]

The other element in the Northern Ireland Government's strategy was the new security initiative. On 7 April Major-General Solly-Flood was appointed as the new military adviser to the Government. He began his task by preparing a rather grandiose defence plan, in which the USC was seen as playing an essentially military role.[57] Solly-Flood's appreciation of the situation was 'generally approved' by the Cabinet, and it was agreed that the 'C' Specials 'should be clothed in Khaki with Military equipment'.[58] A new 'C1' force, in effect a sort of Territorial Army, was created.[59]

The new statutory measure, the Civil Authorities (Special Powers) Act (Northern Ireland) 1922 (the 'Special Powers Act'), received the Royal assent on the day of Solly-Flood's appointment. In its structure and content it was directly derived from DORA.[60] In short, most of the

[53] Final Cabinet conclusions, 19 and 20 June 1922, CAB 4/48, PRONI.

[54] See Boyle, 'Tallents Report', 159.

[55] The details supplied by Collins can be found attached to a memorandum submitted to the NI Cabinet on 18 Apr. 1922, CAB 4/40, PRONI. An amended version of the list prepared by the Northern Government, excluding 10 persons who were already released, two who could not be traced, and two whose cases were inadvertently included twice, can be found in Boyle, 'Tallents Report', 171.

[56] Quoted ibid. 171. Dawson Bates submitted a memorandum to the Cabinet in which he submitted that only two groups could be considered to come within the term 'political prisoner', because these were the only cases which could be considered as having been 'technical breaches of the law'. These were the cases of a firing party at a funeral, and eight Republican Police members arrested in Warrenpoint. CAB 4/40 PRONI.

[57] 'Preliminary Report on the Steps Necessary for the Preservation of Law and Order within the Six Counties, and the City of Belfast', CAB 4/40, PRONI. See also Statement by Maj.-Gen. Solly-Flood, military Adviser to the Cabinet, put up for discussion and Cabinet decision, 18 Apr. 1922, ibid.

[58] Note of decision of Cabinet meeting of 18 Apr. 1922, ibid.

[59] The eventual form of police organization in Northern Ireland, including that of the C1 force, is shown in App. 4.

[60] The derivation of the Special Powers Act and Regulations is set out in App. 3. The provisions governing arrest, detention, internment, and trial by special courts of summary

DORR and ROIR which the British had found useful in combating the IRA, apart from those relating to trial by court martial, were re-enacted, and the Minister of Home Affairs was given power to make new regulations 'for making further provision for the preservation of the peace and maintenance of order'.[61] In place of the CMA, the centrepiece of the Northern Ireland provisions was the 'civil authority', who was to have 'power, in respect of persons, matters and things within the jurisdiction of the Government of Northern Ireland, to take all such steps and issue all such orders as may be necessary for preserving the peace and maintaining order, according to and in the execution of this Act and the regulations'.[62] The civil authority was to be the Minister of Home Affairs for Northern Ireland, who might 'delegate, either unconditionally or subject to such conditions as he thinks fit all or any of his powers under this Act to any officer of police, and any such officer of police shall, to the extent of such delegation, be the civil authority as respects any part of Northern Ireland specified in such delegation'.[63] If DORA amounted to the statutory imposition of martial law, then the Special Powers Act was its civil equivalent—as one commentator later remarked, 'for a government disposed to establish a police state in Northern Ireland, there is a clear way open'.[64]

The Act had come at a time of generally rising violence (Graph F), and on 18 May there began a co-ordinated (though largely ineffectual) series of IRA attacks involving the use of flying columns in rural areas.[65] Though divided on the Treaty issue, the organization still retained some operational capacity in Northern Ireland. In Belfast it switched to arson attacks on commercial targets, and on 22 May was responsible for the assassination of a Unionist MP, W. J. Twadell. This was quickly followed by the 'Pettigo triangle incident', when the IRA drove a force of Specials from a corner of County Fermanagh.

The Northern Ireland Government was quick to take advantage of its new powers. On 20 April the power to hold inquiries (without a jury) in lieu of inquests had been invoked in Belfast,[66] and the Cabinet indicated to the military authorities its willingness to continue to use such powers in

---

jurisdiction are considered in detail on pp. 289–308, 310–13, while the significance of the derivation issue is considered on pp. 327–31. For a detailed analysis of the Special Powers Act and Regulations see B. Jorgensen, 'Emergency Powers in Canada and Northern Ireland' (Ph.D. thesis, University of Cambridge (undated)).

[61] s. 1 (3).
[62] s. 1 (1).
[63] s. 1 (2).
[64] Calvert, *Constitutional Law in Northern Ireland* (London, 1968), 383.
[65] See O'Donoghue, *No Other Law*, 252–3.
[66] Under s. 10. James Graham MD the Belfast Coroner was appointed to conduct the inquiry.

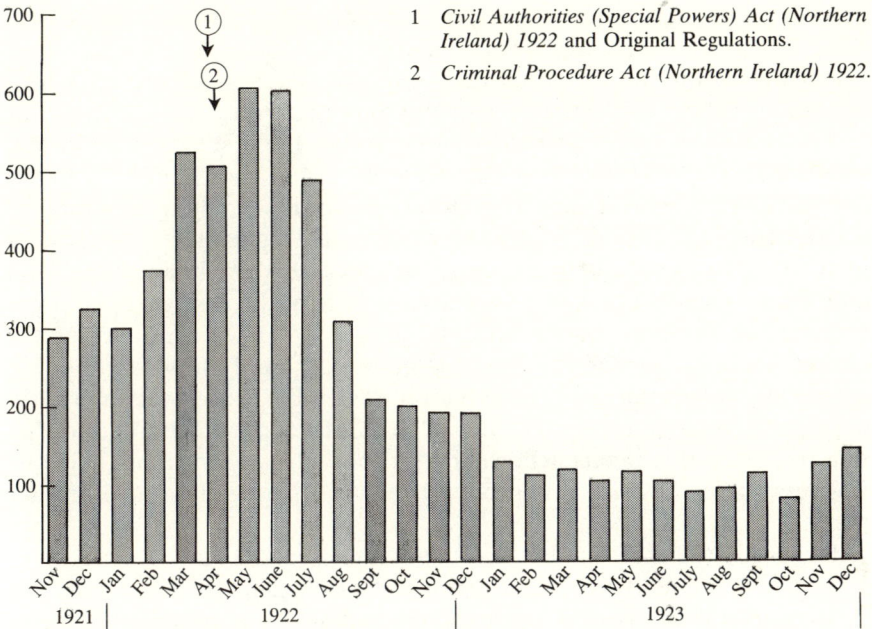

GRAPH F. Northern Ireland monthly 'outrage' totals, November 1921 to December 1923

Source: Derived from graph at CAB 6/11, PRONI.

the future.[67] On 27 April Belfast had been placed under an 11 p.m. to 6 a.m. curfew.[68] Additional restrictions were applied to a part of North Belfast,[69] and then in all of the city[70] the following month (though these were soon relaxed),[71] and May also saw the imposition of an 11 p.m. to 5 a.m.[72] curfew in the rest of Northern Ireland. Restrictions were also placed in May on the opening of public houses in Belfast[73] (though these were lightened the following month,)[74] and some business premises were

---

[67] Spender to Dalrymple, 16 May 1922, HA 8/316, PRONI. The Army, though, seemed keen to reserve its position under ROIA, as Dalrymple (acting for the Major-General Commanding Ulster District) replied: 'In the event of a soldier being killed, or a civilian being killed by a soldier in circumstances of such a nature that a Military Inquiry in lieu of Inquest appears desirable, a notification to that effect will be telegraphed to you from this Headquarters.' Dalrymple to Spender, 23 May 1922, ibid.

[68] *BG* 28 Apr. 1922.

[69] From 9 p.m. to 7 a.m. *BG* 19 May 1922.

[70] From 10 p.m. to 6 a.m. Ibid.

[71] On 8 June the curfew hours were set at 11 p.m. to 6 a.m. *BG* 9 June 1922.

[72] *BG* 26 May and 2 June 1922.

[73] Licensed public houses and spirit groceries were to be closed except between the hours of 12 noon and 7 p.m. *BG* 9 May 1922.

[74] The new restrictions were between 10 a.m. and 9.30 p.m. *BG* 9 June 1922.

ordered to be closed[75] or to have their windows barred up.[76] Elsewhere, the power to ban meetings was invoked.[77]

But the major counter-insurgency initiative was the reintroduction of detention without trial. The first swoop took place on 22 May when over 200 people were held.[78] In the following weeks the numbers in detention grew steadily and detention powers were delegated unconditionally to the police.[79] On 1 June a new regulation specifically granting a power of internment was created.[80] Other newly created regulations gave powers in relation to closure of buildings,[81] to block roads,[82] banned the IRA and some other nationalist organizations (but no loyalist groups),[83] imposed restrictions on the wearing of uniforms,[84] gave members of the Crown Forces a power to stop and question,[85] and enabled residence restrictions to be imposed.[86] Solly-Flood wanted the process taken further, arguing by analogy to the position of the CMA under DORA, that 'full powers under this [Special Powers] Act' be delegated to him.[87] But he was less successful with this proposal than he had been with his earlier plans.

The RIC was then in the last stages of disbandment. The Northern Ireland Government had been distrustful of elements of the force, and in May a bill was rushed through[88] providing for a new police force, the Royal Ulster Constabulary (RUC), which was to be more clearly identified with the new Government than was its predecessor. An establishment of approximately 3,000 was provided for. The USC was also active in policing duties, and it appears that some of its members were also involved in unofficial reprisals.[89] At the end of June the strength of the Special Constabulary stood at 5,500 'A' Specials, 19,000 'B' Specials (of whom 4,215 were mobilized full-time), and 946 full-time 'C' Specials.

---

[75] On 10 June the Duncairn Arms Hotel was closed. *BG* 16 June 1922. The closure was revoked 26 Sept. *BG* 29 Sept. 1922.

[76] On 26 May the Gaiety Picture house was ordered to have its windows barred up. *BG* 30 June 1922.

[77] e.g. on 16 June meetings were banned within a three-mile radius of Belleek railway station. *BG* 23 June 1922.

[78] The use of detention (Reg. 23) and internment (Reg. 23B) powers is considered in detail on pp. 290–308.

[79] The first delegation took place on 10 June (*BG* 16 June 1922). The issue of delegation of these powers is considered in more detail on pp. 294–5.

[80] Reg. 23B.

[81] Reg. 18A. See App. 3.

[82] Reg. 7A. See App. 3.

[83] Reg. 24A, See App. 3.

[84] Reg. 10A. See App. 3.

[85] Reg. 22A. See App. 3.

[86] Reg. 23A. See App. 3.

[87] Solly-Flood to the Ministry of Home Affairs, 13 June 1922, HA 4/1/23, PRONI.

[88] This was enacted as the Constabulary Act (Northern Ireland) 1922.

[89] See M. Farrell, *Arming the Protestants*, 136–7, 158–61.

The 'C1' Specials numbered 7,500, and this force was shortly to rise to a membership of 12,000.[90] The British Army was also increasingly committed, most noticeably in clearing the IRA from the Pettigo triangle in the first week of June. Its strength in Northern Ireland reached a peak of sixteen battalions in the early summer.[91]

The Provisional Government had not been slow in expressing anxiety at the course of events in the North, and at the end of May it had been pressing the British Government for the introduction of martial law in Belfast or for the instigation of a judicial inquiry.[92] Neither request was acceded to, although the British Cabinet did consider the 'question of martial law being imposed in particular areas'.[93] In an attempt to meet some of the concerns which lay behind the request for a judicial inquiry, Tallents, the Imperial Secretary in Belfast, was ordered by the British Government on 19 June to begin an inquiry into the failure of the Craig–Collins pact. But the main focus of attention was shifting away from Northern Ireland. On 22 June Wilson was assassinated in London, and on 28 June the attack on the Four Courts began, signalling the start of the Civil War. Divisions in the IRA ranks meant that at the end of June and the start of July, the campaign against Northern Ireland collapsed. Between 21 June 1920 and 18 June 1922 the Troubles had claimed over 2,000 victims in the six-county area, of whom 1,766 had been wounded and 428 killed.

July 1922 to November 1923: consolidating power

July 1922 did not mark the end of violence in Northern Ireland, though in the following months its intensity decreased steadily (Graph F). Internment under the Special Powers Act survived a judicial challenge at the start of the month[94] and continued to be used. Earlier a new regulation allowing prisoners to be moved between prisons and other detention centres had been introduced,[95] and this was followed by a trickle of amendments and new regulations.[96] On 20 July parts of Belfast were placed under a 9.30 p.m. to 6 a.m. curfew,[97] and although this was relaxed within a few days,[98] curfews remained in force in Belfast and in

[90] See ibid. 143.
[91] See Buckland, *Factory of Grievances*, 197.
[92] See Canning, *British Policy*, 61, and Buckland, *Factory of Grievnces*, 199.
[93] Churchill to Craig, 30 May 1922, CAB 11/2, PRONI.
[94] *R (O'Hanlon)* v. *Governor of Belfast Prison* [1922] 56 *ILTR* 170, (17 July 1922). The case is considered in detail below.
[95] Reg. 23D (6 July 1922). See App. 3.
[96] See App. 3.
[97] *BG* 21 July 1922.
[98] On 24 July this order was revoked leaving these areas under an 11 p.m. to 6 a.m. curfew. *BG* 4 Aug. 1922.

the rest of Northern Ireland. The power to ban newspapers was also invoked. The first victim was a Republican news-sheet,[99] but this was quickly followed by one-month bans on *The Freeman's Journal*,[100] the *Evening Telegraph*[101] and *The Irish Catholic*.[102] Other measures taken included the closing in August of premises at Cupar Street in Belfast,[103] and the continued enforcement of orders made under ROIR[104] (though not the implementation of the regulations generally).

In September there was an outbreak of loyalist violence in Belfast, at least partly, it seems, attributable to the UPA. The threat from this source led to a decision to establish a strict curfew on parts of the city and to search areas of East Belfast, but the Plan was abandoned for fear of alienating Protestant opinion.[105] Indeed curfew restrictions were lightened, first in Belfast,[106] and then in Bangor and in surrounding areas of Belfast.[107] The UPA continued with its campaign, and was broken up only in November following the internment of some of its members.

The other area of security policy to occupy the Northern Ireland Government arose out of the failed Craig–Collins pact. Tallents had submitted a report on 6 July in which he laid much of the blame for the failure of the precise clauses of the Agreement on continued IRA violence.[108] And much to the relief of the Northern Ireland Government, Tallents was also separately expressing the view that a judicial inquiry should not be held into events in Belfast because this would 'lead to a revival of propaganda about matters that are best forgotten'.[109]

One remaining legacy of the pact was the Criminal Procedure Act (Northern Ireland) 1922. The Northern Cabinet had been informed early in July that it was not then possible to introduce in the Imperial Parliament the legislation required to confirm that Act,[110] but replied with a fresh request for its introduction, pointing out that 'a position of grave embarrassment could arise'.[111] The British response was a suggestion that the matter 'might be let slide',[112] a view which it was felt Craig had

---

[99] On 8 July *The Republic of Ireland—Poblacht na h-Eireann* was banned until 7 Apr. 1923. *BG* 21 July 1922.

[100] On 5 Aug. this publication was banned until 5 Sept. *BG* 18 Aug. 1922.

[101] On 5 Aug. this paper was banned until 5 Sept. *BG* 18 Aug. 1922.

[102] Under Reg. 26. *BG* 25 Aug. 1922.

[103] *BG* 25 Aug. 1922.

[104] e.g. the restrictions on homing pigeons under ROIR 21 and 21A. Some correspondence between the authorities and disgruntled pigeon-fanciers can be found at HA 8/810, PRONI.

[105] See Buckland, *Factory of Grievances*, 217.

[106] On 23 Sept. the curfew hours were altered to 11.30 p.m. to 6 a.m. *BG* 29 Sept. 1922.

[107] On 31 Oct. the curfew hours were altered to 11.30 p.m. to 5 a.m. *BG* 3 Nov. 1922.

[108] The Tallents report is reproduced in full in Boyle, 'Tallents Report', 154–75.

[109] Quoted in Canning, *British Policy*, 64. See also Boyle, 'Tallents Report', 152.

[110] Sturgis to Spender, 8 July 1922, CAB 6/56, PRONI.

[111] Spender to Sturgis, 27 July 1922, ibid.

[112] Sturgis to Spender, 28 July 1922, ibid.

acquiesced in. He, however, maintained that what he had had in mind was a temporary holding up of the matter and not the complete dropping of it.[113] At a meeting of the Northern Ireland Cabinet on 9 August 1922 it was decided that as the Imperial Parliament was not sitting, it was impossible to press for legislation on the matter before October.[114] Moreover, the ending of the assizes had taken the urgency out of the matter. The episode eventually came to an end when the Act was repealed in November by the Expiring Laws Act (Northern Ireland) 1922.[115]

That Act also provided that the Special Powers Act was to continue in existence until 31 December 1923.[116] As the Act was not due to expire until April 1923, the move towards its extension took place five months before it could have been considered necessary. Implementation continued, with more internments and bans on Republican newspapers.[117]

On 7 December 1922 both Houses of the Northern Ireland Parliament adopted the resolution required by the Treaty to exclude Northern Ireland from the Free State.[118] The vote was a foregone conclusion; in real terms its effect was to focus attention on the question of the Boundary Commission and on the related issue of the protection of the nationalist minority within Northern Ireland. The prospects of that minority generally had scarcely been enhanced by the abolition in September of proportional representation in local elections by the Local Government Act (Northern Ireland) 1922.[119]

January 1923 opened with a slight relaxation of the curfew in Belfast,[120] and in April the restrictions were further lightened both in Belfast and in the rest of Northern Ireland.[121] In June the restrictions on public houses in Belfast were lifted.[122] January had also seen the appointment of the General Officer Commanding Northern Ireland District as a CMA under ROIA.[123] In July a Committee was appointed under the chairmanship

---

[113] Craig to Spender, 2 Aug. 1922, ibid.

[114] Draft conclusions of Cabinet Meeting, 9 Aug. 1922, CAB 4/51, PRONI.

[115] s. 2, schedule 4.

[116] s. 3 (3), and schedule 3, pt. 5.

[117] On 6 Apr. *Eire—The Irish Nation* and *The Republic of Ireland—Poblacht na h-Eireann* were banned from 8 Apr. 1923 until 31 Mar. 1924. *BG* 13 Apr. 1923.

[118] See p. 166.

[119] The Act provided that local elections in Northern Ireland were to be held under the method of voting in force immediately before the commencement of the Local Government (Ireland) Act 1919 (s. 1). That Act had been the first to introduce proportional representation to Ireland. See, generally, C. Palley, 'The Evolution, Disintegration and Possible Reconstruction of the Northern Ireland Constitution', 1 *Anglo-American Law Review* 368, at pp. 404–6.

[120] The new curfew hours were 11.30 p.m. to 5 a.m. *BG* 5 Jan. 1923.

[121] The order of 6 Apr. set the curfew hours as 12 a.m. to 5 a.m. in Belfast and in the rest of Northern Ireland. *BG* 13 Apr. 1923.

[122] *BG* 29 June 1923.

[123] Mention of the appointment is made in Smith to Martin-Jones, 13 Aug. 1940, CAB 9G/8, PRONI.

of George Talbot to review that Act, and in September, before the Committee reported, a number of orders under DORR and ROIR were revoked in so far as they affected Northern Ireland.[124] This move did not signal an end to reliance on emergency powers, but rather reliance on the Special Powers Act rather than ROIA, for in November there were several amendments to the Special Powers Regulations,[125] and in that month also the Act was extended until 31 December 1924.[126] But this was to be the last amendment to the regulations for some time. By the end of this period, the regulations were in the form in which they were to remain in the years under discussion; the Special Powers Act had been renewed twice, thus indicating the direction of its future development; the bulk of those who were to be interned had been arrested; and the British Army had retreated from major involvement in security duties.

December 1923 to December 1925: the pattern is set

All curfew restrictions in Northern Ireland were temporarily lifted for the Christmas period[127] and in February there was some easing of other restrictions in Belfast,[128] though in Derry city a tighter than normal curfew was imposed for a few weeks in May and June.[129] As emergency legislation became increasingly entrenched, the RUC began to turn its attention to the question of operational practice. This concern was reflected in a series of circulars from the Inspector-General on such subjects as exclusion orders[130] and extradition to and from the Free State.[131]

---

[124] These were The Firearms and Military Arms Order of 17 July 1916, The Explosive Substances Order of 7 Oct. 1916, The Uniforms and Weapons of Offence Order of 25 July 1917, The Motor Cars and Motor Cycles Order of 1 Nov. 1917, The Control and Movement of the Civil Population Order (CB of Londonderry) of 24 June 1920, The Public Meeting Order (Londonderry) of 7 July 1920, The Control of Movements of the Civil Population Order (County of the City of Belfast) of 30 Aug. 1920, The Motor Cars and Motor Cycles Order of 12 Dec. 1920, and The Motor Cars and Motor Cycles Order (Supplementary) of 28 Apr. 1921. *BG* 26 Oct. 1923.

[125] See App. 3.

[126] Expiring Laws Continuance Act (Northern Ireland) 1923, s. 1 and schedule, pt. 4.

[127] *BG* 21 Dec. 1923.

[128] Patrick's Lane was reopened. *BG* 29 Feb. 1924.

[129] On 22 May the city was placed under an 11 p.m. to 5 a.m. curfew (*BG* 23 May 1924), but these special restrictions were lifted on 13 June. *BG* 20 June 1924.

[130] The IG's Circular of 19 June 1924 displayed a noticeable sensitivity about the question of these orders: 'In future when police officers are prosecuting for a breach of an order under this Regulation [23A] and reference is made to deportation, it should be pointed out to the court that the order is not one of "deportation" but of exclusion from certain areas in Northern Ireland, and never from the whole of the Six counties, and that the description of such an order as a "Deportation Order" is inaccurate and misleading.' This probably reflected a concern over the question of domicile. See pp. 331–2. HA 27/1/17, PRONI.

[131] The IG's Circular of 18 Dec. 1924 advised: 'With reference to the execution of warrants issued in Northern Ireland, in the Free State, I am to inform you that all such warrants should be forwarded to headquarters for transmission to the chief officer of the

One factor which tended to keep the attention of the Northern Ireland Government focused on the issue of emergency powers was the question of submissions on the question of ROIA to the Talbot Committee. In January the Government had submitted a note on its use of the Special Powers Act which had emphasized the counter-productive effects of more extreme measures: 'Death sentences or long terms of penal servitude, imposed by specially constituted courts, such as courts martial, are, in the opinion of the Northern Ireland Government, calculated to defeat their own object, and the experience of the Imperial Administration affords striking proof of this view.'[132]

When the Committee reported in August,[133] its main recommendations were that ROIA be repealed as from the end of 1925, that all ROIR be immediately revoked but that a number of regulations relating to search powers be temporarily re-enacted.[134] It also hinted broadly that such search powers and a power to compel the giving of information be made part of the ordinary law of England. The latter suggestion seemed to present few difficulties, as the British Government signalled its agreement to the inclusion of such powers in a Criminal Justice Bill which was then current,[135] but the other recommendations proved more problematic, as the Army objected to the immediate revocation of the regulations.[136]

A memorandum prepared for the Northern Ireland Government on the recent use of ROIR concluded that only a handful of regulations were still applied to the civilian population,[137] and a further memorandum pointed out that 'under an unfriendly Government the powers conferred on the military by the ROIR might be used in a manner which would be very embarrassing to the people of Ulster'.[138] The suggestion was made that 'if it is decided to repeal the ROIR, that we should provide a Court

---

civic guard, on whom will rest the responsibility for seeing that they are duly endorsed by some person having authority to do so.' Ibid. The Circular warned that RUC escorts should not proceed beyond the border, and it made provision for expenses, but it made no mention of political offences.

[132] Note attached to Spender to Tallents, 15 Jan. 1924, CAB 9G/8, PRONI.

[133] Cmnd. 2278 (1924), 'Report of the Committee Appointed to Review the Provisions of the ROIA 1920 and the Regulations Made under the Act'.

[134] ROIR 51, 51A, and 52.

[135] Blackwell to the Imperial Secretary to the Governor of Northern Ireland, 25 Nov. 1924, CAB 9G/8, PRONI.

[136] Cameron to Spender, 13 Jan. 1925, ibid.

[137] These were ROIR 9AA (possession of firearms and explosives—an order under the regulation was still used in the control of explosives), ROIR 21 (keeping of carrier pigeons), ROIR 22 (control of wireless apparatus), ROIR 30 (sale of firearms etc.—two orders of the CMA were still in force and were applied by the police), and ROIR 31 (removal of firearms etc. from Great Britain to Ireland and vice versa—permits were issued for this purpose by the CMA). Memo. by Poynting, included with Sturgis to Craig, 4 Dec. 1924, CAB 9G/8, PRONI.

[138] Memo. by A. P. Magill attached to Sturgis to Craig, 4 Dec. 1924, ibid.

under our [Special Powers] Regulations, and, if necessary, we would be prepared to appoint on that Court, some of his [Army] officers, making them RM's for the purpose'.[139] This was the approach taken when the Northern Ireland Government replied to the 'GOC Ulster Troops' with a secret assurance that he could 'rely upon the Northern Government giving you any facilities, e.g. by appointing your officers temporary resident magistrates in case of necessity, which would to a large extent afford you the powers which you wish to retain'.[140] At the same time it was decided that some provisions of one of the remaining orders should not be enforced.[141] The proposal was never acted upon, and in February 1925 a conference at the Ministry of Home Affairs attended by the police and the military surveyed possible amendments to the Special Powers Regulations which might increase the Army's powers (but the proposal to make soldiers RMs was not mentioned—or at least not recorded), and agreed to recommend that 'ROIR should be retained until there is a reasonable probability that there will be no recurrence of trouble in Northern Ireland'.[142] There the matter seems to have been allowed to rest. The regulations were not repealed in the period under discussion, and the Act proper remained on the statute book for several decades.[143]

The Special Powers Act had again been renewed at the end of 1924.[144] Powers such as those to make exclusion orders[145] and to ban news-

---

[139] Sturgis to Craig, 4 Dec. 1924, ibid.

[140] Spender to Cameron, 6 Dec. 1924, ibid.

[141] Orders of the CMA under ROIR 30 were not to be enforced in relation to (1) the sale of a sporting gun by one registered firearms dealer to another dealer, and (2) the purchase of a sporting gun by registered firearms dealer from a person other than a dealer. Special instructions had already been issued in relation to (a) the sale of sporting guns by a registered dealer to the holder of a firearms certificate (9 Apr. 1924) (b) humane killers (21 Feb. 1924) (c) non-lethal air guns (24 July 1924), and (d) fireworks (30 Jan. 1924). IG's circular, 28 Jan. 1925, HA 27/1/17, PRONI.

[142] Conclusions of Conference Held at the Ministry on 23 Feb. 1925, CAB 9G/8, PRONI.

[143] As late as 1940 the 'General Officer Commanding British Troops in Ireland' was requesting the Army Council that he be appointed a CMA under ROIR 62, in order that he might be able to issue determination orders under ROIR 58D, thus allowing trial of soldiers by court martial for non-military offences. Smith to Martin-Jones, 13 Aug. 1940, ibid. (On the question of use of ROIR 58D for the trial of such offences see p. 310.) The letter makes reference to a conference between the Home Office and the War Office on 4 Feb. 1927 after which it was announced that it had been decided to leave matters in status quo. ROIA was eventually repealed by the Statute Law Revision Act 1953 (s. 1).

[144] The Expiring Laws Continuance Act (Northern Ireland) 1924 kept the Act in force until 31 Dec. 1925 (s. 1, schedule, pt. 3).

[145] e.g. in Nov. 1924 it was reported that certain people from the Free State had taken part in the general election in Northern Ireland and that 'some strong and rather inciting speeches were delivered' ('Memo. on Sinn Fein Activity', RUC Commissioners' Office, Crime Special, 3 Nov. 1924, HA 4/2/36, PRONI). The IG of the RUC, on the recommendation of the special branch, advised that they be excluded and the Minister for Home Affairs made the requisite order under Reg. 23A. Ministry of Home Affairs Northern Ireland Minute Sheet, 20 Nov. 1924, ibid.

papers,[146] continued to be used, a curfew remained in force, and there was more delegation by the Minister of Home Affairs,[147] but overall there was a marked easing in the enforcement of the Act. In the year ending March 1925 all the internees were released—though there was to be a later swoop—and in 1925 also, the number of convictions for breaches of the regulations plummeted.[148] The RUC meanwhile continued the process of development of practice directions, with circulars emanating from the Inspector-General's office relating to such subjects as the tightening up of the use of firearms by the police,[149] treatment of the 'Sinn Féin flag'[150] and insisting on the requirement that permits issued by the CMA be obtained for the bringing in of firearms from Great Britain.[151]

The year 1925 also saw the second elections to the Northern Ireland Parliament. On this occasion the Nationalist Party chose to contest the elections on a participationist ticket. The overall results confirmed the Unionist majority, but ten Nationalists were also elected (and took their seats), as opposed to only two successful Republican candidates. The two were the subject of exclusion orders at the time of their election, and the Ministry of Home Affairs decided against revocation of the orders.[152]

---

[146] On 30 Dec. 1924 the *Sinn Féin* newspaper was banned from 1 Jan. 1925 until 31 Dec. 1925. *BG* 2 Jan. 1925. A circular by the IG on 8 May 1925 drew attention to the fact that a newspaper called *The Loyalist* but containing exactly the same material as *Sinn Féin* was then in circulation. It advised that circulation of *The Loyalist* was in breach of the order against *Sinn Féin* and directed that prosecutions be instituted against any person found circulating *The Loyalist*. HA 27/1/17, PRONI. In Dec. also, the bans on *The Republic of Ireland—Poblacht na h-Eireann* and *Eire—The Irish Nation* were continued for a further year. *BG* 19 Dec. 1924. The ban on the papers had previously been renewed in Mar. 1924. *BG* 21 Mar. 1924.

[147] On 2 Oct. 1925 Dawson Bates authorized Wickham, the IG of the RUC to 'make such Orders from time to time as he may deem necessary under Regulation 4 ... for prohibiting any meetings or processions within any area of Northern Ireland mentioned in any such Order'. *BG* 9 Oct. 1925.

[148] See p. 311.

[149] The circular (dated 15 June 1925) began '1. It has been found necessary to draw the attention of the police to the reckless and unjustifiable use of firearms, and to point out the necessity for extreme caution in having recourse to firing except in cases of urgent or grave necessity. 2. The conditions in Northern Ireland so far as crime is concerned are approaching normal and the necessity for the use of firearms in carrying out police duty is not so great as during the disturbed period.' HA 27/1/1, PRONI. Some issues arising out of this circular are considered on pp. 323–5.

[150] The instructions were: 'Where there is reason to apprehend that the display of the Sinn Fein flag will lead to a breach of the peace it should not be permitted, and unless the police have reason to believe that the display of such a flag will not lead to a breach of the peace it will be well to prevent it.' IG's Circular, 28 Apr. 1925, ibid.

[151] IG's Circular, 9 Nov. 1925, HA 27/1/18, PRONI. The permits were stated to be available through the office of the IG.

[152] Ministry of Home Affairs of Northern Ireland Minute Sheet, 8 Apr. 1925, and Secretary of the Ministry of Home Affairs to the IG RUC, 10 Apr. 1925, HA 4/2/36, PRONI. The two were Eamon Donnelly and Eamonn de Valera. It is not clear whether

One remaining area of 'unfinished business' arising out of the Treaty settlement related to the Boundary Commission. At a meeting of the British, Free State and Northern Ireland Governments in April 1924, Dublin had insisted that the Commission be established. Craig refused to appoint the Northern member, but in October an amending bill was introduced allowing the British to make the appointment,[153] and the following month the Commission began to function. In October of the following year the Commission decided on an award which involved the transfer of minor portions of territory in both directions, but at the last minute the Free State Commissioner resigned. In December the matter was brought to an end when a new pact retaining the existing border was signed, and agreement was secretly reached that the British Government would review the cases of prisoners convicted in Northern Ireland who were serving sentences for politically motivated crimes.[154] While the agreement was being signed there was a temporary round-up under the Special Powers Act, the legislation having been renewed for a further year.[155]

But though the emergency apparatus was not being scrapped, it was being wound down. On 9 December 1925 Craig announced the disbandment on financial grounds of the 'A' and 'C1' classes of USC. This was followed by a minor and unsuccessful mutiny by sections of the Specials which lasted for a few days in December, but early in the new year the 'C1' force was scrapped, and by Easter only 500 'A' Specials remained. The 'B' Specials, however, continued in existence as a reserve force. They, and the Special Powers Act, were still influencing the course of history almost half a century later.

PART II

SECTION (A): ARREST, DETENTION, AND INTERNMENT

The ordinary law of arrest and detention in Northern Ireland in the 1921–5 period remained as it had been prior to partition. A number of

they were excluded from all of Northern Ireland. The minute sheet reads: 'I suggest that the fact of his return to Parliament should not except him from service. If after service he desires to take his seat (which is highly improbable) it is open to him to ask for its revocation.'

[153] This was enacted as the Irish Free State (Confirmation of Agreement) Act 1924.

[154] See M. Farrell, *Arming the Protestants*, 250. The prisoners were released in 1926. The British Cabinet was noticeably sensitive about the classification to be employed in respect of these prisoners 'convicted in Northern Ireland in respect of offences during the period of disturbances in Ireland'. The Cabinet agreed that these cases should be reviewed by one person, 'some doubt having been expressed as to whether it was desirable to admit the distinction between political and other prisoners in the exercise of the Prerogative'. Cabinet Conclusion, 16 Dec. 1925, CAB 23/51, PRO, Kew.

[155] Expiring Laws Continuance Act (Northern Ireland) 1925, s. 1, schedule, pt. 2.

emergency powers of arrest, detention, indefinite detention, and internment were introduced in the Special Powers Act and Regulations, and
because of the way these powers were used, it is necessary to examine
them together. The principal relevant provisions are section 7 (arrest),
Regulation 23 (arrest and indefinite detention), and Regulation 23B
(internment).

There were three broad phases in the use of these powers. In the first,
from May to June 1922, they were employed as the central element in a
co-ordinated counter-insurgency initiative. Over the following two years
there was a steady stream of new internments, though by March 1925 at
the latest all had been released. Finally, there was a brief round-up
towards the end of the period in question.

Arrest under section 7 of the Special Powers Act

Section 7 of the Special Powers Act provided:

any person authorised by the civil authority or any police constable, or any
member of His Majesty's forces on duty may, where it is necessary for the
purpose of effecting an arrest in respect of any crime or any offence against the
regulations, exercise the like powers as may at common law be exercised by a
police constable in effecting arrest in a case where a felony has been committed.

Thus arrest powers were granted to three classes of people: policemen,
on-duty members of the armed forces, and the blanket category of those
'authorised by the civil authority'. This last formula was adopted from
DORR, the original phrase having been 'persons authorised by the competent naval or military authority'.[156] The power was exercisable only in
respect of specific offences and covered not only breaches of the Regulations but also 'any crime'. 'Crime' is given no special definition in the
Act and thus offences in no way connected with civil unrest would appear
to come within the terms of the section. A contrary view would be that it
should be construed as being implicitly restricted to emergency situations,
but it is unlikely that such an argument would have succeeded before a
Northern Ireland court. It would therefore appear that the effect of
section 7 was to make all crimes in Northern Ireland arrestable.

The degree of suspicion required for a section 7 arrest was the same as
that required in relation to the use of 'powers as may at common law be
exercised by a police constable in effecting arrest in a case where a felony
has been committed', that is reasonable suspicion that the arrested person
had committed the offence. This objective test could permit effective
judicial scrutiny.

No extended powers of detention were given under section 7 and it
would therefore appear that the common law position applied, that is that

---

[156] e.g. DORRs 51 and 55 (text in App. 3).

arrested persons were to be charged and brought before a magistrate as soon as reasonably possible. One way in which this provision could possibly have been circumvented was if arrest under section 7 were followed not by charging or by meaningful release, but by rearrest under Regulation 23. Given the attitude of the courts at that time, it seems unlikely that the second arrest *per se* would have been open to judicial challenge.

Section 7 was incorporated in the body of the Act and existed alongside the special arrest powers in the regulation. In this it differed from the precedent set by DORA and ROIA, in both of which arrest powers were found only in the regulations. Section 7 powers were therefore presumably intended to remain available though powers in the regulations might be varied or abolished by ministerial action. This might be taken as internal evidence (though it is scarcely conclusive of the matter) that right from the start it was anticipated that the Special Powers Act would be in existence for longer than its allotted one-year lifespan.

Arrest and detention under Regulation 23

Arrest

The elements of Regulation 23 are set out in Table 24. Its wording was taken directly from DORR 55.[157] Those empowered to arrest under the regulation were the same as under section 7. Three sets of grounds for arrest were incorporated. The first was on reasonable suspicion, not of the commission of a specific offence, but of acting or having acted or of being about to act 'in a manner prejudicial to the preservation of the peace or maintenance of order'. While the reasonableness test could open use of the Regulation to effective judicial scrutiny, the nebulousness of the last quoted phrase would tend to minimize this possibility. In any case, a subjective test was substituted in July 1922 by an amendment to the Regulation.[158] The second ground (Table 24) was essentially an extension of the first providing as it did for arrest where suspicion was grounded on possession of articles, documents, etc.

The third set of grounds (Table 24) incorporated a subjective test of suspicion from the beginning, but unlike the first ground, the suspicion related to the commission of specific offences against the regulations. It also covered suspicion of possession of various items and to this extent was a reinforcement of the combined effects of grounds (1) and (2). Any suspect articles found on an arrested person could be seized or otherwise disposed of.

---

[157] See pp. 41–51.
[158] See *BG* 7 July 1922 and Calvert, *Constitutional Law*, 383 n. 16.

TABLE 24. Regulation 23

Arrester	Grounds for Arrest
(Original Reg. 7 April 1922)	(Original Reg. 7 April 1922)
Any person authorised for the purpose by the civil authority, or any police constable, or member of any of HM's forces on duty when the occasion for the arrest arises	. . . may arrest without warrant any person whose behaviour is of such a nature as to give reasonable grounds for suspecting that he has acted or is acting or is about to act in a manner prejudicial to the preservation of the peace or maintenance of order, or upon whom may be found any article, book, letter, or other document, the possession of which gives ground for such a suspicion, or who is suspected of having committed an offence against these regulations, or of being in possession of any article or document which is being used or intended to be used for any purpose or in any way prejudicial to the preservation of the peace or maintenance of order,

> **Amendment** introduced 6 July 1922
>
> . . . may arrest without warrant any person whom he suspects of acting or of having acted or of being about to act in a manner prejudicial to the preservation of the peace or maintenance of order, or upon whom may be found any article, book, letter, or other document, the possession of which gives ground for such a suspicion, or who is suspected of having committed an offence against these regulations, or of being in possession of any article or document which is being used or intended to be used for any purpose or in any way prejudicial to the preservation of the peace or maintenance of order

cont.

Detention and delegation

An amendment to the Regulation made in June 1922[159] obliged any arrested person to submit to having his fingerprints and photograph taken if ordered by the civil authority or by a police officer of the rank of Chief Officer or above. Under the ordinary law the police had no authority to require a suspect to provide fingerprints.[160]

[159] *BG* 30 June 1922.

[160] An IG's Circular, 20 Oct. 1925, noted that 'the police have no power to compel a prisoner to be finger printed. This, if required, will be done by the prison authorities, after

TABLE 24. *Continued*

Miscellaneous

(Original Reg. 7 April 1922)

... and anything found on any person so arrested which there is reason to suspect is being so used or intended to be used may be seized, and the civil authority may order anything so seized to be destroyed or otherwise disposed of.

Added 23 June 1922

Any person so arrested shall, if so ordered by the Civil Authority, or by a Chief Officer of Police, or by Police Officer of higher rank, be photographed, and finger-print impressions of the fingers and thumbs of both his hands taken and if such person refuses to allow his photograph or such impressions to be taken or obstructs the taking thereof, he shall be guilty of an offence against these Regulations.

Provisions governing Detention

(Original Reg. 7 April 1922)

Any person so arrested may, on the order of the civil authority be detained in any of HM's prisons as a person committed to prison on remand, until he has been discharged by direction of the Attorney General or is brought before a court of summary jurisdiction. Any person to be brought before a court under this regulation shall receive at least twenty four hours notice in writing of the nature of the charge preferred against him. On a person being taken into custody under this regulation he may apply to the civil authority for release on bail, and, if the civil authority so directs in writing, any resident magistrate may discharge the person so in custody upon his entering into a recognizance, with or without, sureties, for a reasonable amount to appear at a time and place to be named in the recognizance. If any person assists or connives at the escape of any person who may be in custody under this regulation, or knowingly harbours or assists any person who has so escaped, he shall be guilty of an offence against these regulations.

Substituted 20 May 1922

Any person so arrested may, on the order of the civil authority, be detained either in any of HM's prisons or elsewhere, as may be specified in the Order, upon such conditions as the civil authority may direct until he has been discharged by direction of the Attorney General or is brought before a court of summary jurisdiction. Any person to be brought before a court under this regulation shall receive at least twenty four hours notice in writing of the nature of the charge preferred against him. On a person being taken into custody under this regulation he may apply to the civil authority for release on bail, and, if the civil authority so directs in writing, any resident magistrate may discharge the person so in custody upon his entering into a recognizance, with or without sureties, for a reasonable amount to appear at a time and place to be named in the recognizance. If any person assists or connives at the escape of any person who may be in custody under this regulation, or knowingly harbours or assists any person who has so escaped, he shall be guilty of an offence against these regulations.

Added 6 July 1922

Any person detained under this Regulation may, without prejudice to any other powers of removal, be removed on the order of the Civil Authority to any place where his presence is required in the interest of justice and may be detained in such place for such time as his presence is so required there, and whilst being so removed or detained he shall be deemed to be detained under the provisions of this regulation.

A general interrogation power of the 'sentry' variety existed under the regulations,[161] but there was no such power specifically in relation to those detained under Regulation 23. Arguably, Regulation 22, which empowered the civil authority to require any person to furnish information, was applicable,[162] and the same could be said of Regulation 17 which made it an offence for any person to 'withhold any information in his possession which he may reasonably be required to furnish from an officer or other person who is carrying out the orders of the civil authority'.[163]

Complaints of ill-treatment, particularly at the hands of the Special Constabulary, were common in 1922. One such account described how a 'middle-aged Catholic farmer', when passing a border post manned by Specials was taken into a dug-out, stripped, blindfolded, and then

He was asked if he was a Sinn Feiner . . . They caught the poor man by the throat and attempted to choke him. Two rifles were put against his breast, one on each side, with the muzzles pressing against the flesh. He was advised to prepare for death and to say his prayers. After threatening to shoot him and making him the victim of other horrible cruelties, the farmer was bundled out of the dug-out.[164]

The account alleged that when the man complained about this treatment to the police, he was told that 'they had nothing to do with these matters',[165] and directed him to the local headquarters of the Specials.

Any arrested person could be detained on the order of the civil authority. No criteria were set out for the exercise of this power and no time-limit was set on the period of detention. The provision was derived from the power in DORR 55 to detain pending completion of the investigation of cases by the CMA, but whereas administrative directions placed time-restrictions on the British provisions, the Northern Ireland measure does not seem to have been subject to such limitations.

A note on the operation of the Regulation included in the Cabinet papers of the period set out that when a man was arrested and taken to gaol, a detention order was handed to the governor of the gaol. The prisoner was then stated to have two rights: to apply for bail and to ask to see a solicitor. In relation to bail, the Regulation provided that detainees

committal to prison on the request of the District Inspector, supported if necessary, by the signature of a magistrate.' HA 27/1/1, PRONI.

[161] Reg. 22A (see App. 3).
[162] The text of Reg. 22 is included in App. 3.
[163] The text of Reg. 17 is included in App. 3.
[164] 'Catholics Tortured', *Irish News*, 14 June 1922. The authorities were clearly displeased with the story. A file on a possible prosecution of the newspaper arising out of its publication (HA 5/1496) remains closed in PRONI.
[165] Ibid.

could apply to the civil authority for release, and if approval was forth-coming, application could then be made to a Resident Magistrate. There seems to have been little awareness of these rights, however, it being noted that 'In many cases persons being detained under this order do not know that they have these rights, and no steps are taken to inform them. Persons have been kept under this order for 6 weeks without trial or knowing what they can do.'[166]

Under the Special Powers Act the civil authority was authorized to delegate his powers under the Act 'either unconditionally or subject to such conditions as he thinks fit . . . to any officer of police',[167] and on several occasions powers under Regulation 23 were thus delegated. On 6 June 1922 Dawson Bates (the Minister for Home Affairs) delegated all his powers under the Regulation throughout the whole of Northern Ireland to the (named) Commissioner of Police for the city of Belfast.[168] The following month, Dawson Bates made a further delegation in the same terms to the Inspector-General of the RUC,[169] and in October 1922, to the Deputy Inspector-General.[170]

The question arises as to whether the Minister was entitled to continue to exercise his powers under the Regulation having thus delegated, and indeed whether he could make further delegations, having previously delegated all his powers unconditionally. It was presumably with a view to these issues that in November 1922 Dawson Bates revoked the orders of July and October of that year, and issued new orders providing that all powers vested in the civil authority under Regulation 23 were to be exercisable by the Inspector-General and the Deputy Inspector-General of the RUC 'concurrently with me and with any other person or persons to whom a similar delegation may have been made or may hereafter be made . . . throughout the whole of Northern Ireland'.[171] Each police officer was then 'for the purpose of the said Regulation [to] be con-currently with me and such other person or persons the Civil Authority for the whole of Northern Ireland'.[172]

Initially, it was provided that detainees could be detained in prison as persons committed to prison on remand, until discharged by direction of the Attorney-General or brought before a court of summary jurisdiction. Any person being brought before such a court was to be given at least twenty-four hours' notice in writing of the nature of the charge preferred

---

[166] Handwritten note entitled 'Special Powers Act', 12 Aug. 1922, CAB 6/56, PRONI.
[167] s. 1 (2). For the full text see App. 3.
[168] *BG* 16 June 1922.
[169] On 24 July 1922. *BG* 4 Aug. 1922.
[170] On 16 Oct. 22. *BG* 20 Oct. 1922.
[171] *BG* 24 Nov. 1922.
[172] Ibid.

against him. In May 1922 the reference to remand was dropped and in its place it was provided that persons could be ordered to be detained in 'prisons or elsewhere as may be specified in the order, upon such conditions as the civil authority may direct'.[173] Presumably this amendment was designed to preclude the possibility of judicial challenge by detainees claiming that they were being subjected to indefinite remand periods, while the provision for detention other than in prisons was to enable detainees to be held in camps and, from June onwards aboard the prison ship *Argenta*.

Later, a further amendment permitted removal of detainees to any place where their presence was required 'in the interests of justice'.[174] This was probably intended legally to copper-fasten detentions where the place of eventual detention was not that specified in the original detention order.

Conditions of detention (and of internment under Regulation 23B) were, from July 1922 onwards, governed by Regulation 23C[175] and by ministerial order. Access to detainees required the permission of the civil authority and it could be stipulated that any meetings would have to take place within sight and earshot of the guards.[176] Likewise, outside communication by detainees required the consent of the civil authority and all correspondence was subject to examination.[177] One effect of these restrictions could be greatly to hinder access to legal advisers.

Detainees held in prison were to be subject to the prison rules governing remand prisoners, except in so far as these rules were inconsistent with this regulation.[178] Different ministerial orders, both made on 24 June 1922,[179] applied to detainees in prison and detainees in camps. The order covering those held in camps provided for such things as hygiene,[180] bedding,[181] etc., and required that all correspondence other than bona fide instructions to a solicitor be sent on postcards,[182] presumably to facilitate censorship. The order relating to those held in prisons was less broad as points of detail were covered by prison rules, but the requirement to use postcards was specifically imposed.[183]

Internment under Regulation 23B

The wording of Regulation 23B, which was derived directly from DORR 14B, is shown on Table 25. The regulation was created some two months after Regulation 23, and its introduction may have been due to fears about the legality of long-term detention under that Regulation.

Regulation 23B empowered the Minister of Home Affairs not only to

---

[173] See *BG* 26 May 1922. [174] See *BG* 7 July 1922.
[175] See App. 3. [176] Reg. 23C (1). [177] Reg. 23C (2). [178] Reg. 23C (5).
[179] See *BG* 30 June 1922.
[180] Clause 1. [181] Clause 2. [182] Clause 5. [183] Clause 3.

TABLE 25. Regulation 23B

Criteria for Use

(Original Reg. 1 June 1922)

When it appears to the Minister of Home Affairs for Northern Ireland on the recommendation of a Chief of Police or of a Police Officer of higher rank, that for securing the preservation of the peace and the maintenance of order in Northern Ireland, it is expedient that a person who is suspected of acting or having acted or being about to act in a manner prejudicial to the preservation of the peace and the maintenance of order in Northern Ireland, shall be subjected to such obligations and restrictions as are hereinafter mentioned . . .

Powers Granted

(Original Reg. 1 June 1922

. . . Minister of Home affairs for Northern Ireland may by Order require that person forthwith, or from time to time, either to remain in, or to proceed to and reside in, such place as may be specified in the order, and to comply with such directions as to reporting to the police, restriction of movement, and otherwise as may be specified in the order,
or
to be interned as may be directed in the order.

If any person in respect of whom any order is made under this regulation fails to comply with any of the provision of the order he shall be guilty of an offence against these regulations, and any person interned under such order shall be subject to such restrictions as the Minister for Home Affairs for Northern Ireland may direct.

Amendment 17 November 1923

When it appears to the Minister of Home Affairs for Northern Ireland on the recommendation of a Chief of Police or of a Police Officer of higher rank, or of an advisory committee, that for securing the preservation of the peace and the maintenance of order in Northern Ireland, it is expedient that a person who is suspected of acting or having acted or being about to act in a manner prejudicial to the preservation of the peace and the maintenance of order in Northern Ireland, shall be subjected to such obligations and restrictions as are hereinafter mentioned . . .

Added 6 July 1922

Any person interned under this regulation may, without prejudice to any other powers of removal, be removed on the Order of the Minister of Home Affairs for Northern Ireland to any place of internment, whether one of HM's Prisons or not, other than that specified in the internment Order, and may be interned there, and whilst being so removed or interned shall be deemed to be interned under the provisions of this Regulation.

Added 30 October 1923

Any person interned under this regulation may, without prejudice to any other powers of removal, be removed on the Order of the Civil Authority to any place where his presence is required for the purpose of entering into a recognisance, or in the interests of justice or for the purpose of any public inquiry, and may be detained in such place for such time as his presence is so required there, and whilst being so removed or detained he shall be deemed to be interned under the provisions of this regulation.

TABLE 25. *Continued*

Appeals	Miscellaneous
(Original Reg. 1 June 1922)	(Original Reg. 1 June 1922)
Provided that any order under this regulation shall include express provision for the due consideration by an advisory committee of any representations which a person in respect of whom the order is made may make against the order.	. . . and if any person so interned escapes or attempts to escape from the place of internment or commits any breach of the rules in force therein, he shall be guilty of an offence against these regulations.
The advisory committee for the purpose of this regulation shall be such advisory committee as is specially appointed by the Minister of Home Affairs for the purposes of this regulation, such committee being presided over by a person who holds or has held high judicial office or is a Recorder or County Court Judge or a practising Barrister of at least ten years standing.	Nothing in this regulation shall be construed to restrict or prejudice the application or effect of Regulation 23a.

order internment but also to impose residence restrictions, and this latter power was in addition to the power to make exclusion orders under Regulation 23A.[184] Orders under Regulation 23B were initially to be made on the recommendation of a Chief of Police or of a police officer of higher rank, but from November 1923 onwards the recommendations of an advisory committee established under the Regulation were also be taken into account.[185] The criteria for the making of an order were that this course appeared expedient 'for securing the preservation of the peace and the maintenance of order in Northern Ireland' where a person was 'suspected of acting or having acted or being about to act in a manner prejudicial to the preservation of the peace and the maintenance of order'. The formulation was 'judge-proof'[186]—there was no requirement for 'reasonable grounds' and the 'expediency' provision effectively prevented the exploitation of any gaps such as might have been created by a 'necessary' test. It seems that it could be only on grounds of *mala fides* that the exercise of the powers given by these provisions could be challenged.

An internee could make representations against the Minister's order to

---

[184] See App. 3.
[185] *BG* 7 Dec. 1923.
[186] See *R (O'Hanlon)* v. *Governor of Belfast Prison* [1922] 56 *ILTR* 170. The case is discussed below.

the advisory committee created under the Regulation. Its members were to be appointed by the Minister for Home Affairs and its chairman was to have certain legal qualifications (Table 25). But the opinion of the committee was not binding on the Minister, and its status as a quasi-judicial body was compromised by the provision from November 1923 that internments could be recommended by the committee, seemingly at first instance. It therefore appeared to be playing the roles of both prosecutor and judge. Perhaps this provision may have been designed to apply in a situation in which the civil authority contemplated renewing an internment order but first chose to obtain the opinion of the committee.

In its original form, the Regulation simply provided that a person could be interned 'as may be directed in the order'. In July 1922 an addition to the Regulation made provision for moving internees between places not mentioned in the original order,[187] and in October 1923 a further addition enabled internees to be moved 'to any place where [their] presence is required for the purpose of entering into a recognisance, or in the interests of justice or for the purpose of any public inquiry'.[188] The Regulation gave no specific power to release on recognizances. It would seem to have been intended that this power was to be taken implicitly to have been created by the last mentioned addition. The only other interpretation of the reference to 'entering into a recognisance' was that it was concerned not with the actual internment but with other criminal matters, but why it should be necessary to make such provision in relation to internees is not clear.

Regulation 23C, which governed conditions of internment, applied to internees as it did to detainees. In addition, an order of 27 September 1922[189] applied only to internees. This covered such things as diet,[190] access to reading material,[191] etc., and it repeated the insistence on the use of postcards originally made in respect of detainees, save that exceptions were made for 'such letters on business or family affairs of an urgent nature as the Officer in charge may permit'.[192] Disciplinary matters were also covered,[193] and provision was made for the infliction of collective punishment 'in case of escape, or attempted escape, by individuals, or disorderly conduct by a number of persons interned'.[194]

Arrest, detention, and internment powers in practice

In 1922 some rural areas of Northern Ireland saw the sort of round-ups that had earlier been a feature of the campaign in the South, particularly in the martial law area. One such operation has been described as follows:

---

[187] *BG* 7 July 1922.   [188] *BG* 2 Nov. 1923.   [189] *BG* 29 Sept. 1922.
[190] Clause 7.   [191] Clause 6.   [192] Clause 2.   [193] Clauses 8–12.
[194] Clause 10.

At the beginning of the month [April] 500 A Specials launched a massive comb-out of the remote valleys of the Sperrin Mountains between Draperstown and Greencastle, rounding up 300 men—almost the entire male population—but holding only three.[195]

The legal basis of this type of activity is problematic. If those rounded up were actually under arrest, then it would presumably have been Regulation 23 which would have been relied upon as having provided the statutory power. But it is difficult to see how even the broad wording of that Regulation would suffice to cover these arrests. Suspicion existed not in respect of individual persons but of a group, that is nationalist males between certain ages living in a given area. If legal authority could be found for these arrests it would presumably have to be in the sphere of residual common law powers.[196] However, it might be argued that those held were not really under arrest but were merely 'helping with enquiries' or some such formulation. But it is clear that those held were not at liberty but were subject to some form of legal or extra-legal restraint.

The first major swoop explicitly under the authority of Regulation 23 took place on 22 May 1922 when 202 people from all over Northern Ireland were arrested.[197] Those detained were initially held in Crumlin gaol, in Larne workhouse, and in a camp near Newtownards. In June they were moved to the prison ship *Argenta*, conditions aboard which were very poor.[198] In that month also, internment under Regulation 23B was introduced. By the end of March 1923, 596 persons had been either detained or interned (Table 26). The following May saw the greatest number held at any one time, when 575 were in detention or internment.

The Advisory Committee (referred to by the Minister for Home Affairs as an 'advisory board'[199]) provided for in Regulation 23B was established in July 1922.[200] In October it consisted of the Deputy Recorder, a barrister, and an ex-soldier.[201] The Minister professed his willingness to follow suggestions for release made by the committee[202] but this was not what always happened in practice.[203]

One of the most striking features of the way in which internment/detention powers were used was the degree of partiality shown. Despite widespread loyalist violence, the vast majority of those held came from

[195] M. Farrell, *Northern Ireland*, 55.
[196] The point is discussed further below.
[197] The breakdown is: Tyrone 63, Antrim 2, Fermanagh 30, Down 10, Armagh 26, Belfast 29, Derry 42. 1 *HCNI Deb.*, col. 599.
[198] See McGuffin, *Internment*, 65.
[199] 1 *HCNI Deb.*, col. 1024.
[200] Buckland, *Factory of Grievances*, 210.
[201] 1 *HCNI Deb.*, col. 1024.
[202] Ibid.
[203] As e.g. in the case of James Mayne, discussed below.

TABLE 26. Numbers interned and detained under Regulations 23 and 23B

	No. of new internments/ detentions	No. released	No. interned/ detained at end of period	Average no. interned/ detained	Internees/ detainees as % of prison populations
21 June 1922– 31 Mar. 1923	596[a]	62	534	408	42.6
1 Apr. 1923– 31 Mar. 1924	132	369	297	380	47.9
1 Apr. 1924– 31 Mar. 1925	n/a	all	0	35	9.7
1 Apr. 1925– 31 Mar. 1926	47	47	0	n/a	n/a

[a] This appears to include the 202 detainees arrested in May 1922. Buckland gives a figure of 728 internees for the period May 1922 to Dec. 1924 (*History*, 210). This corresponds with the sum of the first two entries in the first vertical column of this table. A detainee in respect of whom an internment order was subsequently made is presumably treated as one rather than two cases.

Source: Report of Ministry of Home Affairs on Prisons in Northern Ireland for periods 1 Dec. 1921–31 Mar. 1923.

the nationalist community. It appears that 'a few dozen'[204] of the original internees were loyalists, among them some UPA members,[205] but that these were quickly released and emigrated to Canada and Australia.[206] According to one source, the releases followed threats by those interned that some 'respectable businessmen' behind the gunmen would be named.[207] As the UPA campaign of sectarian assassinations continued, in October 1922 two suspected UPA leaders were interned.[208] They were held for one month and then deported to England on condition that they stayed away for two years.[209] In November four more UPA suspects were interned.[210]

Among the nationalist internees was Cahir Healy, the Sinn Féin MP for the Westminster constituency of Fermanagh South Tyrone. In the opinion of the RUC, he had managed to combine this role with that of IRA

[204] McGuffin, *Internment*, 66.
[205] Buckland, *Factory of Grievances*, 216.
[206] McGuffin, *Internment*, 66.
[207] Ibid.
[208] Buckland, *Factory of Grievances*, 216.
[209] Ibid. 218.
[210] Ibid.

Intelligence Officer, Registrar of the Sinn Féin courts, and Sinn Féin organizer.[211] His internment was an embarrassment to Westminster, and in 1924 pressure from that quarter eventually secured his release, subject, however, to an order excluding him from part of his constituency. Further pressure led to the revocation of that restriction.[212]

In the year ending March 1924 there were 132 new detentions/internments and 369 releases (Table 26). The following year saw the release of all those held but during the year ending March 1926, 47 people were held for various periods.

The case of James Mayne

Perhaps the best way to discover how the internment process worked in practice is to examine one case in detail, although it is difficult to say how typical this case is.[213] James Mayne was a 50-year-old managing clerk in a solicitor's firm in Cookstown, County Tyrone. He also managed to do some farming. On 23 May 1922 he was arrested on suspicion of being an IRA Intelligence Officer and because it was 'rumoured' that he had taken part in a recent ambush.[214]

Two days later Thomas J. Harbison, the Nationalist MP for the local seat of Fermanagh and Tyrone,[215] wrote to Dawson Bates requesting his release, at least until after the forthcoming quarter sessions. He stressed that although he believed that Mayne was a 'Sinn Feiner', he thought he was a 'harmless one'.[216] The matter was referred through the Divisional commissioner of the RUC to the special branch.[217] They repeated the report that Mayne was an Intelligence Officer and that he had been the local leader of the Belfast boycott.[218]

An internment order against Mayne was prepared and signed by Dawson Bates on 19 June 1922 but was apparently not served. A further order was signed on 30 June 1922 and served on 3 July 1922. The order was pre-printed with a recital following the wording of Regulation 23B.[219] Mayne's name, address, and place of internment (the *Argenta*) were typed in, and a certificate of service, signed by Drysdale, the Governor of the *Argenta*, was endorsed on the back.

---

[211] Ibid. 210.

[212] Ibid. 210–11.

[213] The James Mayne file is at HA 8/386, PRONI. All documents referred to below are in this file.

[214] The file does not indicate who gave the order for Mayne's arrest. An undated and unattributed note of a police report in which these allegations are made is on file.

[215] See S. Elliot, *Northern Ireland Parliamentary Elections Results, 1921–1972.* (Chichester, 1973), 16.

[216] Harbison to Bates, 25 May 1922.

[217] Ministry of Home Affairs Northern Ireland Minute Sheet, 10 June 1922.

[218] Ibid. 10 July 1922.

[219] A copy of the order is on file.

The following month Mayne requested parole to attend at a case in the preparation of which he had been involved.[220] The matter was referred to Colonel Topping of the Ministry of Home Affairs who recommended refusal. Topping's observations concentrated on allegations that Mayne's boycott activities had cost Northern traders thousands of pounds, but did not mention IRA activities.[221] Permission was refused.[222] An application for a visit to Mayne by a Mr Ponsonby Staples was likewise refused. The Minister had made a ruling that visits to internees would be restricted to wives, children, and parents.[223]

In February 1923 Patrick Mayne, brother of the internee, wrote to Dawson Bates requesting a visit to discuss the management of the farm. The procedure adopted in this and subsequent requests for visits was that the matter was passed on to the RUC for the area in which the applicant lived and to the central RUC Special Branch for comment on the advisability of allowing the visit to go ahead.[224] Patrick Mayne was favourably considered and the application was granted.[225]

Post to and from the internee was examined and anything considered questionable was referred to the Ministry.[226] Depending on the view taken, the document might then be sent to the RUC for inspection by the Special Branch.[227]

Mayne's former employer wrote to him in October 1923 asking him to apply for release to go to Dublin to discuss business.[228] He himself was 'on the run' from Northern Ireland at the time.[229] The Ministry decided against release on parole, but seemed willing to look favourably on Drysdale's suggestion that Mayne be released on condition that he leave Northern Ireland for good.[230] It was noted, however, that Mayne had never applied to come before the Advisory Committee and it was suggested that no action be taken until he did.[231] A member of the Advisory Committee, Major Shewell, is on record as signifying his agreement with this approach. Shewell (who appears to have been a prison governor[232])

---

[220] Petition of James Mayne of 17 July 1922.

[221] Ministry of Home Affairs of Northern Ireland Minute Sheet, note of 18 July 1922.

[222] Ministry of Home Affairs of Northern Ireland Minute Sheet, 16 Oct. 1922.

[223] Ibid.

[224] Memo. from IG's Office, 2 Mar. 1923.

[225] Ibid.

[226] See e.g. Long (Deputy Governor of the *Argenta*) to the Secretary of the Minister of Home Affairs, 31 July 1923.

[227] e.g. Townshend to IG, 25 Nov. 1922, enclosing letter from A. Mullen.

[228] Mullen to Mayne, 2 Oct. 1923.

[229] Ministry of Home Affairs of Northern Ireland Minute Sheet, 19 Oct. 1923.

[230] Ibid.

[231] Ibid.

[232] The *Belfast and Ulster Directory 1921–22* (Belfast, 1922), lists a Major E. Shewell as Prison Governor of the County Antrim Prison on the Crumlin Road (p. 271).

had earlier concurred with a decision to prevent Mayne sending a letter to the Irish National Foresters, thus indicating that members of the Advisory Committee were involved in the day-to-day administration of internment.

In October 1923, after one and a half years on the *Argenta*, Mayne got in trouble for attempting to have a warder smuggle in a bottle of whisky. The warder took the money offered and then reported the matter to the Governor.[233] The matter was referred to the Ministry with a favourable report from Drysdale.[234] Poynting, the Secretary, decided that the matter should be passed over with a warning.[235]

Later in the month Mayne wrote to Dawson Bates protesting that there was 'absolutely no cause' for his internment and describing conditions as 'miserable'. In his view, application to the Committee was 'out of the question by reason of traditional hostility to such, under other governments and the obligations sought to be imposed for release'.[236] The Minister directed that the internee be told that release was granted only on the recommendation of the Advisory Committee.

The following month Mayne again wrote to Dawson Bates demanding the right to refute any charges against him in court.[237] An application to the Advisory Committee was again ruled out—this would be a 'star chamber proceeding where this right is denied and the vague whisperings of malice and personal spite made to constitute evidence'.[238] The letter was sent to Dawson Bates with a covering note from Drysdale stating that the tone of the letter suggested that Mayne would 'have a powerful influence in deterring weaker men from appearing before the Advisory Committee to have their cases reviewed, and as he is allowed to associate with them his influence will be used in that direction'.[239] Poynting also added a note indicating that although cases were to be brought before the Advisory Committee without the application of the internee, Mayne might still use his influence to prevent internees from accepting the terms offered. Accordingly it was suggested that Mayne be transferred to Derry. On 17 November 1923, a Transfer Internment Order was signed by Dawson Bates[240] and Mayne was moved there.

Around this time a Parliamentary Secretary's conference on internees was held which apparently considered the question of releases, but

---

[233] Statement of the warder to the Governor of 25 Oct. 1923.
[234] Note by Drysdale attached to statement of warder of 25 Oct. 1923.
[235] Ministry of Home Affairs of Northern Ireland Minute Sheet, 29 Oct. 1923.
[236] Mayne to Dawson Bates, 30 Oct. 1923.
[237] Mayne to Dawson Bates, 10 Nov. 1923.
[238] Ibid.
[239] Drysdale to the Secretary of the Minister of Home Affairs, 10 Nov. 1923.
[240] A copy of the Order is on file.

Mayne was not one of those recommended for release.[241] In February he had a meeting with Major Shewell and followed this up with a letter outlining the business losses which he had suffered because of internment and asking for 'a generous consideration' of his case.[242] The Ministry responded by obtaining the opinion of the police.

The report of the District Inspector RUC confirmed that Mayne's business had suffered as a result of his internment and stressed 'he never took part in any violent acts against Crown forces or anything like that, and I don't think would encourage it in others . . . clever propaganda was his forte. He would not countenance violence'.[243] According to the report, Mayne had been frequently writing to the Dublin press complaining about police actions: 'If "B" men made a raid, or searched houses, as they often did, during the troubles, he enquired into their every action and made malicious injury claims when there was the slightest ground and would exaggerate and expose their actions to the trial of these claims'.[244] No mention was made of any IRA activities but it was stated that he was secretary of the local Sinn Féin executive and that boycott notices had been sent to him. Overall the report recommend release.

A report for the county commandant of the Special Constabulary stamped 'HQ Intelligence Branch RUSC' and apparently prepared by the Intelligence Officer took a different view (prose style does not appear to have been one of the Officer's chief concerns):

He was a shrewd propagandist in the interest of the IRA, constantly writing to the southern papers, and when possible after raids being carried out by the police or specials in the Cookstown district done all he could to manufacture malicious claims for the people whose houses were searched by the authorities.[245]

It was also claimed that the office in which Mayne had worked was used as the local headquarters of the IRA, but it was not stated that Mayne had ever been a member. Release was not recommended unless 'he is put over the border'. This report was sent back to the District Inspector, Cookstown for an opinion but he again recommended release.

The RUSC County Commandant supported the view of his Intelligence Officer and suggested that the return of Mayne to Cookstown would disturb the peace of the district. The County Commandant did not alter this view after seeing the reply of the DI Cookstown.[246] The opinion of

---

[241] Ministry of Home Affairs of Northern Ireland Minute Sheet, note by Poynting, 19 Feb. 1924.

[242] Mayne to Shewell, 18 Oct. 1924.

[243] Report of DI Hall, 26 Feb. 1924.

[244] Ibid.

[245] Report of 27 Feb. 1924 to County Commandant Tyrone Special Constabulary.

[246] Note of 29 Feb. 1924.

the Intelligence Officer was again sought and he replied, 'If Mayne is going to be allowed to Cookstown the most stringent conditions that could be imposed would be necessary, from information received from the inhabitants of Cookstown his return might lead to a breach of the peace at any time.'[247] Further reports were then obtained apparently through the RUC Special Branch,[248] and these recommended that if release were granted he should not be allowed back to Cookstown, at least for a couple of months.[249]

A note was then sent to the Governor of Derry gaol by Shewell asking him to check if Mayne wished to appear before the Advisory Committee and the Governor replied that he did. The Committee heard Mayne's case on 27 March 1924. The record includes a statement by Mayne that he never took any action against the Northern Ireland Government and that he could not accept release conditional on exclusion from County Tyrone. Also included is a pre-printed sheet with such questions as 'Are you a loyal subject of His Majesty?' and 'Are you a member of the Irish Republican Army?'[250] The Committee apparently had sight of the various RUC and RUSC reports,[251] but Mayne gave the required answers, and unconditional release was recommended.

Upon receipt of the advice of the Committee, the Ministry requested fresh police reports. The Intelligence Officer of Tyrone RUSC again recommended that Mayne should be the last to be allowed to return unconditionally, while the DI Cookstown suggested release on bail but voiced concern about Mayne's safety on returning to Cookstown.[252] The Inspector-General's office, though, sent a note advising against allowing Mayne to return to County Tyrone on release.[253]

The Ministry decided against Mayne's release[254] but stated that his case would be kept under review.[255] Mayne protested against the refusal of release[256] and it appears that it was agreed to resubmit the case.[257] A civil case in which Mayne was a witness, but unrelated to his internment, came up for hearing in June and Mayne was brought to Cookstown under

---

[247] Report of 27 Feb. 1924.

[248] At least they are stamped 'Inspector General's Office Crime Special Branch'.

[249] Reports of 5, 9, and 12 March 1924.

[250] Headed 'Questions by the Advisory Committee', the form is on file.

[251] Under a heading 'Police Report on Representations' on the pre-printed form, the main points of the report are summarized.

[252] Report of 1 Apr. 1924.

[253] Report of 14 Apr. 1924.

[254] Ministry of Home Affairs of Northern Ireland Minute Sheet, 15 Apr. 1924.

[255] Report of 31 Mar. 1924.

[256] Mayne to Shewell, 25 Apr. 1924.

[257] Ministry of Home Affairs of Northern Ireland Minute Sheet, 28 Apr. 1924. It is not entirely clear whether the file was to be resubmitted to the Minister or to the Committee.

police escort for the hearing.[258] The Ministry again enquired if Mayne would agree to release on bail but he refused.

In that month also Mayne's health deteriorated sharply and he was moved to the prison hospital. The Medical Officer reported that under ordinary circumstances he would recommend the man's release as he was suffering from myocardial degeneration.[259] On 19 June 1924 Mayne petitioned the Governor of Northern Ireland stating that if he was to avoid complete physical breakdown he would require more 'care nursing and building up' than he could get in prison. He outlined how for the past seven months he had been practically in solitary confinement for twenty hours a day and blamed prison conditions for the breakdown in his health. He also enclosed a letter he had received from the Lord Chief Justice dated 24 May 1922 commiserating on his 'trouble' and offering to supply a reference.

Eventually, on 20 June 1924, Mayne's release was ordered, but a further order under Regulation 23A was served on him excluding him from County Tyrone and from Magherafelt rural district.[260] He moved to a nursing home in Belfast and in July he again petitioned the Governor, this time requesting that the exclusion order be revoked. The request was referred to the RUC who recommended non-revocation[261] and with this the Ministry concurred.

By October Mayne's financial position was becoming desperate and for this reason he again requested that the order be revoked.[262] He followed this up with a call to the Ministry during which he offered to give his own personal bail.[263] The RUC recommended that no action be taken until after the forthcoming general election.[264]

Finally, on 25 October 1924 Mayne was informed that the Minister would revoke the order if he entered into bail of £100 without sureties. On 31 October the internee entered into the bail,[265] and four days later the exclusion order was revoked.

Mayne had spent over two years in gaols and in a prison ship. Lesser restrictions had been imposed for four months after his release. The key allegations that had led to his original internment were dropped and can therefore be assumed to have been false. Police reports appear to have carried greater weight than the recommendations of the Advisory Com-

---

[258] Memo. from Minister of Home Affairs to IG RUC, 28 May 1924.

[259] Extract from Medical Officer's Journal of 18 June 1924 submitted to the Secretary of the Minister of Home Affairs.

[260] A copy of the exclusion order is on file.

[261] Memo. from IG's office to the Secretary, Minister of Home Affairs, 17 July 1924.

[262] Mayne to Shewell, 8 Oct. 1924.

[263] Memo. from Shewell to IG RUC, 8 Oct. 1924.

[264] IG RUC to Secretary, Minister of Home Affairs, 17 Oct. 1924.

[265] IG RUC to Secretary, Minister of Home Affairs, 3 Nov. 1924.

mittee; and the process which led to his release might have been the inspiration for Kafka's *The Trial*.

Arrest, detention, and internment: conclusions

The derivation of Regulation 23 can be traced directly to DORR 55, and like that Regulation, it introduced arrest powers which marked a radical departure from the ordinary in three main respects: (1) arrest was authorized where no specific offence was suspected; (2) if a specific offence was suspected, there was no requirement that the suspicion be reasonable; and (3) members of the armed forces were granted arrest powers different from those available to the ordinary citizen (powers which were later held to be *ultra vires*).[266]

Regulation 23 also marked a departure from normal standards in that it permitted extended detention following arrest; indeed, it appears to have permitted indefinite detention. The wording employed in the Regulation in relation to detention was likewise derived directly from DORR 55. But whereas DORR 55 was operated along with the provisions of the Army Act 1881 in a manner which placed some limitation on the length of detention, there were no corresponding provisions in Northern Ireland. It was this absence which was the most invidious feature of the Northern Ireland provisions, particularly in view of the unconditional delegation of powers to senior policemen. In any case, it appears that round-ups took place in 1922 in which even these wide-ranging powers of arrest were exceeded.

Regulation 23B was likewise derived from DORR 14B. As the case examined above illustrates, it could be a crude device, incarcerating political as well as armed opponents, and there is little to suggest that such safeguards as were built into the system operated effectively. It was also used in a highly partisan manner, as virtually all internees came from the nationalist community.

In Northern Ireland constitutional problems in relation to the creation of special courts to try serious offences meant that internment took pride of place in the Government's security strategy. Were these powers effective? A crude indicator might suggest that they were. Northern Ireland survived, and while there was quite a lot of political violence in March 1922 there was very much less in March 1923. This may, however, have been due largely to external factors. As Lyons put it: 'The danger from without was overcome, partly with the help of the British army, partly by the use of emergency powers and the creation of the special constabulary, and most of all, perhaps, because the outbreak of the Civil War in the south relieved the pressure on the north.'[267]

---

[266] See pp. 331–3.   [267] *Ireland since the Famine*, 716.

Had the Civil War not broken out in the South, it is likely that the picture in Northern Ireland would have been quite different; indeed there might well have been a different civil war (as there almost was in March 1922) on a North–South axis. And while resort to emergency powers may have been instrumental in bringing an end to what might be termed 'internal disturbances' in Northern Ireland, the partisan manner in which these powers were used was the stuff of which future conflicts were made.[268]

SECTION (B) SPECIAL COURT PROVISIONS

This section is concerned mainly with the courts of summary jurisdiction (CSJs) established under the Special Powers Act, and with the provision made in the Criminal Procedure Act (Northern Ireland) 1922 for the establishment of a special court. Before examining these in detail, mention must be made of the changes in court structure introduced in Northern Ireland by the 1920 Act and of some other relevant developments.

Ordinary courts and emergency provisions

The 1920 Act abolished the old Supreme Court of Judicature in Ireland and created two new Supreme Courts of Judicature each consisting of a High Court and a Court of Appeal.[269] The High Court was staffed by the Lord Chief Justice and two puisne judges, the Court of Appeal by the Lord Chief Justice and two ordinary judges known as Lords Justice of Appeal.[270] The 1920 Act also created a short-lived High Court of Appeal for Ireland, but with the abolition of that Court, appeal in certain matters lay directly to the House of Lords.

The County courts and the other lower courts continued as before partition, grand juries in Northern Ireland being abolished only in 1926.[271] The great majority of office-holders were Protestants[272] (though the first Lord Chief Justice was a Catholic Unionist[273]), and anti-nationalist bias in the administration of justice was a frequently made charge.[274] Some

---

[268] See, generally, McGuffin, *Internment*.

[269] See, generally, A. S. Quekett, *The Constitution of Northern Ireland* (Belfast, 1933), i. 51–3, upon which this piece is based.

[270] For an impressionistic description of the courts in Northern Ireland see C. de B. Murray, 'Northern Ireland: Its Law Courts and Parliament' [1937] *Scots Law Times* 1919.

[271] By the Jury Law Amendment Act (Northern Ireland) 1926.

[272] Palley, 'Northern Ireland Constitution', 398.

[273] Denis Henry, MP for Londonderry South 1916–21, Solicitor-General for Ireland 1918–19, Attorney-General July 1919–July 1921, Lord Chief Justice of Northern Ireland July 1921.

[274] See P. Hillyard, 'Political and Social Dimensions of Emergency Law in Northern Ireland', in T. Jennings (ed.), *Justice*, 200. Hillyard notes that of the 20 High Court judges appointed since the independent Northern Ireland courts were established, 15 had been

magistrates were also members of the Special Constabulary. A circular issued in August 1924 provided that such magistrates employed full-time in the Constabulary were not to sit and adjudicate at Petty sessions. Those not serving full-time were permitted to exercise their function but were not to adjudicate in any case in which men under their command were concerned.[275]

Emergency provisions

Apart from creating special courts of two RMs (discussed below), the Special Powers Act introduced a number of other changes affecting the court system. Whipping was introduced as a sentencing option for a variety of offences of a type connected with the 'Troubles',[276] and offences against sections 2 and 3 of the Explosive Substances Act 1883 became punishable by death.[277] Following the precedent established in relation to ROIA courts martial,[278] depositions were made admissible in evidence on trial on indictment where it was proved that the witness was so ill as to be unable to travel or where his attendance 'could not be procured owing to the prevalence of a state of disorder or otherwise'.[279] In prosecutions before CSJs for offences against the Firearms Act 1920, the normal geographical jurisdictional limitations were all but dispensed with,[280] and civil procedure was altered to facilitate the service of civil bills where ordinary service was impossible 'owing to the prevalence of a state of disorder or otherwise'.[281]

The Criminal Law and Procedure (Ireland) Act 1887 survived partition to have some slight impact in Northern Ireland.[282] In 1923 there were in the jurisdiction five RMs who were qualified to conduct the special CSJs provided for in the Act.[283] In May of that year it was decided to convene such a CSJ to deal with what the Attorney-General considered 'a very

openly associated with the Unionist Party, while of the 23 County court appointments, 14 had been visibly connected with Unionism.

[275] Circular, 21 Aug. 1924, HA 27/1/1, PRONI.

[276] s. 5. These were: any crime under the Explosive Substances Act 1883 as extended by s. 18 of the Firearms Act 1920, an offence against the Firearms Act 1920 in relation to the having keeping or using of firearms, any offence against s. 30 of the Larceny Act 1916, arson and any indictable offence under the Malicious Damage Act 1861. Whipping could be ordered also for offences against the regulations relating to firearms and explosives offences.

[277] s. 6.

[278] See ROIR 72, app. 3.

[279] s. 9.

[280] Reg. 34. The same position applied to trial by special CSJs of breaches of the Regulation (see below).

[281] Reg. 33.

[282] The measure was repealed in Northern Ireland only by the Northern Ireland (Emergency Provisions) (Amendment) Act 1975, s. 23 (2), schedule 3.

[283] Ministry of Home Affairs of Northern Ireland Minute Sheet, 11 May 1923, HA 8/4, PRONI.

serious case'[284] involving a Special Constable. The local Crown Solicitor was of the opinion that a jury would not convict on the evidence[285] but trial by CSJ secured a conviction.[286]

The question as to whether ROIA courts martial should function after the creation of Northern Ireland had proved a thorny one in the latter part of 1921. A related issue surfaced again in 1924. British soldiers convicted of offences against the civil law and sentenced to imprisonment with hard labour were automatically discharged from the Army. It appears that in some instances this acted as an incentive rather than a deterrent. In February 1924 two soldiers were facing trial in the courts on criminal charges. Prompted by the Army, the Crown Solicitor for the area moved in the High Court to have the cases referred to the CMA under ROIR 58D with a view to trial by court martial. He averred that he had been informed that the offence was committed by the soldiers with the intention of obtaining a discharge from the Army.[287] By ensuring that the soldiers were court-martialled for their crimes the possibility of discharge from the Army was negated. The soldiers were duly handed over for court martial.

Courts of summary jurisdiction under the Civil Authorities (Special Powers) Act (Northern Ireland) 1922

The provisions governing the CSJs established under the Special Powers Act were directly derived from those relating to ROIA CSJs and therefore overlapped considerably with those applicable in trials by ROIA courts martial. The principal difference between trial by ROIA CSJ and trial by CSJ under the Special Powers Act was that the jurisdiction of the former covered both alleged breaches of ROIR and other summary offences, while that of the former was limited to alleged breaches of the Special Powers Regulations.

Prosecutions for alleged breaches of the Regulations could only be brought by persons (usually police officers) authorized by the Attorney-General for Northern Ireland and in accordance with such directions as he might give.[288] Such authorization could be general, and need not have referred to particular cases.[289] This centralized control of prosecutions, a common feature of emergency law, reflected the politically sensitive nature of many of the cases. Similar considerations, it may be assumed,

---

[284] Opinion of AG, 9 May 1923, ibid.
[285] Ibid.
[286] CI RUC (for IG) to Secretary Minister of Home Affairs, 5 July 1923, ibid.
[287] Affidavit in the case of *R (Creery)* v. *Brooks and Wilson*, unreported, papers relating thereto at HA 8/505, PRONI.
[288] s. 3 (4); cf. ROIR 69 (8).
[289] *Sweny* v. *Carroll* [1942] *NILR* 112.

lay behind the great scope given to the prosecuting authorities in deciding on case venue. Normal geographical limitations did not apply since it was provided that the offence in question should be deemed to have been committed either in the place in which the same actually was committed or in any place in which the defendant might be or to which he might be brought.[290] The RM in whose jurisdiction the case was eventually conducted was then empowered to issue witness summonses to persons outside his jurisdiction.[291]

One RM sitting alone was entitled to carry out any business prior to the trial, including committing the defendant to prison or admitting him to bail or adjourning the case.[292] At the actual trial the court was to be constituted of two or more RMs.[293] In practice, the bench usually consisted of only two.[294] The public, or any section of it, could be excluded by the court if the prosecution requested it as being 'in the public interest'.[295] This was a considerable extension of the limited powers inherent in any court to hold cases in camera, and corresponded with the powers of exclusion which seem to have been used with some frequency in ROIA courts martial.[296]

The most usual type of cases tried in this period related to breaches of orders made under regulations relating to curfew etc.[297] In such instances, the prosecution opened its case by proving the making of the order, exhibiting in evidence a copy of a poster or newspaper notice relating to the order.[298] No statistics are available on the numbers of prosecutions in the years 1922–3,[299] but this type of case would have accounted for the bulk of the 3,275[300] convictions in 1924. By 1925 these cases had declined in significance and the number of convictions plummeted to two.[301] This decline, it can be assumed, came about in large measure because of the centralized control of prosecutions.

The Special Powers Regulations, as had been the case with DORR and ROIR, were framed in the widest catch-all fashion, making prosecution

[290] Reg. 34; cf. DORR 58.
[291] Reg. 34.
[292] s. 3 (4); cf. ROIR 77.
[293] s. 3 (4).
[294] See W. A. Carson, *Ulster and the Irish Republic* (Belfast, 1956).
[295] Reg. 32; cf. DORR 58.
[296] See pp. 70–1.
[297] Memo. from Divisional Commissioner Belfast re the Civil Authorities (Special Powers) Act (Northern Ireland) 1922, HA 16/3, PRONI.
[298] Ibid.
[299] At a Ministry of Home Affairs meeting in Jan. 1924 it was noted that judicial statistics were last published in Ireland for the year 1919 and it was 'considered inadvisable to endeavour to compile these statistics for the intervening years which would mean considerable expenditure of time and money'. HA 8/360, PRONI.
[300] *Ulster Year Book 1929*, 148.
[301] Ibid. 148.

and ultimately conviction easier and correspondingly reducing the chances of mounting an adequate defence. Company directors and other officers were liable for breaches of the Regulations by their company unless they proved that the act constituting the offence took place without their knowledge or consent.[302] Withholding information became an offence,[303] but the most notorious example of this type of provision was section 2 (4) which provided:

If any person does any act of such a nature as to be calculated to be prejudicial to the preservation of the peace or maintenance of order in Northern Ireland and not specifically provided for in the regulations, he shall be deemed guilty of an offence against the regulations.

This was derived from ROIR 50, the provision which had been employed in the MLA in 1921 to try breaches of martial law regulations in statutory courts martial.[304] The burden of proof was also reversed in certain instances. But unlike the position under DORR, the accused was made a competent witness in his own defence, since sections 1 to 4 of the Criminal Evidence Act 1898 were made applicable in the case of a person charged with an offence against the Regulations.[305] This move, which corresponded somewhat with contemporaneous developments in the Irish Free State military court system,[306] can be seen as a reaction to the bizarre evidential position which had arisen under DORR and ROIR.[307]

The sentencing powers of the Special Powers Act CSJs were considerably broader than those of their ROIA equivalents. The maximum sentence for breach of a Special Powers Regulation was two years and/or a fine of £100.[308] In addition, whipping could be ordered for any offence against the regulations relating to firearms or explosives offences.[309] An appeal against a decision of a CSJ lay to a court of quarter sessions which was to be constituted of the Recorder or County court judge sitting alone.[310]

The issue of whipping as a sentence, whether or not imposed following conviction by a CSJ, proved a thorny one for the Northern Ireland Government, particularly as the great majority of such sentences were imposed on Catholics.[311] But despite protests from the Provisional

---

[302] s. 2 (5); cf. DORR 48A.
[303] s. 2 (3); cf. DORR 49.
[304] See pp. 85–6. Cf. DORR 50, app. 3.
[305] s. 2 (7).
[306] See pp. 207–8.
[307] See p. 73.
[308] s. 4; under ROIR, a CSJ could impose a maximum sentence of six months.
[309] s. 5 (3).
[310] ss. 3 (3) and 4.
[311] See, generally, Buckland, *Factory of Grievances*, 206–10.

Government, and pressure from the British Government, the execution of such sentences was persevered with.

The Criminal Procedure Act (Northern Ireland) 1922

The provisions of the Criminal Procedure Act were directly derived from clause 4 of the Craig–Collins pact of March 1922, and although the Act was never invoked, the procedures which it sought to establish remain of some significance. The measure was not without historical precedent: broadly similar provisions were incorporated in the abortive Criminal Justice Administration (Ireland) Bill of 1920[312] and in the failed Prevention of Crime (Ireland) Act 1882.

The procedures set out in the Act are illustrated by flow-chart in Figure 6. The measure was concerned with the 'serious crimes'[313] set out in the schedule to the Act. These were any of the following offences punishable by death, penal servitude, or imprisonment for a term exceeding six months:

(1) Treason or treason felony.
(2) Murder or manslaughter.
(3) Assault which either causes actual bodily harm or grievous bodily harm or is committed with intent to cause grievous bodily harm.
(4) Arson whether by common law or by statute.
(5) Any crime or offence cognisable by law involving (a) the breaking into, firing at or otherwise attacking or injuring a dwelling house; (b) larceny or robbery with threats or violence; (c) malicious injury or damage to or destruction of any property whatsoever, including any crime or offence under the Malicious Damage Act 1861.
(6) Any crime against the Explosive Substances Act 1883, or the Firearms Act 1920.
(7) Any attempt or conspiracy to commit any of the said crimes or offences or being accessory to or aiding or abetting the commission thereof.

Committal proceedings for 'serious crimes' were to be held as with other indictable offences. If the accused was committed for trial for a serious offence, however, he had the option to request to be tried by the 'Special Court' provided for in the Act.[314] Such a request was to be made to the justices 'forthwith upon the committal for trial'. This provision was presumably designed to enable nationalist defendants to avoid trial by a jury feared to be biased.

In addition, the Attorney-General for Northern Ireland was empowered to direct that those committed for 'serious crime' be tried by the special court whether they wished it or not.[315] Any such direction was to be given not later than fourteen days after the committal.[316] No criteria were set

---

[312] See fn. 97, pp. 26–7.   [313] s. 1 (3).   [314] s. 2 (5).   [315] s. 1 (1).   [316] s. 2 (6).

```
                          ┌─────────────────────┐
                          │  Indictable offence │
                          └─────────────────────┘
                                     │
                          ┌─────────────────────────┐
                          │ Preliminary examination │
                          └─────────────────────────┘
                    ┌────────────────┴───────────────┐
           ┌─────────────────┐              ┌───────────────────────┐
           │ Returned for trial │           │ Not returned for trial │
           └─────────────────┘              └───────────────────────┘
```

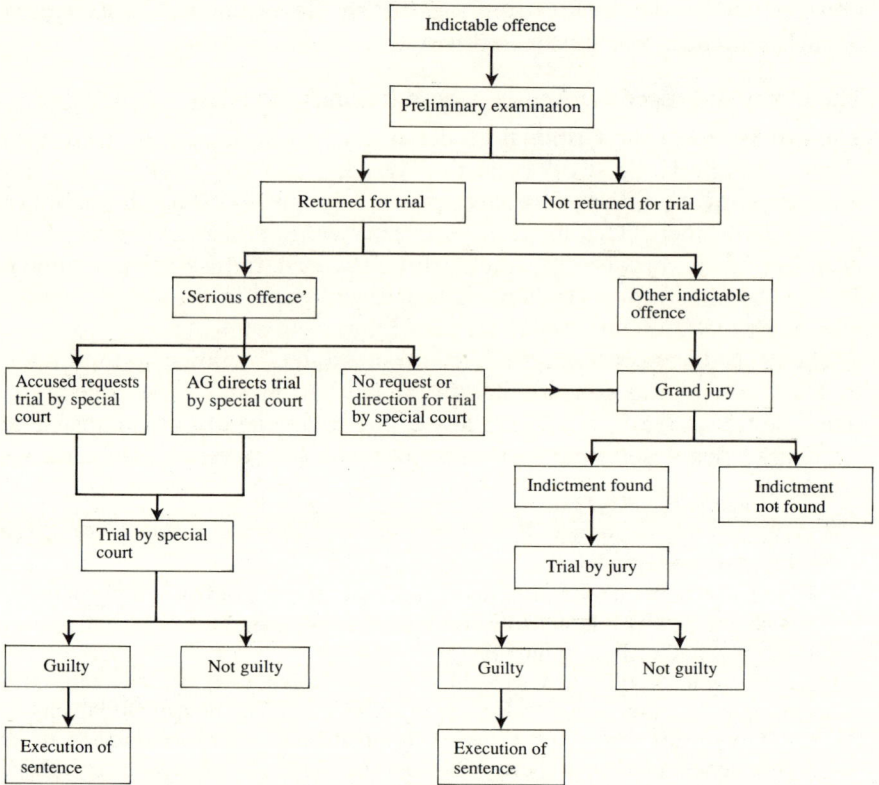

Fig. 6 flowchart: The Criminal Procedure Act (Northern Ireland) 1922

- Indictable offence → Preliminary examination
  - Returned for trial
    - 'Serious offence'
      - Accused requests trial by special court
      - AG directs trial by special court
      - No request or direction for trial by special court → Grand jury
    - Trial by special court
      - Guilty → Execution of sentence
      - Not guilty
    - Other indictable offence
      - Grand jury
        - Indictment found
          - Trial by jury
            - Guilty → Execution of sentence
            - Not guilty
        - Indictment not found
  - Not returned for trial

Fig. 6. The Criminal Procedure Act (Northern Ireland) 1922

out for the exercise of this power. One possible explanation for its existence is that it was designed to cope with situations where loyalist defendants might face perverse acquittals if tried by jury. Speaking in the Northern Ireland House of Commons, however, the Attorney-General gave the distinct impression that the Act was designed primarily to cope with nationalist defendants. The serious crimes were, as he put it, of the type 'committed by people who are dissatisfied with the order of things as they are established at present and who wish to overthrow that order'.[317]

In cases where no request was made by the accused and no direction given by the Attorney-General, those accused of serious crimes would

[317] Apr. 2 *HCNI Deb.*, col. 387.

have their cases tried by jury under the ordinary system of criminal administration. In practice, this was what happened in every case.

The special court, when trying cases, was to consist of the Lord Chief Justice of Northern Ireland and one of the ordinary judges of the Court of Appeal.[318] It was ordinarily to sit in Belfast but could if it wished sit elsewhere.[319] The court was to have the 'powers authorities and jurisdiction'[320] which otherwise have been vested in a court of assize or other court or commission sitting for the trial of the offence in question. As it was to be jury-less, it was empowered to determine any question and to find any issue or verdict which would otherwise have been the prerogative of the jury.

A general power to make rules necessary for carrying the Act into effect was given to the Lord Chief Justice who was to consult in their making with the ordinary judges of the Court of Appeal.[321] In practice, it appears that no such rules were made.[322]

As the court was to sit with only two judges, the question arises as to what was to happen in the event of a disagreement on the bench. A rehearing of the case would necessarily involve one of the judges who had presided at the original hearing. It was considered that it should be left to the Attorney-General to decide whether to enter a *nolle prosequi* or to proceed afresh.[323]

Any sentence of death passed by the special court was to be carried out in such a place as the court directed.[324] It was intended that no appeal should lie against a decision of the court.

Special courts in Northern Ireland: conclusions

CSJs established under the Special Powers Act could be said to have represented a continuation of ROIA summary courts in a manner which did not appear to be in conflict with the 1920 Act.[325] They are therefore susceptible to the kinds of criticism levelled at their predecessors, and in several respects the procedural criticisms are the same as those levelled at ROIA courts martial. There were three main points of departure from ROIA CSJs: an increased sentencing power, an atavistic introduction of corporal punishment as a sentencing option, and a change in the law of evidence which made the accused a competent witness in his own defence.

What has been stated above in relation to the effectiveness of intern-

---

[318] s. 1 (2).   [319] Ibid.   [320] s. 2 (1).   [321] s. 2 (7).
[322] The 1922 *Belfast Gazette* shows no rules or orders made under the Criminal Procedure Act (Northern Ireland) 1922.
[323] 2 *SNI Deb.*, col. 90.   [324] s. 2 (4).
[325] But see pp. 327–33.

ment powers could also be said to apply to the question of special courts. Perhaps the only thing to be added is that constitutional difficulties surrounding the creation of special courts in Northern Ireland ensured that some of the more counter-productive experiences of British rule could not be repeated. As the story of the Criminal Procedure Act (Northern Ireland) 1922 illustrated, Westminster's approval would be forthcoming, if at all, only where the purpose of special courts could be presented as benign. Thus, with the benefit of hindsight, Belfast could lecture London on the general tendency of special courts 'to defeat their own object'.[326]

PART III. JUDICIAL SCRUTINY OF EMERGENCY POWERS

Discussion of the legal basis of emergency powers in Northern Ireland is complicated by two main factors. First, there is the problem of identifying the precise division of functions in this sphere made by the Government of Ireland Act 1920—two Governments and two Parliaments shared responsibility. The second issue is that the scope of delegated legislative authority under the 1920 Act differed somewhat from that of delegated executive power. These differences are particularly relevant to an examination of non-statutory emergency powers.

This part is concerned not only with the limits of the legislative competence of the Northern Ireland Parliament set by the 1920 Act, but also with the question of martial law in Northern Ireland. This latter issue, which has been ignored by most commentators, is mainly of theoretical interest, as there was, of course, no formal assertion of martial law in Northern Ireland. It merits consideration, however, because its imposition in Northern Ireland was a seriously debated issue in 1922, and because an examination of the complexity of the legal issues involved may help to explain why an alternative course was adopted.

The next issue examined in this part is the question of *vires*, particularly in relation to the Special Powers Act. Finally, the extremely limited case law in this area will be discussed and overall conclusions drawn. Throughout, theoretical speculation is tempered by assessment of likely judicial response.

---

[326] See p. 285.

Constitutional limits to emergency legislation in Northern Ireland

The Government of Ireland Act 1920: legislative limits

Subject to certain limitations, the 1920 Act empowered the Parliament of Northern Ireland 'to make laws for the peace order and good government of Northern Ireland'.[327] It has been suggested that this form of words could be construed as permitting judicial review of legislation with a view to testing the conformity of the enactment in question with these authorized purposes. Thus, for instance, the Special Powers Act might have been challenged as having been neither for the peace, order, nor good government of Northern Ireland. The accepted view, however, seems to be that the effect of this wording was to confer plenary legislative power and that therefore such a challenge was precluded.[328] Newark puts it thus: 'we must not approach a consideration of the Parliament's powers by looking to see what it can do; we must look into the Act to see what it cannot do.'[329]

What Parliament could not do was to pass laws *inter alia* discriminating on grounds of religion,[330] or taking property without compensation,[331] or relating to matters which were to fall within the competence of possible all-Ireland institutions—the 'reserved' matters,[332] or relating to matters which were to remain exclusively within the competence of the Westminster Parliament—the 'excepted' matters.[333]

The jurisdiction of the Northern Ireland High Court extended to questions of the validity of legislation, and an appeal lay to the Court of Appeal and thence to the House of Lords. One authority considered this power to be 'analogous to that discharged by an English Court in dealing with subordinate legislation, but more closely resembling the functions of the Supreme Court of the United States with respect to the limits *inter se* of state and federal legislative competence'.[334]

The borderline between the areas within and without the competence of the Northern Ireland Parliament could on occasion prove very difficult

---

[327] s. 4 (1).

[328] For a discussion of these points see Palley, 'Northern Ireland Constitution', 388–9, and H. G. Calvert, *Constitutional Law*, 162–72.

[329] F. H. Newark, 'The Law and the Constitution', 27, in T. Wilson (ed.), *Ulster under Home Rule* (Oxford, 1955). See also F. H. Newark, 'The Constitution of Northern Ireland', in D. G. Neill (ed.), *Devolution of Government: The Experiment in Northern Ireland* (London, 1953), 11.

[330] s. 5 (1).

[331] Ibid.

[332] s. 4.

[333] Ibid.

[334] *Craies on Statute Law*, 423, quoted with approval in relation to Northern Ireland in Quekett, *Constitution*, pt. III, pp. 27–8.

to draw, and the judicial response to this problem was the adoption of the Canadian 'pith and substance' doctrine.[335] Briefly, this test held as valid legislation whose 'true nature and character' came within the express powers of the Northern Ireland Parliament even if it incidentally affected matters outside the authorized field. While it would be an anachronism to apply the doctrine in the 1922–5 period—the test was adopted only in 1937[336]—it would probably be more of a distortion to ignore it.

A number of these reserved and excepted matters are of particular importance for the purposes of this study. Under section 47 of the 1920 Act, the reserved matters encompassed 'all matters relating to the Supreme Court of Northern Ireland'.[337] The interpretation of the words 'all matters relating to' posed a number of problems,[338] and difficulties of interpretation led to a number of declaratory enactments.[339] But it is clear that included under this heading was the criminal jurisdiction of the High Court which extended to trials at first instance at the assizes, or in Belfast under a commission of oyer and terminer and gaol delivery.[340] Among the matters in respect of which the legislative competence of the Northern Ireland Parliament was excepted were 'the making of peace or war, or matters arising from a state of war . . . or the navy, the air force, the territorial army[341] . . . or the defence of the realm or any other naval military or airforce matter . . . or treason, treason felony'.[342]

The Government of Ireland Act 1920: executive powers

In the executive sphere the formula adopted in the 1920 Act was not simply to vest in the Government of Northern Ireland executive authority over those matters in which the Parliament of Northern Ireland was competent. Instead, section 8 (2) of the 1920 Act provided:

as respects Irish services, the Lord lieutenant [from 1922 the Governor of Northern Ireland] or other chief executive officer or officers for the time being appointed in his place, on behalf of His Majesty, shall exercise any prerogative or other executive power of His Majesty the exercise of which may be delegated to him by His Majesty.

---

[335] For a critical discussion see Calvert, *Constitutional Law*, 187–96.
[336] *Gallagher* v. *Lynn* [1937] AC 863.
[337] s. 47 (1).
[338] For a discussion see Calvert, *Constitutional Law*, 245–50.
[339] See e.g. s. 1 of the Northern Ireland (Miscellaneous Provisions) Act 1928, and s. 1 (1) of the Northern Ireland (Miscellaneous Provisions) Act 1932.
[340] Under the Supreme Court of Judicature (Ireland) Act 1887, as adopted by s. 41 of the 1920 Act. See Quekett, *Constitution*, pt. 11, pp. 568–9.
[341] Originally the 'territorial force', but 'territorial army' was substituted by s. 1 of the Territorial Army and Militia Act 1921.
[342] 1920 Act, s. 4.

'Irish services' in turn were defined as 'all public services in connection with the administration of civil government in . . . Northern Ireland'[343] other than with respect to the reserved or excepted matters. Such public services were to be administered through,[344] but not by,[345] Departments of the Northern Ireland Government.

It has been suggested that the effect of the letters patent covering the office of the Governor may have been to increase the sphere of delegated executive competence beyond that merely relating to Irish services.[346] But the point is far from clear and it has not been asserted that additional powers in relation to civil unrest were granted. Indeed, since the 1920 Act expressly removed the power to suspend the Habeas Corpus Act,[347] powers in this area were effectively diminished.

The 1920 Act therefore clearly limited the options available to the Northern Ireland Parliament and Government in the security field. Most importantly, the bar on legislation in respect of the Army precluded the adoption of measures such as had been employed immediately previously by the British (DORA and ROIA). In practice, however, these checks were to a degree circumvented in a manner the constitutionality of which is examined below. In order to place this examination in context, the question of martial law must first be examined.

Martial law

As Calvert points out, both Great Britain and Northern Ireland shared the same common law on the regulation of public order.[348] It does not automatically follow, however, that the non-statutory powers available to the Northern Ireland Government were the same as those available to the British Government. Here the effect of the creation of a subordinate jurisdiction within the United Kingdom on these non-statutory powers is examined. Somewhat different considerations apply with the common law theory than with the prerogative theory, and it is necessary to examine them separately.

The prerogative theory

Prerogative powers are vested in the monarch. In practice, this generally means the Government of the day. In Northern Ireland, prerogative and

---

[343] Ibid. s. 8 (8).

[344] s. 8 (3).

[345] *R* v. *Governor of Maidstone Prison, ex parte Maguire* [1925] 59 *ILTR* 63. The case is discussed below.

[346] See Calvert, *Constitutional Law*, 327–30. The text of the letters patent of 9 Dec. 1922 is included in Quekett, *Constitution*, pt. III, pp. 75–81.

[347] s. 67 of the 1920 Act repealed s. 16 of the Habeas Corpus (Ireland) Act 1781, which allowed for suspension.

[348] *Constitutional Law*, 380. However, the differences noted on pp. 127–8, particularly in the sphere of prerogative powers, should be borne in mind.

other executive powers in relation to 'Irish services' were vested in the Governor of Northern Ireland. It did not automatically follow, however, that the position of the Northern Ireland Government *vis-à-vis* the Governor's delegated prerogative powers was exactly the same as that which obtained between the monarch and the British Government. In practice, there seems to have been some confusion on the issue.

In the case of the Derry IRA prisoners under sentence of death in 1922, the Governor had exercised the prerogative of mercy at the behest of the British Government and against the wishes of the Northern Ireland Government.[349] The justification he advanced for this course was that the advice of the Northern Ireland Government had to be 'modified in the event of my considering the special interests affecting the Empire etc.'.[350] Unionists retorted that 'a grave outrage has been committed against the Northern Parliament and against constitutional law'.[351]

In other circumstances, the Governor might not be permitted to act in defiance of the wishes of the Northern Ireland Government. The question of what these circumstances might be arose for discussion out of the refusal of the Northern Ireland Government to appoint a member to the Boundary Commission. As a result of this refusal, the Judicial Committee of the Privy Council had a number of questions referred to it, among them the query 'Whether . . . it is competent for the Crown, acting on the advice of Ministers of the United Kingdom to instruct the Governor of Northern Ireland, in default of advice from His Ministers, to make an appointment . . . ?'[352] The answer was in the negative (31 July 1924): 'The appointment is not committed to the Governor, who only acts in this matter as the mouthpiece of his Ministers responsible to Parliament.'[353]

The Privy Council was also asked 'Whether it is competent for the Crown, acting on the advice of Minsters of the United Kingdom, to make the appointment . . . ?' The answer was again in the negative:

their Lordships consider that any view of a remanent prerogative in His Majesty to make such an appointment cannot be entertained. In the first place it is not a question of settling boundaries but of supplying a *casus improvisus* in an Act of Parliament, a procedure to which the prerogative could not be held to extend. But further, even supposing it could be looked on as a question of boundary, their Lordships consider that the case of *Attorney General* v. *De Keysers Royal Hotel Ltd* settled that once any matter which includes something which might fall within the prerogative is dealt with in an Act of Parliament to which his Majesty has

---

[349] See p. 274.
[350] Quoted in Buckland, *Factory of Grievances*, 209.
[351] Ibid. 209.
[352] Cmnd. 2214 (1924), 'Report of the Judicial Committee of the Privy Council as Approved by His Majesty in Council of the 31st July 1924, on the Questions Connected with the Irish Boundary Commission referred to the Said Committee', 2.
[353] Ibid. 3.

necessarily assented, all within the ambit of the matter so dealt with can only be dealt with in the future as the Act of Parliament directs and cannot be affected by an exercise of the prerogative outside the provisions of the Act.[354]

In other circumstances the 'mouthpiece' approach might be less emphasized. Thus in *R* v. *Governor of Maidsone Prison, ex parte Maguire*[355] (21 and 22 April 1925) a prisoner who had been convicted of explosives offences in Northern Ireland, and then transferred to England to serve his sentence, sought to challenge his detention before the English King's Bench Division. His principal claim was that the Governor of Northern Ireland, on whose authority the order had been made,[356] was not the person entitled to make the order, on the grounds that under the Government of Ireland Act 1920, the Governor only succeeded to the prerogative powers of the Lord-Lieutenant, whose executive powers were transferred to the Northern Ireland Minister for Home Affairs. Hewart CJ briefly dismissed this argument:

The argument is that . . . the powers which the Lord Lieutenant formerly had as regards prisons have been taken away, and are now vested in the Secretary for the Home Department. In my opinion that contention is erroneous, and pays too little attention to s. 8 (3) of the Government of Ireland Act, 1920, which provides for the exercise of the powers of the Lord Lieutenant 'through', not 'by', the departments. I think that this order was lawfully made.[357]

It appears that two main propositions can be extracted from the foregoing. First, it appears that where in Northern Ireland statutory powers did not exist in the same area as prerogative powers (as for instance in relation to the prerogative of mercy), the Governor of Northern Ireland did not see himself as bound by the wishes of the Northern Ireland Government, despite the fact that his jurisdiction in the matter was grounded in the 1920 Act. Secondly, where statutory powers existed in the same area as the prerogative, the De Keyser principle applied in Northern Ireland as in the rest of the United Kingdom, with the result that the powers could be exercised only in accordance with the statute. It appears that under this rule, the Governor would be bound in relation to matters falling within his sphere of authority just as the monarch would in relation to his.

How does this apply to the question of martial law? It is clear that on the prerogative theory martial law proper could not be imposed solely at the behest of the Northern Ireland Government. This was in practice the

---

[354] Ibid. 4.
[355] 59 ILTR 63.
[356] In fact, the order had been made by two Lords Justices duly appointed to act in the absence of the Governor, but no claim was made as to the validity of this delegation.
[357] At p. 64.

case anyway, as control of the British Army remained with Whitehall. Powers in this area came within the competence of the Governor only if they fell within the definition of 'Irish services'. But 'Irish services' were concerned only with 'civil government' and the Army remained an excepted matter. The question of the role of the Army is of particular importance for the prerogative theory, as unlike the common law theory, it traces the origins of martial law to the Court of the Constable and the Marshal.[358] This did not mean that prerogative powers in the area of civil disorder falling short of the imposition of martial law were denied to the Executive in Northern Ireland. However, because such powers were under the prerogative theory vested in the Governor, it would seem by analogy to the issue of the prerogative of mercy, the Governor might not feel himself bound to follow the wishes of the Northern Ireland Government in the exercise of these powers.

What of the position of the British Government under the prerogative theory? Assuming that 'Irish services' did not include powers in relation to martial law, the relevant provision of the 1920 Act was section 8 (1) which provided: 'The executive power . . . in Northern Ireland shall continue vested in His Majesty the King, and nothing in this Act shall affect the exercise of that power except as respects Irish services as defined for the purposes of this Act.' Clearly this catch-all clause was sufficiently widely phrased to include possible prerogative martial law powers. Therefore, the prerogative theory would effectively vest in the British Government the power to impose martial law in Northern Ireland.

There remains, however, the question of the effect of the De Keyser case and Egan's case on the exercise of this right. ROIA remained on the statute books and Egan's case therefore seems directly applicable. If so, martial law could not be imposed in Northern Ireland. It might be argued that the situation in Northern Ireland in 1922 could be distinguished from that of the South in 1921, in that the creation of a substate in Northern Ireland rendered the enforcement of ROIA politically impossible, as evidenced by the virtual non-application of the Act. But this is primarily a political argument, and would be unlikely to succeed before a court willing, in principle, to follow Egan's case. Even if that argument were accepted, it might still be claimed that once the Special Powers Act had become law, that measure served to place a brake on the prerogative, since it was essentially a version of DORA and therefore of ROIA.[359] The British Cabinet was certainly aware of the overlap between the Special Powers Act and martial law. When in May 1922 the question of martial law in Northern Ireland was discussed, it was noted that the

---

[358] See pp. 125–8.
[359] The point is discussed further below.

effect of the Northern Ireland statute was to create powers similar to those exercised under martial law, the only significant omission being the establishment of military courts.[360] However, comparisons between the Northern Ireland and the British legislation raise further questions of *vires*, which are examined below.

The common law theory

Since the seventeenth century the common law of England in this area had developed in response to civil disorder falling short of insurrection. There existed a body of indigenous English precedent governing legal response to riot, but that relating to armed insurrection proper came mostly from overseas, and it was these overseas precedents which were relied upon when martial law was imposed in parts of the South in December 1920.

The situation in the North differed from that in the South in that the nature of the Northern civil unrest corresponded more with that which had prompted the development of English common law. In the three years of sporadic rioting in Belfast from 1920 to 1922, formal authority for the use of force in its suppression lay with the Lord Mayor of Belfast as the city's Chief Magistrate[361] in the same way as authority and responsibility had lain with the Bristol magistrates at the time of the Bristol riots case.[362]

With the creation of Northern Ireland and the transfer of responsibility for the police to the Northern Ireland Government in November 1921, the question arises as to what powers were vested at common law in the Northern Ireland Government itself and in its agencies for the suppression of disorder. The 1920 Act made no specific mention of common law powers as it had done of prerogative powers, but it may be assumed that the common law was implicitly applicable—certainly the RUC and Special Constables were made aware that the common law rules on the use of firearms (as modified by the Special Powers Act) applied to them.[363] The question is less one of deriving common law powers from the new constitutional arrangements than of fitting these new arrangements into the existing common law framework.

Apologists for the common law theory of martial law have adopted as a

---

[360] See Palley, 'Northern Ireland Constitution', 400 n. 160.

[361] Buckland, *Factory of Grievances*, 182.

[362] *R* v. *Pinney* (1832) 3 B & Ad. 947. Therein, Littledale J., in his address to the jury, stated: 'a party entrusted with the duty of putting down a riot whether by virtue of an office of his own seeking (as in the case of a magistrate) or imposed upon him (as in the case of a constable) was bound to hit the exact line between excess and failure of duty.' For a brief discussion of the case see Greer, 'Military Intervention', 584–5.

[363] See Ministry of Home Affairs Circular of 15 June 1925 on the use of firearms, HA 27/1/1, PRONI. Some details of the circular are given in n. 149 above.

central tenet the proposition that the difference between riot and insurrection is one of degree rather than of substance. According to this view
the 'repelling of force by force' in the suppression of an insurrection by
the imposition of martial law is but a logical extension of the right to use
force in quelling a riot. It might therefore be argued that since the RUC
was clearly empowered at common law to suppress riots, the Northern
Ireland Government was by logical extension empowered during times of
war or armed rebellion to impose a form of martial law administered
perhaps through the use of the Special Constabulary. Indeed, the manner
in which the 'B' Specials sometimes operated (for instance in carrying out
round-ups such as those described above) would suggest that they clearly
exceeded their statutory power and that if any legal basis were to be
found for their actions, it would have to be at common law.

Some support for this viewpoint might be found in Childers' case
wherein O'Connor MR had rejected a challenge to the Free State Army's
military court system holding that the 'right to organize an army for the
protection of the people' was a 'right inherent in any Government. No
government can exist unless there is some physical force behind it'.[364]
Similarly, Pim J., in *R (Johnstone)* v. *O'Sullivan*,[365] had stated in relation
to the powers of the Provisional Government: 'I cannot imagine any person denying the right of every Government, no matter whether absolute
or limited in powers, to protect itself, and in case of hostile attack, to
meet force by force.'[366]

The position of the Provisional Government under the Irish Free State
(Agreement) Act 1922 at the time of those cases was somewhat analogous
to that of the Northern Ireland Government under the 1920 Act. Defence
functions had not then been transferred by Order in Council to the
Provisional Government, and the National Army was without a statutory
basis, while in Northern Ireland, of course, matters connected with defence remained excepted.

But while these arguments might on paper appear at least partially
convincing, the realities of political power would tend to dismiss them. As
Palley points out, 'constitutional schemes . . . must "be in accordance
with political reality" and must conform to the patterns established by
"institutionalized force" '.[367] The decision in Childers' case, essentially a
constitutional one, derived its significance from the degree to which it
accorded with political reality in the legitimization of the institutionalized
force of the Provisional Government.

---

[364] *R (Childers)* v. *Adjutant-General of the Provisional Forces* [1923] 1 *IR* 5, at 14. See
pp. 247–50.
[365] [1923] 2 *IR* 13.
[366] p. 30.
[367] 'Northern Ireland Constitution', 450.

The Northern Ireland Government, on the other hand, was never intended to achieve that degree of independence towards which the South was then moving. The 1920 Act ensured that ultimate responsibility would remain at Westminster, and it is there that responsibility for decisions on the imposition of martial law would lie. For the Northern Ireland Government to have itself invoked non-statutory martial law powers would have amounted to a blatant flouting of the limiting provisions of the 1920 Act (though this did not mean that there was a legal bar on resort to common law powers falling short of martial law in certain circumstances).

Conclusion

It is very difficult to imagine any court validating the imposition of martial law by the Government of Northern Ireland, whether based on common law or on the prerogative. Such a policy option was effectively open only to the British Government and, as Egan's case illustrates, its adoption would have presented formidable constitutional problems as long as ROIA remained on the statute book. But neither would the imposition of martial law by the British Government have been 'in accordance with political reality' as, by undermining the authority of the Northern Ireland Government, it would effectively have set aside the enabling provisions of the 1920 Act.

The position in Northern Ireland, therefore, was that as long as a subordinate Government operated, full-blown martial law was a political impossibility and a lawyer's nightmare. This helps to explain Craig's rejection of martial law in March 1922 in favour of something which lawyers would see as less of an impossibility, but which opposition politicians could regard only as a nightmare: the Special Powers Act.

Statutory emergency powers: the question of *vires*

If analysis of the question of martial law in Northern Ireland highlights the difficulties arising from the complexities of the 1920 Act, the same could be said of the question of statutory emergency powers in that jurisdiction. Some issues appeared clear-cut, others highly debatable. In this section, one relatively clear-cut case, that of the Criminal Procedure Act (Northern Ireland) 1922, is first examined, before moving on to the much more difficult question posed by the Special Powers Act.

The Criminal Procedure Act

As has been noted above, 'all matters relating to the Supreme Court of Northern Ireland'[368] remained reserved matters under the 1920 Act. Even

---

[368] s. 47 (1).

before the formal introduction of the Criminal Procedure Bill in April 1922, it was obvious that, by providing for the creation of a 'Special Court', the measure was of doubtful validity. As Craig put it in a telegram to the Irish Office: 'Grave doubts have arisen . . . as to power of local parliament in a matter affecting High Court of Judicature which is a reserved matter in Act of 1920.'[369]

Shortly thereafter there was a reappraisal, and the Northern Ireland parliamentary draftsman was reported to have decided that the matter was within the scope of the Parliament, although he was 'not quite sure whether there may not be some financial questions which require the confirmation of the Imperial Government'.[370] This emphasis on financial matters appears strange, as a more obvious line of attack would have been to suggest that one effect of the Supreme Court's being a reserved matter was to preclude the Parliament of Northern Ireland from creating any courts designed to exercise a jurisdiction overlapping with, or analogous to, that of the Supreme Court, including the criminal jurisdiction of the High Court. The argument in relation to financial matters was that as the Supreme Court of Judicature was a reserved matter, and as the public services in connection therewith were, under section 8 (8), reserved services, the costs of which were met by deduction from the Irish share of reserved taxes (section 24 (1) (b)), there existed no power in the Parliament of Northern Ireland to provide for the expenses of the special court envisaged by the Act.[371]

The British Parliamentary counsel (Sir Frederick Liddell), and the Secretary to the provisional Government of Ireland Committee (Sir Francis Greer), were clear that confirmatory legislation would be required. Their view seems to have depended more on the overlap with the Supreme Court than on financial points. In the words of Greer: 'The Special Court is to be constituted of Supreme Court Judges and is to have the jurisdiction of a Court of Assize. I think you will agree that these matters may fairly be said to be or to impinge upon Supreme Court Matters.'[372] In the event, the confirmatory bill which was prepared covered all objections, including financial ones.[373] However, the matter was not proceeded with, as no use was made of the Act in Northern Ireland, and it was eventually repealed.

What the episode illustrates is that the Parliament of Northern Ireland

---

[369] Craig to Secretary of State, Irish Office, 3 Apr. 1922, CAB 6/56, PRONI.

[370] Spender to Secretary to the Provisional Government of Ireland Committee of the Cabinet, 6 Apr. 1922, ibid.

[371] These points are set out in Queckett to the AG for NI, 5 May 1922, ibid.

[372] Quoted ibid.

[373] See fn. 52, p. 276 for some of the relevant text. Financial matters were covered in clause 1 (2) of the draft bill.

was constitutionally prohibited from establishing special courts with a jurisdiction overlapping with the assizes (or with that of Belfast Crown Court). Special courts of summary jurisdiction were, however, another matter. This explains reliance on the latter type of court in the Special Powers Act.

The Special Powers Act

In considering the question of *vires* and the Special Powers Act two separate issues arise. The first is the question of whether the Special Powers Act was *intra vires* the 1920 Act; the second is whether the regulations made under the Act and the action taken on foot of them were *intra vires* the Act itself.

The 1920 Act

As noted above, under section 4 (1) of the 1920 Act, legislation in respect of *inter alia* the 'defence of the realm' was made an excepted matter. The expression 'defence of the realm' has a long legislative history but, as Queckett has observed, it is 'not easy to define with exactitude'.[374] Two possible approaches could be adopted in attempting to determine the meaning of the phrase as it is used in the 1920 Act. One would be to concentrate on the content of legislation for the defence of the realm, the other on its purpose.

On the question of content, the starting point would be the Defence of the Realm Acts and Regulations. In App. 3 the derivation of the Special Powers Act and Regulations made up to 31 December 1925 is set out. Of the original thirty-six regulations included as a schedule to the Special Powers Act, thirty-two were directly derived from DORR and two were derived from ROIR for which there was no direct DORR precedent. The remaining two were more Draconian than the DORR covering similar topics. Of the eleven new regulations issued up to December 1925 four were directly based on DORR; three were essentially amendments to, or extensions of, existing Special Powers Regulations; one covered similar ground to that covered by DORR but in different terms; one was based apparently on a martial law regulation (or at least imposing restrictions similar to those imposed under MLA regulations); and the remaining two were without DORR equivalents.

Of the twenty-eight sections and subsections which comprised the Special Powers Act itself, nine were based directly on DORR, three on ROIR for which there were no direct DORR precedents, one was similar in wording to DORR, and one to a section of ROIA. The remaining fourteen were derived neither from DORA/DORR nor ROIA/ROIR.

---

[374] *Constitution*, pt. III. See pp. 1–3 for a discussion of this matter.

In these provisions, as was pointed out in above, powers of arrest, search, and seizure were granted to the armed forces as they had been under DORR. In short, all of the DORR of counter-insurgency value, bar the use of courts martial, were re-enacted, and these were complemented by ROIR which had been developed specifically in response to the Irish situation. These considerations led Palley to observe: 'it is arguable that the legislative history of the Civil Authorities (Special Powers) Act 1922 which is clearly derived from the Defence of the Realm Consolidation Act 1914, shows that it was an Act for the defence of the realm and therefore *ultra vires* section 4 of the Government of Ireland Act.'[375] But it might be argued that the use of courts martial was a key element of DORA and that this omission alone from the Special Powers Act would serve to bring the Act outside the 'defence of the realm' category. To this it can be countered that from 1915 onwards use of DORA courts martial was effectively suspended in England and Wales yet the Act clearly remained an Act for the defence of the realm. In any case, the Second World War equivalents of DORA, the Emergency Powers (Defence) Acts, were clearly Acts 'for the defence of the realm'[376] but did not include the power to court-martial civilians. Instead, provision was made for the establishment of special civil courts.[377] No such courts were established,[378] but in some respects their planned outline was not dissimilar to that of the special summary courts established under the Special Powers Act. It seems clear that if content and derivation alone were the determining factors, then the Special Powers Acts were 'in respect of the defence of the realm' and therefore *ultra vires*.

It might be said, however, that the crucial issue is neither the derivation nor the content of the legislation but rather its purpose—that is its function and not its form. Section 4 of the 1920 Act excepted from the competence of the Northern Ireland Parliament legislation in respect of both 'matters arising from a state of war' and 'the defence of the realm'. Applying the rule of construction *inclusio unius est exclusio alterius*, it might be argued that a distinction was to be made between these two categories and that 'defence of the realm' should be read as 'defence of the realm *apart* from matters arising from a state of war'. A less tortuous construction would be to read the phrase as meaning 'defence of the realm *in addition to* matters arising from a state of war'. Some internal support for this view is provided by the fact that the 'state of war' exception is grouped among others, all concerned with war, whereas

---

[375] 'Northern Ireland Constitution', 401.

[376] s. 1 (1) of the Emergency Powers (Defence) Act 1939 enabled the making of 'defence regulations' for 'securing the public safety [and] the defence of the realm'.

[377] s. 1 (1) of the Emergency Powers (Defence) (No. 2) Act 1940.

[378] See *Halsbury's Laws of England*, fourth edn. (London, 1974), viii. 624 n. 3.

'defence of the realm' is placed among matters which while concerned with war ('the navy, the army, the airforce') are equally applicable in time of peace.

A further point which should be noted is that the prohibition applies to legislation *in respect of* certain matters rather than *for certain purposes*. The importance of this distinction is that legislation whose primary purpose covered matters within the competence of the Northern Ireland Parliament could yet be impugned if it touched upon excepted matters. Bearing in mind what Calvert has referred to as 'the high priority customarily accorded [by the courts] to questions of national security',[379] the pith and substance doctrine would appear to have less application in the present context.[380]

On a reasonable construction, therefore, the 'defence of the realm' exception covered certain matters even when the UK was not at war with a foreign country, and any Northern Ireland legislation which touched upon these matters was constitutionally suspect. It is difficult to be precise about what these matters entail. Queckett considered the category mutable:

the scope of this exception . . . must vary according to the defence policy which may from time to time be adopted by the Imperial Parliament and Government. In other words, a matter which, at any time, is within the scope of measures taken by the Imperial authorities with the object of the defence of the realm would be regarded as being to that extent outside the powers of the Parliament and Government of Northern Ireland.[381]

A narrow view would be that the category includes only defence matters relating to possible or actual conflicts with a foreign country. A broader view would be that it includes defence against both possible or actual external aggression and internal insurrection. A variant of this is that it includes defence against aggression by a foreign country, and at least during the course of such conflict, it also includes defence against internal rebellion. This third approach received judicial approval in *R* v. *Governor of Wormwood Scrubs Prison*,[382] which was concerned with the validity of the use of DORA in dealing with the Irish insurrection. In that case, in the words of the Earl of Reading CJ:

it was said that the power to make regulations at all was limited to the period of the war and to the purpose of securing the defence of the realm, and it was

---

[379] *Constitutional Law*, 225.

[380] In *Morton* v. *Air Ministry*, 1946 NI 136, the court expressed the view (albeit *obiter*) that the terms and conditions under which the department responsible for the Air Force employed civilian personnel constituted an 'Air Force' matter and therefore an excepted one under s. 4. See Calvert, *Constitutional Law*, 225.

[381] *Constitution*, pt. III, p. 3.

[382] 1920 2 KB 305. For a discussion of this case see pp. 117–18.

contended that the meaning of that was that the regulations were to be designed to protect the country against foreign enemies, and not against internal disorder or rebellion . . . To my mind this construction is not right. It gives too limited a meaning to the words of the statute. So long as the war continues . . . acts of rebellion which are in effect military operations against the executive power, must be acts which have the effect of weakening the forces which this country can oppose to the enemy and as such must be acts endangering the public safety and the defence of the realm.[383]

The case is therefore clear authority for the proposition that 'defence of the realm' includes defence during a war both against enemy countries and internal rebellion. The implications for the 1920 Act are that at least during the course of a war in which the UK was involved, legislation dealing with internal rebellion and disorder came under the 'defence of the realm' heading and thus became am excepted matter. Since the Special Powers Act was designed to deal with rebellion and disorder, it seems distinctly arguable that in such circumstances it amounted to legislation 'in respect of the defence of the realm' and was therefore *ultra vires*.

The meaning of 'defence of the realm' in times of international peace was not considered by the court in *R* v. *Governor of Wormwood Scrubs*.[384] It could be argued that 'defence of the realm' should be taken to include laws providing for defence, both during actual international conflict and during peacetime, against potential aggression by another country. If that is so, it would seem to be a corollary of the decision in that case that as rebellion in peacetime would weaken defence capacity against potential external aggression, legislation designed to deal with such disorder should also be considered to be 'in respect of the defence of the realm'. Though this might seem a strained construction, it is at least arguable that the Special Powers Act should be considered to have been *ultra vires* during both peacetime and wartime.

Abdication

Both Palley and the National Council for Civil Liberties' Report on the Special Powers Act (1936)[385] also suggest that the Act might have been challenged on the grounds that in granting such a wide regulation-making power to the Minister of Home Affairs, the Parliament of Northern Ireland was in fact abdicating its power under the 1920 Act. On this view, as Palley has put it:

the validity of the Civil Authorities (Special Powers) Act would depend whether a court was prepared to give flesh to the concept of 'abdication' as opposed to mere

---

[383] pp. 310–11.
[384] [1920] 2 *KB* 305.
[385] *The Special Powers Act of Northern Ireland* (London, 1936), 8–10.

delegation, and whether it would characterise the wide legislative power conferred on the minister as being of such width or scope of uncertainty that it was an endowment of the equivalent of the whole of the legislative power on a new legislative body not created by the Government of Ireland Act.[386]

On this point it is perhaps worth noting that in *Ernest* v. *Metropolitan Police Commissioner*[387] it was held that an alteration to the law by DORR 'was equivalent to an alteration made by Act of Parliament',[388] and that therefore the provisions of the Regulations were capable of overriding statutory provisions. This precedent would probably have been regarded as directly applicable to the Special Powers Regulations.

The Regulations and the 1920 Act

The Special Powers Regulations were open to the test of *vires* in respect of both the 1920 Act and the Special Powers Act. Under the former heading the question is whether the Regulations touched upon reserved or excepted matters or amounted to legislation against which there was a specific prohibition in the 1920 Act.

As the Regulations and parts of the Act conferred powers of search, seizure, and arrest on the armed forces, these provisions were open to challenge as being 'in respect of . . . the army'.[389] Almost fifty years later the Northern Ireland courts were prepared to hold that such powers of arrest were *ultra vires* the 1920 Act.[390] By extension, powers of search and seizure can also be considered to have been *ultra vires* in so far as they conferred powers on the military.

Under the 1920 Act, 'domicile' remained an excepted matter.[391] Regulation 23A[392] empowered the civil authority to make orders (generally referred to as 'exclusion orders') prohibiting persons from entering or residing in certain areas. Often these orders took the form of a bar on

---

[386] 'Northern Ireland Constitution', 403.

[387] [1919] 35 *TLR* 512.

[388] p. 513. See Ch. 2, n. 21.

[389] 1920 Act, s. 4.

[390] *R (Hume)* v. *Londonderry Justices* [1972] *NILR* 91. See K. Boyle, 'Human Rights and the Northern Ireland Emergency', in J. A. Andrews (ed.), *Human Rights in Criminal Procedure* (The Hague, 1982), 144–65. It would be a mistake, however, to draw from the case the conclusion that passage of time was all that was required to ensure a searching application of the test of *vires*. In *McEldowney* v. *Forde* [1970] *NILR* 11 a Regulation (24A) banning Republican clubs and 'any like organization howsoever described' was held to be *intra vires* the Special Powers Act by a majority of the House of Lords. There was, however, one other case on the Special Powers Act in which the courts took a critical approach. In *Great Northern Railway Board* v. *Minister of Home Affairs* [1962] *NILR* 24 it was held that an award of compensation by a County court judge under s. 11 of the Act could not be appealed by the Minister of Home Affairs. It is perhaps significant that the case involved property rather than individual rights.

[391] s. 4 (1).

[392] The text of this regulation is included in App. 3.

entry to and residence in all of Northern Ireland apart from a small specified area.[393] The NCCL Report concluded that this constituted in effect a bar on residence in Northern Ireland and therefore amounted to legislation in respect of domicile: 'there can be little doubt that the employment of "exclusion orders" for this purpose is unconstitutional as violating the provisions of the Government of Ireland Act'.[394] Certainly the Northern Ireland Authorities were sensitive about the issue and were keen to prevent the description of such orders as 'deportation orders'.[395] There is, of course, a difference in law between 'residence' and 'domicile'—questions of intent (the *animus manendi*) being of central importance in the determination of the latter. But it is clear that a bar on residence in a jurisdiction would prevent the establishment of a domicile therein.

In a defence of the Special Powers Act against the NCCL criticisms, Newark did not address the domicile point directly but merely noted that 'certainly none of the persons on whom such orders have been served ever thought it worthwhile to test the point in litigation'.[396] This, however, may be more a reflection of nationalist perception of the judiciary than of the validity of the substantive legal issue. Whether or not a court would be prepared to find the regulation *ultra vires* would depend on the extent to which that court was willing to look behind the form of the regulation at its substance.

Similar considerations apply to the question of habeas corpus. Section 67 of the 1920 Act removed the power to suspend the Habeas Corpus (Ireland) Act 1781. It might be assumed that habeas corpus was intended to be constitutionally entrenched in Northern Ireland. Clearly the framers of the 1920 Act intended to remove from Irish Home Rule Governments the power which the British Government had used in the nineteenth century in Ireland to detain persons without trial by the mechanism of suspending the Habeas Corpus Act.

Yet in Regulations 23 and 23B[397] the same effect was achieved without the explicit suspension of the 1781 Act. The NCCL Report considered that the effect of these Regulations (and those restricting access to detainees and providing for exclusion orders) was 'completely to abrogate the principles of Habeas Corpus which are fundamental to the British Constitution.'[398] Arguably, therefore, it would have been open to a court

---

[393] An example of this type of order can be found at HA 4/2/36, PRONI. See p. 287.
[394] NCCL Report, 19.
[395] See fn. 130, p. 284.
[396] 'Law and the Constitution', 50.
[397] These Regulations are analysed on pp. 290–8.
[398] NCCL Report, 21.

to hold that Regulations 23 and 23B were *ultra vires* the 1920 Act as in effect circumventing section 67. This view was not, however, accepted by a Northern Ireland Divisional Court[399] and parallel arguments also failed in the Irish Free State.[400]

A further point to be considered relates to the prohibition on the taking of property without compensation contained in section 5 of the 1920 Act. While it had been suggested that this prohibition had to do with religious property only, the view which came to be accepted by the courts was that it related to all forms of property.[401] Two Regulations permitted the confiscation of property without compensation, and for this reason the NCCL suggested that they were *ultra vires*.[402] Regulation 18 provided that property seized during a search could be 'destroyed or otherwise disposed of' on the orders of the civil authority, and Regulation 18C provided for the confiscation of money lodged in a bank when the civil authority suspected that 'such money or property has been collected or obtained or is being used, or intended to be used, for any purpose prejudicial to the preservation of the peace or maintenance of order in Northern Ireland'. Under neither Regulation was there a requirement for a court hearing.

The test of vires *with respect to the Special Powers Act*

For two reasons, less scope existed for challenging the Regulations as being *ultra vires* the Act than existed for a challenge in respect of the 1920 Act. First, the initial thirty-six Regulations were enacted as a schedule to the Act. They could not therefore be challenged as being *ultra vires* the Act as they had not been made under the regulation-making power created by the Act. This was presumably the reason for adopting them as a schedule. The practice under DORA and ROIA had been different: the bare statutory provisions were first enacted and then all the Regulations were made under the powers thereby created.

The second reason is that while the 1920 Act contained a check-list of excepted and reserved matters and prohibited purposes against which provisions could be measured, the Special Powers Act merely incorporated a blanket power to make regulations 'for the preservation of the peace and maintenance of order'.[403] While this opened the possibility to a test of *vires*, the number of regulations open to challenge was very small.

---

[399] *R (O'Hanlon)* v. *Governor of Belfast Prison*, 56 ILTR 170. The case is discussed below.

[400] *R (O'Connell)* v. *Military Governor of Hare Park Camp* [1924] 2 *IR* 104. See pp. 262–6.

[401] See Newark, 'Constitution of Northern Ireland', 13.

[402] NCCL Report, 7–8.

[403] s. 3.

In the period in question only the eleven first Regulations made up to the end of 1925, together with the amendments made to the original Regulations, were open to challenge as being *ultra vires* the Act, and bearing in mind the flexible attitude of the courts to the test of *vires* in the DORA cases, it seems unlikely that a court would have been inclined to impugn any of the Regulations.

Arguably, the only viable ground for judicial challenge which the Act itself created was the provision in section 1 (1) (derived from DORR 1[404]) that 'the ordinary course of law and the avocations of life shall be interfered with as little as may be permitted by the exigencies of the steps required to be taken under this Act'. As this provision is included at the end of a section empowering the civil authority 'to take all such steps and issue all such orders' in accordance with the Act and Regulations, it seems properly to refer not to the making of regulations but rather to the exercise of powers under the Regulations and the Act.[405] Thus it would appear that any measure taken under the Act would be open to challenge as not having been strictly required by the circumstances.

The courts and emergency powers: O'Hanlon's case

What the above tends to illustrate is that the legal foundations of the Special Powers Act were far from perfectly secure. The constitutionality of either the entirety of the Act or many of its provisions was open to challenge on several grounds, and had a court been disposed to look critically at the issue, a way was clearly open. In *R (O'Hanlon)* v. *Governor of Belfast Prison*[406] this opportunity was not taken. Were it not for the fact that this is the only Northern Ireland case on emergency law in this period, it is unlikely that this simplistic judgment would receive very much attention.

The applicant, who had initially been detained under Regulation 23, and subsequently interned under Regulation 23B, sought to challenge his internment in habeas corpus proceedings before the Northern Ireland High Court. The report of the case is not a model of clarity but it seems that two main grounds were relied upon. First, O'Hanlon attacked the factual basis of any allegations against him by submitting an affidavit in which he denied involvement in any unlawful association or conspiracy. Secondly, it was submitted that the introduction of internment under the Special Powers Act amounted to the suspension of habeas corpus contrary to the terms of the 1920 Act.

The judgment of the court was delivered by Henry LCJ, a man who

---

[404] See App. 3.
[405] This was the view later taken by the House of Lords in *Forde* v. *McEldowney* [1970] *NILR* 11.
[406] [1922] 56 *ILTR* 170.

was no stranger to emergency law issues.[407] The factual basis of the plaintiff's claim was briefly dismissed: 'the only question the court has to decide in an application of this kind is whether at the moment the matter comes before us O'Hanlon is legally held. We have nothing to do with the consideration of whether there is any evidence against him.'[408]

On the legal issues, the court stated:

this [internment] order is a modification—it is really nothing new—of orders made in England almost every day by the Home Secretary there during the war dealing with persons of hostile origin or hostile associations. The House of Lords in Halliday's case decided that the Home Secretary had power to make such orders, and that the Court was prevented from interfering with them. We decide that . . . the regulations are not *ultra vires*.[409]

Thus the court did not address itself at all to the question of whether or not habeas corpus had effectively been suspended. The assumption that Halliday's case was automatically directly applicable ignored the crucial difference between the unfettered legislative competence of Westminster and the subordinate nature of the Northern Ireland legislature.

Palley criticized the decision on the grounds that the court overlooked the 'apparently objective . . . limitation' contained in the Special Powers Act that 'the ordinary course of law and avocations of life and the enjoyment of property shall be interfered with as little as may be permitted by the exigencies of the steps required to be taken under this Act'.[410]

The decision has also been criticized in *Halsbury's Statutes* (1950) both for its refusal to investigate the factual evidence and for its shortcomings in interpretation.[411] It is pointed out that in Halliday's case Lord Wrenbury expressly stated that if the appellant's case was that he had neither hostile origin nor associates he could have his writ of habeas corpus on the ground that it was so, and if he established that fact he could be discharged'.[412] Thus it is argued that such an investigation was open to the court in Hanlon's case. Against this view it must be said that in *R v. Governor of Wormwood Scrubs Prison*[413] the applicant, an internee, had also sought to challenge the factual basis of the allegations made against him but the English King's Bench Division, purportedly relying on Halliday's case, had refused to go into the matter.

On the question of interpretation, Halsbury's asserts that O'Hanlon's

---

[407] See biographical sketch in n. 273.
[408] p. 172.
[409] Ibid.
[410] 'Northern Ireland Constitution', 401.
[411] *Halsbury's Statutes of England*, second edn. (London, 1950), xvii. 169.
[412] p. 308.
[413] [1920] 2 *KB* 305.

case failed to take into account the material difference between the Defence of the Realm Act and the Special Powers Act:

the power under the Defence of the Realm Act 1914 was wider than that under the present [Special Powers] Act, for it was 'to issue regulations for the public safety and the defence of the realm'. Nevertheless the court in Halliday's case did consider whether the regulation whose validity was attacked was for the public safety and defence of the realm . . . The effect of O'Hanlon's case is to construe 'The civil authority shall have power . . . to take steps . . . as may be necessary' as 'The civil authority shall have power to take all such steps as may appear to him to be necessary'.[414]

Thus viewed, O'Hanlon's case can be considered as marking the virtual abandonment of the test of *vires* in the sphere of delegated emergency legislation, and therefore as the ultimate development of a process begun in the cases on the interpretation of DORA.

Judicial scrutiny: conclusions

The complexities of the 1920 Act meant that whatever emergency measures were taken in Northern Ireland, statutory or non-statutory, were likely to have presented a great many justiciable issues. Martial law, whether on the common law or prerogative theory, is particularly problematical. In Northern Ireland the difficulty arises not only because of the institutional tensions which would have surfaced, as they do in any jurisdiction under martial law, but also because its imposition would effectively have undermined the authority on which the substate was based.

   In the sphere of statutory emergency powers the list of excepted and reserved matters created a framework within which great scope existed for the application of the test of *vires*. The most important limitations were those in respect of the Army and of the defence of the realm. It is distinctly arguable that the Special Powers Act was *ultra vires* the 1920 Act: first, because its content was virtually identical with elements of DORA; secondly, because the phrase 'defence of the realm' was open to the interpretation of covering response to insurrectionary situations such as existed in Northern Ireland. If so, legislation designed to cope with such situations fell to be considered as legislation in respect of the defence of the realm. Since this was clearly the original purpose of the Special Powers Act, the measure could be considered as falling within that category.

   Apart from the possibilities which existed for challenging the Act *in toto*, there also existed grounds for piecemeal challenge. Those sections and regulations which granted powers to the Army were of doubtful

[414] p. 169.

validity, while individual regulations, and actions carried out pursuant to them, were open to the test of *vires* with respect to the main Act.

Had the Northern Ireland courts been disposed to look critically at these issues there can be little doubt that the way was open. Instead, the decision in O'Hanlon's case represented a degree of judicial abdication. In this respect the decision can be seen as marking continuity with the British and Irish emergency law decisions of the previous years.

5. Conclusions

Levels of coercion

Typology of emergency powers

Valid comparison of the emergency measures taken in each of the three jurisdictions under discussion requires the generation of a typology of emergency powers within which the approach adopted in each jurisdiction can be located. This typology (which makes no claims to be applicable beyond the specific measures with which this work is concerned), can be constructed by adopting a series of indicators delineating different 'levels of coercion'. Each succeeding level will generally have all the elements present in lower levels, and will always have certain additional elements.

Each 'measure' adopted in a jurisdiction (typically though not exclusively an Act of Parliament) can be examined for the presence of one or more indicators, and the indicator for the highest level present defines that measure's place in the typology. Thus if a particular piece of legislation is found to contain the second and third indicators it will be located at the third level (L_3).

The 'approach' in any jurisdiction is defined by the highest level of any measure in force. Thus if in a given jurisdiction three measures are employed which are respectively located at L_2, L_3, and L_5, the 'approach' is defined as L_5. If, on the other hand, there are on the statute book measures which locate at L_2 and L_4, but if only the L_2 measure is in operation, the approach is defined as L_2.

Overall, seven indicators can be identified, resulting in seven levels of coercion. The starting point is the ordinary law. Although ordinary legal powers may not have been much used in response to the emergencies with which this work is concerned, they do provide a convenient point of departure. This is particularly so as the ordinary law was virtually identical in all of the jurisdictions under discussion. The first indicator can therefore be described as follows:

L_1. Only the provisions of the ordinary law may be invoked in response to politically motivated crime.

Above the ordinary law comes the situation in which special offences are created, but otherwise the legal system remains unchanged. This leads to the second indicator:

L_2. Special offences exist which penalize certain types of political activity but these offences are tried in the ordinary manner.

At a further level, the trial process will be altered in relation to certain categories of offence or in a discretionary manner. These alterations may range from changes in the composition of juries, to the institution of special courts, but all such changes will be designed primarily to cope with politically motivated crime. The third indicator is therefore:

L_3. Special procedures are applicable for the trial of politically motivated crime.

In the levels defined thus far, adherence to the ideology of the rule of law has been maintained to a greater or lesser degree.[1] A clear break occurs, however, where this adherence is abandoned in favour of internment, or indefinite detention without trial, and there can be no question of this being merely an arbitrarily defined point on a continuum. Internment is clearly a parallel mechanism, operating outside the normal legal system, and permitting all ordinary safeguards in relation to detention to be effectively circumvented. The indicator for this level is simple:

L_4. Persons are subject to indefinite administrative detention.

Since at L_4 suspects can be 'taken out of circulation' simply by administrative act, it might be assumed that this would be the highest level relied upon short of the outbreak of semi-conventional warfare. This, however, is not the case, and states will rarely rely solely on an L_4 mechanism, unless prohibited for constitutional reasons from going further. The reasons why will be examined further below, suffice to say at this stage that a desire to confer legitimacy on the process will frequently lead states to the next level, which is where a parallel apparatus of such breadth is created, that this apparatus could be said to constitute a parallel legal system. The criteria which can be employed in determining whether this apparatus constitutes a system are as follows: (1) Was there a special rule-making process? (2) Were the offences thereby created enforced through special tribunals or courts? (3) Were special executive powers granted under the special rule-making power? Typically, these special executive powers will include powers in relation to indefinite detention. Typically also, there will be special rules in force in relation to inquests, and this will correspond with an apparent policy of assassination of suspected insurgents by the state's security forces. The indicator for L_5 is therefore as follows:

L_5. A parallel legal system is created under statutory powers.

(1) There exists a special rule-making process.

---

[1] In this context, 'rule of law' is taken to have not Dicey's traditional meaning (supremacy of regular law, equality before the law, and the Constitution as the result of the ordinary law of the land), but rather to connote a broad political doctrine involving government according to law. See Wade and Bradley, *Constitutional and Administrative Law*, 91–104.

(2) Offences are created by this special rule-making process which are triable through special courts or tribunals.

(3) Special executive powers are granted under the special rule-making process.

L_5 is truly legal in the sense that it is based on statutory authority. The system under martial law differs in that specifically martial law measures have no basis in statute. Although legal form may be maintained (for example in the institution of military courts), it is form devoid of substance. For this reason it can be categorized as 'pseudo-legal'. At L_6 the breadth of this pseudo-legalism is such that, under the criteria outlined above, it could be said to constitute a pseudo-legal system. The indicator is as follows:

L_6. A pseudo-legal system is created under non-statutory powers.

(1) There exists a special rule-making process, but rules thus created have no standing in strict law.

(2) Offences are created by this special rule-making process which are triable through pseudo-courts or tribunals.

(3) Special executive powers are granted under the special rule-making process.

L_6 could probably fairly be described as the ultimate counter-insurgency mechanism. The terms in which the conflict is defined are taken to require some adherence to legal form. Where, however, the nature of the fighting has progressed beyond that implicit in the 'counter-insurgency model' and corresponds with conventional warfare a new level has been reached. Concern with legal form (even pseudo-legal form) will be absent. Typically this occurs in a civil war situation or in the final phase of an insurrection. Domestic legal standards will not be referred to, consequently this level can be described as 'infra-legal'. International humanitarian law may or may not be applicable, and the question of its applicability or otherwise is certain to be politically contentious and hotly debated. Thus:

L_7. No domestic legal standards are applied. The situation corresponds with conventional warfare. International humanitarian law may be applicable.

British rule

If this typology is applied to the emergency measures adopted under British rule in the years 1918–21 it is obvious that the Criminal Law and Procedure (Ireland) Act 1887 is located at L_3 by virtue of its provisions permitting alteration to jury trial. This does not define the approach, however, since the 1887 Act coexisted with DORA and ROIA. ROIA incorporated a special rule-making power (the power to create ROIR), and offences created under this power were tried by a variety of special courts (courts martial). In addition, special executive powers were granted to the CMA. Because these three criteria are met, ROIA can be said to have constituted a parallel legal system. This was also true of DORA as applied to Ireland, particularly from January 1920 onwards. It was because DORA amounted to a complete system that its introduction has been described as 'a statutory imposition of martial law'.[2]

Reliance on DORA and ROIA therefore constituted an L_5 approach. The declaration of martial law under non-statutory powers in December 1920 signalled a shift to L_6. Pseudo-legal courts and tribunals were created (military courts, summary courts, and drumhead courts), a special rule-making procedure was invoked (the martial law proclamation), and special executive powers became exercisable by the Military Governor-General and by his subordinate Military Governors. Thus a pseudo-legal system was created.

The Irish Free State

At the start of the Irish Civil War the approach can be defined as infra-legal (L_7) in that the conflict corresponded with conventional warfare, and domestic legal standards whether truly legal or pseudo-legal were not relied upon in the conduct of this stage of the conflict. With the switch to guerrilla warfare there was a shift to L_6 with the adoption of the Army Emergency Powers Resolution. The military courts and committees established on foot of the Resolution can be considered to have been pseudo-legal because they were without statutory authority. The apparatus as a whole met the criteria for a system set out above, because (1) there was a special rule-making power in two senses (the parliamentary resolution and the subordinate power to make general orders given to the Army Council); (2) the special offences thus created were tried by military courts and committees; and (3) the Army Council was given special executive powers (for example in relation to firearms).

The constitutional prohibition on the creation of special courts, except during a period of war or armed rebellion, meant that there could be no introduction in the Irish Free State of a parallel legal system, so that with the ending of martial law there was a drop from L_6 to L_4. At L_4 comes the Public Safety (Emergency Powers) (No. 2) Act 1923 and the Public Safety (Powers of Arrest and Detention) Temporary Act 1924, both of which provided for internment without trial. At L_3 comes the Public Safety (Punishment of Offences) Temporary Act 1924, which incorporated special procedural trial provisions, though without internment powers. However, since for most of the period during which this Act

---

[2] See p. 118.

was in operation the Public Safety (Powers of Arrest and Detention) Temporary Act 1924 was simultaneously in force, the overall approach remained at L$_4$. The lapse of the Public Safety Acts was followed by the enactment of the Treasonable Offences Act 1925, a measure which although it did create a number of special offences, did not alter trial procedures, and can thus be located at L$_2$.

Northern Ireland

In Northern Ireland the Criminal Procedure Act (Northern Ireland) 1922 can formally be located at L$_3$ in the proposed typology by virtue of its provisions allowing for trial of a range of offences by a special court, but the fact that these provisions were never invoked means that this classification is without practical significance. The important issue is where the Special Powers Acts and Regulations are to be located, and the question to be answered is whether or not these measures constituted a parallel legal system.

In order to answer this question the first issue to be tackled is whether there was a special rule-making power, and the answer is clearly in the affirmative, as such a power was given in the regulation-making power under the Act. The issue of the second criterion for the existence of a system, the question of resort to special courts, is answered by the provision for the creation of special courts of two Resident Magistrates to try breaches of the regulations, provisions which were extensively used in the years 1922–4. The third question is whether special executive powers were granted under the special rule-making power. Again the answer is in the affirmative. The civil authority was given a range of such powers which were in line with those granted to the CMA under ROIA, and he in turn was authorized to delegate these powers, and on occasion so delegated to the police.

Calvert's comment in relation to the Special Powers Act that 'for a government disposed to establish a police state in Northern Ireland, there is a clear way open' has been noted above.[3] In the years 1922–4, during which the Special Powers Act and Regulations were being vigorously enforced and developed, the institution of a parallel legal system at L$_5$ of the proposed typology could be said to have amounted to the creation of a police state in the same way as varieties of statutory and non-statutory martial law were being used under British rule and in the Irish Free State.

Three kinds of police state have been identified by Chapman:[4] the first is the 'traditional police state' a phenomenon which emerged in the eighteenth century, the founding fathers of which were Frederick William and Frederick II of Prussia and Joseph II of Austria. Its predominant feature was a paternalistic modernism. The second is the 'modern police

---

[3] *Constitutional Law*, 383. See p. 278.
[4] B. Chapman, *Police State* (London, 1970).

'state', a typical example of which is Germany in the 1933–9 period. In this form of organization, institutions which may be in conflict with the police, especially the political police, are either removed or neutralized, though the force or forces remain subject to the will of the political elite. Finally, there is the 'totalitarian police state', of which Germany in the years 1940–5 provides a prime example. Once this level is reached, the police *apparat* replaces the dominant party as the ideologues of the state.

As regards its emergency legal code, Northern Ireland in the years 1922–4 approximated most closely to the modern police state. The delegation of indefinite detention powers to the police, coupled with the vast array of sweeping police powers also granted by the Special Powers Act, removed the regular police (RUC) and the paramilitary reserve (Specials) from the normal constraints of the law. And as O'Hanlon's case illustrated, the judiciary was in effect neutralized in this sphere. Political analysis of the nature of the Northern Ireland state is outside the scope of this work, suffice it to say that continuous single-party rule in Northern Ireland meant that Parliament would place only such brakes on the security *apparat* as the dominant elite would allow it to.

The struggle for legitimacy

The elements of the emergency law of the three jurisdictions under discussion can now be illustrated according to the suggested seven-level typology (Table 27). But if this typology is useful for assessing the relative severity of the measures adopted, there are limits to the answers it, of itself, can provide. Why, for instance, was it that the measures which the Irish Free State took at L_6 and L_7 appeared to work (in the sense that the Free State side won the Civil War), while the measure taken by the British at L_6 seemed ineffectual and often counter-productive? And why is it that the measures taken in Northern Ireland at L_5 have generally attracted more criticism than those taken by the Irish Free State at L_6? The answer must lie in the different bases of legitimacy in the three jurisdictions; in emergency law the question of 'who was responsible' is at least as important as that of 'what was done?'

British rule: a crisis of legitimacy

It is a truism that the assembly of the first Dáil and the emergence of the Republican guerrilla campaign in 1919 and 1920 heralded a crisis of legitimacy for British rule in Ireland. The electoral successes of Sinn Féin meant that a mandate for the maintenance of the union was almost entirely lacking outside the North-East. In order to explain away the phenomenon, the activities of the Irish Volunteers were dismissed as 'a conspiracy' which was 'terrorising the majority of the community'.[5]

---

[5] See pp. 20–1.

TABLE 27. Levels of coercion

	L₁ Ordinary law	L₂ Special offences	L₃ Special procedures	L₄ Administrative detention	L₅ Parallel legal system	L₆ Pseudo-legal system	L₇ Infra-legal
Indicator	Only the provisions of the ordinary law may be invoked in response to politically-motivated crime.	Special offences exist which penalize certain types of political activity but these offences are tried in the ordinary manner.	Special procedures are applicable for the trial of politically motivated crime.	Persons are subject to indefinite administrative detention.	A parallel legal system is created under statutory powers. 1 There exists a special rule-making process which are triable through special courts or tribunals. 2 Offences are created by this special rule-making process 3 Special 'executive' powers are granted under the special rule-making process.	A pseudo-legal system is created under non-statutory powers. 1 There exists a special rule-making process, but rules thus created have no standing in strict law. 2 Offences are created by this special rule-making process which are triable through pseudo-courts or tribunals. 3 Special 'executive' powers are granted under the special rule-making process.	No domestic legal standards are applied. The situation corresponds with conventional warfare. International humanitarian law may be applicable
Measures	Treasonable Offences Act 1925	Criminal Law and Procedure (Ireland) Act 1887 Public Safety (Punishment of Offences) Temporary Act 1924 Criminal Procedure Act (Northern Ireland) 1922	Public Safety (Emergency Powers) (No. 2) Act 1923 Public Safety (Powers of Arrest and Detention) Temporary Act 1924	DORA ROIA Special Powers Act	Martial Law (British) Army Emergency Powers Resolution	Civil War measures, pre-October 1922	

This categorization depended for its validity on contrast with the actions of the Crown Forces, whose activities were presented as being subject to the 'rule of law'. Thus, insofar as British concepts of legitimacy were keyed to a matrix in which the rule of law was an important constituent element, the progressive shift from this standard, and its ultimate abandonment in the move from L_5 to L_6, was bound to be profoundly damaging. Not that the imposition of martial law signalled the abandonment of legal form but rather, as has been indicated above, a shift from legalism to pseudo-legalism. Some adherence to legal form had a role to play in the process of legitimation, if only because it was more 'acceptable' to shoot a prisoner after trial by military court or even by drumhead court, than it was to shoot him without any such 'trial'. But this was force only thinly mediated by legal form. Dysfunctional elements have traditionally been seen as central to the legitimating function of legal process ('it is better that the guilty go free than that the innocent suffer'),[6] but under the martial law regime there was little role for such dysfunctionality. The martial law system for dealing with prisoners resembles nothing so much as a series of hoppers (see especially Figure 3). A prisoner might be interned or tried, and if tried he might still be interned if the trial process seemed unlikely to achieve the desired 'result'. What is clear is that he could be 'caught' at whatever level of the system the authorities deemed appropriate.

Above all, though, it was the reprisals, both official and unofficial, which served to undermine British conceptions of legitimacy. As definition had depended to a large extent on contrast with the Republican assassination campaign, this categorization was bound to fragment in the face of indiscriminate action by the Crown Forces. The growth of reprisals was facilitated by the substitution of military courts of inquiry for coroners' inquests at L_5, and was partly validated by the institution of 'official reprisals' at L_6. It was suggested in Chapter 2 that the IRA campaign depended in large measure on raising the cost to Britain to an unacceptable level; in terms of international opinion, the reprisals did just that.[7]

Ironically, these developments corresponded with an increasing legalism on the part of the Republicans. The leaders of the 1916 Rising had seen no necessity for obtaining a prior democratic mandate for their actions, and in that regard, their thinking formed part of a stream of Irish nation-

---

[6] However, for a criticism of this view see A. Hyde, 'The Concept of Legitimation in the Sociology of Law', 1983 *Wisconsin Law Review* 379.

[7] As Conor Cruise O'Brien and Maire O'Brien have commented on the practice of reprisals, 'it horrified many people in Britain—as well as in Canada and Australia—and many of Britain's supporters in Ireland and was seriously damaging to Britain's relations with America' (*A Concise History of Ireland* (London, 1972), 144–5).

alist thought, in which the idea of a Republic was seen as in a sense 'self-legitimating'. The meeting of the first Dáil and the formal endorsement of the Republic therefore represented a departure within that tradition. It owed a lot to the post-World War insistence on the democratic right to national self-determination. It is in that context that the (unsuccessful) attempt by the Dáil Government to obtain representation at the Paris Peace Conference should be seen. This attempt to tie the Irish Republican tradition with the newly emerging post-war international law norms also found expression in the Irish Volunteers' claim concerning the applicability of the Hague Convention and Rules of 1907. Behind these assertions was a claim to legitimacy founded (in a Weberian sense) on such charismatic authority as attached to those who had taken part in, or claimed continuity with, the 1916 Rising. But this was an authority mediated and signified by law.

In practical terms, international legal norms were bound to be less important than concrete visible steps in breathing life to the paper Republic. Given the conditions of the time, the practical effects of the Dáil's legislative programme was bound to be limited; of far more importance was the work of the Dáil courts. As Kohn remarked: 'More effectively than any of the quasi-governmental activities of the revolutionary State, these judicial agencies succeeded in establishing the legitimacy of the new order in the minds of the people and of observers abroad.'[8] This was a view also shared by the Republicans. As one of them was later to write: 'nothing conveyed proof in America of existence of [the] Republic here so much as the establishment and work of courts'.[9]

The Irish Free State and the emergence of the new norms

The acceptance of the Treaty by the second Dáil signalled the end of the marriage of Republican dogmatism and democratic mandate, and thus the break-up of the coalition of ideologies and groups which only a few years previously seemed to have fused into a nationalist monolith.[10]

The dual constitutional position occupied by the pro-Treaty group from January 1922 onwards (Dáil Government and Provisional Government) reflected internal contradiction in the basis of legitimacy of this group. In its initial stages, the pro-Treaty faction was heavily reliant on the charismatic authority of those leaders (particularly Collins) who had played important roles in the struggle against the British. The contradiction

---

[8] *Constitution*, 38–9.

[9] Captured Republican Civil War document headed 'No. 2', 29 Aug. 1922, Mulcahy papers, P7/B/86.

[10] Cf. J. Prager's analysis of the two sides in the Civil War in terms of 'Irish-enlightenment values' and 'gaelic-romantic values' (*Building Democracy in Ireland: Political Order and Cultural Integration in a Newly Independent Nation* (Cambridge, 1986), 50–66.

arose from the fact that in order to maintain this authority it was necessary to present the new constitutional entity as a continuation of the revolutionary assertions of 1919 (hence Collins's support for the Treaty on the basis that it offered the 'freedom to win freedom'), yet the acceptance of the Free State necessarily meant the abandonment of the Republic. It was these contradictions which underlay the conflict in British and Irish law as to the basis of the 1922 Constitution. To have presented the Constitution as deriving its validity from an Act of the British Parliament would have been politically impossible since it was the forcible rejection of British rule which had brought the Free State leaders to the position they then enjoyed.

If the pro-Treaty faction faced difficulties, these were minor compared with those which assailed the Republicans. The break-up of nationalist unity left the Republicans with dogmatism deprived of a mandate. For the military-minded, this resulted in the rejection of the Treaty at the IRA convention of 1922 and in the decision that the organization would work for Republican objectives answerable only to itself. The response of Republican politicians was encapsulated in de Valera's formula that 'the people never had a right to do wrong'.[11] As the Dáil had exceeded its powers by accepting the Treaty and thus disestablishing the Republic, legitimate authority was taken to rest only with those elected representatives of the second Dáil who had rejected the Treaty. This analysis found expression with the assembly of a rival Republican Dáil in October 1922. In essence the Republicans first reverted to a pre-1919 concept of the Republic as in some sense 'self-legitimating', and later attempted to maintain the form of a democratic mandate, even if the substance proved elusive.

When the Civil War began it is probably true to say that neither side was over-concerned with legal niceties, although on the Free State side at least, there was a concern with the formal assertion of civil primacy. Fighting, and ultimately winning, were more important, thus explaining an approach which has been categorized as L_7. Such norms as had been established under the fledgling Republic were shattered; British rule was being dismantled and the new norms had yet to emerge, indeed the outcome of the Civil War would determine what form these new norms would take.

With the switch to L_6 in the Army Emergency Powers Resolution, it might have been expected that the reprisal executions carried out under the Resolution would prove as damaging to the Free State as earlier reprisals had been to the British, yet this was not the case. This can be explained by a number of factors, but principally because of the different

---

[11] See p. 151.

bases of legitimacy in the Free State and under British Rule. Adherence to the rule of law could scarcely be the foundation of the legitimacy of the Provisional Government in September 1922, since the legal position was in a state of flux, and the Provisional Government and Parliament suffered from a number of formal legal incapacities, some of them self-imposed.[12] Instead, the basis was charismatic authority, validated (at least partly) by electoral success. On such a basis, lack of adherence to the rule of law was less significant, and once this pattern was set, it carried through even for the first half of 1923 when the new Constitution had come into force.

Allied to this was the question of cost. The British Government had to balance the cost of fighting what had become a 'dirty' counter-insurgency campaign against the benefits of maintaining its rule in a troublesome neighbouring island. Its own existence was never threatened. In the Free State, however, what was at stake was the very existence of the state. No cost was therefore likely to prove to be too high. Related to this is the international factor: world opinion tends to be much more critical of emergency measures taken in a conflict which is viewed as colonial or quasi-colonial than in the post-independence situation. Two other factors can be mentioned: the Free State reprisals were discriminate, that is they were directed solely against Republican prisoners and therefore were unlike those carried out by the Crown Forces, many of which were directed against, or impinged upon, civilians. Finally, there was a general feeling in the population of war-weariness, or at least that the differences between the Republic and the Free State were not worth fighting over. While the executions did create a degree of revulsion, this did not result in increased support for the Republicans.

The effective ending of martial law by the courts in August 1923 can be taken as representing the concretization of the norms of the new legal order. The shift was from L_6 to L_4, because the Constitution prohibited reliance on special courts such as would have been entailed in reliance on any parallel legal system (L_5). What is significant about this is that the Executive Council felt itself bound by the rulings of the courts and by the Constitution in a way which would have seemed impossible a year earlier.

When the Public Safety Acts expired, there was a drop to L_2. Thus, overall, it is possible to see developments in emergency law in the Irish Free State in the period 1922–5 as indicating a shift from legitimacy founded upon charismatic authority to one founded on law, though as the history of the state in the following twenty years was to show, adherence to the ideology of the rule of law would be partial and contingent.[13]

---

[12] See pp. 243–7.
[13] See M. Farrell, *Apparatus of Repression*, and Mulloy, *Dynasties of Coercion*.

Northern Ireland and constitutional government

The manner in which the Northern Ireland state was created ensured that the new entity would be beset by crises from its inception. Yet in the light of subsequent events, it is ironic that the Northern state faced less of an internal threat than arose in the other jurisdictions. The acceptance of the Treaty settlement by the Dáil confirmed partition, and by the end of 1922, when it had become clear that the Free State/Republican split was a permanent one, and that the Free State would win the Civil War, the military menace was effectively ended, leaving the Boundary Commission as the only real 'threat'.

Some parallels can be drawn between the position of the Northern Ireland Government and that of the Provisional Government. While in British law the status of the Provisional Government was derived from the Irish Free State (Agreement) Act 1922, in fact it owed its existence to the partial success of the Republican campaign of 1919–21. Similarly, while the Government of Ireland Act 1920 provided the legal basis for partition, it was the loyalist revolt of 1912–14 and the tentative moves towards the formation of a Provisional Government of Ulster which paved the way for the partition of the country.

There is a sense in which Northern Ireland in the period in question can be considered a semi-constitutional entity. It was prohibited by the Government of Ireland Act from creating its own army, yet by the establishment of its various special forces and the appointment of a military adviser it very nearly did just that. It was prohibited from enacting legislation in respect of the 'defence of the realm',[14] yet in the Special Powers Act and Regulations, the bulk of the key Defence of the Realm Regulations were enacted with minor amendments. Arrest powers were given to the British Army, powers which were later found to be *ultra vires*. Activities by the Special Constables were tolerated even when these went far beyond the law and when there was no declaration of martial law and Act of Indemnity with which to cloak them. Comparisons can also be drawn between the minor mutinies in the National Army in 1924 and that in the Specials in 1925. Groups which had formed a government's power base were unlikely quietly to allow themselves to be demobilized into political oblivion.

To some extent all this represented a degree of historical continuity. The dichotomy in the British response of 1920–1 between statutory powers (ROIA) and non-statutory martial law powers can be seen as having been mirrored in the enactment of the Special Powers Act in Northern Ireland and the adoption of martial law powers by the Provisional Government and their retention by the Executive Council of the

---

[14] See pp. 317–19.

Irish Free State. In none of the jurisdictions was a concern with legalism uppermost. This was particularly true in the period 1920–3 during which the approach in all three jurisdictions was between L_5 and L_7 of the typology.

Ultimately, Northern Ireland's claim to legitimacy was founded on the assertion of a right of self-determination by the Ulster loyalists. In the nationalist analysis there were not two but one 'people' in Ireland (as the phrase is used in international law), and therefore the unit for self-determination was the whole island. Consequently, the action of the Ulster loyalists was not self-determination but secession by a minority intent on the preservation of its privilege. Whichever view is accepted, it is clear that the function of emergency law in Northern Ireland was seen as that of protecting the interests of those for whose benefit the state had been established.

This also provides a key as to why the judgments on Northern Ireland have been quite different from those on the Irish Free State. During the Civil War, although there were marginal class differences between the two sides, an oppositional position was defined simply in terms of being in opposition and not by reference to any wider distinctive feature. Thus there were plenty of examples of members of the same family supporting different sides. In Northern Ireland, however, the conflict over the question of self-determination meant that the opposition was identifiable as having a separate national (and religious) outlook. Particularly in view of its partisan application, resort to emergency law in that jurisdiction was readily categorizable as oppression of a national or religious minority.

The role of the judiciary

Although the context in each jurisdiction was different, the attitude of the judiciary towards emergency powers was remarkably similar in all three. For that reason, and because of the shared common law tradition, the role of the judges can be analysed thematically by reference to the suggested typology of emergency powers rather than separately for each jurisdiction.

Definition of the emergency

If a state responds to an emergency by reliance only on ordinary powers (that is at L_1), the issue of definition of the emergency obviously cannot come before the courts, since the existence of the emergency is not being recognized in law. This may also be true for L_2. Since at this level ordinary criminal procedure is being neither altered nor circumvented (for example by reliance on internment powers), there may be no divergence from simultaneously existing ordinary powers. The point can be illustrated by contrasting the approach under L_2 and L_3. Under L_3, there may be provisions allowing trial venue to be altered in certain circumstances but these provisions are marked out as special by virtue of the fact that trials may also proceed in the ordinary manner. By contrast, the Treasonable Offences Act 1925 (L_2) redefined certain acts as treason at all times and in all circumstances.

Because the procedures at L_3 are clearly identifiable as extraordinary they will usually also be marked out as temporary. This may be achieved either by placing a specific lifespan on the legislation in which the power is incorporated (for example, in the cases of the Public Safety (Punishment of Offences) Temporary Act 1924 and the Criminal Procedure Act (Northern Ireland) 1922), or by having the legislation permanently on the statute books, though brought into force, in part or in whole, only by proclamation (as in the case of the Criminal Law and Procedure (Ireland) Act 1887). The importance of the difference between the two mechanisms is that in the former the decision on the existence or otherwise of the circumstances justifying resort to emergency powers is made by Parliament, whereas in the latter it is a question for the Government of the day.

One or other of these mechanisms was also used at L_4 and L_5. In the Irish Free State, all the Public Safety Acts during the relevant period were marked as emergency provisions by their limited lifespan, but in this jurisdiction there were also the provisions of a written Constitution to be considered. The 1922 Constitution prescribed a particular formula for the enactment of legislation by an emergency procedure, and the courts demanded that that procedure be adhered to,[15] although there were limits to the importance which the courts were willing to attach to possible procedural irregularity.[16]

Procedure was one thing, but the existence or otherwise of the factual circumstances justifying resort to emergency powers was quite another. DORA made use of both of the mechanisms mentioned above, in that the legislation was temporary ('during the continuance of the present war'[17]), and there was provision for the making of a proclamation suspending the right to jury trial 'In the event of invasion or other special military emergency arising out of the present war'.[18] The courts, however, refused to adjudicate on the validity of continuing reliance on either mechanism even after the factual circumstance originally advanced as justification had come to an end. Instead, the artificial statutory definition given to the ending of the war by the Termination of the Present War (Definition) Act 1918 was accepted, and it was held that the decision on

---

[15] *R (O'Brien)* v. *Military Governor NDU* [1924] 1 *IR* 32.
[16] *R (Murphy)* v. *Military Governor of Mountjoy Prison* [1924] 58 *ILTR* 1.
[17] Defence of the Realm Act 1914, s. 1.
[18] Defence of the Realm (Amendment) Act 1915, s. 1.

the continuing existence of the section 1 emergency was solely a matter for the Government.[19]

At L_6 precisely the opposite course was taken. The existence or otherwise of the circumstances justifying resort to martial law was taken to be a justiciable matter,[20] and while the view of the military was persuasive it was not binding on the court.[21] When the state of war or rebellion was over, an act of the military could be challenged as not having been justified by the circumstances and necessities of the particular case, unless protected by an Act of Indemnity.[22] Prior to the introduction of the 1922 Constitution, the same position was held to apply in the south of Ireland,[23] and subsequently constitutional provisions were interpreted as being in line with the pre-partition position, as the courts asserted their right to bring martial law to an end.[24] The one decision running contrary to this line of authority was that of O'Connor MR in *Egan* v. *Macready*.[25] While modern legal opinion seems to be moving in the direction of a positive reappraisal of the merits of that decision, and while plenty of support for the 'prerogative theory' upon which Egan's case was founded can be found in the Irish legal tradition, at the time it was viewed as eccentric, and O'Connor later refused to follow it.[26] The institutional conflict which Egan's case provoked illustrates that there are effective practical limits to the power of the judiciary in situations of severe civil conflict. Viewed in these terms, the main line of authority can be seen as a legal rationalization of the realities of political power.

The test of vires *and constitutional review*

The issue of judicial rationalization also arises in relation to the application of the test of *vires*. This is particularly important at L_5, since one of the defining characteristics of the approach at that level is the existence of a special rule-making power. Subordinate legislation thus created could be tested for *vires* by reference to its parent statute. In the case of DORA, however, the test was not applied in the normal manner. Particularly during the course of the actual fighting in Europe, judicial application of the test of *vires* seemed geared towards validating whatever claim the Executive might wish to make.[27] With the end of the fighting,

---

[19] *R* v. *Governor of Wormwood Scrubs Prison* [1920] 2 *KB* 305.

[20] *R* v. *Allen* [1921] 2 *IR* 241.

[21] *R (Garde and Others)* v. *Strickland* [1921] 2 *IR* 317.

[22] *R (Ronayne and Mulcahy)* v. *Strickland* [1921] 2 *IR* 333; *Higgins* v. *Willis*, [1921] 2 *IR* 386.

[23] *R (Childers)* v. *Adj.-Gen.* [1923] 1 *IR* 5; *R (Johnstone)* v. *O'Sullivan* [1923] 2 *IR* 13.

[24] *R (O'Brien)* v. *Military Governor NDU* [1924] 1 *IR* 32.

[25] [1921] 1 *IR* 265.

[26] *R (Childers)* v. *Adj.-Gen.* [1923] 1 *IR* 5.

[27] *R* v. *Halliday* [1917] *AC* 260.

however, a more stringent approach was taken, at least in relation to property rights.[28]

In Ireland, as the case law on procedural irregularity and the powers of ROIA courts martial illustrate, the attitude of the courts corresponded more with the pre-armistice position in Britain.[29] And this was also true of the attitude of the Northern Ireland courts to the test of *vires* in relation to the Special Powers Act.[30]

Perhaps not surprisingly, the approach adopted in relation to *vires* also seems to have coloured the attitude of the judiciary in the Irish Free State to the question of constitutional review of legislation. As Kelly has remarked of this power, 'the only judicial function even remotely similar had been the testing of administrative orders for vires'.[31] While the courts were prepared to insist that constitutional provisions on procedure be adhered to,[32] substantive review was a different matter. Post-Civil War context was given precedence over ordinary meaning, with the result that constitutional provisions were interpreted in such a way as to cause minimum friction with the Executive.[33]

Characteristics of emergency law

Judge-proof drafting and accountability

The virtual absence of meaningful judicial scrutiny of the emergency powers under discussion was not, however, solely the result of self-imposed judicial restraint. Partly it came about because of the way in which emergency powers were deliberately drafted in a way designed to minimize the possibility of judicial scrutiny. In the words of C. K. Allen, they were 'judge-proof'.[34] Typically this was achieved by omitting any requirement of 'reasonableness' in the exercise of emergency powers.[35] Another device was to make primary emergency powers (for instance in relation to arrest) exercisable where no specific offence was suspected. This was particularly true of the statutory measures adopted in pre-partition Ireland and in Northern Ireland at L_5.[36] In the Irish Free State the position under statutory powers was somewhat different, in that

---

[28] *AG* v. *Wilts United Dairies Ltd.* [1921] 37 *TLR* 884; *Chester* v. *Bateson* [1920] 1 *KB* 829; *AG* v. *De Keyser's Royal Hotel Ltd.* [1920] *AC* 508.
[29] *R* v. *Murphy* [1921] 2 *IR* 190; *Whelan* v. *Rex* [1921] 2 *IR* 310; *R (Rodgers)* v. *Campbell and Others* [1921] 55 *ILTR* 192.
[30] *R (O'Hanlon)* v. *Governor of Belfast Prison* [1922] 56 *ILTR* 170.
[31] *Fundamental Rights*, n. 4.
[32] *R (O'Brien)* v. *Military Governor NDU* [1924] 1 *IR* 32.
[33] *R (O'Connell)* v. *Military Governor of Hare Park Camp* [1924] 2 *IR* 104.
[34] *Law in the Making*, 564.
[35] *R* v. *Denison* [1916] 32 *TLR* 528.
[36] e.g. DORR 55, ROIR 55, and Special Powers Regulation 23.

statutory powers never exceeded L$_3$, and such powers were generally tied to the suspected commission of a specific offence.[37]

If emergency powers, particularly at L$_5$, in areas such as arrest could be said to have been 'loosely textured', this can also be said to have been the case in relation to follow-up powers, exercisable as a consequence of the use of primary powers. To take the example of detention, ROIR 55 incorporated no definite time-limit on detention and neither did Special Powers Regulation 23. The deliberate exclusion of provisions which might have facilitated judicial scrutiny of the use of these powers meant that, in effect, accountability in their exercise was limited to an administrative process, there having been virtually no legal requirement for parliamentary scrutiny of this or any other emergency powers in the period in question.

In cases where there was an administrative willingness to permit abuses to occur, as for instance where brutality during interrogation was tolerated (as it seems to have been under British rule from mid-1920 onwards), no effective remedy existed. This lack of legal accountability reached its ultimate development under martial law, and as the way in which prisoners were treated during the Irish Civil War illustrates, the consequences for victims of abuse of emergency powers under martial law could be dire. It is striking that the worst allegations of ill-treatment occurred only from L$_5$ upwards, suggesting strongly that the increased legal accountability present at the lower levels acted as a brake on any such tendencies which may have been present.

The other sphere in which lack of accountability had particularly marked consequences was in relation to the use of lethal force. Accountability in this sphere was greatly diminished by the substitution of special procedures for the investigation of deaths in place of coroners' inquests at L$_5$ under British rule and in Northern Ireland. The piecemeal holding of inquests during the Irish Civil War seems to have had much the same effect. It is no mere coincidence that this occurred at times in all three jurisdictions when unofficial reprisal assassinations seem to have been receiving a degree of official tolerance. It is probably not overstating the case to say that tinkering with the inquest process was the prime legal mechanism facilitating the development of reprisals.

Catch-all drafting and function

Closely related to the issue of 'judge-proof' drafting is that of 'catch-all' or 'fall back' drafting. This means that, for instance, emergency arrest

---

[37] e.g. arrest powers under s. 2 (1) of the Public Safety (Emergency Powers) (No. 2) Act 1923, and s. 2 (1) of the Public Safety (Powers of Arrest and Detention) Temporary Act 1924.

powers were typically drafted in a manner designed to cover all situations in which it might be thought expedient or convenient to arrest someone. The role of such powers was less to mediate between the individual and state power than to render the individual accessible to discretionary administrative action.

It is possible to see this as one example of a general tendency of the 'catchment area' of emergency powers to increase at each level of coercion, indicating generally that emergency law was functionally differentiated from the ordinary law. Thus with the rise from L_1 to L_2 a range of political activity is brought within the ambit of the criminal law which would not otherwise be so. Similarly, the institution of special procedures at L_3 might have the effect of increasing the numbers tried and/or convicted. But the big shift occurs at L_4, since the institution of administrative detention means that a person may be detained (and therefore 'caught') without the necessity for criminal proceedings.

At L_5 this was supplemented by provisions designed to broaden the scope of criminal or quasi-criminal procedure (for example, courts martial) so as to ensure that in addition to the use of administrative detention, suspects would be 'caught' by the imposition of sentences of judicial or quasi-judicial tribunals. These tribunals were also designed to function in a 'catch-all' manner, but only against those whose removal was deemed politically expedient, since the institution of prosecutions was centrally controlled. A number of mechanisms were employed to 'enhance the efficacy' of these tribunals. Typically these included the reversal of the burden of proof in cases involving alleged possession of contraband material, but the most blatant example of this type of device was ROIR 50 which provided:

If any person does any act of such a nature as to be calculated to be prejudicial to the restoration or maintenance of order in Ireland and not specifically provided for in the foregoing regulation, he shall be deemed to be guilty of an offence against these regulations.

This was the Regulation which was used to enforce offences against martial law regulations in statutory courts martial. With minor amendments the Regulation also appeared as part of the Special Powers Act.[38]

The question which has been adverted to above needs to be asked: why was it thought necessary to alter criminal procedure thus when administrative detention powers were also available, and therefore when suspects could in any case be 'caught' without the necessity for any form of trial? Two related answers can be given. The first is that, as has been discussed above, adherence to legal form expressed in quasi-criminal

---

[38] Civil Authorities (Special Powers) Act (Northern Ireland) 1922, s. 2 (4).

procedure might be seen as conferring legitimacy on the process in a way which administrative detention could not. The second is that the imposition of a variety of sentences by such quasi-judicial tribunals could be taken to confer legitimacy on death sentences, in that such sentences could be justified as having been reached by something approximating to legal process. And as the British Cabinet debates of the summer of 1920 illustrate, great importance was attached to the need to generate such sentences by some members of the British Government.

These trends were intensified at L_6, hence the reference above to the martial law regime resembling a series of hoppers. The issue of the role of legal form in the legitimation of the execution of prisoners at this level is perhaps best illustrated by the way in which reprisal executions without trial were abandoned in the Irish Free State in favour of the system whereby sentences of military courts might be conditionally suspended, or military committees might be used in a way calculated specifically to generate such sentences. At L_7 this process reached its ultimate development in that notions of individual guilt were largely abandoned in favour of the strategic concerns of conventional warfare. Thus a person would be taken prisoner or shot merely because he was taken to belong to the 'enemy' and not by reference to any quasi-legal or pseudo-legal provisions.

Conclusions

In each of the three jurisdictions under discussion, the legal response to political violence went beyond mere alteration of the law to the point at which a parallel legal system and/or a pseudo-legal system was created. Where the legitimacy of the politico-legal order was based at least partly on the ideology of the 'rule of law', this creation, and the growth of reprisals which it facilitated, served to delegitimize that order. Where other bases of legitimacy were relied upon, such delegitimization did not necessarily occur. It is the different bases of legitimacy in the various jurisdiction that explain why broadly similar measures could have quite different affects in each.

That there were obvious similarities in the measures taken is without doubt. The link between the Special Powers Act and DORA and ROIA is clear, as is the link between the British and the Irish Free State versions of martial law. Not only were there similarities in broad strategy, there were also more specific points of comparison. Emergency powers tended to be structured in a judge-proof and catch-all fashion in a way which minimized legal accountability and therefore contributed to abuse. And this effect was exacerbated by a self-imposed judicial restraint resulting from a concentration on context at the expense of meaning.

The period 1918–25 was clearly one of momentous constitutional change, and this was reflected in the very different bases of legitimacy in each of the jurisdictions under discussion. However, the fearful symmetry of the measures adopted in the various jurisdictions means that in terms of the mechanics of coercion the period can be considered to have been one of continuity rather than of disjunction.

Appendix 1. *Disputed Police and British Army Killings, 1918–1921*

Dáil Statistics: Killings by Police and the British Army Described as 'Murder' in the *Irish Bulletin*

Year	Period (w/e)	No.
1918	Full year	6
1919	Full year	7
1920	3 Jan.–19 Aug.	28
TOTAL		41
1920	21 Aug.	5
	28 Aug.	1
	4 Sept.	2
	11 Sept.	4
	18 Sept.	4
	25 Sept.	9
	2 Oct.	4
	13 Nov.	10
	20 Nov.	10
	27 Nov.	36
	4 Dec.	10
	11 Dec.	9
	18 Dec.	8
	24 Dec.	12
	1 Jan.	16
1921	8 Jan.	10
	15 Jan.	5
	22 Jan.	16
TOTAL		171

Source: *Irish Bulletin* weekly surveys from w/e 12 July 1919 to w/e 22 Jan. 1921 and retrospective figures for 1918 and Jan.–Sep. 1919 published in *Irish Bulletin* w/e 27 Sept. 1919. National Library Dublin.

British Army Statistics: Findings of Military Courts of Inquiry in lieu of Inquests on Civilians (from 13 August 1920)

	No.
Death caused by Crown Forces in execution of their duty	233
Justifiable homicide by Crown Forces	4
Death caused accidentally by Crown Forces	6
Death caused feloniously by Crown Forces	2
Reasons for deaths caused by Crown Forces in execution of their duty	
Armed attack on Crown Forces or resisting arrest with arms	108
Attempting to escape	30
Failing to halt or evading arrest	78
On streets after curfew	3
Misadventure during conflict with rebels	14
TOTAL	233

Source: Townshend, 107. Categories are Townshend's.

Appendix 2. National Army
Civil War Executions

Name	Status	Charge[1] (date of offence)	Tried/investigated by (date)	Place of execution (date of execution)
Bagnell, Patrick	IRA	Poss. without proper authority of 10 rifles, 200 rounds ammo. 4 Bomb detonators & 1 exploder.	Committee	Dublin (19 Dec. 1922)
Barrett, Richard	IRA	No charge—administrative reprisal execution.		Dublin (8 Dec. 1922)
Bourke, Martin (or Burke)	IRA	Poss. without proper authority of arms and ammo.	Committee	Athlone (20 Jan. 1923)
Brady, Terence	Ex-National Army private	Treachery, in that at Leixlip he assisted certain armed persons in using force against the National Troops, and Treacherously communicating and consorting with the armed persons mentioned in the first charge, in the place and at the time mentioned.	General court martial	Dublin (8 Jan. 1923)
Brosnan, Michael	IRA	Poss. of arms and ammo. without proper authority.	Military court	Tralee (20 Jan. 1923)
Burke, Frederick	IRA	Poss. without proper authority of 2 Rifles, 35 rounds of ammo. and one Thompson gun without proper authority (23 Dec. 1922).	Committee	Roscrea (15 Jan. 1923)
Burke, Luke (alias Henry Keenan)	Civilian[2]	Taking part in armed raid on the Hibernian and Northern banks Oldcastle (27 Feb. 1923), Poss. of £385/19/11 stolen money.	Committee	Mullingar (14 Mar. 1923)

Name	Status	Charge[1] (date of offence)	Tried/investigated by (date)	Place of execution (date of execution)
Byrne, Joseph	IRA	Poss. without proper authority of one Webley revolver (10 Nov. 1922).	Committee	Portlaoise (27 Jan. 1923)
Cassidy, Peter	IRA	Poss. without proper authority of a revolver (27 Oct. 1922).	Military court (9 Nov. 1922) (Dublin)	Dublin (17 Nov. 1922)
Childers, Erskine	IRA	Poss. without proper authority of automatic pistol (10 Nov. 1922).	Military court (17 Nov. 1922) (Dublin)	Dublin (24 Nov. 1922)
Clifford, John	IRA	Poss. arms and ammo. without proper authority.	Military court	Tralee (20 Jan. 1923)
Collins, Herbert	IRA	Poss. without proper authority of arms and ammo.	Committee	Athlone (20 Jan. 1923)
Conroy, William	IRA	Poss. firearms (21 Nov. 1922), feloniously and Burglariously [*sic*] entering into intent [*sic*] the houses of several residents in Tullamore and stealing therefrom a silver watch, several sums of money with other goods and chattels.	Military court (5 Jan. 1923) (Roscrea)	Birr (26 Jan. 1923)
Creane, John	IRA	Poss. without proper authority of a revolver (15 Feb. 1923).	Committee	Wexford (13 Mar. 1923)
Cunnane, Francis	IRA	Poss. without proper authority of a rifle and ammo. (21 Feb. 1923).	Committee	Tuam (11 Apr. 1923)

Name	Affiliation	Charge	Court	Place (Date)
Cunningham, Patrick	IRA	Poss. firearms (21 Nov. 1922), feloniously and Burglariously [sic] entering into intent [sic] the houses of several residents in Tullamore and stealing therefrom a silver watch, several sums of money with other goods and chattels.	Military court (5 Jan. 1923) (Roscrea)	Birr (26 Jan. 1923)
Daly, Charles	IRA	Poss., together with 5 other persons of 3 rifles, 1 revolver, 300 rounds of .303 ammo., 6 rounds of .45 ammo., 1 German Egg Bomb, without proper authority.	Military court (18 Jan. 1923) (Drumboe)	Drumboe (14 Mar. 1923)
Daly, James	IRA	Poss. of arms and ammo. without proper authority.	Military court	Tralee (20 Jan. 1923)
Dowling, Leo	Ex-National Army Corporal	Treachery, in that at Leixlip he assisted certain armed persons in using force against the National Troops, and Treacherously communicating and consorting with the armed persons mentioned in the first charge, in the place and at the time mentioned.	General court martial	Dublin (8 Jan. 1923)
Enright, Daniel	IRA	Poss., together with 5 other persons of 3 rifles, 1 revolver, 300 rounds of .303 ammo., 6 rounds of .45 ammo., 1 German Egg Bomb, without proper authority.	Military court (Drumboe) (18 Jan. 1923)	Drumboe (14 Mar. 1923)
Farrelly, Patrick	IRA	Poss. without proper authority of a bomb.	Military court (14 Nov. 1922) (Dublin)	Dublin (30 Nov. 1922)

Name	Status	Charge[1] (date of offence)	Tried/investigated by (date)	Place of execution (date of execution)
Ferguson, Joseph	IRA	Poss. without proper authority of arms and ammo. (7 Jan. 1923).	Committee	Dundalk (22 Jan. 1923)
Fisher, James	IRA	Poss. without proper authority of one revolver.	Military court (8 Nov. 1922) (Dublin)	Dublin (17 Nov. 1922)
Fitzgerald, Michael	IRA	Poss. without proper authority of arms and ammo. (4 Dec. 1922).	Committee	Waterford (25 Jan. 1923)
Gaffney, John	IRA	Poss. without proper authority of one revolver.	Military court (8 Nov. 1922) (Dublin)	Dublin (17 Nov. 1922)
Geraghty, Patrick	IRA	Poss. without proper authority of one automatic pistol	Committee	Portlaoise (27 Jan. 1923)
Gibson, Thomas	Ex-National Army private	Treachery in as much as that on the 19th November 1922, being then on active service, he left Portlaoise Barracks and took with him five rifles and one grenade cap.	General court martial	Maryborough (27 Feb. 1923)
Greaney, Edward	IRA	Attack on members of National Forces in which members of the National Forces were killed (18 Apr. 1923).	Committee (18 Apr. 1923)	Tralee (25 Apr. 1923)
Greery, Michael (or Grealy)	Civilian	Taking part in armed raid on the Hibernian and Northern banks Oldcastle (27 Feb. 1923). Poss. of £385/19/11 stolen money.	Committee	Mullingar (14 Mar. 1923)

Name	Affiliation	Charge	Court	Place (Date)
Hanlon, James	IRA	Poss. without proper authority of arms and ammo.	Military court	Tralee (20 Jan. 1923)
Hathaway, Reginald	IRA	Attack on National Forces in which members of National Forces were killed (18 Apr. 1923).	Committee (18 Apr. 1923)	Tralee (25 Apr. 1923)
Healy, William	IRA	Conspiracy to murder (8 Mar. 1923), conspiracy with and encouraging persons to damage and destroy property by fire, aiding and abetting an attack on National Troops, Poss. without proper authority of revolver.	Unclear	Cork (13 Mar. 1923)
Heaney, Sylvester	Ex-National Army Corporal	Treachery, in that at Leixlip he assisted certain armed persons in using force against the National Troops, and Treacherously communicating and consorting with the armed persons mentioned in the first charge, in the place and at the time mentioned.	General court martial	Dublin (8 Jan. 1923)
Hennessy, Patrick	IRA	Poss. without proper authority of ammo., being implicated in the destruction of the railway at Ard Solus (14 Jan. 1923), Poss. of articles taken from Ard Solus station.	Committee	Limerick (20 Jan. 1923)
Hogan, Patrick	IRA	Poss. without proper authority of a revolver (15 Feb. 1923).	Committee	Wexford (13 Mar. 1923)
Hughes, Thomas	IRA	Poss. without proper authority of arms and ammo.	Committee	Athlone (20 Jan. 1923)

Name	Status	Charge[1] (date of offence)	Tried/investigated by (date)	Place of execution (date of execution)
Johnston, Joseph	IRA	Poss. without proper authority of 10 rifles, 200 rounds ammo. 4 bomb detonators, 1 exploder.	Committee	Dublin (19 Nov. 1922)
Joyce, Stephen	IRA	Poss. without proper authority of arms and ammo.	Committee	Athlone (20 Jan. 1923)
Kelly, Colum	IRA	Poss. firearms (21 Nov. 1922), feloniously and Burglariously [sic] entering into intent [sic] the houses of several residents in Tullamore and stealing therefrom a silver watch, several sums of money with other goods and chattels.	Military court (5 Jan. 1923) (Roscrea)	Birr (26 Jan. 1923)
Larkin, John	IRA	Poss. without proper authority of 3 rifles, 1 revolver, 300 rounds of .303 ammo., 6 rounds .45 ammo. 1 German Egg Bomb (2 Nov. 1922).	Military court (18 Jan. 1923) (Drumboe)	Drumboe (14 Mar. 1923)
Lennon, Thomas	IRA	Poss. without proper authority of arms and ammo (7 Jan. 1923).	Committee	Dundalk (22 Jan. 1923)
Lillis, James	IRA	Poss. without proper authority of a rifle (14 Nov. 1922), poss without proper authority of ammo. (14 Nov. 1922), Taking part in attack on National Forces (24 Oct. 1922).	Military court (Kilmainham)	Carlow (15 Jan. 1923)

Name		Charge	Authority	Place (date)
McInerny, James	IRA	Attack on members of National Forces in which members of National Forces were killed (18 Apr. 1923).	Committee (18 Apr. 1923)	Tralee (25 Apr. 1923)
McKelvey, Joseph	IRA	No charge—administrative reprisal execution.		Dublin (8 Dec. 1922)
McKeown, Thomas	IRA	Poss. without proper authority of one revolver and 100 rounds of ammunition (3 Jan. 1923).	Military court	Dundalk (13 Jan. 1923)
McMahon, Cornelius	IRA	Poss. without proper authority of ammo., being implicated in the destruction of the railway at Ard Solus (14 Jan. 1923), Poss. of articles taken from Ard Solus station.	Committee	Limerick (20 Jan. 1923)
McNamara, Patrick	IRA	Poss. without proper authority of one rifle and ammo. (24 Dec. 1922)	Military court (23 Dec. 1922) (Roscrea)	Roscrea (15 Jan. 1923)
Mc Nulty, John (alias Joseph Murphy)	IRA	Poss. without proper authority of one revolver and 12 rounds ammo. (9 Jan. 1923).	Military court	Dundalk (13 Jan. 1923)
Maguire, John	IRA	Poss. without proper authority of a rifle and ammo. (21 Feb. 1923).	Committee	Tuam (11 Apr. 1924)
Mahoney, Patrick	IRA	Poss. of partially loaded revolver (21 Apr. 1923), Being implicated in an attack in which members of National Army were killed.	Committee (23 Apr. 1923)	Ennis (26 Apr. 1923)
Mangan, Patrick	IRA	Poss. without proper authority of 10 rifles, 200 rounds ammo., 4 bomb detonators, 1 exploder.	Committee	Dublin (19 Nov. 1922)

Name	Status	Charge[1] (date of offence)	Tried/investigated by (date)	Place of execution (date of execution)
Melia, James	IRA	Poss. without proper authority of arms and ammo. (7 Jan. 1923).	Committee	Dundalk (22 Jan. 1923)
Mellowes, Liam	IRA	No charge—administrative reprisal execution.		Dublin (8 Dec. 1922)
Monaghan, Michael	IRA	Poss. without proper authority of a rifle and ammo. (21 Feb. 1923).	Committee	Tuam (11 Apr. 1923)
Moore, Brian	IRA	Poss. without proper authority of 10 rifles, 200 rounds of ammo. 4 bomb detonators, 1 exploder.	Committee	Dublin (19 Dec. 1922)
Moylan, Martin (or Nolan)	IRA	Poss. without proper authority of a rifle and ammo. (21 Feb. 1923).	Committee	Tuam (11 Apr. 1923)
Murphy, John	IRA	Poss. without proper authority of 2 bombs.	Military court (14 Nov. 1922) (Dublin)	Dublin (20 Nov. 1922)
Murphy, John	IRA	Poss. without proper authority of arms and ammo. and being concerned in a raid on Shenstown House, when property to the value of £189 was taken.	Committee	Kilkenny (29 Dec. 1923)
Murphy, Michael[3]	Unclear	n/a	n/a	Tuam (11 Apr. 1923 or 30 May 1923)

Name	Organisation	Charge	Court	Place (Date)
Murray, Charles (or Thomas Murray)	IRA	Poss. without proper authority of one revolver and 6 rounds ammo. (9 Jan. 1923).	Military court	Dundalk (13 Jan. 1923)
Nolan, Patrick	IRA	Poss. without proper authority of 10 rifles, 200 rounds ammo. 4 bomb detonators, 1 exploder.	Committee	Dublin (19 Dec. 1922)
Newell, James	IRA	Poss. without proper authority of a rifle and ammunition (21 Feb. 1923).	Committee	Tuam (11 Apr. 1924)
O'Connor, James	IRA	Poss. without proper authority of 10 rifles, 200 rounds ammo. 4 bomb detonators, 1 exploder.	Committee	Dublin (19 Dec. 1922)
O'Connor, Rory	IRA	No charge—administrative reprisal execution.		Dublin (8 Dec. 1922)
O'Malley, James	IRA	Poss. without proper authority of a rifle and ammo. (21 Feb. 1923).	Committee	Tuam (11 Apr. 1924)
O'Reilly, Anthony	Ex-National Army private	Treachery, in that at Leixlip he assisted certain armed persons in using force against the National Troops, and Treacherously communicating and consorting with the armed persons mentioned in the first charge, in the place and at the time mentioned.	General court martial	Dublin (8 Jan. 1923)
O'Reilly, Patrick	IRA	Poss. without proper authority of arms and ammo. (4 Dec. 1922).	Military court	Waterford (25 Jan. 1923)
O'Rourke, James	IRA	Taking part in an armed attack on members of the National Army in Jury's Hotel, Dublin (21 Feb. 1923), Poss. without proper authority of 1 revolver and three rounds of ammo.	Committee	Dublin (13 Mar. 1923)
O'Rourke, Joseph	Unclear	n/a	n/a	Tuam

Name	Status	Charge[1] (date of offence)	Tried/investigated by (date)	Place of execution (date of execution)
O'Shea, Martin	IRA	Poss. without proper authority of 2 rifles, 35 rounds of ammo. and one Thompson Gun without ammo. (23 Dec. 1922).	Committee	Roscrea (15 Jan. 1923)
O'Sullivan, Timothy	IRA	Poss. without proper authority of 3 rifles, 3 revolvers, 3 bandoliers containing .303 ammo., 1 pouch of .45 ammo. (2 Nov. 1922).	Military court (18 Jan. 1923) (Drumboe)	Drumboe (14 Mar. 1923)
Parle, James (or Pearle)	IRA	Poss. without proper authority of a revolver (15 Feb. 1923).	Committee	Wexford (13 Mar. 1923)
Phelan, John	IRA	Poss. without proper authority of arms and ammo. and being concerned in a raid on Shenstown House, when property to the value of £189 was taken.	Committee	Kilkenny (29 Dec. 1923)
Quinn, Christopher	IRA	Murder of a member of the National Forces (21 Apr. 1924), Poss. of revolver.	Military tribunal	Ennis (2 May 1923)
Russell, Patrick	IRA	Poss. without proper authority of 2 rifles, 35 rounds ammo., and one Thompson Gun with ammo. (23 Nov. 1922).	Committee (2 Jan. 1923)	Roscrea (15 Jan. 1923)
Shaughnessey, Will.	IRA	Murder of a member of the National Forces (21 Apr. 1923), Poss. without proper authority of one revolver.	Committee	Ennis (2 May 1923)

Sheehy, Laurence	Ex-National Army private	Treachery, in that at Leixlip he assisted certain armed persons in using force against the National Troops, and Treacherously communicating and consorting with the armed persons mentioned in the first charge, in the place and at the time mentioned.	General court martial	Dublin (8 Jan. 1923)
Spooner, Joseph	IRA	Poss. without proper authority of revolver (30 Oct. 1922).	Military court (14 Nov. 1922) (Dublin)	Dublin (30 Nov. 1922)
Twohig, Richard	IRA	Poss. without proper authority of a revolver (23 Oct. 1922).	Military court (Dublin)	Dublin (17 Nov. 1922)
Walsh, Michael	IRA	Poss. without proper authority of arms and ammo.	Committee	Athlone (20 Jan. 1923)
White, Stephen	IRA	Poss. without proper authority of 10 rifles, 200 rounds ammo., 4 bomb detonators and 1 exploder.	Committee	Dublin (19 Nov. 1922)

[1] Description of charges taken from press releases (see source).

[2] This case and that of the other person listed as a civilian (Michael Greery), do not figure in Macardle's list of 'Executed Republicans'. Sources indicate that the two were non-politically-motivated bank robbers.

[3] This case and that of Joseph O'Rourke are not listed by Macardle, *Irish Republic*, nor do they appear in the collection of Army press releases. Both cases are, however, included in the lists in the SPO, but different dates of execution are given in the two lists.

Source: Prepared from lists of 'Executions' and 'Executed Irregulars' at S1 184, SPO, list of 'Executed Republicans' in Macardle, *Irish Republic*, 1023–4, copies of press releases issued by the National Army after the executions, in Military Archives, A/0770, Dublin, and list of military court trials attached to Deputy Judge Advocate General to Director of Intelligence, 15 Nov. 1923, Military Archives, P/7, Dublin.

Appendix 3. The Derivation of the Civil Authorities (Special Powers) Act (Northern Ireland) 1922 and Regulations up to 31 December 1925

1(1) The civil authority shall have power, in respect of persons, matters and things within the jurisdiction of the Government of Northern Ireland, to take all such steps and issue all such orders as may be necessary for preserving the peace and maintaining order, according to and in the execution of this Act and the regulations contained in the Schedule thereto, or such regulations as may be made in accordance with the provisions of this Act (which regulations, whether contained in the said Schedule or made as aforesaid, are in this Act referred to as 'the regulations'):

Provided that the ordinary course of law and avocations of life and the enjoyment of property shall be interfered with as little as may be permitted by the exigencies of the steps required to be taken under this Act.

Derived from

S. 1 (1) Defence of the Realm Consolidation Act 1914 (part of)

His Majesty in Council has power during the continuance of the present war to issue regulations for securing the public safety and the defence of the realm, and as to the powers and duties for that purpose of the Admiralty and Army Council and of the members of His Majesty's forces and other persons acting in his behalf . . .

DORR 1 (part of) (introduced 28 Nov. 1914)

The ordinary avocations of life and the enjoyment of property will be interfered with as little as may be permitted by the exigencies of the measures required to be taken for securing the public safety and the defence of the Realm, and ordinary civil offences will be dealt with by the civil tribunals in the ordinary course of law.

(2) For the purposes of this Act the civil authority shall be the Minister of Home Affairs for Northern Ireland, but that Minister may delegate, either

unconditionally or subject to such conditions as he thinks fit, all or any of his powers under this Act to any officer of police, and any such officer of police shall, to the extent of such delegation, be the civil authority as respects any part of Northern Ireland specified in such delegation.

DORR 62 (part of) (introduced 28 Nov. 1914, amended 29 Feb. 1916)

The Admiralty or Army Council may appoint any commissioned officer of His Majesty's Naval, Military or Air Forces, not below the rank of lieutenant-commander in the Navy or field officer in the Army or Air Force, to be a competent naval or military authority and may authorise any competent naval or military authority thus appointed to delegate, either unconditionally or subject to such conditions as he thinks fit, all or any of his powers under these regulations to any officer qualified to be appointed a competent naval or military authority, and an officer so appointed, or to whom the powers of the competent naval or military authority are so delegated, is in these regulations referred to as a competent naval or military authority. Where the holder of a designated office has been appointed to be a competent naval or military authority, or any powers of the competent naval or military authority have been delegated to the holder of a designated office, then, unless express provision is made to the contrary, the appointment or delegation shall be deemed to extend, and shall be deemed always to have extended, to the person for the time being performing the duties of the office designated, if he is so qualified as aforesaid.

---

(3) The Minister of Home Affairs shall have power to make regulations:

(*a*) for making further provision for the preservation of the peace and maintenance of order, and

(*b*) for varying or revoking any provision of the regulations;

and any regulations made as aforesaid shall, subject to the provisions of this Act, have effect and be enforced in like manner as regulations contained in the Schedule to this Act.

See s. 1 (1) Defence of the Realm Consolidation Act 1914 (above)

---

(4) All regulations made as aforesaid shall be laid before both Houses of Parliament as soon as may be after they are made, and, if an address is presented to the Lord Lieutenant by either House within the next fourteen days on which such House shall be sitting after any such regulation is laid before it praying that the regulation may be annulled, the Lord Lieutenant may annul that regulation and it shall thenceforth be void, without prejudice to the validity of anything done thereunder, or to the power of making a new regulation; and regulations made as aforesaid shall not be deemed to be statutory rules within the meaning of section one of the Rules Publication Act, 1893.

S. 1 (1) ROIA (part of)

Provided that all regulations so made shall be laid before both Houses of Parliament as soon as may be after they are made, and, if an address is presented to His Majesty by either House within the next fourteen days during the session of Parliament after any such regulation is laid before it praying that the regulation may be annulled, His Majesty may annul the regulation and it shall thenceforth be void, without prejudice to the validity of anything done thereunder, or to the power of making a new regulation; and the regulations shall not be deemed to be statutory rules within the meaning of section one of the Rules Publication Act, 1893.

2(1) It shall be the duty of every person affected by any order issued by the civil authority or other person in pursuance of the regulations to comply with that order, and if he fails to do so he shall be guilty of an offence against the regulations.

DORR 47 (introduced 28 Nov. 1914)

It shall be the duty of every person affected by any order issued by the competent naval or military authority or other person in pursuance of these regulations to comply with that order, and if he fails to do so he shall be guilty of an offence against these regulations.

---

(2) Any person who attempts to commit, or solicits or incites or endeavours to persuade another person to commit, or procures, aids or abets, or does any act preparatory to, the commission of, any act prohibited by the regulations, or any order, rules or other instrument made thereunder, or harbours any person whom he knows, or has reasonable grounds for supposing, to have acted in contravention of the regulations, or any order, rules, or other instrument made thereunder, shall be guilty of an offence against the regulations.

DORR 48 (introduced 28 Nov. 1914, amended 28 June 1917, 8 Aug. 1917)

Any person who attempts to commit, or solicits or incites or endeavours to persuade another person to commit, or procures, aids or abets, or does any act preparatory to, the commission of, any act prohibited by these regulations, or any order, rules, or other instrument made thereunder, or harbours any person whom he knows, or has reasonable grounds for supposing, to have acted in contravention of these regulations, or any order, rules, or other instrument made thereunder, shall be guilty of an offence against these regulations, or, if the Act constituted or would have constituted a summary offence against these regulations, of a summary offence against these regulations.

---

(3) It shall be the duty of any person who knows, or has good reason for believing, that some other person is acting, has acted, or is a about to act, in

contravention of any provisions of the regulations to inform the civil authority of the fact, and if he fails to do so he shall be guilty of an offence against the regulations.

DORR 49 (introduced 28 Nov. 1914, amended 23 Mar. 1915)
It shall be the duty of any person who knows or has good reason for believing that some other person is acting in contravention of any provisions of these regulations to inform the competent naval or military authority of the fact, and if he fails to do so he shall be guilty of an offence against these regulations.

(4) If any person does any act of such a nature as to be calculated to be prejudicial to the preservation of the peace or maintenance of order in Northern Ireland and not specifically provided for in the regulations, he shall be deemed to be guilty of an offence against the regulations.

DORR 50 (introduced 28 Nov. 1914)
If any person does any act of such a nature as to be calculated to be prejudicial to the public safety or the defence of the Realm and not specifically provided for in the foregoing regulations, with the intention or for the purpose of assisting the enemy, he shall be deemed to be guilty of an offence against these regulations.

(5) Where the offence against the regulations is committed by a corporation or company, every director and officer of the corporation or company shall be guilty of the like offence, unless he proves that the act constituting the offence took place without his knowledge or consent.

DORR 48A (introduced 17 July 1917)
Where the person guilty of an offence or a summary offence against these regulations is a corporation or company every director and officer of the corporation or company shall be guilty of the like offence unless he proves that the act constituting the offence took place without his knowledge or consent.

(6) Where under the regulations any act if done without lawful authority or without lawful authority or excuse is an offence against the regulations, the burden of proving that the act was done with lawful authority or with lawful authority or excuse shall rest on the person alleged to be guilty of the offence.

DORR 58B (introduced 10 June 1915)
Where under these regulations any act if done without lawful authority or without lawful authority or excuse is an offence against these regulations, the burden of proving that the act was done with lawful authority or with lawful authority or excuse shall rest on the person accused.

(7) Sections one to four, inclusive, of the Criminal Evidence Act, 1898, shall apply in the case of a person charged with an offence against the regulations.

No DORA or ROIA Equivalent
Under DORR neither the accused nor his wife was, in Ireland, a competent witness in his own defence.

3(1) A person alleged to be guilty of an offence against the regulations may be tried by a court of summary jurisdiction constituted in accordance with this section, and not otherwise.

DORR 56 (1) (part of) (introduced 23 Mar. 1915)
Except as otherwise provided by this regulation, a person alleged to be guilty of an offence against these regulations may be tried either by court-martial, or by a civil court with a jury, or by a court of summary jurisdiction.

DORR 58A (part of) (introduced 23 Mar. 1915, amended 28 July 1915)
Whenever His Majesty by Proclamation suspends the operation of section one of the Defence of the Realm (Amendment) Act, 1915, either generally or as respects any specified area, then, as respects all offences committed against these regulations, or (as the case may be), all such offences committed within the specified area, so much of Regulation 56 as relates to trial by a civil court with a jury, and in particular paragraphs (6) to (9) and (13) thereof, shall, so long as the Proclamation remains in force, cease to have effect . . .

---

(2) An offence against the regulations shall not be prosecuted except by such officer or person as may be authorised in that behalf by the Attorney General for Northern Ireland, and in accordance with such directions as may be given by the said Attorney General.

ROIR 68 (8) (introduced 13 Aug. 1920)
(8) A crime, the investigation of which has been referred to the competent naval or military authority, shall not be prosecuted before a court of summary jurisdiction by any person other than the competent naval or military authority or a person authorised by him, or a police officer or constable, an officer of customs and excise, or a person authorised by the Government department concerned except with the consent of the Attorney General for Ireland, or a person authorised by him.

---

(3) Any person aggrieved by a conviction of a court of summary jurisdiction for any such offence may appeal in manner provided by the Summary Jurisdiction (Ireland) Acts.

DORR 58 (part of) (introduced 28 Nov. 1914)

Any person aggrieved by a conviction of a court of summary jurisdiction under these regulations may appeal in England to a court of quarter sessions, and in Scotland under and in terms of the Summary Jurisdiction (Scotland) Acts, and in Ireland in manner provided by the Summary Jurisdiction (Ireland) Acts.

---

(4) A court of summary jurisdiction when trying a person charged with an offence against the regulations shall be constituted of two or more resident magistrates, but one resident magistrate may act alone in doing anything antecedent to the hearing of the charge under this Act, or in adjourning a court or the hearing of a case, or in committing the defendant to prison or admitting him to bail, until the time to which the court or case has been adjourned; and a court of quarter sessions, when hearing and determining an appeal against a conviction of a court of summary jurisdiction for any such offence, shall be constituted of the recorder or county court judge sitting alone.

ROIR 76 (introduced 13 Aug. 1920)

11. A court of summary jurisdiction, when trying a person charged with a crime the investigation of which has been referred to the competent naval or military authority, or when hearing and determining an application for an order to estreat a recognisance, shall, except in the Dublin Metropolitan Police district, be constituted of two or more resident magistrates, and a court of quarter sessions, when hearing and determining an appeal against a conviction of a court of summary jurisdiction for any such crime or against an order made on any such application, shall be constituted of the recorder or county court judge sitting alone.

---

4 A person convicted of an offence against the regulations shall be liable to be sentenced to imprisonment with or without hard labour for a term not exceeding two years or to a fine not exceeding one hundred pounds or to both such imprisonment and fine, and the court may, in addition to any other sentence which may be imposed, order that any goods or articles in respect of which the offence has been committed shall be forfeited.

DORR 58 (part of) (introduced 28 Nov. 1914)

A person convicted of an offence against these regulations by a court of summary jurisdiction shall be liable to be sentenced to imprisonment with or without hard labour for a term not exceeding six months or to a fine not exceeding one hundred pounds, or to both such imprisonment and fine, and the court may, in addition to any other sentence which may be imposed, order that any goods in respect of which the offence has been committed shall be forfeited.

5 Where after trial by any court a person is convicted of any crime or offence to which this section applies, the court may, in addition to any other punishment which may lawfully be imposed, order such person, if a male, to be once privately whipped, and the provisions of subsection (6) of section thirty-seven of the Larceny Act, 1916, as to sentences of whipping shall apply accordingly.

The crimes and offences to which this section applies are as follows:

(1) Any crime under the Explosive Substances Act, 1883, as extended by section eighteen of the Firearms Act, 1920.

(2) Any offence against the Firearms Act, 1920, in relation to the having, keeping or using of firearms.

(3) Any offence against the regulations in relation to the carrying, having or keeping of firearms, military arms, ammunition or explosive substances.

(4) Any offence against section thirty of the Larceny Act, 1916, (which relates to demanding with menaces, with intent to steal).

(5) Arson, whether by common law or by statute, and any offence punishable on indictment under the Malicious Damage Act, 1861.

Provided that this section shall not be deemed to apply to any crime or offence committed before the passing of this Act.

No DORA or ROIA Equivalent

---

6 A crime under section two or section three of the Explosive Substances Act, 1883, shall be a crime punishable by death: provided that this section shall not apply to any such crime committed before the passing of this Act.

Where a sentence of death is pronounced by the court upon conviction for a crime to which this section applies, the sentence may be pronounced and carried into execution, and all other proceedings thereupon and in respect thereof may be had and taken, in the same manner as sentence might have been pronounced and carried into execution, and proceedings might have been had and taken, upon a conviction for murder.

No DORA or ROIA Equivalent
Under the martial law regulations issued 12 Dec. 1920 unauthorized possession of explosives was a capital offence.

---

7 Any person authorised by the civil authority, or any police constable, or any member of any of His Majesty's forces on duty may, where it is necessary for the purpose of effecting an arrest in respect of any crime or any offence against the regulations, exercise the like powers as may at common law be exercised by a police constable in effecting arrest in a case where a felony has been committed.

No DORA or ROIA Equivalent

8 Where any enactment or other provision of law (including this Act or the regulations) provides for the exercise of any power by, or imposes any duty on, any inspector, head-constable, sergeant, or constable of the Royal Irish Constabulary in connection with the arrest, prosecution, remand, trial or conviction of any person for any crime or offence, whether punishable on indictment or summary conviction, that enactment or provision shall in Northern Ireland have effect as if the said power were also exercisable by, or the said duty were also imposed on, the corresponding officer or member (by whatever title designated) of any police force under the management and control of the Government of Northern Ireland; and references in any such enactment or provision to any inspector, head-constable, sergeant, or constable of the said constabulary, shall be construed accordingly.

No DORA or ROIA Equivalent

9 The provisions of section fourteen of the Petty Sessions (Ireland) Act, 1851, in relation to the reading of depositions as evidence upon the trial of a person charged with an indictable crime or offence, shall extend so as to authorize the reading of such depositions as evidence, where it is proved that a witness is so ill as to be unable to travel or where the attendance of the witness cannot be procured, owing to the prevalence of a state of disorder or otherwise.

ROIR 72A (introduced 14 Feb. 1921) (see also s. 2 (1) Evidence Amendment Act 1915)

On the trial by court martial of a person alleged to be guilty of a crime or of an offence against these regulations, the statement on oath of any witness which is included in the summary of evidence taken by or by the direction of the competent naval or military authority to whom the case has been referred for investigation shall be admissible in evidence, if it is proved that the statement was signed by the witness and taken in the presence of the accused and that the witness is dead or has been forcibly and unlawfully carried away or is unable to attend owing to sickness or injuries. The foregoing provisions shall be in addition to and not in substitution for, the provisions of any Act, regulation or rule of law as to the admission of evidence.

10(1) For the purpose of preserving the peace and maintaining order, the Minister of Home Affairs may by order:

(*a*) Prohibit the holding of inquests by coroners on dead bodies in any area in Northern Ireland specified in the order, either absolutely or except in such circumstances or on such conditions as may be specified in the order; or,

(*b*) Prohibit the holding of any particular inquest specified in the order; and

(*c*) Provide for the duties of a coroner and a coroner's jury (or of either of them) as respects any inquest prohibited by the order being performed by such officer or court as may be determined by the order.

(2) Any such officer or court shall have and may exercise, for the purposes of any inquiry directed to be held in pursuance of such order or any report thereon, all or any of the powers which might have been exercised by the coroner or coroner's jury for the purposes of the inquest which has been prohibited and the finding thereon, whether conferred by statute or at common law.

ROIR 81 (introduced 13 Aug. 1920)

(1) The Lord Lieutenant, for the purpose of securing the restoration or maintenance of order in Ireland, may by order:

(*a*) prohibit the holding of inquests by coroners on dead bodies in any area in Ireland specified in the order; or

(*b*) prohibit the holding of any particular inquest specified in the order; and

(*c*) provide for the duties of a coroner and a coroner's jury as respects any inquest prohibited by the order being performed by a court of inquiry constituted under the Army Act instead of by a coroner and jury.

(2) Any court of inquiry directed to be held in pursuance of such order for the purposes of the inquiry and the declaration thereon shall have, and may exercise, all or any of the powers which might have been exercised by the coroner or coroner's jury for the purposes of the inquest which has been prohibited and the finding thereon, whether conferred by statute or at common law.

11(1) Where, under the powers conferred by this Act or the regulations, any lands, buildings, goods, chattels or other property are taken, occupied or destroyed, or any other act is done involving interference with private rights of property, compensation shall, subject to the provisions of this section, be payable by the civil authority out of moneys provided by Parliament.

(2) If any question arises as to such compensation, such question, if not settled by agreement, shall be referred for settlement to the county court or an arbitrator to be appointed by that court, and all questions in dispute shall be settled in accordance with such procedure as may be prescribed by rules made by the Lord Chief Justice of Northern Ireland after consultation with the civil authority.

(3) Nothing in this section shall be construed as giving to any person, where an offence against the regulations has been committed, any right to compensation in respect of lands, buildings, goods, chattels or other property taken, occupied or destroyed in connection with such offence.

No DORA or ROIA Equivalent

A Royal Commission was appointed on 31 Mar. 1915 to enquire as to payments out of public funds in respect of direct loss or damage to property and business in UK through the exercise by the Crown of its rights and duties in the defence of the Realm.

12 This Act shall continue in force for one year and no longer, unless Parliament otherwise determines.

See s. 1 (1) Defence of the Realm Consolidation Act 1914 (above)

13 This Act may be cited as the Civil Authorities (Special Powers) Act (Northern Ireland), 1922.

Comparisons inapplicable

(*b*) *The original Regulations as amended up to 31 Dec. 1925*

Reg. 1 (as amended 27 Apr. 1922)

1 The civil authority may by order require every person within any area specified in the order to remain within doors between such hours as may be specified in the order, and in such case, if any person within that area is or remains out between such hours without a permit in writing from the civil authority or some person duly authorised by him, he shall be guilty of an offence against these regulations.

For the purpose of this Regulation a person within such area shall be deemed to be or to remain out between such hours if he is found between such hours elsewhere than at his usual place of abode.

Provided that a person shall not be deemed to be or to remain out between such hours if he is found in a hotel or registered lodging house in which he is duly registered according to law, or if he has given previous notice to the police at the police station nearest to the house at which he intends to stay, of his intention to stay therein.

DORR 13 (introduced 9 Oct. 1919)

In any area in respect of which the operation of section one of the Defence of the Realm (Amendment) Act, 1915, is for the time being suspended, the competent naval or military authority may by order require every person within any area specified in the order to remain within doors between such hours as may be specified in the order, and in such case, if any person within that area is or remains out between such hours without a permit in writing from the competent naval or military authority or some person duly authorised by him, he shall be guilty of an offence against these regulations.

2 The civil authority may by order:

(1) Require all or any licensed premises within any area specified in the order to be closed, either altogether, or subject to such exceptions as to hours and purposes, and to compliance with such directions, as may be specified in the order;

(2) Make such provisions as he thinks necessary for the prevention of the practice of treating in any licensed premises within any area specified in the order.

Any order of the civil authority under this regulation may be made to apply either generally or as respects all or any members of the police or other forces mentioned in the order, and may require copies of the order to be exhibited in a prominent place in any licensed premises affected thereby.

If any person contravenes or fails to comply with any of the provisions of an order made under this regulation or any conditions or restrictions imposed thereby, he shall be guilty of an offence against these regulations, and the civil authority may cause such steps to be taken as may be necessary to enforce compliance with the order.

In this regulation the expression 'licensed premises' includes any premises or place where the sale of intoxicating liquor is carried on under a licence.

DORR 10 (introduced 22 Dec. 1916)

The competent naval or military authority or the Minister of Munitions may by order:

(1) require all or any licensed premises within any area specified in the order to be closed, either altogether, or subject to such exceptions as to hours and purposes, and to compliance with such directions, as may be specified in the order;

(2) make such provisions as he thinks necessary for the prevention of the practice of treating in any licensed premises within any area specified in the order.

Any order of the competent naval or military authority or the Minister of Munitions under this regulation may be made to apply either generally or as respects all or any members of His Majesty's forces or of the forces of any of His Majesty's Allies mentioned in the order, and may require copies of the order to be exhibited in a prominent place in any licensed premises affected thereby.

If any person contravenes or fails to comply with any of the provisions of an order made under this regulation or any conditions or restrictions imposed thereby, he shall be guilty of an offence against these regulations, and the competent naval or military authority or the Minister of Munitions may cause such steps to be taken as may be necessary to enforce compliance with the order.

In this regulation the expression 'licensed premises' includes any premises or place where the sale of intoxicating liquor is carried on under a licence.

3(1) The civil authority may make orders prohibiting or restricting in any area:

(*a*) The holding of or taking part in meetings, assemblies (including fairs and markets), or processions in public places;

(*b*) The use or wearing or possession of uniforms or badges of a naval, military or police character, or of uniforms or badges indicating membership of any association or body specified in the order;

(*c*) The carrying in public places of weapons of offence or articles capable of being used as such;

(*d*) The carrying, having or keeping of firearms, military arms, ammunition or explosive substances; and

(*e*) The having, keeping, or using of a motor or other cycle, or motor car by any person, other than a member of a police force, without a permit from the civil authority, or from the chief officer of the police in the district in which the person resides.

(2) Any order under this regulation may be made so as to apply generally to the whole of the area aforesaid or to any special localities in that area, and so as to prohibit all or any of the Acts and matters aforesaid absolutely or subject to such exceptions or save upon such conditions as may be specified therein.

(3) If any person contravenes, or fails to comply with, any provision of any order made under this regulation, or fails to comply with any condition subject to which anything is authorised under any such order, he shall be guilty of an offence against these regulations.

(4) The civil authority, or any person authorised by him in writing, or any police constable, or any member of His Majesty's forces on duty (without prejudice to the powers given by any other regulation):

(*a*) If he suspects that any firearms, military arms, motor or other cycles or motor cars, ammunition or explosive substances are, or are kept, in or upon any house, building, land, vehicle, vessel, or other premises in contravention of an order under this regulation, or otherwise unlawfully, may enter, if need be by force, the house, building, land, vehicle, vessel, or premises, at any time of the day or night and examine, search and inspect the same or any part thereof, and may seize any firearms, military arms, motor or other cycles or motor cars, ammunition or explosive substances found therein or thereon which he suspects to be, or to be kept, therein or thereon in contravention of the order, or otherwise unlawfully; and

(*b*) If he suspects that any person is carrying any firearms, military arms, ammunition, or explosive substances in contravention of any such order, may stop that person and search him; and

(*c*) May seize any firearms, military arms, ammunition, explosive substances or other articles carried by any person in contravention of any such order, or otherwise unlawfully, or any motor or other cycle or motor car used by or in the possession or custody of any person in contravention of any such order.

Any firearms, military arms, ammunition, explosive substances, motor cycles, motor cars, or other articles seized under this regulation may be destroyed or otherwise disposed of as may be ordered by the civil authority or chief officer of police.

DORR 9AA (introduced 28 June 1917, amended 5 Feb. 1918, 19 July 1918, 27 Sept. 1918, 23 Oct. 1918, 9 Oct. 1919)

(1) In any area in respect of which the operation of section one of the Defence of the Realm (Amendment) Act, 1915, is for the time being suspended, the competent naval or military authority may make orders prohibiting or restricting:

(*a*) the holding of or taking part in meetings, assemblies (including fairs and markets), or processions in public places;

(*b*) the use or wearing in public places of uniforms of a naval or military character, or of uniforms indicating membership of any association or body specified in the order;

(*c*) the carrying in public places of weapons of offence or articles capable of being used as such;

(*d*) the carrying, having or keeping of firearms, military arms, ammunition or explosive substances; and

(*e*) the having, keeping or using of a motor cycle or motor car by any person, other than a member of His Majesty's Forces, or of the Forces of any of His Majesty's Allies, or a police constable, without a permit from the competent naval or military authority, or from the chief officer of the police in the district in which the person resides.

(2) Any order under this regulation may be made so as to apply generally to the whole of the area aforesaid or to any special localities in that area, and so as to prohibit all or any of the acts and matters aforesaid absolutely or subject to such exceptions or save upon such conditions as may be specified therein.

(3) If any person contravenes, or fails to comply with, any provision of any order made under this regulation, or fails to comply with any condition subject to which anything is authorised under any such order, he shall be guilty of an offence against these regulations.

(4) The competent naval or military authority or any person authorised by him, or any police constable (without prejudice to the powers given by any other regulation):

(*a*) if he suspects that any firearms, military arms, motor cycles or motor cars, ammunition or explosive substances are, or are kept, in or upon any house, building, land, vehicle, vessel, or other premises in contravention of an order under this regulation, may enter, if need be by force, the house, building, land, vehicle, vessel, or premises, at any time of the day or night and examine, search and inspect the same or any part thereof, and may seize any firearms, military arms, motor cycles or motor cars, ammunition or explosive substances found therein or thereon which he suspects to be, or to be kept, therein or thereon in contravention of the order; and

(*b*) if he suspects that any person is carrying any firearms, military arms, ammunition or explosive substances in contravention of any such order, may stop that person and search him; and

(*c*) may seize any firearms, military arms, ammunition, explosive substances or other articles carried by any person in contravention of any such order, or any motor cycle or motor car used by or in the possession kept, therein or thereon in contravention of the order; and

Any firearms, military arms, ammunition, explosive substances, motor cycles, motor cars or other articles seized under this regulation may be destroyed or otherwise disposed of as may be ordered by the competent naval or military authority or chief of police.

4 Where there appears to be reason to apprehend that the assembly of any persons for the purpose of the holding of any meeting will give rise to grave disorder, and will thereby cause undue demands to be made upon the police forces, or that the holding of any procession will conduce to a breach of the peace or will promote disaffection, it shall be lawful for the civil authority, or for any magistrate or chief officer of police who is duly authorised for the purpose by the civil authority, or for two or more of such persons so authorised, to make an order prohibiting the holding of the meeting or procession, and if a meeting or procession is held or attempted to be held in contravention of any such prohibition, it shall be lawful to take such steps as may be necessary to disperse the meeting or procession or prevent the holding thereof; and every person taking part in any such prohibited meeting or procession shall be guilty of an offence against these regulations.

DORR 9A (introduced 3 Oct. 1916)

Where there appears to be reason to apprehend that the assembly of any persons for the purpose of the holding of any meeting will give rise to grave disorder, and will thereby cause undue demands to be made upon the police or military forces, or that the holding of any procession will conduce to a breach of the peace or will promote disaffection, it shall be lawful for a Secretary of State, or for any mayor, magistrate, or chief officer of police who is duly authorised for the purpose by a Secretary of State, or for two or more of such persons so authorised, to make an order prohibiting the holding of the meeting or procession, and if a meeting or procession is held or attempted to be held in contravention of any such prohibition, it shall be lawful to take such steps as may be necessary to disperse the meeting or procession or prevent the holding thereof.

Where His Majesty by Proclamation has suspended the operation of section one of the Defence of the Realm (Amendment) Act, 1915, this regulation shall have effect in any place in the United Kingdom in respect of which the operation of that section is so suspended as if references to a Secretary of State included references to the competent naval or military authority.

In the application of this regulation to Scotland, references to the Secretary for Scotland and to a provost shall be substituted respectively for references to a Secretary of State and a mayor.

In the application of this regulation to Ireland, references to the Lord Lieutenant shall be substituted for references to a Secretary of State.

5(1) The Minister of Home Affairs may, by order, declare this regulation to be in force in any area, and in any such area no person other than a member of the police forces, shall, subject to any exceptions for which provision may be made in the order, practise, take part in, or be concerned in any exercise, movement, evolution, or drill of a military nature, or be concerned in, or assist the promotion or organisation of any such exercise, movement, evolution, or drill, by persons other than members of the police forces.

(2) If any person acts in contravention of this regulation he shall be guilty of an offence against these regulations.

(3) The provisions of this regulation are in addition to and not in derogation of any other provision of law relating to the same subject-matter.

DORR 9E (introduced 23 Nov. 1916, amended 29 Nov. 1916)

(1) A Secretary of State or the Army Council may by order declare this regulation to be in force in any area, and in any such area no person other than a member of His Majesty's naval, military or air forces, or a constable, shall, subject to any exceptions for which provision may be made in the order, practise, take part in, or be concerned in any exercise, movement, evolution, or drill of a military nature, or be concerned in, or assist the promotion or organisation of any such exercise, movement, evolution, or drill, by persons other than members of His Majesty's naval, military, or air forces, or constables.

(2) If any person acts in contravention of this regulation he shall be guilty of an offence against these regulations.

(3) The powers of a Secretary of State under this regulation may be exercised as respects Ireland by the Chief Secretary.

(4) The provisions of this regulation are in addition to and not in derogation of any other provision of law relating to the same subject-matter.

---

6 The civil authority, and any person duly authorised by him shall have right of access to any land or buildings or other property whatsoever.

DORR 3 (introduced 28 Nov. 1914)

The competent naval or military authority and any person duly authorised by him shall have right of access to any land or buildings or other property whatsoever.

---

7 The civil authority, if he considers it necessary so to do for the purposes of any work of defence or other defended work, or for any other purpose for which it is deemed necessary for preserving the peace or maintaining order to afford protection, may, by order, close, stop, or divert any road, lane, passage, pathway, or ferry, for so long as the order remains in force:

Provided that where any public road or ferry is so closed, stopped or diverted the civil authority shall publish notice thereof in such manner as he may consider best adapted for informing the public, and where any road is stopped by means of any physical obstruction he shall cause lights sufficient for the warning of passengers to be set up every night whilst the road is so stopped.

DORR 5 (introduced 28 Nov. 1914)

5 The competent naval or military authority may by order if he considers it necessary so to do for the purposes of any work of defence or other defended military work, or of any work for which it is deemed necessary in the interests of public safety or the defence of the Realm to afford military protection, stop

up or divert any road or pathway over or adjoining the land on which such work is situate for so long as the order remains in force:

Provided that where any such road or pathway is so stopped up or diverted the competent naval or military authority shall publish notice thereof in such manner as he may consider best adapted for informing the public, and where any road or pathway is stopped up by means of any physical obstruction he shall cause lights sufficient for the warning of passengers to be set up every night whilst the road or pathway is so stopped up.

8 It shall be lawful for the civil authority and any person duly authorised by him, where for the purposes of this Act it is necessary so to do:

(*a*) To take possession of any land and to construct works, including roads, thereon, and to remove any trees, hedges, and fences therefrom;

(*b*) To take possession of any buildings or other property, including works for the supply of gas, electricity or water, and of any sources of water supply;

(*c*) To take such steps as may be necessary for placing any buildings or structures in a state of defence;

(*d*) To cause any buildings or structures to be destroyed, or any property to be moved from one place to another, or to be destroyed;

(*e*) To take possession of any arms, ammunition, explosive substances, equipment, or stores intended or liable to be used for purposes prejudicial to the preservation of the peace or the maintenance of order; to take possession of any horses, vehicles or mechanically propelled vehicles, or other means of transport, or require them to be placed at the disposal of any Government Department or person specified by the Civil Authority in that behalf, either absolutely or by the way of hire, and either for immediate or future use.

(*f*) To do any other act involving interference with private rights of property which is necessary for the purposes of this Act.

If, after the civil authority has issued a notice that he has taken or intends to take possession of any movable property in pursuance of this regulation, any person having control of any such property sells, removes or secretes it without the consent of the civil authority, he shall be guilty of an offence against these regulations.

DORR 2 (introduced 28 Nov. 1914, amended 10 May 1916)

It shall be lawful for the competent naval or military authority and any person duly authorised by him, where for the purpose of securing the public safety or the defence of the Realm it is necessary so to do:

(*a*) to take possession of any land and to construct military works, including roads, thereon, and to remove any trees, hedges, and fences therefrom;

(*b*) to take possession of any buildings or other property, including works for the supply of gas, electricity, or water, and of any sources of water supply;

(*c*) to take such steps as may be necessary for placing any buildings or structures in a state of defence;

(*d*) to cause any buildings or structures to be destroyed, or any property to be moved from one place to another, or to be destroyed;

(*e*) to take possession of any arms, ammunition, explosive substances, equipment, or warlike stores (including lines, cables, and other apparatus intended to be laid or used for telegraphic or telephonic purposes);

(*f*) to do any other act involving interference with private rights of property which is necessary for the purpose aforesaid.

If, after the competent naval or military authority has issued a notice that he has taken or intends to take possession of any movable property in pursuance of this regulation, any person having control of any such property sells, removes, or secretes it without the consent of the competent naval or military authority he shall be guilty of an offence against these regulations.

9 Every person who uses or keeps motor spirit, whether for the purpose of supplying motive power to motor-cars or for any other purpose, shall supply such information in relation to the motor spirit used or kept by him, and the purposes for which and the manner in which it is used or kept by him, as the civil authority may by any general or special order require, giving such particulars in such form and at such times as the civil authority may by order direct; and if any person fails to comply with this regulation, or with any order made thereunder, or knowingly gives any false information, he shall be guilty of an offence against these regulations.

For the purposes of this regulation 'motor spirit' has the same meaning as in section eighty-four of the Finance (1909–10) Act, 1910.

DORR 15A (introduced 1 June 1916)

Every person who uses or keeps motor spirit, whether for the purpose of supplying motive power to motor-cars or for any other purpose, shall supply such information in relation to the motor spirit used or kept by him, and the purposes for which and the manner in which it is used or kept by him, as the Board of Trade may by any general or special order require, giving such particulars in such form and at such times as the Board of Trade may by order direct; and if any person fails to comply with this regulation, or with any order made by the Board of Trade thereunder, or knowingly gives any false information, he shall be guilty of a summary offence against these regulations.

For the purposes of this regulation, 'motor spirit' has the same meaning as in section eighty-four of the Finance (1909–10) Act, 1910.

10 No person shall, without lawful authority, collect, record, publish or communicate, or attempt to elicit, any information with respect to the movement, numbers, description, condition, or disposition of any police force, or with respect to the plans or conduct, or supposed plans or conduct, of any operations by any such force, or any information of such a nature as is calculated to be or might be directly or indirectly useful to persons hostile or opposed to the preservation of the peace or maintenance of order, and if any person contravenes the provisions of this regulation, or without lawful authority or excuse has in his possession any document containing any such information as aforesaid, he shall be guilty of an offence against these regulations.

DORR 18 (part of) (introduced 28 Nov. 1914, amended 10 June 1915, 14 Oct. 1915, 25 June 1918)

No person shall without lawful authority collect, record, publish or communicate, or attempt to elicit, any information with respect to the movement, numbers, description, condition, or disposition of any of the forces, ships, or aircraft of His Majesty or any of His Majesty's allies, or with respect to the plans or conduct, or supposed plans or conduct, of any operations by any such forces, ships, or aircraft, or with respect to the supply, description, condition, transport, or manufacture or storage or place or intended place of manufacture or storage, of war material, or with respect to any works or measures undertaken for or connected with, or intended for the fortification or defence of any place, or any information of such a nature as is calculated to be or might be directly or indirectly useful to the enemy, and if any person contravenes the provisions of this regulation, or without lawful authority or excuse has in his possession any document containing any such information as aforesaid, he shall be guilty of an offence against these regulations.

---

11 No person without lawful authority shall injure, or tamper or interfere with, any wire or other apparatus for transmitting telegraphic or telephonic messages, or any apparatus or contrivance intended for or capable of being used for a signalling apparatus, either visual or otherwise, or prevent or obstruct or in any manner whatsoever interfere with the sending, conveyance or delivery of any communication by means of telegraph, telephone, or otherwise, or be in possession of any apparatus intended for or capable of being used for sending messages, or tapping messages sent, by wireless telegraphy or otherwise, and if any person contravenes the provisions of this regulation he shall be guilty of an offence against these regulations.

DORR 20 (introduced 28 Nov. 1914)

20 No person without lawful authority shall injure, or tamper or interfere with, any wire or other apparatus for transmitting telegraphic or telephonic messages, or any apparatus or contrivance intended for or capable of being used for a signalling apparatus, either visual or otherwise, or prevent or obstruct or in any manner whatsoever interfere with the sending, conveyance or delivery of any communication by means of telegraph, telephone, or otherwise, or be in possession of any apparatus intended for or capable of being used for tapping messages sent by wireless telegraphy or otherwise, and if any

person contravenes the provisions of this regulation he shall be guilty of an offence against these regulations.

12 If any person, without lawful authority or excuse, uses or has in his possession or under his control any cipher, code, or other means adapted for secretly communicating information which may be prejudicial to the preservation of peace or the maintenance of order he shall be guilty of an offence against these regulations, unless he proves that the cipher, code, or other means of secret communication is intended and used solely for commercial or other legitimate purposes.

Any person who has in his possession or under his control any cipher, code, or other means of secret communication shall, if required by the civil authority, or any person authorised by him, or by any police constable, supply the key or other means for deciphering it, and if he fails to do so shall be guilty of an offence against these regulations.

DORR 22A (introduced 10 June 1915)

If any person, without lawful authority or excuse, uses or has in his possession or under his control any cipher, code, or other means adapted for secretly communicating naval, military or air-force information, he shall be guilty of an offence against these Regulations, unless he proves that the cipher, code, or other means of secret communication is intended and used solely for commercial or other legitimate purposes.

Any person who has in his possession or under his control any cipher, code, or other means of secret communication shall, if required by the competent naval or military authority, or any person authorised by him, or by any police constable, supply the key or other means for deciphering it, and if he fails to do so shall be guilty of an offence against these regulations.

13 If any person does any injury to any railway, or is upon any railway, or on, under or near any tunnel, bridge, viaduct, or culvert, or loiters on or in any road or path or other place near a railway tunnel, bridge, viaduct or culvert, with intent to do injury thereto, he shall be guilty of an offence against these regulations.

DORR 28 (introduced 28 Nov. 1914, amended 24 Jan. 1917)

If any person does any injury to any railway, or is upon any railway, or on under or near any tunnel bridge viaduct or culvert, or loiters on or in any road or path or other place near a railway tunnel bridge viaduct or culvert, with intent to do injury thereto, he shall be guilty of an offence against these regulations.

13a Where a person employed by a Government Department or by a municipal authority or by any company or contractor upon whom is imposed by Act of Parliament the duty, or who have otherwise assumed the duty of supplying any city, borough, town or place, or any part thereof, with electricity, gas, or water, wilfully and maliciously breaks a contract of service with that department, authority, company, or contractor, knowing or having reasonable cause to believe that the probable consequence of his so doing, either alone or in combination with others, will be to deprive the inhabitants of that city, borough, town, place or part, wholly or to a great extent of their supply of electricity, gas or water, he shall be guilty of an offence against these regulations.

DORR 43C (introduced 5 Feb. 1919)

With a view to affording to the public similar protection in relation to the supply of electricity to that conferred in relation to the supply of gas and water by section four of the Conspiracy and Protection of Property Act, 1875, the following provision shall have effect:

Where a person employed by a Government Department or by a municipal authority or by any company or contractor upon whom is imposed by Act of Parliament the duty, or who have otherwise assumed the duty of supplying any city, borough, town or place, or any part thereof, with electricity, wilfully and maliciously breaks a contract of service with that department, authority, company, or contractor, knowing or having reasonable cause to believe that the probable consequences of his so doing, either alone or in combination with others, will be to deprive the inhabitants of that city, borough, town, place, or part, wholly or to a great extent of their supply of electricity, he shall be guilty of a summary offence against these regulations.

---

14 The civil authority may by order prohibit any person from approaching within such distance as may be specified in the order of any camp, barrack, work of defence or other defended work, or any work or place to which it is deemed necessary in the interest of the preservation of the peace or maintenance of order to afford protection, and if any person contravenes any such order he shall be guilty of an offence against these regulations.

DORR 29 (part of) (introduced 28 Nov. 1914)

The competent naval or military authority may by order prohibit any person from approaching within such distance as may be specified in the order of any camp, work of defence or other defended military work, or any work to which it is deemed necessary in the interest of the public safety or the defence of the Realm, to afford military protection, and if any person contravenes any such order he shall be guilty of an offence against these regulations.

---

15 If any person by the discharge of firearms or otherwise endangers the safety of any police officer or constable or other person who is charged with the execution of any duties under these regulations, he shall be guilty of an offence against these regulations.

DORR 32 (introduced 28 Nov. 1914, amended 14 Apr. 1917)

If any person by the discharge of firearms or otherwise endangers the safety of any member of any of His Majesty's forces or any police constable or other person who is charged with the execution of any duties under these regulations he shall be guilty of an offence against these regulations.

16 If any person attempts or does any act calculated or likely to cause mutiny, sedition, or disaffection in any police force or among the civilian population, or to impede delay or restrict any work necessary for the preservation of the peace or maintenance of order he shall be guilty of an offence against these regulations.

DORR 42 (introduced 28 Nov. 1914, amended 30 Nov. 1915, 15 Feb. 1916, 22 Mar. 1918)

If any person attempts or does any act calculated or likely to cause mutiny, sedition, or disaffection among any of His Majesty's forces, or any of the forces of any of His Majesty's Allies, or among the civilian population, or to impede, delay, or restrict the production, repair, or transport of war material, or any other work necessary for the successful prosecution of the war, he shall be guilty of an offence against these regulations.

17 No person shall obstruct, knowingly mislead or otherwise interfere with or impede, or withhold any information in his possession which he may reasonably be required to furnish from an officer or other person who is carrying out the orders of the civil authority, or who is otherwise acting in accordance with his duty under these regulations, and if he does so shall be guilty of an offence against these regulations.

If any person obstructs, impedes, or otherwise interferes with any member of any police or other authorised force in the execution of his duties, he shall be guilty of an offence against these regulations.

DORR 43 (introduced 28 Nov. 1914, amended 23 Mar. 1915)

No person shall obstruct, knowingly mislead, or otherwise interfere with or impede, or withhold any information in his possession which he may reasonably be required to furnish from, any officer or other person who is carrying out the orders of the competent naval or military authority, or who is otherwise acting in accordance with his duty under these regulations, and if he does so shall be guilty of an offence against these regulations.

18 The civil authority, or any person duly authorised by him, or any police constable, or any member of any of His Majesty's forces on duty, may, if he has reason to suspect that any house, building, land, vehicle, vessel, aircraft, or other premises or any things therein are being or have been, or are about to be, constructed, used or kept for any purpose or in any way prejudicial to the preservation of the peace or maintenance of order, or that a crime or an offence against these regulations is being or has been committed thereon or therein, enter, if need be by force, the house, building, land, vehicle, vessel, aircraft, or premises at any time of the day or night, and examine, search and inspect the same or any part thereof, and may seize anything found therein or any such vehicle or vessel which he has reason to suspect is being used or intended to be used for any such purpose as aforesaid, or is being kept or used in contravention of these regulations, and the civil authority may order anything so seized to be destroyed or otherwise disposed of.

DORR 51 (introduced 28 Nov. 1914, amended 10 June 1915, 22 Apr. 1916, 16 Nov. 1917, 21 Dec. 1917)

The competent naval or military authority, or any person duly authorised by him or any police constable may, if he has reason to suspect that any house, building, land, vehicle, vessel, aircraft, or other premises or any things therein are being or have been constructed used or kept for any purpose or in any way prejudicial to the public safety or the defence of the Realm, or that an offence against these regulations is being or has been committed thereon or therein, enter, if need be by force, the house, building, land, vehicle, vessel, aircraft, or premises at any time of the day or night, and examine, search, and inspect the same or any part thereof, and may seize anything found therein which he has reason to suspect is being used or intended to be used for any such purpose as aforesaid, or is being kept or used in contravention of these regulations (including, where a report or statement has appeared in any newspaper or other printed publication, or where a leaflet has been printed in contravention of any of these regulations, any type or other plant used or capable of being used for the printing or production of the newspaper or other publication or of the leaflet), and the competent naval or military authority, with the consent of the Admiralty or Army Council, or a chief officer of police with the consent of a Secretary of State, the Secretary for Scotland, or the Chief Secretary in Ireland (as the case may be), may order anything so seized to be destroyed or otherwise disposed of.

19 Where the civil authority, or any superior officer of police, is of opinion that a meeting or assembly is being or about to be held of such a character that an offence against these regulations may be committed thereat, he may authorise in writing a police constable or other person to attend the meeting or assembly, and any police constable or person so authorised may enter the place at which the meeting or assembly is held and remain there during its continuance.

In this regulation the expression 'superior officer of police' means an officer of police of a rank superior to that of constable.

The powers given by this regulation shall be in addition to and not in derogation of any powers of the civil authority, constables, or superior officers of police.

DORR 51B (introduced 6 Feb. 1917)

Where a competent naval or military authority, or any superior officer of police, is of opinion that a meeting or assembly is being or about to be held of such a character that an offence against these regulations may be committed thereat, he may authorise in writing a police constable or other person to attend the meeting or assembly, and any police constable or person so authorised may enter the place at which the meeting or assembly is held and remain there during its continuance.

In this regulation the expression 'superior officer of police' means an officer of police of a rank superior to that of sergeant.

The powers given by this regulation shall be in addition to and not in derogation of any other powers of competent naval or military authorities, constables, or superior officers of police.

20 If a justice of the peace is satisfied, by information in writing upon oath laid before him by any person duly authorised by the civil authority, that any house, land, building, or other premises are being or are about to be used for any purpose or in any way prejudicial to the preservation of the peace or maintenance of order by persons suspected of attempting to cause mutiny, sedition, or disaffection among the police forces or among the civil population, the justice may by order require the premises either to be closed altogether or · not to be used for any purpose prohibited by the order, or not to be used except in accordance with conditions and restrictions imposed by the order, and if the owner or occupier of the premises or any other person contravenes or fails to comply with any of the provisions of the order or any conditions or restrictions imposed thereby, he shall be guilty of an offence against these regulations, and the civil authority may cause such steps to be taken as may be necessary to enforce compliance with the order.

DORR 51C (introduced 14 Apr. 1917, amended 19 July 1918)

If a justice of the peace is satisfied, by information in writing upon oath laid before him by any competent naval or military authority, or any person duly authorised by him, or by an officer of police of a rank not below that of inspector, that any house, land, building, or other premises are being or are about to be used for any purpose or in any way prejudicial to the public safety or the defence of the Realm, by persons of hostile origin or association, or by persons suspected of attempting to cause mutiny, sedition, or disaffection among His Majesty's forces or among the civil population, the justice may by order require the premises either to be closed altogether or not to be used for any purpose prohibited by the order, or not to be used except in accordance with conditions and restrictions imposed by the order, and if the owner or occupier of the premises or any other person contravenes or fails to comply with any of the provisions of the order or any conditions or restrictions imposed thereby, he shall be guilty of an offence against these regulations, and the competent naval or military authority may cause such steps to be taken as may be necessary to enforce compliance with the order.

In the application of this regulation to Scotland references to a justice of the peace shall be construed as references to the sheriff.

---

21 Any police officer or constable may stop any vehicle travelling along any public road, and, if he has reason to suspect that any vehicle upon any public road is being used for any purpose or in any way prejudicial to the preservation of the peace or maintenance of order, or otherwise unlawfully, may search and seize the vehicle and seize anything found therein which he has reason to suspect is being used or intended to be used for any such purpose as aforesaid.

DORR 52 (introduced 28 Nov. 1914)

Any officer, or any soldier, sailor or airman engaged on sentry patrol or other similar duty, and any police officer, may stop any vehicle travelling along any public highway, and, if he has reason to suspect that the vehicle is being used for any purpose or in any way prejudicial to the public safety or the defence of the Realm, may search and seize the vehicle and seize anything found therein which he has reason to suspect is being used or intended to be used for any such purpose as aforesaid.

---

22 The civil authority may by order require any person or persons of any class or description to furnish him, either verbally or in writing, with such information as may be specified in the order, and the order may require any person to attend at such time and such place as may be specified in the order for the purpose of furnishing such information, and if any person fails to comply with the order he shall be guilty of an offence against these regulations.

DORR 53 (introduced 28 Nov. 1914, amended 23 Oct. 1917, 21 Dec. 1917, 25 Nov. 1918)

The competent naval or military authority, or any person duly authorised in that behalf by the Admiralty, Army Council, Air Council or Director-General of National Service, may by order require any person or persons of any class or description to furnish him, either verbally or in writing, with such information as may be specified in the order, and the order may require any person to attend at such time and such place as may be specified in the order for the purpose of furnishing such information, and if any person fails to comply with the order he shall be guilty of an offence against these regulations.

Reg. 23 (amended 20 May 1922, 23 June 1922, 6 July 1922)

Any person authorised for the purpose by the civil authority, or any police constable, or member of any of His Majesty's forces on duty when the occasion for the arrest arises, may arrest without warrant any person whom he suspects of acting or of having acted or of being about to act in a manner prejudicial to the preservation of the peace or maintenance of order, or upon whom may be found any article, book, letter, or other document, the possession of which gives ground for such a suspicion, or who is suspected of having committed an offence against these regulations, or of being in possession of any article or document which is being used or intended to be used for any purpose or in any way prejudicial to the preservation of the peace or maintenance of order, and anything found on any person so arrested which there is reason to suspect is being so used or intended to be used may be seized, and the civil authority may order anything so seized to be destroyed or otherwise disposed of.

Any person so arrested may, on the order of the civil authority, be detained either in any of His Majesty's prisons or elsewhere, as may be specified in the Order, upon such conditions as the civil authority may direct, until he has been discharged by direction of the Attorney-General or is brought before a Court of Summary Jurisdiction. Any person to be brought before a Court under this regulation shall receive at least twenty-four hours notice in writing of the nature of the charge preferred against him.

Any person so arrested shall, if so ordered by the Civil Authority, or by a Chief Officer of Police, or by Police Officer of higher rank, be photographed and finger-print impressions of the fingers and thumbs of both his hands taken, and if such person refuses to allow his photograph or such impressions to be taken or obstructs the taking thereof he shall be guilty of an offence against these Regulations.

On a person being taken into custody under this regulation he may apply to the civil authority for release on bail, and, if the civil authority so directs in writing, any resident magistrate may discharge the person so in custody upon his entering into a recognizance, with, or without, sureties, for a reasonable amount to appear at a time and place to be named in the recognizance.

Any person detained under this Regulation may, without prejudice to any other powers of removal be removed on the order of the Civil Authority to any place where his presence is required in the interest of justice and may be detained in such place for such time as his presence is so required there, and whilst being so removed or detained he shall be deemed to be detained under the provisions of this Regulation.

If any person assists or connives at the escape of any person who may be in custody under this regulation, or knowingly harbours or assists any person who has so escaped, he shall be guilty of an offence against these regulations.

DORR 55 (introduced 28 Nov. 1914, amended 27 Jan. 1916, 29 Feb. 1916, 12 Apr. 1916, 27 June 1916, 28 Aug. 1918, 14 Jan. 1919)

Any person authorised for the purpose by the competent naval or military authority, or any police constable or officer of customs and excise or aliens officer may arrest without warrant any person whose behaviour is of such a nature as to give reasonable grounds for suspecting that he has acted or is acting or is about to act in a manner prejudicial to the public safety or the defence of the Realm, or upon whom may be found any article, book, letter, or other document, the possession of which gives grounds for such a suspicion, or who is suspected of having committed an offence against these regulations, or of being in possession of any article or document which is being used or intended to be used for any purpose or in any way prejudicial to the public safety or the defence of the Realm; and anything found on any person so arrested which there is reason to suspect is being so used or intended to be used may be seized, and the competent naval or military authority may order anything so seized to be destroyed or otherwise disposed of.

Any person so arrested may be detained either in civil custody or in military custody; and without prejudice to any other powers of detention any such person may, on the order of the competent naval or military authority, be detained in any of His Majesty's prisons as a person committed to prison on remand, or, in Scotland, for further examination, until it has been determined whether or not he is to be proceeded against for an offence under these regulations and, if the offence for which he is to be proceeded against is not a summary offence, until it has also been determined in what manner he is to be tried.

Any person so arrested shall, if so ordered by the competent naval or military authority, or by the chief officer of police for the district, be photographed and finger-print impressions of the fingers and thumbs of both of his hands taken, and if any person refuses to allow such photograph or impressions to be taken, or obstructs the taking thereof, he shall be guilty of a summary offence against these regulations:

Provided that—

(a) no photograph of a person so taken shall be published except for the purpose of tracing that person, nor shall a copy of any such photograph be shown to any person except a person officially authorised to see it; and

(b) If the person arrested neither has been nor is subsequently convicted of an offence against these regulations, all photographs (both negatives and copies) and finger-print impressions so taken shall be destroyed as soon as they are no longer required for the purposes of these regulations, and in any case forthwith after the termination of the present war.

On a person being taken into custody under this regulation he may apply to the competent naval or military authority for release on bail, and, if the competent naval or military authority so directs in writing, any officer of police, who under the Summary Jurisdiction Acts has power to release on bail any person apprehended without warrant, may discharge the person so in custody upon his entering into a recognizance, or, in Scotland, finding caution, with or without sureties, for a reasonable amount to appear at such time and place, to be named in the recognizance or caution, as may be fixed by the competent naval or military authority. Provided that a person so taken into custody as having committed a summary offence against these regulations may be released on bail in manner aforesaid without application to or direction from the competent naval or military authority.

The power given by this regulation to an officer of the police to discharge any person in custody shall in Ireland be exerciseable by a resident magistrate or in the police district of Dublin Metropolis by a divisional justice of that district.

If any person assists or connives at the escape of any person who may be in custody under this regulation, or knowingly harbours or assists any person who has so escaped, he shall be guilty of an offence against these regulations.

24(1) Any person who does any act with a view to promoting or calculated to promote the objects of an unlawful association within the meaning of section 7 of the Criminal Law and Procedure (Ireland) Act, 1887, shall be guilty of an offence against these regulations.

(2) If any person, without lawful authority or excuse, has in his possession any document relating or purporting to relate to the affairs of any such association, or emanating or purporting to emanate from an officer of any such association, or addressed to the person as an officer or member of any such association, or indicating that he is an officer or member of any such association, that person shall be guilty of an offence against these regulations unless he proves that he did not know or had no reason to suspect that the document was of any such character as aforesaid or that he is not an officer or member of the association.

Where a person is charged with having in his possession any such document, and the document was found on premises in his occupation, or under his control, or in which he has resided, the document shall be presumed to have been in his possession unless the contrary is proved.

ROIR 79 (introduced 13 Aug. 1920)

(1) Any person who does any act with a view to promoting or calculated to promote the objects of an unlawful association within the meaning of section seven of the Criminal Law and Procedure (Ireland) Act, 1887, shall be guilty of an offence against these regulations.

(2) If any person without lawful authority or excuse has in his possession any document relating or purporting to relate to the affairs of any such association, or emanating or purporting to emanate from an officer of any such association, or addressed to the person as an officer or member of any such association or indicating that he is an officer or member of any such association, that person shall be guilty of an offence against these regulations unless he proves that he did not know or had no reason to suspect that the document was of any such character as aforesaid or that he is not an officer or member of the association.

Where a person is charged with having in his possession any such document, and the document was found on premises in his occupation, or under his control, or in which he has resided, the document shall be presumed to have been in his possession unless the contrary is proved.

25 No person shall by word of mouth or in writing, or in any newspaper, periodical, book, circular, or other printed publication:

(*a*) spread false reports or make false statements; or

(*b*) spread reports or make statements intended or likely to cause disaffection to His Majesty, or to interfere with the success of any police or other force acting for the preservation of the peace or maintenance of order in Northern Ireland; or

(*c*) spread reports or make statements intended or likely to prejudice the recruiting or enrolment of persons to serve in any police or other force enrolled or employed for the preservation of the peace or maintenance of order in Northern Ireland, or to prejudice the training, discipline, or administration of any such force; and no person shall produce any performance on any stage, or exhibit any picture or cinematograph film, or commit any act which is intended or likely to cause any disaffection, interference or prejudice as aforesaid, and if any person contravenes any of the above provisions he shall be guilty of an offence against these regulations.

If any person without lawful authority or excuse has in his possession or on premises in his occupation or under his control, any document containing a report or statement the publication of which would be a contravention of the foregoing provisions of this regulation, he shall be guilty of an offence against these regulations, unless he proves that he did not know and had no reason to suspect that the document contained any such report or statement, or that he had no intention of transmitting or circulating the document or distributing copies thereof to or amongst other persons.

DORR 27 (introduced 23 May 1916, amended 28 July 1916, 23 Nov. 1916, 22 Aug. 1917, 21 Dec. 1917, 4 Mar. 1918)

No person shall by word of mouth or in writing or in any newspaper, periodical, book, circular, or other printed publication.

(*a*) spread false reports or make false statements; or

(*b*) spread reports or make statements intended or likely to cause disaffection to His Majesty or to interfere with the success of His Majesty's forces or of the forces of any of His Majesty's Allies by land or sea or to prejudice His Majesty's relations with foreign powers; or

(*c*) spread reports or make statements intended or likely to prejudice the recruiting of persons to serve in any of His Majesty's forces, or in any body of persons enrolled for employment under the Army Council or Air Council or entered for service under the direction of the Admiralty, or in any police force or fire brigade, or to prejudice the training, discipline or administration of any such force, body or brigade; or

(*d*) spread reports or make statements intended or likely to undermine public confidence in any bank or currency notes which are legal tender in the United Kingdom or any part thereof, or to prejudice the success of any financial measures taken or arrangements made by His Majesty's Government with a view to the prosecution of the war;

and no person shall produce any performance on any stage or exhibit any picture or cinematograph film or commit any act which is intended or likely to cause any such disaffection interference or prejudice as aforesaid, and if any person contravenes any of the above provisions he shall be guilty of an offence against these regulations.

If any person without lawful authority or excuse has in his possession or on premises in his occupation or under his control any document containing a report or statement the publication of which would be a contravention of the foregoing provisions of this regulation, he shall be guilty of an offence against these regulations, unless he proves that he did not know and had no reason to suspect that the document contained any such report or statement, or that he had no intention of transmitting or circulating the document or distributing copies thereof to or amongst other persons.

---

26 The civil authority may by notice prohibit the circulation of any newspaper for any specified period, and any person circulating or distributing such newspaper within such specified period shall be guilty of an offence against these regulations.
None

DORR 27C (introduced 16 Nov. 1917, amended 21 Dec. 1917) made provision for censorship). See also DORR 27 (above).

---

27 If any person in any newspaper, periodical, circular or other printed publication, or in any public speech, without lawful authority shall publish the contents of any confidential document belonging to, or of any document which has in confidence been communicated by, or any confidential information obtained from, any Department of the Government of Northern Ireland, or any person in the service of that Government, such first mentioned person shall be guilty of an offence against these regulations.

DORR 27A (introduced 22 Apr. 1916, amended 27 Feb. 1918)
If either House of Parliament in pursuance of a resolution passed by that House holds a secret session. it shall not be lawful for any person in any newspaper, periodical, circular or other printed publication, or in any public speech, to publish any report of, or to purport to describe, or to refer to, the proceedings at such session, except such report thereof as may be officially communicated through the Directors of the Official Press Bureau.

It shall not be lawful for any person in any newspaper, periodical, circular or other printed publication, or in any public speech, to publish any report of, or to purport to describe, or to refer to, the proceedings at any meeting of the Cabinet, or without lawful authority to publish the contents of any confidential document belonging to, or of any document which has in confidence been communicated by, or any confidential information obtained from, any Government department, or any person in the service of His Majesty.

If any person contravenes any provision of this regulation he shall be guilty of an offence against these regulations.

---

28 Every document purporting to be an order or other instrument issued by the civil authority and to be signed by that authority shall be received in evidence and be deemed to be such an order or instrument without further proof unless the contrary is shown, and the Documentary Evidence Act, 1868, as amended by the Documentary Evidence Act, 1882, shall apply as if the civil authority were mentioned in the first column of the schedule to the first-mentioned Act, and as if the civil authority or any person authorised by the civil authority to act on his behalf were mentioned in the second column of that schedule.

DORR 58C (introduced 28 July 1915)
Every document purporting to be an order or other instrument issued by a competent naval or military authority and to be signed by such an authority shall be received in evidence and be deemed to be such an order or instrument without further proof unless the contrary is shown.

---

29 The powers conferred by these regulations are in addition to and not in derogation of any powers exerciseable by the civil authority and other persons to take such steps as may be necessary for securing the preservation of the peace or maintenance of order, and save as otherwise expressly provided by these regulations nothing in these regulations shall affect the liability of any person to trial and punishment for any offence or crime otherwise than in accordance with these regulations. Provided that no person shall be liable to be punished twice for the same offence or crime.

DORR 59 (introduced 28 Nov. 1914)
The powers conferred by these regulations are in addition to and not in derogation of any powers exercisable by members of His Majesty's naval, military and air forces and other persons to take such steps as may be necessary for securing the public safety and the defence of the Realm, and nothing in these regulations shall affect the liability of any person to trial and punishment for any offence or war crime otherwise than in accordance with these regulations.

---

30 The civil authority, or any other person by whom an order is made in pursuance of these regulations, shall publish notice of the order in such manner as he may consider best adapted for informing persons affected by the order, and no person shall, without lawful authority, deface or otherwise tamper with any notice posted up in pursuance of these regulations, or any other notice, advertisement or placard, relating to any matters connected with the preservation of the peace or maintenance of order, exhibited or posted up under lawful authority, and if he does so shall be guilty of an offence against these regulations.

DORR 60 (introduced 28 Nov. 1914, amended 14 Oct. 1915, 16 Nov. 1917)

The competent naval or military authority, or any other person by whom an order is made in pursuance of these regulations, shall publish notice of the order in such manner as he may consider best adapted for informing persons affected by the order, and no person shall without lawful authority deface or otherwise tamper with any notice posted up in pursuance of these regulations, or any other notice, advertisement or placard, relating to any naval, military or air-force matters or any matters connected with any financial or other measures taken or any financial or other arrangements made by or on behalf of His Majesty's Government with a view to the prosecution of the war or otherwise connected with the public safety or the defence of the Realm exhibited or posted up under lawful authority, and if he does so shall be guilty of an offence against these regulations.

---

31 Any person claiming to act under any permit or permission granted under or for the purposes of these regulations shall, if at any time he is required to do so by the civil authority or any person authorised by him, or by any officer of police, produce the permit or permission for inspection, and if he refuses to do so he shall be guilty of an offence against these regulations.

Any permit or permission granted under or for the purposes of any provision of these regulations may at any time be revoked.

DORR 61 (introduced 28 Nov. 1914)

Any person claiming to act under any permit or permission granted under or for the purposes of these regulations shall, if at any time he is required to do so by the competent naval or military authority or any person authorised by him, or by any naval, military or air-force officer, or by any sailor, soldier or airman engaged on sentry patrol or other similar duty, or by any officer of customs and excise, officer of police or alien's officer, produce the permit or permission for inspection, and if he refuses to do so he shall be guilty of an offence against these regulations.

Any permit or permission granted under or for the purposes of any provision of these regulations may at any time be revoked.

---

32 In addition and without prejudice to any powers which a court may possess to order the exclusion of the public from any proceedings, if in the course of such proceedings application is made by the prosecution on behalf of the civil authority that in the public interest all or any portion of the public shall be excluded during any part of the hearing, the court may make an order to that effect.

DORR 58 (part of) (introduced 10 June 1915)

In addition and without prejudice to any powers which a court may possess to order the exclusion of the public from any proceedings, if in the course of proceedings before a court of summary jurisdiction against any person for an offence against these regulations or the proceedings on appeal, application is made by the prosecution, in the public interest, that all or any portion of the public shall be excluded during any part of the hearing, the court may make an order to that effect, but the passing of sentence shall in any case take place in public.

---

33 If it is made to appear to a county court judge or recorder that personal service of any civil bill returnable to his court, or such other service as is by law prescribed, cannot be effected owing to the prevalence of a state of disorder or otherwise, he may, in addition and without prejudice to any other powers in that behalf, make such order for substituted or other service, or for the substitution for service of notice by advertisement or otherwise as may seem just, or may declare the service actually effected sufficient.

ROIR 83 (introduced 13 Aug. 1920)

If it is made to appear to a county court judge or recorder that personal service of any civil bill returnable to his court, or such other service as is by law prescribed, cannot be effected owing to the prevalence of a state of disorder or otherwise, he may, in addition and without prejudice to any other powers in that behalf, make such order for substituted or other service or for the substitution for service of notice by advertisement or otherwise as may seem just, or may declare the service actually effected sufficient.

---

34 For the purposes of the trial of a person for an offence under these regulations, or under the Firearms Act, 1920, by a court of summary jurisdiction and the punishment thereof, the offence shall be deemed to have been committed either at the place in which the same actually was committed or in any place in which such person may be or to which he may be brought, and the trial, or any proceedings antecedent thereto or connected therewith, may take place on any date appointed by a resident magistrate having jurisdiction in such place, and a summons may be issued by a justice to a witness who is not within his jurisdiction, and any such summons may be issued, served and enforced in the same manner as a summons to a witness within the jurisdiction of the issuing justice.

DORR 58 (part of) (introduced 28 Nov. 1914, amended 29 Feb. 1916)

For the purpose of the trial of a person for such an offence the offence shall be deemed to have been committed either at the place in which the same actually was committed, or at any place in which the offender may be, and the court in Scotland shall be the sheriff court. In Ireland for the purposes of such trial a summons may be issued by a justice to a witness who is not within his jurisdiction and any such summons may, in Ireland, be issued, served and enforced in the same manner as a summons to a witness within the jurisdiction of the issuing justice.

---

35 These regulations shall not, save as therein expressly provided, be construed as applying to members of His Majesty's forces when acting within the scope of their duties.

No DORA or ROIA Equivalent
Under DORR it was the practice to exempt the police from restrictions imposed by particular orders made under the regs.

(c) *The additional Regulations (up to 31 Dec. 1925)*

Reg. 18A (introduced 18 May 1922)
Where for any purpose prejudicial to the Preservation of the Peace and Maintenance of Order in Northern Ireland any house, yard or other premises is, or has been, used, adapted of fitted up for or contains any device calculated to facilitate the discharge of firearms, or the throwing of bombs therefrom, or the escape of persons from arrest, or the obstruction of the forces of the Crown in searching such premises, or the commission of any other act prejudicial to the Preservation of the Peace or the Maintenance of Order in Northern Ireland, every person owning, having control of, frequenting or occupying such house, yard or other premises, shall be guilty of an offence against these Regulations unless he proves that he did not know and had no reason to suspect that the house, yard or other premises was, or had been so used, adapted or fitted up for, or contained any such device, as aforesaid. For the purpose of this Regulation every person for the time being entitled to the receipt of the rack rent of the premises, shall be deemed to be a person owning such premises.

The Civil Authority may by Order require every person residing in or occupying such house, yard or other premises forthwith to vacate the same, and, whether so requiring or not, may by Order require such house, yard or other premises either to be closed altogether, or such alterations to be made therein as may be specified in such Order, as being necessary for preventing any such unlawful use as aforesaid of such house, yard or other premises, or not to be used except in accordance with conditions and restrictions imposed by the Order, and it shall be lawful to take such steps to restore the premises to proper condition and generally as may be necessary to enforce compliance with the Order.

If any person contravenes or fails to comply with any provision of any Order made under this Regulation, he shall be guilty of an offence against these Regulations.

No DORA or ROIA Equivalent
This reg. is essentially an extension of reg. 20 (above).

Reg. 7A (introduced 18 May 1922, amended 1 June 1922)

Any Military or Police Officer in any case where he considers it necessary so to do for the purpose of preventing an armed attack on His Majesty's Forces or on a Police Force or on the civilian population, and in any other case where he considers it necessary so to do, having regard to the Military or Police necessities of the situation, may close, stop or otherwise render impassable any road, lane, passage, pathway or ferry, or may cut trenches in such road, lane, passage or pathway, or may demolish or otherwise render impassable any bridge without publishing or giving any notice thereof or setting up any warning lights, but any Military or Police Officer taking such action as aforesaid shall immediately give notice thereof to the Civil Authority.

Provided that where at any time, or by any person or under any circumstances whatsoever, any road, lane, passage, pathway, or ferry has been closed, stopped or otherwise rendered impassable, or trenches have been cut in any road, lane, passage or pathway, or any bridge has been demolished or otherwise rendered impassable, and where any Military or Police Officer considers it necessary for the purposes aforesaid or having regard to the aforesaid necessities to keep such road, lane, passage, pathway or ferry closed, stopped or otherwise rendered impassable, or to keep open such trenches so cut as aforesaid, or to keep demolished or otherwise rendered impassable such bridge, such military or police officer may keep such road, lane, passage, pathway or ferry closed, stopped or otherwise rendered impassable, or may keep open any trenches so cut as aforesaid or may keep demolished or otherwise rendered impassable any such bridge, and any such closing, stopping or rendering impassable any road, lane, passage, pathway or ferry, cutting of trenches or demolishing or rendering impassable any bridge shall be deemed to have been done under the provisions of this Regulation.

No DORA or ROIA Equivalent
This reg. is essentially an amendment to reg. 7 (above).

Reg. 24A (introduced 22 May 1922)

Any person who becomes or remains a member of an unlawful association or who does any act with a view to promoting or calculated to promote the objects of an unlawful association or seditious conspiracy shall be guilty of an offence against these Regulations.

If any person without lawful authority or excuse has in his possession any document relating to or purporting to relate to the affairs of any such association or emanating or purporting to emanate from an officer of any such association or addressed to the person as an officer or member of any such association or indicating that he is an officer or member of any such association that person shall be guilty of an offence against these Regulations unless he proves that he did not know or had no reason to suspect that the document was of any such character as aforesaid or that he is not an officer or member of the association.

Where a person is charged with having in his possession any such document, and the document was found on premises in his occupation, or under his control, or in which he is found or has resided, the document shall be presumed to have been in his possession unless the contrary is proved.

The following organisations shall for the purposes of this Regulation be deemed to be unlawful associations:

> The Irish Republican Brotherhood,
> The Irish Republican Army,
> The Irish Volunteers,
> The Cumann na m'Ban,
> The Fianna na h'Eireann.

See *ROIR 79* (above). See also s. 6 and s. 7 Criminal Law and Procedure (Ireland) Act 1887.

Reg. 10A (introduced 25 May 1922)
If:

(a) any unauthorised person uses or wears any naval, military, air force, police, or other official uniform, decoration, or medal (whether such uniform, decoration or medal is British or Foreign), or any badge supplied or authorised by the Admiralty, Army Council, Air Council or Minister of Munitions or by the police or other official authority, or any uniform, decoration, medal, or badge so nearly resembling the same as to be calculated to deceive or any miniature or other representation of any such decoration or medal, or any brooch or personal ornament designed to imitate any such decoration or medal; or

(b) any person falsely represents himself to be a person who is or has been entitled to use or wear any such uniform, decoration, medal, or badge as aforesaid; or

(c) any person without lawful authority or excuse has in his possession, supplies or offers to supply any such uniform, decoration, medal, or badge as aforesaid or any such representation, brooch or ornament as aforesaid to any person not authorised to use or wear the same;

such person shall be guilty of an offence against these Regulations.

Provided that nothing in this Regulation shall be deemed to prohibit the wearing or supply of ordinary regimental badges, or any brooch or ornament representing the same.

DORR 41 (introduced 28 July 1915, amended 30 Mar. 1917, 21 Dec. 1917, 28 July 1918)
If,

(a) any unauthorised person uses or wears any naval, military, air-force, police, or other official uniform, decoration, or medal (whether such uniform decoration or medal is British or foreign), or any badge supplied or authorised by the Admiralty, Army Council, Air Council or Minister of Munitions or by the police or other official authority, or any uniform, decoration, medal, or badge so nearly resembling the same as to be calculated to deceive or any miniature or other representation of any such decoration or medal, or any brooch or personal ornament designed to imitate any such decoration or medal; or

(*b*) any person falsely represents himself to be a person who is or has been entitled to use or wear any such uniform, decoration, medal, or badge as aforesaid; or

(*c*) any person without lawful authority or excuse supplies, or offers to supply, any such uniform, decoration, medal, or badge as aforesaid or any such representation, brooch, or ornament as aforesaid to any person not authorised to use or wear the same;

such person shall be guilty of an offence against these regulations.

Provided that nothing in this regulation shall be deemed to prohibit the wearing or supply of ordinary regimental badges, or any brooch or ornament representing the same.

Reg. 22a (introduced 1 June 1922)

It shall be the duty of any person, if so required by any member of any of His Majesty's Forces when on duty or by a police constable, to stop and to answer to the best of his ability and knowledge any questions which may reasonably be addressed to him, and if he refuses or fails to stop or if he refuses or fails so to answer such questions he shall be guilty of an offence against these Regulations.

DORR 53 (part of) (introduced 28 Nov. 1914, amended 23 Oct. 1917, this part revoked 25 Nov. 1918)

It shall be the duty of any person, if so required by an officer, or by a soldier, sailor or airman engaged on sentry patrol or other similar duty, or by a police constable, or any person duly authorised in that behalf by the Director-General of National Service to stop and answer to the best of his ability and knowledge any questions which may be reasonably addressed to him, and if he refuses or fails to do so he shall be guilty of an offence against these regulations.

Reg. 23A (introduced 1 June 1922)

Where a person is suspected of acting, or of having acted, or of being about to act in a manner prejudicial to the preservation of the peace and the maintenance of order in Northern Ireland, and it appears to the Civil Authority that it is desirable that such person should be prohibited from residing in or entering a certain area or areas, the civil authority may by order prohibit him from residing in or entering any area or areas which may be specified in the order and upon the making of such an order the person to whom the order relates shall, if he resides in any specified area, leave that area within such time as may be specified by the order, and shall not subsequently reside in or enter any area specified in the order, and if he does so, he shall be guilty of an offence against these regulations. Any order made as aforesaid may require the person in respect of whom it is made to comply with such conditions as to residence, reporting to the police, restriction on movements, or otherwise as may be imposed on him, and if any person in respect of whom such an order is made fails to comply with any such condition he shall be guilty of an offence against these regulations.

Any such order may further require the person to whom the order relates to report for approval his proposed place of residence to the civil authority and to proceed thereto and report his arrival to the police within such time as may be specified in the order, and not subsequently to change his place of residence without leave of the civil authority, and in such case if he fails to comply with the requirements of the order he shall be guilty of an offence against these regulations.

If any person remains in or enters any area in contravention of an order under this regulation he may be removed therefrom by the direction of the civil authority.

DORR 14 (introduced 28 Nov. 1914, amended 23 Mar. 1915, 24 Sept. 1915, 28 June 1917)

Where a person is suspected of acting, or of having acted, or of being about to act in a manner prejudicial to the public safety or the defence of the Realm and it appears to the competent naval or military authority that it is desirable that such person should be prohibited from residing in or entering any locality the competent naval or military authority may with the consent of the Admiralty or Army Council by order prohibit him from residing in or entering any area or areas which may be specified in the order and upon the making of such an order the person to whom the order relates shall, if he resides in any specified area, leave that area within such time as may be specified by the order, and shall not subsequently reside in or enter any area specified in the order, and if he does so, he shall be guilty of an offence against these regulations. Any order made as aforesaid may require the person in respect of whom it is made to comply with such conditions as to residence, reporting to the police, restriction on movements, or otherwise as may be imposed on him, and if any person in respect of whom such an order is made fails to comply with any such condition he shall be guilty of an offence against these regulations.

Any such order may further require the person to whom the order relates to report for approval his proposed place of residence to the competent naval or military authority and to proceed thereto and report his arrival to the police within such time as may be specified in the order, and not subsequently to change his place of residence without leave of the competent naval or military authority, and in such case if he fails to comply with the requirements of the order he shall be guilty of an offence against these regulations.

If any person remains in or enters any area in contravention of an order under this regulation he may be removed therefrom by the direction of the competent naval or military authority.

The Admiralty or Army Council may from time to time revoke or vary any order made under this regulation.

Reg. 23B (introduced 1 June 1922, amended 6 July 1922, 30 Oct. 1923, 17 Nov. 1923)

When it appears to the Minister of Home Affairs for Northern Ireland, on the recommendation of a Chief Officer of Police or of a Police Officer of higher rank or of an advisory committee: that for securing the preservation of the peace and the maintenance of order in Northern Ireland it is expedient that a person who is suspected of acting or having acted or being about to act in a manner prejudicial to the preservation of the peace and the maintenance of order in Northern Ireland, shall be subjected to such obligations and restrictions as are hereinafter mentioned, the Minister of Home Affairs for Northern Ireland may by order require that person forthwith, or from time to time, either to remain in, or to proceed to and reside in, such place as may be specified in the order and to comply with such directions as to reporting to the police, restriction of movement, and otherwise as may be specified in the order, or to be interned as may be directed in the order.

Provided that any order under this regulation shall include express provision for the due consideration by an advisory committee of any representations which a person in respect of whom the order is made may make against the order.

If any person in respect of whom any order is made under this regulation fails to comply with any of the provisions of the order he shall be guilty of an offence against these regulations, and any person interned under such order shall be subject to such restrictions as the Minister of Home Affairs for Northern Ireland may direct, and if any person so interned escapes or attempts to escape from the place of internment or commits any breach of the rules in force therein he shall be guilty of an offence against these regulations.

The advisory committee for the purposes of this regulation shall be such advisory committee as is specially appointed by the Minister of Home Affairs for the purposes of this regulation, such committee being presided over by a person who holds or has held high judicial office or is a Recorder or County Court Judge or a practising Barrister of at least ten years' standing.

Any person interned under this regulation may, without prejudice to any other powers of removal, be removed on the Order of the Civil Authority to any place where his presence is required for the purpose of entering into a recognisance, or in the interests of justice or for the purpose of any public inquiry, and may be detained in such place for such time as his presence is so required there, and whilst being so removed or detained he shall be deemed to be interned under the provisions of this Regulation.

Any person interned under this Regulation may, without prejudice to any other powers of removal, be removed on the Order of the Minister of Home Affairs for Northern Ireland to any place of internment, whether one of His

Majesty's Prisons or not, other than that specified in the internment Order, and may be interned there and whilst being so removed or interned shall be deemed to be interned under the provisions of this Regulation.

Nothing in this regulation shall be construed to restrict or prejudice the application or effect of Regulation 23A.

DORR 14B (introduced 10 June 1915, amended 8 June 1916, 16 Nov. 1917, 20 Apr. 1918, 4 Sept. 1918, 9 Feb. 1920)

Where on the recommendation of a competent naval or military authority or of one of the advisory committees hereinafter mentioned it appears to the Secretary of State that for securing the public safety or the defence of the Realm it is expedient in view of the hostile origin or associations of any person that he shall be subjected to such obligations and restrictions as are hereinafter mentioned, the Secretary of State may by order require that person forthwith, or from time to time, either to remain in, or to proceed to and reside in, such place as may be specified in the order, and to comply with such directions as to reporting to the police, restriction of movement, and otherwise as may be specified in the order, or to be interned in such place as may be specified in the order.

The Secretary of State may make any such order as aforesaid with respect to any alien in any case where in his opinion the making of the order is calculated to secure the safety of any British subject in any foreign country.

Provided that any order under this regulation shall, in the case of any person who is not a subject of a state at war with His Majesty, include express provision for the due consideration by one of such advisory committees of any representations he may make against the order.

If any person in respect of whom any order is made under this regulation fails to comply with any of the provisions of the order he shall be guilty of an offence against these regulations, and any person interned under such order shall be subject to the like restrictions and may be dealt with in like manner as a prisoner of war, except so far as the Secretary of State may modify such restrictions, and if any person so interned escapes or attempts to escape from the place of internment or commits any breach of the rules in force therein he shall be guilty of an offence against these regulations.

The advisory committees for the purposes of this regulation shall be such advisory committees as are appointed for the purpose of advising the Secretary of State with respect to the internment and deportation of aliens, or any committee specially appointed by the Secretary of State for the purposes of this regulation, each of such committees being presided over by a person who holds or has held high judicial office.

In any area in respect of which the operation of Section one of the Defence of the Realm (Amendment) Act, 1915, is for the time being suspended, this regulation shall apply in relation to any person who is suspected of acting or having acted or of being about to act in a manner prejudicial to the public safety or the defence of the Realm, as it applies in relation to persons of hostile origin or association.

In the application of this regulation to Scotland and Ireland, references to the Secretary for Scotland and references to the Lord Lieutenant or Chief Secretary shall respectively, be substituted for references to the Secretary of State, but an order under this regulation may require the person to whom the order relates to reside or to be interned in any place in the British Islands.

Nothing in this regulation shall be construed to restrict or prejudice the application and effect of Regulation 14, or any power of interning aliens who are subjects of any State at war with His Majesty.

Reg. 23C (introduced 6 July 1922)

(1) A person detained or interned under the Regulations shall not, except with the sanction of the Civil Authority, be permitted to be visited by any person other than an officer of the place of detention or internment:

Provided that in any case where the Civil Authority considers it necessary so to do for the purpose of the prevention of crime or of the preservation of the peace or of the maintenance of order or for the purposes of the security, good order and government of the place of detention or internment, and of the persons detained or interned therein, or for the purpose of preventing any tampering with evidence, or any plans of escape or for other like considerations, he may direct that no person whether an officer of the place of detention or internment or not may visit a person detained or interned except in the presence and if so directed, the hearing of such person as the officer in charge of the place of detention or internment may nominate.

(2)(*a*) Except with the consent of the Civil Authority no communication may be sent by a person detained under the regulations whilst so detained. All communications from or to such person shall be examined by the said officer in charge or by another officer appointed by him for the purpose.

(*b*) No communications may be sent or received by a person interned under the Regulations except such as have been examined and passed by the said officer in charge or by another officer appointed by him for the purpose.

(3) Nothing in this Regulation shall be construed to prevent the Civil Authority from giving directions as to the conditions upon which persons are to be detained under Regulation 23 of these Regulations provided always that if such conditions are inconsistent with this Regulation, this Regulation shall prevail.

(4) Nothing in this Regulation shall be construed to prevent the Minister of Home Affairs for Northern Ireland from giving directions as to the restrictions to which a person interned under Regulation 23 (*b*) shall be subject or to prevent rules being made to be in force in the place of internment provided always that if such restrictions or such rules are inconsistent with this regulation, this Regulation shall prevail.

(5) Persons detained or interned in any of His Majesty's Prisons shall be subject to any rules for the government of prisoners awaiting trial, including such general prison rules as are applicable to such prisoners, for the time being in force, except in so far as the said rules are inconsistent with this Regulation.

No direct DORA or ROIA Equivalent
Some restrictions relating to internees (and prisoners of war) imposed by
DORR 46A (introduced 8 Nov. 1918).

Reg. 23D (introduced 6 July 1922, amended 30 Oct. 1923)
Any person undergoing a sentence of imprisonment in Northern Ireland may
without prejudice to any other power of removal be removed by order of the
Minister of Home Affairs for Northern Ireland to or from any of His Majesty's
Prisons in Northern Ireland, and any such person may on the like order be
brought to any place where his presence is required in the interests of justice
and may be detained in such place for such time as his presence is so required
there, and whilst being so detained shall be deemed to be in legal custody.

This regulation shall apply to all prisoners in Northern Ireland in like
manner as it applies to persons undergoing a sentence of imprisonment in
Northern Ireland. For the purposes of this regulation, the expression 'prisoner'
shall have the same meaning as that assigned to it in Section 11 of the Prison
Act, 1898.

No DORA or ROIA Equivalent

Reg. 18B (introduced 20 Sept. 1922)
The Civil Authority may by Order as regards any area specified therein
require the occupier or manager of every building or portion of a building
where lodging is provided on payment to keep a book, in which he shall
require each lodger therein or other inmate thereof himself to enter his correct
name, address and occupation, and if such lodger or other inmate refuses or
fails so to make the required entries such occupier or manager shall forthwith
notify the police at the nearest police station of such refusal or failure.

And any such Order as aforesaid may require such occupier or manager to
produce such book on demand by any person authorised for the purpose by
the Civil Authority, or by any police officer or constable or by any member of
any of His Majesty's Forces when on duty. And where any such Order as
aforesaid has been made by the Civil Authority, each such lodger or inmate
shall himself enter his correct name, address and occupation in such book, and
such entry shall be made in the case of such lodger immediately on his arrival,
and in the case of such inmate on the date succeeding the date of the making
of such Order if he is then an inmate and otherwise immediately on his
becoming an inmate.

The Civil Authority may by Order, as regards any area specified therein,
require the occupier of every dwelling house or portion of a building used as a
dwelling house other than as hereinbefore described to keep posted on the
inside of the principal entrance door thereof a list, in which he shall have
entered or caused to be entered the correct name, address and occupation of
each inmate for the time being thereof.

Where any such Order, as is mentioned in this Regulation, has been made, any person authorised for the purpose by the Civil Authority, or by any police officer or constable, or any member of any of His Majesty's Forces when on duty, may enter if need be by force, any such building, dwelling house, or portion of a building, as is hereinbefore mentioned in this Regulation, at any time of the day or night, and may interrogate any person found therein.

Nothing in this Regulation shall require any entry to be made with respect to any lodger or inmate under fourteen years of age.

The Civil Authority may exempt any class or classes of buildings from the operation of an Order made under this Regulation.

If any person contravenes or fails to comply with any of the provisions of this Regulation or of any Order made thereunder, he shall be guilty of an offence against these Regulations.

No DORA or ROIA Equivalent
Similar obligations and restrictions imposed by martial law regulations introduced Jan. 1921.

Reg. 18C (introduced 13 Mar. 1923)

The Civil Authority, if he has reason to suspect that any money or other property has been lodged or deposited with any Bank or person, and that such money or property has been collected or obtained or is being used, or intended to be used, for any purpose prejudicial to the preservation of the Peace or maintenance of Order in Northern Ireland may

(a) By Order authorise any person or persons named in such Order to enter the premises of such Bank or person and to examine and take extracts from the books and documents of such Bank or person as to any such lodgment or deposit by or to the credit or account of any person or persons named in such Order, and to examine the accounts of any such last named person, and all vouchers and documents relating thereto;

(b) By Order require such Bank or person to retain for the disposal of the Civil Authority any such sums of money or other property so lodged or de- posited, and such vouchers and documents. Such Order of the Civil Authority shall, as from the service of a copy thereof upon such Bank or person, operate as a legal transfer to the Civil Authority of any debt, obligation, or chose in action arising out of any such deposit or lodgment.

(c) By Order direct how such money, property, vouchers and documents are to be disposed of—whether by forfeiture or otherwise.

In this Regulation the word 'Bank' shall include any Banking Company, and the word 'person' shall include any firm or partnership.

If any Bank or person contravenes or fails or refuses to comply with the terms of any such Order, such Bank or person shall be guilty of an offence against the Regulations.

No DORA or ROIA Equivalent

Appendix 4. Organization of the Constabulary in Northern Ireland (May 1925)

Inspector-general

RUC
- Commander or County Inspector
- District Inspector
- Head Constable or Sergeant in charge Station

Constabulary Depot
- Commander — 1 Adjutant
- Company Commander District Inspector
- Schools of Instruction

Special Constabulary, Classes A, B, and C
- County Commandant — 2 Adjutants, Paymaster, Assistant Paymaster
- Area Commandant
- Platoon Commander
- District Commandant (B)
- Sub District Commandant (B)

Special Constabulary, Class 'C1'
2 Brigades of 4 Battalions
1 Brigade of 3 Battalions
- Commandant 'C1' — 2 Staff Officers, 3 Instruction Officers, (Musketry, Signalling, Lewis Gun) Paymaster, Assistant Paymaster
- Group (Brigade) Commander — 1 Staff Officer
- District (Battalion) Commander (unpaid) — 1 Adjutant, 1 Quarter Master

Transport (Motorized Branch)
- 1 Senior Inspector Transport
- 2 Adjutants
- Transport Depot
  - 1 Store Office
  - 1 Repair Office
- LRUS 2 Officers (Clogher & Belfast)
- County Transport Officers 5

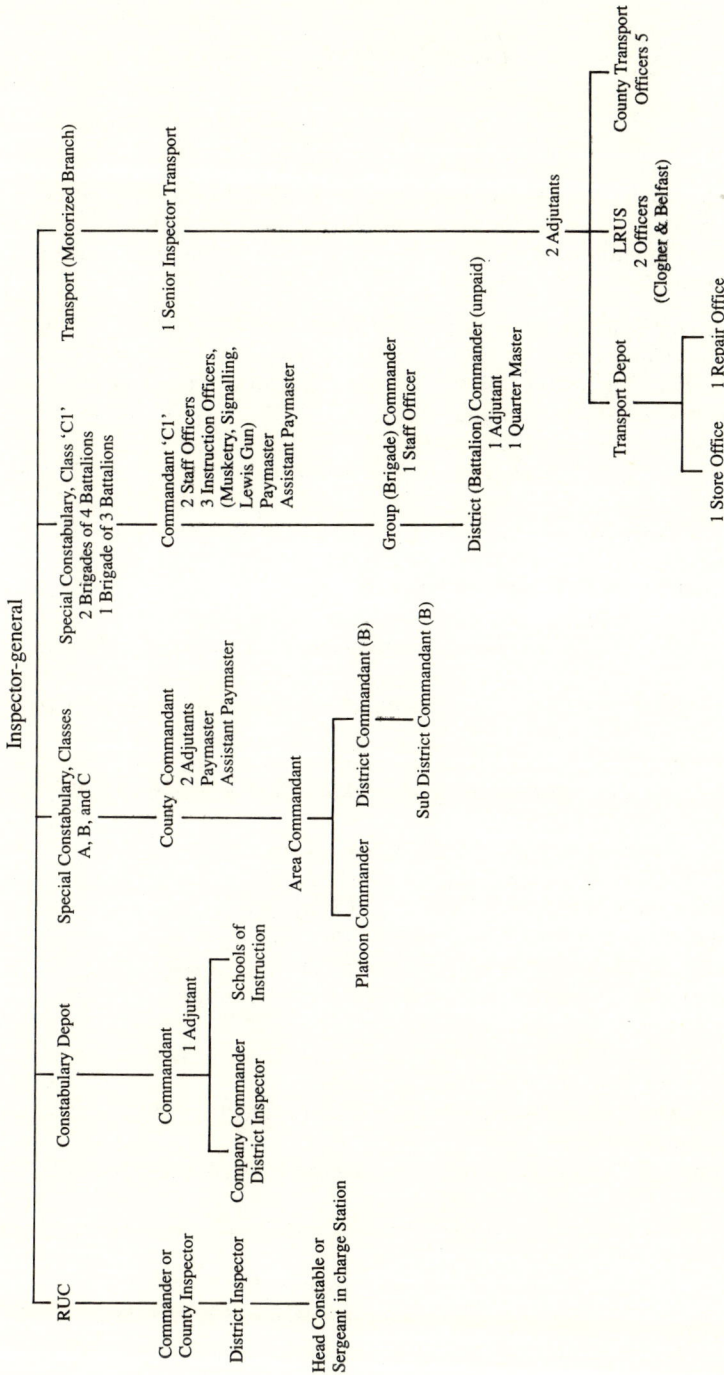

Source: Organizational table attached to Inspector-General RUC to Secretary, Ministry of Home Affairs, 15 May 1925, HA 20/B/2/6, PRONI.

Bibliography

BOOKS, ARTICLES, AND THESES

Where other than the most recent edition of a work has been referred to, this was either in order to trace the development of a particular doctrine, or to assess the state of legal opinion in a period as close as possible to that with which this work is concerned.

AKENSON, D. H., and FALLIN, J. F., 'The Irish Civil War and the Drafting of the Free State Constitution', 5 *Eire-Ireland* 2 (1970), p. 42; 4, p. 28.

ALLEN, C. K., 'Regulation 18B and Reasonable Cause', [1942] 58 *LQR* 232.

—— *Law in the Making* (London, 1964).

—— *Law and Orders* (London, 1965).

ANDREWS, J. A. (ed.), *Human Rights in Criminal Procedure* (The Hague, 1982).

ANON., 'Confessions and Admissions Allowable in Evidence', 52 *ILT & SJ* 89 (1918) (reprinted from *Justice of the Peace*).

—— 'Statements by Prisoners or Suspects,' 52 *ILT & SJ* 242 (1918) (reprinted from *Law Journal*).

—— 'The War Emergency Laws (Continuance) Act 1920', 54 *ILT & SJ* 121 (1920).

—— 'The War Emergency Laws (Continuance) Act 1920', [1920] 54 *ILT & SJ* 121.

—— 'The Legal Effect of the Termination of the War', [1921] 55 *ILT & SJ* 203.

BABINGTON, A., *For the Sake of Example: Capital Courts-Martial 1914–18* (London, 1983).

BARRY, T., *Guerilla Days in Ireland* (Dublin, 1949).

BISHOP, J. W., *Justice under Fire* (New York, 1974).

—— 'Law in the Control of Terrorism and Insurrection: The British Laboratory Experience', 42 *Law and Contemporary Problems* 140 (1978).

BONNER, D., *Emergency Powers in Peacetime* (London, 1985).

BOWMAN, H. M., 'Martial Law and the English Constitution,' 15 *Michican Law Review* 93 (1916).

BOWYER BELL, J., *The Secret Army: The IRA 1916–1979* (Dublin, 1979).

BOYD, A., *Holy War in Belfast* (Belfast, 1987).

BOYLE, K., 'The Tallents Report on the Craig–Collins Pact of 30 March 1922', 12 *Ir. Jur.* 148 (1977).

—— HADDEN, T., and HILLYARD, P., *Ten Years On in Northern Ireland* (London, 1980).

BREAKEY, W. A., *Handbook of the Common and Statute Law of Ireland* (Dublin, 1895).

BREEN, D., *My Fight for Irish Freedom* (Dublin, 1981).

BUCKLAND, P., *The Factory of Grievances: Devolved Government in Northern Ireland* (Dublin, 1977).

BUCKLAND, P., *A History of Northern Ireland* (Dublin, 1981).

CALVERT, H. G., *Constitutional Law in Northern Ireland: A Study of Regional Government* (London, 1968).

CANNING, P., *British Policy towards Ireland 1921–1941* (Oxford, 1985).

CAPUA, J. V., 'Early History of Martial Law in England from the 14th Century to the Petition of Right', 36 *Cambridge Law Journal* 152 (1977).

CARSON, W. A., *Ulster and the Irish Republic* (Belfast, 1956).

CASEY, J. P., 'Republican Courts in Ireland, 1919–1922', 5 *Ir. Jur.* 321 (1970).

—— 'The Genesis of the Dáil Courts', 9 *Ir. Jur.* 326 (1974).

CHAPMAN, B., *Police State* (London, 1970).

CLUTTERBUCK, R., *Guerrillas and Terrorists* (Chicago and London, 1977).

—— (ed.), *The Future of Political Violence: Destabilization, Disorder and Terrorism* (London, 1986).

COOK, C. (ed.), *Defence of the Realm Manual*, sixth edn. (London, 1918).

—— *Defence of the Realm Manual*, seventh edn. (London, 1919).

—— *Defence of the Realm Manual*, eighth edn. (London, 1919).

Craies on Statute Law, by W. S. Scott, fourth edn. (London, 1936).

CRAWFORD, J. C., 'Origins of the Court of Castle Chamber: A Star Chamber Jurisdiction in Ireland', 24 *American Journal of Legal History* 22 (1980).

CURRAN, J. M., *The Birth of the Irish Free State* (Tuscaloosa, Ala., 1980).

CURTIS, L. P., *Coercion and Conciliation in Ireland 1880–1892* (Princeton, 1963).

DAVITT, C., 'The Civil Jurisdiction of the Courts of Justice of the Irish Republic 1920–22', 3 *Ir. Jur.* 112 (1968).

DEASY, L., *Towards Ireland Free: The West Cork Brigade in the War of Independence, 1917–1918* (Dublin, 1973).

—— *Brother against Brother* (Dublin, 1982).

DELANEY, V. T. H., *The Administration of Justice in Ireland* (Dublin, 1970).

DE SMITH, S. A., *De Smith's Judicial Review of Administrative Action*, fourth edn. by J. M. Evans (London, 1980).

—— *Constitutional and Administrative Law*, fifth edn. by H. Street and R. Brazier (Harmondsworth, 1985).

DICEY, A. V., *The Law and the Constitution* (London, 1885).

DODD, C., 'The Case of Marais', 18 *LQR* 143 (1902).

ELLIOTT, S., *Northern Ireland Parliamentary Election Results, 1921–1972* (Chichester, 1973).

ERLE-RICHARDS, H., 'Martial Law', 18 *LQR* 133 (1902).

EVELEGH, R., *Peace-Keeping in a Democratic Society: The Lessons of Northern Ireland* (London, 1978).

FANNING, R., *Independent Ireland* (Dublin, 1983).

FARRELL, B., 'A Note on the Dáil Constitution, 1919', 4 *Ir. Jur.* 127 (1969).

—— 'The Drafting of the Irish Free State Constitution', 5 *Ir. Jur.* 115 (1970).

—— 'The Legislation of a "Revolutionary" Assembly: Dáil Decrees, 1919–22', 10 *Ir. Jur.* 122 (1975).

FARRELL, M., *Northern Ireland: The Orange State* (London, 1980).

—— *Arming the Protestants: The Formation of the Ulster Special Constabulary and the Royal Ulster Constabulary, 1920–27* (London, 1983).

—— *The Apparatus of Repression*, Field Day Pamphlet, 11 (Derry, 1986).

FEELY, F. M., *The Criminal Law and Procedure (Ireland) Act 1887* (Dublin 1888).

FERGUSON, K. P., 'The Army in Ireland from the Restoration to the Act of Union' (Ph.D. thesis, Trinity College, Dublin, 1980).

Field Service Pocket Book (London, 1914).

FIGGIS, D., *The Irish Constitution* (undated (1922?)).

FINLASON, A., *A Treatise on Martial Law* (London, 1866).

FORDE, M., *Constitutional Law of Ireland* (Dublin, 1987).

GREER, S. G., 'Military Intervention in Civil Disturbances: The Legal Basis Reconsidered', 1983 *Public Law* 573.

Halsbury's Laws of England, fourth edn. (London, 1974).

Halsbury's Statutes of England, second edn. (London, 1950).

HANNA, J., *The Statute Law of the Irish Free State* (Dublin, 1929).

HARKNESS, D., *Northern Ireland since 1920* (Dublin, 1983).

HENNESSEY, R. M., *Molloy's Justice of the Peace for Ireland* (Dublin, 1910).

HEUSTON, R. F. V., *Essays in Constitutional Law* (London, 1964).

HEZLETT, A. R., *The 'B' Specials: A History of the Ulster Special Constabulary* (London, 1972).

HIGHAM, R., *A Guide to the Sources of British Military History* (London, 1972).

HOGAN, G., and WALKER, C., *Political Violence and the Law in Ireland* (Manchester, 1989).

HOLDSWORTH, W. S., 'Martial Law Historically Considered', 18 *LQR* 117 (1902).

HOPKINSON, M., *Green against Green: The Irish Civil War* (Dublin, 1988).

HUMPHREYS, H., *The Criminal Law and Procedure (Ireland) Act 1887* (Dublin, 1887).

HYDE, A., 'The Concept of Legitimation in the Sociology of Law', 1983 *Wisconsin Law Review* 379.

International Committee of the Red Cross, 'The International Committee of the Red Cross and Internal Disturbances and Tensions' (Geneva, 1986).

IRWIN, L., 'Irish Presidency Courts 1569–1672', 12 *Ir. Jur.* 106 (1977).

JENNINGS, A. (ed.), *Justice under Fire* (London, 1988).

JONES, T., *Whitehall Diary, iii. Ireland 1918–1925*, ed. K. Middlemas (London, 1971).

JORGENSEN, B., 'Emergency Powers in Canada and Northern Ireland' (Ph.D. thesis, University of Cambridge (undated)).

KALSHOVEN, F., *Constraints on the Waging of War* (Geneva, 1987).

KEE, R., *Ourselves Alone* (London, 1982).

KEIR, D., and LAWSON, F., *Cases in Constitutional Law* (Oxford, 1979).

KELLY, J. M., *Fundamental Rights in the Irish Law and Constitution* (Dublin, 1961).

KELLY, M., O'DOWD, L., and WICKHAM, J. (eds.), *Power, Conflict and Inequality* (Dublin, 1982).

KENNA, G. B. (pseud.), *Facts and Figures of the Belfast Pogrom* (Dublin, 1922).

KENNEDY, D., *The Widening Gulf: Northern Attitudes to the Independent Irish State 1919–49* (Belfast, 1988).

KITSON, F., *Low Intensity Operations: Subversion, Insurgency and Peace-Keeping* (London, 1971).

KLAYMAN, B. M., 'The Definition of Torture in International Law', 51 *Temple Law Quarterly* 449 (1978).

KOHN, L., *The Constitution of the Irish Free State* (London, 1932).

LAWLOR, S. M., 'Civil–Military Relations in Ireland 1921–23' (MA thesis, University College, Dublin, 1976).

LONG, D., 'The Army of the Irish Free State, 1922–24' (MA thesis, University College, Dublin, 1983).

LOWRY, D. R., 'Terrorism and Human Rights: Counter-Insurgency and Necessity at Common Law', 53 *Notre Dame Lawyer* 49 (1977).

LYONS, F. S. L., *Ireland since the Famine* (London, 1985).

MACARDLE, D., *The Irish Republic* (London, 1937).

MC COLGAN, J., *British Policy and the Irish Administration 1920–22* (London, 1983).

MCELDOWNEY, J. F., 'Irish Jury Trial: A Survey of Some Eighteenth and Nineteenth Century Statutes', *Warwick Law Working Papers*, 3/4 (1979).

MCGUFFIN, J., *Internment* (Tralee, 1973).

MACREADY, C. F. N., *Annals of an Active Life* (London, 1924).

MANSERGH, N., *The Government of Northern Ireland: A Study in Devolution* (London, 1936).

Manual of Military Law (London, 1914).

MARAN, R., 'Against Torture', 4 *Human Rights Review* 85 (1979).

MATHEWS, A. S., *Freedom, State Security and the Rule of Law: Dilemmas of the Apartheid Society* (Cape Town, 1986).

MILLER, D. W., *Queen's Rebels: Ulster Loyalism in Historical Perspective* (Dublin, 1978).

MOLLOY, C., *The Justice of the Peace for Ireland* (Dublin, 1890).

MORRIS, G. S., 'The Emergency Powers Act 1920', 1979 *Public Law* 317.

MULLOY, E., *Dynasties of Coercion*, Field Day Pamphlet, 10 (Derry, 1986).

MURRAY, C. DE B., 'Northern Ireland: Its Law Courts and Parliament' [1937] *Scots Law Times* 191.

National Council for Civil Liberties, *The Special Powers Act of Northern Ireland: Report of a Commission of Enquiry Appointed to Examine the Purpose and Effect of the Civil Authorities (Special Powers) Acts (Northern Ireland) 1922 and 1933* (London, 1936).

NEESON, E., *The Civil War in Ireland* (Dublin, 1989).

NEIL, D. G. (ed.), *Devolution of Government: The Experiment in Northern Ireland* (London, 1953).

O'BRIEN, CONOR CRUISE, and O'BRIEN, MAIRE, *A Concise History of Ireland* (London, 1972).

OCCLESHAW, M., *Armour against Fate: British Military Intelligence in the First World War* (London, 1989).

O'CONNOR, J., *The Irish Justice of the Peace* (Dublin, 1911).

O'DONOGHUE, F., *No Other Law* (Dublin, 1986).

O'HIGGINS, P., 'Wright v Fitzgerald Revisited', 25 *MLR* 413 (1962).

—— 'English Law and the Irish Question', 1 *Ir. Jur.* 59 (1966).

O'MALLEY, E., *The Singing Flame* (Dublin, 1978).

—— *On Another Man's Wound* (Dublin, 1979).

O'MALLEY, E., *Raids and Rallies* (Dublin, 1982).

O'NEILL, D. G. (ed.), *Devolution of Government: The Experiment in Northern Ireland* (London, 1953).

OSBOROUGH, W. N., 'Law in Ireland 1916–26', 23 *Northern Ireland Legal Quarterly* 48 (1972).

O'SULLIVAN, D., *The Irish Free State and its Senate* (London, 1940).

O'SULLIVAN, R., *Military Law and the Supremacy of the Civil Courts* (London, 1921).

PALLEY, C., 'The Evolution Disintegration and Possible Reconstruction of the Northern Ireland Constitution', 1 *Anglo-American Law Review* 368 (1972).

PHILLIPS, O. HOOD, and JACKSON, P., *Hood Phillips' Constitutional and Administrative Law*, seventh edn. (London, 1987).

POLLOCK, F., 'What is Martial Law?', 18 *LQR* 152 (1902).

PRAGER, J., *Building Democracy in Ireland: Political Order and Cultural Integration in a Newly Independent Nation* (Cambridge, 1986).

QUEKETT, A. S., *The Constitution of Northern Ireland*, 3 parts (Belfast, 1933).

Report of the Labour Commission to Ireland (London, 1921).

SCHLUETER, D. A., 'Courts-Martial: An Historical Survey', 87 *Military Law Review* 129 (1980).

SCORER, C., SPENCER, S., and HEWITT, P., *The New Prevention of Terrorism Act: The Case for Repeal* (London, 1985).

STALLYBRASS, W. T. S., *Salmond's Law of Torts* (London, 1936).

STEWART, A. T. Q., *The Ulster Crisis: Resistance to Home Rule, 1912–14* (London, 1969).

SUPPERSTONE, M., *Brownlie's Law of Public Order and National Security* (London, 1981).

SWIFT MAC NEILL, J. G., *Studies in the Constitution of the Irish Free State* (Dublin, 1925).

TOWEY, T., *Hugh Kennedy and the Constitutional Development of the Irish Free State 1922–23*, 12 *Ir. Jur.* 355 (1977).

TOWNSHEND, C., *The British Campaign in Ireland 1919–1921* (Oxford, 1975).

—— 'Martial Law: Legal and Administrative Problems of Civil Emergency in Britain and the Empire, 1800–1940', 25 *Historical Journal* 167 (1982).

—— *Political Violence in Ireland* (Oxford, 1983).

VANSTON, G. T. B., *The Criminal Law and Procedure (Ireland) Act 1887* (Dublin, 1887).

VILLIERS-TUTHILL, K., *Beyond the Twelve Bens: A History of Clifden and District 1860–1923* (Galway, 1986).

WADE, E., and BRADLEY, A., *Constitutional and Administrative Law*, tenth edn., with T. St J. N. Bates and C. Himsworth (London, 1985).

WADE, E. C. S., and PHILLIPS, G. GODFREY, *Constitutional Law*, seventh edn., by E. C. S. Wade and A. W. Bradley (London, 1965).

WALKER, C., *The Prevention of Terrorism in British Law* (Manchester, 1986).

WEST, N., MI5 (London, 1983).

WILKINSON, P., *Terrorism and the Liberal State* (London, 1986).

WILLIAMS, G., 'The Interpretation of Statutory Powers of Arrest without Warrant', [1958] 543 *Crim. LR* 73.

WILSON, T. (ed.), *Ulster under Home Rule: A Study of the Political and Economic Problems of Northern Ireland* (Oxford, 1955).

WINFIELD, P. H., 'Courts-Martial from the Lawyer's Point of View', 34 *LQR* 143 (1918).

YOUNGER, C., *Ireland's Civil War* (London, 1970; 1986 reprint).

COMMAND PAPERS AND OFFICIAL PUBLICATIONS

Cmnd. 1534 (1921), 'Arrangements governing the Cessation of Active Operations in Ireland which Came into Force on July 11, 1921'.

Cmnd. 1560 (1921), 'Article of Agreement for a Treaty between Great Britain and Ireland'.

Cmnd. 1684 (1922), 'Correspondence between His Majesty's Government and the Provisional Government of Ireland relating to the Liability for the Relief of Irish Refugees'.

Cmnd. 1688 (1922), 'Draft Constitution of the Irish Free State'.

Cmnd. 2214 (1924), 'Report of the Judicial Committee of the Privy Council as Approved by His Majesty in Council of the 31st July 1924, on the Questions Connected with the Irish Boundary Commission referred to the Said Committee'.

Cmnd. 2278 (1924), 'Report of the Committee Appointed to Review the Provisions of the ROIA 1920 and the Regulations Made under the Act'.

Cmnd. 7608 (1946), 'Report of Army and Air Force Courts-Martial Committee'.

Dublin Gazette, published by authority.
Belfast Gazette, published by authority.
Iris Oifigiúil, published by authority.
Irish Bulletin, journal of Dáil Eireann.
An tOglach, official organ of the Irish Volunteers.
Ulster Year Book.

Parliamentary Reports

United Kingdom
    House of Commons Debates, fifth series, vols. 126, 136, 138, 140, 141.

Irish Free State
    Dail Debates, vols. 1, 2.

Northern Ireland
    House of Commons of Northern Ireland Debates, vols. 1, 2.
    Northern Ireland Senate Debates, vol. 2.

A NOTE ON SOURCES

Chapter 2 (Ireland 1918–21) relies heavily on material from the Imperial War Museum London, and from the Public Records Office, Kew. Of the Museum material, the papers of Major-General Sir Peter Strickland, GOC 6th Division and martial law Military Governor, proved a particularly useful source of material. Included among them are the 'Notes on the Administration of Martial Law for the Use of Commanding Officers', 'The Irish Rebellion in the Sixth Divisional Area from after the 1916 Rebellion to December 1921', 'Notes on the Organization and Methods of Sinn Fein', and '17th Infantry Brigade, Summary of Important Instructions'. The other collection accessed in the Museum was that of Lieutenant-General Sir Hugh Jeudwine, GOC 5th Division. From that source came the 'Record of the Rebellion in Ireland in 1920–21 and the Part Played by the Army in Dealing with It' (vol. i, 'Operations', and vol. ii, 'Intelligence'), and the 'History of the 5th Division in Ireland, November 1919–March 1922'.

Two sets of material in the Public Record Office were made use of. First, the War Office Irish records located at WO 35, including the General Routine Orders for the period, and the 'Circular Memorandum on Martial Law'. Secondly, the records of the Cabinet Office, particularly the weekly surveys of the GOC and of the Chief Secretary held at CAB 24. Some Irish material on the period came from the *Irish Bulletin* in the National Library, Dublin.

For Chapter 3 (Irish Free State 1922–5), the material from the Military Archives, Cathal Brugha Barracks Dublin entitled 'Civil War Series, Prisoners' Files' P/2–P/8, proved invaluable in filling gaps in the reconstruction of the Civil War martial law regime. Another useful source was the collection of General Risteard Mulcahy's papers, held in the University College, Dublin, Archives. For much of the Civil War, General Mulcahy combined the posts of Minister for Defence and Commander-in-Chief of the National Army. Some use was also made of the papers of Ernie O'Malley who held the rank of an IRA Divisional Commander in the Civil War, and which are also held in the UCD Archives. Other sources of material were the Cabinet Minutes of the Provisional Government (G1/1–G1/3) and the Executive Council of the Irish Free State (G2/1–G2/4), and the cabinet 'S' files kept at the State Paper Office, Dublin Castle.

The Public Record Office of Northern Ireland provided much of the material on which Chapter 4 (Northern Ireland 1921–5) is based. The Northern Ireland Cabinet Conclusion and Cabinet papers (principally those at CAB 4) proved a useful source, as did Ministry of Home Affairs files (coded 'HA') including the RUC Inspector-General's circulars for the period. Some use was also made of Ministry of Finance ('FIN') files.

Index